Some of the Books by Jerome Agel

DELIVERANCE IN SHANGHAI (A NOVEL WITH EUGENE BOE)
22 FIRES (A NOVEL WITH EUGENE BOE)
IS TODAY TOMORROW?
TEST YOUR WORD POWER
PREDICTING THE PAST (WITH DR. HUMPHRY OSMOND)
THE MAKING OF KUBRICK'S 2001
DR. COTT'S HELP FOR YOUR LEARNING DISABLED
CHILD (WITH DR. ALLAN COTT)
I SEEM TO BE A VERB (WITH BUCKMINSTER FULLER)
HERMAN KAHNSCIOUSNESS
AMERICA AT RANDOM
SPORTS AT RANDOM
TEST YOUR BIBLE POWER
FASTING: THE ULTIMATE DIET (WITH DR. ALLAN COTT)

Some of the Books Produced by Jerome Agel

THE MEDIUM IS THE MASSAGE (WITH MARSHALL MCLUHAN)
THE COSMIC CONNECTION (WITH CARL SAGAN)
OTHER WORLDS (WITH CARL SAGAN)
THE LUNAR EFFECT (WITH DR. A. L. LIEBER)
IT'S ABOUT TIME & IT'S ABOUT TIME (WITH ALAN LAKEIN)
MAXIMIZING YOUR POTENTIAL THROUGH THE ART OF BREATHING
(WITH JAMES LOEHR AND DR. JEFFREY MIGDOW)

BEYOND TRIVIA

Jerome Agel

SIMON AND SCHUSTER
New York

1   3   5   7   9   10   8   6   4   2
LIBRARY OF CONGRESS CATALOGING IN PUBLICATION DATA
AGEL, JEROME.
BEYOND TRIVIA.
1. TRIVIAL PURSUIT (GAME)—DICTIONARIES.   I.   TITLE.
GV1469.T77A36   1984   031'.02   84-27579
ISBN: 0-671-54128-5

INTRODUCTION

Thou, Trivia, Goddess, aid my song,
Thro' spacious streets conduct thy bard along.

Trivia doesn't need to be trivial. It can make you want to go beyond the simple fact and learn lots more, broadening the horizon of the inquiring mind. Who wrote *In Cold Blood?* Right! But by digging a bit one learns that Truman Capote lost a bet with Kenneth Peacock Tynan as to whether the malicious mite's nonfiction novel would have been released if the accused murderers hadn't been executed. Who starred in television's *Your Show of Shows?* Right, Sid Caesar. By digging a bit one learns that the comedian once received a telephone call from Albert Einstein—yes, *that* Albert Einstein—who wanted to meet him and discuss the human condition. Who has been depicted more often than any other woman? The Virgin Mary. The gospel according to Saint Mark tells us that she gave birth to at least four other sons and to at least two daughters.

Leonard Bernstein knows the score: "A known fact is like a dry, dead thing. But when connections are made, wham! All those facts become fun to know instead of a drag."

ANSWERS LEAD TO QUESTIONS:

- The telephone number of the White House is (202) 456-1414. What happens when you ring up and ask to speak with the President?
- Gene Tunney was the world's heavyweight boxing champion. What turned him on to Shakespeare?
- Gavrilo Princip's shots in Sarajevo were heard 'round the globe. Whatever became of the youth who ignited World War I?
- Hank Aaron is baseball's home run king. How did his brother Tommie do at the plate?
- Ray Bradbury wrote *Fahrenheit 451,* a classic about book burning. Why did his publisher put out a censored edition?
- Walt Disney animated *Snow White*. What names did the Grimm folklorists give the seven dwarfs?
- Albert DeSalvo confessed that he was the Boston Strangler. Did the police ever prove it?

5

- Why was the *Mona Lisa* hidden under a bed in Italy for two years, earlier this century?
- June 16 is the most famous date in all of English literature. Why did James Joyce pick it for the day that everything happens in *Ulysses?*
- Stonewall Jackson was killed by friendly fire. Wasn't Barbara Fritchie nearly a centenarian when their alleged confrontation occurred?
- Why did Gandhi exhort all of Europe's Jews to commit suicide?
- *Nineteen Eighty-Four* preempted for itself a calendar year in the history of man. How many of the book's major themes derive from Eugene Zamiatin's *We?*
- Why was Jacqueline Kennedy criticized by a congressman just before J.F.K. was assassinated?
- Why was Picasso nearly dumped into a garbage pail when he was born?
- What was the name of the *Merrimack* when it clashed with the *Monitor?*
- Why was membership of the Supreme Court reduced to eight during President Andrew Johnson's administration?

Fascinating facts flourish when answers to America's most loved trivia game are expanded: ''The Star-Spangled Banner'' was set to the tune of a popular English drinking song . . . Alfred C. Kinsey, who blabbed about America's sex life, was the world's foremost authority on the gall wasp . . . John le Carré believes that a great part of one's adult life is concerned with getting even for the slights suffered as a child . . . Carry Nation's mother was mad . . . Louisa May Alcott, who forced *Huckleberry Finn* off the Concord library's shelves, wrote thrillers for a steamy weekly . . . King George III was crazy during the last decade of his sixty-year reign . . . Alice Liddell was acting as ''cox'' of his gig when Lewis Carroll began making up Alice's adventures in wonderland . . . Cervantes' *Don Quixote* is a classic, but Mark Twain and Sigmund Freud didn't want their ladyfolk reading it . . . Some Dead Sea Scrolls were sold through a classified advertisement in the *Wall Street Journal* . . . Columbus was probably Jewish . . . Ty Cobb was expelled from baseball, yet led all nominees in the first Hall of Fame balloting . . . Chaucer was a prisoner in the Hundred Years' War . . . Lillian Carter: ''When I look at my children, I say, 'Lillian, you should have stayed a virgin!' '' . . . Twenty percent of gay men interviewed in San Francisco had attempted suicide . . . Ted Williams outhit Joe DiMaggio (.412–.408) during DiMag's historic 56 consecutive-game hitting streak.

Headwords in *Beyond Trivia* were inspired by answers and some questions in America's ''hottest cardboard entertainment'' (*Time* magazine) If the question concerned the initials S.N.C.F. on a railroad train's engine, the headword here is S.N.C.F. rather than the answer (France). If the question concerned what Moses did for a living before he was called by God, the headword is Moses rather than Shepherd. If the question

6

concerned a mosquito's teeth, the headword is Mosquito rather than Yes. If the question concerned the number of Gutenberg bibles, the headword is Gutenberg rather than Forty-seven. Invariably, headwords refer to proper names or nouns.

To update the Declaration of Independence: Seek and ye shall be endowed with the trivial pursuit of happiness. To the strains of *La Triviata*, of course.

(*Mr. Agel grew up in Burlington, Vermont at a "tri-via"—at the junction of three roads—North, School, and Hyde Streets—wishing, of course, that it had been Jekyll and not Hyde.*)

A

A—THE SCARLET LETTER

" 'Mercy on us, goodwife,' exclaimed a man in the crowd, 'is there no virtue in woman, save what springs from a wholesome fear of the gallows? That is the hardest word yet! Hush now, gossips! for the lock is turning in the prison-door, and here comes Mistress Prynne herself.' " Critics have called Nathaniel Hawthorne's mid-nineteenth-century novel *The Scarlet Letter* the greatest book that's been written in the Western Hemisphere. Mistress Hester Prynne makes a clean breast of her shame as Hawthorne traces the effect of A for Adultery on the lives of four people in Puritan Massachusetts, including Hester's bastard daughter, Pearl—*there's* a question for trivial pursuers! "On the breast of her gown, in fine red cloth, surrounded with an elaborate embroidery and fantastic flourishes of gold-thread, appeared the letter A. It was so artistically done, and with so much fertility and gorgeous luxuriance of fancy, that it had all the effect of a last and fitting decoration to the apparel which she wore; and which was of a splendor in accordance with the taste of the age, but greatly beyond what was allowed by the sumptuary regulations of the colony . . . the SCARLET LETTER . . . had the effect of a spell, taking her out of the ordinary relations with humanity, and enclosing her in a sphere by herself. 'She hath good skill at her needle, that's certain,' remarked one of her female spectators; 'but did ever a woman, before this brazen hussy, contrive such a way of showing it! Why, gossips, what is it but to laugh in the faces of our godly magistrates, and make a pride out of what they, worthy gentlemen, meant for a punishment?' "

AARON, HANK

Major league baseball's King of Klout hung up his swatter with a total of 755 round-trippers and (the sport's most important stat) 2,297 runs-batted-in. (Babe Ruth struck 714 HRs.) Getting a fastball past Aaron was like the morning sun trying to get up past a rooster. He's the only athlete who's been honored on the floor of the House of Representatives; the

Flag Day committee, in 1974, the year Aaron ruthlessly exceeded the Bambino's mark, saluted the Alabama-born slugger (.314 BAV) as "America's number-one athlete, a great competitor, and a sportsman in the finest American tradition . . . a humanitarian unsurpassed as well." His late brother Tommie wasn't in the same league—13 HRs and a .229 BAV.

ABACUS

This ingenious ancestor of the computer is probably of Babylonian origin —it may be as old as 4,000 years. In various forms, it was used in eastern Asia and in ancient Rome and, in the Middle Ages, in Europe and the Arab world. Where the abacus was replaced, it gave way first to the Hindu-Arabic notation system with its flexible place values and its zero, later to calculators, finally to computers. The most common abacus still used—chiefly in Japan and in parts of the Middle East—is the Chinese version: In a portable frame, wires (or strings) of beads are divided at a right angle by a bar toward which the counted beads are moved—five beads at one side of the bar, each representing 1, and two beads at the other side, each representing 5. If, for example, one "5" bead and three "1" beads on the first wire are moved to the bar, they stand for an 8; on the second wire, the same combination of beads would stand for 80; on the third wire, for 800, etc. The values are carried from wire to wire. An expert operator of the abacus can compete with many of the mechanical calculating machines. (In architecture, an abacus is the flat layer of stone on top of the capital of a column.)

"ABDICATION!"

The one-word, page-wide headline of the London *Star* in December 1936 blared that King Edward VIII had given up his throne (after 325 days) for the woman he loved, the first English monarch to relinquish his crown voluntarily. The government had opposed his marriage to the twice-divorced American Wallis Warfield. A few other sensational newspaper screamers: "FORD TO N.Y.: DROP DEAD" "LINDBERGH DOES IT! TO PARIS IN 33½ HOURS" "JAPAN WARS ON U.S. AND BRITAIN; MAKES SUDDEN ATTACK ON HAWAII" "THE WAR IN EUROPE IS ENDED! SURRENDER IS UNCONDITIONAL; V-E DAY WILL BE PROCLAIMED TODAY" "FIRST ATOMIC BOMB DROPPED ON JAPAN; MISSILE IS EQUAL TO 20,000 TONS OF TNT; TRUMAN WARNS FOE OF A 'RAIN OF RUIN' " "JAPAN SURRENDERS TO ALLIES, SIGNS RIGID TERMS ON WARSHIP; TRUMAN SETS TODAY AS V-J DAY" "U.S. IMPOSES ARMS

BLOCKADE ON CUBA ON FINDING OFFENSIVE-MISSILE SITES; KENNEDY READY FOR SOVIET SHOWDOWN" "MEN WALK ON MOON—ASTRONAUTS LAND ON PLAIN; COLLECT ROCKS, PLANT FLAG" "NIXON RESIGNS—HE URGES A TIME OF 'HEALING'; FORD WILL TAKE OFFICE TODAY" "AGEL COMPOSES 'BEYOND TRIVIA'—1,500 MANUSCRIPT PAGES IN TEN WEEKS" "REAGAN: AVALANCHE"

ABEL, RUDOLF

He had many aliases, Emil Robert Goldfus among them, and he was said to have been the Soviet Union's master spy in the United States for nine years. The nature of the information that the "painter-photoengraver" passed has never been disclosed. Shaving brushes, tiepins, coins, flashlight batteries, cufflinks, screws, bolts, and pencils were converted into containers used for smuggling microfilmed and microdotted material to Moscow. Defection of an assistant led to Abel's arrest by the Federal Bureau of Investigation in 1957. In 1962, Abel was exchanged at Glienicker Bridge between East Berlin and West Berlin for U-2 reconnaissance spy Francis Gary Powers, shot down over Russia on the eve of a summit meeting in 1960. Abel was awarded the Order of Lenin on his return to Russia. Powers became a traffic-helicopter broadcaster for a radio station in Los Angeles and died in a crash. Abel's pigeon, Reino Hayhanen, died mysteriously in the United States. Abel died in Russia nine years after his return there.

ABOMINABLE SNOWMAN

Yeti means "all-devouring creature" in the vernacular of the Sherpa tribespeople of Nepal. In Tibetan, it's *metoh kangmi,* or "abominable snowman." Yeti, Abominable Snowman, Big Foot, Sasquatch—are there really seven-foot-tall, 500-pound, hairy beasts with a human face and an apelike body and a size-16 foot (at least) making tracks in the Himalayas and the Pacific Northwest? In 1960, Sir Edmund Hillary, one of the first two men to top Everest, went on the track of the chimerical monster because it might be there, and returned with no Sir-prize.

ABORTION

The expulsion—spontaneous or induced—of an embryo or fetus before it has matured to live outside the uterus. The Soviet Union, in legislation in 1920, both recognized the equal status of women and protected their health from the ravages of illegal procedures, and thus became the first country to legalize in-hospital abortion on request of the woman in the first trimester of gestation. In 1935, abortion became a criminal offense in Russia again, then in 1955 legal again. A modified abortion law was passed in Iceland in 1935. Legal history was made in London in 1938 when the precedent was established that a physician could perform an abortion if he believed that continuation of the pregnancy would endanger the woman's life or make her "a physical and mental wreck." The Nazis in 1943 made abortion punishable by the death penalty. In 1948, Japan made abortion widely available for a broad range of indications. Seven years later, the People's Republic of China adopted a policy of elective abortion. In 1965, Tunisia became the first Moslem nation to permit abortion on request. In the United States, beginning with Colorado in 1967, about a dozen states liberalized their statutes. In 1973, the Supreme Court declared that a woman could have an abortion during the first trimester if she had the approval of her physician.

ACHILLES

Achilles, in Greek mythology, was the foremost Greek hero of the Trojan War, in which he was fated to die. His mother, the sea goddess Thetis, had attempted to make the baby Achilles immortal by bathing him in the magic waters of the river Styx. But the right heel, by which she had dunked him, remained vulnerable, and Paris, the son of Hecuba, inflicted a fatal wound in that heel. After slaying Achilles, Paris was fatally wounded by Philoctetes, the son of Poias, who had acquired, as a gift, Hercules' bow and arrow by lighting the pyre on which the superman was consumed alive. An "Achilles' heel" refers to a person's vulnerable point.

ADAM

Once upon a time, on the sixth day, in His own image, there was Adam, and then from a rib made He a Woman, Eve. "And Adam knew Eve his wife; and she conceived, and bare Cain, and said, I have gotten a man from the Lord. And she again bare his brother Abel. [After a jealous Cain had risen up against Abel, his brother, and slain him] Adam knew his wife again; and she bare a son, and called his name Seth: For God, said she, hath appointed me another seed instead of Abel, whom Cain slew. And to Seth, to him also there was born a son; and he called his name Enos; then began men to call upon the name of the Lord."—Genesis 4.

ADAMS, JOHN

One of the Revolution's most devoted patriots, the lawyer successfully defended the British captain and eight soldiers who had been charged with murder after the Boston Massacre of 1770. His belief in justice led him to accept their defense. Six of the defendants were acquitted and the other two were found guilty only of manslaughter—they were branded on their thumbs and released. He was the first United States minister to Britain, in 1785. He was the first Vice-President and the second President. He was the first President to reside in the President's House. He once said, "The history of our Revolution will be one continued lie from one end to the other. The essence of the whole will be that Dr. Franklin's electrical rod smote the earth and out sprang General Washington. That Franklin electrified him with his rod—and thenceforward these two conducted all the policies, negotiations, legislatures, and war." Some historians believe that Adams may have been a manic-depressive. The longest lived President—he died on July 4, 1826, at the age of 90—he is the only President to father another President, John Quincy Adams, the sixth President.

ADAMSON, JOY

At first it was reported that the naturalist and author had been killed by one of her beloved animals in the remote game preserve in Central Kenya, probably by a lion. The Silesian-born wife of a British-Irish game warden had raised a lioness (Elsa), a cheetah (Pippa), and leopard cubs almost from their birth and had written about her 43 years in the East African wilds in the popular books *Born Free, Living Free, Forever Free.* She was tight with her pets. It turned out that she had been mauled with a twin-edged African sword wielded by a disgruntled former aide.

ADDER

The European viper or adder, *Vipera berus,* is the only venomous snake in England; fatalities are rare. It also slithers throughout the European continent and in northern Asia. The adder is small, rarely longer than two feet. Its fangs are folded back against the roof of its mouth except when it strikes. A light zigzag pattern down the back is a characteristic; sometimes the markings are ill-defined or broken up into a series of dots. The pit vipers of the Americas, which include the rattlesnake, the copperhead, the water moccasin, the fer-de-lance, and the bushmaster, are classified in a separate family.

ADOLESCENCE

One of the word's roots is *adolescens,* the present participle of the Latin *adolescere,* to grow up. Adolescence—the state or process of growing up—the period of life from puberty to maturity terminating legally at the age of majority—in girls, physiologically, the years roughly span the ages 12 to 21; in boys, 13 to 22. Major, and often disturbing, changes occur at varying rates in sexual characteristics, body image, sexual interest, social roles, intellectual development, self-concept. Herman Melville observed that "there is no steady unretracing progress in this life; we do not advance through fixed gradations, and at the last one pause: through infancy's unconscious spell, boyhood's thoughtless faith, adolescence' doubt (the common doom), then skepticism, then disbelief, resting at last in manhood's pondering repose of If. But once gone through, we trace the round again; and are infants, boys, and men, and Ifs eternally. Where lies the final harbor, whence we unmoor no more?"

AEGEAN SEA

Archipelago is Greek for "chief sea" and it was the name, long ago, of the Aegean Sea, the southeast European arm of the Mediterranean. Now, archipelago means a sea containing numerous islands, or the islands themselves. The longest archipelagos are Malay, separating the Pacific Ocean from the Indian Ocean; 1,400-mile-long Japan; Lofoten and Vesteralu in the Norwegian Sea; and ice-bound islands in the Arctic north of Canada and in the Antarctic south of Tierra del Fuego. The Aegean civilization is the term for the Bronze Age culture of pre-Hellenic Greece.

AESOP

He may have been a fable, himself; he may never have existed. The stories are much older than the sixth century B.C., in which, it is said, the black slave lived and attached himself, when freed, to the court of Croesus, king of Lydia. In the fourteenth century a monk, Maximum Planudes, collected 144 fables, and from these all the later collections known as Aesop's have been taken. Animal characters behave and speak like human beings, showing the weaknesses and foibles of human nature: "The Ant and the Grasshopper," "The Fox and the Grapes," "The Dog and the Bone," "The Lion and the Mouse," "King Log and King Stork." Aesop's morals include "Don't count your chickens before they hatch."

AFRICA

There are fifty-one countries in the world's warmest, second-largest-in-size, third-largest-in-population continent, slow to emerge into the modern world for many reasons, among them: the emphasis in the rapid emergence from colonialism was on political independence rather than on economic development; industrialization did not include development of agriculture—there was a large rural-to-urban migration and university graduates did not want to return to their villages; technically knowledgeable persons who could run the countries were few in number; tribal competition continued; leaders did not set the best examples for the brightest young people—they indulged in luxury, making the up-and-comers reluctant to sacrifice; the necessity for foreign aid often meant agreeing to purchase unnecessary or overpriced goods from the lender.

AFRIKAANS

A combination of Dutch, some Hottentot, some Bantu, and English, Afrikaans is, with English, the official language of the Republic of South Africa. It came into being when Dutch migrated there 300 years ago; written Afrikaans, however, dates only from 1861. Afrikaans is considered an independent language rather than a dialect or a variant of Dutch, and is spoken by close to 3 million people, most of whom are South African.

AGING

Man is living longer than ever. An "ancient" Roman had an average life expectation of twenty years, but he who lived beyond a few weeks could expect to live for quite a long time. The average American today will live into his seventies, even into his eighties. Fewer people now die prematurely from infectious disease. Medical research, which has learned to prevent early death, is striving to combat degenerative diseases. Age changes that affect blood vessels or the endocrine glands produce widespread effects out of all proportion to their extent.

AGNEW, SPIRO

The son of Theofrastos Spiro Anagnostopoulis, a Greek immigrant who changed his name to Agnew, was not our first Vice-President to quit.

John C. Calhoun, the only Vice-President in two different administrations, resigned from the Jackson administration in 1832 so that he could ardently defend states's rights and slavery as an appointed senator from South Carolina. (He had been John Quincy Adams' Vice-President as well.) Agnew, celebrated for his criticism of "nattering nabobs of negativism" (his speech writer William Safire's coinage to describe newsmen) and for his remark "You see one slum, you've seen them all," left the Nixon administration in 1973 while under investigation for a kickback scheme in Maryland, where he had been county executive and governor, and for accepting bribes while Vice-President; in a 40-page document, the prosecution detailed Agnew's alleged misdeeds. Agnew later claimed that he had resigned not to avoid prosecution but because he believed that Alexander Haig, President Richard M. Nixon's Chief of Staff in the White House, might have him killed if he stayed on. A court order required Agnew to pay $268,000 to Maryland as reimbursement and penalty for his misdeed as governor.

ALASKA

The largest state since 1958 (it is one-fifth the size of the rest of the 49 states combined) has the least population—every resident could have a square mile of Alaska all to himself. The population is 438,000 and the square mileage is 569,600. (By comparison, Manhattan has a population density of 64,337 persons per square mile.) Alaska is the number-one magnet state today—more people are moving in than out. The first known European to set boot in Alaska was Vitus Bering, a Danish explorer in the employ of Russia—the year was 1741. (Bering Strait separates by 51 miles Alaska and the Soviet Union's eastern fringes.) Juneau is the capital, but maybe not for long; a more central location is being sought. Anchorage is the largest city; Fairbanks, named for an Indiana senator, is the second largest. When bought in 1867 for two cents an acre by a determined United States Secretary of State, William H. Seward, Russian America was derisively known as "Seward's icebox" because little financial return was envisaged. In 1964, the strongest earthquake ever recorded in North America killed 114 Alaskans and destroyed several cities almost totally. Mount McKinley in the southcentral part of the North to the Future state is the highest point in North America. It was named in 1896 for the President-elect; its former names were Bolshaya Gora, "big mountain" in Russian, and Denali, "big one" or "high one." Famous Alaskans include Ernest Gruening, Joe Juneau, Sydney Laurence, James Wickersham, and Carl Eielson. About 22,000 of the world's 70,000 Eskimos live in Alaska. Violent winds known as williwaws assault the barren Aleutian Islands.

ALBATROSS

"He thought he saw an albatross that fluttered round the lamp: he looked again, and found it was a penny postage stamp. 'You'd best be getting home,' he said. 'The nights are very damp.'" Lewis Carroll, of course. The largest aquatic bird—the albatross made famous by Samuel Taylor Coleridge's haunting *Rime of the Ancient Mariner*—has a wingspread of from ten feet to twelve feet. Man seems to be the bird of good omen's only enemy—tens of thousands of albatrosses have been slaughtered for their feathers. "God save thee, ancient Mariner! From the fiends, that plague thee thus!—Why look'st thou so?" "With my crossbow I shot the Albatross."

ALCATRAZ

La Isla de los Alcatraces—the isle of the pelicans—successively a military prison, an army disciplinary barracks, an impregnable, escape-proof federal pen, an American Indian stronghold, and today part of Golden Gate National Recreation Area: twelve desolate acres on a craggy escarpment rising 135 feet out of the swirling currents of San Francisco Bay, a mile and a quarter off Fisherman's Wharf, a grim bastion of dungeons and doors when it was a 450-cell prison—claustrophobic cells (9' × 5'), steel-plated doors, "deep six" solitary dark holes. Al Capone and Machine Gun Kelly were locked up in The Rock.

ALCOTT, LOUISA MAY

The author of the two volumes of *Little Women* surprised visitors by being tall. Before the novels of warmth and sensibility about Jo March and her sisters, drawn on the life of her own family, made the Alcotts financially comfortable, she churned out swashbucklers in thrillers for Frank Leslie's steamy weekly newspaper. They appeared under the by-line A. M. Barnard, and are collected today in *The Unknown Thrillers of Louisa May Alcott* and *Plots and Counterplots: More Unknown Thrillers of Louisa May Alcott*. *Little Men* was based on experiences of Miss Alcott's nephews. During the Civil War she served as a nurse in the Union hospital in Georgetown. She argued to keep Mark Twain's *Huckleberry Finn* off the shelves of her library in Concord, Massachusetts. His masterpiece was not proper reading for "our pure-minded lads and lassies," because its realistic description of life on the Mississippi and its use of common language were not morally uplifting.

ALEXANDRIA

The center of Hellenistic and Jewish culture and the capital of the Ptolemies (304–30 B.C.) was founded in northern Egypt in 332 B.C. by one of history's greatest generals at age twenty-three. King Alexander of Macedon was only thirty-two years old when he died, after gobbling up more territory than any aggrandizer before him: from Greece to India, including the Persian Empire. Napoleon remarked that Alexander the Great was the greatest military genius of all time. He was also a social reformer: In a universal society, all people would be equal—under certain conditions. Alexander put on Persian dress and the manners of an Oriental despot and asked his fellow Greeks to treat him like a god. There were two celebrated royal libraries in Alexandria containing, counting duplicates, about 700,000 scrolls. The city regained importance in the nineteenth century, and in World War II it was the Allies' chief naval base in the eastern Mediterranean.

ALI, MUHAMMAD

The world heavyweight boxing champ's contract to play the title role in the Broadway "black power" musical *Buck White* (1969) was unique. He could censor the script for profanity. He could skip a performance if there was a professional boxing bout he wanted to attend. He might even have to quit the show: He was threatened with a jail term for refusing—on religious grounds—induction into the armed services. (He had been stripped of his heavyweight crown for refusing induction.) Reviews were respectful, especially for his second-act number "Mighty Whitey," the favorite of the "Greatest." The show was kayoed after seven performances.

ALICE—LEWIS CARROLL

Because of a stammer, Lewis Carroll (the pseudonym of the Oxford deacon-mathematician Charles Lutwidge Dodgson) said he was comfortable only in the company of children, especially little girls, one of whom was Alice Liddell, to whom, with her siblings, he told stories of nonsense. Two became the classics *Alice's Adventures Under Ground* (1865) and its sequel, *Through the Looking-Glass* (1872). Carroll gaily improvised the opening chapters of *Alice's Adventures* while drifting in a boat with Canon Robinson Duckworth and the three young Liddell sisters in July 1862, never for a moment—as biographer Derek Hudson has pointed out —knowing, "poor fellow, that falling down a well would be called a symbol of coitus, or that a little door with a curtain in front of it might be interpreted as a female child and her clothes." Canon Duckworth remembered the genesis: ". . . I was 'stroke' of the 'pair' of which he was 'bow' in the famous voyage from Oxford to Godstow. . . . The quaint story floated over my shoulders to the pretty trio of sisters, daughters of Dean Liddell, on that beautiful summer afternoon in the Long Vacation . . . [it was] actually composed . . . for the benefit of Alice Liddell, who was acting as 'cox' of our gig. I remember turning round and saying, 'Dodgson, is this an extempore romance of yours?' And he replied, 'Yes, I'm inventing as we go along.' " The beginning of the deacon's invention: "Alice was beginning to get very tired of sitting by her sister on the bank and of having nothing to do: once or twice she had peeped into the book her sister was reading, but it had no pictures or conversations in it, 'and what is the use of a book,' thought Alice, 'without pictures or conversations?' So she was considering, in her own mind (as well as she could, for the hot day made her feel very sleepy and stupid), whether the pleasure of making a daisy-chain would be worth the trouble of getting up and picking the daisies, when suddenly a White Rabbit with pink eyes ran close by her. There was nothing so *very* remarkable in that; nor did Alice think it so *very* much out of the way to hear the Rabbit say to itself 'Oh dear! Oh dear! I shall be too late!' (when she thought it over afterwards it occurred to her that she ought to have wondered at this, but at the time it all seemed quite natural); but, when the Rabbit actually *took a watch out of its waistcoat-pocket,* and looked at it, and then hurried on, Alice started to her feet, for it flashed across her mind that she had never before seen a rabbit with either a waistcoat-pocket, or a watch to take out of it, and burning with curiosity, she ran across the field after it, and was just in time to see it pop down a large rabbit-hole under the hedge. In another moment down went Alice after it, . . ." Dodgson had met Alice six years earlier, when she was four years old; he noted in his diary, "I mark this day with a white stone." He made many photographs of her. On the fateful odyssey, she was a pretty child with an oval face, dark hair, and shy, fawnlike eyes. Dodgson conducted the children back to their home, and Alice is said to have said, "Oh, Mr. Dodgson, I wish you would write out Alice's adventures for me." When he "fell asleep" in 1898, aged 65 years, there was a wreath from "Alice."

ALICE—CROQUET IN WONDERLAND

"Alice thought she had never seen such a curious croquet-ground in her life: it was all ridges and furrows: the croquet balls were live hedgehogs, and the mallets live flamingoes, and the soldiers had to double themselves up and stand on their hands and feet, to make the arches. . . . 'I don't think they play at all fairly,' Alice began, in rather a complaining tone, 'and they all quarrel so dreadfully one ca'n't hear oneself speak—and they don't seem to have any rules in particular: at least, if there are, nobody attends to them—and you've no idea how confusing it is all the things being alive: for instance, there's the arch I've got to go through next walking about at the other end of the ground—and I should have croqueted the Queen's hedgehog just now, only it ran away when it saw mine coming!' 'How do you like the Queen?' said the Cat in a low voice. 'Not at all,' said Alice: 'she's so extremely—' Just then she noticed that the Queen was close behind her, listening: so she went on '—likely to win, that it's hardly worth while finishing the game.' The Queen smiled and passed on.''

ALICE—HUMPTY-DUMPTY

From Chapter VI, Lewis Carroll's *Through the Looking-Glass:* "However, the egg only got larger and larger, and more and more human: when she had come within a few yards of it, she saw that it had eyes and a nose and mouth; and, when she had come close to it, she saw clearly that it was HUMPTY-DUMPTY himself. 'It ca'n't be anybody else!' she said to herself. 'I'm as certain of it, as if his name were written all over his face!' It might have been written a hundred times, easily, on that enormous face. Humpty-Dumpty was sitting, with his legs crossed like a Turk, on the top of a high wall—such a narrow one that Alice quite wondered how he could keep his balance—and, as his eyes were steadily fixed in the opposite direction, and he didn't take the least notice of her, she thought he must be a stuffed figure, after all . . . so she stood and softly repeated to herself:—'Humpty-Dumpty sat on a wall: Humpty-Dumpty had a great fall. All the King's horses and all the King's men couldn't put Humpty-Dumpty in his place again.' '' '' '. . . Yes, all his horses and all his men,' Humpty-Dumpty went on. 'They'd pick me up again in a minute, *they* would!' '' Humpty-Dumpty broke onto the literary scene about 1803, in *Mother Goose's Melody.*

ALICE—A MAD TEA-PARTY IN WONDERLAND

"There was a table set out under a tree in front of the house, and the March Hare and the Hatter were having tea at it: a Dormouse was sitting between them, fast asleep, and the other two were using it as a cushion, resting their elbows on it, and talking over its head. 'Very uncomfortable for the Dormouse,' thought Alice; 'only as it's asleep, I suppose it doesn't mind.' 'Have some wine,' the March Hare said in an encouraging tone. Alice looked all round the table, but there was nothing on it but tea. 'I don't see any wine,' she remarked. 'There isn't any,' said the March

Hare. 'Then it wasn't very civil of you to offer it,' said Alice angrily. 'Take some more tea,' the March Hare said to Alice, very earnestly. 'I've had nothing yet,' Alice replied in an offended tone: 'so I ca'n't take more.' 'You mean you ca'n't take *less*,' said the Hatter: 'it's very easy to take *more* than nothing.' 'Nobody asked *your* opinion,' said Alice. 'Who's making personal remarks now?' the Hatter asked triumphantly. . . . she got up in great disgust, and walked off: the Dormouse fell asleep instantly, and neither of the others took the least notice of her going, though she looked back once or twice, half hoping that they would call after her: the last time she saw them, they were trying to put the Dormouse into the teapot. 'At any rate I'll never go *there* again!' said Alice, as she picked her way through the wood. 'It's the stupidest tea-party I ever was at in all my life!' "

ALLEN, WOODY

The cleverest scene in an Allen movie may have been the last scene in the sequence in *Everything You Ever Wanted to Know About Sex* in which a sheep and Gene Wilder have a profound zoophilic affair—"ewe do something to me" social intercourse. When the sheep takes it on the lamb and returns to Europe, his distraught, beWildered lover becomes down and out, reduced to begging on Manhattan's Fifth Avenue—his receptacle for coins a can of Woolite. In Allen's futuristic movie, *Sleeper,* the orgasmatron is the cylindrical booth with the teatillating msnomer. ("There are four things to stay away from in movies, Woody baby: boats and water; animals; kids; and futurism.") The little nebbish gets into the orgasmatron—or-gas-matron—and closes the door. A bit of whirring schtick and he is ejected looking all shook up. Easy come, easy go. "I was thinking about *Sleeper* today in terms of how I hate machines in real life," Woody said one night during production. "I have no patience with them. I break them. That's an honest thing with me. People close to me will confirm how many toasters I've broken." The toast of the town said he noticed in *Sleeper* one of the recurrent themes is that advanced technology doesn't work. Which may be what future shock really means.

ALLIED CONFERENCES IN WORLD WAR II

August 1941—President Franklin D. Roosevelt and British Prime Minister Winston Churchill meet off the coast of Newfoundland and promulgate the Atlantic Charter, pledging allegiance to democratic principles and promising to work for political and economic equality among nations "after the final destruction of the Nazi tyranny." January 1943—the Casablanca Conference—Roosevelt and Churchill agree that the Axis must surrender unconditionally. May 1943—Roosevelt and Churchill meet in Washington and decide on a cross–English Channel invasion of the continent for the spring of 1944. October 1943—the Moscow Conference—The four principal Allies (the United States, Great Britain, China, and the Soviet Union) proclaim "the necessity of establishing at the earliest practicable date a general international organization." August 1943—Roosevelt and Churchill meet in Quebec and review detailed plans for the invasion of Europe. November 1943—Tehran Conference—Roosevelt and Churchill inform Joseph Stalin of their invasion plans and Dwight D. Eisenhower is appointed to direct the Allied Expeditionary Force. November 1943—Roosevelt, Churchill, and China's Chiang Kai-shek proclaim the dismemberment of the Japanese empire as a war aim; Manchuria, Formosa, and the Pescadores Islands are to be returned to China. August–October 1944—Dumbarton Oaks Conference—Plans are drafted by the Allies for a general international organization. February 1945—the Yalta Conference—Roosevelt, Churchill, and Stalin make additional decisions forming the United Nations and Stalin is promised membership for Belorussian and Ukrainian Soviet Socialist Republic; they agree that only nations declaring war on the Axis will be invited to the charter conference in San Francisco. April 1945—San Francisco Conference—Poland is denied membership in the new world organization; Denmark, Argentina, Turkey, Egypt, and Saudi Arabia are welcomed—they had declared war against the Axis by the March 1 deadline. (Sweden, Switzerland, Spain, Eire, and Portugal were still neutral.) The U.N. charter was signed on June 26, 1945. Summer 1945—Potsdam Conference—The borders of Poland are drawn and a council of foreign ministers created to draft peace treaties for Italy, Rumania, Bulgaria, Hungary, and Finland; Japan was to surrender unconditionally.

ALLIGATOR

It has a broader, blunter snout than the related crocodile, and the lower fourth tooth does not protrude when its mouth is closed. A large-type (up to nine feet) alligator is found in the southeastern United States. A nearly extinct, smaller type (up to six feet) is found in the Yangtze River valley near Shanghai. Alligators hunt by night and attack humans only in self-defense. They hibernate from October to March. The crocodile is aggressive. The Nile and the Orinoco crocodiles are commonly twelve feet long and have been known to attack innocent humans. The marsh crocodile is a fresh-water species of India and Ceylon and is regarded as sacred in some regions. The Congo dwarf crocodile averages three and a half feet in length. The alligator Old Moses, at the New York zoological park, could swallow an eight-pound chicken in a single gulp.

"ALL IS NOT GOLD THAT GLISTERS"

The observation was not original with the Spanish novelist Miguel de Cervantes in *Don Quixote*. Eighteen years earlier, in *The Merchant of Venice,* Shakespeare wrote, "All that glisters is not gold—Often have you heard that told." Often, indeed. Spenser in *The Faerie Queene* had written, "Gold all is not that doth golden seem." Lydgate: "All is not golde that outward shewith bright." Chaucer, "The Canon's Yeoman's Tale," in *The Canterbury Tales:* "But al thyng which that shineth as the gold Nis nat gold, as that I have herd it told." De Lille, who died in 1202, wrote, "Do not hold as gold all that shines as gold." The phrase may have been coined by Aristotle, who said, "Yellow-colored objects appear to be gold." To put a fine carat on the nugget: More than two tons of South African rock must be processed to produce about an ounce of gold. To get at every ounce of gold the earth might yield, miners have dug as deep as 2½ miles.

"ALOHA"

It was "aloha" to the Aloha state, Hawaii, when it became the fiftieth to join the Union, in 1959. Aloha is a Janus word—in addition to meaning hello, it can mean goodbye. It is also an expression of love, affection, kindness. It can be said while wearing your aloha shirt.

ALOU BROTHERS

There were three of the Dominican Republic baseball-playing brothers in the big leagues—Felipe Alou, Jesus Alou, Matty Alou—and together they outhit the three DiMaggio brothers—Joltin' Joe, Dom (the "Little Professor"), and Vince. Matty batted a career .307; Felipe, .292; Jesus, .279. The Yankee Clipper was the only one of the three DiMaggios to break .300: He hit .325; Dom, .298; Vince, .249. Baseball's best-hitting brothers were Paul "Big Poison" Waner's .333 and Lloyd "Little Poison" Waner's .316, for a combined average of .3245.

AMAZONS

Did these hulking, strong, masculine women exclude men from their lives? Did they make men scrub the floors while *they* did the governing and warred abroad? Aeschylus called them "the warring Amazons, men-haters." An expert on Greek mythology: The Amazons banned all men from their kingdom. Says another: Each Amazon had to kill a man before she could marry, and all male children were killed or maimed at birth or exiled. The legendary race of superwomen dwelled on the coast of the Black Sea in Asia Minor, and each cut off her right breast in order to employ her bows and spears more effectively. Their queen was the golden-girdled Hippolyte. Hercules' ninth labor as humble slave to the ingenious Eurystheus, king of Mycenae, was to obtain the girdle for Eurystheus' daughter, Admeta. The strongest man on Earth, with the supreme self-confidence that magnificent physical strength gives, considered himself a peer of the gods—indeed, they needed his help to conquer giants. And Hippolyte? Turns out that she received Hercules kindly and consented to yield her girdle. A troublemaker (Zeus' wife) persuaded the Amazons that the powerful stranger was carrying off their queen. Hercules, believing that Hippolyte had acted treacherously, killed her, made off with the girdle, and sailed homeward.

AMBASSADOR BRIDGE

Once (during the late 1920s) the bridge with the longest suspension span and the longest span of any bridge in the world, it is today "only" the world's longest suspension bridge between two countries: the United States and Canada, over the Detroit River. It was also the first bridge with a suspension span that exceeded the length of a cantilever. Construction had proceeded smoothly when the failure of the steel wire in the cable was discovered. Breaks were of such magnitude that the entire cable system had to be dismantled and restrung with cold-drawn wire. Cold-drawn wire is used now in the construction of all suspension-bridge cables. Despite the setback, the 1,850-foot-long Ambassador Bridge opened seven months ahead of schedule, on Armistice Day 1929.

AMERICAN INDIANS

Oklahoma (156,501), Arizona (152,145), and New Mexico (106,840) are the states with the largest Indian populations. The major tribes and/or natives in Oklahoma are the Cherokee, Creek, Choctaw, Chickaw Chickasaw, Osage, Cheyenne, Arapahoe, Kiowa, and Comanche. There are also federal Indian reservations in twenty-four other states: Alaska, California, Colorado, Florida, Idaho, Iowa, Kansas, Louisiana, Maine, Michigan, Minnesota, Mississippi, Montana, Nebraska, Nevada, New York, North Carolina, North Dakota, Oregon, South Dakota, Utah, Washington, Wisconsin, and Wyoming. Tribally owned land in Arizona totals 19,555,053 acres. There are 19,946 Indians in seventy-eight reservations in California. In 1838, federal troops under General Winfield Scott evicted the Cherokee from their homes in the southeast and marched, or escorted, them at gunpoint 1,000 miles to Indian land in Oklahoma—the Trail of Tears. A minority of the nation, over the protest of the majority, had surrendered the Cherokee land in Georgia by the Treaty of New Echota, in 1835.

AMERICAN REVOLUTION

Five days after the Battle of Lexington had ignited the war for independence, in 1775, word came from England that Parliament would allow the colonies to tax themselves to provide for their own civil administration and defense. Three months later, the Continental Congress tried to stop the war. It adopted John Dickinson's Olive Branch Petition asking King George III to use his authority to cease hostilities; the British monarch refused to accept the rebels' petition. Tories outnumbered the American patriots in New York City, probably in Philadelphia, and in certain parts of the Carolinas and Georgia. Six thousand militiamen deserted and returned to their homes, forcing the revolutionaries to abandon a plan to attack the British at Newport, Rhode Island. A year before the war's end, General George Washington's army was shattered at Charleston, South Carolina—about 5,400 men were slain there. Eight months later, more than 1,000 soldiers quit because they had not been paid. One reason that Washington's army had starved at Valley Forge: Pennsylvania farmers preferred to sell food to the British for ready cash. After Yorktown, Congress fled Philadelphia when Pennsylvania troops mutinied, demanding back pay. Canada was invited to become a member of the Confederation, the only colony outside the original thirteen invited to do so. It declined.

AMERICAN REVOLUTION—THE SHOT HEARD 'ROUND THE WORLD

"By the rude bridge that arched the flood/Their flag to April's breeze unfurled/Here once the embattled farmers stood/And fired the shot heard 'round the world." A hymn sung at the dedication of a monument at Concord, Massachusetts, on Independence Day 1837. But it will never be known if an embattled farmer—a minuteman—or a Redcoat fired the shot on the New England green that early morning hour of April 19, 1775. A small number of Americans were on hand in Lexington to greet a column of royal infantry seeking colonial military stores. As the minutemen, realizing that armed resistance would not be the better part of valor, were dispersing, a shot was fired. There was another. And another. And an exchange. Several minutemen were killed. Singing "Yankee Doodle," Major John Pitcairn's Redcoats marched on to Concord, destroyed military supplies, fought again, then retreated under harassing fire to Boston. In May, the Second Continental Congress assembled in Philadelphia. Though blood had been shed, most of the delegates still hoped the rights previously declared might yet be acknowledged by the mother country.

AMERICA'S CUP

Sports's longest winning streak—132 years, 24 successful defenses— ended when *Australia II* (with a controversial keel) outsailed *American Liberty* in the seventh and final 24.3-mile sailing race in the Atlantic Ocean off Newport, Rhode Island, in the summer of 1983. Not since the schooner *America* had won the 27-inch-high trophy in a 53-mile run around the Isle of Wight off England's southern coast in the first international yachting meet, in 1851, had a challenger copped more than two races. *Australia II* was two and a half tons lighter than America's defender. A patent for the controversial keel had been publicly registered in England before the competition.

AMETHYST

Known as bishop's stone, it is a violet to purple variety of quartz used as an ornamental or gem stone; it has been used for episcopal rings. In Greek, amethyst means nondrunkenness. Among the superstitions with which amethyst is associated, there's one that guarantees drinking wine out of a cup made of amethyst won't make you intoxicated. Amethyst is also regarded as a love charm, a potent influence in improving sleep, and a protection against thieves. It is the February birthstone. Much fine amethyst comes from the Soviet Union.

AMIN, IDI

Full name: Idi Amin Dada Oumee. Uganda's heavyweight boxing champion 1951–60. Once a private in the Ugandan army. Fought in the jungles of southeast Asia and Africa. Became commander in chief. Became Moslem president-dictator of Uganda in 1971: "I am not an ambitious man; I am just a soldier with a concern for my country and its people." His eight-year reign was filled with terror, violence (he had about 300,000 Ugandans slaughtered), and sudden and inexplicable changes and re-

versals in policy. The "Hitler of Africa" was ousted in 1979 by Tanzanian troops and Ugandan exiles. Living in Jeddah, Saudi Arabia, he devises plans for his return home: "I need money, arms, and political support, and no one is giving me anything. Allah will reward me with success. It is only a matter of time."

ANCHORAGE

The largest city in the forty-ninth state (population: about 173,000) was founded in 1914 as a shipping depot during construction of the Alaska Railroad, and it grew as a railroad town. Water was sold for five cents a bucket and garbage was heaved into the outgoing tide. Located at the head of Cook Inlet in southcentral Alaska, it suffered monumental damage in the severe earthquake of 1964. A point of interest is Earthquake Park.

ANDERSON, JOHN

When he realized he wasn't going to be the Republicans' nominee for President in the 1980 national election, the moderate 10-term Illinois congressman mounted an independent campaign. His running mate was a Democrat, Wisconsin Governor Patrick J. Lucey. The ticket called for lower Social Security taxes, ratification of the Salt II treaty, a cap on federal spending at one-fifth of the gross national product, and a gasoline tax (50¢) to discourage use of imported oil. It opposed a constitutional amendment banning abortion. Anderson-Lucey was endorsed by the Liberal Party of New York State. The pair received no electoral votes in Ronald Reagan's rout of the incumbent, Jimmy Carter, but did net 5,719,437 votes—seven percent of the popular vote. Carter received 41 percent of the popular vote and 49 electoral votes; Reagan: 51 percent of the popular vote, 489 electoral votes.

ANDORRA

Smuggling is an important economic activity in this semifeudal state nestled in 191 square miles, high in the eastern Pyrenees Mountains between France and Spain, to which homage is paid annually through a nominal gift. The country is under the joint suzerainty of the President of France and the Bishop of Urgel (Spain). Andorra has iron, lead deposits, marble quarries, and extensive pine forests, and more than half a million visitors each year.

ANDROMEDA

Every second brings this 200-billion star galaxy and the Earth 50 miles closer together. In a few billion years, we'll be only half as far apart— 1.1 million light-years—as we are today and Andromeda will loom twice as large in our skies. (A light-year is about 6 million million miles.) Like our Milky Way, the Andromeda galaxy, or Great Nebula, is a spiral; but with a diameter of roughly 100,000 light-years it is only about half the mass of the Milky Way. Andromeda is the only galaxy visible to the naked eye in the Northern Hemisphere; it reaches its highest point there in the evening sky in November. There are red and yellow stars in the central regions of Andromeda and younger blue stars in the realm of the spiral arms.

ANGEL FALLS

A gold hunter, Jimmy Angel was the discoverer of the highest uninterrupted waterfall in the world (3,212 feet) when he flew through one of the canyons of the plateau Auyan Mesa in southeastern Venezuela in 1935. An old prospector had told the American pilot about Auyan Mesa and showed him gold from a stream at its top; they planned to visit the area together, but the prospector died and Angel was not able to find the stream on his own. Angel Falls is about 800 feet higher than the second highest falls, Yosemite, in the United States.

ANGELS

They've been where the action was. "And in the sixth month the angel Gabriel was sent from God unto a city of Galilee, named Nazareth, to a virgin espoused to a man whose name was Joseph, of the house of David; and the virgin's name was Mary. And the angel came in unto her, and said, Hail, thou that art highly favored, the Lord is with thee: blessed art thou among women." . . . "And, behold, there was a great earthquake: for the angel of the Lord descended from heaven, and came and rolled back the stone from the door, and sat upon it . . . And the angel answered and said unto the women, Fear not ye: for I know that ye seek Jesus, which was crucified. He is not here: for he is risen, as he said. Come, see the place where the Lord lay." . . . "And when the morning arose, then the angels hastened Lot, saying, Arise, take thy wife, and thy two daughters, which are here; lest thou be consumed in the iniquity of the city." Angel: Greek for messenger. In Christianity, the order of the celestial hierarchy: the seraphim are the highest order of angels, the celestial beings surrounding God's throne. Cherubim are the second order of angels, heavenly beings usually represented as winged children. Thrones are the third highest class. There are also dominions, virtues, powers, principalities, archangels, and angels. Bodiless, immortal spirits. Except by implication (Revelation 4:8), there is no mention of seraphim in the New Testament. Lucifer, or Satan, was the rebellious archangel who was cast out of heaven: "How art thou fallen from heaven, O Lucifer, son of the morning! How art thou cut down to the ground, which didst weaken the nations! For thou hast said in thine heart, I will exalt my throne above the stars of God . . ." Angelology burgeoned in the eleventh to thirteenth centuries—thousands upon thousands of new angels came into being.

ANIMAL GROUPS

Whales travel in pods. Pod: a small herd or "school" of seals or whales, or sometimes of other animals; sometimes a small flock of birds. Daniel Webster, in a letter on September 14, 1832: "We saw several small pods of coots go by." F. D. Bennett, in 1840: "The Sperm Whale is gregarious; and usually occurs in parties, which are termed by whalers 'schools' and 'pods'." There are also: an army of frogs; a corps of giraffes; a dray of squirrels; a stud of mares; a bed of oysters; a knot of toads; a swarm of eels; a peep of chickens; a bevy of swans; a descent of woodpeckers; a clutch of newborn snakes; a labor of moles; a smack of jellyfish; a school of hippos; a rag of colts; a gang of elks; a murder of crows; a siege of bitterns; an ambush of tigers; a shoal of pilchards; a crash of rhinoceros; a mustering of storks; a gam of dolphins; a convocation of eagles; a drift of swine; a desert of lapwings; a band of gorillas; an exaltation of larks; a mob of cattle. Not to mention a heap of living.

ANIMALS, WARM-BLOODED

If the temperature in your body falls on a cold day and rises on a warm day, you are a cold-blooded animal. You are not a bird and you are not a mammal. Birds and mammals are warm blooded; their/our body temperature is the same on a cold day as on a hot day. The cold blooded include animals that have no blood at all, such as jellyfish and sponges.

ANNO DOMINI (A.D.)

Medieval Latin for "in the year of the Lord," that is, Jesus Christ. But Jesus was actually born from four to eight years before he was "born."

He was delivered of the Virgin Mary while Herod was king, and Herod died in 4 B.C. In 534 A.D., the first man to calculate the year of Jesus' birth made a mistake—and that's the way it's been for 1,450 years (at this writing).

ANTARCTICA

Entombed under the continent's ice are mountains, hundred-mile-long lakes, and deep troughs. The Ross Ice Shelf, hundreds of feet thick, is equal in area to that of France. Some valleys are the driest spots on the planet, but they have more water than does any place on or above the surface of Mars. Tiny ponds of water exhibit microscopic life in the summer—tiny wingless insects in patches of moss and lichens and two types of plants that send forth flowers. One pond, San Juan, has enough water to fill a half dozen average-sized American living rooms; the only form of life in the pond is one species of bacterium. The geographic South Pole, at an altitude of 9,816 feet above sea level, does not coincide with the magnetic South Pole—they are about 5° apart—and it has six months of uninterrupted daylight and six months of total darkness every year. The geographic Pole was first reached by the Norwegian Roald Amundsen in 1911: "Washing was a luxury never indulged in on the journey, nor was there any shaving; but, as the beard has to be kept short, to prevent ice accumulating from one's breath, a beard-cutting machine which we had taken along proved invaluable. Another article taken was a tooth extractor, and this also proved valuable, for one man had a tooth which became so bad that it was absolutely essential that it should be pulled out. . . . For food we relied entirely on pemmican, biscuits, chocolate, powdered milk, and, of course, dog meat." In 1929, Richard E. Byrd became the first man to have flown over both the North and South Poles. He claimed Marie Byrd Land for the United States, as Charles Wilkes had claimed Wilkes Land for the United States ninety years earlier.

ANTHONY, SUSAN B.

As someone has to have said, "If George Washington really threw a silver dollar across the Potomac, it must have been the Susan B. Anthony, and he was throwing it away." The quarter-sized, eight-sided coin, introduced on July 2, 1979, was so unpopular that some banks made a big scene before handling it. A savings and loan office near Chicago peddled some of the coins for only fifty cents. Why so unpopular? It felt too much like the two-bit piece, and it looked awful. Miss Anthony was a vigorous leader in the nineteenth century for women's rights in politics, education, and industry. She asserted the rights of women in industry on the ground that "a man's clumsy fingers would never be nimble enough to master the [sewing] machine that was invented for women." She was a force in getting women admitted to the University of Rochester on the same conditions as men. In Rochester, New York, she tested the right of women to the franchise under the terms of the Fourteenth Amendment, and was denied by the United States Supreme Court. (Her illegal vote, in 1872, was cast for the Republican presidential incumbent, Ulysses S. Grant. She refused to pay a fine of $100 or to go to jail, and the sentence was not carried out.) The Nineteenth Amendment, guaranteeing women the right to vote, was adopted in 1920, fourteen years after Miss Anthony's death.

AORTA

A mammal's primary artery of the circulatory system delivers oxygenated blood to all other arteries except those of the lungs. At the hips, it divides into the two iliac arteries, which carry blood to the pelvis and to the legs. The human aorta is about one inch in diameter and originates at the left ventricle of the heart.

APENNINES

The 840-mile-long marble and limestone backbone of Italy, from the Colle di Cadibona in the northwest, close to the Maritime Alps, to the Egadi Islands to the west of Sicily. (The system continues in the Sicilian mountains.) Vesuvius and Etna are active volcanos in the Apennines and the river Tiber rises in the range. Because it's a relatively young mountain system, still settling, it is prone to earthquakes and landslides. The Appian Way is in the Apennines, as is the scenic Autostrada del Sole, the "highway of the sun," with an imposing series of tunnels and embankments, the main artery of the peninsula.

APHRODITE

The Greek goddess of love, beauty, fertility, sea, and war was a busy body. Hesiod says she was born of the foam of the sea ("aphros" is "foam" in Greek). In Homer's *Iliad,* she is the daughter of Zeus and Dione. In the *Odyssey,* she marries the lame and deformed blacksmith of the gods, Hephaestus, and is the lover of Ares. In some legends she is the mother of Eros and Aeneas by a mortal, a shepherd named Anchises. Her romance with the handsome hunter Adonis (he had been restored to life by Zeus) explained the changing seasons to the Greeks: When the two lived together, the weather was sublime, the plants flourished; when they were apart for six months of the year, the weather was unpleasant, the vegetation expired. It was to Aphrodite that Paris awarded the apple of discord which led to the dispute that in turn led ultimately to the Trojan War. Aphrodite was similar in many of her attributes to the Oriental goddesses Astarte and Ishtar; in Roman mythology, she was identified with Venus.

APPIAN WAY

All roads led to Rome. The Appian was the first of them to be built—the *longarum regina viarum,* the queen of long roads, the brainchild of the arrogant censor Appius Claudius Caecus to cement Rome's grip upon lands conquered to the south along the Adriatic. Its stone blocks marched south from a gate in the first masonry wall of Rome, struck into the heart of its biggest, most dangerous neighbor, the Samnite League, coasted the eastern slope of the Apennines to Tarentum (Taranto) on the Ionian Sea, then slashed across the heel of the Italian boot to Brundisium (Brindisi) —about 360 miles, a 68-year project completed in 244 B.C. It was used by Mark Antony in courtship of Cleopatra, by Hannibal, the apostle Paul, Spartacus, the poet Horace in 38 B.C.—"From Rome to Brindisi, with Stops"—no other highway trafficked in as much bloodshed and glory and turbulence and trade and gossip of early Western civilization. There is a second Appian Way, parallel with the original road from Rome to Albano, ordered built by Pope Pius VI in 1784.

APPLE—GRANNY SMITH

On the family's farm at Eastwood, near Sydney, Down Under, Maria Ann "Granny" Smith planted seeds from rotting Tas apples (found in a gin case at market). One of them grew into a tree that produced splendid fruit, and soon Ms. Smith was the apple of everyone's eye. The fruit of the genus Malus of the family Rosaceae (Rose family) was named for her. At first, the tart, green Granny Smith was used exclusively for cooking; it was found to keep better than other varieties. All Granny Smith apple trees in Australia and overseas originate from grafted fragments of the original tree. Some other apple names: Wealthy, Paradise, Northern Spy, Gloria Mundi, Primate, and Grenadier. At one time, the apple was considered a species of the pear genus *Pyrus,* with which it shares the characteristic pome fruit. It is native to the Caucasus Mountains of western Asia. The forbidden fruit in the Garden of Eden was the apple. In classical mythology, the apple was sacred to Aphrodite. The "love apple" is a tomato.

ARABIAN SEA

Cochin, Aden, Karachi, and Bombay are among the cities that front the Arabian Sea, the 1,800-mile-wide northwest part of the Indian Ocean between Arabia (Africa) and India. It has four elongated arms—the Red Sea, the Gulf of Aden, the Gulf of Oman, the Persian Gulf. A dominating feature, if not *the* dominating feature, is the monsoon—it blows from the southwest in the summer, from the northeast in the winter. Arab dhows (150 tons–200 tons) still ply the ancient shipping routes. The port of Socotra, in northeast Ethiopia, was for centuries a haven for pirates. There are few islands in the Arabian Sea.

ARCARO, EDDIE

"Banana Nose" rode two hundred and fifty losers before his mount was the first across the finish line. But then he kept on being a winner—4,779 times a winner. The jockey won the Kentucky Derby five times (in 1938, 1941, 1945, 1948, 1952), the Preakness six times, the Belmont Stakes six times—and the Triple Crown of racing in 1941 (Whirlaway) and 1948 (Citation). He was inducted into the National Museum of Racing Hall of Fame in 1958. (If you're a horse player, according to psychologists, you probably have an inordinate fear of dying and a constitutional need for stimulation.)

ARC DE TRIOMPHE

More egotestical than arch—he wanted to demonstrate his manhood—Napoleon ordered construction of this imposing commemoration of French war triumphs—i.e., Napoleon's war triumphs. It took three decades to build. The height of a 16-story building and 148 feet wide and 72 feet deep, it dominates the intersection of a dozen radiating avenues at the head of the Champs Elysées in Paris. Interred beneath the arch is the body of an unknown French soldier of the Great War; the tomb is surmounted by a perpetual flame.

ARCHIMEDES

The celebrated Greek mathematician and engineer was about seventy-five years old when he was murdered by a Roman soldier at Syracuse, Sicily. The story goes that he was bending over geometrical figures he had marked in sand. The soldier told him to move on. Archimedes replied, "Don't disturb my circles." They were his last words. The Roman general Marcellus ordered that an honorable burial be given the greatest

Greek—nay, *the* greatest—scientist and mathematician of ancient times. His equal did not arise for nearly two thousand years. Archimedes hit on the principle of buoyancy—he ran through the streets shouting "I've got it! I've got it!"—*Heureka* in Greek. He worked out the principle of the lever in full mathematical detail: "Give me a place to stand on and I can move the world." He invented the "screw of Archimedes." He calculated a value for "pi." He took an educated guess as to the number of grains of sand required to fill the entire Universe. It has been said that he would have discovered calculus if he had had a decent system of mathematical symbols to work with—discovery had to wait for Newton.

ARCH OF HADRIAN

Hadrian was a busy Roman emperor for twenty-one years in the second century. He was accomplished in music and poetry and learned in Greek. He pacified Moesia. He kept the Jews out of Jerusalem. He gave alms to the poor and put on a few circuses. He built great protective walls in Germany and the 73-mile-long Hadrian's Wall dividing England and Scotland. He rebuilt the Pantheon in Rome and expanded the Roman Forum. He built the Arch of Hadrian in Athens, which is extant. It was the gateway to the new city of Novae Athenae, which rose around the Olympieum. Under Hadrian (his full name was Publius Aelius Hadrianus, and he was an orphan before becoming the ward of Emperor Trajan), Athens ceased to be politically important. It was a great university city of the Roman world and it revived as an important commercial center. Still, Hadrian had time for young Antinous.

ARCTIC CIRCLE

Arctic from *arktos,* the Greek name for the "Great Bear" or "Ursa Major," the principal constellation above the Arctic Circle. Antarctic means "opposite the bear." The Arctic and the Antarctic Circles are the imaginary lines around the Earth parallel to the Equator at 66°32′ latitude north and south. The Arctic Circle crosses Scandinavia, Iceland, Greenland, Canada, Alaska, and the Soviet Union. The Antarctic Circle touches only one continent—Antarctica, the fifth largest. The world's northernmost city of size, Trömso (twice the area of Los Angeles), in Norway, is never out of sight of the Sun from May 21 to July 23: Most people act like little kids who never want to go to bed, they fly around like butterflies, they even wash their cars at two in the morning. During *morketiden,* when the Sun has gone away, quite a few Trömsonians fly off to southern Norway just to get a glimpse of that golden ball, that furnace in the sky.

ARGENTINA

South America's second-largest nation in size—1,072,150 square miles—borders five other countries (Brazil, the largest; Uruguay; Paraguay—the spectacular Iguacu Falls are in a national park where Argentina, Brazil, and Paraguay meet—Bolivia; and Chile) and is the third-largest (behind Brazil and Colombia) in population—about 30,000,000—85 percent of European ancestry, about 15 percent of mixed Indian-European ancestry: mestizos. The symbol of the Sun on both the nation's flag and coat of arms represents Argentina's freedom from Spain. The blue and white colors in the flag were worn by patriots who fought off British invaders in the early 1800s. May 25 is the Argentine national holiday; on that date in 1810 revolutionists deposed the Spanish viceroy. The legendary national symbol is the gaucho, or cowboy, the nomadic herdsman of the fertile Pampas—portrayed in *Martin Fierro,* the classic Argentine folk epic by Jose Hernandez. Military duty is compulsory: a year in the army or in the air force, 14 months in the navy. When the military government took control in 1976, parts of the Constitution (adopted in 1853) were suspended.

ARLINGTON NATIONAL CEMETERY

Two Presidents—John F. Kennedy and William Howard Taft—are among the more than 188,000 dead buried there under standard Government Issue tombstones of white marble, 13 inches wide, 4 inches thick, 42 inches high (24 inches above ground, 18 below). ("I had not thought," T. S. Eliot wrote in *The Waste Land,* "death had undone so many.") An eternal flame burns near Mr. Kennedy's grave. The Virginia hills and the mansion overlooking the white-marbled District of Columbia were originally part of an 1,100-acre tract purchased in the year of America's independence from England by Mrs. George Washington's son by her first marriage. Her only grandchild married Robert E. Lee, the West Pointer who was to become the Confederacy's general-in-chief, and for thirty years the mansion there, Arlington House, was the Lees's home. The curator of Arlington House today has said, "People don't like to talk about this particular thing, but if it hadn't been Lee's home, the land wouldn't have been turned into a cemetery." During the Civil War, the Virginia estate was confiscated for nonpayment of $92.07 (plus penalty) in taxes. Ownership passed to the government for $26,800 in a subsequent "sale for default." The Supreme Court then ordered the estate restored to Lee's heirs, who sold it to the government for $150,000. Both Confederate and Union dead were buried in the new cemetery, as were thousands of slaves who had migrated to Washington and died there in the

Freedman's Village. Remains of soldiers in the American Revolution and the War of 1812 have been reburied there. The 585 acres are thought to be enough for the next 35 years, though there are more than a dozen burials each day. An active-duty member of the military at the time of death or a career retiree is qualified to be buried there. Exceptions, such as for Joe Louis, are granted.

ASHE, ARTHUR

He was a lieutenant in the Army in 1968 when he won the first U.S. Open tennis championship, the most notable achievement in the sport by a black male athlete. (Althea Gibson, who won 10 straight black women's singles championships, had gained the U.S. and the Wimbledon women's singles championships.) Ashe exploded 26 aces in defeating the blond Tom Okker of the Netherlands, 14–12, 5–7, 6–3, 3–6, 6–3. He was ineligible to receive the $14,000 top prize because he was an amateur. He had copped the U.S. amateur singles championship two weeks earlier. At Forest Hills, Ashe was the first men's winner from the United States in 13 years; he had been seeded fifth, behind four Aussies. "I am a sociological phenomenon," he said, when he was denied a visa by South Africa on racial grounds in 1970; he appeared at the United Nations to oppose South Africa's apartheid policy. Ashe won the Australian Open in 1970, then defeated Jimmy Connors in the Wimbledon final in 1975. He is the nonplaying (heart condition and age) captain of the U.S. Davis Cup team.

ASH WEDNESDAY

"Earth to earth, ashes to ashes, dust to dust; in sure and certain hope of the Resurrection unto eternal life."—*The Book of Common Prayer*. In the Old Testament, ashes and dust are symbols of sorrow and repentance, mortality and worthlessness. In the Western Church, since the early Middle Ages, ashes are reminders of death, sin, the need to upgrade one's life. Ashes are placed on the foreheads of the faithful on the first day of Lent—Ash Wednesday—the seventh Wednesday before Easter. The first prayer for the blessing of the ashes gives them a sacred character as sacramentals for healing from sin ("healing remedy"); three other prayers and the formula of imposition express their symbolism of mortality. The practice of receiving ashes on the forehead has been universal since the Synod of Benevento in 1091. Ashes are also used in dedicating a church.

ASIMOV, ISAAC

The biochemist and science and fiction writer has authored more than 300 books since *Pebble in the Sky,* in 1950, but he didn't make best-seller lists until his 262nd, *Foundation's Edge* (1982), the fourth in the series that began in 1951 with *Foundation.* His first sale of a short story was "Marooned off Vesta" to *Amazing Stories,* in 1939. He isn't sure when he was born in Russia: "The date of my birth, as I celebrate it, was January 2, 1920. It could not have been later than that. It might, however, have been earlier. Allowing for the uncertainties of the times, of the lack of records, of the Jewish and Julian calendars, it might have been as early as October 4, 1919. There is, however, no way of finding out. My parents were always uncertain and it really doesn't matter." He loves to compose limericks. He composed his first on July 13, 1953, not quite three months after his first extramarital sexual experience (which had left him riddled with guilt—and triumphant): "A priest with a prick of obsidian/Was a foe to the hosts of all Midian./Instead of immersion/Within a young virgin/'Twas used as a bookmark in Gideon."

ASPIRIN

What if Felix Hoffmann's father didn't have rheumatoid arthritis and young Hoffmann, a chemist in Germany, didn't seek a way to relieve his father's pain? $C_9H_8O_4$—the acetyl derivative of salicylic acid—wasn't a new compound, but Hoffmann used it in a new way, to answer prayers. We now know that by interfering with the synthesis of specific prostaglandins in the body, it can relieve pain associated with arthritis and other pain, inflammation, and fever. A basic constituent of the analgesic comes from the spirea plant, which led to the trade name aspirin, the most widely used drug of all time.

ASTROLOGY

Baloney! That's how nearly 200 scientists, including a fistful of Nobel Prize winners, in a 1975 survey, saw the divination that treats of the supposed influences of the stars upon human affairs and of foretelling terrestrial events by their positions and aspects. (The author of *Beyond Trivia,* for example: Sun in Gemini, Moon in Aries, Cancer rising.) Astrology arose in Babylonia but needed to fuse with Greek mathematics before it could make a decisive advance. Before invention of the zodiac, omens were everywhere: the birth of a lion, the fluttering of a bird, the appearance of a scorpion, the bite of an ass. "When a woman bears a child with small ears, the house will fall into ruin." Hitler, Himmler, Hess, and other Nazi bigwigs took off their hats to astrology. Rudolf Hess confided to the American prison psychiatrist during the Nuremberg war crime trials that he had been prompted to fly to the British Isles when one of his astrologers read in the stars that Hess was ordained to bring about peace.

ASWAN HIGH DAM

When the United States and Great Britain withdrew their offer to finance the project, Egyptian president Gamal Abdel Nasser angrily and revengefully nationalized the Suez Canal, in 1956. The Soviet Union took over much of the financing and technical supervision of the 10-year construction project about four miles south of Aswan Dam, which had been built by the British in 1902 and enlarged in 1934. Aswan High Dam is 375 feet high and 11,811 feet long, and Lake Nasser, its reservoir, is now one of the world's largest artificial lakes, about 2,000 square miles. Its waters have the potential for expanding agriculture by about 2 million acres in Egypt and by about 5 million acres in Sudan to the south. Creation of the reservoir required relocation of 90,000 people. Under UNESCO auspices, the threatened Nubian temples at Abu Simbel were moved to a cliff 200 feet above their former site. The cycle of ruinous floods is now part of Egypt's past.

ATHENS

The Greek capital's oldest residential area, the Pláka, lies behind the Acropolis. Amid narrow, winding streets are relics of the classical, Byzantine, and Turkish periods. They include the church of St. Theodore and the octagonal Tower of the Winds. Every Greek city had an acropolis, which in Greek means "high point of the city." Athens' Acropolis, on its acropolis, was devoted to religious purposes rather than to customary defensive purposes.

ATLANTA

Katie Scarlett O'Hara said that the capital of the Peachtree State was full of mighty pushy people. "Why was the place so different from the other Georgia towns? Why did it grow so fast? After all, they thought, it had nothing whatever to recommend it—only its railroads and a bunch of mighty pushy people . . . restless, energetic people from the older sections of Georgia and from more distant states were drawn to this town that sprawled itself around the junction of the railroads in its center. They came with enthusiasm."

ATLAS, CHARLES

There really was a Charles Atlas, the former ninety-seven-pound weakling who was always getting sand kicked into his face at the beach in full-page mail-order advertisements on the back cover of periodicals. He became a body builder when he saw a muscular statue of Hercules and then a zoo's lion stretch and ripple its muscles. "Dynamic tension" led to the title of "the world's most perfectly developed man" in a contest sponsored by *Physical Culture* magazine. He adopted the name Atlas— he was born Angelo Siciliano—when he began to resemble a statue of the Greek god who held up the heavens. The physical culturist was a model for the sculptors of the statues of George Washington in Washington Square in New York City and Alexander Hamilton at the Treasury Building in Washington.

ATLAS MOUNTAINS

The European Alpine system extends and constitutes northwest Africa's Atlas system of ranges and plateaus. The Atlas run about 1,500 miles. The highest point is Jebel Toubkal, at 13,671 feet, in southwest Morocco. The Strait of Gibraltar separates the Atlas from the Sierra Nevada of Spain; the Mediterranean Sea separates the Atlas from Sicily and the Apennines of Italy. If there were no Atlas Mountains, there probably would not be a Sahara. Rain coming in from the north is effectively stopped by the Atlas, whose northern slopes are generally well-watered. The name comes from Atlas, the Greek god who held the heavens on his shoulders.

ATLAS SHRUGGED

"Who is John Galt?" the objectivist-novelist Ayn Rand asks on page one of the novel. There was a real John Galt, appropriately a self-made moneyman. He was born in Newburgh, New York, in 1867, and attended Siglars Academy there. Moved to Honolulu in 1899 and spent thirty-six years as a banker with the Hawaiian Trust Company. A lifelong Republican. Retired in 1936 and died in Orange, New Jersey, at the age of seventy-four. Miss Rand's John Galt was modeled on her dearly held concept of man as a heroic being, with his own happiness as the moral purpose of his life, with productive achievement as his noblest activity and reason as his only absolute. Galt said that he would stop the motor of the world, and he did. The book's last line: Galt "raised his hand and over the desolate earth he traced in space the sign of the dollar."

ATTICA

Thirty-nine citizens of New York State—29 inmates, 10 hostages—were shot dead at Attica Correctional Facility between September 9 and 13, 1971. Nearly 90 others—3 hostages, 85 inmates, 1 trooper—were wounded during the 15 minutes it took the State Police to quell the prisoner uprising and retake the violence-ripped prison. With the exception of Indian massacres in the late nineteenth century (according to the official report of the New York State Special Commission on Attica), the assault was the bloodiest one-day encounter between Americans since the Civil War. The prisoners had pressed their grievances: the shortage of trained personnel and the inadequacy of facilities made rehabilitation an impossible dream; idleness was the principal occupation; most correction officers were not equipped by training to communicate with their inmate charges. The Special Commission, directed by the dean of the law school of New York University, Robert B. McKay, placed responsibility for the bloody encounter on Governor Nelson A. Rockefeller, who had refused to go to the prison, on prison officials, and on conditions within the prison system: "It is not even clear that rehabilitation was then, or is now, a real objective of the American prison system." President Richard M. Nixon supported Governor Rockefeller's suppression of the revolt: "When a man is in a hard place and makes a hard decision and steps up to it, I back him up."

ATTILA

He was no fun, this son of a Hun! The Huns rode out of Asia on their ponies and roughshod through the lower Volga valley and over the Ostrogoths, the Visigoths, and the Eastern Roman Empire, vandalizing, brutalizing, sodomizing, ravaging, looting, plundering, pillaging, savaging, slaughtering. The short, swarthy, broadchested, snub-nosed Attila even murdered his brother, co-King Bleda, in 445 A.D., or had him murdered —same thing. "The Scourge of God" set up his palace in Hungary and received in tribute the territories that now constitute Poland, Germany, and European Russia. A funny thing happened on the way to the Forum: the Huns were routed at Maurica by Aetius, in 451. Two years later,

Attila died of a nasal hemorrhage suffered at a banquet celebrating his marriage. The prisoners who buried him in coffins of gold, silver, and iron, one within another, were put to death so they could not reveal the location of the grave. ("Work Makes One Free.") Legend has it that Attila isn't half-bad when he is compared with his fore- and aft-fathers.

AUCKLAND ISLANDS

A depot nearly two centuries ago for sealers and whalers, they are today uninhabited, 234 square miles of igneous rocks and glacial moraine about 300 miles south of South Island, New Zealand, to which they belong.

AUERBACH, RED

He's had a real first name all these years: Arnold. He's been a cog in the wheel of the fortunes of the National Basketball Association since its beginning after World War II. He coached Washington and Tri-Cities to 143 victories in the late 1940s, then took the reins of the Boston Celtics —their "auer" had come! The victory-cigar-smoking mentor became the first, and only, N.B.A. pilot to land more than a thousand triumphs, as the Celtics raised nine division championships and eight consecutive world championships (1959–66) to the roof of Boston Garden. As Celtics' major domo, Auerbach wasn't able to persuade Virginia's Ralph Sampson to join the team—the seven-footer later joined the Houston Rockets in the N.B.A.

AUSTRALIA

Five continental states—Queensland, New South Wales, Victoria, South Australia, Western Australia—and two territories—the Northern and the Australian Capital—and one island state—Tasmania, separated from Victoria by Bass Strait—comprise the smallest continent, the island continent, the only country that is a continent, the commonwealth of Australia (*australis terra,* Latin for southern land). There are more people in New York State than there are in all of the basically flat, dry, Down Under land, which is almost as large as the continental United States. Britain considered the entire continent the perfect, faraway dumping ground for convicts and other undesirables. There are preserves in the Northern Territory for the native dark-skinned, economically disadvantaged aborigines and part-aborigines. In 1907, a 1,000-mile-long fence was built from the North to the South coasts to prevent the proliferating rabbit population in the East from harassing the West. There are animal species that are found nowhere else in the world: the kangaroo, koala, platypus, dingo (wild dog), Tasmanian devil (raccoonlike marsupial), wombat (bearlike marsupial), the flying opossum, the wallaby, the spiny anteater, and the barking and frilled lizards. Germaine Greer is an Australian. A. B. "Banjo" Paterson's song "Waltzing Matilda" was nominated to replace "God Save the Queen" as the national anthem.

AUTOMOBILES

Britain may boast of having the most cars per mile of paved road, but the United States has by far the most cars. A recent figure: in one year 147-million vehicles were driven 1,480,000 *million* miles, or 206.2 miles per week per driver, and there were 138,000,000 drivers. What hath Benz wrought? John Kenneth Galbraith asked if this indeed is the American genius: "The family which takes its mauve and cerise, air-conditioned, power-steered, and power-braked automobile out for a tour passes through cities that are badly paved, made hideous by litter, blighted buildings, billboards, and posts for wires that should long since have been put underground. They pass on into a countryside that has been rendered largely invisible by commercial art. . . . They picnic on exquisitely packaged food from a portable icebox by a polluted stream and go on to spend the night at a park which is a menace to public health and morals. Just before dozing off on an air mattress, beneath a nylon tent, amid the stench of decaying refuse, they may reflect vaguely on the curious unevenness of their blessings. Is this, indeed, the American genius?" It *is* enough to give one car-diac arrest.

AUTOMOBILE ACCIDENTS

"Never buy a car built on a Monday." The National Highway Traffic Safety Administration, a division of the U.S. Department of Transportation, says you might not want to drive a car on a Saturday: it's the day of the week on which most fatal highway accidents occur in the United States. The safest day: Tuesday. California and Texas are by far the most lethal states. The month with the most accidents: July. Then August, then October. February is the safest month, January the second safest, no doubt because they are hazardous winter months, there are fewer vehicles on the road, drivers tend to be extra-cautious. (The data were compiled for the year 1982, when there were 39,092 road deaths.) Half of all American households will be affected by alcohol-related automobile accidents. If it takes you two full days to read this book, *140* more Americans will be the victims of drunk drivers.

AUTOMOBILE FIRSTS

Another spinoff from the invention of the automobile: the automatic parking meter, designed to make money for both the inventor, Carlton Cole Magee, and for the cities that installed it. First to give the Park-O-Meter the green light: Oklahoma City, Oklahoma, in July 1935. Twenty-foot spaces were painted at the curb and a nickel-in-the-slot meter was installed at each space. The parking meter became nationally popular—at least with Depression cities. The first traffic lights were installed in Cleveland in 1914. Or were they? Another source says that traffic lights were not installed until 1920, in Detroit. In Cleveland, it is said, the system featured crossarms 15 feet above the ground which were equipped with red and green lights and buzzers. In Detroit, the electric light system used the three colors familiar to the railroads: green for go, red for stop, amber for caution. The first automobile accident occurred in New York in 1896: A Duryea Motor Wagon collided with a bicycle rider—the woman cyclist fractured a leg. The yell "Hey, watch where you're goin', lady" probably originated at the same moment. Three years later, the first fatality also occurred in New York City—a 68-year-old real estate broker was run over as he alighted from a southbound streetcar at Central Park West and 74th Street. The first driver arrested for speeding was doing 12 miles an hour on Lexington Avenue in New York, in 1899. New York was the first state to require registration and license tags, in 1901; the tags carried the owner's initials. St. Louis historians claim that the first drive-in gasoline station opened in their city in 1905. The first Indianapolis 500 was staged in 1911; the winning speed was 74.7 m.p.h. In 1914, an advertising agency convinced Gulf Oil to give away road maps, it'd be good advertising. The first drive-in movie theater opened in New Jersey, in 1933.

AVIATION FIRSTS

Some aviation firsts: fatality, Thomas Selfridge, in 1908 (Orville Wright was badly hurt in the crash); moving picture projected, in a Ford transport, at 5,000 feet, 1929; bombed battleship to the bottom, a test, 1921; sleeping berths, 1933; jet, 1942; broke the sound barrier, 1947; transatlantic solo westward, 1932, five years after Lindbergh flew west to east; trans–United States, forty-nine days, 1911—a train with spare parts kept pace; transpacific nonstop, 1931; jet round-the-world nonstop, 1957; parachute jump, 1912; woman passenger, 1909. *Wings* was the first motion picture, and the only silent film ever, to win the best picture Academy Award, 1927.

AVOCADO

Pearlike, it is a fruit, not a vegetable, first cultivated by the Aztecs. It is also called an alligator pear. The super-caloric avocado has a high oil content. A 3⅛″ California avocado has 369 calories. A 3⅝″ Florida avocado has 389 calories. A boiled medium-sized artichoke, by comparison, has 125 calories. (A 2½″-diameter apple eaten with the skin has 77 calories.)

B

BABAR

From stories that his wife, Cecile, told their children, the French painter and writer Jean de Brunhoff created books about the lovable elephant. The first, *The Story of Babar, the Little Elephant,* was published in 1932, and follows Babar from his hammock in the jungle to a solid bourgeois life in Paris and his return to the jungle, where he is chosen king because of his aristocratic aplomb and his wardrobe. "Distinguished nonsense," wrote the *Horn Book* reviewer. De Brunhoff died of tuberculosis in 1937, at the age of 38. His son, Laurent, continued the stories, producing *Babar's Cousin, Babar's Visit to Birds Island, Babar and the Professor,* and so on. Laurent says he has "never been able to paint and do Babar books at the same time. Only when a book was finished would I pick up my brushes and engraving tools again." He created characters based on his daughter and his son: "They were quite pleased to recognize themselves and regard it as perfectly normal that they should be in the book along with Babar."

BACALL, LAUREN

Seeing Katharine Hepburn—so beautiful, so funny, so mysterious, so wonderful, so touching—in *The Philadelphia Story* convinced the former Ms. Betty Perske that being an actress should be the *only* goal in life. Her first notice from the theater critic George Jean Nathan appeared in *Esquire* in 1942: "The prettiest theatre usher—the tall slender blonde in the St. James Theatre, right aisle, during the Gilbert & Sullivan engagement—by general rapt agreement among the critics, but the bums are too dignified to admit it." She was screen-tested and signed by the director Howard Hawks: "Saw the test on Wednesday," she wrote her mother. "It's the weirdest feeling to see yourself move around and talk. I didn't think it was exceptionally good. I didn't look beautiful. Anyway, I'm the first girl Howard has ever signed personally . . . I'm his protegée." Hawks told the sultry neophyte that he intended to wait for just the right part for her introduction to movies—and he expected her to work on her voice. Her most anxious moment during Humphrey Bogart's courtship? Revealing her religion.

BAILY'S BEADS

Named for the prosperous English stockbroker Francis Baily, who had retired in 1825 and taken up with his intellectual mistress—astronomy— they are the row of brilliant points of sunlight shining through valleys on the edge of the Moon that are seen for a few seconds just before and just after the central phase in an eclipse of the Sun. Baily was a founder of the Royal Astronomical Society and its perennial president or vice-president. His discovery of the broken bits of sunlight renewed astronomical interest in eclipses.

BAJA PENINSULA

The 760-mile-long peninsula in northwest Mexico separates the Gulf of California from the Pacific Ocean, and the northern border separates San Diego and Tijuana: beaches, lagoons, waving green palms, some of the best fishing in the world, vast wilderness, crags of mountains, deserts (once sea bottoms), salt beds on which nothing exists. "Green Angels" cruise the highway system to help motorists in distress or to remind them not to drive there at night. ". . . a handful of people who, besides their physical shape and ability to think, have nothing to distinguish them from animals," an early, German missionary observed. Within 125 miles of Los Angeles Bay is the only place on Earth to see the so-called "boojum tree," which resembles an "upside-down carrot with pencil-like branches helter-skelter up their 40- and 50-foot height, while they can often bend over like a giant croquet hoop and root their top in the soil again." The warm lagoons of Baja California in the north (the southern section is called Baja California Sur) are a lure for gray whales, which travel annually the 7,000 miles—80 miles a day, ten minutes below water, blowing, then another ten—from the glacial waters of the Arctic to mate, roll with apparent delight in the breakers, and a year later to deliver their calves. In the 1850s, the whaler Charles *Melville* Scammon slaughtered grays. When his competitors learned of "Scammon Lagoon," off the Bay of Bizcaino, they had a whale of a picnic, nearly extinguishing the mammal.

BAKER'S ITCH

People earning their bread as bakers face several sources of dermatitis. Wet, sticky dough is a common cause, as are soaps and detergents used to remove the dough. The persulfate flour improvers, which activate yeast, are a cause of contact allergy; they are banned in most countries.

BALBOA, VASCO NÚÑEZ de

The Spanish conquistador was the first European (1513) to see the eastern shore of the Pacific Ocean, which he claimed, along with all shores washed by it, for the crown. "Then felt I like some watcher of the skies When a new planet swims into his ken; Or like stout Cortez when with eagle eyes He star'd at the Pacific—and all his men Look'd at each other with a wild surmise—Silent, upon a peak in Darien." On orders from Spain, Balboa was summarily seized, accused of treason, and beheaded. John Keats was also to be bemused.

BALDING

The human scalp contains about 100,000 hairs. The part of a hair that is below the surface of the skin sits in a baglike structure called the follicle. The length of a single hair depends on the duration of the growing phase of the follicle. Follicles in the human scalp are active for two to six years; then they rest for about three months. A hair grows less than half an inch per month. The color is determined largely by the amount and the distribution of a brown-black pigment called melanin. When pigment no longer forms, hair becomes gray or white. Baldness occurs when the follicles die. The most common cause of follicle death is heredity.

BALI

Ha'i. The westernmost of the six Lesser Sunda Islands in 13,600-island Indonesia floats in the sunshine where the sky meets the sea, nearly twice as many square miles as Rhode Island, with more than 2 million people (Hindus in a predominantly Muslim nation), many noted for their artistic skill, physical beauty, and high level of culture—the hills are alive with the sound of culture—volcanic (actively), mountainous (Mount Agung is 10,308 feet high), tigers and deer abound, the giant waringin tree is sacred. Oscar Hammerstein observed, "Bali Ha'i may call you any night, any day." The five other Lesser (known) Sundas are Flores, Lombok, Sumba, Sumbawa, and Timor. The Greater Sunda Islands are Borneo, the third largest island in the world (after Greenland and New Guinea); Celebes; Java, the most heavily populated island of Indonesia; and Sumatra, the sixth largest island in the world. The seasons throughout Indonesia are based on differences in rainfall, not in temperature change. Denpasar is the capital of Bali.

47

BALLESTEROS, SEVERIANO

The youngest golfer, at barely twenty-three, to win the prestigious Masters, in April 1980. He carded an even par in the final round and a total of 275 on the Augusta (Georgia) National course to finish 13 strokes under par and four strokes better than the pair tied for second. A year earlier, the Spaniard had won the British Open with his beautiful swing and his muscle and instinct. Ballesteros copped the Masters again in 1983.

BALLPOINT PEN

The Hungarian brothers Biro—Georg, a chemist, and Ladislao J., a hypnotist, a sculptor, a journalist, a painter—agreed on the advantage of a quick-drying ink for use in pens. They constructed the prototype ballpoint and in 1938 applied for a patent. They fled the encroaching Nazi menace, moved to Paris, then to Argentina, where they received a patent in 1943. A British financial backer, on a mission in Buenos Aires for the British government, acquired British rights and began producing ballpoints for the R.A.F. in a disused aircraft hangar near Reading. An American, Milton Reynolds by name, developed a gravity-fed pen without infringing the Biro patents. It went on sale on October 29, 1945, at Gimbels, the Manhattan department store; nearly 10,000 pens were sold in a single day, at a price of $12.50 each. In the late 1950s, Bic Crystal breached the pentup need for a throwaway ballpoint pen.

BALTIC SEA

It's between Riga and Stockholm, between Goteborg and Copenhagen, between Rostock and Malmo, between Gdansk and Oland, a 163,000-square-mile crooked arm of the Atlantic Ocean in northern Europe and the scene of the worst maritime disaster ever. In 1945, a Russian submarine, the S-13, torpedoed the German vessel *Wilhelm Gustloff* in the relatively shallow sea. Close to 8,000 people drowned, most of them women and children, fleeing the last days of the Third Reich.

BALTIMORE ORIOLES

Baseball's winningest team from 1957 to 1983, by .014 over the second-place New York Yankees. Since 1969, when division play was instituted in the major leagues, the Orioles have won the pennant the most times: five. Manager Earl Weaver stressed pitching and went for the big inning;

he wasn't much for the sacrifice bunt or for the hit-and-run, one-run tactic. During his nearly 15 years as skipper, Weaver was ejected from 89 games. The Orioles were once (since 1902) the St. Louis Browns, which sent a midget to bat in a publicity stunt in 1951. Eddie Gaedel wore number "⅛" on his little uniform and without prior announcement—no batting practice, no nothing—went to bat in the bottom half of the first inning of the second game of a doubleheader against the Detroit Tigers. The twenty-six-year-old righthanded swinger never got an official time at bat because he was walked, on four laughable pitches; he then was pinch-run for. Two days later, Gaedel's contract was voided in the best interests of baseball. The Browns subsequently moved to Baltimore.

BANFF NATIONAL PARK

Eighty miles west of Calgary cow country, Banff is the oldest (founded in 1887) of the national parks in Canada's jagged Rocky Mountains: together, the parks are a reserve larger in size than the state of Massachusetts. Banff, on the Bow River, and Jasper, the largest park, are in the province of Alberta. The others—Mt. Assiniboine, Kootenay, Yoho, Glacier, Hamber, and Mt. Robson—are in British Columbia. In all, Canada has 31 national parks. The Canadian Pacific's granite, baronial hotel in the town of Banff has 600 rooms.

BANKS, ERNIE

The best power hitter to play shortstop, Mr. Cub never played in a World Series. (Through 1984, it was 39 years since the Cubs had been in Series play.) He played a record-setting 424 consecutive games at the start of his career, in the mid-fifties. He was the National League's most valuable player two years in a row, 1958–59, and his 47 home runs in '58 represent the most struck in a season by any shortstop. His 41 homers in 1960 were tops in the league. In 19 campaigns, the All-Star infielder (shortstop and first base) played 2,528 games, banged out an average of more than a hit a game (2,582 in all, including 512 home runs) and knocked across 1,636 runs. He's been in the Hall of Fame since 1977.

BANNISTER, ROGER

He was like a man going to the electric chair that day in 1954 when he became the first person in history to break the "unbreakable" physical and psychological barrier of the four-minute mile. After all, the art of running the mile consists, in essence, of reaching the threshold of unconsciousness at the instant of breasting the tape. The tall, pale-skinned British neurologist did it outdoors, in 3:59.4, in Oxford. The next year, Jim Beatty went under four minutes indoors. Sebastian Coe has held the outdoor-mile record at 3:47.33 and Eamonn Coghlan the indoor mark, 3:49.78.

BANTRY BAY

The head of the picturesque twenty-one-mile-long inlet of the Atlantic Ocean in Cork County, southwest Republic of Ireland, was the site of tragedy in the early hours of January 8, 1979. Fifty people were killed when the French oil tanker *Betelgeuse* exploded close to the Gulf Oil terminal at Whiddy Island. The tanker was accessible to firefighters only by boat or by rubber rafts. The terminal had been built in 1968 to handle and store crude oil transported in supertankers from the Middle East.

BARBADOS

Originally Los Barbados, for the bearded fig trees the Portuguese found there, the 166-square-mile island state in the Windward Islands in the easternmost West Indies is a land without a river. George Washington contracted smallpox there. The constabulary in the capital, Bridgetown, wear the same uniform as did British limeys under Horatio Nelson. The densely populated island is about 90 percent black, and the "poor whites" are known locally as "redshanks." A delicacy is the flying fish caught in the nearby Caribbean.

BAR MITZVAH

Literally, "son of the commandment," that is, one who is responsible to perform the commandment. Ceremony marks the passage of a thirteen-year-old Jewish male into the religious community. It is comparatively recent; it was not held before the thirteenth or fourteenth century. The boy reads from the Scroll of the Law on the Sabbath at his thirteenth birthday and is addressed in the synagogue by the rabbi. The initiation of a thirteen-year-old girl is called Bat Mitzvah.

BAROMETER

The instrument for measuring atmospheric pressure—a change in pressure usually means the weather will change—was invented by Galileo's last secretary and companion, the Italian physicist Evangelista Torricelli, who had been profoundly affected when he first read the blind old man's works, in 1638. Torricelli attributed the day-by-day changes in the height of mercury in a tube to the fact that the atmosphere must possess a slightly different weight at different times. He was right. The atmospheric pressure at sea level is 29.92 inches of mercury, or 14.7 pounds per square inch. The decrease with elevation is approximately one inch for every 900 feet of ascent. A rising barometer means that fair weather is on the horizon—usually. A falling barometer means that foul weather is probably on the way.

BARTLETT, ENOCH

In France and England, a particular pear has been known for centuries as the "bon chrétien." A Captain Thomas Brewer brought one of the pear's trees back with him to the New World and planted it on his farm in Roxbury, Massachusetts. A Dorchester merchant, Enoch Bartlett, bought Brewer's farm, in the nineteenth century, and began distributing what is today his popular eponym, or epearnym, to the peachy punster.

BASEBALL

The 1953 season marked the first time in half a century that there was a new major-league baseball city. The Boston Braves pulled up stakes in Beantown and became the Milwaukee Braves. They later became the Atlanta Braves, and Milwaukee got a new club, the Brewers, which made it to the seventh game of the World Series in 1982. Air transportation made major moves and expansion possible. The Brooklyn Dodgers and the New York Giants moved to greener pastures in Los Angeles and San Francisco in 1958. The American League increased from eight teams to ten in 1961 and the National League followed suit in 1962. Ten more major league teams were added in the last two decades. In 1969, each league had 12 clubs—two six-team divisions—and for the first time major league baseball was an international game: Montreal joined the National League. A second Canadian club, Toronto, joined the American League in 1977. The English game of "rounders" evolved into baseball; under rules established by Alexander J. Cartwright, a surveyor and an amateur athlete, who umpired, the New York Nine defeated the Knickerbockers, at the Elysian Fields, in Hoboken, New Jersey, on June 19, 1846, in a form of the game no one had ever seen—the seeds were sown for organized baseball. Abner Doubleday did not invent baseball in Cooperstown, New York. The West Point graduate should be a national figure, however; he fired back the first shot from the Union's Fort Sumter, in Charleston bay, in the first duel in the Civil War, in April 1861.

BASEBALL—ATTENDANCE

Baseball—the major leagues, the minor leagues, the colleges—is the current number-one spectator sport in the United States, overtaking horse racing, thoroughbred and harness combined. In 1983, baseball attendance was 78,051,343 and racing attendance was 75,784,430. Racing still outdrew baseball in eight major cities—Detroit, Baltimore, Philadelphia, New York, Boston, Los Angeles, Chicago, and San Francisco. Football, basketball, and hockey were the third, fourth, and fifth most popular sports with exact attendance figures. Automobile racing drew 55,122,329, but it's an estimated figure and thus does not move the sport into the third slot in national popularity.

BASEBALL FIRSTS—GLOVE, ETC.

First designated hitter, 1973; first night World Series game, 1971; first Canadian team (Montreal), 1968; first domed stadium, 1965; first black in the Hall of Fame, 1962; first expansion in modern times, 1961; first franchises on the West Coast, 1958; first franchise shifts of modern times, 1953; first black players, 1947; first team to wear helmets at bat, 1941; first telecast, 1939; first commissioner, 1921; first Sunday game in New York, 1919; first use of cork center in the baseball itself, 1910; first U.S. President at opening game, 1909; first shin guards for catcher, 1907; first American League game, 1901; first catcher to work continuously behind bat, 1887; first use of chest protectors for catchers and umpires, 1885; first use of reserve clause in player contract, 1879; first glove, 1875; first catcher's mask, 1875; first calling of balls and strikes, 1863; first player's uniform, 1849; first match game, 1846.

BASEBALL HALL OF FAME

Ty Cobb, with the most votes, Babe Ruth, Christy Mathewson, Honus Wagner, and Walter Johnson were the first immortals selected for the National Baseball Hall of Fame, in Cooperstown, New York. Baseball writers did the voting in 1936 and induction took place in 1939, when the Hall was dedicated. (Unsubstantiated data led a baseball committee in 1907 to conclude that the game had been created in Cooperstown by a West Point cadet, Abner Doubleday. It was first designed somewhat as we know it at the Elysian Fields, in Hoboken, New Jersey, on June 19,

1846, by a surveyor and amateur athlete, Alexander J. Cartwright.) Cobb: the game's most dynamic and fiercest competitor, the dominant figure for twenty-four years, the career batting champ who hit .323 in his final season when he was forty-one years old. Ruth: the most fabulous figure in baseball, an outstanding pitcher (89 wins in six seasons) who became the greatest power hitter and the highest paid player of his time and brought baseball a lush period. Mathewson: an All-American boy from Bucknell who pitched 373 victories in the National League from 1900 to 1916 (20 or more wins in a dozen straight years) and 3 shutouts in the 1905 World Series, Big Six (for a famous New York fire engine) had his career aborted by being gassed in World War I and by tuberculosis. Wagner: the greatest all-around player, the best shortstop, the National League's best hitter (better than .300 for seventeen straight seasons), the bowlegged Flying Dutchman had a ponderous chest and gorilla-like arms. Johnson: The Big Train, the fastest express of them all: 416 sidearming victories with the cellar-dwelling Washington Senators, 3,508 strikeouts, 5,924 innings pitched, 531 complete games, 113 shutouts.

BASEBALL—HOMESTEAD GRAYS, OTHER BLACK TEAMS

The Grays of Pittsburgh, the Monarchs of Kansas City were top black baseball teams, but the dominant team in the first three years of the Negro National League, formed in 1920, was the Chicago American Giants. Tracing the course of the organized black leagues has been likened to trying to follow a single black strand through a ton of spaghetti. The author of *Only the Ball Was White* has observed that (1) the black leagues (and most of the teams) were consistently underfinanced and (2) there was little leadership, and (3) the leagues in their three decades never approached in stability or discipline the level of white organized baseball because of (1) and (2). Stars in the Negro leagues now in baseball's Hall of Fame: Cool Papa Bell, who played for both the Grays and the Monarchs, Oscar Charleston, Martin Dihigo, Rube Foster, Josh Gibson (a stupendous home-run clouter), Monte Irvin, Judy Johnson, Buck Leonard, John Lloyd, and Satchel Paige. Rube Foster, who organized the Negro National League, was black baseball's best pitcher for nearly a decade with the Cuban Giants and the Philadelphia Giants. In 1910, he managed the Chicago Leland Giants and posted a 123–6 record.

BASEBALL—NO-HITTERS

Vickers? Worcester? Barker? They're among the 17 pitchers of perfect games in baseball's major leagues through the 1984 season. Only one was a World Series game, the Yankees' Don Larsen's 2–0 shutdown of the

Brooklyn Dodgers at Yankee Stadium on October 8, 1956. (This author was a witness in the leftfield mezzanine.) Only three pitching greats are in the pantheon: Cy Young, Boston vs. Philadelphia (A.L.), 3–0, May 5, 1904; Sandy Koufax, Los Angeles vs. Chicago (N.L.), 1–0, Sept. 9, 1965; Catfish Hunter, Oakland vs. Minnesota (A.L.), 4–0, May 8, 1968. Harvey Haddix lost a perfect game in extra innings. The Boston Red Sox's Ernie Shore's perfect game (4–0 over Washington, 1917) has an asterisk next to it because he didn't pitch the whole game. Babe Ruth had pitched to the first Senator, Ray Morgan, walking him, then argued the base on balls so vociferously that he was thumbed out of the game. Shore came on to pitch. Morgan was thrown out stealing second and Shore retired the 26 Senators he faced. Perfect pitchers include: John Richmond, Worcester vs. Cleveland (N.L.), 1–0, June 12, 1880; John Ward, Providence vs. Buffalo (N.L.), 5–0, June 17, 1880; Ed Karger, St. Louis vs. Boston (N.L.), 4–0, 7 innings, Aug. 11, 1907; Harry Vickers, Philadelphia vs. Washington (A.L.), 5–0, 5 innings, Oct. 5, 1907; Addie Joss, Cleveland vs. Chicago (A.L.), 1–0, Oct. 2, 1908; Charles Robertson, Chicago vs. Detroit (A.L.), 2–0, April 30, 1922; Harvey Haddix, Pittsburgh vs. Milwaukee (N.L.), 0–1, 13 innings, May 26, 1959; Jim Bunning, Philadelphia vs. Mets (N.Y.), 6–0, June 21, 1964; Dean Chance, Minnesota vs. Boston (A.L.), 2–0, 5 innings, Aug. 6, 1967; Len Barker, Cleveland vs. Toronto (A.L.), 3–0, May 15, 1981; David Palmer, Montreal vs. St. Louis (N.L.), 4–0, 5 innings, April 21, 1984; Mike Witt, California vs. Texas (A.L.), Sept. 30, 1984.

BASEBALL—TRIPLE CROWN

Only thirteen times has a player led one of the major baseball leagues in homers, runs batted in, and batting percentage in the same year, and only Ted Williams (1942, 1947) and Rogers Hornsby (1922, 1925) have won the crown two times apiece. The other triple crown winners: Carl Yastrzemski (the most recent winner, 1967), Frank Robinson, Mickey Mantle, Joe Medwick, Lou Gehrig, Jimmy Foxx, Chuck Klein, Henry Zimmerman, and Ty Cobb. Mantle hit the most home runs in a triple crown year: 52; Gehrig, the most RBIs, 165; Hornsby had the best BAV, .403.

BASTILLE

French for "fortress," which is what the massive structure with eight great towers and a moat was when it was built in the fourteenth century to command one of the gates of Paris. It became a state prison with a generally undeserved reputation as a place of horrors. Among its celebrated residents were the Man in the Iron Mask—if there really was such

a prisoner—Voltaire, and the Marquis de Sade with writing (and writh-
ing) tools in hand. By July 14, 1789, the Bastille had become a hated
symbol of tyranny. Lower-class Parisians spontaneously seized arms
from the Invalides and stormed the Bastille for its stores of ammunition,
then razed the structure—the French Revolution was afire. "Bastille
Day" acquired symbolic significance and became the national holiday of
republican France.

BATON ROUGE

It's French for "red stick." In a 1722 report received in Paris: ". . . because there is in this place a reddened post, which the savages have
placed, to mark the division of the lands of two nations, namely: that of
the Bayogoulas from which we came, and the other about 30 leagues
higher than Baton Rouge, called the Oumas." The city was built along
the fifty-foot Istrouma Bluff on the east bank of the Mississippi River and
has been French, English, Spanish, West Floridian, Louisianan, Confederate, and American. It became Louisiana's capital city in 1849 after the
capital had been New Orleans, Donaldsonville, and New Orleans a second time. The seat of state government moved thrice when the South
rebelled: to Opelousas, then to Alexandria, then to Shreveport, before
returning for good to Baton Rouge in the 1880s.

BATTERY

Battery is from the Middle French *battre,* to beat. An electric battery is
a group of two or more cells connected together to furnish electric current. A cell consists of two electrodes immersed in an electrolyte, which
acts chemically upon the electrodes to produce the current. Thomas Edison did his best to make an electric-storage battery for the early electric
cars. When his much-heralded unit didn't work, he recalled every single
one of them and made prompt and full refunds from his own pocket. The
Wizard of Menlo Park eventually produced an improved, rechargeable
battery, but by that time the internal combustion engine was lord of the
road. Edison's battery became the workhorse in mining, on shipboard,
and for telegraphy, submarines, and railway signaling.

BATTLE OF THE BULGE

Hitler's last gasp on the western front in World War II. On December 16,
1944: The German Fifth and Sixth Panzer armies under Marshal Karl von
Rundstedt surprisingly and massively counterattack the thinly held forty-

mile American front in the Belgian Ardennes; their goal is the port of Antwerp, already being pounded heavily by V-2 missiles. Dec. 17: Allied reinforcements rush to the Ardennes. About 90 American prisoners of war are shot dead—possibly by mistake—in the Nazis' "Malmédy Massacre." Dec. 17–18: German troops advance deep into Belgium, creating a "bulge" in the lines of outnumbered American regiments. Dec. 19: Bastogne is all but surrounded. Dec. 20: German troops pressure American forces at St.-Vith. Dec. 21: American Brigadier General Anthony C. McAuliffe responds "Nuts" when issued an ultimatum to surrender his besieged Bastogne forces. Dec. 23: Supplies are air-dropped to the Bastogne garrison. Dec. 24: Reinforcements begin arriving—two American armies temporarily under British Field Marshal Bernard Montgomery in the North, the U.S. Third Army under General George S. Patton in the South. Christmas Day: The Bastogne perimeter holds against German pressure, but German tanks advance to within four miles of the Meuse. Dec. 26: The Bastogne siege is lifted. The Nazis' tactical victory delayed by six weeks the Allied drive on the Fatherland. January 28, 1945: The last Germans are expelled from the Ardennes bulge and the battle line is restored to the status of December 16. Casualties: the Germans—100,000 dead and wounded and up to a thousand planes. Allies: twenty-nine American and four British divisions suffer 75,000 dead and wounded. On March 7, the Allies cross the Rhine.

BATTLE OF HASTINGS

William, Duke of Normandy, secured the support of the Pope and led an army of 5,000 men across the English Channel, landing without opposition at Pevensey, near Hastings, slew King Harold II in a momentous clash on October 14, 1066, established Norman rule of England, became known as William the Conqueror and, on December 25 of that same year, he was crowned the proud, ruthless King of England, putting the lords under his direct control. He directed the preparation (1085–86) of the *Domesday Book,* an economic survey of all regions in his kingdom for purposes of more accurate taxation.

BATTLE OF MIDWAY

Japanese Admiral Isoruku Yamamoto—"the sword of my emperor"— had planned the devastating attack on Pearl Harbor. Now, in June 1942, he planned to destroy the last United States carriers, near Midway Island in the mid-Pacific. He went into battle with eight carriers, eleven battleships, eighteen cruisers, and sixty-five destroyers. The United States had three carriers, no battleships, eight cruisers, and fifteen destroyers, yet made it an early turning point of the war in the Pacific by handing the Japanese their first naval setback since 1592 (when the Koreans whipped the Japanese). The United States lost one carrier, the *Yorktown;* the Japanese lost four carriers. How did the Americans do it? The Navy could read the Japanese codes.

BATTLE OF NEW ORLEANS

It made Major General Andrew Jackson famous, a national hero. American rifle fire slaughtered crack British troops. It was January 1815—two weeks after the War of 1812 was over, after the Treaty of Ghent was signed. Another couple of weeks passed before news of the war's end even reached Louisiana. The war had started because of lagging communications—the United States opened hostilities because it did not know that British orders interfering with U.S. commerce had been repealed. For ignoring a federal judge's writ of habeas corpus during his emergency control of New Orleans, the future President was fined $1,000. Thirty years later, and a year before Jackson died, Congress refunded the money.

BATTLE OF THE SOMME

The Great War: on reclaimed marshland in Picardy, on the English Channel, in northern France, and along the river Somme, terrible, terrible carnage in 1916. There were no major strategic objectives and the task of excavating trenches in the chalk was immense. After a seven-day bombardment, the Allies attacked the Germans' strongest defenses on the western front. On the very first day, July 1, British units suffered 57,450 casualties and a great defeat. On September 15, they attacked on a ten-mile front with thirty-six units of the "weapon of the future"—the tank. By November, Allied forces had gained a few thousand yards. More than 1 million men, on both sides, died in the Battle of the Somme. Though exhausted, the Allies and the Central Powers killed each other all over the place for two more years. The war ended without a truly decisive battle having been fought and with German troops still occupying territory from the Crimea to France.

BAY OF PIGS

"The greatest mistake of my administration"—that's what President John F. Kennedy called his failure to cancel the planned invasion of the west coast of Cuba in 1961 by anti-Castro Cuban exiles who had been encouraged by the Eisenhower administration and funded and trained by the Central Intelligence Agency. Two weeks before Kennedy was sworn, the United States had broken relations with Castro. It's been called a curious gesture for a lame-duck administration to make, but many of Eisenhower's associates, notably in the C.I.A., were eager that the Bay of Pigs operation go forward: "Severing diplomatic relations with Cuba made it harder for Kennedy and Castro to communicate," insider William Attwood has written, "let alone negotiate the differences that led to the Bay of Pigs fiasco." Several hundred of the invaders were killed, at least a thousand were captured and imprisoned, and the Cuban masses did not rise up and sweep communism from the country.

BAYONET

The town of Bayonne in the Pyrenees-Atlantiques department, in southwest France, in Gascony, on the Adour River near its entrance into the Bay of Biscay, is famous for at least three historic events: it successfully resisted a British siege at the close of the Peninsular War, Charles IV and Ferdinand VII of Spain abdicated there to Napoleon, and a steel dagger was attached to the muzzle of a rifle there—the first "bayonnet," or bayonet.

BEACH BOYS

The first public performance of the extended Wilson family was at a New Year's Eve 1961 memorial concert in Long Beach, California, and there were good vibrations. Six months later, they recorded "Surfin'." Shy Brian Wilson was conceptually responsible for the rock-'n'-roll band. One reason for its longevity: "You can tell your brother or your cousin that he's a jerk," Mike Love has explained, "where you couldn't even a good friend. You know his strengths and weaknesses, and he knows yours, and you can't fire your family." The high, tight wall of harmony, counterpoint, and background, with rich vocals and orchestration leaning in and out of rising balanced music with a shape and an energy of its own, clear and powerful, was music that the beach and sunshine culture of Southern California could ride—the perfect wave curled even around the Ronald Reagans.

BEAN, JUDGE ROY

"The law west of the Pecos" had been a cattle rustler in Mexico, and during the Civil War he joined a band of lawless irregulars fighting with the Confederacy. He followed the construction camps of the Southern Pacific Railroad across the desolate parts of southwestern Texas and gained a reputation as a saloonkeeper and a gambler. In 1882, he settled in Vinegaroon, had it renamed Langtry (for the vivacious English actress Lillie Langtry), and set up in the Jersey Lily a combination saloon and courtroom. He handed down justice with a law book in one hand and a six-shooter in the other—his decisions were arbitrary and unorthodox. In 1896, he arranged to have the Bob Fitzsimmons–Peter Maher prize fight staged near Langtry. Bean has been portrayed in the movies by Walter Brennan, Edgar Buchanan, and Paul Newman.

BEATLES

Ringo Starr: "I was in the greatest show on earth, for what it was worth; now I'm only thirty-two and all I want to do is boogaboo." Paul Mc-Cartney: "Sophie Tucker was our favorite group." George Harrison: "Anywhere is paradise!" John Lennon: "None of us would've made it alone, because Paul wasn't quite strong enough, I didn't have enough girl appeal, George was too quiet, and Ringo was the drummer. But we thought everyone would be able to dig at least one of us, and that's how it turned out . . . The Beatles made it, and they stopped touring and they had all the money they wanted, and all the fame they wanted and they found out they had nothing. . . . The hardest thing is facing yourself. It's easier to shout 'Revolution' and 'Power to the People' than it is to look at yourself and try to find out what's real inside you and what isn't, when you're pulling the wool over your own eyes. That's the hardest one." The Beatles were first called the Quarrymen. John was the leader while studying at Liverpool College of Art. Paul gave up the trumpet—the trumpet hurt his lips—and joined the group and brought in George, his longtime friend. The Beatles took their name from the new beat music. At one time they all but threw in the towel. Pickings were thin—"It's getting hard to be someone . . ." Decca didn't offer a recording contract in January 1962, after the Beatles had been voted the number-one group by Liverpool's *Merseybeat* magazine. Another Beatle, in the Hamburg days, was Stu Sutcliffe, a former schoolmate of John. He was bass guitar, and he died at age 21, in 1962, from a burst blood vessel in the brain. He was an abstract painter, and was considered exceptionally talented.

BEAU GESTE

Gary Cooper was the French Foreign Legionnaire in the 1939 movie. He had starred in the first motion picture to win a best picture Academy Award—*Wings* (1927)—the only silent movie to win one; "Coop," himself, twice won a best actor Oscar, for *Sergeant York* (1941) and *High Noon* (1952). (Alvin York agreed to let his heroism in World War I be the subject of a movie only when he was assured that he would be portrayed by Cooper.) The six-foot-three All-American male was the son of a justice of the Montana Supreme Court. He learned to ride, shoot, and punch cows on the family's small (450 head) ranch. He was inspired by Tom Mix and began his film career playing cowboy extras. In *Beau Geste,* directed by William A. Wellman, Cooper's brothers were played by Ray Milland and Robert Preston (Donald O'Connor played Beau as a young man), and the martinet officer was Brian Donlevy; for honor's sake, the Gestes leave England and join up with the Foreign Legion.

BEAVER

The second-largest living rodent (a member of a gnawing family)—the four-foot capybara in Central America and much of South America is the largest—is indeed an eager beaver. It is always doing something, such as cutting down trees with its four curved front teeth and dragging them to a nearby pond to build a dam. The aquatic engineer-geographers sleep by day, work by night. They can swim underwater up to 15 minutes at a time. They do not eat fish. Baby beavers are born in the spring and are called kits or pups. When the beaver was nearly trapped out of existence —12 skins could be traded for a rifle—the ecology in North America changed. Laws now protect the furry animal with the wide, flat tail that looks like a paddle. Now they can be killed and skinned only at prescribed times.

BEER

"Throw all the beer and spirits into the Irish Channel, the English Channel, and the North Sea for a year, and people in England would be infinitely better. It would certainly solve all the problems with which the philanthropists, the physicians, and the politicians have to deal." So said the eminent physician Sir William Osler in 1905. Over the past 20 years, people around the world have been drinking more and more, and mostly it's been beer. The World Health Organization says it's enough to drive the tea totaler to drink: "In virtually all countries for which statistics are available, cirrhosis, which is often used as an index of the extent of alcohol damage, now ranks among the five leading causes of death among males aged 26 to 64." Production of beer has foamed up 500 percent in Asia, 400 percent in Africa, and 200 percent in Latin America. West Germany drinks the most beer per head. Officials of W.H.O. say that the human costs are incalculable while acknowledging that production and sales of alcoholic beverages create jobs. Too, taxes on drink are a source of revenue: "Economically, alcohol is an important commodity." Give an Irishman lager for a month, and he's a dead man, Mark Twain said. "An Irishman is lined with copper, and the beer corrodes it. But whiskey polishes the copper and is the saving of him."

BEES

They are pollinators. Nearly 100 crops (e.g., red clover, orchids) in the United States alone are dependent on pollination by the honeybee. Some forest and range plants must be pollinated by bees to produce seeds on which birds and other wildlife are dependent. There are 20,000 species of this flying insect of the superfamily *Apoidae*. The honeybee is naturally a social bee. Nectar is converted to honey in its digestive tract. There are the female workers in the hive, maybe 50,000 of them. There are the male drones, 1,000 or so. And there is one more bee: the queen. The Germans call her mother-bee, which is exactly what she is: the mother of the colony. She mates and she lays eggs, about 2,000 a day during the height of the summer. She does nothing else. But without her, the orderly functioning of the colony falls into chaos and disintegration. When four or five drones put the bee on her, their genital organs are torn away and remain in the body of the queen, and the males die. The queen won't fly again until she leaves the colony with a swarm. Only one federal law pertains to bees; adult bees carrying the mite *Acarapis woodi* cannot be imported into the States—such bees are unable to fly and they have disjointed wings and distended abdomens. Beekeeping is called apiculture. Sherlock Holmes retired to a farm and became an apiculturist. The bee is the only insect that makes a food that man eats—alimentary, dear Watson. To bee or not to bee, there is no question—if you're a wasp.

BEETLES

If that bug crawling on your arm has tough, armorlike forewings covering the membranous hind wings, which are used for flying, it's a beetle, the order of insect that contains the most species. Coleoptera ("sheath wings") is the largest order in the animal kingdom—a third of all known insects—300,000 known species worldwide, about 30,000 in North America, ranging in size from 5⅛" long to less than ¹⁄₁₆". Most species produce one generation every year; some, as many as four generations. Many beetles are predators, others are scavengers, a few are parasites. Some species attack plants and stored foods; others pollinate flowers and eat plant pests. The habitat of the dull black tumblebug is wherever dung of large mammals is underfoot. The tumblebug helps to convert the dung into fertilizer for plants.

BELGIUM

"Belgians" have been pushovers for warring armies. Conquerors of the small northwest European country have included Rome, the Franks, Burgundy, Spain, Austria, France—and Germany in both World Wars. During World War I, Allied propagandists claimed that the Huns were bayoneting and eating Belgian babies. The list of notable Walloons and Flemish is long: Jan van Eyck, Hans Memling, Hugo van der Goes, Hieronymus Bosch, Pieter Bruegel the Elder, Peter Paul Rubens, Anthony Van Dyck, Henri Evenepoel, James Ensor, Paul Delvaux, René Magritte, Henry van de Velde, Johannes Ockeghem, Josquin Des Prés, Heinrich Isaac, Pierre de la Rue, Adrian Willaert, Roland de Lassus, Andre Cluytens, Charles de Coster, Camille Lemonnier, Emile Verhaeren, Georges Simenon, Suzanne Lilar, and six Nobel Prize winners: Maurice Maeterlinck, Jules Bordet, Corneille J. F. Heymans, Auguste Beernaert, Henri Lafontaine, and Father Dominique Pire. Belgian literacy is 99 percent: either Flemish in the North or the French dialect Walloon in the South, or even both languages.

BELL, ALEXANDER GRAHAM

It was almost the Gray System. Elisha Gray's description of his invention arrived in the U.S. Patent Office only a few hours after Bell's. "It is a strange fact," the Scottish-born Bell once said, "that important inventions are often made almost simultaneously by different persons in different parts of the world." (While Charles Darwin was evolving his concept of evolution, another English naturalist, Alfred Russel Wallace, a few miles down the road, was evolving a similar concept from his study of comparative biology in Brazil and in the East Indies. Wallace, without knowledge of Darwin's work, sent his paper for comment to Darwin, always a worrywart. Darwin was thunderstruck—and offered to publish jointly with Wallace.) When Bell cried out, on March 10, 1876, that he needed his assistant, Thomas Watson, the apparatus on which Bell was working was so far developed that Watson elsewhere in the building got the message. The telephone was introduced to the world at the U.S. Centennial celebration in Philadelphia later that year. In 1915, Watson didn't come when he again heard Bell's call; this time, Bell was in New York and Watson was in San Francisco and they were demonstrating the first coast-to-coast telephone linkup. Sixteen years before Bell received U.S. patent 174,465, a German, Philipp Reis, had invented what, too, could be a telephone. The Reis System? At first, the ringing telephone was answered with "Ahoy!" Many Europeans today answer a call with a double hello—"Hello, hello."

BELLADONNA

A Janus word. Two-faced. Italian for "fine lady" or "fair lady," from *bella*, the feminine of *bello*, beautiful, from the Latin *bellus + donna*, lady. Belladonna is also the name of a perennial European poisonous plant, *Atropa belladonna*, which is grown extensively in the United States. It has reddish bell-shaped flowers and shining black bee berries. It is also called deadly nightshade. The flower yields atropine, variously used in medicine, as to relieve pain and check spasms. (Atropine from the Greek fate Atropos, who cut the thread of life.) Here's an eyeopener: Belladonnas used atropine as an eyedrop.

BELLOW, SAUL

The much-honored novelist—*Humboldt's Gift* (Pulitzer Prize, Nobel Prize), *Henderson the Rain King, Herzog, The Dean's December, The Dangling Man,* and most recently *Him With His Foot in His Mouth and Other Stories*—asks, "How could I be anything but a dissenter? Who wants the opinion of a group?" In an interview with D. J. R. Bruckner, the nearly 70-year-old Canadian-born Bellow, who grew up in slums in Montreal and Chicago and is now also a teacher in the Committee on Social Thought at the University of Chicago, revealed himself a bit—he never bellows: "My life would be terribly abstract if I didn't have my students to talk with about what I am reading. . . . Why should I look for honorable standards in the literary world now? They haven't been there for a long time. . . . Who would not prefer the vulgarity of Chicago to the finesse of the East Coast literary establishment? You have to count your blessings, you know . . . It is certainly hard to see how modern man could survive on what he gets from his conscious life—especially now that there is a kind of veto against impermissible thoughts, the most impermissible being the notion that man might have a spiritual life he's not conscious of." Bellow told "60 Minutes," "You write a book, you put the force of your imagination into it, then you hand it over to lots of people who have no imagination for writing or for their own enterprise, and you're up against it."

BENNY, JACK

For 64,000 silver dollars, who was the only contestant on "The $64,000 Question" television quiz program who quit after the first question?

Okay, a hint. He knew a terrific publicity idea when he thought of it. Okay, another hint. His public persona adored money. Getting warm? He was Mr. Pinchpenny. Right! Mr. Benny. When "The $64,000 Question" was reaping reams of publicity and contestants were walking off with bundles, the nationally loved comedian—"Jello again, it's Jack Benny"—called Hal March, the master of ceremonies, and arranged to go on the program. His category would be the violin. The first question, for $64, typically was easy: "Who was the famous eighteenth-century violin maker whose first name was Antonio?" Jack answered promptly: "Stradivari." "Right," March said. "You now have $64, Mr. Benny. Would you like to try for $128?" "No," Jack responded. The studio audience screamed, and March protested, "*No one* stops at $64." But Jack stopped. He was taking no chances; $64 were $64 in those days. And he didn't leave the stage until March took $64 out of his own pocket and handed it to him. Benny and the subject of money also got radio's biggest laugh. "Your money or your life," the stickup man said. For two minutes, Benny said nothing as the audience roared. "Quit stalling—I said your money or your life," the stickup man barked. Finally, Benny responded, to thunderous laughter, "I'm thinking it over." It was a purely radio joke; it died when Benny tried it on television. Another scene: Rochester took a quarter out of a pocket of Benny's pants in the dressing room to tip a Western Union boy. About a minute later, Jack entered and picked up his trousers to change into them. As he held up his trousers, he "weighed" them for a couple of seconds, then turned to his valet and asked, "Rochester, who took a quarter out of my pants' pocket?" That was worth a long audience scream. Benny didn't like his television programs to be called specials. To him, a special was "when coffee goes from ninety-eight cents a pound to forty-nine cents."

BENZ, KARL

Karl, Karl! Warum kaufste denn kein Pferd? Three wheels, an electric ignition, differential gears, rear engine, water-cooled—it was a 0.75-horsepower Benz, the first automobile powered by an internal-combustion engine—German engineer Karl Benz's baby. First driven in Mannheim, in 1885, patented in 1886. The single front wheel was steered by a handle, which also operated the brake. The Benz didn't immediately hit the open road. It immediately hit a wall, when the steering proved inadequate. (That's all right: eighteen years later, Wilbur didn't even get off the ground on the boys's first try at flying.) On his second start, Benz went a few hundred yards. His wife, Berta, in a tour de force, drove sixty-two miles from Mannheim to Pforzheim—the first journey ever by car. Business picked up when Benz agreed the tricar was both unstable and uncomfortable, a four-wheeler would be the ticket. In 1893, the Viktoria proved a triumph—forty-five of the double rack-and-pinion-steering, 3-h.p. cars were snapped up as if they were going out of style.

BERGEN, EDGAR, AND CHARLIE McCARTHY

Candice Bergen's impudent "sibling" was based on a quick-witted, brassy, cocksure, redheaded Irish boy named Charlie, who sold newspapers on a corner in Decatur, Illinois. A barkeep named Mack who was something of a woodcarver worked with Edgar on creating Charlie McCarthy: "The head, made of pine, was empty but for a rubber band that ran from the inside top of the skull to the back of the neck. The backbone was a broomstick, nine inches long, that terminated in a semi-disc hinged to the neck. Along the hickory spine, trail cords were attached to the lower jaw." Charlie weighed forty pounds, wore a perfect size 4, and took size 2AAA shoes. Ventriloquist Bergen was no dummy. When Mae West told Charlie that if he came up and saw her sometime, she'd let him play around in her woodpile, it made headlines, and radio ratings soared. Charlie spent years threatening, in his cocky cackle vow, to "*mow* you *down*, Bergen, so help me, I'll *mmooww ya' down*." In 1937, a wooden Oscar was given to Bergen. In 1938, Northwestern University awarded Charlie an honorary college degree. Charlie holds his peace today in the Smithsonian Institution.

BERLIN, IRVING

He wrote a melody, not used, for the all-soldier show *Yip, Yip, Yaphank* during World War I. He dusted it off in 1938 and wrote to it the lyrics "God Bless America." Kate Smith sang it on a radio program on Armistice Day and it became even more popular than the national anthem. Berlin divides the royalties among the Boy Scouts, the Girl Scouts, and the Campfire Girls. To celebrate the publication of his song "Marie of Sunny Italy"—in 1907—he changed his name from Israel Baline. *Annie Get Your Gun* needed a song. Doing what came naturally, he knocked off "Doin' What Comes Naturally" during a taxicab ride from a rehearsal to his home. Many of his 3,000 compositions will be standards forever: "White Christmas," "Alexander's Ragtime Band," "Easter Parade," "Let's Face the Music and Dance," "I Left My Heart at the Stage Door Canteen," "Puttin' on the Ritz," "A Pretty Girl Is Like a Melody" (the hit of the Follies of 1919), "Everybody's Doin' It." Nobody has done it quite like the little Russian immigrant whose marriage to a New York blueblood, Ellin Mackay, heiress of the Postal Telegraph, caused a sensation—but they danced cheek to cheek into the sunset. There's no business like Berlin business.

BERLIN WALL

It's now more than a score of years since the concrete barrier with its steel girders, dog-runs, watchtowers, tank traps, and electronic "death strips" was erected. On August 13, 1961, barbed wire, heavily armed troops, and teams of Volkspolizei first controlled the passage of East Germans to the western sector of Berlin. Construction of the formal 100-mile symbol of the Cold War began apace a few days later. Among the obstacles are trenches with camouflaged steel meshes that can swallow any vehicle, or anything else, that attempts to pass over them. It was from a platform at the wall that President John F. Kennedy announced that he, too, was a Berliner.

BERMUDA BOWL

It is the trophy at stake in the World Team Contract Bridge Championship. It was in Bermuda, in 1950, that the first post-World War II world contract bridge team championship was played, at the initiative of Norman M. Bach. Teams represented Europe (a combined Sweden-Iceland team), Great Britain (the European champion), and the United States (the winner). During the early qualifying stages of the Bermuda Bowl's 25th anniversary tourney, two players were accused of using foot signals. The World Bridge Federation was unable to find a correlation between the foot movements and the team's play and dismissed the charge with a reprimand; the players were found guilty only of "improper" foot movements. Coffee tables were placed beneath the card tables to block the future possibility of foot-movement signals. Italy has been the Bermuda Bowl champion the most times.

BERMUDA TRIANGLE

The mystery began in December 1945. Five TBM Avengers, U.S. torpedo bombers equipped with navigational and radio equipment, disappeared over the Atlantic off the coast of Florida. A sixth plane searching for the five also vanished. The Navy searched the ocean floor but found no debris. The ocean separating Florida and Bermuda and Puerto Rico is said to be characterized by magnetic and gravitational anomalies. Did the planes have a close encounter of the third kind? Did they pass into the fourth dimension? Was there a conspiracy and did the six pilots by design fly to a Central American country so they could begin new lives?

BERNSTEIN, LEONARD

He was hung over from an all-night party when he got the call that changed his life—he had to go on in a few hours for the indisposed Bruno Walter. Going on meant that he would have to conduct the New York Philharmonic in a Sunday afternoon concert at Carnegie Hall. He knew the score—the critics were alerted and were on hand *en masse*—and he's been at the top of the charts ever since, as conductor (the first American on the rostrum at La Scala in Milan), composer (symphonic, operatic, musical comedy), and lecturer. He excited "Omnibus" viewers by walking all over the first measures of Beethoven's *Fifth:* da-da-da-smart. "Some people *have* 'explained' the glory of a thunderstorm—now and then, with varying degrees of success—and such people are called poets. Only artists can explain magic; only art can substitute for nature. By the same token, only art can substitute for art. And so the only way one can really say anything about music is to write music." Thus spake—and does—Lenny.

BIATHLON

"It's a bitch" is the way that a polite biathloner speaks of his Olympic event in a family book. Skiing over a twenty-kilometer cross-country course, sometimes in dastardly weather, the competitor stops at designated points to fire his rifle at a stationary target. He races the clock. Time is added to the run as a penalty for a missed target.

THE BIBLE

From the Greek for "the books," the Bible is the name used by Christians for their Scriptures. It is the world's most widely distributed book. Portions have been translated into more than 1,600 languages. United Bibles Societies reports that more than 6 billion copies were printed in the last four decades alone. By contrast, the crime novels of the two top-selling authors, Erle Stanley Gardner and Agatha Christie, have barely reached the combined figure of 600 million copies. Before the New Testament was composed, the Old Testament was called The Law and the Prophets. There are sixty-six books in the King James Version: thirty-nine in the Old Testament, twenty-seven in the New Testament. (Jesus wrote none of the books.) Two of the books begin with the words "In the beginning. . . .": Genesis 1:1, John 1:1. The first five books of the Old Testament are known collectively as the Torah. Deuteronomy takes the form of three farewell speeches by Moses. There are 436 "missing" years between the last book of the Old Testament and the first book of the New Testament. In Greek, the language of the New Testament, the word "gospel" means "good news." The New Testament does not record Jesus' life between the age of twelve, when he was at the Temple, and his baptism at the age of thirty. There is no mention of the Virgin Birth or of the Sermon on the Mount in the Gospels according to Mark and John. Jesus' cry upon the cross, "My God, my God, why hast thou forsaken me?," first appears in Psalms. On learning of the miracles of Jesus, King Herod Antipas averred that they must be the work of John the Baptist risen from the dead. Mass extermination of Jews was not an original idea with Germany's Third Reich. In the book of Esther, Haman proposed a "final solution" to Persia's King Ahasuerus.

THE BIBLE—THE OLD TESTAMENT

Not everyone in Jericho was killed when the walls came tumblin' down and the massacre took place. The prostitute Rahab and her family were spared. "And they utterly destroyed all that was in the city, both man and woman, young and old, and ox, and sheep, and ass, with the edge of the sword. But Joshua had said unto the two men that had spied out the country, Go into the harlot's house, and bring out thence the woman, and all that she hath, as ye sware unto her. And the young men that were spies went in, and brought out Rahab, and her father, and her mother, and her brethren, and all that she had; and they brought out all her kindred, and left them without the camp of Israel. . . . and she dwelleth in Israel even unto this day; because she hid the messengers, which Joshua sent to spy out Jericho . . . the Lord was with Joshua; and his fame was noised throughout all the country." The twenty-fourth, and last, chapter in Joshua is regarded as one of the most important passages in the Old Testament—the covenant ceremony in which Joshua said, "Put away . . . the strange gods which are among you, and incline your heart unto the Lord God of Israel. And the people said unto Joshua, The Lord our God will we serve, and his voice will we obey. So Joshua made a covenant with the people that day, and set them a statute and an ordinance in Shechem. And Joshua wrote these words in the book of the law of God, and took a great stone, and set it up there under an oak, that was by the sanctuary of the Lord."

"BIG BERTHA"

Two different sets of long-range German howitzers of immense caliber were named during the Great War in "honor" of the ample waistline of

Frau Bertha Krupp von Bohlen, a scion of the munitions maker. She was the daughter interested in the financial rather than in the technical aspects of the Krupp works. She married von Bohlen und Halbach, who assumed the name Krupp and took over management of the firm, which later put muscle into Hitler's rearmament. The Big Berthas were not built by Krupp, however; they were produced by Skoda, in Austria-Hungary. Their 100-foot-long barrels hurled one-ton projectiles a distance of seventy-six miles, pounding Liège, Antwerp, and Verdun.

BIG SUR

A winding ninety-four-mile California highway across canyons on towering bridges between William Randolph Hearst's massive San Simeon and the village of Carmel in the north, rugged mountain flanks forming rocky, misty headlands alternating with deep coves in the Pacific, a wild and windswept coastline, dramatic clashing of solid land and surging sea —a gloriously scenic stretch. Freestanding rocks and pinnacles offshore are eroded remnants of headlands that once extended much farther out to sea.

BIKILA, ABEBE

Not only did this Ethiopian soldier in the Palace Guard of Emperor Haile Selassie win the Olympic Marathon in Rome, in 1960, and become the only man to win it a second time, in Tokyo, in 1964, and both times in record times, he ran the twenty-six-plus miles along the Appian Way in his bare feet. Some feat! Only two Americans have won the Marathon: Tommy Hicks in 1904 and Sullivan Award-winner (America's best amateur athlete) Frank Shorter, of Yale, in 1972. Hicks had finished second, but he was awarded the gold medal when the apparent winner admitted that he had gotten a lift in an automobile (!) a part of the way.

BINARY SYSTEM

This simple, nondecimal system uses only two symbols, usually 0 and 1. One is 1, two is 10, three is 11, four is 100, five is 101, six is 110, seven is 111, eight is 1000, and so forth. Early computers used O and C, for open and closed. Because the system is so simple and the two symbols can be translated easily into electric impulses (just "on" and "off"), binary arithmetic is used in computers.

69

"BIRDMAN OF ALCATRAZ"

"Since my former work, *Diseases of Canaries,* was hastily executed and badly garbled in the hands of the publisher, and because a number of important investigations have been carried to completion since its publication, I now desire to take another step along the road I entered with its conception—the road leading to a complete description and classification of the diseases and ailments of pet birds and to the development of a practical and effective system of avian therapeutics." Thus began Robert Stroud's introduction to his *Digest of the Diseases of Birds*. Stroud was the "birdman of Alcatraz," a two-time murderer who became an authority on the care and breeding of canaries and other caged birds during his fifty-four years behind bars. He was in solitary for forty-two years. He had killed his mistress' former lover in Alaska and later a prison guard in front of 1,200 witnesses in Leavenworth Federal Prison, in Kansas. Parole boards found him antisocial, uncooperative, a hard case. Rescuing baby sparrows in the prison yard nurtured his life's interest, and he was allowed to have scientific equipment in his cell. When he was transferred to Alcatraz, he became fluent in French, Spanish, and Greek, and he wrote a confiscated book on American prisons: "It is not only my hope that this material in the hands of bird breeders, poultrymen, and stockmen may eventually lead to the complete eradication of a number of serious bird and animal diseases; but, in the hands of competent investigators, that it may open up new avenues for an attack upon some of the more stubborn diseases of man which have, up until this time, resisted all attacks." Stroud died in prison in Springfield, Missouri, a year after Attorney General Robert F. Kennedy said he could not recommend commutation of Stroud's sentence and six months after parole was denied without comment by the Federal Board of Parole.

THE BIRTH OF A NATION

The first movie ever shown in the White House, during Woodrow Wilson's administration, it was based on a best-selling book, the militant Southerner Thomas Dixon's *The Clansman,* which at one time was going to be also the title of the historic film. Director D. W. Griffith's father had been in the Confederate army and the family was Civil War-impoverished. Eight years after working in Thomas A. Edison's studio in West Orange, New Jersey, Griffith made his technically innovative and controversially racist Civil War drama. There was no script. The night riding of the Ku Klux Klan looks like a company of avenging spectral crusaders sweeping along moonlit roads. Griffith was stung by much of the criticism of the film, and in defense wrote a pamphlet, "The Rise and Fall of Free Speech." His next opus, *Intolerance,* was made in response to the more

70

violent of his critics, who had attempted to have *The Birth of a Nation* banned. The redneck preacher William J. Simmons got the idea for forming the modern K.K.K. after seeing Griffith's silent classic. In a "vision," Simmons saw the Klansmen of yore riding in their inquisition-style white robes, and he got down on those knees of his and swore to the Almighty that he would resurrect that gallant old fraternity and they would go out and get themselves some niggers. Thomas Dixon's income from the movie became the largest sum any author has received for a motion-picture story. When Griffith ran out of money and could pay only $2,500 of the $10,000 due for the movie rights, he offered Dixon a 25 percent interest in the picture. Dixon reluctantly agreed—and made several million dollars.

BISMARCK

"She was a terrific ship," the former naval person (British Prime Minister Winston Churchill) telegraphed President Franklin Roosevelt on May 28, 1941, "and a masterpiece of naval construction." The ship was the *Bismarck,* Germany's newest (one month) and largest battleship—it displaced 42,000 tons of water—and it had just been sunk in the North Atlantic by the British seeking revenge for the sinking by the *Bismarck* four days earlier of England's cherished large battle cruiser H.M.S. *Hood:* Churchill wrote that loss of the *Hood* was a bitter grief. The *Bismarck* was pulverized by gunfire from pursuing British battleships. Dead in the water, she finally went under when struck by torpedoes from the cruiser *Dorsetshire*. Only three limeys had survived the sinking of the *Hood*. About 115 Nazis survived the sinking of the *Bismarck*. Expunging of the *Bismarck* eased England's naval situation, prompting Churchill to cable Roosevelt, "The effect upon the Japanese will be highly beneficial. I expect they are doing all their sums again."

BIT

It's a contraction of *b*inary dig*it,* a digit in the binary number system represented by a 0 or a 1: It is the smallest unit of storage in the computer. Groups of bits form other units of storage, such as a nibble, a byte, or a word.

BLACK GENERAL—DAVIS, BENJAMIN OLIVE

The first black general in the United States Army. A fifty-year military career begun in the Spanish-American War included duty in the Philippines, professorship in military science and tactics at Wilberforce University, military attaché in Liberia, garrison and border patrol in the West. His promotion to the rank of general a month before the 1940 presidential election aroused intense controversy for a time—had Franklin Delano Roosevelt, the Commander in Chief, been politically motivated? Davis's all-black 99th Fighter Squadron (later the 332nd Fighter Group) flew 1,575 missions from North Africa and Italy, and he was honored with the Silver Star, Legion of Merit, Distinguished Flying Cross, and Air Medal with four Oak Leaf clusters. Benjamin Davis, Jr., became the first black general in the Air Force.

BLACK HILLS

There was gold in them thar hills and an expedition headed by General George Custer found it in 1874. The Homestead Mine there is the largest gold mine in the country. Deadwood, Spearfish, Custer, Lead, Rapid City —the towns sprang up in the Black Hills. From afar, from the surrounding Great Plains, the heavily forested slopes of the low mountain range sprawling 6,000 square miles between South Dakota and northeastern Wyoming appear black, thus their name. Harney Peak, at 7,242 feet, is South Dakota's tallest peak. Mount Rushmore National Memorial with its enormous busts of four U.S. Presidents visible for sixty clear miles is an attraction. Another is the limestone caverns in Wind Cave National Park, where the elk and the buffalo are encouraged to play.

BLACK HOLE OF CALCUTTA

The British East India Company founded Calcutta about 1690—it is now the capital of West Bengal state, in East India, on the Hooghly River, the second-largest city in India and one of the largest cities in the world. In the mid-1750s, French and British interests supported rival claims of local princes for power there. The Indian governor, or nawab, of Bengal, Siraj-ud-daula, captured Calcutta, took 146 British prisoners, and stuffed them into a small, suffocating prison known as the Black Hole. The next morning, only twenty-three were still alive. The reckless and rapacious British administrator Robert Clive, governor of Fort St. David, near Madras, avenged the deaths of his countrymen—he was also a reckless and rapacious soldier—recovered Calcutta, and captured the provinces of Behar and Bombay. This action marked the beginning of nearly two centuries of British ascendency throughout India. In 1786, Britain's governor general there was Lord Cornwallis, fresh from defeat in the American Revolutionary War.

72

BLACK HOLES

These hypothetical stars are invisible because their gravitational pull is so intense that light cannot escape from them. The existence of these stars was predicted in 1907 by the German astronomer Karl Schwarzschild. The most likely place to look for a black hole might be in the company of a normal star. A black hole might be detected in terms of its influence on material that is close by. A peculiar star in the binary system Epsilon Aurigae may be a black hole. It seems to have a mass twenty-three times that of the Sun and it emits no visible light.

BLACKJACK

The most popular gambling card game is also known as twenty-one or *vingt-et-un* or, in Britain and Australia, pontoon. Rules can vary from place to place. The player must beat the dealer's hand without exceeding 21. (An ace counts as 1 or 11, a face card as 10, and all other cards according to their face value.) A score of 21 on the first two cards is the perfect hand—blackjack! You feel as though you've been blackjacked—struck by a small leather-covered club with a flexible handle—if it's the other guy who has the face card and the ace.

BLACKOUT

Everyone involved remembers where he was on the evening of November 9, 1965, the night of the electrical short in an 80,000-square-mile area of the northeastern United States and two provinces of southeastern Canada. Maine and Staten Island, New York, were not affected by the power collapse, which originated along the Niagara frontier in upper New York State; Canadian electricity was accidentally diverted onto overloaded New York lines. There weren't even any lights at Manhattan's Hotel Edison, which had been dedicated in 1931 by Thomas Alva Edison, the man who made the blackout possible. Eight hundred thousand New York subway riders were stranded underground for hours. A fireman reached a stalled elevator high up in the Empire State Building and asked if there were any pregnant women in the car. "We've hardly even met," one of the male passengers responded. The crime rate was lower than normal during the 13½-hour blackout. The only major incident was a two-hour riot by inmates of the state prison in Walpole, Massachusetts.

"BLACK TUESDAY"

In September 1929, stock market prices leaped to all-time highs. In October, the president of New York's National City Bank declared, "I know of nothing fundamentally wrong with the stock market or with the underlying business and credit structure." Two days later, Black Thursday, the market collapsed; about 13 million shares were sold at declining prices. Wealthy investors such as J. P. Morgan and John D. Rockefeller bought, bought, bought, hoping to prop up Wall Street. The crash came on October 29—Black Tuesday—the most catastrophic day in the market's history—about 16 million shares were sold at declining prices—it was the forerunner of the Depression. By mid-November, some $30 billion in the value of listed stocks had been wiped out. On December 3, President Herbert Hoover, in his annual message to Congress, declared that confidence in the nation's business had been restored. The Secretary of the Treasury, the fabulously wealthy Andrew Mellon, averred that the Depression might be a good thing: "People will work harder, live a more moral life. Values will be adjusted and enterprising people will pick up the wrecks from less competent people." Twelve million people were out of work and uncounted savings—and lives—were yielded up during the Depression.

BLANDA, GEORGE

The six-foot-two quarterback-placekicker played in the National Football League until he was forty-eight years old: twenty-six seasons, 340 games. He booted 335 field goals (three points each) and scored a record 2,002 points. His 4,007 passes clicked for 26,920 yards and 236 TDs. With the Houston Oilers in 1961 he passed for seven touchdowns in one game and for 36 in all; he completed 51.7 percent of his year's passes. When he was forty-three years old, during the 1970 season, Blanda made headlines for his last-minute heroics in five straight games for the Oakland Raiders.

BLARNEY STONE

Kissing the Blarney Stone at the Blarney Castle is not the easiest thing in the world to do—you need the luck of the Irish to pull it off. Triangular in shape, it's a block of limestone some 20 feet from the top of a tower of the castle which was built near Cork, Ireland, in 1446. The only way to reach and kiss the stone is to hang downward in a dangerous manner. If you can do that, you're entitled to the gift of clever, flattering, coaxing, expressive, convincing speech that legend says you'll receive. It may all be just so much blarney.

BLONDIN, CHARLES

The French acrobat put his best foot forward on an 1,100-foot-long tight-rope 160 feet above Niagara Falls between the United States and Canada in 1855, and, after a period of retirement, in 1860. He did it on stilts, he did it carrying a man on his back, he did it blindfolded while pushing a wheelbarrow; once, he even carried a stove to the middle of the line, where he then cooked and ate an omelette.

THE BLUE ANGEL

Judy Garland loved to tell the story of how the ageless *femme fatale* Marlene Dietrich would invite friends to her hotel suite and they'd sit around all night listening to an LP—the only thing on it was applause recorded at Dietrich performances. Dietrich was something else. She began her show biz career as a violinist. She was irresistible to men, and went everywhere with a monocle and a boa, sometimes with five red-fox furs. She got her movie start in *Tragedy of Love* in the early twenties; she claimed she looked like a potato with hair. She was so sensational as Lola-Lola, the heartless cabaret singer, in *The Blue Angel* (original title: *Professor Unrat*), that Emil Jannings as the enamored college professor nearly strangled her during one scene; her genuine terror is recorded indelibly. One thing she couldn't do was to sing the word "moths." The haunting "Falling in Love Again" came out, "Men cluster to me/Like moss around a flame." Director Josef von Sternberg made her sing it 235 times over two days; she couldn't do it, so there's a yelled "voice over" when she gets to "moss"—listen for it. Her father was a German cavalry officer in the Franco-Prussian War of 1870. During World War II, the blonde Venus entertained Allied troops around the world and German prisoners of war in the United States.

BLUE GROTTO

The Italians call it Grotta Azzurra. "Lost" for centuries, the most famous of the isle of Capri's caves along a high, precipitous coast was rediscovered in 1826. Spectacularly blue water in the cave results from the play of the Sun's rays through a huge natural arch to the bottom of sand and white stone. Capri also has a green grotto. The isle, in the Bay of Naples, is a gigantic block of limestone that broke off from the promontory of

Sorrento. The remains of the XII villas built there by the Roman emperors Augustus and Tiberius are a tourist attraction.

BLUE, VIDA

The big lefthander has been the only pitcher to start for both the American League and the National League in major league baseball's midsummer All-Star game. He was with the Oakland A's when he started for the A.L. in 1971 and 1975 and with the San Francisco Giants when he started for the N.L. in 1978. Not until the 50th anniversary All-Star game, in 1983, was there a grand slam home run: Fred Lynn of the California Angels clouted it out in Chicago in the American League's first triumph in a dozen years and only its third in twenty-four. The 13–3 score was the most lopsided in thirty-seven years, and the seven-run A.L. third was the most tallies scored by one team in one inning. The National League returned to its winning ways in 1984.

BLUE WHALE

The fastest-growing thing in either the plant or the animal kingdom is already a giant at birth. The newborn averages about 2 short tons in weight and twenty-three feet in length. It then gains about 200 pounds a day. The blue, which is toothless, nurses up to seven months. The breast muscles of the mother pump milk into the baby's mouth. It is richer in fat, protein, and minerals than the milk of other mammals, and is highly concentrated. Fifty-year-old blue whales have been known to reach a length of 100 feet—ten feet longer than it is from home plate to first base—and to weigh as much as 120 short tons. They are the largest and the heaviest mammals the planet has seen.

BOCK'S CAR

The name of the B-29 American superfortress bomber that dropped an atomic bomb on Nagasaki on August 9, 1945. The pilot was Major Charles Sweeney, in place of Captain Frederick Bock. The bombardier was Captain Kermit K. Beahan. Navy Commander Frederic L. Ashworth assembled and armed the bomb en route to the Japanese city. *Enola Gay* was the name of the B-29 that had unleashed an atomic bomb on Hiroshima three days earlier. Its pilot was Colonel Paul Tibbets, Jr., who named the bomber for his mother. The bombardier was Major Thomas W. Ferebee. Navy Captain William S. Parsons assembled and armed the bomb en route to the target. *Bock's'* Major Sweeney had piloted the B-29

Great Artiste in tandem with the *Enola Gay* on the Hiroshima raid. Col. Tibbets had piloted the first B-17 to cross the English Channel and bomb German-occupied Europe, in the Rouen-Sotteville raid, the initial mission of the Eighth Army Air Force in World War II. He was at the controls of the first B-17 to bomb North Africa during the Allied invasion in November 1942.

BOGART, HUMPHREY DeFOREST

"Mr. Tough Guy" was born on a Christmas Day in the late nineteenth century, his parents were socially prominent, and he made his stage debut in drawing-room comedies. His sinister, tough gangster Duke Mantee, in Robert E. Sherwood's *The Petrified Forest,* both on the stage and in films, catapulted him into stardom. Louise Brooks thought that too much dialogue in *The Maltese Falcon* "betrayed the fact that his miserable theatrical training had left him permanently afraid of words . . . his eyes glazed and invisible comic-strip balloons circled his dialogue." Bogie won his lone Oscar as best actor for the sympathetic Mr. Olney opposite Katharine Hepburn's Rosie in James Agee's *The African Queen*. He died more than twenty-five years ago.

BOHEMIA

It is today a district or milieu of unconventional artists and writers. The original Bohemian lived in the province of Bohemia in western Czechoslovakia, and by foreigners was often thought to be a gypsy. A Bohemia bohemian, like a gypsy, was said to go his own way, protesting against or indifferent to social conventions. The high point of Bohemia's glory was reached during the reign of Charles I of the Luxemburg Dynasty. He was crowned Holy Roman Emperor Charles IV in 1355 and he made Prague the empire's capital. Celtic tribes had inhabited much of Bohemia before the birth of Christ. It was from one of those tribes, the Boii, that the name Bohemia was derived. The province's patron saint is Vaclav (St. Wenceslas), who was instrumental in spreading Christianity there.

BOLEYN, ANNE

The witness in 1522 was ambidextrous: "Anne Boleyn was rather tall of stature, with black hair and an oval face of a sallowish complexion, as if troubled with jaundice. She had a projecting tooth under the upper lip and on her right hand six fingers. There was a large wen under her chin, and therefore to hide its ugliness she wore a high dress covering her throat." On the other hand, "she was handsome to look at, with a pretty mouth, amusing in her way, playing well on the lute, and was a good dancer. She was the model and mirror of those at Court, for she was always well dressed and every day made some change in the fashion of her garments." She was the handmaiden of Henry VIII's barren Queen Katharine. When Hanky-panky began playing around, she was the sister of one of his mistresses. Inexorably, he had a hankering for the betrothed Anne as well. Elizabeth was delivered but no son. It's never been determined if Henry's second wife (for whose hand Henry broke from the Church) was indeed guilty of the adultery and incest for which she was condemned and executed in 1536, the first of Henry's two wives to lose their heads over him.

BOLIVAR

The basic monetary unit of Venezuela is named for the "George Washington" of South America, the revolutionary Simon Bolivar, who was the most powerful man on the continent in the 1820s. He was born in Venezuela, educated in Spain, and he directed the ouster of Spain from Venezuela, Ecuador, Colombia, and Peru. Peru made its southern lands a separate republic and named them Bolivia in honor of "The Liberator." In November 1984, it took twelve bolivars to equal the value of an American dollar.

BOLOGNA

It's no baloney: the large seasoned sausage got its name from this commercial and industrial center in northcentral Italy. Hamburger, by the way, is for Hamburg, West Germany, the largest seaport in continental Europe, on the North Sea. Homburg, the man's soft felt hat with a dented crown and a rolled brim, is named for a central West German spa and resort.

BOMBAY

India's largest teeming city—about 7,000,000 people—oppressively hot in the summer—Maharashtrians, Gujaratis, South Indians, Parsees, Goans: once they see Bombay, in the Arabian Sea, they don't want to go back to their muluk, or home region. The city was given as a gift to Charles II of England when he married Catherine of Braganza. The British occupied the seven islands that constitute the garden city and established a fort and trading post. Bombay expanded during the U.S. Civil

War to meet the world demand for cotton, becoming a spinning and weaving center. It has the only natural deepwater harbor in western India.

BONAVENA, OSCAR

"The toughest fighter I ever met," Muhammad Ali said after TKOing the hulking, beetle-browed Argentine heavyweight boxer in the last round of a non-title bout. Bonavena responded in his halting English: "You no chicken. Frazier no win you." The thirty-three-year-old granite block of a man was shot dead outside a legal Nevada brothel in May 1976 by a security guard. Three months earlier, "Ringo" had married a Mustang Ranch prostitute; the marriage was annulled ten days later.

BOND, JULIAN

He's been the only black man whose name has been put in nomination for the vice-presidential slot on the national ticket of a major political party. (Congresswoman Shirley Chisholm's name was placed in nomination to be the Presidential standardbearer of the Democratic Party in 1972 and Jesse Jackson's was put forward at the Democratic convention in 1984.) Bond was constitutionally ineligible for the position: The Georgia legislator was only twenty-eight when a Wisconsin delegate, Ted Warshafy, put Bond's name in nomination at the Democratic conclave in riot-torn Chicago, in 1968. (To be President or Vice-President, a person must be at least 35 years of age.) Still, he received 48½ votes, including 21 from delegates of the District of Columbia and 12½ from Minnesotan delegates. The black members of the Georgia delegation claimed that they had all voted for Bond and that their white chairman had announced the vote incorrectly. Bond declined the nomination during the roll call, declaring, "I am deeply gratified by the honor, but unfortunately I have not yet reached the age and must therefore ask that my name be removed." The nomination of Bond was an attempt by forces opposing Hubert Humphrey to gain the microphone and to declare their opposition to the ongoing Vietnam War, the brutality of the Chicago police in the streets, and the way that Vice-President Humphrey had controlled the convention to garner the Presidential nomination.

BONES

There are 206 bones in your body. There are 28 bones in the skull (8 cranial, 14 facial, 6 ossicles of the ear); 30 in each extremity. There are paired bones (such as the 12 ribs on each side, the 8 wrist bones, the 7 ankle bones, the 14 toe bones) and single bones, such as the 26 vertebrae. The bony skeleton acts as a support and a protective framework for the vital organs of the body. Next to tooth enamel, bone is the hardest and strongest structure in the human body. Bone develops from cartilage (gristle) by a physiological process called ossification. It is hollow and is easily maneuvered by the muscles attached to the ligaments that hold it together. Some bones fuse as you get older. A pole vaulter, when he lands, may safely absorb up to ten tons of pressure per square inch on the joints of his tubular thigh bones.

BORDEN, GAIL

He lived two distinct lives. He was a surveyor in Mississippi, and he directed the survey of Austin, Texas. He surveyed and plotted the site of the city of Galveston and was the collector of customs there. He farmed and raised stock in Texas and was copublisher, with his brother, of the *Telegraph and Texas Land Register,* which promoted and unified the revolutionary fervor of the American settlers. Borden then became interested in the problem of keeping food wholesome and fresh during long journeys. Returning East, he saw how the Shaker community in New Lebanon, New York, used a vacuum-pan method of making maple sugar. He used a similar process to condense milk to an easily transportable state. (Condensed milk is evaporated milk with sugar added.) He made a killing in the Civil War. He also patented a method of condensing fruit juices.

BORDEN, LIZZIE

She took an axe and gave her stepmother forty whacks; and when she saw what she had done, she gave her father forty-one. Or did she? Lizzie and her sister had been anxious as to the eventual disposition of their father's wealth—he was a well-to-do businessman and married again after the girls' mother had died. Though there was circumstantial evidence—the accused murderess was seen burning a dress in the kitchen stove after the grisly murders had been discovered—she was acquitted after a sensational trial in Fall River, Massachusetts, in 1893. Lizzie lived the rest of her life (35 years) in Fall River, but was ostracized. The case is still open.

BORG, BJORN RUNE

A man of his word, the Swedish tennis star cannot call himself a great player. Mr. Cool once said he could describe himself thus only after he had won the U.S. Open championship. He played in the finals four times, in 1976, 1978, 1980, and 1981, and lost all four times, twice each to Jimmy Connors and John McEnroe. He did win Wimbledon an unprecedented five straight years (and lost in the finals in the sixth year to McEnroe) and the French Open six times, including four straight, and he paced Sweden to its first Davis Cup cup. Under pressure he has *is i magen* ("ice in the stomach"). He also has a revolutionary two-handed backhand. "You'd better do a lot with your approach when you play Borgie, because he's the world's best counterpuncher," Vitas Gerulaitis said. "Others may be flashier . . . but Bjorn does more with the ball—more often—than anyone else in the game's history." Borgie is one of the richest men in sports. His marriage in 1980 to Mariana Simionescu, a Romanian tennis pro, was a major social event. A photo unit paid 100,000 pounds to shoot exclusive pictures at the ceremony and the reception in Bucharest. The marriage lasted four years.

BOSTON

Wanna lose ten pounds in a hurry? In two hours ten minutes? Or even in three hrs ten mins? Without amputation? Run the Boston Marathon! You'll also be badly dehydrated, blistered, and cramped—but 10 pounds! Another reward, some contestants exude, is the "sheer joy and internal beauty" that the run brings on. This American tradition got a leg up on the New York Marathon way back in 1897. At the turn of the century, the course crossed railroad trackage; once, a ninety-seven-car freight train separated the front-runners from the rest of the pack. The marathon is held on Patriot's Day, April 19, a state holiday. Women ran for the first time in 1974. About fifty minutes have been clipped off the winner's time in the nine decades of the run. Boston itself is the largest city in New England, and the Common downtown (forty-five acres) is the nation's oldest public park.

BOSTON BRUINS

In 1924, they became the first United States professional team in the National Hockey League. In only five years, the Bruins were the champs, and they were again a year later. The Big Bad Bears then really got good, winning the coveted Stanley Cup three times in a row, 1939–41. But they were not the first U.S. team to cop the Stanley Cup—the New York Rangers did it in 1928.

BOSTON CELTICS

The team's National Basketball Association championship in 1984 was its fifteenth. Bill Russell was on ten of the teams. "Some teams come to play. The Celtics come to win," the long-time coach and general manager Red Auerbach has said. It's the last franchise to have won the championship in consecutive years: 1968–69. Three businessmen bought ownership from Harry Mangurian in 1983 for an estimated $15 million. The team's current star, Larry Bird, is paid about $20,000 a game.

"BOSTON STRANGLER"

At first he was the "Measuring Man," claiming he worked for a model agency, talking his way into the apartments of gullible women, getting his kicks from touching them while he took their measurements. Then he was the "Green Man"—he wore green work pants—sexually assaulting a thousand women in New England. He was being held in a Massachusetts maximum security asylum for another series of crimes, including sex offenses against four women, when he confessed also to being the Boston Strangler—between 1962 and 1964, thirteen women died at the Strangler's hands, most of them choked with a stocking. The prisoner did not match any psychiatric profile, any ESP forecast, any psychometrist revelation. He had not been programmed into a computer. Albert Henry DeSalvo was a semiskilled factory hand, the father of two children. He may have raped 2,000 women while a G.I. in Allied occupation forces in Germany. Massachusetts never tried him for the Strangler's crimes, and he later retracted the confession. (A cellmate told authorities that DeSalvo had been tutored for the Strangler role by another convict.) He became skilled in making costume jewelry, and his products were on display in the prison lobby. DeSalvo was murdered by another inmate in 1973; he had been trafficking in drugs. He may not have been the Strangler, but there were no more Strangler-type murders once DeSalvo was locked up.

BOTTICELLI, SANDRO

It is in the *Spring* (the *Primavera*) and *The Birth of Venus* of the "little barrel" (which is what "Botticelli" means) that the Florentine Renaissance sense of beauty appears in its most evolved and peculiar form. He was a marvelous colorist, a master of rhythmic line, the favorite painter of the Medici (the Ford Foundation of the period), a former apprentice to Fra Filippo Lippi, and his works will be admired as long as there are eyes: *Mars and Venus, Pallas Subduing a Centaur, Last Communion of St. Jerome, Pieta, Fortitude, Madonna del Magnificat, Adoration of the Magi, Chigi Madonna, Portrait of a Young Man, Madonna of the Pomegranate,* and the three narrative scenes he painted in the Sistine Chapel: two episodes in the life of Moses and *The Temptations of Christ.* But eventually the Renaissance passed him by; he was no longer the state of the art. Michelangelo and Leonardo and the Raphaelites were the new kids on the canvas, with new perspectives. Easel come, easel go even then.

BOUQUET

The first perfume from a newly opened bottle of wine is the bouquet. The later, more lingering odor is the aroma. Volatile acidity brings on the bouquet. The scent, which should be clean, with no trace of moldiness, results from the vaporization of esters and ethers, elusive chemical components that the wine contains. The bouquet is faint and hard to identify if the wine is cold. France continues as the wine-consumption-per-capita leader.

BOURGEOISIE

"Civilized society is one huge bourgeoisie," George Bernard Shaw observed; "no nobleman dares now shock his greengrocer." Bourgeois: a middle-class person, one of the social class whose income derives from the profits of commercial and industrial enterprise, especially as distinguished from the landed gentry, the wage earners, and farmers, and sometimes the professions. His social behavior and political views are determined or influenced by private property interest. H. L. Mencken, the Baltimore iconoclast, took the words "boob" and "bourgeoisie" and coined the word "booboisie," to refer to people who are stupid and gullible.

BOW, CLARA

"The It Girl"—It: personal magnetism, charm—won a "fame and fortune" contest in 1921 and presently found herself playing a flapper in

Hollywood. She also played a manicurist, a shopgirl, a waitress, an usherette, a dance hall hostess. (Others said to have had "It" in Tinseltown: the actor Tony Marone, the wild stallion Rex, the doorman at the Ambassador Hotel.) Her hair was flame red, and she had seven chow dogs to match. Men in tow included Gary Cooper. She made a comeback in 1933 playing a sexy dancer in *Hoopla*. She became racked with insomnia and depression. In 1947, she was "Mr. Hush" on the radio program "Truth or Consequences." She died of a heart attack while watching television.

THE BOWERY

It became New York's "Street of Forgotten Men" because the neighborhood had the cheapest beer in the city. One could put down five-cents-a-glass whiskeys until one passed out. Half of the cheap lodging houses were there, south of Houston Street on the lower East Side. A 15-cents "bum's roost" was a bunk in a dormitory. Twenty-five-cents "hotels" were rooms with head-high partitions. One could sleep on the floor in a "flop house." In the 1870s, 105 Bowery was noted as a resort for some of the toughest characters abroad: "There, the blind man recovered his sight, the cripple laid aside his crutches and straightened his twisted leg, the one-armed man released the arm that had been bound tightly to his body all the day, the boiler explosion victim removed his bandages."

BOWLING

Close to 60,000 perfect 300-games (12 strikes) have been sanctioned by the American Bowling Congress for its male members since the turn of the century. But not until July 1, 1982, was a perfect 900-series—three consecutive 300-games—rolled in sanctioned league competition. But the Congress has not approved Glenn Allison's feat. Mr. Allison scored 36 consecutive strikes with his 15-pound ball, at La Habra 300 Bowl, in La Habra, California. All thirty-six balls were in the 1–3 pocket. Earlier in the evening, he had bowled a three-game 578. His book average was 214. The previous three-game "untouchable" high of 886 was bowled in 1949 by Allie Brandt, of Lockport, New York. The world's largest bowling hall sported 252 lanes: the Tokyo Lanes Bowling Center. The largest today may be Edison Lanes (112 lanes) in Edison, New Jersey. Another fascinating 10-strike: Martin Luther—*that* Martin Luther—was so interested in the game that he experimented with the best number of pins, and that, it is said, gave birth to ninepin bowling.

BOWLING BALLS

Up to 8½ inches in diameter, 27 inches in circumference, and 16 pounds in weight, they have three holes and most bowlers use all three holes—the three-finger grip is the thumb, the middle finger, and the ring finger. Some bowlers only use two of the holes—the two-finger grip is the thumb and the middle finger. Most bowlers slip their thumb and finger(s) into the holes up to the second knuckle. Others use a "fingertip" grip, that is, the fingers extend into the holes only up to the first knuckle. The ball is made of hard rubber, sometimes plastic, never metal. In league play the ball must weigh from 10 to 16 pounds and have a circumference of not more than 27 inches. The maple and pine lane is nearly 63 feet long and 41–42 inches wide. The gutter is 9 inches wide.

BOWLING SPLITS

It's not easy "punching the ticket" of a railroad split, that is, knocking over with your second ball, for a spare, the remaining two pins in this difficult split, such as the 8–10, the 7–10, or even the 4–6. Trying can lead to gutter language 60 feet long. Another "popular" bowling split is known as the Christmas tree: for a righthander, it's the 3–7–10 split; for a lefty, it's the 2–7–10 split. A 1–7–10 split is sometimes called a Christmas tree—or a How In the World Did That Happen?

BOXING—QUEENSBERRY RULES

John Sholto Douglas, the ninth marquis of Queensberry, became especially famous for two kinds of bouts: for KOing boxing's unsportsmanship and for exposing Oscar Wilde's immoral conduct with the marquis's son Lord Alfred Douglas; the scandal led to Wilde's conviction and imprisonment. The boxing rules that the British nobleman sponsored—they were devised by John Graham Chambers, in 1867—are the rules under which bouts are staged to this day. Three-minute rounds. Padded gloves. A boxer must return to his corner when his opponent goes down. The decked boxer must rise unaided and be ready to continue the round within ten seconds or lose the tiff. And no belting below the belt. In the early days, everything went: biting, butting, kicking, wrestling, and that shot that was heard 'round the world—the low blow.

BOY SCOUTS

The organization dedicated to the mental, moral, and physical development of boys over twelve years of age was founded in 1908 by a British soldier and former Inspector General of the South African constabulary, Robert Baden-Powell. Two years later, and with the assistance of his sister Agnes, he founded the Girl Guides, or Girl Scouts. In training army recruits, Baden-Powell had developed self-reliance, resourcefulness, and courage; on return to Great Britain from South Africa, he was asked to develop a program for boys based on the same principles. In 1910, he was persuaded by King Edward VII to retire from the army and devote himself exclusively to furthering the Scout movement; he was made a baron in 1922 and a peer in 1929. In the United States, the Boy Scouts absorbed the organizations Sons of Daniel Boone and the Woodcraft Indians. James E. West was chief Scout in the United States for thirty-two years, until 1943. The first international gathering of Boy Scouts, the jamboree, was held in London in 1920.

"BOZO AND THE PINEAPPLE"

Gerald R. Ford and Senator Robert Dole! The Republican Presidential and Vice-Presidential ticket in the 1976 national election. Ford has been the only Chief Executive not to win a national election as a Presidential or a Vice-Presidential candidate. Senator Dole was renowned as a Republican hatchet man—he liked to accuse the Democrats of all the wars of the century. Ford had been appointed Vice-President when Spiro Agnew resigned in disgrace and he became President when Richard M. Nixon resigned in 1974. He had to beat back Ronald Reagan's challenge for the '76 nomination, and he did it on the very first ballot in the convention: Ford, 1,187 votes; the former California governor, 1,070 votes. Because the Democratic candidate, Jimmy Carter, was more than 30 points ahead in the polls, Ford made an unprecedented offer: He would debate the "Georgia peanut" on television. Republican Senator Robert P. Griffin, of Michigan, once said, "The nicest thing about Jerry Ford is that he just doesn't have enemies." President Lyndon B. Johnson: "He's a nice fellow but he spent too much time playing football without a helmet." The long-time congressman almost pulled out the election: He garnered 48 percent of the popular vote. The electoral vote was Carter, 297, and Ford, 240. (Carter became the first President from the Deep South since Zachary Taylor.)

BRADLEY, BILL

"I think Bradley's happiest whenever he can deny himself pleasure," Princeton coach Butch van Breda Kolff said about his basketball star many years ago. Whenever Bradley discussed basketball, he frequently repeated the words "concentration" and "discipline." The college All-American and Rhodes Scholar played with the gold medal United States Olympic quintet in 1964 and with two championship New York Knickerbocker teams (1970, 1973) in the National Basketball Association. In 1984, he was reelected a U.S. Senator from New Jersey. His principal goal is restoration of integrity to the tax system "and, by so doing, to begin restoring confidence in government." His Fair Tax would "lower the tax rates of all Americans and eliminate the special interest tax provisions that reward the few at the expense of higher rates for the many. Four out of five taxpayers would pay 14 percent. About 70 percent of the taxpayers would be paying less tax than they do now; 30 percent would be paying more. The special interests that benefit from tailor-made tax loopholes are hoping the idea will simply die." Bradley remembers that when he started to play professional basketball, he just wanted to play and be paid well. His tax attorney told him it wasn't so simple. He told "Dollar Bill" that he could take his pay as salary, or defer all or part of it, or take it as property, or take it as a long-term consulting contract, or take it as employer-paid life insurance and pension plans, or take it as payment to his own corporation, or take . . .

BRAHE, TYCHO

The sixteenth-century Danish nobleman of Swedish descent had planned to go into politics, but that plan was forever eclipsed when he observed an eclipse of the Sun. Tycho became a mathematician and the greatest of the naked-eye astronomers. He corrected almost every important astronomical measurement, and determined the length of the year to less than the time it took you to read this part of this sentence—that is, he was less than a second off. His nose for discovery smelled out people, too. He engaged as an assistant Johann Kepler, himself soon to be a star in astronomical circles—he accurately described the revolutions of the planets around the Sun. Tycho was a belligerent, spiteful fellow. When he was still in his teens, he got into a foolish feud over a point in mathematics, and presently found himself in a midnight duel, where his nose was sliced off. He wore a false nose, of metal, for the last thirty-six years of his life.

BRAIN

Tomes that might give some of us tomaine poisoning have been written about the brain and will continue to be—new worlds are constantly being discovered there. (Like, what made him think "Tomes that might give some of us tomaine poisoning. . . ."?) Even the brain doesn't know what the brain doesn't know. It is the largest part of your central nervous system. Its tens of billions of interconnected neurons, or brain cells, have innumerable extensions, telling your muscles, glands, and other organs what to do; it is the site of your emotions, memory, self-awareness, and thought. There are two hemispheres. The right hemisphere works in the areas of music, artistic ability, creativity, and emotions. The left hemisphere tends to be responsible for producing and understanding speech, logical thinking, writing, and reading. Brain cells deprived of oxygen will die in less than five minutes; they do not reproduce.

BRASILIA

Brazil's capital since 1960 was laid out unconventionally—from the air it looks like an airplane. Or is it a bent bow and arrow? Creation of an inland capital had been talked about for more than a century. Brasilia, in the once unpopulated uplands of Goias, deep in the heart of the undeveloped Sertao, where the humidity is sometimes even lower than in the all but humidity-less Sahara, quickly had a population of more than half a million. Rio de Janeiro, 600 miles to the southeast, had been the capital for 125 years, and it is still the country's chief tourist attraction. Brazilians say that God made the world in six days and spent the seventh making Rio.

BRASSIERE

The woman's undergarment for supporting her breasts might have been known today even more appropriately as a teatsling if its inventor—a man named Titzling—had taken out a patent in the 1910s for the chest halter providing uplift and shapeliness he had devised for "Swanhilda Olafsen," an opera singer who had complained of discomfort and the lack of support that corsets gave to her huge breasts. Titzling, an immigrant from Germany, was working at the time for an uncle in the women's undergarment business in New York. The word brassiere is from the French brassière, for bodice, but it also happened to be the surname of a

Frenchman, Philippe de Brassière, who brazenly made the invention his own in the late 1920s. When Titzling sued for infringement, the court pointedly decided that Seventh Avenue was a tit-for-tat place and left Titzling holding the bag. The falsie, or padded brassiere, was invented by an Englishman in the late 1920s to protect breasts from injuries in athletic competition. Now, let's make a clean breast of this entry: One might have to be in his, or her, cups to believe it.

BRAZIL

It's big. It is nearly half of the entire continent of South America, yet it is not as big in square mileage as the United States. It borders all but two of the continent's ten other independent countries—Chile and Ecuador are the exceptions. The equator crosses Brazil in the north, as does the Tropic of Capricorn in the south. Recife on the eastern bulge, Cabo de Sao Roque, is South America's easternmost city, and São Paulo is its largest city. The capital was moved more than twenty years ago from Rio de Janeiro to a city carved out of the interior by architect Oscar Niemeyer —Brasilia. The new "race" of Brazilians is an amalgam of Indian, Negro, and European strains—it is said that Negro slaves had to be imported when the native Indians were not adaptable to the backbreaking labor of the cane fields. Brazil joined the Allies in both world wars. It is the continent's only country in which Spanish is not the official language— it's Portuguese. Some of the junglelike forests, *silvas,* are still unexplored; the boa, the cougar, the jaguar there have given the region the name Green Hell.

BRAZIL'S—AND OTHERS'—NATIONAL ANTHEMS

"Hino ·Nacional Brasiliero," music by Francisco Manoel da Silva, in 1831, is Brazil's national anthem: "On the peaceful banks of the Ypiranga . . ." Words, 1922. Japan's national anthem is "May Our Sovereign Lord Remain." Egypt's: "The Khedive March." Hungary's: "Lord Bless the Hungarian." Peru's: "We Are Free, So Let Us Remain Forever." Argentina's: "Mortals, Hear the Heavenly Call." Denmark's: "King Christian Stood by the Lofty Mast." Sweden's: "From the Bottom of Swedish Hearts." Ecuador's: "We Greet Thee, Our Fatherland." Finland's: "Our Fatherland." Switzerland's: "To the Fatherland." The national anthem of Yugoslavia is made up of a combination of the Serbian "Boze Pravde," the Croatian "Liepa Nasa Domvina," the Slovene "Napred Zastava Slave."

BREAD—"THE STAFF OF LIFE"

And seeing the multitudes, Jesus went up into a mountain: and when he was set, his disciples came unto him. And he opened his mouth, and taught them, saying . . . "Give us this day our daily bread." Earlier, after a forty-day fast and being tempted—as the Son of God—by the devil to command "that these stones be made bread," He said, "It is written, Man shall not live by bread alone, but by every word that proceedeth out of the mouth of God." Christ's kingdom was foretold in the book of the prophet Isaiah (3): "For, behold, the Lord, the Lord of hosts, doth take away from Jerusalem and from Judah the stay and the staff, the whole stay of bread, and the whole stay of water." It was Jonathan Swift who, in 1704, wrote, "Bread is the staff of life."

BRIDGE—CONTRACT

The most popular form of the card game was thought up by the yachtsman and railroad financier (the Penn Central) Harold Stirling Vanderbilt on a cruise (probably on the bridge) from Los Angeles to Havana in the mid-1920s. It is almost the same game as the popular auction bridge, created in 1904; the major difference—altering the strategy of the game —is that only the amount of the bid in contract bridge is scored "below the line" whereas in auction bridge all the tricks won in play, not merely those bid, contribute to winning the game. Mr. Vanderbilt had adopted a principle from the kindred French game of plafonde. Contract bridge (played by four in two partnerships) is the only card game with official laws recognized and used everywhere. In 1940, Charles H. Goren introduced the point count system, replacing the honor count. In 1928, Mr. Vanderbilt (who thrice defended America's Cup successfully) established a trophy for an annual national contract bridge championship; *he* won it in 1932. The Vanderbilt Cup is the most sought-after trophy in the bridge world.

THE BRIDGE OF SAN LUIS REY

"On Friday noon, July the twentieth, 1714, the finest bridge in all Peru broke and precipitated five travelers into the gulf below." The five in Thornton Wilder's novel were an ugly, eccentric Marquesa (who, the night before her death, looked at "the stars that glittered above the Andes. Throughout the hours of the night, though there had been few to hear it, the whole sky had been loud with the singing of these constellations"); the Marquesa's unhappy companion; a former dramatic teacher

90

of a famous actress; his ward, the actress's illegitimate son; and a man deeply devoted to his dead twin brother, lover of the actress. The Pulitzer Prize-winning novel is purportedly based on the eyewitness account of the accident by Brother Juniper, whose purpose it was to show that the tragedy, at a crisis of love in each of the five lives, was a scientifically explainable example of Divine Providence. Wilder was inspired by Prosper Mérimée's drama *La Carosse du Saint-Sacrement* (1829)—the famous actress Camila Perichole presents her luxurious coach, extorted from the viceroy, to the church so that priests, when they set out to administer extreme unction to the dying, need travel on foot no longer. It is in Wilder's account (1927) that we learn that "all families lived in a wasteful atmosphere of custom and kissed one another with secret indifference." The suspension bridge was woven of osiers in Incan times and was much used and considered indestructible.

THE BRIDGE ON THE RIVER KWAI

It was said to have been the largest single set ever constructed for a Hollywood motion picture—the bridge (built by Ceylonese army engineers as an exercise) was a third longer than a football gridiron and as high as a six-story building. It was made of hewn logs moved from nearby jungles by a force of twenty-five elephants and hundreds of workers. David Lean's Cinemascope production was inspired by the bridging of the Kwai in Thailand by the Japanese conquerors for the Burma-Thailand "death railway" built by European POWs during World War II. Alec Guinness, as a proud disciplinarian of the British India Army service, spurs his men to build a bridge of which they can be proud and thereby prove they are better men than their captors—at the same time, Allied commandoes are plotting to blow it up. The Oscar-winning movie (1957) was spectacularly photographed and thrillingly acted.

BRIGADOON

The mythical Scottish town that comes to life for one day every 100 years in the musical comedy of the same name by Alan Jay Lerner and Frederick Loewe. There was a strong, probably coincidental plot similarity to the German classic *Germelshausen*. First produced in 1947, *Brigadoon* ("in thy valley there'll be lovers") fulfilled the theater ideal of weaving dance, music, and story into a single fabric of brightness and enchantment. It was named best musical by the New York Drama Critics. Four producers had turned it down. Lerner and Loewe went on to create *My Fair Lady, Camelot,* and *Gigi.* It was almost like being in love.

BROADWAY—"THE GREAT WHITE WAY"

"A bouquet of luminous advertising," a visitor from France lit up in New York's Times Square in 1903. By decade's end, it was "an immense blaze of legends and pictures, most of them in motion . . . the finest free show on earth." Electricity turned on the Great White Way, the theater district from 42nd Street, Times Square, to 48th Street and Broadway, in New York City—Broadway, the longest of the modern streets in the world, has run as much as 150 miles, from Bowling Green in lower Manhattan to Albany, the state capital; it was the principal street of New Amsterdam, and the Dutch kept extending it northward. "Fabulous glow-worms crawl up and down," a British visitor wrote in 1917. "Zig-zag lightnings strike an acre of signboard—and reveal a panacea for overeating! A four-story Highlander dances a whiskey-fling; another pours out a highball, with a hundred feet between his bottle and the glass. Household words race with invisible pen across a whole city block. . . ." It was—it sometimes still is—luminous epilepsy, incandescent hypnotism. "Pity the sky with nothing but stars." (The longest streets in the ancient world were broad ways, too: the Appian Way, 350 miles from Rome to Brundisium; the Romans' Watling Street in England, 100 miles from London north, then southwest, then westerly to Wroxeter.)

BROCA, CONVOLUTION OF

The nineteenth-century French pathologist, neurologist, and anthropologist Paul Broca was an authority on aphasia, the loss of the power to use or understand words, the impairment of the ability to articulate ideas. He located the brain center for articulate speech in a small region in the third convolution of the left frontal lobe of the cerebral cortex. It is known today as the convolution of Broca, or Broca's area. It was, as Carl Sagan has pointed out, "one of the first discoveries of a separation of function between the left and right hemispheres of the brain . . . that specific brain functions exist in particular locales in the brain, that there is a connection between the anatomy of the brain and what the brain does, an activity sometimes described as mind." Broca's own brain, with its convolution of Broca, is floating in formalin and in fragments in the Musée de l'Homme, the Museum of Man, in Paris.

BROOKLYN

When the glorious Brooklyn Bridge linking the boroughs of Brooklyn and Manhattan was opened to vehicular traffic by President Chester A. Arthur at 2 P.M. on May 24, 1883, the vehicles did not include automobiles. There weren't any yet. But there were plenty of wagons. In 1890, the bridge carried 37,677,411 people. New Yorkers did not see their first automobile until Decoration Day 1896. Brooklyn, at the southwestern tip of Long Island, has been known as the city of churches. Its population is 2,231,000.

BROWN, EDMUND GERALD, JR. (JERRY)

The erstwhile Jesuit seminarian and California governor and Democratic Presidential hopeful (he is also the brother-in-law of a CBS News major domo) would tell his staff to work "in the spirit of Ho Chi Minh." He did not believe "that janitors should be paid more than judges, but I think the gap between them is too great. If work is interesting and challenging, people should be paid less. Those are the people who get great psychic rewards. Their lives are better because they have the privilege of interesting work." Brown was buddy-buddy with the publisher of the *Whole Earth Catalog*. "Hot lunches for school children? No one ever gave me a hot lunch." In 1976, he said he should be President because he saw the need of coming to terms with "the era of limits—economically, ecologically, and even humanly—that we're entering into." He has been seen in Africa with Linda Ronstadt.

BROWN, HELEN GURLEY

Nearly a score of years ago, *The* Cosmo Girl said, "I really don't know how ladies raised in Little Rock and in most provincial cities can wind up with any interest in sex. People do their very best to disinterest you. They say, 'It's all right to make love after you get married. Then the fireworks start and the heavens light up.' But before that time you're supposed to feel nothing whatever, so how a girl reared in a Midwestern town maintains her interest in sex is beyond me." Mrs. Brown's *Cosmopolitan* magazine is pitched at unmarried working women. One of the magazine's memorable tips to women on the make: Put perfume on the light bulbs.

BROWN, JIM

Even the ultra-neutral Pro Football Hall of Fame hails him as the "most awesome runner in history." The Jim-dandy Cleveland Brown, an All-American at Syracuse University in 1956, and the Browns's number-one draft selection in 1957, led National Football League rushers eight of his nine years . . . was all-N.F.L. eight years . . . N.F.L.'s most valuable player, 1958, 1965 . . . rookie of the year, 1957 . . . played in nine straight pro bowls . . . career marks: 12,312 yards rushing, 262 receptions, 15,459 combined net yards, 756 points scored. In his late forties, in 1983, Brown threatened to come out of retirement when Franco Harris, of the Pittsburgh Steelers, threatened to eclipse the rushing record. But the record turned out to be broken by the Chicago Bears's Walter Payton, in October 1984. In the sixth game of his tenth N.F.L season, Payton (off to the best start of his career) reached 12,400 yards rushing in the fifty-ninth 100-yard-plus game of his career. By game's end he held twenty-one Bear records and four league records, with another five league career marks within his reach. Payton had needed 436 more carries and 18 more games than Brown to surpass Brown's rushing mark.

BROWN, JOHN

The fierce, radical free-soiler pledged that he would "die fighting" for abolition. "There will be no peace in this land until slavery is done for. I will give them something else to do than to extend slave territory. I will carry the war into Africa." He settled his family of twenty in a black community in North Elba, New York, and with other abolitionists revengefully massacred five suspected proslavers in Lawrence, Kansas, for burning homes of free-staters. In 1859, Brown and a band of followers seized the federal arsenal at Harpers Ferry, Virginia. It was retaken by a militia company commanded by Col. Robert E. Lee; John Wilkes Booth was a member of the militia. There was considerable evidence that Brown was insane. He was convicted of murder, promoting slave insurrection, and treason against Virginia: "Now if it is deemed necessary that I should forfeit my life for the furtherance of the ends of justice and mingle my blood further with the blood of my children and with the blood of millions in this slave country whose rights are disregarded by the wicked, cruel, and unjust enactments—I submit; so let it be done!" And so it was, on December 2, 1859. "John Brown's Body" was a popular Union song during the Civil War.

BROWNING, ELIZABETH BARRETT AND ROBERT

"I love your verse with all my heart, dear Miss Barrett." The much-younger poet's first, impetuous letter threw the semi-invalid dear Miss Barrett, of 50 Wimpole Street, into ecstasies. Four months, ten days, three hours, two minutes, eight seconds later, on May 20, 1845, the two poets met for the first time. A secret courtship—"My daughter should be thinking of another world," her father proclaimed—and eighteen months later, they undertook a fifteen-year marriage made in heaven. "We are happy as two owls in a hole," Robert Browning wrote, "two toads in a tree stump." "How do I love thee? Let me count the ways. I love thee to the depth and breadth and height My soul can reach, when feeling out of sight For the ends of Being and ideal Grace." "Ah, but a man's reach should exceed his grasp, Or what's a heaven for?" Browning's literary masterpiece was a murder story, the four-volume poem *The Ring and the Book*—a seventeenth-century Italian Rashomon: "Life is an empty dream."

BRUCE, LENNY

Before a nightclub act could get away with "four-letter words," Lenny Bruce was repeatedly busted for obscenity. The nation's culture mavens, like Lionel Trilling, William Styron, James Baldwin, and Norman Mailer, supported him as a social satirist "in the tradition of Swift, Rabelais, and Twain." Typical Bruce: "Eichmann really figured, you know, 'The Jews —the most liberal people in the world—they'll give me a fair shake.' Fair? *Certainly*. 'Rabbi' means lawyer. He'll get the best trial in the world, Eichmann. Ha! They were shaving his leg while he was giving his appeal! That's the last bit of insanity, man." The "sick comedian" limned one reason he got busted: "I picked on the wrong god. If I had picked on the god whose replica is in the whoopee cushion store—the Tiki god, the Hawaiian god, those idiots . . . but I picked on the Western god—the cute god, the IN-god, the Kennedy-god—and that's where I screwed up." Bruce was DOA from a drug overdose in 1966.

BRUNDAGE, AVERY

A star athlete at the University of Illinois, and a decathloner (with Jim Thorpe) in the Olympics in Stockholm in 1912, he was America's amateur all-around champion in 1914, 1916, and 1918. He was president of the Amateur Athletic Union of the United States seven times, president of the U.S. Olympic Association 1929–53, and president of the International Olympic Committee 1952–72. He successfully stemmed the burgeoning movement for U.S. athletes to join a boycott of the "Nazi Olympics" in Berlin in 1936; at the same time, he dismissed Eleanor Holm from the team for breaking training rules. (She had won the backstroke swimming competition in the Olympics in Los Angeles in 1932.) He was dedicated to the principle of amateurism, and he battled to keep questions of politics and international rivalry out of the games. (He died in 1975, before President Carter withdrew the U.S. team from participation in the Olympics in Moscow in 1980 and before the Soviet Union and Eastern bloc nations, in revenge, withdrew from the Olympics in Los Angeles in 1984.) Mr. Brundage, as IOC chief, ordered the games to go on in the wake of the kidnapping and massacre of Israeli athletes at the Olympics in Munich in 1972.

BRYANT, ANITA

When Miss Bryant was the Sunshine Tree Girl for the Florida Citrus Commission, Governor Reubin Askew quipped, "People connect orange juice, Florida, and Anita Bryant so much that it becomes difficult to decide which to visit, which to listen to, and which to squeeze." Ancestry was French, Dutch, English, Scottish, Irish, Cherokee Indian. Baptism at the age of eight "stands out for me beyond almost everything else that has happened in my life." She used to pray nightly, "Lord, I really do want to become a star." In 1959, she was Miss Oklahoma and the second runner-up for the Miss America title; she was co-Miss Congeniality. Her records "Till There Was You," "Paper Roses," and "My Little Corner of the World" were gold. "Honey," Lyndon B. Johnson reportedly said to her, "I want you to sing 'The Battle Hymn of the Republic' when they lower me in the ground." She did. Miss Bryant has been an outspoken critic of homosexuality.

BUFFET, JIMMY

The good-time, "hopelessly likable" singer-songwriter was wastin' away again in Margaritaville, searchin' for his lost shaker of salt. Some people claimed that there was a woman to blame, "but I know—it's nobody's fault . . . it's my own damn fault." "Margaritaville" was a big hit in 1977. His songwriting, it is said, exhibits a "journalist's eye": "The Great Filling Station Holdup," "My Head Hurts, My Feet Stink and I Don't Love Jesus," and the infamous "Why Don't We Get Drunk (and Screw)." To an awful lot of people, the Margarita is the salt of the earth. Juice of ½ lime, drop hull (approximately ½ oz. juice). 1 jigger sweetened lemon juice. ¼ jigger pineapple juice. ¼ barspoon orgeat syrup. ½ jigger triple sec. 1 jigger tequila. Frappe with shaved ice and strain into chilled 6 oz. glass (or other specialty glass) that has been rimmed with fresh lime and dipped in special kosher crystal salt.

BULLFIGHTING

The national sport and spectacle of Spain. *Death in the Afternoon:* "Those passes were designed to show the matador's skill and art with the cape, his domination of the bull and also to fix the bull in a certain spot before the entry of the horses. They are called veronicas after St. Veronica who wiped the face of Our Lord with a cloth and are so called because the saint is always represented holding the cloth by the two corners in the position the bullfighter holds the cape for the start of the veronica.'' Veronicas. Corrida de toros. Plaza de toros. Matador. Toro. Picadors. Peones. Banderilleros. Banderillas. Paseillo. Capas. Pic. Muleta. The bull must weigh at least 1,194 pounds and be four or five years old. The Portuguese bullfighter fights the bull from horseback, and the bull is not killed. Bullfighters in Spain used to fight from horseback, but the torero Francisco Romero changed all that a long time ago, in the 1720s, when he chose not to be cowed, got off his high horse, and fought man-to-bull.

BURMA ROAD

It was a close shave. In the late 1930s, Japanese soldiers were plunging south and blockading China's coast. Materiel had to come in through the ''back door'' if China was going to survive the rising of the Rising Sun. Under prodigious hardships, nearly 200,000 Chinese and Burmese laborers built a 700-mile road through subtropical mountains from the Burmese railhead of Lashio to K'un-ming, in Yunan province, in China—a base of rocks was filled with crushed stone and topped with mud. In places, it followed the ancient Marco Polo trail. In 1942, the Japanese captured the Burmese part of the trail. Toward war's end, Allied soldiers united the road with a new road from Ledo, India: The combined length was 1,079 miles.

BURNETT, CAROL

What would make the actress yelp, ''There is a God''? Among several things: a Los Angeles jury, after three days of deliberation, awarded her $1.6 million in damages in her libel suit against the *National Enquirer*. It took a long time to get the magazine into court: ''I'm very happy to be here,'' Miss Burnett said. ''It's like a five-year-old toothache and I'm finally at the dentist.'' In 1976, the *Enquirer,* implying that she had been drinking, wrote that ''at a Washington restaurant a boisterous Carol Burnett had a loud argument with another diner, Henry Kissinger. Then she traipsed around the place offering everyone a bit of her dessert'' and ''accidentally knocked a glass of wine over one diner and started giggling instead of apologizing.'' The *Enquirer* later admitted the ''events did not occur,'' but the actress was not satisfied: It was like ''being in the hospital and the hit-and-run driver sends you a bouquet of crabgrass.'' (Both of

Miss Burnett's parents had died of alcoholism.) An *Enquirer* reporter testified that his editor had insisted on running the item despite the reporter's misgivings about its accuracy. The jury was convinced that the *Enquirer* had acted with reckless disregard for the truth. The award was later reduced by one-half.

BURR, AARON

The disgruntled third Vice-President killed former U.S. Treasurer Alexander Hamilton in a pistol duel, in 1804, after Hamilton had helped to frustrate Burr's plans to become governor of New York and have New York and the New England states secede from the Union; Burr would have become president of the new nation. (The Federalist Hamilton, a major mover in the call for the Constitutional Convention, had wanted to make the nation "the united state of America," doing without individual states altogether.) Hamilton had also helped to deny Burr the Presidency when a tie in the electoral college between Veep Thomas Jefferson and Burr threw the election of 1800 into the House of Representatives; Burr lost and became Jefferson's Vice-President, on the thirty-sixth ballot. Murder charges against Burr were dropped; the first governor of New York, George Clinton, was Vice-President during Jefferson's second term. In 1808, Burr was charged with treason because (or so it was said) he had tried to separate the western lands from the rest of the country and establish his own rule there. In a trial over which Chief Justice John Marshall presided, he was acquitted; but his image was forever tarnished.

BUTTERFLY

It is an insect with two pairs of wings. With the moths, butterflies comprise the order *Lepidoptera*. There are about a dozen families of butterflies. All of them were once caterpillars. The genus *Polygonia* can be recognized by deeply notched borders on the wings and a brown marbled underside of the hindwings and a conspicuous white mark near the center. In the Comma, *Polygonia c-album,* this mark is in the form of a white comma or c-mark. In the Southern Comma, *Polygonia egea,* it is L-shaped. The species are widespread in Europe.

C

CABER-TOSSING

Caber is Scandinavian for "pole" or "spar." Caber-tossing—the tossing of a long, heavy, slightly tapered wooden pole—originated in Scotland and is today a feature of the Highland Games. McClure Caber is the most widely used caber. It measures 17 feet in length and weighs about 100 pounds. To keep weight standard, cabers are usually buried in the mud of a creek bed between contests; they are removed and dried off only hours before they are used. At the start, the tosser, with the help of another person, lifts his caber to a vertical position. He then picks up the pole on the slender end and runs with it. When he believes he has gained sufficient momentum, he halts suddenly and flips the caber into the air in a manner that the pole turns 180 degrees in flight. The thicker end hits the ground and the pole falls directly away from him, hopefully. A perfect throw is called a twelve o'clock toss. Caber-tossing is not restricted to musclemen. It is a sport where balance, dexterity, strength, even speed are factors.

CABLE CARS

It was once said that hills in San Francisco are so steep that a dime dropped on the crest of California Street would gather speed enough to kill a horse on Market Street, unless it hit a Chinaman on Grant Avenue. More than one horsepower was needed to get the wealthy back to their homes on the city's peaks every night. The first cable car began operating in 1873. The moving cable followed the contour of the street and the grip did not tear the cable apart by too sudden a jerk—it was an engineering achievement. In the press, a visiting English noblewoman mimicked the newly arrived Oriental: "No pushee, no pullee, no horsee, no steamee; Melican man heap smart."

CADILLAC

The beaver led the eager beaver Antoine de la Mothe Cadillac to found Detroit. The French King wore a high hat one day—the *first* high hat of record—it was made of the fine inner fur of the beaver—and there was suddenly a demand for beaver among the high hats of Europe. To keep English traders from hogging the beaver market, Cadillac, for several years commandant of the French fort at Mackinac, was authorized by Paris to found a settlement on the Detroit River and to build a fort there, garrison it, and hold it as a barrier against the invasion of the English traders from Fort Orange. The French language has two words signifying "straight." The adjective word is *etroit*. The noun is *detroit*. Therefore, the name of Detroit signifies that it is the "city of the strait." The first two white women in Detroit were Madame Cadillac and Madame Tonty —Tonty was Cadillac's lieutenant. "The first women were given a grand reception as they came up the river. The cannon was fired from the parapet of the fort, the soldiers discharged their muskets in a salvo, and all the white men and a horde of Indians made as much noise as possible while the ladies were helped ashore and conducted to the fort on the bluff." A decade later, Cadillac served for three years as governor of the territory of Louisiana. Back in France, he was stuffed into the Bastille for a time, falsely charged as a counterfeiter, franctly trying to make ha' while the Sun King shone. The Cadillac Automobile Company was founded in Detroit more than eighty years ago by Henry Leland.

CAESAR, SID

The comedian received a telephone call from Albert Einstein, who suggested they meet and discuss the human condition. Einstein died before the historic confab could take place. The modern Pagliacci has been a self-described alcoholic and a pill addict for most of his adult years.

CAIRO

Almost nothing happens in Egypt that does not happen in Cairo. The most populous city in the Middle East and Africa—over 5 million people —was known as On in antiquity, then Heliopolis, the city of the Sun. The Nile flows past Cairo and to the north, where it divides to form the great delta and pour into the Mediterranean. To the east, behind the soaring minarets of the Muhammad Ali mosque and the Mukattam Hills, the desert stretches to Arabia. To the west, beyond the pyramids, more Sahara. Cairo was founded in 969 to replace nearby Al Qatai as the capital. The ancient Egyptian capital Memphis was almost directly across the Nile, and the Roman fortress city Babylon was where Old Cairo is today, in the southeast section of the capital. Al Azhar, the center of Koranic studies, is the oldest university in the world.

CALEDONIA

It's what the conquering Romans called Britain north of the firths of Clyde and Forth—today, it's Scotland, or the Scottish Highlands. The name first occurred in the works of Lucan, in the first century, about the time that a Roman general named Agricola marched against the Caledonians, or Picts. The natives were little more than savages, naked, wild, their bows and arrows and small shields finally bowing before the metal-clad invaders. When one night fell, ten thousand Caledonians lay dead upon the battlefield. In the fifth century, after the Romans had retired to the continent, the rejuvenated Caledonians ruined parts of the seventy-three-mile-long Hadrian's Wall separating Scotland and England and plunged south as far as London.

CALIGULA

His real name was Caius Caesar Germanicus. As a child, he wore little boots, *Caligulae,* hence Caligula (the singular). The Roman Senate conferred absolute power upon him after he had had Tiberius done in. He caused the names of his sisters to be included in all oaths: ". . . I will not value my life or that of my children less highly than I do the safety of the Emperor Caius and his sisters." He committed incest with his sisters at large banquets. Crazed, he made his horse Incitatus a consul and a member of a priestly college. He fed criminals, rather than expensive butcher's meat, to his collection of wild animals. He made parents attend their sons' executions. "Let them hate me, so long as they fear me." He invented new kinds of baths. He was terrified of thunderstorms, but insomnia was his worst torment. His four-year reign of terror and insanity ended when a tribune of the Praetorian Guard drove a sword into him repeatedly.

CALLAS, MARIA

Real name: Maria Kalogeropoulos. The spellbinding diva was once chubby, painfully shy, clumsy, unpopular, and would never look at herself in a mirror. The "ugly duckling" became the magnificent Greek-American soprano under her mother's drive. "There should be a law against that kind of thing," Maria once said bitterly. "A child treated like this grows old before its time. They shouldn't deprive a child of its childhood! Only when I was singing did I feel loved." She wore for years a Bulova watch she had won in a national amateur talent contest on a radio network. She made her operatic debut in Athens in *Cavalleria Rusticana* at the age of fourteen. But nearly a score of years passed before she first sang at the Metropolitan Opera in New York City. Her *Norma* on opening night there in 1956 drew a record audience. The next year, she met Aristotle Onassis at a party given in Venice by Elsa Maxwell; their turbulent affair was aborted by Onassis' involvement with Jacqueline B. Kennedy. On the day that President John F. Kennedy was shot in Dallas, Miss Callas' touring partner was scheduled to sing *The Masked Ball* there —the opera is about the assassination of a king. Miss Callas' last operatic performance was in *Tosca* at the Met in 1965. She died at the age of 53, in 1977.

CALLEY, WILLIAM L.

"It was a massacre all right," President Richard M. Nixon agreed. "And under no circumstances was it justified." When no enemy soldiers were found in the South Vietnamese hamlet of Mylai, in 1968, U.S. Army First Lieutenant Calley ordered his infantry platoon to round up the residents, men, women, and children. Calley began to shoot them and ordered his men to shoot them, too, shoot anything that moved. The massacre of maybe 500 Vietnamese went on for several hours. Three years later, Calley was convicted of murdering twenty-two unarmed civilians. Eleven other soldiers were acquitted or the charges against them were dismissed. Calley was sentenced to life at hard labor, but served only three years, after President Nixon had reviewed the case, and that under house arrest at Fort Benning, Georgia. He has worked in his father-in-law's jewelry store in Columbus, Georgia, and been described as the store's most popular salesman. Lieutenant General William R. Peers, who led the Army's inquiry, has said, "To think that out of all those men, only one, Lieutenant William Calley, was brought to justice. And now he's practically a hero. It's a tragedy."

CAMPBELL, GLEN

"There's got to be a captain of this ship and there's got to be a first mate," the more-than-one-time-loser country-pop crooner crooned about bride number four—you can count 'em—"I was put on this earth as a male and I function and do that for which God created me as a male, and she's a female and she does that. She never picks arguments and we don't bitch at each other." Campbell told *People:* "I consider that a blessing." He had cotton-pickin' hands as a kid—to earn money to go to the movies, in Delight, Arkansas; "It's a lot easier pickin' a guitar"— and with true grit he's picked up a mine of golds and Grammies and box-office records since his first national hit, "Turn Around—Look at Me." Yes, that's a dagger tattooed on his left arm. He doesn't think his songs fall into any particular category: "If there's anything about them, I think it's the lyrics . . . they're meaningful and I hope they say something to all people." That's gentle on our mind.

CANADA

"It's only a few acres of snow," Voltaire jibed. It's the "great lone land." It's also the second largest country in the world (six time zones). It has the world's longest coastline: 151,488 miles; the province of British Columbia's is a complex of winding, twisting waterways, islands, bays, inlets, fjords, rugged cliffs, sandy beaches of white, gray, even black. Two of the 10 provinces—Yukon and Northwest Territories—constitute more than a third of the land area but they have less than one percent of the population of about 25 million. Nearly 90 percent of the nearly 4 million square miles is economically useless for any purpose other than growing trees or providing minerals (e.g., nickel, zinc, asbestos, potash, uranium). A million square miles is tundra. But Canada has about half of the fresh water of the world. It was invited to join the Union after the American Revolution. From the War of 1812 until Theodore Roosevelt's presidency, it feared American military invasion. *That* fear has been superseded by the fear of American economic and cultural domination. Nearly every Maple Leafer can read and write. Canada's official animal is the beaver.

CANARY ISLANDS

A Spanish archipelago of seven large (2,808 square miles) islands of volcanic origin in the Atlantic off the Spanish Sahara, they may have been the Fortunate Isles of really ancient Romans. *Canariae insulae*—Late Latin for "dog islands"—the Canary Islands. In Roman times, they were noted for a breed of large dogs—dog in Latin is *canis*. *Canaria* was the Latin name of one of the group of Canaries. The side facing Africa is savage and barren, the Atlantic side luscious and gentle. It only rains three or four days a year. Mount Teide is the highest point (12,162 feet) in Spanish territory, and is often above the clouds. It was from the Canaries that Columbus finally set out for the New World. The British naval person Horatio Nelson was repulsed at Santa Cruz there, in 1797, and lost an arm. Aviation's greatest passenger tragedy occurred at Tenerife Airport in 1977; two airliners collided on the ground and 574 people were killed; 70 survived.

THE CANTERBURY TALES

"May, with alle thy floures and thy grene, Welcome be thou, faire, fresshe May"—from the knight's tale, one of the eighteen *Canterbury Tales*. Geoffrey Chaucer had planned to relate fifty-eight—the twenty-nine pilgrims who had assembled at the Tabard, an inn in Southwark, a London suburb, agreed to help pass the time, to tell one tale each on the journey to the shrine of St. Thomas à Becket at Canterbury and one each on the return journey; the pilgrim telling the best tale would be treated by the others to a supper at the Tabard. ("For dronkenesse is verray sepulture Of mannes wit and his discrecioun"—from the pardoner's tale.) The unfinished work, about 17,000 lines, is one of the most brilliant works in all literature, a panorama of fourteenth-century English life. The poet was a soldier on one of the English's intermittent forays into France that made up so large a part of the Hundred Years' War. He was taken prisoner near Rheims and later ransomed. During the 1370s, he was frequently employed on diplomatic missions to the Continent, visiting Italy on two occasions; his Italian period of literary activity was modeled primarily on Dante and Boccaccio. His *House of Fame* recounted the adventures of Aeneas after the fall of Troy; his *Parliament of Fowls,* which tells of the mating of fowls on St. Valentine's Day, is thought to celebrate the betrothal of Richard II to Anne of Bohemia. He introduced the heroic couplet into English verse and perfected the seven-line stanza, called rhyme royal. In civil jobs, he supervised repair of walls, ditches, sewers, and bridges. But Chaucer is best known for the tales of the earthy wife of Bath, the worldly prioress, the evil summoner, the gentle knight. He was the first poet to be buried in Westminster Abbey.

CAPONE, AL—"SCARFACE"

Big Al. Snorky. Scarface. He tried to conceal with talcum powder the scar (source unknown) on his left cheek. He wore silk pajamas. He showered friends with gifts. He gave football-game tickets to Boy Scouts. He established a soup kitchen in Chicago during the Depression which doled out 20,000 meals a week. He was a lavish tipper. "Public service is my motto." He had many friends. He had even more enemies. In 1919, he moved from New York to Chicago because he was needed there by a gangster and because he was a suspect in several murders in New York. He became a bootlegger and he fixed elections and he became the city's crime syndicate boss. Chicago police said he was responsible for twenty-five murders, including the rub-out of seven Bugs Moran associates in a warehouse on St. Valentine's Day in 1929. At times he didn't have a heart. A Cadillac was custom-made for the big man: plush upholstery, half a ton of armor plate, a steel visor over the gas tank, thick, bulletproof glass windows, a removable rear window that converted the back seat into a machine-gun emplacement. The Caddie was preceded by a scout car and tailed by a car bristling with marksmen. Capone once said, "A woman's home and her children are her real happiness. If she would stay there, the world would have less to worry about"—but that's not why he needed the guard-all shield. The competition had nicknames like Machine Gun and Greasy Thumb and The Enforcer and The Bomber and The Terrible. In restaurants and in theaters, Capone was surrounded by trusted henchmen. When he walked along a street or through a lobby, he was in a huddle of bodies. His office had secret exits and entrances. His swivel chair had an armor-plated back. When he learned that lieutenants were conspiring to dethrone him, he first partied them, then beat them to death with a baseball bat. The Feds got him on twenty-two counts of income tax evasion. He was fined $50,000 and nailed with an eleven-year prison term. While waiting for the appeals decision, he resided in a cell in Chicago's Cook County jail made comfortable by a friendly warden. He conferred there with colleagues; when meetings required extreme privacy, he was allowed to use the death chamber. He was sent to the federal prison in Atlanta—#40,822—then transferred to impregnable Alcatraz because he was "incorrigible." He was stabbed and nearly strangled by other prisoners. Given time off for good behavior, and because he was shattered by syphilis, he retired to Miami—"as nutty as a fruitcake," a former henchman claimed. When Capone died, he was denied a requiem mass by the Church.

CAPOTE, TRUMAN

Kenneth Peacock Tynan declared that "for the first time, an influential writer of the front rank has been placed in a position of privileged intimacy with criminals about to die, and—in my view—done less than he might have to save them," and he wasn't alone in that opinion. A "prominent Manhattan lawyer" agreed that Truman Capote did not do all he might have to save the lives of Richard Eugene Hickock and Perry Smith, the murderers literarily captured in Capote's electrifying best-selling nonfiction novel, *In Cold Blood*. "I would doubt whether *In Cold Blood* would have been released prior to the decease of the accused," Mr. Tynan quoted the lawyer as having said. Mr. Capote said that if Mr. Tynan indeed could prove he had such an opinion, he would donate $500 (of the millions of dollars he made on the book) to "Mr. Tynan's favorite charity (if so uncharitable a spirit has a favorite charity)." The late Mr. Tynan proved it—the lawyer provided a sworn affidavit—and the late Mr. Capote forwarded his personal check to the Howard League for Penal Reform. Five years before Hickock and Smith senselessly and brutally slaughtered four members of the Herbert W. Clutter family, in Holcomb, Kansas, *The New York Times Magazine* published a three-page feature on a typical Kansas farmer—Herbert W. Clutter: "There is little evidence of the wealth this land produces. In fact, the teen-age daughters who are doing the housekeeping while the mother is away convalescing from a stay in the hospital complain about 'that old refrigerator,' which Mr. Clutter ruefully admits needs replacing." Mr. Capote did not mention *The Times*'s feature in his book, and it will never be known if Hickock and Smith read the article and intentionally sought out the "tidy, efficient, and unpretentious" layout.

CARCINOGEN

It's from the Greek *karkinos,* "cancer," and connotes a substance or agent that produces or incites cancerous growth. Among many known carcinogens are asbestos, additives in processed meat, alkylating agents, cigarette smoke, X rays, radioactive elements, and, in light-skinned people, sunlight.

CARIBOU

Place a female caribou among a herd of other female deer and you can pick her out from miles away. She's the one with the antlers. The caribou are the only deer in which both genders have antlers. The caribou is the native reindeer of North America, in both arctic and subarctic regions: the barren-ground caribou of the tundra, the woodland caribou of the bogs and coniferous forests. The animal has two toes on each foot and, like a cow and a camel, a four-part stomach. It chews regurgitated food in the form of cud.

CARLOS, JUAN

The royal wedding of Prince Charles and Lady Diana Spencer in London, in 1981, was snubbed by King Juan Carlos and Queen Sofia of Spain. The reason: the honeymooners planned to board the royal yacht *Britannia* at Gibraltar for a two-week honeymoon cruise in the Mediterranean. The Rock has been a British naval base and crown colony since the early eighteenth century and long the subject of dispute between Britain and

Spain. Spain claims the Jurassic limestone fortress as its own territory. The royal visit to Gibraltar was considered "inopportune, gratuitous, and mistaken" by the Spanish Foreign Ministry, for whom Gibraltar was its most emotional political issue. The border between Gibraltar and Spain had been closed for more than a decade. In England the Spanish monarchs were to have watched Prince Charles play polo against Spain and then to have marched with other continental sovereigns in the wedding procession in St. Paul's Cathedral.

CARLSBAD CAVERNS

The Green Lake Room, the King's Palace, the Queen's Chamber, the Papoose Room—four of the reasons that New Mexico is "the land of enchantment"—are hundreds and hundreds of feet underground in the state's most famous tourist attraction, the limestoned, stalactited, stalagmited Carlsbad Caverns, a national park in the foothills of the Guadalupe Mountains since 1930. The floor of the Big Room is as expansive as fourteen football fields, its ceiling as high as a twenty-two-story building; the trail around its perimeter is 1¼ miles long. The temperature throughout is a constant fifty-six degrees F. A lunchroom for tourists is 749 feet underground. Even more spectacular than the myriad shapes and sizes is the nocturnal flight from the cave, April through October, by "millions" of bats that feed on insects in the valleys of the Black and Pecos rivers. They return at dawn, diving swiftly into the entrance and back to their lair, where they spend the day hanging head-downward. (The bats migrate to warmer regions in the winter.) All that bat guano, a nitrate-rich fertilizer, attracted miners at the turn of the century. How did Carlsbad start hundreds of million years ago? The limestone originated as an organic reef around the edge of a warm shallow sea in what is now southeast New Mexico.

CARROLL, DIAHANN

She wasn't television's first black star—Bill Cosby, in 1965, played the second lead to Robert Culp in the action-adventure hour "I Spy"—but she was the first black star in a sit-com, "Julia," 1968–71, on NBC. Playing Julia Baker, a widowed nurse (her husband was killed in Vietnam) raising a young son (Corey) and living in an integrated housing project, she was the first black to carry a series on the same terms as a white star—good ratings and ample advertiser support. The series' pilot had been rejected at NBC at first, but it was put on when the network needed programming opposite the long-time CBS hit "The Red Skelton Show." NBC decided to "salvage something from the loss—the appearance of having tried to do a program with a black lead." Les Brown, the television industry chronicler, has written that to NBC's, "and the industry's, surprise, 'Julia'—with all its faults—turned out to be a hit." The program was criticized as being unrealistic and unrepresentative of black life.

CARSON CITY

Unearthing of the nearby Comstock Lode, the richest known silver deposit in the United States, was a "goldmine" for Nevada's capital city, the smallest (16,000 pop.) in the country. Carson City, named for frontiersman-guide-Indian fighter-brigadier general Kit Carson, became the terminus of the railroad carrying the ore. It was also a station on the short-lived Pony Express and the terminus of a telegraph line, from San Francisco, whose dots and dashes replaced the galloping hooves. Old-timers still recall the world heavyweight championship fight there in 1897 —Bob Fitzsimmons beat up Jim Corbett and a motion picture was made of the bout. It had a bluish tint, and it flickered and it shifted without warning, but it was considered a marvel and made a lot of money, some say a goldmine.

CARSON, RACHEL

Her *Silent Spring*, in 1962, was a thunderbolt. What was killing the birds might kill man next. She introduced to general consciousness the idea of ecology. She had written *The Sea Around Us, Under the Sea-Wind,* and *The Edge of the Sea*. She dove into *Silent Spring* when she learned that a private bird sanctuary near Cape Cod was being pesticided out of existence. More than fifty pages of sources were cited as she detailed the effects of man-made poisons on the environment: The environment was being altered, with unforeseen and possibly disastrous consequences. "I am not afraid of being thought a sentimentalist," she said, "when I say that I believe natural beauty has a necessary place in the spiritual development of any individual or any society. I believe that whenever we . . . substitute something man-made and artificial for a natural feature of the earth, we have retarded some part of man's spiritual growth." Miss Carson died of cancer at the age of fifty-six.

CARTER, "MISS LILLIAN"

"When I look at my children, I say, 'Lillian, you should have stayed a virgin.' " Jimmy Carter's late mother had lots more to say: "There was really nothing outstanding about Jimmy as a boy." "I never did like the

White House. It was boring." "Hunger and poverty are things I cannot live with, and I cannot live with myself unless I work to do something about them." "I know folks have a tizzy about it, but I like a little bourbon of an evening. I don't much care what they say about it. I'm a Christian, but that doesn't mean I'm a long-faced square." She shocked and scandalized white neighbors in Georgia by receiving black guests in her parlor. At the age of sixty-seven, she was a Peace Corps volunteer in India; it meant more to her than any other one thing in her life. She regretted not taking her late husband's seat in the Georgia legislature when it was offered. During the 1976 presidential campaign, she told her candidate son to "quit that stuff about never telling a lie." Jody Powell, President Carter's press secretary, believes Carter had relationship problems with journalists because he was a small-town Southern Baptist with a set of values and beliefs that made many of them decidedly uncomfortable: "The sad fact is that many political reporters are a good bit more familiar and comfortable with politicians who lie, cheat, and steal than with one who prays—particularly if he prays in private and with conviction." Powell also believes that the press found it "unforgivable" that Carter did not fit the southern-pol stereotype: "Not only did he practice as well as preach his religion, he did not tell racist jokes, even in private, and he did not drink large quantities of bourbon and pat strange women on the fanny."

CARVER, GEORGE WASHINGTON

An agricultural chemist, a botanist, a member of the Royal Society of London, a treasured friend of Thomas A. Edison, many times a guest of Henry Ford, and a former slave. From red clay and sandy loam, he developed ink, pigments, cosmetics, paper, paints, and many other articles. From the sweet potato, he produced tapioca, molasses, dyes, starch, and flour. He created sixty products from the pecan. When he began research into the possibility of making rubber from sweet potatoes, Carver was invited by Edison to join him at Menlo Park in Orange, New Jersey, at a salary representing a princely advance over the "peanuts" he was getting at Tuskegee Institute in Alabama—Carver passed; he was devoted to helping his fellow blacks. His laboratory was his head. He was also an accomplished artist. His sketch of Yucca Gloriosa won a first prize in the World's Columbian Exposition, in 1893.

CASABLANCA

The 1943 motion picture was directed by Michael Curtiz from a screenplay by Howard Koch and the twins Julius J. and Philip G. Epstein, based on an unproduced play, *Everybody Comes to Rick's*, by Murray Burnett and Joan Alison. Herman Hupfeld's song "As Time Goes By" (sung by Dooley Wilson, as Sam) had been used in an earlier movie, *Everybody's Welcome*. Ronald Reagan was at one time scheduled to play the role of Rick Blaine, who runs a gambling casino in Nazi-occupied French territory in Moroccan Casablanca ("white house" in Spanish). There was no final shooting script for the film. Humphrey Bogart, playing Blaine, had many lines quotable four decades later: "What's your nationality?" *"I'm a drunkard."* "You despise me, Rick, don't you?" *"If I gave you any thought, I probably would."* Sydney Greenstreet was the fezzed, amiably corrupt proprietor of the Blue Parrot. *Casablanca* won Oscars for best picture, best direction, best screenplay. The best actress award that year went to Jennifer Jones, *The Song of Bernadette,* not to Ingrid Bergman, who played Ilsa Laszlo in *Casablanca,* and the best actor award went to Paul Lukas, for *Watch on the Rhine,* not to Bogie.

"CASEY AT THE BAT"

The National League was only twelve years old when Ernest Lawrence Thayer, a journalist, an editor, a poet, published in the San Francisco *Examiner* what is still, nearly a century later, the best-known poem about the national pastime: "Oh! somewhere in this favored land the sun is shining bright; the band is playing somewhere, and somewhere hearts are light; and somewhere men are laughing and somewhere children shout, But there is no joy in Mudville—mighty Casey has struck out." Later that year, 1888, the light-opera singer DeWolf Hopper recited it at Wallack's Theater, in New York City. Over the years he was to sing it about 9,999 more times before hanging up his voice. Thayer's score has been frozen at 4–2.

CASPIAN SEA

What large, very large lake, a.k.a. sea, is 92½ feet below sea level? What large, very large lake, a little less than the square mileage of California, is up to 3,200 feet deep toward its southern end and has an average depth of only 17 feet at its northern end? What is the largest salt water lake in the world? What is the largest inland body of water, with no outlet? The Caspian Sea. The Caspian Sea. The Caspian Sea. The Caspian Sea. Three sides of the lake, the beluga caviar sides, the offshore oil and gas drilling sides, lie within the Soviet Union; the southern side, the deep side, is Iran's. It may once have been linked with the Arctic Ocean far to the north—there are seals in the Caspian, as there are both saltwater and freshwater fish. At one time, the northern Caspian, near the oilfields of

Baku, was the most beautiful bathing site in all of Russia. But the lake's been at sea for years—pollution makes it a sight for sore eyes.

CASTRO, RAUL

He is second only to his revolutionary brother Fidel as the most powerful official in Cuba. He is first vice-premier, a Communist party official, and spokesman for Cuba's unique form of Marxism-Leninism. He was educated in Jesuit schools and the University of Havana, then linked his future with his older brother's: "I had had enough of prayer. I liked sports and deviltry." The Castros's attack on an army post at Santiago de Cuba in 1953 was unsuccessful, and they were imprisoned. After a general amnesty, they went into exile in Mexico, where they organized the 26th of July Movement that toppled the Batista regime on New Year's Day 1959. Raul's wife, Vilma Espin, is the official hostess of the Castro regime.

THE CATCHER IN THE RYE

When nobody at Harcourt, Brace had read his manuscript of adolescent rebellion after a week, or so the story goes, the author retrieved it and took it to Little, Brown, which has been in clover ever since. Jerome David Salinger's only novel was published in 1951. "The final scene is as good as anything that Salinger has written," the reviewer for the *New Republic* wrote, "which means very good indeed. So are a number of other episodes. But the book as a whole is disappointing, and not merely because it is a reworking of a theme that one begins to suspect must obsess the author." *Saturday Review of Literature:* "This is a book to be read thoughtfully and more than once." *New York Herald Tribune:* "Recent war novels have accustomed us all to ugly words and images, but from the mouths of the very young and protected they are peculiarly offensive. There is probably not one phrase in the whole book that Holden Caulfield would not have used upon occasion, but when they are piled upon each other in cumulative monotony, the ear refuses to believe." *San Francisco Chronicle:* "Mr. Salinger's novel is funny, poignant, and, in its implications, profound. It is literature of a very high order. It really is." A copy of the book was being carried by Mark David Chapman, a former mental patient, when he shot and killed the Beatle John Lennon in New York, in 1980, and he thumbed through Holden Caulfield's near-breakdown while waiting for the police. "This is my statement," Chapman has said of the book. Reading it would help anyone "understand what has happened."

CATCH-22

Joseph Heller's gift to the vernacular—the term describes the self-contradictory, endlessly circular, even insane snag that modern bureaucracy effortlessly produces—was almost Catch-18. It's what he originally planned to call his novel about the lunacy of lunacy. But there was a catch. As Heller was readying his book for publication, Leon Uris came out with a novel about the Warsaw-ghetto uprising he called *Mila 18*. Yipes, Yossarian! It was anything but love at first sight. Heller changed his title. Now when captain-bombardier John Yossarian of an American bomber squadron in Italy during World War II seeks to be grounded for medical reasons, he suffers Catch-22 when the Doc explains that he can ground anyone who is crazy—but, God knows, anyone who wants to avoid combat duty must be sane.

CATS

Many people do not find the carnivorous mammals constituting the family *Felidae,* specifically the domestic cat, *Felis catus,* to be the cat's meow. They do not have an abnormal fear or dread of the cat—they do not suffer ailurophobia—but given a choice they doggedly insist there is no choice, even if it's a Siamese and comes in on little fog's feet. Not to be catty, but—these men would rather not have been in Felidelphia: Napoleon, President Eisenhower, Johannes Brahms (an avowed cat hater), the French king Henry III, the French poet Pierre de Ronsard. A famous British military man would become, well, catatonic when his kids asked him to read "Puss in Boots." The punishment for killing a feline in ancient Egypt was capital. The sacred animal, probably a derivation of the North African wildcat, stood between death and life for millions because it rid granaries of rodents, the cause of disease and famine. It was also illegal to ship cats abroad. The cat has been domesticated for about five millennia. Only the cat, the camel, and the giraffe walk by moving their front and hind legs on one side, then on the other. The cat was also venerated in the Norse religion. It was burned as a witch in the Middle Ages.

CAVIAR

It is the roe of various species of sturgeon that abound in Russian rivers and the Caspian and Black Seas. The ovaries are beaten and strained through a sieve to clear the eggs of membranes, fibers, and fatty matter; salt is added. The most common caviar comes from the beluga. (*Hamlet:*

"His play . . . pleased not the million, 'twas caviar to the general.") The superb rare albino beluga produces the "imperial" caviar. Caviar spoils if it is kept at over 40°F. for more than a few hours.

CB

"Got your ears on? Do it to me." In CB talk, that's "Are you listening to your CB? Answer me." Some of the 2,000 or so CB (citizens band) radio slang expressions that have evolved: Pregnant rollerskate = VW (Volkswagen). Kiddie car = school bus. Bear bite = speeding ticket. Motion lotion = fuel. Pavement princess = prostitute who works the truck stops. Reefer = refrigerator truck trailer. Bulldog = Mack truck. Bubblegummer = teenage CBer. Cold coffee = beer. Bone box = ambulance. Zoo = police headquarters. That's all from blessed event = the new CB unit.

CELSIUS SCALE

Anders Celsius was the Swedish astronomer who was the first to try to determine the magnitude of stars by measuring the intensity of their light with something other than the human eye. His contribution to science has nothing to do with astronomy. In 1742, he divided the temperature difference between the boiling point and the freezing point of water into an even one hundred degrees, or steps. (On Gabriel Daniel Fahrenheit's scale, there are 190 degrees between the two points.) At first, Celsius placed the boiling point at 0° and the freezing point at 100°; a year later, he reversed the two extremes. If your body temperature is 37° and it's been taken with a centigrade (the word means "divided into 100 parts") thermometer, you're absolutely normal—it's 98.6° on the familiar (in the United States) F. thermometer. To change a temperature on the Celsius scale to one on the Fahrenheit scale, multiply the Celsius temperature by $\frac{9}{5}$, then add 32. Multiply by $\frac{9}{5}$ because 1 Celsius degree equals 1.8 (or $\frac{9}{5}$) Fahrenheit degrees. Add 32 because 0° C. equals 32°F. To change Fahrenheit readings to Celsius readings: °C. = $\frac{5}{9}$ (°F. −32). In the upscale scientific community, even in the United States, the Celsius scale is preferred because it is part of the favored metric system of measurement.

CERBERUS

The mythical three-headed watchdog of the underworld, he had a snake's tail and a row of serpent heads sprouting from his back. He was so hideous that any man who looked on him turned to stone. Cerberus devoured any inmate who tried to escape from the realm of Hades. To get past him and into the underworld, Sibyl of Cumae threw him a sop—a cake soaked in drugged wine—hence the expression a "sop for Cerberus," bribing or calming a difficult person. Hercules' twelfth labor was to fetch Cerberus. By sheer strength, the most popular of all Greek heroes carried the brute to Mycenae, terrifying Eurystheus with the sight, then returned it to Hades.

CEREBRAL PALSY

The greatest child crippler in the United States is a paralysis caused usually by injury at birth and characterized by poor muscular control and spasms and by mental retardation. CP cannot be cured. It cannot be inherited. Most physical forms can be helped with therapy. About half of one percent of all people in the world suffer cerebral palsy. Preventing brain damage to the baby before and during birth and immediately after birth is the best way to head off the disorder.

CERVANTES SAAVEDRA, MIGUEL DE

Can a burlesque of the popular romances of chivalry be an immediate and enormous success? Cervantes' *Don Quixote* was, when it was published in the early seventeenth century. But nearly three centuries later, two eminent Victorians didn't want their ladyfolk reading it. "It pains me to think of your reading that book just as it stands," Mark Twain wrote his intended. "I have thought of it with regret time and again. If you haven't finished it, Livy, don't do it. You are as pure as snow, and I would have you always so—untainted, untouched even by the impure thoughts of others." Justin Kaplan, who is family, has recorded Sigmund Freud's admonition to his fiancee, Martha Bernays: "It is no reading matter for girls. I had quite forgotten the many coarse and in themselves nauseating passages when I sent it to you. No doubt it achieves its aim in a remarkable manner, yet even this is somewhat remote from my princess." Neither Twain nor Freud were themselves quixotic.

CHAMBERLAIN, WILT

"The Stilt" played 798 hours in the National Basketball Association—that's 47,859 minutes over thirteen years—and never once fouled out of a game, and he was in 1,045 of them. The league's second highest all-time scorer netted 31,419 points—12,681 field goals, 6,057 foul throws (but at the end of his career he may have been the world's worst free thrower)—and pulled down 23,924 rebounds—and he is still the only NBAer to score 100 points in a single game. (It's also the only game in which two players on the same team together scored at least 100 points.) Chamberlain once scored 78 points in a game, 73 points in a game twice, and 72 once. He scored at least 50 points in 72 NBA games and retired with a 30.1 points per game average. Only two other players have once each exceeded 70 points in a game: David Thompson (73) and Elgin Baylor (71).

CHAN, CHARLIE

Mystery-novelist Earl Derr Biggers' humble, courteous, charming Chinese-Hawaiian-American sleuth fingered his first case in 1925—rich, handsome, genial, and dead Dan Winterslip had a past in *The House Without a Key*. The Honolulu police detective sergeant (later inspector) cum sage lived in a house on Punchbowl Hill, was married, and had eleven children, including number-one son, Lee. "Pop" loved to quote aphorisms: "Bad alibi like dead fish. Cannot stand test of time." "If strength were all, tiger would not fear scorpion." Chan's accusatory "You the murderer" echoes through the stories that Biggers wrote until 1932: *The Chinese Parrot, Behind That Curtain the Black Camel, Charlie Chan Carries On,* and *Keeper of the Keys*. Under the pseudonym Dennis Lynds, Michael Collins wrote *Charlie Chan Returns*. "The Amazing Chan and the Chan Clan" was a TV cartoon series in which the offspring tried their hand at solving the mystery; often their hands were tied.

CHANEY, LON

The silent screen star (more than 150 flicks) was "the man of a thousand faces." He was a master of the grotesque. His parents were deaf and dumb, and for several years his mother was helpless from inflammatory rheumatism. Exchanging thoughts with his parents by means of sign language led to extraordinary skill as an actor and unusually expressive gestures, particularly body language. He first gained national "recognition" by playing a frog in *The Miracle Man*. He reshaped his face with plastic gum. He twisted his body with a straitjacket to play Quasimodo in *The Hunchback of Notre Dame*. He could throw a shoulder out of joint. He made himself "legless" for *The Penalty*. In *The Blackbird,* he curved his spine by drawing up one leg and having the tailor accentuate the apparent bodily deformity by making one side of his clothes longer than the other. He "scarred" himself, he "wounded" himself, he "burned" himself. The *Encyclopedia Britannica* had him write its article on make-up. He didn't have to make anything up.

THE CHANNEL ISLANDS

The bailiwick of Jersey and the bailiwick of Guernsey, which includes Alderney, Sark, Herm, Brechou, Jethou, and some islets with no permanent inhabitants—seventy-five square miles off the northwest coast of France—the Channel Islands, the only portions of the duchy of Normandy belonging to the Crown since the Norman Conquest, more than nine centuries ago. (The official language on Jersey is French; on Guernsey, English.) During the reign of Queen Elizabeth I, the knitted woolen ''jerseys'' were first made. The cattle Jerseys and Guernseys, renowned for their milk, are kept pure by laws prohibiting other breeds. The Nazis occupied the Channel Islands in June 1940; the Allied armies invading Europe went right by them; both captor and captee suffered during a long blockade. The Germans raised the white flag just before V-E Day.

CHARLESTON

The South Carolina city was named for King Charles II of England, Scotland, and Ireland (as was Carolina, which in the mid-seventeenth century encompassed all the land between Virginia and Florida). (Lincoln and Douglas debated in Charleston, Illinois, in 1858, and Daniel Boone lived in the Charleston that is now the capital of West Virginia.) Charleston was once Charles Town, and a repository of genteel tradition. Holding out for accommodation with England were the aristocrats Laurens, Rutledge, Drayton, Pinckney, and Cotesworth. The British held the city for a year after Yorktown. In 1720, slaves suspected of rebellious intent were burned alive near the city. In 1822, the freed preacher Denmark Vesey and more than thirty other blacks were suspected of rebellious intent and hanged in the noonday sun. There was to be no monkey business. The Civil War was ignited in Charleston—Confederate artillery had Union troops at bay in Fort Sumter. Three years later, the Union nearly leveled the city with bombardment and siege, shell and shall-not. An earthquake devastated the city in 1886, and storms have done severe damage. It's a tourist's delight through which one could Charleston: the Old Slave Mart Museum and Gallery, the Charleston Museum, Fort Sumter National Monument, Cabbage Row, Magnolia Gardens, Cypress Gardens, St. Michael's Episcopal Church, the Miles Brewton house, Old Powder magazine, the Citadel, the College of Charleston (the first municipal college in the country), and the waterfront, called the Battery. *The Charleston* began as a black dance in the early 1900s: outward heel kicks combined with an up and down movement achieved by bending and straightening the knees in time to the syncopated 4/4 rhythm of ragtime. The city has shown a lively interest in the arts. It is the home today of

"John Colleton" (the polymath Robert Marks), the intellectual/writer who has authored multimillion-copy paperbacks.

"CHARLIE'S ANGELS"

Charlie of "Charlie's Angels" was never seen by his three private-sleuthing Angels nor by the television viewer. Only the Angels' immediate superior, played by Tom Bosley, saw Charlie, and he didn't say much. Yes, Charlie lived in lavish splendor. Yes, he was surrounded by beautiful women. Yes, he liked champagne and song. And here are his latest directives, girls—and a tape recording would be turned on. The voice of Charlie was the actor John Forsythe's—he *is* seen in the current television rage "Dynasty."

CHAVEZ, CESAR

The agrarian labor-union organizer and maverick leader of California's table-grape pickers—he had been a migrant worker himself—became so popular in the late 1960s that it was said that "most liberals would rather eat a cyanide pellet than a California grape these days." His United Farm Workers Organizing Committee was the first viable agricultural union in the country. Robert Kennedy called Chavez "one of the heroic figures of our time."

CHECKERS

The two-player, sixty-four-square board game is called draughts in Britain, *dama* in Italy, *la jeu de dames* in France, *aracaby* in Poland, and *da Damenspiel* in Germany. Its origin is lost in history. The Egyptians were playing checkers about 6000 B.C. The first book about checkers (1547) is in the Royal Library of Madrid, Spain. The first book in English seems to have been written by a London mathematician, William Payne, in 1756.

CHEESE

Cheese brings a smile to every Frenchman's face. He eats more of it every year than does a person in any other country, though the United States is the biggest producer. The Paris restaurant Androuet's has offered 250 varieties made from the milk of cows, sheep, and goats. The cheese can be classified scientifically in seven major groups: fresh or unripened soft cheese; ripened soft curd types; semi-hard (pressed), hard (pressed), high temperature cooking (scalding), soft, surface-mould ripened, and internal (blue) mould ripened. The government controls the industry in France. The cheese must have at least 23 percent total solids. If milk other than cow's milk is used, it must be named; there are exemptions, such as good old favorite Roquefort. Charles De Gaulle complained, "It's impossible in normal times to rally a nation that has 265 kinds of cheese."

CHEETAH

The fastest four-legged animal, it can achieve bursts of speed of over 60 miles per hour. Its tremendous sprints are accompanied, however, by a great energy loss that leads quickly to near-exhaustion. Over long stretches, the cheetah can be overtaken by a horse. The carnivore of the cat family, unique among cats in having nonretractile claws, the cheetah can be tamed easily. Properly trained, it can be a valuable hunting companion. The cheetah has been called a hunting leopard. Large cheetah populations are now seen only in reserves in eastern Africa and in the Etosha region in southwestern Africa.

CHESAPEAKE BAY

"The noblest bay in the Universe," an early colonist swooned. The largest bay in the United States, the Atlantic arm is the largest inland body of water on the East Coast: 3,237 square miles; the deepest point: only 156 feet; 195 miles long; 22 miles at its widest; 3 miles at its narrowest; 48 principal tributaries; and a drainage area about the combined area of the six New England states. "No cruising waters in the United States have more to offer the boatman than Chesapeake Bay," writes a modern boatman. James A. Michener composed an enthralling novel of more than a thousand pages centered on the "glorious" bay while his wife, Mari, cared for the geese, the herons, the ospreys, and the cardinals. The drowned mouth of the Susquehanna River separates Delmarva Peninsula and the mainland, eastern Maryland and eastern Virginia. The shoreline is about 6,000 miles in length.

CHESTERFIELD

Philip Dormer Stanhope, fourth earl of Chesterfield, gave his English royal family name to an overcoat, a sofa, and a cigarette, and he gave advice to his son that the boy of course didn't take. So synonymous is his name with courtly manners that it is possible to forget that he had a distinguished career in public affairs: an ambassadorship to The Hague (1728–32), a negotiator of the second Treaty of Vienna, a seat in Parliament, a successful tenure as lord lieutenant of Ireland. In letters to his illegitimate son, Philip Stanhope, he reviewed the easy elegance of manner—such as his own—that could be a guide to the fashionable world. But the offspring went off and married a woman of low birth and never assumed the position for which his father had tried to prepare him. Lord Chesterfield himself married the illegitimate daughter of George I, and he quarreled famously with Samuel Johnson on the publication of Johnson's seminal lexicographical work on English. Neither had the last word.

CHESTERTON, GILBERT KEITH

The English reactionary, the prince of paradox, wrote fifty-one whodunit stories featuring the Roman Catholic priest Father Brown. His biographies (Browning, Dickens) and his essays were famous, and he was the editor of a weekly that advocated the small-holding system. He was a friend of Hilaire Belloc, whose books he illustrated. Chesterton uncovered an inventive scheme for disposing of a body: As a forest eclipses a single tree, he reasoned that a battlefield would obscure a single corpse. In *The Sign of the Broken Sword,* he had a body dumped in a war zone. Chesterton also wrote a nonlethal detective story, *The Flying Stars*—it's a Christmas story.

CHICAGO

It was the birthplace of American architecture, in the wake of the great Chicago fire of 1871. "The Lake is there, awaiting, in all its glory; and the sky is there above, awaiting in its eternal beauty; and the Prairie, the ever-fertile Prairie is awaiting. And they, all three, as a trinity in one, are dreaming—some prophetic dream." So said the design genius Louis Sullivan, whose buildings for Chicago were great in influence and power and "summed up all truth in Art." Skyscrapers became possible when William Le Baron Jenney observed how a large birdcage of thin metal ribs worked and figured out how a skeleton framework of metal could thus bear both the floors and the exterior masonry walls—the 10-story high Home Insurance Building, of 1883. Burnham, Root, Richardson, Adler, and Frank Lloyd Wright were proponents of the Chicago school of architecture that expunged the Windy City's edifice complex. The 1,559-foot-tall Sears Tower in Chicago is the tallest building in the world today.

CHICAGO CUBS

There hasn't been a World Series game in the Windy City since the White Sox were beaten by the Los Angeles Dodgers in 1959. The Cubs last won the National League pennant in 1945, only to lose the Series to Hank Greenberg and the Detroit Tigers. Over the years, the Cubs have had outstanding players: Ernie Banks, "Mr. Cub" himself, and Ron Santo and Billy Williams, among them, but the team hasn't fared well. In 1961, the club tried something really different with the hope of catching fire: Three men managed the team at the same time. The team led the league in total bases, Billy Williams was voted the National League's rookie of the year, and Ron Santo was voted sophomore of the year. But the Cubs finished with only sixty-four wins, seventh in an eight-team division, twenty-nine games behind the pennant-winning Cincinnati Reds. In 1984, the Cubs won the eastern division but lost the pennant to the never-say-die San Diego Padres after winning the first two games in the five-game play-off.

CHIHUAHUA

It is the tiniest dog, a five-inch tall toy weighing from 1 to 6 pounds. (The St. Bernard weighs as much as 150 pounds.) It is probably of oriental origin. The pooch is named after the capital city, Chihuahua, of the largest (and chief agricultural) state in Mexico.

CHIMPANZEE

The most intelligent subhuman primate has been known to make a monkey out of man. The third-largest ape (five feet tall, 150 pounds), after the gorilla and the orangutan, it has both an excellent memory and reasoning power, and it enjoys performing. In the earliest stage of development, an infant chimp matures at a rate equal to that of a human baby, sometimes even faster. Its native home is the equatorial forests of central and west Africa. In captivity it may develop affection for humans, but it can be dangerous. Chimps have been taught "signing." At Washington University, the chimp Washoe learned more than 130 signs: good, me, out, white, red, and so on. Washoe in turn taught signing to human actors playing apes. No chimp has put a sentence together—the test of cognitive thinking—and none has even by chance aped a bard and typed King Kong.

CHINA AND JAPAN (AT WAR)

It was, in the words of the Chinese novelist Lin-Yutang, "the most terrible, the most inhuman, the most brutal, the most devastating war in all of Asia's history." The ultimate toll may have reached 10 million people. The historian Dick Wilson, tracing the conflict surrounding the Marco Polo Bridge incident, in July 1937, to Japan's surrender eight years later, has noted that "China represented the passive, aristocratic element in east Asian civilization, Japan the brash and energetic newcomer, newly modernized and dying to proselytize. China was a huge reservoir of humanity, Japan a relatively small island state, with only about one-tenth the population of China. A tragic and wasteful episode which did no good to anyone, a negative example of the unwise use of military power." In 1931–32, the Japanese had swept over Manchuria and renamed it Manchoukuo, a puppet state. In 1937, Hirohito's armies sought total conquest, and presently occupied the Chinese sections of Shanghai and all of Nanking and pushed up the Yangtze. By 1939, they had Peking, Tientsin, the Yangtze Valley, Hankow, and Canton in hand. It then took seven years for the Chinese—strongly supported by the American war effort after Pearl Harbor—to rout the emperor's forces and stall their global aspirations. While battling the Japanese, Generalissimo Chiang Kai-shek's Nationalists were also fighting a civil war with Mao's cadres.

CHINOOK

It sometimes is indeed an ill wind that blows no good. Occurring mainly in winter, the Chinook is a warm, dry air mass that loses moisture by condensation over the western slopes of the United States and Canadian Rocky Mountains and then descends the eastern slopes, raising temperatures by forty degrees in a few hours. Cattlemen welcome the chinook sometimes because it melts the snow cover quickly. Sometimes, however, confused animals begin to shed their winter coats and discombobulated plants begin to germinate and there can be disastrous consequences if there is a sudden return to very cold weather. Oregon settlers were the first to call it the chinook—a moist Pacific wind was blowing at them from a Chinook Indian camp. In the Alps, a similar wind is known as *foehn*.

CHISHOLM, SHIRLEY

The first black woman to serve in the House of Representatives (1969–83) declared in 1972 for the Presidency "in the full knowledge that, as a black person and as a female person, I do not have a chance of actually gaining that office in this election year." Her name was put in nomination at the Democratic National Convention: "I ran because someone had to do it first. In this country everyone is supposed to be able to run for President, but that's never been really true. I ran *because* most people think the country isn't ready for a black candidate, not ready for a woman candidate. Someday. . . ." She had taught nursery school, directed day-care centers in New York City, and served in the state assembly before her congressional stint. The first woman member of the House was Jeannette Rankin, of Montana, the only member of congress to vote against United States entry into both World Wars—she had become a congress-person in 1916, four years before women got the franchise nationally. Not until 1932 was a woman elected to a full term in the Senate; in 1943, Senator Hattie W. Caraway, of Arkansas, cosponsored an equal rights amendment. The nation didn't have its first woman governor until 1926: Nellie Tayloe Ross succeeded her late husband as Wyoming's chief executive, and was elected in her own right a month later. She became a vice-chairman of the Democratic National Committee and the first woman to be director of the United States Mint.

CHLOROPHYLL

From Greek words meaning "green leaf." The compound that makes plants green, it supervises the chemical processes whereby green plants convert sunlight into chemical energy (photosynthesis), thereby supporting themselves and the entire animal kingdom, including man. Man was ignorant until 1817 that all life depended upon chlorophyll; it was isolated that year by the French chemists Pierre Joseph Pelletier and Joseph Bienaime Caventou. The German botanist Julius Sachs learned that chlorophyll is not evenly spread throughout the plant, although leaves and other plant parts appear uniformly green. Chlorophyll is confined to certain discrete bodies within a cell, chloroplasts within which the chlorophyll is formed and in which starch grains appear when the leaf is first exposed to light. The German chemist Hans Fischer, who was awarded the 1930 Nobel Prize in chemistry for his work on blood, worked out the complete structure of the chlorophyll molecule. In 1960, the American chemist Robert Woodward synthesized chlorophyll, and in 1965 he was awarded the Nobel Prize for chemistry—he would have flunked out of Massachusetts Institute of Technology as a green teenager if the faculty had not recognized his promise.

CHOW CHOW

It was an all-purpose hunting dog in China 2,000 years ago. Its name may have come from the pidgin-English term for miscellaneous cargo, of which the dog formed a part, hauled from China to England in the late eighteenth century. Or it may have come from the Chinese Chaou, a large, primitive, undomesticated dog of great strength. The chow chow is today a compact dog—up to twenty inches high at the shoulder and fifty to sixty pounds—and it is raised as a companion and house pet. The hungry have been known to wolf down one of these dogs for chow. (Dog meat is popular chow in Hong Kong.)

CHRISTIAN, FLETCHER

What in the world in 1789 was the *Bounty* doing out in the middle of nowhere—the South Pacific five thousand miles east of Australia—anyway? Under William Bligh's command, it was to carry breadfruit trees from Tahiti to Jamaica for transplanting there in the hope that a substitute could be developed for American flour, which had been denied England by the American Revolution. Bligh knew his way around the Pacific; his notable career included service as sailing master on Captain James Cook's last voyage. But his was an irascible nature and he was a strict disciplinarian, which led to mutiny on the *Bounty*. Fletcher Christian seized command, and Bligh and eighteen loyal crew members were cast adrift in a 23-foot launch. Incredibly, the launch made it to Timor, 3,618 miles and more than a month and a half away. The mutineers sailed the *Bounty* to small (2 square miles), isolated Pitcairn Island, which had been first sighted by an English ship twenty-three years earlier. On Bligh's return, England dispatched the H.M.S. *Pandora* and rounded up some of the mutineers—three were hanged after a trial. It is not known what became of master's mate Christian. Most of the people living on Pitcairn today are descendants of the mutineers and their Polynesian wives. Pitcairn islanders were converted to the Seventh-day Adventist faith in 1871. The novel *Mutiny on the Bounty,* by Charles Nordhoff and James Norman, has thrice been made into a major motion picture, starring in turn Clark Gable, Marlon Brando, and Mel Gibson. The Bounty Islands, in the South Pacific and named by Captain Bligh, were once the home of large herds of fur seals. Christian's older brother Edward was a jurist and a professor of laws at Downing College, Cambridge.

A CHRISTMAS CAROL

Four ghosts appear to Ebenezer Scrooge on Christmas Eve in the English novelist's classic. *Marley's Ghost:* "The same face: the very same. Marley in his pigtail, usual waistcoat, tights and boots; the tassels on the latter bristling, like his pigtail, and his coat-skirts, and the hair upon his head. The chain he drew was clasped about his middle. It was long, and wound about him like a tail; and it was made (for Scrooge observed it closely) of cash-boxes, keys, padlocks, ledgers, deeds, and heavy purses wrought in steel. His body was transparent; so that Scrooge, observing him, and looking through his waistcoat, could see the two buttons on his coat behind." *Spirit of Christmas Past:* "It was a strange figure—like a child: yet not so like a child as like an old man, viewed through some supernatural medium, which gave him the appearance of having receded from the view, and being diminished to a child's proportions. Its hair, which hung about its neck and down its back, was white, as if with age; and yet the face had not a wrinkle in it, and the tenderest bloom was on the skin . . . It wore a tunic of the purest white; and round its waist was bound a lustrous belt, the sheen of which was beautiful. It held a branch of fresh green holly in its hand; and, in singular contradiction of that wintry emblem, had its dress trimmed with summer flowers. But the strangest thing about it was, that from the crown of its head there sprung a bright clear jet of light . . ." *Spirit of Christmas Present:* "It was clothed in one simple deep green robe, or mantle, bordered with white fur. This garment hung so loosely on the figure, that its capacious breast was bare . . . on its head it wore no other covering than a holly wreath, set here and there with shining icicles . . . Girded round its middle was an antique scabbard; but no sword was in it, and the ancient sheath was eaten up with rust." *Spirit of Christmas to Come:* "It was shrouded in a deep black garment, which concealed its head, its face, its form, and left nothing of it visible, save one outstretched hand . . . the Spirit did not speak or move." The grasping old cheapskate Scrooge learns how to keep Christmas well. "God Bless Us, Every One."

CHROMOSOME

The 23d pair are the sex chromosomes. You—and everyone else, male or female—have 46 chromosomes, or 23 pairs, half from your father, half from your mother. They are the structural carrier of hereditary characteristics found in the nucleus of every cell. Twenty-two of the 23 pairs are the same in males and females. These are the autosomes. Only the 23d pair is different. In the female, there are two X chromosomes; in the male, there is one X chromosome, which is just the same as the two in the female, but its partner is the much smaller Y chromosome. A human being originates in the union of two gametes, the ovum and the spermatozoon. It is the Y chromosome that determines if the human being will be male or female. The German anatomist Walther Flemming discovered the threads of chromatin material that form during cell division, and another German anatomist, Heinrich Wilhelm Waldeyer, coined the name "chromosome." A certain number of chromosomes is characteristic of each species of plant and animal. A potato has 48 chromosomes. The fruit fly has 8.

CHURCHILL, WINSTON S.

His mother was the American-born Jennie Jerome, who created the Manhattan cocktail, and he and Franklin Delano Roosevelt, who led the Allies to victory in World War II, were seventh cousins once removed. The personification of John Bull was *Time* magazine's "Man of the Century," in 1950, and he was the first of the two foreigners who have been made honorary American citizens. (The other is Raoul Wallenberg, the Swedish diplomat who helped to save thousands of Hungarian Jews from deportation and probable death in the last year of World War II.) Churchill's was the first commoner's funeral attended by the reigning British sovereign.

CITATION

The first equine millionaire, by Bull Lea out of Hydroplane by Hyperion out of Toboggan (English Oaks), bred at Calumet Farm and ridden by Eddie Arcaro. Citation won thirty-two out of forty-five races, including the Triple Crown, the American Derby, and the Jockey Club Gold Cup, and was "out of the money" only once. His first-place finish in the Hollywood Gold Cup Handicap at Hollywood Park, in Inglewood, California, in July 1951, put him over the million mark in earnings.

CITIZEN KANE

Orson Welles, the genius producer-director-actor-writer, doesn't consider this motion picture masterpiece his best film. He considers *Chimes at Midnight,* which was made a quarter of a century later, in 1966, by far his best. *Kane* was a synthesis and an extension of everything innovative in film to the early 1940s, and it is considered by most cinemas and pas to be the most important American movie ever made. The imaginary biography of a newspaper tycoon and American sultan (Charles Foster Kane), it was based on the life of the flamboyant, highly controversial publisher William Randolph Hearst, whose newspapers were known to manipulate the news. Hearst didn't want the movie shown, and threatened a lawsuit if it were, but one of Welles' lawyers noted, "Hearst is going to have to say, the reason I know that SOB is me is because I'm that SOB, which he is not likely to do." Cinema history's most fascinating symbol was the device that knotted together the series of Kane reminiscences into a plausible story line. Welles had unenthusiastically offered a long quote from Coleridge. His co-writer, Herman Mankiewicz, a former drama critic of *The New York Times,* substituted the search for "Rosebud"—the sled young Charles was riding in a blizzard the day that his mother bound him over to the bank executive. Mank's biographer, Richard Meryman, considers Rosebud to be the symbol of the parental love denied to both Charles Kane and Herman Mankiewicz.

CLARKE, ARTHUR C.

In 1945, the British science-fiction writer was a flight lieutenant in the Royal Air Force when he thought up the idea of a communications satellite—a relay station hovering over a fixed point 22,000 or so miles above the planet—and he described it in a paper in the British journal *Wireless World.* He didn't think to apply for ownership, and the idea lay dormant for nearly a decade. When Telstar and Echo were launched, Clarke was out a bundle. In 1947, he predicted that a rocket would be launched to the Moon in 1959—he was right on the money. His short story "The Sentinel" was the basis for the book and the motion picture *2001: A Space Odyssey.* "As soon as you mention science fiction," Clarke says in the book *The Making of Kubrick's 2001,* "most people think of bug-eyed monsters and weird apparitions. There has been little attempt at integrity on the part of filmmakers in dealing with the possibility of extraterrestrial life. This is what makes *2001* so unique, I think. It poses metaphysical, philosophical, and even religious questions. I don't pretend that we have the answers. But the questions are certainly worth thinking about." Clarke thinks all of the following might happen: levitation, immortality, invisibility, communication with the dead. Stay tuned.

CLEMENS, SAMUEL LANGHORNE (MARK TWAIN)

He was a fresh, new journalist who "needed a nom de guerre." Captain Isaiah Sellers, in *The New Orleans Picayune,* had used the pen name Mark Twain, and Clemens, a Mississippi riverboat pilot, decided that he would, too. "Mark twain" was a phrase used in making soundings in the Mississippi: It meant two fathoms, or twelve feet deep. He created his new identity when he was a feature writer with the Virginia City (Nevada) *Territorial Enterprise.* When the Civil War put an end to river traffic, he and his brother set out for Nevada partly to avoid war service. He later worked on the San Francisco *Call* and contributed to *The Californian* and the *Golden Era.* Publication of his shaggy frog story, "The Celebrated Jumping Frog of Calaveras County," accelerated a career as a humorist during the Gilded Age (his coinage), joking to punch across the

126

truth: "A baby is an inestimable blessing and bother . . . Put all your eggs in the one basket and—WATCH THAT BASKET. . . . Familiarity breeds contempt—and children . . . Let us be thankful for the fools. But for them the rest of us could not succeed. . . . When in doubt, tell the truth. . . . Everything human is pathetic. The secret source of humor itself is not joy but sorrow. There is no humor in heaven."

CLEMENTE, ROBERTO

The Pittsburgh Pirate outfielder and most valuable player was an unreconstructed hypochondriac, Mr. Aches and Pains himself. He was also four times the batting champion of the National League (MVP in 1966) and twelve times both a league All-Star and a Golden Glover for his fielding. In the 1971 World Series (MVP), he hit .414 and all but single-handedly made the Baltimore Orioles an endangered species. After eighteen storied seasons, he was batting .317, highest among active players. He was killed in the crash on New Year's Eve 1972 of an airplane in which he was taking twenty-six tons of food and $150,000 in relief from Puerto Rico to earthquake victims in Managua, Nicaragua, where he had coached and played with Puerto Rican teams during the off-season. Puerto Rico's governor-elect said, "Roberto died serving his fellow man. Our youth loses an idol. Our people lose one of their glories." Clemente got a hit his very first time at bat in the biggies and he got a hit—a ringing double to deep left centerfield—his very last time at bat in his very last regular season game. In all, he registered exactly 3,000 hits.

CLEOPATRA

She was not the last ruler in the Egyptian dynasty of Ptolemies. Her son by Julius Caesar, Ptolemy XIV, with whom she shared rule, briefly survived her suicide by asp; but the boy was presently put to death by the Roman Octavian, who feared Ptolemy might gain popular support. Cleopatra was married three times: to two younger brothers, then to Marc Antony after her affair with Julius Caesar took her to Rome (she was there on the infamous Ides of March), and bore Ptolemy. Antony lived and died by the sword—he and Cleopatra were defeated by the Romans at Actium and again in Alexandria. Rome bossed Egypt until 640 A.D.

CLEOPATRA (THE MOVIE)

Marc Antony and Cleopatra's love affair ended in suicides after twelve years. Richard Burton and Elizabeth Taylor's two marriages to each other ended in two divorces. Gossip about the modern two on the Nile spread quickly after the stars crossed in the early 1960s, during production of the Joseph L. Mankiewicz-directed $28 million epic: "Elizabeth and Burton are not just playing Antony and Cleopatra." Miss Taylor added fuel to the conflagration: "He was like Prince Charming kissing the sleeping princess." That was no pea under her mattress: In turn, it was the 33-carat Krupp diamond, the 69-carat Cartier diamond, the lustrous Peregrina pearl that King Philip II of Spain had given Mary Tudor in 1554. But not all the king's men could put old Humpty back together again.

CLEVELAND BROWNS

The Cleveland franchise in professional football was named for its coach-owner, Paul Brown: 1946–49 in the All-American Football Conference, 1950–62 in the National Football League. Brown went on to coach the Cincinnati Bengals and was enshrined in the Pro Football Hall of Fame in 1967. He was an exceptionally successful coach at all levels of the game. His Cleveland dynasty sported a 158W–48L–8T record: four A.A.F.C. titles, three N.F.L. titles. He had only one losing season in seventeen campaigns.

CLIFT, MONTGOMERY

The ethereal actor's sensational movie debut as a cowboy in *Red River* was released after he had made a second film, *The Search,* in which he played an American soldier. He had appeared in a dozen or so dramas on Broadway, including five performances in *Life With Father*—he was dismissed because he was "not suited to the role." Amoebic dysentery, contracted in Mexico, made him ineligible for service in the military. "Acting is make-believe," he admitted, "but you can carry it too far. To be convincing, an actor must share, or at least be aware of, experiences familiar to the audience. Otherwise, you're making faces in an emotional vacuum and nobody knows what . . . you're trying to express." After a trip to Israel, he said, "It's inconceivable to me that any young actor who has the fare doesn't go there. Everything is dramatic and challenging —perfect source material for acting." Clift was a twin—sister Ethel. And like Hollywood's number-one screen lover in the 1930s, Robert Taylor, he was from Nebraska. (Other famous Cornhuskers: Johnny Carson, Henry Fonda, Dick Cavett, the Astaires, Harold Lloyd, Willa Cather, William Jennings Bryan, and Malcolm X.)

A CLOCKWORK ORANGE

"What's it going to be then, eh? There was me, that is Alex, and my three droogs, that is Pete, Georgia, and Dim, Dim being really dim, and we sat in the Korova Milkbar making up our rassoodocks what to do with the evening, a flip dark chill winter bastard though dry." Droogs—friends. Rassoodocks—minds. Flip—wild. The language is Nadsat, created by Anthony Burgess for his nightmarish fantasy of a future England where the hoodlums take over after dark (brilliantly filmed by Stanley Kubrick). Lubbilubbing—making love. Krovvy—blood. Choodessny—wonderful. Malchick—boy. Bratchny—bastard. Cheena—woman. Chepooka—nonsense. Appy polly loggy—apology. Bog—God. Plenny—prisoner. Mozg—brain. Pretty polly—money. Shoom—noise. Neezhnies—underpants. Yahoodies—Jews. Smeck—laugh. Synthemesc—a drug. In-out in-out—copulation. Filly—to play or fool with. Dama—lady. Millicent—policeman. Cancer—cigarette. Charles—chaplain. Jeezny—life. Rozz—policeman. Oobivat—to kill.

CN TOWER

"To be polite," says the ladylike Canadian author Margaret Atwood, "it looks like a giant icicle." The tallest building outside the United States, the Canadian National communications tower in Metro Centre in Toronto is the world's tallest self-supporting tower (as opposed to a guyed mast), rising 1,822 feet one inch. Taller TV antennas are supported. A 416-seat restaurant and disco revolve in the Tower's Sky Pod at 1,140 feet. Lightning strikes the top about two hundred times (in about thirty storms) each year. The tallest guyed structure is the Warszawa Radio mast at Konstantynow near Gain and Plock in Poland—the tallest pole in the world is more than four-tenths of a mile high. The mast is so high that anyone falling off the top would reach terminal velocity and no longer be accelerating as he smashed into the ground.

COBB, TY

He was kicked out of baseball for a time—the charge of misconduct was unsubstantiated—and when the first ballot was taken for the National Baseball Hall of Fame, in 1936, the Georgia Peach led all other nominees, including the Babe. When "baseball's greatest player" retired at age forty-one, in 1928, he had amassed fifty-eight records in twenty-four seasons. Some still stand: a career average of .367; 4,192 hits; twelve batting titles; three .400 seasons, topped by .420 in 1911; eight slugging percentage titles, six in succession. He hit .357 when he was forty years old and .323 the next season, his last. (Rogers Hornsby, of the St. Louis Cardinals, batted .358 over twenty-three seasons—"only" .009 points under Cobb's high—but knocked out 1,262 fewer hits.) Cobb's 892 career stolen bases stood up for nearly half a century: He'd hit the base with spikes flying; he was a fierce competitor. Cobb was player-manager of Detroit's Tigers for six seasons, winning more games than he lost but no pennant. As a youth, he had had to make a choice: Accept an appointment to West Point or play baseball.

COCCYX

At one time, you had 33 vertebrae; when you were a child, the lower nine in the spinal column became fused into two immovable bones, the sacrum and the coccyx, forming the back of the pelvis; as an adult, you thus have only 26 separate bony segments in your spinal column, or main structural support. Twenty-four are movable: 7 cervical (neck), 12 dorsal (back of the chest), and 5 lumbar (loin). An 18-inch spinal cord of nervous tissue runs lengthwise through your spinal column from the first lumbar vertebra to the medulla at the base of the brain.

COCKFIGHTING

The word "crestfallen" originated in this bloody sport of fighting roosters, or gamecocks. Crestfallen: with drooping crest or hanging head. The beaten rooster's crest droops or hangs over: "slinking back into the club somewhat crestfallen after his beating"—Thackeray.

"COCK ROBIN"

How did the Sparrow kill Cock Robin?
With my bow and arrow, I killed Cock Robin, said the Sparrow
The Fly saw Cock Robin die
the Fish caught his blood
the Beetle made his shroud
the Owl will dig his grave
the Rook will be the parson
the Lark will be the clerk
the Linnet will carry the link
the Dove will be the chief mourner
the Kite will carry the coffin
the Wren will bear the pall

the Thrush will sing a psalm
the Bull will toll the bell

All the birds of the air
Fell a-sighing and a-sobbing
When they heard the bell toll
For poor Cock Robin

COFFEE

Italian churchmen opposed the beverage as an infidel drink, until it was Christianized by Pope Clement VIII. The coffee tree originally grew wild in Ethiopia, which today is about number nine among the leading coffee-growing countries. Brazil is number one, producing billions of pounds every year. Americans drink hundreds of millions of cups every day. The caffeine in coffee acts as a stimulant to mental and physical energy. Coffee became popular in the United States only after tea met with rejection following the Boston Tea Party.

COLLINS, MICHAEL

He was the "other" astronaut who made the historic flight to the Moon in July 1969. While Neil Armstrong and Edwin Aldrin, Jr., were landing and walking on Earth's only natural satellite, Collins was circling the Moon in the command module of *Columbia*. The lunar module (LM) was cast adrift in space after Armstrong and Aldrin had soared in it out to the *Columbia* for the return voyage to Earth. The astronauts carried the torn halves of four $1 bills. On their return, their halves were compared with the four other halves to prove that the men were the same who had been launched from Cape Kennedy eight days earlier. President Richard M. Nixon had telephoned the men on the Moon: "This certainly has to be the most historic telephone call ever made." He later greeted them on the aircraft carrier *Hornet:* "This is the greatest week in the history of the world since Creation. . . ."

COLORADO

The highest state. Fifty-three snow-capped Rocky Mountains there rise higher than 14,000 feet; the highest is Mount Elbert, 14,433 feet. Twelve peaks in Alaska are higher (the highest in the United States is Alaska's Mount McKinley: 20,300 feet), as is one in California (Mount Whitney: 14,494 feet); but Colorado's average elevation of 6,800 feet is tops for a state. Other states with at least one mountain at least five figures high: Arizona, Hawaii, Idaho, Montana, Nevada, New Mexico, Oregon, Utah, Washington, Wyoming. A bit peaked beside these altitudinal high points are Delaware, the District of Columbia, Florida, Louisiana, Mississippi, Rhode Island—no place is even a thousand feet above sea level. "Colorado" is Spanish for "red or colored." It was first applied to the Colorado River. Called the Territory of Jefferson before joining the Union in 1876 —the Centennial State—it is the eighth largest state in area. Early civilizations (Indian cliff dwellers) centered around Mesa Verde two millennia ago. The state's most valuable mineral is molybdenum, a difficultly fusible polyvalent metallic element. Gold was discovered where mile-high Denver now sits. Explorer–army officer Zebulon Montgomery Pike made it only halfway up the 14,110-foot-high mountain on the edge of the Great Plains in central Colorado that bears his name. Pikes Peak was topped fourteen years later, in 1820, by Major Stephen Harriman Long. One of the highest meteorological stations in the world is there. (Pike was exonerated in Aaron Burr's plot to detach western territory from the United States, and he was killed while commanding his troops during the successful assault on York (now Toronto), Canada, in the War of 1812.) Colorado mountains spawn six large river systems: the Colorado, the Arkansas, North Platte, South Platte, Republic, and Rio Grande. Famous Coloradoans have included Byron R. White, Jack Dempsey, and Douglas Fairbanks.

COLOR BLINDNESS

A sloppy English chemist, John Dalton by name, was the first (in 1794) to describe color blindness, also called daltonism. He was sloppy because he was color-blind, a disadvantage to a chemist, who must be able to see color changes when he works with chemicals. In a world where 8 percent of the men and one-half of one percent of the women are color-blind, color is still used extensively to convey education and information. Many texts, for example, use color to emphasize meaning. The red-green color-blind behave toward red and green as all humans behave toward ultraviolet light—they don't see the colors. They don't see Greenland. (Birds see ultraviolet light.) Daltonism is inherited. Much of the literature on color blindness stems from the concern of the navies of the world to avoid having watchkeepers and lookouts who cannot distinguish red from green. A color-blind automobile driver with dyslexia is a menace.

COLOSSEUM

"Go thou to Rome—at once the Paradise, the grave, the city, and the wilderness," Shelley exhorted. If one took thou to Rome, one saw the imposing, four-storied, oval Flavian Amphitheater, the formal name of the Colosseum, near the southeast end of the Forum, between the Palatine and Esquiline hills. "Colosseum" from the colossal (150 feet tall) statue of Emperor Nero once nearby. One hundred and fifty years to build, it was inaugurated in A.D. 80 with games lasting 100 days and the slaughtering of 9,000 animals. About 45,000 spectators packed the marble seats to watch gladiator duels to the death, Christians thrown to the lions, and mock naval engagements. Stone was later carried off to build medieval palaces. There is an ancient prophecy: "While stands the Colosseum, Rome will stand; When falls the Colosseum, Rome will fall; And when Rome falls, the world!"

COLUMBUS, CHRISTOPHER

The Admiral of the Ocean Sea and the governor-general of all lands he discovered in his odysseys West to the East—a man who changed the shape of the world and the course of history—was probably Jewish. It is known that as a lad, in Italy, he quoted the Jewish prophets and mystics, and his early exercise books (as well as his later letters) displayed a style of writing much influenced by the Old Testament. When he lived in Portugal and then in Spain (Italy was not in the exploration and discovery business), he probably became a *converso,* a convert to Christianity, as did so many Jews in those days of Spanish inquisition and expulsion, but he always retained his Genoese citizenship. He postponed his historic departure, in August 1492, for a whole day—the original sailing date coincided with Tishah B'ab, the Jewish holy day of fasting and mourning that commemorates the destruction of the First and the Second Temples of Jerusalem. In his last letters to his son, he wrote a *beit-hay,* the Hebrew symbol "Praised be the Lord." His will adhered to Jewish traditions in disposing of worldly goods. In the late fifteenth century, the Jews of Spain were expelled by the Catholic rulers; it has been argued that Columbus' personal mission was finding a homeland in Asia for his brethren. He undoubtedly knew of the large Jewish community in Kaifeng, China, once the world's largest city. (See my co-authored nonfiction novel *Deliverance in Shanghai.*) It had taken the Genoese eight years of persistent supplication to get three ships and 90 men out of the monarchs, Ferdinand and Isabella, who were up to their armaments with Moors. His second expedition, in 1493, consisted of seventeen ships and 1,500 colonists; he returned to Spain with 500 Indians, whom Isabella sent back to Haiti. Columbus made four trips in all to the New World. On his third, in 1498, he carried convicts as colonists, and sailed as far south as Venezuela. An independent governor sent by Ferdinand charged Columbus with tyrannical mismanagement of Haiti and returned him to Spain in chains. In 1502, he sailed toward Asia with four ships, and was for a time marooned on Jamaica. He died in 1506.

COLUMBUS, OHIO

There's Columbus, the second largest city in Georgia, captured by Union troops a week after Lee's surrender at Appomattox. There's Columbus, the Indiana city known for its outstanding architecture; buildings were put up there by world-famous architects from the late 1930s onward. There's Columbus, the site of many of Mississippi's most beautiful antebellum homes. There's Columbus, the seat of Platte County, Nebraska. And there's the capital of Ohio. Almost all of the Buckeye State is within 150 miles of Columbus. Many state leaders in the 1810s wanted to name it Ohio City, but General Joseph Foos, a legislator from Franklin County, in which the city is located, suggested that the discoverer of the New World be honored. A 20-foot-tall bronze statue of the Admiral of the Ocean Sea, a gift of Christopher Columbus' home city, Genoa, Italy, stands in a plaza at city hall, on a shore of the Scioto River. Many Italians now reside in Columbus. It is an educational center—Ohio State University alone is spread over more than 300 buildings. It is the headquarters of the American Rose Society, with one of the world's largest rose gardens.

COMANECI, NADIA

Her gymnastics career lasted eight fabulous years. When she was a solemn, five-foot-tall, 86-pound fourteen-year-old, in 1976, she stunned the sports world by turning in a series of perfect 10 scores and winning three gold medals in the Olympics in Montreal—they were the first 10s ever recorded in the Olympics. She collected twenty-one gold medals in international competition before retiring in 1984. "I regret," the now-103-trim-pound Rumanian sobbed on quitting, "that from now on I will never know the excitement of competition."

COMMA

In Greek, "clause." The most frequently used punctuation mark in English indicates a slight separation in ideas of construction. Misuse gets states and political parties into hot water. In 1850, the state of Michigan's constitution read, "Neither slavery nor involuntary servitude, unless for the punishment of crime, shall ever be tolerated in this state." Not until 1963 was the comma shifted from its position after servitude—where it legalized slavery as an appropriate punishment for crime—to a position after slavery—where it outlawed slavery. In 1984, the National Republican Party's platform subcommittee on economic policy declared that Republicans "oppose any attempts to increase taxes which would harm the recovery and reverse the trend to restoring control of the economy to individual Americans." Only harmful tax increases, not all tax increases, were thus opposed. Conservative firebrands proposed to insert a comma after the word *taxes*. The party should "oppose any attempts to increase taxes, which would harm the recovery and reverse the trend to restoring control of the economy to individual Americans." All tax hikes were harmful. The subcommittee put a period to debate by approving the comma without dissent!

COMPIEGNE

Hitler forced France to capitulate in 1940 at the same little clearing in the woods at Compiegne where the German Empire had capitulated on November 11, 1918. Nazi army engineers demolished the wall of the museum where the old *wagon-lit* of French Marshal Foch was on display and moved it to tracks in the center of the clearing. William L. Shirer says it was one of the loveliest summer days he ever remembered in France: "A warm June sun beat down on the stately trees—elms, oaks, cypresses, and pines—casting pleasant shadows on the wooded avenues leading to the little circular clearing." As soon as the preamble to the armistice terms had been read to the French, Hitler and his entourage left the *wagon-lit,* allowing others to handle the negotiations. At the Führer's order, a three-foot-high granite block at the site was destroyed. The script on the block had read: "Here on the eleventh of November 1918 succumbed the criminal pride of the German empire—vanquished by the free peoples which it tried to enslave."

COMPUTER LANGUAGE

Barf, flag, garbage, alias, jump, nybble, mung, mode, boot, bulletproof, Pascal, prom, write—some of the vocabulary of the new electronic life. COBOL—COmmon Business-Oriented Language, a programming language for business, developed two decades ago. FORTRAN—FORmula TRANslation, a scientific and engineering language, developed by IBM, originally conceived for use on scientific problems. Pascal—the computer language in which instructions appear like sentences, making concepts as simple and as clear as possible. It was named for Blaise Pascal, the seventeenth-century mathematician who invented the mechanical "cash register." The Department of Defense initiated a "programming language to end all programming languages" and dubbed it Ada, for Lady

Ada Lovelace, Lord Byron's daughter who supported Charles Babbage's search for a mechanical calculating machine. There were about 5,000 desk-top computers in the United States six years ago. In another six years there may be 80 million.

CONCORDE

Three hours and twenty-five minutes—that's all it takes to fly London–New York in the world's fastest luxury airliner, the supersonic British-French Concorde. New York–Paris is also under four hours. At 1,400 miles per hour, it far outdistances the speed of sound—a shocker when it came on the market. "Cruises" at an altitude of 55,000 feet and, fully loaded, carries about one-fourth the number of passengers that a Boeing 747 does—at double the price. The 747's flying time between Heathrow and Kennedy is 7 hrs 40 mins.

CONGREVE, WILLIAM

The Way of the World (1700) is one of the great comedies in the English language, and the Restoration dramatist enjoyed the friendship of Swift, Steele, Pope, Voltaire, and Sarah, duchess of Marlborough, and vice versa. The leading roles in Congreve's many plays were written for Anne Bracegirdle, probably his mistress. In the tragedy *The Mourning Bride* (1697), he wrote, "Heaven has no rage like love to hatred turned, Nor hell a fury like a woman scorned." And, "Music hath charms to soothe the savage breast, To soften rocks, or bend a knotted oak." In a letter, Congreve exhorted, "Defer not till tomorrow to be wise, Tomorrow's sun to thee may never rise."

CONKERS

A popular game played with chestnuts or hazelnuts by children in England. Each player swings a horse chestnut threaded on a knotted string to try to break one held by his opponent. The term "conker(s)" derives from the Greek for "conch" and through the Latin *concha* for "shell" (of a snail); the game was first played with snail shells. Serious conker players have been known to prepare their nuts with great care, soaking them in vinegar or in salt and water and then baking them for about half an hour. A victory is notched when no part of a foe's conker remains on the string.

CONNOLLY, MAUREEN

Talk about a force in sports! "Little Mo" was a one-woman tennis dynasty. In her teens she won the U.S. tennis singles championship three consecutive times (1951–53). She won Wimbledon three consecutive times (1952–54). In the calendar year 1953 she won the grand slam—the four major titles: the French, Wimbledon, the U.S., and the Australian. (Margaret Court is the only other woman to win the four titles in one year. Martina Navratilova won the titles over two years. Ron Laver, twice, in 1962 and in 1969, and Don Budge, in 1938, are the only men to win the grand slam.) Miss Connolly was forced to retire in 1955 after breaking a leg in a horseback accident, and she died of cancer in 1969.

CONNORS, CHUCK

Before he became an actor, television's "Rifleman" played first base in 67 major league baseball games: one in 1949 with the Brooklyn Dodgers, sixty-six in 1951 with the Chicago Cubs. His batting average was .238. His forty-eight hits included two homers, five doubles, and one triple. He was marooned on a desert island for five years with Doris Day in *Move Over, Darling*.

COOLIDGE, CALVIN

The only President to be born on Independence Day, in 1872. When Warren G. Harding died suddenly in California, Vice-President Coolidge was administered the Presidential oath by his own father, a notary public and justice of the peace in Vermont. The former Massachusetts governor enjoyed horseback riding but as President gave it up for an electric steed. He met his future bride when she happened to see him shaving in front of a mirror with nothing on but long underwear and a hat. He believed that four-fifths of all our troubles in this life would disappear if we would only sit down and keep still. Silent Cal liked to sleep at least eleven hours a day. Laissez faire, indeed. Once after waking from a long nap in the White House, the thirtieth Chief Executive asked, "Is the country still here?" The country kept cool with Cal.

COOPER, ALICE

School's been out since the Queen of Schlock 'n' Rouge changed his name from Vincent Furnier (son of a preacher) to the nom de freak Alice

Cooper—it's "a fine old American name." His art form is chaos and confusion, a nightmare. He wears a boa constrictor and his act is the living end: He's guillotined and resurrected. At home, he's Andy Hardy, cooking and listening to Burt Bacharach records.

COPERNICUS, NICHOLAS

It wasn't a new idea. The ancient Greek astronomer Aristarchus had suggested the notion, and German Cardinal Nicholas of Cusa had, too: All the planets, including Earth, revolved around the Sun. The heavenly bodies were not rotating around the third planet from the Sun. The Pole had studied mathematics (and painting) at Cracow. In East Prussia, where he had been nominated canon of the cathedral and practiced medicine, he set about working out his system in full mathematical detail, to demonstrate how planetary positions could be calculated. He determined the length of the year to within twenty-eight seconds. His treatise was completed in 1530 but it was not published—though it had a public-relations dedication to Pope Paul III—until he was on his deathbed, in 1543. *De revolutionibus orbium* was banned until 1835 by the Catholic Church, which in the seventeenth century persecuted Galileo for supporting the heliocentric planetary theory. Copernicus freed astronomy from the Ptolemaic geocentric viewpoint. Kepler then promulgated his laws of planetary motion and Newton his embracing theory of universal gravitation, which describes the force that holds the planets in their orbits. When a statue to Copernicus was unveiled in Warsaw—a gesture stimulated by the conquering Napoleon—no Catholic priest would officiate on the occasion.

CORRIGAN, DOUGLAS

Maybe the pilot-mechanic had been reading his George Moore, who in 1900 said, "The wrong way always seems the more reasonable." Discombobulation certainly made the flying Irishman a celebrity, and the subject of a movie, *The Flying Irishman*. In mid-July 1938, he set a nonstop transcontinental speed record of less than twenty-eight hours in his Curtis Robin J-6 monoplane, which he had picked up at auction six years earlier for $900. The next day, he took off in a fog from New York's Floyd Bennett Field for the return flight to Long Beach, California. For twenty-four hours he was in the soup. He didn't have a radio and his compass was faulty. He didn't realize that he had made a wrong turn in the fog. When he could see the earth again, he saw that "all the houses were made of stones, the roofs were grass, and the streets were cobblestones," my God, it's Ireland. He returned a hero. There was a ticker-tape parade and he had a nickname: "Wrong-Way" Corrigan. He ran for the Senate on the Prohibition ticket in 1946.

COSELL, HOWARD

The mid-60ish Mouth worked in the trenches for more than a decade before gaining a rep as an outspoken ABC sportscaster. The Phi Beta Kappa-former lawyer once said, "My constituency is blacks, kids who are sick and tired of all the nonsense, and intelligent people everywhere." Most of his critics (who claim he's made a career out of insufferability) "are not men of education, and it hasn't been an easy thing for those people to see life pass by in philosophical terms they don't even understand." The CBS television program "60 Minutes" shot lots of tape of Cosell but couldn't put together a tell-it-like-it-is segment worth airing. "He for whatever reason decided to play marshmallow," Mike Wallace told Barbara Walters on "20/20." "He decided to play bland. If you can believe that a profile undertaken at some expense by '60 Minutes'—lots of time on both coasts—that interview was unusable."

COSMOLOGY

Kosmos, Greek for "the world." Cosmology is the story of the world—specifically, it is the branch of astronomy that deals with the overall structure of the Universe—theory and philosophy about its origins and its constitution and its future. The "steady state" Universe implies continuous creation, for matter must be created continuously out of nothing to make it work. The big-bang theory declares that at the beginning of time, between 12 and 15 billion years ago, all the matter and energy in the Universe were concentrated in a very small volume that exploded—the resultant expansion and cooling continues to this very moment. On the average, the physicist-journalist Jeremy Bernstein has reported, there are in every cubic centimeter of the Universe some four hundred low-energy, microwave photons, or light quanta, that originated in the big bang. The residual noise of the big bang can be *heard* in those photons.

COWARD, NOEL

Asked if he was the wittiest man alive, the wittiest man alive said, "There might be someone at this very moment being witty as all get-out in Urdu." Well, let's see. "Certain women should be struck regularly like gongs." "Keir Dullea, gone tomorrow." "I'm not very keen on Hollywood, I'd rather have a nice cup of cocoa really." "*Amanda*: Heaven preserve me from nice women. *Sybil*: Your reputation will do that." "If you're a star, you should behave like one. I always have." ". . . the public on the whole prefer to see extraordinary people on the stage rather than ordinary ones; fantastic situations rather than familiar, commonplace ones and actors of outsize personality and talent rather than accurately competent mediocrities." "Dear 338171," Coward wrote to the shy T. E. Lawrence, who was in the Royal Air Force, "may I call you 338?" The English playwright, actor, composer, and director was on stage from the age of twelve. Five of his twenty-seven plays were hits in London in 1925. He wrote *Private Lives* in four days in a hotel room in Shanghai: "I write at high speed because boredom is bad for my health." Civilized interest in this blithe spirit was revived when he published a book about the agony of an aging homosexual writer who had to write dishonestly about his private life—*Song at Twilight* was Sir Noel's autobiography.

COWPUNCHER

In the American Revolution, a cowboy was a Tory marauder, an adherent to the British cause who fought the skinners, or revolutionaries, in the contested area of Westchester county, north of New York City. Less than a century later, a cowboy was a mounted employee of a ranch who herded and tended and punched cattle. Some of these cowpunchers were darn good at coining words. A hanging was a Texas cakewalk or a necktie social. Whiskey was neck oil or tonsil paint. A book of cigarette papers was the Bible. Death was the big jump. Any kind of a hard fall, but especially one when thrown from a horse, was a fartknocker. An old, skinny cow or steer was a Nellie. A fugitive or a wild person was a cimarron.

COW'S STOMACH

Cattle, goat, deer, camels—they are ruminants (from Latin "to chew again"), grazing, split-hoofed mammals that chew their cud. They have four stomachs, or sections! They swallow their food, then regurgitate it in the form of cud. They chew the cud thoroughly; when they swallow it, the cud moves into their "real" stomach and is digested. The word pecuniary is derived from the Latin *pecus,* "cattle"; the words cattle, chattel, and capital are related. The number of cattle that a person owns has been the measure of his wealth.

CRANE, STEPHEN

The fourteenth child of a Methodist minister wrote *Maggie: A Girl of the Streets* (she "blossomed in a mud puddle"), *The Red Badge of Courage, The Black Rider, War Is Kind, The Open Boat and Other Tales,* and *The Monster and Other Stories*—his collected works fill twelve volumes—he was the first modern American writer—he pioneered realism—he served as a foreign correspondent in Cuba and Greece—and he was dead at the age of twenty-eight of tuberculosis. It is said that his genius was for dissidence, he naturally saw everything in contradiction to what he was supposed to say: "Of course, I am admittedly a savage. I have been known as docile from time to time but only under great social pressure." Two years before he died in the Black Forest, he wrote to a friend: "When I was the mark for every humorist in the country I went ahead; now, when I am the mark for only 50% of the humorists of the country, I go ahead, for I understand that a man is born into this world with his own pair of eyes, and that he is not at all responsible for his vision—he is merely responsible for his quality of personal honesty. To keep close to this personal honesty is my supreme ambition."

CRAWFORD, JOAN

"Mommy dearest" loved having "a hundred people clutching at my coat, clamoring for autographs." After a string of blue movies—she looked sexed to the gills—she scored as the good-hearted flapper in *Our Dancing Daughters,* a 1928 silent. She was Fred Astaire's first dancing partner in the movies. She won an Oscar as best actress in *Mildred Pierce,* in 1945. She appealed to women—she seemed to embody their secret sufferings. "I won't kid you. I was from the absolute bottom," she said in so many words. "If you work as hard, you can be me, too." Her real name was Lucille Le Sueur, she was five-feet three, and she married four times: Her first husband was the elegant Douglas Fairbanks, Jr., her last was the chairman of the board of Pepsi-Cola.

CRAZY HORSE

The Sioux's greatest war chief was known as Curly when he was a kid. His given name was His Horse Looking. His father, an Oglala holy man, passed on his name of Crazy Horse, adopting in turn the name Worm. The blue-eyed, pale-skinned Crazy Horse stole a Black Buffalo woman from her husband, No Water; No Water, heap big mad, shot Crazy Horse in the face. The Sioux vigorously defended their land in the mineral-rich

Black Hills, in the Dakota territory, against the encroachment of whites. Crazy Horse was the best Indian cavalry tactician, victorious in battle after battle. With Sitting Bull and Gall, he defeated General George Armstrong Custer (who had stood last in his West Point class) in the battle of Little Bighorn, in Montana—Custer's Last Stand. Crazy Horse was imprisoned after he and his followers were surrounded and nearly starved, and he was fatally stabbed with a bayonet while trying to escape. A doctor tried to take his photograph, but the dying Indian turned his face to the wall—no one must take away his shadow.

CRICKET

From the Middle French *criquet,* "goal post"—England's and the Commonwealth's national pastime. Two eleven-man teams, a long flat-sided, paddle-like bat, a ball, a large field, and two wickets 66 feet apart. The batsman hits the ball—if he hits it right, if the noise is like a trout taking a fly, the ball will travel 600 feet in four seconds—and he runs back and forth between the wickets, trying to score as many runs as possible before the ball is fielded and returned. A team's inning ends when ten of the players have been put out. A match can consist of one or two innings, it can last several days, and a team can score hundreds of points. The uniform is a peaked cap, white or cream trousers, open-necked shirt, and white spiked or crepe-soled boots. Batsmen and wicketkeepers are equipped with protective leg pads and gloves. Cricket is about six centuries old. The first printed rules, making everything cricket, appeared in 1744.

CROSSBOW

A triggered bow set on a grooved stock, it was used by the Chinese of the Han period, 200 B.C., and by the Romans, but didn't come into its own until the Middle Ages. Ammunition included arrows, darts, stones, and a square-headed, ten-inch-long bolt known as a "quarrel"—hence the admonition that one shouldn't quarrel with a crossbow. Richard the Lionhearted, seeking to recapture Jerusalem, was triumphant in the battle of Arsuf (1191) during the Third Crusade when his Christian crossbowmen stuck it to the sultan Saladin's Muslim forces. Genoese crossbowmen served as mercenaries in armies all over Europe, but at the battle of Crecy (1346) the Genoese fighting for the French were so outclassed by English longbowmen firing from fixed positions that the crossbow was put on the shelf as the dominant projectile weapon in European warfare.

CUBA

President Thomas Jefferson (1801–09) could have purchased our "Antilles heel" in the West Indies for $3 million, but the United States didn't have the pesetas. (It had just purchased Louisiana for $15 million.) In the early 1850s, the American ministers to England, France, and Spain—James Buchanan (to be President Abraham Lincoln's immediate predecessor in the White House), John Y. Mason, and Pierre Soule, slaves to their ideal—met in Ostend, Belgium, and sent word to President Franklin Pierce's Secretary of State, William L. Marcy, to offer Spain up to $120 million for Cuba: If Spain refused to sell, "then, by every law, human and divine, we shall be justified in wresting it from Spain. . . ." Because Cuba would have become a slave state, abolitionists were outraged. Secretary Marcy refused to accept the recommendation of the ministers. When the Civil War erupted after Buchanan's Presidential stint—"I will be the last President," he had averred—only three countries in the Western world still condoned slavery: the United States, Cuba, and Brazil. The Spanish overseers were vicious in their suppression of sporadic slave revolts in Cuba—one reason they were sporadic.

CUBAN MISSILE CRISIS

Eleven days after astronaut Wally Schirra had orbited the planet nearly six times in a Mercury capsule and two days before the New York Yankees had captured still another World Series championship and three weeks before former Vice-President Richard M. Nixon would be defeated in his bid to become governor of California and vow that the press wouldn't have him to kick around anymore, an American U-2 spy plane on routine reconnaissance over Cuba discovered the construction of missile bases capable of launching nuclear warheads. The United States Joint Chiefs of Staff, in secret meeting, in mid-October 1962, argued for an immediate air strike and an invasion that would get rid of Cuban premier Fidel Castro once and for all. President John F. Kennedy's brother, the Attorney General, Robert, argued that an invasion so soon after the Bay of Pigs disaster would destroy the U.S. moral position in the world. President Kennedy, however, ordered a naval quarantine that would block the entry of additional offensive weapons. October 22—J.F.K. on television announces the existence of the missile bases. Soviet ships with additional missiles continue steaming toward Cuba. October 23–25—Intense negotiations continue at the United Nations, where Adlai Stevenson is the chief U.S. spokesman. October 26—The Soviet Union lets it be known that it would dismantle the bases in exchange for a public promise by the U.S. not to invade Cuba. J.F.K. agrees to the proposal.

The cold-war confrontation ends as suddenly as it began. November 20 —The U.S. ends its naval blockade. By year's end, Soviet missiles and bombers had been removed from the Pearl of the Antilles. (The big Broadway musical during the Cuban Missile Crisis happened to be *Stop the World, I Want To Get Off*.)

CUBE ROOT

A number or quantity whose cube is the given number or quantity. 3, for example, is the cube root of 27. 4 is the cube root of 54. 53 is the cube root of 148,877.

CUBIT

"And God said unto Noah [shortly after the Great Experiment known as Earth was begun], The end of all flesh is come before me; for the earth is filled with violence through them; and, behold, I will destroy them with the earth. Make thee an ark of gopher wood; rooms shalt thou make in the ark, and shalt pitch it within and without with pitch. And this is the fashion which thou shalt make it of: The length of the ark shall be three hundred cubits, the breadth of it fifty cubits, and the height of it thirty cubits. A window shalt thou make to the ark, and in a cubit shalt thou finish it above; and the door of the ark shalt thou set in the side thereof; with lower, second, and third stories shalt thou make it"—Genesis 6. A cubit was an ancient unit of measurement based on the length of the forearm from the elbow to the tip of the middle finger and was equal to about 20 inches. Noah's ark was thusly 500 feet long, 84 feet wide, and 50 feet high.

CURIE, MARIE

It wasn't easy being the French scientist—because she was a woman. The only person to win two Nobel Prizes in the sciences became the first woman ever to teach at the Sorbonne only after her scientist husband, Pierre, had been killed in a traffic accident (he was run over by a horse-drawn vehicle). However, the august French Academy still refused her membership because she was a woman. She was awarded the Nobel Prize in physics in 1903 for her studies of radioactive radiations and the Nobel Prize in chemistry in 1911 for her discovery of two new elements. The Curies' daughter, Irène, and her husband, Frederic Joliot, shared the Nobel Prize in chemistry in 1935. Both Marie Curie and Irène Joliot-

Curie died of leukemia, brought on undoubtedly by their years of work with hard radiation.

CURLING

It resembles shuffleboard or lawn bowling, and is the sport in which stones are thrown at a house. It is played on a 138-foot-long, 14-foot-wide strip of ice by two teams of four players, each player in turn sliding two curling stones along the ice toward a series of four concentric circles— or houses—at the opposite end of the rink. The stone is a large polished circular stone, about a foot in diameter, usually of granite or hone, specially quarried from the Scottish island of Ailsa Craig. It weighs 38 pounds and has a gooseneck handle at the top, making the ellipsoid look like a tea kettle. In curling, teams, not individuals, win. The game, which originated in Scotland and is popular in Canada, demands practice, practice, practice, and an unselfish attitude.

D

DALI, SALVADOR

"I have never seen a more complete example of a Spaniard. What a fanatic!"—the dying Freud's view of the Spanish surrealist painter during a meeting in London. "The young Spaniard, however, with his candid fanatical eyes and his undeniable technical mastery" made Herr Doktor reconsider his opinion that surrealists were cranks. (Surrealists hailed Freud as their patron saint.) "It would in fact be very interesting to investigate analytically how a picture like this [a surrealist picture] came to be painted. . . ." During their conversation, Dali sketched Freud's head but dared not show it to the Master—he had incorporated death into the picture. Dali's brilliant draftsmanship was touted by his one-man publicity band: He never dallied at telling the world about himself. He was suspended and then permanently expelled from the Madrid School of Fine Arts for subversive behavior and he was jailed for political activity. He painted in several distinct and conflicting styles: realism, cubism, abstraction, Neo-Classicism. Whatever worked. In 1927, he completed *Blood Is Sweeter Than Honey,* which announced the fantastic art of subconscious obsessions for which he has become best known. His famous works have included *Helena Rubinstein's Head Emerging from a Rocky Cliff, Persistence of Memory, Christ of St. John of the Cross, The Dream of Christopher Columbus, Face of the Great Masturbator, Man with Unhealthy Complexion Listening to the Sound of the Sea, Girl Sewing.* The man with the waxed mustache designed and executed the dream sequences in Alfred Hitchcock's movie *Spellbound.*

DALLAS

The Texas city of nearly a million people was probably named for the American statesman who was James K. Polk's Vice-President (1845–49), George Mifflin Dallas—the Democrat Polk's campaign platform had called for the annexation of Texas and "reoccupation" of Oregon. Dallas read law, was admitted to the bar, and then was secretary to Albert Gallatin (the Swiss-born financier and public servant), solicitor of the Bank of the United States, city attorney and mayor of Philadelphia, district attorney, Pennsylvania senator, state attorney general, and from 1837 to 1839 minister to Russia. Seven years after leaving the second highest elective office, Dallas was appointed minister to Great Britain. In five years, he convinced the British to drop their long-standing claim to the right to search foreign ships during peacetime, and he arranged for the settlement of contretemps in Central America. He died seven years before "Big D" was founded as a cotton market.

DARROW, CLARENCE

He renounced a lucrative corporate law practice to defend the underdog —he had dropped out of law school after a year to study on his own. His famous clients included Eugene V. Debs, William D. Haywood, the McNamara brothers, Leopold and Loeb, Navy Lieutenant Tommy Massie, and Charles Darwin—he took the Scopes "evolution" case in Tennessee in 1925 to "show up fundamentalism, to prevent bigots and ignoramuses from controlling the educational system of the United States." He didn't believe in God because he didn't believe in Mother Goose. "I do not consider it an insult but rather a compliment to be called an agnostic. I do not pretend to know where many ignorant men are sure—that is all that agnosticism means." None of the tens of accused murderers whom he defended was ever sentenced to death. In April 1936, Darrow confessed, "There is no such thing as justice—in or out of court."

DARTS

The game with its small, pointed missiles evolved directly from warfare: the shooting of arrows, the pegging of spears. Anne Boleyn gave her husband Henry "Biscayan fashion, richly ornamented dartes" for use in tournaments at court. Passengers killed time aboard the *Mayflower* shooting darts. In Great Britain, where darts is especially popular in the public houses, the target with twenty scoring sectors is nine feet away; in the United States, it's eight feet. "Three in bed" is a darter's term for three darts in the same number. Bunghole: the bull's-eye. Hard cheddar: tough luck. In England, bed and breakfast means a score of 26 in the combination of 20/1/5—coinage right on target.

DARWIN, CHARLES—GALAPAGOS TORTOISES

The volcanic Islas de los Galapagos, "Tortoise Islands," were discovered in 1535, about 650 miles west of Ecuador, by the bishop of Panama, who thought God "had caused it to rain stones." The tortoise is one of the planet's longest-lived creatures, up to 150 years. It may reach a length of over four feet and weigh over 500 pounds. The dozen races of the Galapagos tortoise roam isolated on the thirteen separate islands of the Galapagos. "I frequently got on their backs," Charles Darwin wrote about the Galapagos tortoises, "and then giving a few raps on the hinder part of their shells, they would rise up and walk away—but I found it very difficult to keep my balance." The Galapagos, celebrated for odd reptilian fauna, including giant iguanas, were the source of Darwin's theory of evolution. There are also giant tortoises on islands in the Indian Ocean.

DARWIN, CHARLES—*THE ORIGIN*

Irving Stone's saga suggests that England made a monkey of itself by not knighting the originator of the revolutionary theory of organic evolution —Darwinism. But the man who "had made such a noise in the world," his cousin-wife Emma's phrase, was honored with burial in Westminster Abbey. The pallbearers were Thomas Huxley, Alfred Russel Wallace ("the origin of species belongs solely to Mr. Darwin"), John Lubbock, James Russell Lowell (the American minister to the Court of St. James), Joseph Hooker, William Spottiswoode, Canon Farrar, the Duke of Devonshire, the Earl of Derby, the Duke of Argyll—each in his own way a survivor of the fittest. Because Darwin had wanted nothing on his tomb, Thomas Huxley's suggestion to carve on it Emerson's potent quote was to no avail: "Beware when the great God lets loose a thinker on this planet." The thinker was also a punster. He suffered profound seasickness. When a shipmate asked, "Still alive, Darwin? How do you feel?," Darwin managed to reply, "Retch-edly." He admitted it was a bad pun, "but the best I can conjure up." Whoops.

DAVY JONES'S LOCKER

Toward the end of the eighteenth century, it was writ, "The great bugbear of the ocean is Davie Jones. . . . At the crossing of the line . . . [they call] out that Davie Jones and his wife are coming on board and that everything must be made ready." A little later, in a naval chronicle: "The . . . seamen would have met a watery grave; or, to use a seaman's phrase, gone to Davy Jones's locker." Davy Jones is a sailor's devil, and his locker is the bottom of the sea, and that's where drowned sailors go, that's their grave.

DDT

Paul Muller, a Swiss scientist, was awarded the 1948 Nobel Prize in Physiology or Medicine for discovering nine years earlier the properties of the first man-made insecticide. DDT was used to control lice in World War II; it helped to turn back an outbreak of typhus in Naples. Mosquitoes eventually developed a resistance to the chemical (2,2-bis (p-chlorophenyl)-1,1,1-trichloroethane, chlorinated hydrocarbon compound). DDT is toxic to many animals, including man, and not easily degraded into nonpoisonous substances. Rachel Carson's book *Silent Spring,* published in 1962, brought to public awareness the dangers of DDT. Since 1972, it has been banned in the United States for all but emergency use.

DEAD SEA SCROLLS

Ancient manuscripts written in Hebrew, Aramaic (the language of Jesus), and Greek, they were discovered in 1947, and later, in caves at Qumran, near Jericho, northwest of the Dead Sea, by young Bedouin goat-tenders. Fragments include the oldest Bible manuscripts known—they were written or copied between the first century B.C. and the first half of the first century A.D. The complete and the incomplete books of Isaiah are almost a millenium older than any biblical manuscript previously known. There are commentaries on various books of the Bible and fragments of apocryphal and apocalyptic works. They portray a milieu that probably influenced Christ. Many of His doctrines, previously thought to derive from Hellenistic sources, are seen in the light of the Dead Sea scrolls to derive from Jewish sectarian circles. The scrolls first discovered traveled with a Bedouin tribe for a time, perhaps as long as two years. Eventually, four arrived in the United States and were sold by Syrians through a classified advertisement in the Wall Street Journal: "THE FOUR DEAD SEA SCROLLS: Biblical Manuscripts dating back to at least 200 B.C. are for sale. This would be an ideal gift to an educational or religious institution by an individual or group." Most of the scrolls are housed today in the Shrine of the Book in the Israel Museum, in Jerusalem. The thousands of fragments are housed mostly in the Rockefeller Museum, also in Jerusalem. It is uniformly believed that they are not hoaxes.

DEAN, DIZZY AND DAFFY

Jay H. "Dizzy" Dean has been in baseball's Hall of Fame since 1953. Brother Paul D. "Daffy" Dean is not going to make it. Dizzy began a distinguished career with the St. Louis Cardinals in 1932; he started one game for the St. Louis Browns in 1947, after being off the mound for the six years since leaving the Chicago Cubs. He averaged twenty-four wins a season over his first five campaigns. He was 30–7 in 1934 and the National League's most valuable player when he and brother Paul led the Cardinals to the World Series championship. The brash fireballer topped the league in strikeouts four times and set the single-game record of seventeen. Dizzy refused to pitch for a time, "striking" for higher pay for Paul. A batted ball broke Dizzy's toe in the 1937 All-Star game; it led to a changed delivery and an arm injury and a shortened career. He hung up his glove with a .644 winning percentage; he had completed 154 of the 230 games he started. Paul Dean joined the Cards in their 1934 championship season—Dizzy swore that Paul was a better pitcher than even he was—but an arm injury early-on crippled Paul's career. Daffy won 19 games in each of his first two seasons, then only 12 more in seven seasons of varying lengths. But he did something that Dizzy never did: He pitched a no-hit game, against Brooklyn in 1934.

DEAN, JOHN WESLEY, III

The White House counsel to President Richard M. Nixon blew the whistle on Watergate. It was he who disclosed there was a growing cancer, a lethal cancer, close to the Presidency. Two months after Republican aides broke into Democratic Party headquarters at the Watergate in Washington, Mr. Nixon said, [Mr. Dean's] "investigation indicates that no one in the White House staff, no one in this administration, presently employed, was involved in this bizarre incident. . . . What really hurts in matters of this sort is not the fact they occur, because overzealous people in campaigns do things that are wrong. What really hurts is if you try to cover it up." A year after the break-in, Mr. Dean testified, "I had no advance knowledge that the President was going to indicate that I had investigated the matter and found no complicity on the part of anybody at the White House or anyone presently employed in the Administration. I first learned of . . . it on a television news broadcast." Mr. Dean, terrified at the prospect, served a prison term, albeit a brief one. His book was titled *Blind Ambition*.

DEATH OF A SALESMAN

The original title: *The Inside of His Head*. "No one goes to a play with the word 'death' in the title, Artie." It was written in six weeks, and centered on the last days of sixtyish salesman Willy Loman, brilliantly created by Lee J. Cobb. Thirty-five years later, in 1984, the Pulitzer

150

Prize-winning drama was revived on Broadway, and Mr. Miller grossed $63,000 a week as the author and a producer. It was not his first play. In 1944, *The Man Who Had All the Luck;* in 1947, *All My Sons* won the New York Drama Critics' Circle Award. He is the nation's leading playwright: *After the Fall, A View from the Bridge, Incident at Vichy, The Price, The Crucible.* He was married to Marilyn Monroe, and wrote the screenplay for her and Clark Gable's last movie, *The Misfits.*

DEATH VALLEY

If you're terrified of heights, Death Valley in southeast California and southwest Nevada is made for you—if you don't mind heat and being below sea level. The ground temperature gets well up into the 100s and Badwater, in the southcentral desert of the nearly 2 million square acres nearly rimmed by high mountains, is 282 feet below sea level, the lowest point in the hemisphere. (To the northwest in the Sierra Nevadas is Mt. Whitney, at 14,496 feet the highest point in the United States.) Like the Dead Sea and the Great Rift of North Africa, the 140-mile long, 6- to 14-mile-wide Death Valley is the result of dislocation of rock strata along a plane of fracture through prolonged strain in a certain stratum. At Stovepipe Wells in Grapevine Canyon is Walter—"Death Valley Scotty" —Scott's $2 million Moorish castle. Seeing it may be the only reason to pass through the valley. Less than two inches of rain falls there during a year.

DECLARATION OF INDEPENDENCE

Between June 11 and June 28, 1776, Thomas Jefferson composed the most important of all American historical documents. Benjamin Franklin, John Adams, and Jefferson himself revised it, and the Second Continental Congress, meeting in Philadelphia, revised the revision. Among eighty-six changes from Jefferson's draft was the deletion of his indictment of George III for trafficking in slaves, but it may have been the only committee work ever that didn't end up with a camel. Jefferson said that his purpose was "not to find new principles, or new arguments, never before thought of, not merely to say things which had never been said before; but to place before mankind the common sense of the subject, in terms so plain and firm as to command their assent, and to justify ourselves in the independent stand we are compelled to take . . . and to give that expression the proper tone and spirit called for by the occasion." For several years after promulgation of the Declaration, Jefferson sent to friends for comment his draft and the published version. Signing of the Declaration took place over half a year. Fifty of the fifty-six signators, including John Hancock, affixed their names on August 2 to the document adopted on July 4, and toasted the event with Madeira, the colonists' favorite wine.

DE GAULLE, CHARLES

When the six-foot-five leader of the Free French, who had unsuccessfully advocated mechanization of France's peacetime army in the 1930s, arrived at the 1943 Casablanca Conference with President Franklin D. Roosevelt and Prime Minister Winston S. Churchill, "he thought he was Joan of Arc and the following day he insisted that he was Georges Clemenceau," President Roosevelt later commented. Churchill was to give the Great Uncompromiser grudging admiration: "A great man? Why, he's selfish, he's arrogant, he thinks he's the center of the universe . . .He . . . Yes, you're right, he's a great man!" General De Gaulle for his part admired Churchill, distrusted F.D.R. He was driven by one idea: "France cannot be France without greatness." He got the country out of Indochina and Algeria, withdrew from military integration in the North Atlantic Treaty Organization, vetoed British membership in the Common Market. The first president of the Fifth Republic (1959–69) accumulated gold—it's now worth about $200 billion, one reason any French leader can be cavalier with the French economy. He once wrote: "How could I not have learned by now that what is good for the nation is not achieved without disapproval from public opinion and losses in elections?" He was not assassinated by the Jackal. No one was surprised to learn he was playing solitaire when he died of a heart attack, in 1970.

DENMARK

Europe's oldest monarchy, the Scandinavian country jutting out from northwest Europe is made up of the Jutland peninsula and nearly 500 islands, including the largest island in the world, semiautonomous Greenland far to the west in the Atlantic. There doesn't seem to be much rotten in Denmark. The impossible-to-please Evelyn Waugh described the Danes as "the most exhilarating people in Europe." Life expectancy is threatened by overeating. Wages go up automatically when holidays in the Canary Islands become more expensive. A proper wedding still calls for a horse-drawn bridal carriage. One in three children is born out of wedlock. Tivoli Gardens in Copenhagen and "Hamlet's castle" at Elsinore, on the narrow sound between Jutland and Sweden, are tourist magnets. Five Viking ships were found at the bottom of the fjord at Roskilde. Hans Christian Andersen was born in the third largest town, Odense, the provincial capital of Funen. Denmark's nineteen volcanic

Faroe islands mark the northern limit of the Atlantic Ocean. Union with Sweden was dissolved in 1523, with Norway in 1814. The national flag is one of the oldest flags in continuous use, if not the oldest, and is called the Dannebrog: a red field with a pair of intersecting white stripes. Legend says it fell from heaven as a victory symbol at the battle of Lyndanisse, in June 1219, as King Valdemar was leading his troops against the pagan Livionians. Dannebrog literally translated means "Danish cloth"; It is the spirit of Denmark. Helping the country's Jews escape Nazi tyranny—the king declared, "We are all Jews"—was also in the spirit of Denmark.

DESDEMONA

The villainous ensign Iago was sexually jealous of Othello, the Moor in the military service of Venice whose happiness with Desdemona seemed ideally perfect: "I hate the Moor; and it is thought abroad that twixt my sheets he has done my office. I know not if 't be true; but I, for mere suspicion in that kind, will do as if for surety. . . . and I dare think he'll prove to Desdemona a most dear husband. Now, I do love her too; not out of absolute lust, though peradventure I stand accountant for as great a sin, but partly led to diet my revenge, for that I do suspect the lusty Moor hath leap'd into my seat; the thought whereof doth, like a poisonous mineral, gnaw my inwards; nothing can or shall content my soul till I am even'd with him, wife for [wife]; or failing so, yet that I put the Moor at least into a jealousy so strong that judgement cannot cure." When Othello enters Desdemona's chamber to kill her—once the embodiment of purity, she now seems to him corrupted and defiled—he conceives of himself as the agent not of vengeance but of divine justice. To gnawing jealousy had been added the force of shattered idealism.

"DESMOND AND MOLLY JONES"

Molly is a singer in a band, always was, always will be. Desmond liked her face and gave Molly a twenty-carat golden ring. Presently, the belle was ringing, bells were ringing, and they had a home sweet home with a couple of kids running in the yard. If you, too, want some fun happily ever after, the Beatles say, "take Obladi, Oblada."

DEVILS ISLAND

One of the three Iles du Salut—"health islands"—the hot, humid, escapeproof French penal colonies in the Caribbean off French Guiana, within six degrees of the equator—so called because they were free from malaria; the anopheles mosquito could not cross the shark-infested strait that separates the three from the mainland. Devils Island's first prisoner, in 1894, was Alfred Dreyfus; other "elite," political Frenchmen were to follow. But for the five years he was there, Dreyfus was truly in solitary confinement—there was no other prisoner on the spit in the ocean. France's cutthroats were imprisoned in hell holes on claustrophobic Ile Royale and St. Joseph. The penal colonies were closed down by 1951. Captain Dreyfus, who had been a general staff officer, was exonerated of the charge of "Jewish treason" and decorated with the Legion of Honor.

DEWEY DECIMAL SYSTEM

During a long Sunday sermon by President Stearns of Amherst College, "the solution flasht over me [Dewey] so that I jumpt in my seat and came very near shouting 'Eureka!' " Melvil Dewey, a twenty-one-year-old student, and acting librarian, had figured out how to arrange books in a library orderly and efficiently. Arabic numerals would be used decimally (from 000 to 999) to cover the general fields of knowledge and the decimal point would designate more specific subjects. Two years later, in America's centennial year, Dewey published anonymously "A Classification and Subject Index for Cataloguing and Arranging the Books and Pamphlets of a Library," 42 pages. A conference of librarians in Philadelphia immediately hailed his classification of the printed records of human knowledge. Dewey was also keen on "speling" reform, and he is credited with invention of the vertical office file.

DEW POINT

Dew is a thin film of water that has condensed on the surface of objects near the ground. The dew point is the temperature at which moisture in the air begins to condense. It is either lower than the temperature of the air or it is the same as the air temperature when the relative humidity is 100 percent. If a dew point temperature below 32°F. is reached, sublimation occurs; that is, the water vapor converts directly to frost. (What did one thin film of water say to the other thin film of water? Funny, you don't *look* dewish.)

DIAMONDS

Three thousand one hundred and six carats, about 1⅓ pounds—the Cullinan, the largest gem diamond that's ever been discovered. And there it was, just lying around the Premier mine in South Africa, where it was literally stumbled across in 1905. Two years later, the Transvaal government bought it and sent it by post to England as a gift for King Edward VII on his sixty-sixth birthday. (Talking about gift to come!) The world's two largest cut diamonds are from the Cullinan—the Great Star of Africa, a pear-shaped diamond weighing 530.20 carats, and Cullinan II, weighing 317.40 carats. They are among the British crown jewels on display in the Tower of London. The 44.5-carat Hope is the most famous diamond in the United States; it's in the Smithsonian Institution. The Hope was probably cut from a 112.50-carat blue diamond found in India. Another British crown jewel is the Koh-i-noor, the diamond with the longest history. It was first reported in the possession of the Raja of Malwa, one of the Indian states south of Delhi. The year was 1304. A diamond is the hardest known substance, and the simplest gem in chemical composition.

DICK, ALBERT BLAKE

Thomas Alva Edison was indeed a wizard. He held over 1,300 United States and foreign patents. That light bulb was always going on in his head. While experimenting with paraffin paper for possible use as telegraph tape, he discovered that he could use a wax stencil in a duplicating process. On August 8, in the centennial year of the inventive nation, he obtained U.S. Patent No. 180,857 on a "method of preparing autographic stencils for printing." Four years later, he obtained a patent for an improved model. That's where the Chicago lumberman Albert Blake Dick Albert Blake Dick got into the duplicating business. He bought the patent and made a flat-bed duplicator. A wax stencil was placed into a wooden frame and a stylus was used to inscribe the text. Ink was applied to the stencil with a roller and squeezed through and onto the copying sheet beneath. The A.B. Dick Co. sold its first Diaphragm Mimeograph in 1887. A modern stencil is good for 10,000 copies.

DIEN BIEN PHU

"Sortie failed. Stop. Can no longer communicate with you. Stop and end." The last message that a Frenchman would send from the fortress, near the Laotian border, the last bastion of French colonial power in Indochina—it fell on May 7, 1954, after a fifty-six-day siege by the Viet Minh forces of Ho Chi Minh and when desperate pleas for United States intervention were unsuccessful. Prime Minister Joseph Laniel, sixty-five years old, bull-necked, told the French people "that for seven years now the Army of the French Union has unceasingly protected a particularly crucial region of Asia and has alone defended the interests of all. All of France shares the anguish of the families of the fighters of Dien Bien Phu. Their heroism has reached such heights that universal conscience should dictate to the enemy—in favor of the wounded and of those whose courage entitles them to the honors of war—such decisions as will contribute more than anything to establish a climate favorable to peace."

DILLINGER, JOHN

It was like taking coals to Newcastle—Public Enemy Number One, in disguise, was at a gang-and-gun movie in Lincoln Avenue on Chicago's North Side. *Manhattan Melodrama* starred Clark Gable and William Powell, and its moral was crime doesn't pay. The outlaw knew from crime. After deserting the Navy—he served on the battleship *Utah*, bombed two decades later at Pearl Harbor—he went on an eleven-year bank-robbing and killing tear. Twice, he escaped sensationally from jail. In April 1934, he and his gang shot their way out of a police trap in Little Bohemia, Wisconsin, slaying two would-be captors. Three months later, the outlaw went to the movie with Mrs. Anna Miller, who was wearing a red dress, and Mrs. Rita Keele, his current lover. The Federal Bureau of Investigation had been tipped off and waited for two hours. To this day, it is believed that the "woman in red" was the finger. July 22, 1984, marked the fiftieth anniversary of the mow-down.

DIONNE QUINTUPLETS

Monday, May 28, 1934. The backwoods of northern Ontario, Canada. "Gosh!" "Gosh!" "GOSH!" said the doctor. "Holy Mary!" said the mother. The doctor was Allan Roy Dafoe, the mother was Elzire Dionne. She was delivering five identical baby girls, the world's first quints to survive, to this day the only quints to be born from a single egg. The largest of the two-months-premature girls weighed only 2½ pounds, the smallest, 1 pound 8½ ounces. None was more than nine inches long— grotesque creatures with the legs of insects, disproportionately large heads, bright blue eyes with long lashes, appreciable shocks of hair. The last two born were still imprisoned in their amniotic sacs. The quints' only nourishment for the first twenty-seven hours was a few drops of warm water from an eyedropper. They lived in a "goldfish bowl" for the first nine years, exhibited daily in Quintland, separated from parents and their other siblings. (The Dionnes had already had six children when the quints were born.) When they were eighteen, the sisters entered a convent school. Emilie suffered an epileptic seizure and suffocated to death in 1954. Marie, who married in 1958, died in 1970 from a brain clot. Yvonne, Cecile, and Annette live today in the Montreal suburb of St. Bruno.

DISMAS AND GESTAS

"And set up over His head His accusation written, THIS IS JESUS THE KING OF THE JEWS. Then were there two thieves crucified with him, one on the right hand, and another on the left." Gestas pleaded, "If you're Christ, save yourself and us as well." But Dismas said, "We deserved our sentence. Jesus has done nothing to deserve it. Jesus, will you remember me when you come into your kingdom?" "I promise you," Jesus replied, "that today you will be with me in paradise." The four Gospels do not identify either of the thieves by name, but apocryphal literature invented a number of names for both. Matthew and Mark speak of the robbers who upbraided Jesus, but "Dismas" in Luke does not rail against Him. A portion of the cross on which "Dismas" is said to have died is preserved at the Church of Santa Croce in Rome, and he is the patron of those condemned to death.

DISTRICT OF COLUMBIA

The Father of His Country himself picked the site. "Federal City" would be geographically at the mid-point between the Northern financiers and the Southern farmers. Maryland and Virginia were willing to grant malarial swampland on each bank of the Potomac River. Alexandria County was returned to Virginia in 1846. When Georgetown became part of the city of Washington in 1878, the District of Columbia and Washington became one and the same. (The Constitution had left unresolved the location of the national capital. Secretary of State Thomas Jefferson, Treasury Secretary Alexander Hamilton, and Congressman James Madison, in the second year of George Washington's first presidential term, in New York, moved to move the seat of the government.) The population doubled during the Civil War—thousands of freed black slaves moved there—and between 1950 and 1980 it grew faster than any other large city. It has more residents than at least twenty members of the United Nations. Citizens have been allowed to vote in Presidential elections in the last two decades, and they can elect local government officials. States are debating a constitutional amendment that would allow Districters to elect voting delegates to the House and to the Senate. In *Captive Capital,* published by Indiana University Press, Sam Smith writes that what "lies beyond the community that supports this pageant [of cultural D.C.] is considered a strange and fearful place inhabited by muggers and rapists. The tourists heed the advice of room clerks, cab drivers, and tour guides not to stray far from the Mall or their hotels." The first residents were Piscataway Indians.

DIVORCE

Impotence has been a ground for divorce in twenty-four states. Some other grounds for divorce: crime against nature—Alabama; gross misbehavior and wickedness—Rhode Island; mental incompetence for at least three years—Florida; abuse or neglect of a child—West Virginia; sodomy or buggery outside the marriage—Virginia; deviant sexual conduct without consent of spouse—New Jersey; marriage entered into as a result of fraud—Connecticut; maliciously turning spouse out-of-doors—North Carolina; unexplained absence of spouse for seven years, public defamation, attempt on spouse's life—Louisiana; husband did not know that wife was pregnant by another man at time of marriage—several states; any grounds the court deems sufficient—Nebraska.

DNA

The master heredity chemical of all living things. Genes are composed of molecules of DNA, or deoxyribonucleic acid; grouped around chromosomes, they are the carriers of heredity. All life forms have been created from the same basic genetic material, a fact that supports the theory of evolution strongly. Totally new creatures, totally new forms of life can be created through the combining of genes—yes, the genes of a pear can be combined with the genes of a lion. The secret of the structure of the DNA molecule was unveiled in 1953 by two biochemists, James Watson of the United States and Francis Crick of England. The U.S. Supreme Court has ruled that a live human-made organism is patentable by genetic engineers.

DOLDRUMS

They're a place, too—the area around the Earth centered slightly north of the equator between the two belts of trade winds. Severe weather is sometimes spawned in the doldrums because of intense heating by solar radiation. The Doldrums are also known as the equatorial belt of calms —days or weeks can go by when there isn't a breath of air, when nothing moves. When you're in the Doldrums, you can be in the doldrums.

DOLOMITE(S)

Dolomite is a mineral composed of calcium and magnesium and it is a rock containing the mineral as a principal constituent. The Dolomites, or Dolomite Alps, are a mountain group in the eastern section of the northern Italian Alps, eighteen peaks rising over 10,000 feet—all named for the French geologist Deodat Guy Silvain Tancrede Gratet de Dolomieu, who first studied the mineral in the Dolomites, where Lenin was to walk. Dolomite crystals are widespread: Joplin, Missouri; Alston, Cumberland, England; Spain; Brazil; and so on. They are used as a source of magnesia and as building stone. Dolomieu wrote his celebrated treatise on mineralogy (1801) while imprisoned at Messina for being a Bonapartist.

DOLPHIN

There are more than fifty species of the aquatic, hairless, small-toothed, warm-blooded mammal. Most are gregarious . . . playful . . . friendly . . . very intelligent . . . they look merry . . . they look as though they are smiling . . . they are capable of imitation and memorization. Computers are still trying to crack the dolphin language and dolphin echolocation, which would have military applications; some dolphin frequencies are up to ten times those that can be heard by a human being. The Japanese are the last still to hunt the dolphin for food, and there is still no record of a dolphin attacking a person.

DONALD DUCK

It's been said that he is every child who has not yet learned that it's often more prudent to hold one's temper than to turn rose-red with anger and let the fury fly. He is loudmouthed, excitable, impatient, shortsighted, and accident-prone. Donald's only human. He made his Hollywood debut in "The Wise Little Hen," a Walt Disney–Silly Symphony cartoon, and he won an Oscar in 1943. "In Der Fuehrer's Face," Disney's most popular wartime cartoon, his heils were contemptuously punctuated with overripe raspberries; prints were smuggled into Europe. A painting of Donald on crutches was on the fuselage of the *Ruptured Duck,* the B-25 piloted by Captain Ted W. Lawson in Jimmy Doolittle's surprise raid on Tokyo four months after Pearl Harbor. He was also patriotic in the extreme, racing from California to Washington with red, white, and blue flags in his eyes to pay his income tax in person in the film *The New Spirit* that the Secretary of the Treasury had asked Disney to make to "help us sell people on paying their tax." At first, the Treasury's movie critics

159

were dismayed. "Well, I, uh—I always visualized, Mr. Disney, that you would create a little character who would be called Mr. Taxpayer. I don't like Donald Duck." Disney exploded: "I've given you Donald Duck. At our studio, that's like giving you Clark Gable out of the M-G-M stable." The production bill was $80,000. The Secretary said he would have to go to Congress for a deficiency appropriation. The cartoon was held up as an example of boondoggling, or boonduckling, and Disney was accused of being a war profiteer. For all of Donald's 50-plus-years career, his voice has been supplied by Clarence "Ducky" Nash.

DOSTOEVSKI, FEODOR

The Russian novelist and *de facto* editor of the magazine *Time (Vremya)* boldly introduced a major new theme into the political prose of the 1860s, the theme of the disinherited in the capitalist world who are no longer passive and wordless but who take up arms against their oppressors. "The ideal of beauty is useful because it is beauty, because mankind always has a need for beauty and for beauty's highest ideal." He believed that Russia's salvation lay in the soil and the people. His father, an alcoholic military surgeon of despotic temperament, was brutally murdered by his own serfs. "Man is a pliable animal, a being who gets accustomed to everything," Dostoevski wrote of prison life in Siberia, where he suffered prodigious physical and mental pain in four years at hard labor for having had an illegal printing press. A nightmarish life and then a contented marriage to his young secretary led him to *Notes from the Underground, Crime and Punishment, The Idiot, The Possessed, A Raw Youth,* and *The Brothers Karamazov:* "We have all come out of Gogol's *Overcoat*."

DRAFT

In the United States military draft lottery in 1917 the first number—258 —was held by Alden C. Flagg. In the peacetime lottery in 1940 the first number—158—was held by Flagg's son Alden, Jr. The process of selection of some of the male population for compulsory military service is a peculiarly American concept. In Europe, the entire male population, generation after generation, is conscripted for training. Until 1863, American military manpower was based entirely on volunteers. The Civil War draft led to bloody riots over the provision for money payments in lieu of service. The Selective Service Act of 1917 outlawed both the hiring of substitutes and the payment of bounties; over half of America's 4 million men in arms in World War I were draftees. With the exception of one year (March 1947–48), the draft was in continuous operation from 1940, when the blindfolded Secretary of War, Henry Stimson, pulled the first number (158) out of a fishbowl, to January 27, 1973.

DR. SEUSS

Theodor Seuss Geisel, now eightyish, had no formal training in art. His nonsense and rhymes and drawings have been charming children—and their parents—since he "saw it on Mulberry Street" in 1937. He created the "Quick Henry, the Flit!" series of advertisements in cartoon form for an advertising agency. He won three Oscars: for the Army film *Hitler Lives,* in 1946; for *Design for Death,* a feature-length documentary on Japanese history, in 1947; and for a film cartoon starring his original character Gerald McBoing-Boing, in 1951. No doubt he shared his 1984 Pulitzer Prize with the cat in the hat and the Grinch who stole Christmas. Seuss books are the rare children's books that parents can read night-afternight to their children without becoming bored.

DR. STRANGELOVE

Peter Sellers was also to be the cowboyish American bomber pilot in the black-humored movie, but he broke a leg—there goes *that* show biz "good luck" wish—after playing Dr. Strangelove himself, the American President, and a British officer before the bomber sequences were filmed. Stanley Kubrick, the director and co-writer, didn't miss a beat. He considered Slim Pickens the only authentic cowboy actor in the world and immediately contacted Pickens' agent. It was a typical Kubrick selection —perfect. *Dr. Strangelove* was based on Peter George's novel *Red Alert.* Kubrick and George talked frequently about the book's potential. In a taxicab in The Bronx one day, Kubrick slapped George's leg and said, "What if we made it a comedy!" Release of the film was delayed until early 1964 because of the assassination of President John F. Kennedy, in late 1963.

DRURY LANE

On Catherine Street, at Russell, it is England's oldest theater. Nell Gwynn trod there, actor-manager David Garrick innovated there, Edmund Kean electrified audiences there, Sir Augustus Harris introduced melodrama there, Rex Harrison taught Julie Andrews English English there—that the rain in Spain stays mainly in the plain. Drury Lane is also the name of the English theater district—in the environs are the Duchess, Aldwych, Shaftesbury, Strand (*Arsenic and Old Lace* charged through

1,337 performances there), the Royal Opera House–Covent Garden, the Royalty, the Fortune, the London. For a time in the mid-seventeenth century, the monarchy kept London's theaters closed—the conscience of the king was not going to be caught *there*.

DUCK-BILLED PLATYPUS

One of only two mammals that lays eggs rather than live young—the other is the echidna, a toothless, spiny, burrowing nocturnal anteater somewhat larger than the groundhog and, like the platypus, indigenous to Tasmania and Australia. Brown, furry, up to two feet long, it is called the duckbill or the duckbilled platypus because its rubbery muzzle or snout—broad, flat, hairless—resembles the bill of a duck. Its webbed five-toed feet and broad, flat, four-to-five-inch-long tail aid in swimming. It has no teeth. The hollow heel of the male secretes a defensive poison. The female platypus lays one or two or three eggs at a time.

DULCINEA DEL TOBOSO

Don Quixote's imaginary love—he never met the buxom peasant wench famous for her skill in salting pork. He believed she was enchanted, and he dedicated his deeds of valor to her. The quixotic one wrote her of both his acts of penance and his fasting for her love, and he dispatched those he "defeated" to inform her of his brave deeds. Miguel de Cervantes' lancing of the books of chivalry has been described as the best novel ever written, beyond comparison.

DUMDUM

The name of an airport in Calcutta, the name of a fever, and once best known as the name of a vertically-slit lead-nosed bullet that expands upon impact and causes a terrible ripping wound. The first Hague Conference, in 1899, outlawed the bullet. Dumdum, from *Dum-Dum,* a suburb of Calcutta, in the state of West Bengal in eastcentral India. The arsenal in Dum-Dum was the first to produce the dumdum bullet.

DUNGRI

Eponym is from the Greek word for "giving one's name." Dungarees got their name, it is said, from the Bombay suburb of *Dungri*. (But it may have been derived from the Hindi word *dungri,* for "coarse.") A cudgel, traditionally of blackthorn or oak, is a shillelagh, from the Irish town of

162

Shillelagh. Coarsely or vulgarly abusive language—billingsgate—is from the fishmarket *Billingsgate* in London. A small seedless raisin—the currant—is from the Greek port *Corinth*. The fur of young lambs, with lustrous, closely curled wool—astrakhan—is from the city *Astrakhan* in Russia. The official residence of a sovereign or bishop, any large and stately building—a palace—is from the hill *Palatium* in ancient Rome.

DUROCHER, LEO

Was there a more outspoken baseball player and manager from 1925 to 1973 than Leo the Lip? "Show me a good loser in professional sports and I'll show you an idiot. Show me a sportsman and I'll show you a player I'm looking to trade to Oakland. Win any way you can as long as you can get away with it. When you're playing for money, winning is the only thing that matters. A buffoon is a drunk on a hitting spree. A drunk is a pitcher who's lost his fastball. A confirmed drunk is a pitcher with a sore arm. An incurable drunk is a pitcher who hasn't won a game all season." He's in *Bartlett's* for his remark "Nice guys finish last." The Brooklyn Dodgers' manager was sizing up the New York Giants as they appeared for batting practice in the Polo Grounds: Ott, Cooper, Mize, Marshall, Kerr, Gordon, Thomson. "Take a look at them," he said to Frank Graham of the New York *Journal-American*. "All nice guys. They'll finish last. Nice guys. Finish last . . . Give me some scratching, diving, hungry ballplayers who come to kill you. Now, [Eddie] Stanky's the nicest gentleman who ever drew breath, but when the bell rings you're his mortal enemy. That's the kind of guy I want playing for me." In 1941, Durocher piloted the Dodgers to their first pennant in twenty-one years, and in seven of nine seasons kept them in the first division in the National League. He switched subway lines and managed the Giants to pennants in 1951 and 1954 and to the World Series title in '54. His nineteen-year managerial career with three clubs was 1,616W, 1,343L, .546. He sat out the 1947 season, suspended by Commissioner Happy Chandler (coincidentally on the day before the Dodgers placed Jackie Robinson on their roster) for conduct detrimental to the national pastime—there had been dice games, constant rows with umpires, three marriages—it was the most drastic action ever taken against a major league manager—it was also thought to be the outgrowth of a feud between the Dodgers and the Yankees, whose new president was a former president of Dem Bums.

DYLAN, BOB

Real name: Robert Allen Zimmerman. The folk/rock singer and composer adopted the surname Dylan from the Welsh poet Dylan Thomas. He "bummed" around the country, making "my own Depression." He was a new morning: "Visions of Johanna," "It Ain't Me, Babe," "A Hard Rain's A-Gonna Fall," "Like a Rolling Stone," "Blowin' in the Wind." He made his electric debut at The Newport Folk Festival on August 24, 1965. Bob Dylan's dream: "We thought we could sit forever in fun." He no longer has the subterranean blues; indeed, he is said to be deeply involved with the Hasidic Lubavitcher movement.

E

E

Gadsby is a 50,000-word novel with no words with the letter "e"—the device is called a lipogram. The author, in the late 1930s, was a California musician, Ernest Vincent Wright. "E" is the most commonly used letter in the English alphabet. (T is the second most commonly used letter, then a, then i, s, o, n, h. . . .) In 1969, the French novel *La Disparitim (The Disappearance)*, by George Perec, did not contain the letter e, -ither; "e" is also the most commonly used letter in French. James Thurber published a story about a country in which the letter "o" could not be used. The prolific Spanish playwright Lope de Vega Carpio wrote five novels, each in turn minus one of the vowels. The German poet Gottlob Burmann wrote 130 poems without using the letter "r." For seventeen years, he didn't use or speak any word with the letter "r" in it, presumably not even his own name. There have been books with absolutely no words and Samuel Beckett has staged a play called *Breath* in which there were not only no words but no actors; it ran thirty seconds. Here's why *Gadsby* sold only fifty copies or so: "Upon this basis I am going to show you how a bunch of bright young folks did find a champion; a man with boys and girls of his own; a man of so dominating and happy individuality that youth is drawn to him as is a fly to a sugar bowl. It is a story about a small town. It is not a gossipy yarn; nor is it a dry monotonous account. It is . . . a practical discarding of that worn-out notion that 'a child doesn't know anything.' "

EAGLETON, THOMAS

A Missouri senator since 1968—he plans to retire in 1986—the "Jim Farley" of his class at Amherst College was (in George McGovern's presidential-campaign director Gary Hart's words) "a last-minute entry put on primarily because he was Catholic, urban, and an unknown from a border state." He was the Vice-Presidential candidate for two weeks! Though the top of the ticket had announced that McGovern was supporting him 1,000 percent, Eagleton was forced off the ticket after it was learned that he had been "voluntarily" hospitalized for "nervous exhaustion" three times over the previous twelve years, twice after tough election campaigns. Eagleton later said that he took the heat, "and I endured. I endured very well," and he campaigned indefatigably for the McGovern ticket (R. Sargent Shriver had replaced Eagleton). He had been Missouri's youngest lieutenant governor: "The way other kids wanted to be farmers or firemen or cowboys, I wanted to be a politician."

EARDRUM

Now hear this! The cliche goes back six centuries: "Oon ere it herde, at tothir out it wente." Chaucer. Some "earie" facts: It still is not known how the movement of the 20,000 sensory hair cells stimulates nerve impulses or how the brain distinguishes high-pitched sounds from low-pitched sounds or how the brain distinguishes between loud and soft sounds. The smallest of the 216 bones in your body are your ear bones. The three bones, or ossicles, in your middle ear (which is separated from the outer ear by the eardrum) are the hammer (malleus), the anvil (incus), and the stirrup (stapes), named for their shapes. Your chief organs of balance and orientation are the utriculus and the sacculus in the inner ear. Another earie fact: The function of the sacculus is still not fully understood.

EARHART, AMELIA

She was no fly-by-night heroine. She set aviation mark after mark over nine years and won accolade after accolade, including the Distinguished Flying Cross. She was the first woman passenger on a transatlantic flight (aboard the trimotor *Friendship*, in 1928). She was the first woman to fly solo across the Atlantic, from Newfoundland to Ireland in a record fourteen hours, fifty-six minutes in 1932. She made three record-setting and -breaking trans–U.S. flights and in 1935 the first solo flight by any pilot from Hawaii to the mainland and the first nonstop Mexico City–New York flight. With Frederick J. Noonan as copilot and navigator, she was seeking another record when she took off from Miami in June 1937. Her goal was to return to Miami after flying around the world at the equator. An accident in Honolulu made her start out a second time from Miami. The twin-engined Lockheed Electra vanished without a trace between New Guinea and Howland Island in the central Pacific.

EARTH

Columbus was right: The planet is shaped like a pear, roughly spherical in shape, with an average diameter of 7,918 miles. There's a slight bulge at the equator, giving an equatorial diameter 26.6 miles greater than that from Pole to Pole. Mass is 5.976×10^{21} tons, and average density is 5.52 times that of water. Seventy percent is covered with water. It is the fifth largest planet of the solar system and it is warmed by one of the about 100 billion stars in the Milky Way Galaxy—the Sun is 93 million miles away. Under the continents is a crust with an average thickness of 20 miles; the crust is only about three miles thick under the oceans. The fact that Earth rotates, at 66,000 miles per hour, wasn't clearly demonstrated until 1851. A force equal to that of a thirty-four-megaton atomic bomb struck northern Arizona when a meteorite impacted there about 27,000 years ago. Atomic dating determined that rocks found in Greenland were 3.7 billion to 3.9 billion years old. The magnetic field has flipflopped, North and South, at least 171 times. Half of the world's population lives in four countries: China, India, the Soviet Union, the United States. Experiments representing the first systematic search by physicists for intelligent life beyond the planet are under way. Hundreds of millions of people living in India and in Africa have never heard of the United States.

EARTHQUAKES

Seventy-five percent of the 850 active volcanoes in the world are within the "ring of fire"—a zone running along the west coast of the Americas from Chile to Alaska and along the east coast of Asia from Siberia to New Zealand. Twenty percent of these volcanoes are located in Indonesia, where Krakatoa blew its top in 1883—the 2,640-foot-high peak of the volcano collapsed to 1,000 feet *below* sea level. Ash from the eruption, the largest in recent centuries, colored sunsets around the world for two years and the tidal wave that was generated broke on English shores. The ring of fire is also the site of destructive earthquakes caused by shifting rock in the crust of the planet. The Tangshan quake in China in 1976 wiped out 650,000 persons. Killer quakes have struck Tokyo thrice in the last two centuries. The year 1812 was known in California as the year of earthquakes. In 1906, at least eight quakes in the ring of fire registered a magnitude of 8 on the Richter scale of 0 to 9. A magnitude of 8.9 was registered in a Colombia-Ecuador shock. About six thousand scary tremors are reported annually: Few take lives.

EASTER

It has been traditionally said that the resurrection of Jesus took place on a Sunday (the first day of the week). The ecumenical Nicaea Council of Eastern and Western bishops and papal legates, convened in 325 A.D. by the Roman Emperor Constantine the Great, determined to fix a consistent time for commemoration—Easter. They consulted the Hebrew calendar and settled on the first Sunday after the first full moon following the vernal equinox—the Sunday would be between March 22 and April 25. Some Eastern Orthodox churches still determine the date for Christ's resurrection by other methods.

EASTER ISLAND

The entire 46-square-mile Chilean dependent 2,200 miles out in the eastern Pacific Ocean west of Chile is today a historic monument. Volcanic in origin, grasslanded, trade-wind swept, it is triangularly shaped, with an extinct volcano perched near each of the three corners. It was indeed discovered on Easter Day, in 1722, by a Dutch navigator. Six hundred or so monolithic stone heads ranging in height from ten to forty feet and each weighing tens of tons were probably carved from tufa, a soft volcanic stone, by Polynesian ancestors of the present residents. They are not extraterrestrial droppings! The islanders, who are not taxed by Chile, call their home Te-Pito-o-te-Henua, "the navel of the world."

"EAST IS EAST"

Did England's first Nobel Prize winner in literature think in 1889 that East and West would meet? "Oh, East is East, and West is West, and never the twain shall meet," Rudyard Kipling wrote, in "The Ballad of East and West," "Till Earth and Sky stand presently at God's great Judgment Seat: But there is neither East nor West, Border, nor Breed, nor Birth, When two strong men stand face to face, though they come from the ends of the earth!"

EBONY

It's a black-created, black-oriented, general, picture magazine dealing primarily with contemporary topics. Total paid circulation after forty years is 1,659,243, and it is read, say the advertising department's demographers, by 3,157,000. The total black consumer market is $163 billion, says the United States Bureau of Labor Statistics.

ECUADOR

"Equator" in Spanish. In 1832, Ecuador claimed 13 large islands (about 3,029 square miles) 650 miles due west on the equator, the Galapagos, "tortoises" in Spanish, 500-pound tortoises. The United States built an airfield in the Galapagos to help protect the Panama Canal during World War II. There are about 3,000 permanent residents there today—human residents—and thousands of survivors of species reflecting various evolutionary stages. Darwin went "bananas" in the Galapagos. Earthquake-prone Ecuador was in the northern Inca empire and encompassed four times more land than it does today. The snowcapped volcanic peaks Chimborazo (20,577 feet) and Cotopaxi (19,347 feet) are Andes, which strut through the country in two ranges. Fifty-five percent of the population (about 7 million) are mestizo. Ecuador is Latin America's second largest oil producer.

EDISON, THOMAS

"Genius is one percent inspiration and ninety-nine percent perspiration." "There is no substitute for hard work." He found Braille preferable to visual reading. The electrical Wizard of Menlo Park established an "invention factory," the first industrial research laboratory. He patented more than 1,300 inventions, including the electric light with carbon filament. His favorite accomplishment: the phonograph. He tested the prototype by yelling "Mary Had a Little Lamb" into the recording device. He made only one purely scientific discovery: the "Edison effect," which involves the flow of electricity across a vacuum. He patented the effect, but could think of no use for it and went on to other things. The Edison effect turned out to be the basis of the whole electronics industry—radio, television, and all. When Congress awarded Edison a gold medal in 1928, it was estimated that his inventions were worth $25 billion to humanity.

EIFFEL TOWER

The French engineer Alexandre Gustave Eiffel used 5,000 sheets of paper, each nearly a yard square, to lay out his plans for the world's tallest building, which the 985-foot 11-inch eyeful soaring out of Paris' Champ-de-Mars was until the Chrysler Building went up in East 42nd Street, in New York City, 41 years later. (The exact height varies according to the temperature.) Twelve thousand pieces of metal and 2.5 million rivets were used to put together the iron framework—four open-lattice wrought iron columns uniting in one shaft. The Eiffel Tower was inaugurated by Edward VII, then Prince of Wales, at the Centennial Exposition of 1889. There are 1,792 steps to the top. Today, a high-tech restaurant, *the* place to be seen, is on the second level—a polished, sparkling black and white Jules Verne room decorated by Slavik. There has always been a committee of Parisites lobbying to abolish the "eyesore." Eiffel was a noted bridge engineer, and he had designed the interior of the Statue of Liberty. He was to contribute to the science of aerodynamics. (The Eiffel Tower had a love nest at its peak so the designer could carry on his trysts at a higher level.) "Shepherdess, O Eiffel Tower, your flock of bridges is bleating this morning."

EINSTEIN, ALBERT

One of the greatest physicists, he refused the Presidency of Israel because, he said, he had no head for human problems. If he had known that the Germans would not succeed in making an atomic bomb, he would have done nothing to further its development by the United States. The root of his intellectual development of relativity grew from his wonder at what light waves would look like to him if he moved as fast as they did. He revolutionized physics with three historic papers in 1905—he was at the time a clerk in a Swiss patent office—but it took him four more years to land a professorship, and a poorly paying one at that, at the University of Zurich. "The most beautiful experience we can have is the mysterious. It is the fundamental emotion which stands at the cradle of true art and true science. Whoever does not know it and can no longer wonder, no longer marvel, is as good as dead, and his eyes are dimmed. A knowledge of the existence of something we cannot penetrate, our primitive perceptions of the profoundest reason and the most radiant beauty—it is this knowledge and this emotion that constitute true religious feeling." His last words will never be known. He spoke them in German, and the attending nurse did not understand German.

EISENHOWER, DWIGHT D.

The two-term thirty-fourth President, whose smile and simple frontier approach to complex problems made him to Supreme Court Justice William O. Douglas "as American as apple pie," was buried in military uniform in an army coffin. Former President Harry S Truman declared that "Ike didn't know anything, and all the time he was in office he didn't learn a thing. . . . In 1959, when Castro came to power down in Cuba,

Ike just sat on his ass and acted like if he didn't notice what was going on down there, why, maybe Castro would go away or something." As a chef, Ike liked to make vegetable soup, charcoal-broiled steaks, and corn-meal pancakes. To relax, he read westerns and watched "The Fred Waring Show" on television. The childhood heroes of the Supreme Commander of Allied armies in Europe 1944–45 were Hannibal and George Washington. His early ambition was to become a railroad engineer. His mother was a pacifist. When he was President, he suffered a heart attack, bursitis, ileitis, and, in 1957, a slight stroke that impaired his speech for a brief time. He was one of six professional soldiers who have been President; the others: Washington, Jackson, William Henry Harrison, Taylor, and Grant.

EL ALAMEIN

Five hundred and twenty-seven years to the week before British General Bernard L. Montgomery sent out from this northern Egyptian town his beleaguered Eighth Army against German Field Marshal Erwin ("the Desert Fox") Rommel's Afrika Corps, King Henry V of England sent his longbowmen into battle against a much larger, heavily armored French army at Agincourt. Surely Shakespeare's version of the turning point in the 116-year Hundred Years' War rang in the heads of the backs-to-the-Suez British in the turning point of the North African struggle in the six-year World War II: "Once more unto the breach, dear friends, once more, or close the wall up with our English dead . . . imitate the action of the tiger; stiffen the sinews, summon up the blood, disguise fair nature with hard-favour'd rage; then lend the eye a terrible aspect . . . show us here the mettle of your pasture . . . we in it shall be remembered, we few, we happy few, we band of brothers . . . and gentlemen in England now a-bed shall think themselves accurs'd they were not here, and hold their manhoods cheap whiles any speaks that fought with us upon Saint Crispin's day . . . The game's afoot! Follow your spirit, and upon this charge cry, 'God for Harry! England and Saint George!'." October 1942, after stalling Rommel for four months, Montgomery began his attack shortly before midnight, after meticulous preparation. At stake: the British presence in North Africa, control of the eastern Mediterranean, support of Middle Eastern countries dearly tempted to ally themselves with Hitler. A tremendous air and artillery bombardment leads within two weeks to a breakthrough by the British X Corps. Casualties on both sides are high. The Eighth Army takes 30,000 prisoners. On November 8, Operation Torch commences—the Allies invade French North Africa on the Atlantic coast. The German armies, east and west, are pincered in Tunisia. For the desert victory, Montgomery was made a viscount with the title Montgomery of Alamein.

171

ELBA

"Able was I ere I saw Elba," the eighty-six-square-mile mountainous island of iron ore six miles west of Tuscany in the Tyrrhenian Sea. Syracuse, Pisa, Spain, Naples held it, and for a brief time, May 1814–February 1815, it was the abdicated, exiled Napoleon's sovereign principality. He improved the island's roads and agriculture, then, during the Congress of Vienna, the former emperor of the French took his leave. With a handful of followers, he landed near Cannes and soon began his ephemeral rule of the Hundred Days in Paris. When he met his Waterloo, Elba was restored to the Grand Duke of Tuscany; in 1860, the island was incorporated into the new kingdom of Italy.

ELDER, LEE

The first black golfer to tee off in the prestigious Masters' tournament created by Bobby Jones. On the PGA tour since 1967, he qualified by having copped the Monsanto Open the previous year (1974) with an 18-foot birdie putt on the fourth hole of the playoff. He didn't do well in his Augusta debut, falling out before the final two rounds. Elder, who was born in 1934, looks like Flip Wilson and plays cross-handed. He learned to play golf by sneaking onto courses at *night*. He refined his game in the Army. In 1968, he became famous by matching "the Golden Bear," Jack Nicklaus, for four holes of the sudden-death playoff in the American Gold Golf Classic, in Ohio. He admires Jackie Robinson: "If I had to look up to one man, it would be to him. He took the hard knocks."

EL DORADO

Spanish for "the gilded man," which is what once each year a Muisca among the Chibcha Indians in the Andes, in what is now Colombia, would be. He was rolled in gold flakes, then rowed into the middle of a sacred lake, where he would wash them off. The custom had gone the way of all flesh by the time the conquistadors began to plunder South America, but the word was out. El Hombre Dorado became El Dorado, the golden city. Francisco Pizzaro's brother Gonzalo was among many who went in search of streets paved with gold. Sir Walter Raleigh postponed his beheading by promising to find the pot at the end of the rainbow. Coronado walked thousands of miles through the American southwest, but again El Dorado proved to be a land of nowhere, utopia. Candide visited El Dorado in Voltaire's imagination. Milton mentioned it in *Paradise Lost*. The besotted Edgar Allan Poe asked, "Where can it be—this land of Eldor-

ado? Over the Mountains of the Moon, down the Valley of the Shadow."
Explorers among the Chibcha did dig another kind of goldmine: the potato, which they introduced to Europe. El Dorado may have been what
is now Guyana. The Rev. Jim Jones sought El Dorado there—in a different sense.

ELEMENTS

Just over 100 are known—substances composed of atoms all having the
same number of protons in their nuclei; this number, called the atomic
number, defines the element. Ninety-two are known to occur naturally
on Earth. A few have been known since antiquity, but recognition did
not occur until relatively modern times. Only a dozen were known before
the eighteenth century. The Greek philosopher Empedocles had said that
all things were made up of combinations and arrangements of water, air,
fire, and earth. The first synthetic element was technetium, discovered in
1937. The first transuranium element to be synthesized was neptunium
(atomic number 93), in 1940. Among the elements: iodine, iron, zinc,
radium, oxygen, gold, mercury, argon, americium, aluminum, silicon,
silver, potassium, neon, tin, tungsten, xenon, yttrium, krypton, lead,
magnesium, calcium, boron, arsenic, and nickel.

ELEPHANT AND CASTLE

It's a traffic center in London these days, a communications hub for both
British rail and the underground, a terminus for the Bakerloo line. It was
formerly the site of a public house called Enfanta de Castile, which, in a
typical dysphemistic transformation of the late seventeenth century, be-
came Elephant and Castle. Why Enfanta de Castile in the first place?
Two years before acceding to the throne of Great Britain and Ireland,
Charles I made a visit to Madrid with the hope of concluding a marriage
treaty with the languorous princess the Enfanta de Castile. When the
Spanish government insisted that Charles convert to Roman Catholicism,
Charles crossed her off his list and mounted expeditions against Spain.

"ELEPHANT MAN"

John Merrick, England's famous "elephant man" of the Victorian 1880s,
told his doctor, "I am happy every hour of the day." For anyone who
was willing to be friendly with this twisted, grotesque, hideous-looking,
neurofibromatosis-stricken individual—the most disgusting specimen of
humanity anyone had seen—he radiated oceans of affection and grati-

tude. He must have been much loved in his early years, for he grew up with the most noble, loving, and delicate sensibilities and certain skills, such as reading and woodcarving. It is very likely that he received much love from his mother during the first three or four years of life.

EL GORDO

"The Fat One"—Spain's annual pre-Christmas lottery (December 22). First prize has been 2,400,000,000 pesatas, about $15 million. Invariably, many people hold the winning number and must share the loot. Invariably, winners, if they are the family breadwinners, immediately quit their jobs; the lottery there, as well as here, as well as everywhere, if the prize is fat enough, opens up job opportunities. In America, the first public announcement for a lottery was in Philadelphia, in 1720. Three hundred and fifty tickets at 20 shillings each were offered. The prize: a new house. Benjamin Franklin and friends sponsored a 3,000-pound lottery (that's British pounds) to raise money for cannon needed to defend the City of Brotherly Love; Philadelphia itself, after overcoming Quaker objections, took 2,000 tickets. John Hancock managed a lottery in 1761 to raise funds to repair Boston's Faneuil Hall, damaged by fire. George Washington managed a lottery to raise funds for construction of a road over the Cumberland Mountains. Harvard bought an orrery, an astronomical device, through a lottery. Lotteries were preferred to taxes. New Jersey ran one to pay Indians for land, another to build a jail. There's been one national lottery. The Continental Congress announced a $10 million lottery. But drawings were postponed and the lottery faded out, arousing much anger. The town of Lotteryville, Rhode Island, came into being through a lottery. The largest state lottery, Louisiana's, was terminated in 1890 by a federal statute prohibiting the movement of lottery tickets or prizes by mail or in interstate commerce. If your great-grandfather then bet that state lotteries would be legalized some day, he was a winner; in 1963, New Hampshire became the first of many states to authorize a sweepstakes lottery.

ELIOT, GEORGE

"Whatever may be the success of my stories," Mary Ann (or Marian) Evans wrote to the publisher, "I shall be resolute in preserving my incognito, having observed that a *nom de plume* secures all the advantages without the disagreeables of reputation. Perhaps, therefore, it will be well to give you my prospective name, as a tub to throw to the whale in case of curious inquiries, and accordingly I subscribe myself, Yours very truly, George Eliot." She chose the name, she informed her husband,

John W. Cross, because "George was Mr. Lewes' Christian name, and Eliot was a good mouth-filling, easily pronounced word." (Lewes had been her long-time lover.) And so the name of George Eliot appeared on the title page of the popular mid-nineteenth-century English novels *The Mill on the Floss* and *Adam Bede* and *Silas Marner* and *Middlemarch,* a portrait of life in a provincial town that is considered the frequently depressed woman's masterpiece.

ELIZABETH II

The princess was up a tree in Kenya, when she learned that her father, King George VI, had died in his sleep in wintry Sandringham and that she was the Queen of England, Defender of the Faith. The twenty-five-year-old Princess Elizabeth and distant cousin Prince Philip were staying at Treetops Hotel in Kenya, a resthouse with three bedrooms and a dining room that had been built into the branches of a giant mgumu, or wild fig tree. Below the platform was a salt lick and a large pool visited nightly by rhinos, warthogs, deer, and other wild animals of East Africa. The royal couple were planning to go on to New Zealand and Australia, when the news arrived. They walked together along the bank of the peaceful Sagana stream where they had fished for trout that morning. She was wearing a white summer dress and the tropical sky was clouding over as they planned their return to their blessed plot, their precious stone set in the silver sea, the teeming womb of royal kings. She was crowned four months later, in June 1952. She has had four children (two after becoming the monarch) and she was, in January 1953, *Time*'s "Woman of the Year."

ELY, RON

There he was, the former Tarzan, emceeing the 1980 Miss America Pageant, in Atlantic City, New Jersey, in place of the venerable host, Bert Parks, who had been dumped unceremoniously—he got the word on returning home from a party celebrating his sixty-fifth birthday—he hadn't posed in the buff for *Playgirl,* he just didn't have a modern, contemporary image in the middle of his seventh decade and you know, Bert baby, you aren't a spring chicken anymore and there are nearly 100 million Americans out there watching. Johnny Carson mounted a nationwide "We want Bert" protest, admitting that he admired anyone who worked only one night a year. Ely, host of the "Face the Music" television quiz show, faced the music himself: But at forty-two years of age, six foot six inches tall, 220 pounds, it was suggested that he looked better than some of the contestants.

E = MC²

Albert Einstein's famous equation states that energy contained in matter is equal in ergs to its mass in grams multiplied by the square of the velocity of light in centimeters per second. The velocity of light (C) being what it is, a very small amount of mass (M) is equivalent to a vast amount of energy (E). In 1921, in Prague, Einstein was approached by a young man wanting to produce a weapon from nuclear energy based on the famous equation. "You haven't lost anything if I don't discuss your work with you in detail," Einstein told the young man. "Its foolishness is evident at first glance. You cannot learn anything more from a longer discussion." In 1939, Einstein, an ardent pacifist, stressed in a letter to President Franklin Roosevelt the urgency of investigating the possible use of atomic energy in bombs. He later said that he would not have advocated the development of "extremely powerful bombs of a new type" if he had realized or known that Nazi Germany's experiments with uranium would not produce The Bomb. Still popping up in books is the dubious story that Nazi scientists decided not to build The Bomb so "the world would be safe."

EMPIRE STATE BUILDING

It was the world's tallest office building in 1931—its 1,250 feet are now eight stories shorter than the world's tallest building, the 110-story Sears Tower in Chicago, but that's another story. The construction stats are awesome. It was built in less than a year: 6,400 windows, 67 elevators, one million bricks, 450 tons of aluminum, 210 columns, 600 million pounds distributed so evenly that the weight on any given square inch is no greater, it is said, than that normally borne by a French heel. In all, 37 million cubic feet on a plot about 200 feet by 425 feet. Fourteen men died during construction. During the day, the skyscraper is a city of 25,000 permanent residents, plus tens of thousands of visitors. The $52 million building in midtown Manhattan (it replaced the old Waldorf-Astoria Hotel) was dedicated from the nation's capital: President Herbert Hoover pressed an electric button that "turned on" the heavens-piercing pinnacle. Former governor and presidential candidate Alfred E. Smith, the building's major domo, read a radiogram from a Europe-bound liner: "One day out and I can still see the building." There was one rub in the day's excitement. Visitors to the fifty-fifth floor showroom were met by a crude but genial mural drawn in pencil. The reporter for *The New Republic* was "grateful to the man who drew the pictures: he is a public benefactor. He has done something to take the curse off the opening of the building." That something: "A large male figure is seen standing upright and fornicating, *Venus aversa,* with a stooping female figure, who has no arms but pendulous breasts. The man is saying. 'O, man!' Further along is a gigantic vagina with its name in four large letters written under it.'' The Empire State is now the world's fourth tallest building. The Sears Tower is 1,559 feet tall and the twin towers of the World Trade Center in lower Manhattan are 1,350 feet tall.

EMPIRE STATE BUILDING—BOMBER CRASH

Lieutenant Colonel William F. Smith, Jr., a graduate of West Point in 1942, had flown two years' combat in Europe and wore two Distinguished Flying Crosses and four Air Medals. On July 28, 1945, he was on home duty, flying a twin-engined B-25 bomber named "Old Feather Merchant" through the soupy overcast shrouding the skyline spires of Manhattan. He became lost over Rockefeller Center and flew downtown at too low an altitude. He flew right into the 78th and 79th floors of the then world's tallest building, the 102-story Empire State, at Fifth Avenue and 34th St. The building rocked. A great bud of flame flowered in a gray cloud and a cascade of fiery gasoline rushed down the sides of the building. One of the bomber's motors ripped clear through the building. The other lodged in an elevator shaft, and two elevators plunged from the 80th floor to the basement. Though it was a Saturday, it was a work day. Fourteen people were killed and twenty-five injured.

ENAMEL

The hardest substance in the human body, the enamel of teeth is 96 percent inorganic material and 4 percent organic matter and water. It seems to be composed of fine, hexagonal prisms arranged at right angles to the outer surface of the tooth and extending to the underlying dentin. Enamel, which has no nerve supply, receives its slight nourishment from the dentin that it covers. Radioisotope tracer materials have shown some circulation of fluids.

ENGLISH

The mother tongue, the second-most-spoken language. Over there, in Britain, a garbageman is a dustman. An amusement park is a funfair. An automobile hood is a bonnet. A maid for all work is a slavey. Corn is called maize. Liable to taxation is ratable. Subway is the underground. A person holding a concert ticket for standing room only is a rover. A flashlight is a torch. Why *can't* the English learn to speak? There are at least 396 words in English that cannot be rhymed with another simple word. Some examples: kitchen, angel, film, sofa, budget, gossip, bargain, and that good old reliable, orange. Mandarin Chinese is the most-spoken language in the world. In the Federal Court of the United States, English is the principal language, and Spanish is second. The third-most-used language is—Thai. Don't ask.

ENGLISH CHANNEL

In French, *La Manche*—the sleeve—the channel between France and England is an arm of the Atlantic Ocean. The North and the Irish Seas were covered by the Pleistocene ice sheet and received glacial debris, but the English Channel lay beyond the farthest extent of the ice front. It is about 350 miles long and about 150 miles at its widest. Its 645 cubic miles of water is replenished completely every 500 days or so by an influx of water from the Atlantic. The direction of flow upchannel, through the Straits of Dover, and into the southern North Sea is reversed occasionally by wind conditions. Since 1930, the herring has virtually disappeared there and been replaced by the pilchard, the change coinciding with alterations in the phosphorus and plankton content of the waters. The Channel was William the Conqueror's route to Hastings in 1066. The English (and storms) broke up the "invincible" Spanish Armada of 130 ships in the Channel before the intended invasion could overthrow the Protestant Elizabeth I and establish the Catholic Philip on the English throne. The Allies mounted in the Channel the greatest invasion force in history for D-Day, in 1944.

ENOLA GAY

It was Japan's industrial city of Hiroshima all the way for the *Enola Gay* that day, August 6, 1945—there was no alternative target. Colonel Paul Tibbets, Jr., who had named the United States B-29 Superfortress to honor his mother, and his crew had two worries: arming "Little Boy," The Bomb, in flight, and getting the hell out of there after releasing it. The weatherman had forecast clear skies over the target, and they were —until the uranium bomb burst at 8:16 A.M. Japanese War Time. There were 320,000 casualties, including 80,000 instant dead. Hiroshima had not been previously attacked. Nagasaki's luck ran out three days later. Kokura, on the northern coast of the island of Kyushu, was to have been the second city in the history of the world to be atomized. But smoke and haze obscured Kokura when *Bock's Car* flew over it not once, not twice, but three times—and so it was on to an appointment in Nagasaki. A hole was found in the cloud cover there and the 10,000-pound plutonium bomb "Fat Man," the last atomic weapon in the United States' arsenal, was released. The bull's-eye was missed by three miles. Nagasaki's broken terrain checked the effect of the blast, and so only 30,000 or so people were immediately killed and not every building was blown away. The Soviet Union opportunistically entered the war against Japan two days after Hiroshima, or six days before Emperor Hirohito surrendered unconditionally, ending World War II. The Son of Heaven on the Chrysanthemum Throne had a tax-exempt annual salary of $1.6 million and a household staff numbering 5,000.

ERVIN, SAM

He had been a North Carolina jurist for a score of years and a United States senator for nearly another twenty years before gaining national attention as chairman of the Senate Select Committee to Investigate Presidential Campaign Practices that investigated the Watergate affair which led to the resignation of President Richard M. Nixon. He had been sworn as senator in 1954 by Vice-President Nixon. "I found that an apt story is worth an hour of argument," he likes to say. "A story that fits a point that you're trying to make sort of tends to arouse your audience, to get their attention if you're about to lose it. And a good story is a good way to relieve tension." In the 1970s he believed that the Constitution should be taken like mountain whiskey—undiluted and untaxed.

ESPERANTO

"Nu, mi sendas koran saluton kaj bondeziron al vi kah via familio." "I send hearty greetings and good wishes to you and your family." An artificial universal language based on Romance languages, it was created by a Polish oculist and linguist, Dr. Ludwig L. Zamenhof, in the late nineteenth century, to help break down barriers separating people speaking different languages. It was not designed to replace national languages. All nouns end in "o," adjectives in "a." There are twenty-eight letters; there is no Q, W, X, or Y. There are sixteen fundamental rules with no exceptions. Amiko is friend. Lago, lake. Multaj, many. Muziko, music. Jaro, year. Historio, history. Kara, dear. Kolegio, college. Fiŝo, fish. Dankas, thanks. Kial, why. Plezuro, pleasure. Tempo, time. Venas, comes. Informo, information. The Esperanto League, P.O. Box 1129, El Cerrito, California 94530. There are a thousand members.

ETHIOPIA

The Queen of Sheba is said to have been the midwife of the northeast African nation—her son by Solomon, Menelik I, founded the kingdom in the tenth century B.C. Documentary evidence, rather than tradition, points to establishment of the first kingdom in the first century A.D. by immigrants from southern Arabia. Abyssinia in the Bible. Ethiopia, from the Greek word meaning "sunburned faces." Cities along the Red Sea are among the hottest spots in the world. The country is about twice the size of Texas, and it was never a European colony. The Great Rift Valley traverses the country. There is only one navigable river, the Awash. The rural highlands, where most of the 25 million people live, are free of malaria-carrying mosquitoes. There are no large-scale mineral deposits. The "Falashas," black Jews, live north of Lake Tana. In the mid-1930s, Italy captured Ethiopia in Mussolini's campaign to establish an Italian empire. Twice, Emperor Haile Selassie (Amharic = power of the Trinity), supposedly the 111th descendant of King Solomon and the Queen of Sheba to rule, appealed in vain to the League of Nations for effective action against Italy. In late 1984, Ethiopia's Marxist government needed the help of a worldwide airlift flying in food and other supplies to millions of famine victims.

EUCHRE

It's a card game of the trumps family, a forerunner of five hundred and bridge, and it was once popular in the United States. In its most common form, it is a game for four players in two partnerships. The four-hand game uses a deck of only thirty-two cards—the regular fifty-two-card deck minus the ranks from 2 to 6. Among the unique features is the rank of cards in the trump suit. The right bower—the jack of trumps—is the most powerful card. The second-highest-ranking card is the left bower—the jack of the next suit or suit of corresponding color.

EUCLID

"There is no royal road to geometry." The fourth-century Greek's textbook on geometry has been, with some modifications, the standard for 2,300 years—he codified into a single work two and a half centuries of others' work. Tradition ascribes to him only one theorem, the proof he presented for the Pythagorean theorem. He proved that the number of primes is infinite. He proved neatly that the square root of two was irrational.

"EUREKA!"—STATES' MOTTOES

"I have found it!"—it's the State motto of California. From the Greek *heureka*. Found was gold! And California itself. Why is Connecticut known as the Nutmeg State? There's no nutmeg in the Constitution State, another nickname for Connecticut. Maybe it's because the early inhabitants had the reputation of being so ingenious and shrewd that they were able to make and sell wooden nutmegs. The motto of Oklahoma is "Labor conquers all things." Montana: "Gold and silver." Minnesota: "The star of the north." Wyoming: "Let arms yield to the gown." On Wyoming's state seal is the motto "Equal Rights," referring to the political position of women in the state. Texas adopted its motto in February 1930: "Friendship." The Indian (Spanish) word *Tejas* is the source of the name Texas—*Tejas* means "friendship."

EVERGLADES

About 5,000 square miles of jungle, prairie, and water, millions of years of vegetable decay, much of the lower part of the Florida peninsula. No point is more than seven feet above sea level. Spectacular wildlife abounds, particularly in the southernmost sector, in the 1,400,533-acre Everglades National Park, the third largest national park; spoonbills, herons, pelicans, ibises, and egrets are among 300 species of birds. The United States chased the Seminole Indians out of the Everglades in the late 1830s.

EXXON

America's largest industrial corporation—it took in $84.8 billion dollars in 1983. Repeat: $84.8 billion. Repeat: $84.8 billion. Second place General Motors took in only $74.5 billion. The chairman and chief executive of Exxon, Clifton C. Garvin, Jr., made $842,000 overseeing operations in nearly 100 countries. He is not a workaholic. Repeat: not. He likes to play golf and to fish and to watch birds, but he *does* spend about 140 days on the road. Number three on the Fortune 500 list is Mobil, followed by Ford Motor, International Business Machines, Texaco, E. I. du Pont de Nemours, Standard Oil (Indiana), Standard Oil of California, and number ten, General Electric. Were it not for the carmakers' extraordinary comeback, real profits for the top 500 corporations would have dropped in '83 for the fourth straight year. In 1984, Americans bought 14.1 million cars and light trucks, the auto industry's best year since 1979; record-setting profits were about $10 billion. General Motors, despite a strike, posted a 43.7 percent share of the total sales.

F

FAHRENHEIT 451

In Ray Bradbury's 3-million-copy novel firemen start the fires: They burn books. (451°F. is the temperature at which paper burns.) At first, "the books were burned by minorities, each ripping a page or a paragraph from this book, then that, until the day came when the books were empty and the minds shut and the libraries closed forever." The science-fiction writer presently learned that life was once again imitating art: "I discovered that, over the years, some cubbyhole editors at Ballantine Books, fearful of contaminating the young, had, bit by bit, censored some 75 sections" in *Fahrenheit 451*. A new editor there ordered the book reset as written and published properly.

FAHRENHEIT, GABRIEL D.

The boiling point of a liquid varies with atmospheric pressure. Water can be cooled below its freezing point without solidifying. Both were discoveries of this German-Dutch physicist, who devised the thermometric scale that bears his name. He used mercury in a glass rather than spirits of wine (alcohol) to make the first accurate thermometer. In devising a scale for his thermometer, he chose as his zero point the coldest temperature obtainable with a water-ice-salt mixture. As his second fixed point, he chose the temperature of human blood. (Refined measurements showed the temperature of human blood to be 98.6° on the Fahrenheit scale.) He divided the interval between these into twelve equal parts or degrees; later, as a measure of convenience, he made ninety-six equal parts. Which is why pure water freezes at 32°F. and boils at 212°F. Shortly after Fahrenheit's death, in 1736, the Swedish astronomer Anders Celsius divided the temperature difference between the boiling point and the freezing point of water on the temperature scale into an even hundred degrees—the centigrade scale ("hundred steps"). Temperatures on the Fahrenheit scale can be converted to equivalent temperatures on the Celsius scale (favored by scientists) by subtracting 32° from the Fahrenheit temperature, then multiplying the result by $\frac{5}{9}$, according to the formula $(F. - 32)\frac{5}{9} = C$.

FALCONRY

The sport of kings was known around the world in ancient times. The Kubla Khan boasted of his 500 gyr-falcons and hawks and an army of 1,000 beaters armed with whistles to flush out small animals or other birds. Falconry was popular in late medieval and early modern Europe, especially with local monarchs in southern England in the fifth and the sixth centuries. Trained predatory birds were a symbol of power, and such symbols were emblazoned on crests and coats of arms. The patron saint of falconers is St. Bavo of Valkenswaard, traditional home in Holland of the great Dutch falconers. In 1954, hawking was made a lawful sport again in France after a prohibition of nearly a hundred years. There is a Falconers' Club of America. Thousands of acres of land or extensive moors are no longer a requirement to be a falconer.

FALSTAFF

Shakespeare's great, gross comic figure—"I am not only witty in myself, but the cause that wit is in other men," Sir John brags in *Henry IV, Part II*, act one. In both *Henry IV* plays, he has the longest role: jesting, flamboyant in *Part I,* less sympathetic and seen with his inferiors in wit in *Part II*. He is reduced to a comic butt in *The Merry Wives of Windsor* and his demise is reported by Pistol in *King Henry the Fifth:* ". . . he's not in hell. He's in Arthur's bosom, if ever man went to Arthur's bosom." Nym: "They say he cried out of sack." Hostess: "Ay, that 'a did." Bardolph: "And of women." Hostess: "Nay, that 'a did not." Boy: "Yes, that 'a did; and said they were devils incarnate." Hostess: " 'A could never abide carnation; 'twas a colour he never lik'd." S. F. Johnson, of Columbia University, has noted that in the first version of the *Henry IV* plays, the name was not Falstaff, but Oldcastle—the name of one of the disreputable companions of Prince Hal (later Henry V) in the old play *The Famous Victories of Henry V,* from which Shakespeare adapted incidents for his plays on Henry IV and Henry V. When descendants of the real Oldcastle objected to the caricature of their ancestor, the Bard changed the name, modifying it from that of a cowardly knight, Fastolfe, in his *King Henry the Sixth, Part I,* to suggest that he was a "false staff" for Prince Hal to rely on.

FANDANGO

Did it or didn't it originate in Spain? Was it originated in Spain by non-Spaniards? ¿Quién sabe? At least, who knows absolutely? There is the probability that the fandango was a Moorish dance that beat its way into

Europe about a century and a half after the Moors were beaten back by the Ferdinands. What is known, even by tomfoolers, is that lively Spanish couples have been doing it in triple time for centuries to the accompaniment of castanets, guitars, and songs sung by the dancers, freezing when the music stops at the end of certain measures, melting and dancing again when the music resumes. ¡Ole!

FANEUIL HALL

The "cradle of liberty," so named because Bostonians in the years before the Revolution protested unpopular British measures in the public meeting hall of the market. It was Beantown's only polling place from 1743, the year after a wealthy merchant of Huguenot extraction, Peter Faneuil, made a gift of it to the community, to 1817. During the Revolution, British troops used it as a theater. In 1784, the Marquis de Lafayette had dinner there. Charles Bulfinch restructured it in 1805, adding a third floor. It was draped in mourning a month after Presidents John Adams and Thomas Jefferson had died coincidentally on the same day, July 4, 1826; Daniel Webster delivered the memorial speech. In 1837, Wendell Phillip made his first speech against slavery there. In 1972, the Democratic National Committee held platform hearings in Faneuil Hall.

FARMER, FANNIE MERRITT

Yes, Mr. Whitman, there was a real Fannie Farmer. She turned to cooking when a paralytic stroke prevented her from going to college. She wrote one of the best-known and most-popular of American cookbooks, the *Boston Cooking School Cook Book*. Miss Farmer's School of Cookery was a blue-ribbon training ground in cookery for nurses and housewives. Insistence on the accurate measurement of ingredients (teaspoonful, cupful) earned her the sobriquet "mother of level measurements."

FARROW, MIA

Sucking on a string of pearls between her lips, she graced the first cover of *People* magazine, in 1974—she was appearing as Daisy Buchanan in *The Great Gatsby*, "the year's next big movie." The daughter of the director John Farrow and the actress Maureen O'Sullivan (Jane to Johnny Weissmuller's Tarzan) likened her bony frame to an "elephant's graveyard." By twenty-three, the saucer-eyed, sparrow-thin, freckled actress had been wed and shucked by fiftyish crooner Frank Sinatra. She had three children with André Previn, including twins conceived before he had divorced songsmith Dory Previn, who then wrote *Beware of Young Girls*. The Previns also adopted three children. Her new leading man is Woody Allen, who cast her brilliantly in *Zelig* and *Broadway Danny Rose*.

FATHER TIME

Subtle thief of youth, a maniac scattering dust, the mercy of eternity, a bloody tyrant, a lovely gift, the soul of the world, a winged chariot, an illusion perpetrated by the manufacturers of space, a mental device to give order to events by identifying them as coexisting or successive, the great conundrum—Time! Time is life. To be alive is to be ticking—like clockwork. We are all time capsules. The interaction of the brain (with its 10 billion cells) and the mind cannot proceed without the human time it creates. A stroke victim is a clock gone cuckoo. Your state is only fair if you're as restless as a willow in a windstorm and as jumpy as a puppet on a string—and it's November 15 in the Northern Hemisphere. Time is the music of our being. It is to man what water is to fish. As Alan Lakein and I have written, "We are time and time is we and we are all together. Imagine a time without time." Time will tell.

"FEAR OF THE LORD"

"Praise ye the Lord. I will praise the Lord with my whole heart, in the assembly of the upright, and in the congregation. The works of the Lord are great, sought out of all them that have pleasure therein. His work is honorable and glorious: and his righteousness endureth for ever. He hath made his wonderful works to be remembered: the Lord is gracious and full of compassion. He hath given meat unto them that fear him: he will ever be mindful of his covenant. He hath shewed his people the power of his works, that he may give them the heritage of the heathen. The works of his hands are verity and judgment; all his commandments are sure. They stand fast for ever and ever, and are done in truth and uprightness. He sent redemption unto his people: he hath commanded his covenant for ever: holy and reverend is his name. The fear of the Lord is the beginning of wisdom: a good understanding have all they that do his commandments: his praise endureth for ever."—Psalm 111.

FEMUR

Your bones perform five functions for your body: support, protection, movement, mineral reservoir, blood cell formation. Your longest bone is also your heaviest bone, and there are two longest, two heaviest. They are the femurs, or thigh bones—femur from the Latin for "thigh." Technically, several prominent markings characterize the femur. For example, three projections are conspicuous at each epiphysis: the head and greater and lesser trochanters proximally and the medial and lateral condyles and adductor tubercle distally. (The largest sesamoid bone, and you have two of them, is the kneecap.)

FEZ

Once again it's hat's off to necessity. The fez—brimless, felt, cone-shaped, flat-topped—allows the wearer to touch his forehead on the floor in prayer and still keep his hat on. Which is one reason it's so popular with Mohammedan men in the central Moroccan religious city for which the fez was named—there are more than 100 mosques there. The old city of Fez was founded in 808 by Idris II, the new city four centuries later; the two are connected by walls. Fez was the capital of several dynasties and reached its zenith under Marinid sultans—seven centuries ago.

F.I.A.

The Fédération Internationale de l'Automobile governs international motor racing. (F.I.S.A. governs rowing—Fédération Internationale des Societes de Aviron.) The rules vary from year to year so that no manufacturer can dominate the competition. Fuel capacity, number of cylinders, wheelbase, and weight are specified. The key parts of the scantily constructed racing car must be commercially available, not a one-time creation. The rear-placed engine usually forms a major part of the structure; the driver lies almost on his back in the "cockpit," striving to reduce air drag to a minimum. Motor racing is a really dangerous sport—the mechanically propelled land vehicles fly at 200 miles per hour over a point-to-point course or closed circuit with corners and turns banked. The top races are designated Grand Prix races. The Indianapolis 500 is the most famous American race.

FIELDS, W.C.

President Ronald Reagan, as he was being patched up by surgeons following an assassin's attempt on his life, quoted W. C. Fields' epitaph: "On the whole, I'd rather be in Philadelphia." Fields ran away from home when he was eleven years old and never looked back, juggling his fortunes as best he could. A vaudevillian, he performed far afield, even at Pago Pago in the South Sea Islands. The comedian's raspy remarks and "know-it-all" perspective made him a nationwide character. He was a master mimic. His voice alone carried him to a great cinematic triumph as Humpty-Dumpty—in *Alice in Wonderland*—no egg on that bulbous nose. His movies are classics: *Never Give a Sucker an Even Break, You Can't Cheat an Honest Man, My Little Chickadee, The Bank Dick.* His original name was Claude William Dukenfield, which he must have said wasn't fit for man nor beast. He loved to hit the bottle. Also kids and dogs: "Anyone who hates children and dogs can't be all bad." He died on Christmas Day 1946, and left a part of his estate for the benefit of orphans. Go figure.

FINGER LAKES

There are eleven of them in long, narrow, fingerlike north–south valleys in westcentral New York State. In the imagination of Indians, the Great Spirit laid his hand in benediction upon the countryside and left the crystal-blue waters as his print. Geologists believe the fingers are pre-glacial valleys whose south-flowing rivers were bottled up by glacial debris. The biggest of the lakes is Cayuga: 40 miles long, 2 miles wide, 435 feet deep—life on the shores was the heart of novels by Grace Miller White. Seneca is more than 35 miles long. High above Cayuga is Cornell University and Ithaca College. The highest waterfall east of the Rockies is Taughannock Falls near the head of Cayuga Lake—it plunges 215 feet. Keuka Lake is at the center of the state's wine industry. (New York is the only state that touches both the Atlantic Ocean and the Great Lakes.)

FISCHER, BOBBY

His sister introduced him to chess when he was six years old. Nine years later, in 1958, he was chess's youngest international grandmaster. He may be the grandest grandmaster of all time. The World Chess Championship was established in 1866, and Fischer, at the age of twenty-nine, became the first American to hold the title when he defeated the Soviet Union's Boris Spassky, 12½ to 8½, in Reykjavik, Iceland, in 1972. He was stripped of his title in 1975 for not defending it. Fischer is said to have an IQ of 187. He has been hibernating in Pasadena, California, for several years.

FISH—ON FRIDAYS

Roman Catholics have been able in good conscience to eat meat on Fridays since November 1966. On February 23, 1966, the Church autho-

187

rized that a substitution of other works of penance could take the place of the observance of abstinence and fast on appointed days of the year. The National Conference of Bishops in the United States designated Ash Wednesday and Good Friday as days of fast and abstinence and all Fridays of Lent as days of abstinence. The Church had long set Friday as a weekly day of fasting to underscore the centrality of Jesus' crucifixion. It is believed that Friday was the day that Christ was crucified. Believers were also expected to engage in acts of penance and even of physical mortification. Christians turned to fish because meat was forbidden on the fast day, and Church councils decreed that all products of the sea, even mammalians, were fish rather than meat.

FISH—SYMBOLISM

As a food and as a symbol, the fish has held an important position in the history of religions and in the cults of the gods and the dead. The symbol probably originated in pagan cults; Jews and then Christians (=Christ) adopted it. It appeared as an acrostic, derived from the Greek words for "Jesus Christ, Son of God, Savior," and yielding the word *ichthus,* meaning "fish," and as a symbol in early Christian art and literature. It appeared in pictures showing Christ and the Apostles at the Last Supper: fishermen catching fish. In Syrian culture, the fish was a symbol of happiness and life.

FLEMING, ALEXANDER

While performing research on influenza, in 1928, the Scottish bacteriologist left a culture of staphylococcus germs uncovered in a dish for some days. When he was about to discard the dish, he noticed that some specks of mold had fallen into it and that a ring free of bacteria had formed around each speck and there had been no new growth. Obviously, the mold contained a substance that killed bacteria: "I had no suspicion that I had got a clue to the most powerful therapeutic substance yet used to defeat bacterial infections in the human body. But the appearance of that culture plate was such that I thought it should not be neglected." A pure culture of the mold thrived best in meat broth, and in bread and in cheese. When Fleming could not isolate or identify the substance that inhibited bacterial growth and which he labeled penicillin, he received help from others. Penicillin was the first important example of germ-killing antibiotics, literally a life-saver during World War II and beyond. "People called it a miracle," Dr. Fleming said. "For once in my life as a scientist I agree. It is a miracle."

FLYNN, ERROL

The matinee idol's biographer called him "a prince of liars." "Robin Hood," "Captain Blood," "Don Juan" was not born of a noble Irish family. He was not, as he boasted, on an Australian Olympic boxing team. He did not swim an Irish channel. He did not have his first erection as a babe in the cradle. He could not drink twenty-five glasses of ale without slurring a syllable. He *was* born in Tasmania and his father *was* a professor of biology at the University of Tasmania and he *was* descended on his mother's side from Fletcher Christian of *Bounty* fame. He hated Jews. He was a lifelong kleptomaniac. He was turned on by the German mystique, by the sexual fascination of Nazism. A boy hustler confessed that "Errol was so handsome, superbly built and passionate that for the first time in my career as a male prostitute I was genuinely excited by a client"; he was amazed by the actor's staying power, virility, and sheer energy in bed. Flynn experimented with drugs, including kif. *Life* magazine in 1938 reported that Flynn periodically irked his film bosses by "running away to sail his boat or get into a war." With whom was Flynn in like Flynn? His biographer writes that Flynn and just-married fellow-actor Tyrone Power "met at obscure motels, at the private home of a trusted homosexual director friend, at the West Coast home of a prominent New York orchestra conductor." Flynn's autobiography (1959) was appropriately entitled *My Wicked, Wicked Ways*. Ronald Reagan called himself "the Errol Flynn of B movies."

FOOTBALL

There were twenty-five students on each side when Rutgers scored a 6–4 victory over Princeton, at New Brunswick, New Jersey, on November 6, 1869, in the first intercollegiate game; Princeton won the return game, 8–0. At one time, unlimited use of hands, fists, and feet was permitted in getting and keeping control of the ball. In 1895, the president of Harvard averred that "it has become perfectly clear that the game as now played is unfit for college use." Theodore Roosevelt countered, "Is there a boy in college that would not gladly risk a broken bone for the honor and glory of being on one of the great teams?" Rules were modified in the wake of many deaths on the college gridiron. In the 1970s, James Michener observed that "football is a game; it need not be so grim an occupation that one needs shriving before the whistle blows."

FOOTBALL—CANADIAN

There are twelve men on a team, one more than there are on a team in American football. The extra man plays in the backfield or as a flanker on offense or as a linebacker or a defensive back on defense. These are some of the other differences in the Canadian rules: The receiver of a punt may not make a fair catch. A team is allowed only three downs in which to advance the ball 10 yards for a first down. There are only three 15-yard penalties (clipping, unnecessary roughness, unsportsmanlike conduct). The field is 110 yards long and the goalposts are on the goal lines. If the receiving team does not run a punt out of the end zone, which is 25 yards deep, the punting team scores a point, called a "rouge." The defensive linemen must line up one yard away from the ball—there is a three-foot "neutral zone" between the opposing linemen. There is no restriction on the number of backs that may be in motion at the snap of the ball nor on the direction in which they may run. The pass was introduced in American college football in 1906 but was not officially recognized in Canada until 1931. The principal trophy in the Canadian Football League is the Grey Cup, donated in 1909 by Lord Grey, then governor-general of Canada. On a roster of thirty-two active players, a team may have only fourteen Americans.

FOOTBALL—FORWARD PASS

The short, chunky end and captain, twenty-five-year-old Knute Rockne, and the quarterback, Gus Dorais, worked at it in secret all summer at a beach in the Midwest. Dorais would throw the pigskin, Rockne would catch it. All summer long. The forward pass was a legal football weapon but it had been little used until the Notre Dame pair unwrapped its potential that Saturday afternoon in 1913 when the Fighting Irish took the field against a college it'd never beaten: West Point was expecting another breather. Dorais threw seventeen passes, completed thirteen of them, most of them to his buddy Rockne, and the South Bend school scored a 35–13 upset victory. The pair then passed a few days at West Point to demonstrate the possibilities to the Army players. Rockne had been delayed in going to college by the need to earn entrance fees. He was "looking only for an education—to my mind, college players were supermen to whose heights I could never aspire." He had planned to attend the University of Illinois, but friends at Notre Dame persuaded him to join them. The chief inducement: It was cheaper to live in South Bend than in Urbana.

FOOTBALL—GOALPOST

First recorded mention of "H-shaped" poles and scoring above the horizontal bar between the two vertical bars: ". . . a sort of gigantic gallows of two poles 18 feet high, fixed upright in the ground some 14 feet apart, with a cross bar running from one to the other at the height of 10 feet or thereabouts . . . the match is for the best of three goals . . . it won't do . . . just to kick the ball through these posts—it must go over the cross bar; any height'll do, as long as it's between the posts." The game was rugby and the reporter was at Rugby from 1834 to 1842. In American football, the goalpost is centered at the back of the end zone; in Canadian football, it is on the goal line. The crossbar is 10 feet above the ground.

FOOTBALL—OVERTIME GAMES

December 28, 1958—Pro football history was made: The first sudden-win overtime game. The Baltimore Colts vs. the New York Giants in Yankee Stadium for the championship of the National Football League. Two months earlier, the Giants had topped the Colts, 24–21; the Colts' star quarterback, Johnny Unitas, was out of action—he had suffered fractured ribs and a punctured lung in a 56–0 rout of the Green Bay Packers. He was back for the playoff game. The Colts led, 14–3, at the half, and it was 17–17 after sixty minutes, the Colts's Steve Myhra kicking a 20-yard field goal with seven seconds to go. The Giants won the toss and naturally chose to receive the overtime kickoff. They moved the ball only nine yards on three plays and punted. Baltimore took over on its 20-yard line. Unitas connected on four of five passes and the Colts, on twelve plays, were on the Giants's one-yard line. Alan Ameche stepped through a gaping hole on the right side and the Colts were 23–17 winners and the champs. There were three more sudden-win overtime playoff games before the NFL adopted the crowd-pleaser for all games beginning in 1970. A regular-season game can end in a deadlock after five periods; a playoff game must have a winner. But the day must come soon, if not sooner, when both teams get at least one crack at the ball—no more one team getting the luck of the coin toss and receiving the kickoff in the OT and scoring—and ergo winning—while the other team does not even get to touch the pigskin.

FORD, WHITEY

Major league baseball's All-Star lefthander was the "money pitcher" with the New York Yankees in the 1950s and early 60s. His winning percentage of .690 (236W–106L) is the best of any pitcher in the modern era. His World Series records included ten triumphs, 33⅔ consecutive scoreless innings, and ninety-four strikeouts. He started three games in the many-times-rain-delayed World Series in 1962. In the first outing, his shutout string was cut, but the Yankees won, 6–2; Ford yielded ten hits, but only four after the third inning. (The shutout string had included fourteen shutout innings in the '61 Series and 18 in the '60 Series.) He left the fourth game after giving up two runs in six innings; the Yankees' 1956 World Series no-hit, no-run artist, Don Larsen, was the Giants's winning pitcher. Ford lost the sixth game, 5–2; the turning point was a pickoff play at second base—he threw the ball into the outfield. The Yankees won the seventh game, 1–0, and the Series, second baseman Bobby Richardson spearing a smash off the bat of Willie McCovey with runners on second and third in the ninth inning.

FORMICARY

It's the dwelling of a colony of ants—an anthill or an ant nest. From the Middle Latin *formicarium* via the Latin *formica:* ant + *-arium* -ary. As in you can't go formicary again. Formica is a genus of hymenopterous insects formerly including all the ants but now restricted to various typical ants (such as the mound-building ants and the sanguinary ant).

FOSBURY, DICK

He executed his backward "Fosbury Flip" and won the gold medal in the high jump at the Olympics in Mexico City in 1968. His winning mark was a record 7'4½". Among other highlights of the international games that year: Bob Beamon's astonishing broad jump of 29 feet 2½ inches—nearly two feet farther than anyone had yet jumped; the American never jumped more than 27 feet again. Mexico City's thin air should have helped all the leapers—Beamon out-broadjumped the silver medalist by two feet. During the playing of "The Star-Spangled Banner," two black sprinters raised blacked-gloved, clenched fists, and were ordered back to the States. Seven horses died during a three-day equestrian endurance test. The United States won ninety-five medals.

FOURTH ESTATE

Thomas Carlyle said, "Burke said there were Three Estates in Parliament; but, in the Reporters' Gallery yonder, there sat a Fourth Estate more important far than they all. It is not a figure of speech, or witty saying; it is a literal fact—very momentous to us in these times." Thirteen years earlier, in 1826, Thomas Macaulay had coined the phrase: "The gallery in which the reporters sit has become a fourth estate of the realm." The fourth estate: a group other than the first, second, and third estates of the clergy, nobility, and commons that wields political power, specifically the public press. W. S. White wrote, "The fourth estate . . . has genuine being in Congress and in national politics generally." William Makepeace Thackeray, never one to have made peace with the press of his day, the mid-nineteenth century, said his piece: "Of the Corporation of the Goosequill—of the Press . . . of the fourth estate . . . There she is —the great engine—she never sleeps. She has her ambassadors in every quarter of the world—her courtiers upon every road. Her officers march along with armies, and her envoys walk into statemen's cabinets. They are ubiquitous." "The power of the press in America is a primordial one," Theodore H. White wrote in 1973. "It sets the agenda of public discussion; and this sweeping political power is unrestrained by any law. It determines what people will talk about and think about—an authority that in other nations is reserved for tyrants, priests, parties, and mandarins." President Ronald Reagan's reelection directors were successful in setting the agenda of public discussion in 1984—the press couldn't lay a hand on 'em. There is now a fifth estate, a class or group existing in addition to the traditional four—scientists!

FRANK, ANNE

She and her family hid out from the Nazis for twenty-five months in an attic in a warehouse at 263 Pricengracht, in Amsterdam, before being turned in for a small bounty. Sergeant Silverbauer, of the Green Police, plundered the Secret Annex, stuffed silverware and a Hanukkah candlestick into a briefcase, and left. Among the papers left behind was the diary a young girl had started on June 14, 1942, when her family was still free: "On Friday, June 12, I woke up at six o'clock and no wonder; it was my birthday. But of course I was not allowed to get up at that hour, so I had to control my curiosity until a quarter to seven. . . . [Later] I have strings of boyfriends, anxious to catch a glimpse of me and who, failing that, peep at me through mirrors in class. . . . As soon as a boy asks if he may bicycle home with me and we get into conversation, nine out of ten times I can be sure that he will fall head over heels in love immediately and simply won't allow me out of his sight . . . you get some [boys] who blow kisses or try to get hold of your arm, but then they are definitely knocking at the wrong door." In March 1945, two months before Holland was liberated, Anne died in the concentration camp at Bergen-Belsen. Her *Tales from the Secret Annex* has just been translated: "The war raged about us . . . I cannot describe it; I don't remember that tumult quite clearly, but I do know that all day long I was in the grip of fear." *The Diary of a Young Girl* was first published, unnoticed and in a tiny edition, in French. More than twenty American and English publishers rejected the manuscript before Otto Frank, Anne's father and the lone survivor in the Frank family, was able to secure an English-language edition with the aid of Meyer Levin. In December 1942, the U.S. State Department revealed that 2 million Jews had already died in German concentration camps and that millions more were facing the same fate.

FRANKENSTEIN

The author "passed the summer of 1816 in the environs of Geneva. The season was cold and rainy, and we occasionally amused ourselves with some German stories of ghosts, which happened to fall into our hands. These tales excited in us a playful desire of imitation. Two other friends (a tale from the pen of one of whom would be far more acceptable to the public than anything I can ever hope to produce) and myself agreed to write each a story founded on some supernatural occurrence. The weather, however, suddenly became serene; and my two friends left me on a journey among the Alps, and lost, in the magnificent scenes which they present, all memory of their ghostly visions. . . . Swift as light and as cheering was the idea that broke in upon me. 'I have found it! What terrified me will terrify others; and I need only describe the spectre which had haunted my midnight pillow.' On the morrow I announced that I had thought of a story. I began that day with the words, 'It was on a dreary night of November,' making only a transcript of the grim terrors of my waking dream." The author was Mary Wollstonecraft Shelley, her two friends were her husband, Percy Bysshe Shelley, and Lord Byron, who was writing the third canto of *Childe Harold*. Her offspring was *Frankenstein, or The Modern Prometheus*. The story of Dr. Victor Frankenstein's eight-foot creation without love or friend or soul is told with little skill, but it has lived as the most famous of all horror stories. Mary Shelley, who had had a tumultous affair with the poet before their marriage, wrote a second novel, *The Last Man*, in 1826.

FRANKLIN, BENJAMIN

The youngest son of the seventeen children of a Boston candlemaker was a one-man phenomenon. He was a polymath, a genius. He was protean. He did whatever struck his fancy—everything struck his fancy. His last public act: signing a memorial to Congress for the abolition of slavery. (One blotch: His illegitimate son William, the last royal governor of New

Jersey, was arrested as a loyalist and imprisoned.) Benjamin initiated municipal police and fire forces, a circulating library, a national postal service. He gained international recognition for his scientific experiments concerning lightning—the first two men who tried to repeat Franklin's experiment of charging a Leyden jar with electricity drawn from "thunder gusts" were electrocuted. He had many words for the wise: "Necessity never made a good bargain. Eat to live, and not live to eat. Three may keep a secret, if two of them are dead. There are three faithful friends—an old wife, an old dog, and ready money. Some are weather-wise, some are otherwise. He that riseth late must trot all day. Lost time is never found again. He that lives upon hope will die fasting. There never was a good war or a bad peace." At the signing of the Declaration of Independence, he said, "We must all hang together, or assuredly we shall all hang separately." Thirty-six years of politics and diplomacy included twenty-five years' service in London and in Paris. The "wisest American" helped to direct the compromise that brought the Constitution of the United States into being: "Our Constitution," he wrote a year before his death, "is in actual operation; everything appears to promise that it will last; but in this world nothing is certain but death and taxes."

FRAZIER, JOE

It was billed as the fight of the century—heavyweight champ Smokin' Joe Frazier vs. the contending Louisville Lip, Muhammad Ali, at Madison Square Garden in New York, March 8, 1971. A big hook in the eleventh round left Ali rubber-legged. In the twelfth, Frazier folded the undefeated Ali "like a carpenter's rule" with successive shots to the belly and the head. In the thirteenth, Ali appeared in a trance in a neutral corner, oblivious to the hoarse scream, "You got God in your corner, Champ." In the fifteenth, a murderous left hook put Ali down for a four-count and nailed his first professional loss. Frazier was right: "Clay is good, but he isn't good enough to escape." It was a unanimous decision. Ali won the rematch, the thrilla in Manila, in October 1975, a knockout in the fourteenth round.

FREUD, SIGMUND

It has been reported that Sigmund Freud had erotic dreams about American women, that they really turned him on. It *is* known that he interpreted a dream about his American niece Hella as covering a sexual wish toward his eldest daughter. The intimate biographer Ernest Jones has summarized the Viennese's character and personality: "There was a striking contrast between the rather unflattering picture he revealed to the world concerning his inner life, notably in the analysis of his dreams, and the quite complete reticence on the matter of his love life. The sacredness undoubtedly centered there, and [he took] quite extraordinary precautions to conceal a most innocent and momentary emotion of love in his adolescence. . . .'' On learning that his most promising protégé had committed suicide—strangulating himself and shooting out his brains at the same time—Herr Doktor declared, ''Good riddance. He was going to cause trouble anyway.'' The cofounder of psychoanalysis—he claimed never to have met the historic first patient treated successfully, in 1880, by Josef Breuer's ''talking cure,'' Bertha Pappenheim, or ''Anna O.,'' a friend of Freud's wife and a visitor to the Freud home—was saved from bleeding to death by the cretin who happened to be sharing a hospital room with him. Taught by numerous experiences, Freud systematically refrained from granting interviews; most strenuously he avoided American newspaper correspondents. He rejected additional invitations to visit America after his Clark University lectures of 1909. Both the *Chicago Tribune* and William Randolph Hearst—Citizen Hearst!—said he could name his own price, including a private chartered ocean liner, if he would go to Chicago and psychoanalyze the ''thrill'' killers (1924) Richard Loeb and Nathan Leopold. Columbia University wanted him as a lecturer; he could meet with private patients in the afternoon; Freud declined, averring that he'd lose too much money in the arrangement. He hated to travel. In the early 1930s, Albert Einstein, lamenting man's ''lust for hatred and destruction,'' asked him if he thought that mankind could somehow evolve out of its predisposition for war, and Freud replied, ''In some happy corners of the earth, where nature brings forth abundantly whatever man desires, there flourish races whose lives go gently by, unknowing of aggression or constraint. . . .'' At the age of sixty-seven, Freud tried to overcome the death instinct by mobilizing the life instinct. He underwent surgery to rejuvenate his testicles; it didn't work. To help Freud escape imprisonment and certain death (the fate of his four sisters, and of Kafka's three sisters), a ransom, or bribe, of roughly £20,000 was delivered to the Nazi conquerers of Vienna for his freedom. He died a year later in England.

FRIEDAN, BETTY

Ladies' Home Journal, McCall's, and *Redbook*—the latter said in its rejection it wouldn't publish an article about ''a few neurotic housewives''—all said no, no, a thousand times no. Her book publisher, frankly tired of the overbearing woman (*summa cum laude* graduate of Smith, a graduate fellow in psychology, a mother of three) already years late in delivering her manuscript, put out 3,000 copies and expected to mark off a small loss for *The Feminine Mystique*. ''Being born a woman with a brain in America today can seem a handicap," Mrs. Friedan said. "You feel like a freak. I used to think I might have enjoyed life more if I'd been born a Frenchwoman in the time of Mme. de Stael, a bluestocking with salons and lovers and lots of good talk. Now I think now is fine, now is great . . . Men are victims of the feminine mystique, too, because it keeps them from knowing women as human beings. . . . Some people think I'm saying 'Women of the world unite—you have nothing to lose but your men.' It's not true. You have nothing to lose but your vacuum cleaners." When President Richard M. Nixon's White House wondered how schemes would play in Peoria, it didn't have Peoria-born Ms. Friedan in mind.

FRISBEE

Once known as the Pluto Platter, the plastic saucer-shaped disk has been scaled by the likes of Neil Armstrong (not on the Moon), Pierre Trudeau, and Richard Burton. There's frisbee competitive play; the championships are supervised by the International Frisbee Disc Association. The world record for outdoor distance has been 444 feet. The indoor distance record has been 316 feet. Wham-o!

FROST, ROBERT LEE

New England's four-time Pulitzer Prize winner—"Home is the place where, when you have to go there, They have to take you in"—was born in California—"I met a Californian who would Talk California—a state so blessed, He said, in climate, none had ever died there A natural death" —and he lived for three years in England. He inevitably took the road less traveled by, which indeed made all the difference: "To me the thing that art does for life is to clean it, to strip it to form." His verse was as simple and honest as an axe or a hoe, a way of taking life by the throat: "It is only a moment here and a moment there that the greatest writer has." He had promises to keep and miles to go before he slept. Irascible, to put it mildly, he believed appropriately that good fences make good neighbors.

FROZEN FOODS

Like a bird, Clarence Birdseye had an eye for seeing things no one else could. The only way that he could keep vegetables fresh for his family while they were on a fur-trading expedition in Labrador in the early 1910s was to place the food in barrels of water and let it freeze solid. Another light bulb went off, another Eureka! was shouted. When he returned to his home in Springfield, Massachusetts, he experimented with the commercial application of frozen foods. In 1930, the first packages of Birds Eye frozen foods went up into refrigerated cases of ten grocery stores in Springfield. They sold like coldcakes. Birdseye had hit the target, and founded a whole new industry.

FULLER, R. BUCKMINSTER

What was the comprehensive designer, inventor, engineer, mathematician, architect, cartographer, philosopher, poet, cosmogonist, choreographer, visionary—celebrated for developing geodesic houses that fly and for dymaxion ways of living—trying to do? "As a conscious means of hopefully competent participation by humanity in its own evolutionary trending while employing only the unique advantages inhering exclusively to the individual who takes and maintains the economic initiative in the face of the formidable physical capital and credit advantages of the massive corporations and political states I seek through comprehensively anticipatory design science and its reduction to physical practice to reform the environment instead of trying to reform man also intend thereby to accomplish prototyped capabilities of doing more with less whereby in turn the wealth-regenerating prospects of such design-science augmentations will induce their spontaneous and economically successful production by world-around industrialization's managers all of which chain reaction-provoking events will both permit and induce all humanity to realize full lasting economic and physical success plus enjoyment of all the Earth without one individual interfering with or being advantaged at the expense of another." Bucky was a verb.

FULTON, ROBERT

He didn't invent the steamboat. He was an expert gunsmith and a jeweler and a painter and a miniaturist and he developed a practical submarine and invented torpedoes and he made steam propulsion commercially practical, but he didn't invent the steamboat. John Fitch did. A score of years before Fulton's North River Steam Boat, based at Clermont, New York, steamed and paddlewheeled along the Hudson River from New York City to Albany and back again, a sixty-two-hour round-trip, Fitch (who had been engaged in surveying and real-estate speculation in Kentucky and the Northwest Territory) demonstrated a 45-foot boat with steam-powered oars for propulsion. The site was the Delaware River, and witnesses included delegates to the Constitutional Convention. Fitch for a time in 1790 maintained a regular schedule of trips between Philadelphia and Trenton, New Jersey. Financial difficulties and various misfortunes led to a failure, and he committed suicide.

G

GAGARIN, YURI ALEKSEYEVICH

April 12, 1961, Radio Moscow: "The world's first satellite spaceship, the *Vostok*, with a man on board, has been put into orbit round the Earth in the Soviet Union. . . . The pilot-space navigator of the satellite spaceship *Vostok* is a citizen of the U.S.S.R., Flight Major Yuri Alekseyevich Gagarin." The twenty-seven-year-old cosmonaut—history's first—flew around the world once. He radioed at 9:22 A.M. that he was over South America and was fine—at 10:15, he was over Africa, "the flight is normal. . . . I withstand well the state of weightlessness"—he safely landed after 108 minutes, including 89.1 in orbit, "in the pre-arranged area of the U.S.S.R." *Vostok* [it means East] weighed five tons and reached apogee at 188 miles. Gagarin's early schooling had been interrupted when Nazi panzer units overran Gzhatsk, where he lived, 100 miles east of Moscow. Before the rocketed launch from the spacedrome near Baykonur, he had had water and eaten a jelly. He was awarded the Soviet Union's highest honor—the title of Hero of the Soviet Union with the Order of Lenin and the Gold Star. In 1968, he was killed when a plane he was testing crashed.

GALILEO

The Vatican is still examining the "heresies" of the seventeenth-century Italian astronomer and physicist. Pope John Paul II has disputed the Church's official view that the Earth is the center of the Universe: Yes, he says, the planet revolves around the Sun. Galileo was forced to recant his heliotropic view under the threat of torture he had suffered at the hands of the Church. Yes, but perhaps Galileo was partly responsible for his plight: He had pursued his research independent of Catholic centers that were also studying astronomy and astrophysics. When Church inquisitioners forced Galileo to sign a retraction, he is said to have muttered under his breath, *"E pur si muove"*—"Nevertheless, it does move." Galileo was born in 1564, three days before Michelangelo died, "a kind of symbolic passing of the palm of learning from the fine arts to science," and two months before Shakespeare was born. His nickname as a student was "the wrangler," because he was argumentative and a nonconformist. His studies of the Sun damaged his eyes, and in old age he went blind. He had a visit from John Milton.

GANDHI, INDIRA

India's first woman prime minister (and P.M. for fifteen of the eighteen years 1966–84) was not related to the Mahatma, or Great Soul. Her aunt Mrs. Vijay Lakshmi Pandit was the first woman to be president of the General Assembly of the United Nations. Her father was Jawaharlal Nehru, who guided India to independence from Great Britain. Her early heroine had been Joan of Arc; Mrs. Gandhi had also been imprisoned. She became unpopular because her late son, Sanjay, had proposed a campaign of compulsory sterilization for men. (There are nearly 750 million Indians.) She served as president of the Indian National Congress party. She served as minister of information. She faced an inadequate nationwide supply of food. She agreed to the creation of a separate state for the western Punjab's 7 million Sikhs. She helped to direct India's defeat of Pakistan and the establishment of Bangladesh. Her ruthless and autocratic methods were often at variance with her democratic principles. Thousands of opponents were arrested and press censorship was imposed. "I have lived in crisis since earliest childhood," Mrs. Gandhi once remarked. "Perhaps that's why problems don't overwhelm me." In October 1984, the right-wing Bharatiya Janata Party sought the overthrow of Mrs. Gandhi's government: "She talks of political morality, but she is the most immoral politician we have in this country." Madam, Madamji, Mrs. G., Indiraji, Amma (Mother), "She"—on October 31, 1984, was shot dead (more than 20 bullets) by two Sikh members of her personal bodyguard—another murder motivated by religious hatred.

GANDHI, MOHANDAS KARAMCHAND

The nonviolent civil-disobedience proponent (an erstwhile cross-examining lawyer in Johannesburg and a *bon vivant* in London) led India to independence from Great Britain and was assassinated on January 30, 1948, by a Hindu fanatic angered by the Mahatma's solicitude for the Muslims. (Gandhi had vigorously opposed establishment of the separate Muslim state of Pakistan.) January 30 also marked both the birthdate of Franklin D. Roosevelt, America's most-often-elected President, and the ascension to power, in 1933, of Adolf Hitler. After Nazi Germany's Crystal Night (Kristallnacht), in November 1938, a night of incalculable savagery without precedent since the Thirty Years' War three centuries earlier . . . hundreds of synagogues torched . . . looting, raping, wholesale murdering . . . Walpurgisnacht! . . . Gandhi once again deplored violence as the resolution of any problem. But he had a modest proposal for the German-Jewish victims of Nazi thuggery: They should all commit suicide. Collective suicide would dramatize the horrors of Hitler's Germany and Nazism, and the whole world would rise in righteous wrath. The moral victory of good over evil would be secured forevermore. Gandhi also proposed that England lay down her arms and let the Nazis win —better that than to have all those historic monuments destroyed and all those people killed.

GANGES

Hindu India's sacred river, from the river *Ganga,* was originally confined to the celestial regions. It flowed from the toe of Vishnu to the sundry paradises and made fertile the spheres of heaven. Its water would have flooded the Earth had not Siva allowed it to flow through his hair, calming the torrent. And so from the head of Siva and then from the ear of the sage Jahnu it arrived as the *Sapta-sindhavan,* seven streams, or the seven sacred rivers of India, and to this day the Ganges is personified as the goddess Ganga, a name of Austric derivation. It is said to have healing powers. Voluntary death by drowning in the Ganges assures a place in paradise. Depositing the bones and ashes of a deceased person in the river ensures his entry into bliss. Gandhi was cremated on a bank of the Ganges. The river is believed to enter the nether regions at the island of Sagar near its mouth, at the Bay of Bengal. It really rises in an ice cave in the Himalayas and flows generally east for about 1,560 miles.

GARBO, GRETA

"The best actress of the half-century" and one of the world's most beautiful women nearly came out of self-imposed retirement in 1949. She went to Italy under contract to the producer Walter Wanger to star in a movie of Balzac's *La Duchesse de Langeais;* alas, it wasn't made. In her native Sweden, Greta Gustafson had been a latherer in a barbershop while striving to become an employed actress. She put a toe into the cinematic waters as a bathing beauty in the comedy *Peter the Tramp,* in 1922. It is said that when Sweden's foremost movie director, Mauritz Stiller, was offered a three-year contract to work with M-G-M in Hollywood, he insisted that the studio give a contract to Garbo as well; no Garbo, no Stiller. Her portrayal of sexual passion in *Flesh and the Devil* (1927) was hailed. (From the moment that Garbo's first American film went into production, no contemporary actress was ever again to be quite happy in herself. The career of several Hollywood stars ended up permanently on the cutting-room floor. So says Louise Brooks.) Her first sound picture was advertised with the slogan "Garbo Talks." A close-up in *Queen Christina* was a high point in cinema achievement to that date (1933). *Anna Karenina* (1935), *Camille* (1936). When she made the unsuccessful *Two-Faced Woman* (1941), she retired to legendary seclusion. She walks mid-Manhattan (she lives in River House, overlooking the East River) and has used the pseudonym Harriet Brown.

GARSON, GREER

Her Oscar-acceptance speech of more than half an hour prompted the Academy of Motion Picture Arts and Sciences to impose a time limit on thank-yous. She had been voted best actress, in 1942, for the title role in M-G-M's story of an ideal middle-class English family in World War II, *Mrs. Miniver,* which was also acclaimed best production of the year, best written screenplay, and best achievement in black-and-white cinematography. Directed by William Wyler and co-starring Walter Pidgeon, it was "a great war picture that photographs the inner meaning instead of the outward realism" of the War.

GATLING, RICHARD JORDAN

Early in the Civil War, the inventor of agricultural implements and former medical student witnessed "almost daily the departure of the wounded, sick, and dead. Most of the latter lost their lives not in battle but by sickness and exposure incident to the service. It occurred to me if I could invent a machine—a gun—which by its rapidity of fire enabled one man to do as much battle duty as a hundred that it would, to a great extent, supersede the necessity of large armies, and, consequently, exposure to battle and disease would be greatly diminished." And so Gatling invented the precursor of the modern machine gun. Ten or more breech-loading rifles were fixed round a crank-operated central shaft. One man rotated the shaft and a second loaded the guns with cartridges, and 400 rounds a minute could be fired. The Army bought 100 in 1866, and by 1882 a Gatling could fire 1,200 rounds a minute; eventually, 3,000 rounds a minute. Gatling's justification—cleaner carnage and a life-saver (it could help to end wars quicker)—was used by the United States for unleashing the atomic bomb on Japan.

GEESE

A goose is no silly goose. A gander tends to mate for life, which can be for thirty years or so. These days, that's worth a celebration with *paté de foie gras*. Mother goose breeds when she is three years old, and broods for about a month. With but one exception, what was good in the latter part of the Stone Age for the wild European greylag goose has been good for all barnyard geese ever since. The exception is the Chinese goose, which was developed, by selective breeding, from the Asiatic swan goose, *anser cygnoides*. The fireballing major league relief moundsperson "Goose" Gossage is celebrated for laying golden eggs.

GEHRIG, LOU

From June 1, 1925, to May 2, 1939—that's nearly 14 full years—"the iron horse" took the field in every game the New York Yankees played —2,130 consecutive games, a record that's never been approached. The previous record was Everett "Deacon" Scott's 1,307 consecutive games, for the Boston Red Sox and the Yankees. (The National League record is 1,207, set between September 2, 1975, and July 29, 1983, by Steve Garvey, first baseman with the Los Angeles Dodgers and the San Diego Padres.) The Bronx Bomber once hit four home runs in a game, and twenty-three times he struck grand-slam home runs, by far the big-league record. In seventeen glorious seasons, Gehrig swatted 493 round-trippers (outhomering Babe Ruth in 1934 and 1936) and batted in 1,990 runs. He was the American League's most valuable player four times, in 1927, 1931, 1934, and 1936. He suffered from a rare and fatal form of paralysis —amyotrophic lateral sclerosis, known now as "Lou Gehrig's disease" —and had to quit the game. His was the first number (4) retired by a team, in an emotional ceremony at Yankee Stadium in 1939. The pride of the Yankees was quickly elected to the Hall of Fame.

GELDING

A gelding is a male horse, a stallion, whose testicles have been removed. Castration mitigates impulses, and the horse, of course, is no longer available as a stud. For his fertility, Devil's Bag was syndicated at $36 million.

GENESIS

Through the static of 231,000 miles, the three astronauts of *Apollo 8* read in turn the Biblical version of the creation of their home base: "In the beginning, God created the heaven and the Earth. And the Earth was without form and void; and darkness was upon the face of the deep . . .

And God called the light day, and the darkness He called night . . . And God called the dry land Earth; and the gathering together of the water called He Seas: and God saw that it was good." It was Christmas Eve 1968 and the astronauts Colonel Frank Borman, of the Air Force, Captain James A. Lovell, Jr., of the Navy, and Major William A. Anders, of the Air Force, were the first men to orbit the Moon. Ten times they circled that desolate realm of dream and scientific mystery, the first terrestrials to have a close look (within seventy miles) at our nearest celestial neighbor and to witness a lunar sunrise. Colonel Borman described the Moon as a "vast, lonely and forbidding sight . . . not a very inviting place to live or work." On the fifty-seven-hour return flight from the most far-reaching voyage of the Space Age to that date, one of the astronauts radioed, "Please be informed there is a Santa Claus." Seven months later, the *Eagle* landed at Gordy base in the Sea of Tranquility and USAstronauts Neil Armstrong and Edwin Aldrin, Jr., walked on the Moon for mankind.

GEORGE III

The British monarch succeeded his grandfather, George II, in 1760, and reigned for sixty years—the last ten while he was insane—during a series of epochal events: the American Revolution, the French Revolution (which threatened England's very existence), the act of union that in 1801 brought Ireland into the United Kingdom of Great Britain and Ireland, and the unprecedented social and economic changes brought on by the satanic mills of the Industrial Revolution. He harassed the American colonists by calling assemblies at peculiar locations and difficult hours, and so there was another grievance in 1776: "He has called together legislative bodies at places unusual, uncomfortable and distant . . . for the sole purpose of fatiguing [us] . . ." On July 4, in '76, he wrote in his diary, "Nothing of importance happened today"—he had no way of knowing what had occurred in the City of Brotherly Love far across the sea.

GEORGIA

The Peachtree State, the Goober State, a land of magnolias and moss-draped trees, is the largest state (58,876 square miles) east of the Mississippi River, but only twenty-first in size among all the states. It was named for King George II of England. Of the thirteen colonies that fought in the Revolutionary War, it was the last to have been founded and the fourth to join the Union, on January 2, 1788.

GERONIMO

It was the enlightened West Point graduate and career soldier George Crook who convinced Geronimo (Spanish for "Jerome") to throw in his headdress and surrender. Crook was then censured, and he voluntarily quit the Army without reservation after the Apache chief didn't keep his word and fled. (Geronimo gave himself up for good two years later to Crook's successor.) Crook had performed exploration and frontier defense duties in the Northwest, fought the Confederacy all over the place, and spent twenty years fighting and dealing with the Apache, the Sioux, the Cheyenne, the Paiute, the Snake—discovery of gold in the Black Hills made even more manifest America's destiny to encroach. Crook negotiated where he could, fought where he had to. The government let George do it until Geronimogate. Geronimo himself, after years in captivity, marched in President Theodore Roosevelt's inaugural parade in Washington, in 1905, appeared at the St. Louis World's Fair, was a prosperous farmer, sold pictures of himself at two dollars each, and adopted Christianity—after he and a small Chirahua band of Apaches had terrorized the Southwest for going on twenty years. Geronimo's easygoing nature had been incited to a homicidal pitch by the slaying, by Mexicans, of his wife and three children.

GERSHWIN, IRA

George's older brother was an incredibly modest lyricist, everyone's one and only—he rhymed "delishious" and "caprishious." During a work session with colleagues in the Hollywood vineyards, he volunteered to telephone their favorite restaurant and reserve a table for lunch at one o'clock. He came back from the phone and said the restaurant was full up, he'd have to try elsewhere, any suggestions? "Here, let me try that place," colleague Jerome Kern said. When *he* came back from the phone, he announced there would be a table for all of them at one o'clock. "How'd you do that, Jerry?" Ira asked. "They told me they were fully booked." "Easy, Ira. I used your name." The lyric that gave him special pleasure, the one he was proudest of, was written for *Funny Face* (1927) and was about trotting in little velvet panties and being kissed by sisters and cousins and aunties—it was "an Inferno worse than Dante's." He was inactive for the last twenty-nine years of his life. His loving wife, Lee, whom Truman Capote noted was devoted to diamonds, used to call him a stick-in-the-mud—"he hates to go from one room to the next"—unless it was to pick up an etymological or rhyming dictionary. Ira was entitled. He viewed the morning with alarm because the British Museum had lost its charm. When he died in 1983, the world noted that in time the

Rockies might crumble, even Gibraltar might tumble, because they're only made of clay, but its love for Ira Gershwin was here to stay.

GESTAPO

Geheime Staatspolizei, the Nazis' secret state police, was established as the Prussian political force under Hermann Goering at 8 Prinz-Albrecht-strasse in Berlin on April 26, 1933, three months after Hitler had grabbed power; the address became notorious as an interrogation center and a prison. Under Heinrich Himmler, the Gestapo wielded virtually absolute power. It established and controlled the concentration camps and the killing camps. The Nuremberg trials indicted the Gestapo as a criminal organization involved in every aspect of Nazi terrorization, and its agents were collectively condemned as war criminals. The S.S. loyalty oath: "I swear loyalty and valor to you, Adolf Hitler, as Fuhrer and Chancellor of the German Reich. I solemnly promise you and the superiors appointed by you obedience to the death. So help me God."

GIBBON, EDWARD

One of the great historians, the short, bulbously fat, vain, affected Englishman had little formal education. He was forced to leave Oxford as a teenager when he converted to Roman Catholicism. His family shipped him to Lausanne, where he returned to Protestantism. Among the ruins of Rome he got the idea for the panoramic story of thirteen centuries of Roman power, *The Decline and Fall of the Roman Empire.* He was a captain for three years in the Hampshire militia and a member for nine years, 1774–83, of Parliament, then withdrew to Lausanne to complete his twenty-year work on his masterpiece. In the second century of the Christian era, in Gibbon's view, the Empire of Rome comprehended the fairest part of the Earth, and the most civilized portion of mankind: "After a diligent inquiry, I can discern four principal causes of the ruin of Rome, which continued to operate in a period of more than a thousand years. The injuries of time and nature; the hostile attacks of the barbarians and Christians; the use and abuse of the materials; the domestic quarrels of the Romans. . . . The winds and waves are always on the side of the ablest navigators."

GILLETTE, KING CAMP

It was the real name of the inventor of the safety razor. "If I had been technically trained, I would have quit," he said after spending eight frustrating years striving to make a razor with pre-sharpened, disposable blades and a guard to keep the man from cutting himself. Within a year, his company had produced 90,000 razors and more than 12,000,000 blades, and made beards less fashionable. In 1910, the inventor vainly offered former President Theodore Roosevelt a million dollars to be president of an experimental "world corporation" in Arizona.

GINZA

Tokyo's Ginza district, south of the business and financial center, and some distance from Emperor Hirohito's palace, is the city's shopping and entertainment center, world-famous for its stores and nightclubs, and the world's most expensive real estate. One futuristic apartment building there is the essence of capsule living. Each apartment unit of twenty cubic meters (approximately ten feet by ten feet with a seven-foot-high ceiling) has a bed, a bathroom, a desk, and a bookshelf—minimum space, maximum equipment.

GIRAFFE

It's a camelopard—*Giraffa camelopardalis*—the tallest land animal on the planet. The male may be eighteen feet from hoof to crown (it may be six feet tall at birth). Its neck, which has the usual number (seven) of vertebrae for a mammal, may be seven feet in length. The same pressure generated in its brain by a giraffe when it raises its head from the ground would cause unconsciousness in humans. Its tongue is about a foot and a half long, the better to graze on leaves of acacia and mimosa in treetops. The all-but-speechless animal—what's "How's the weather up there?" in giraffe?—lives in the open savanna south of the Sahara, in Africa, and belongs to the order of ungulates called *Artiodactyla,* cloven-footed, even-toed, hoofed animals. Its affinities are closest to the deer. It can run like the wind, up to thirty miles per hour, and with one kick a giraffe can kill a lion. Egyptians, about 1500 B.C., believed that the giraffe was a crossbreed between a female camel and a male panther. Americans (unless they'd been to Africa) didn't see a giraffe until Ulysses S. Grant was President, when the first one was imported into the States.

GISH, LILLIAN AND DOROTHY

At first, their director-discoverer D. W. Griffith couldn't tell them apart, so he had Lillian wear a blue ribbon in her hair, younger sister Dorothy a red one. Later, he said, "Lillian Gish is not only the best actress in her profession, but she has the best mind of any woman I have ever met." Dorothy read Proust and was the life of the party. The Gishes starred in *Hearts of the World, Orphans of the Storm,* and *Romola,* and their names will be associated always with the golden days of the silent motion picture. In the 1950s, they were reunited in *The Chalk Garden* on Broadway. Their childhood playmate Gladys Smith also did well in the movies—she became Mary Pickford.

GLACIATION

It's the process of becoming ice; the formation of ice sheets; the formation of glaciers: the condition of being covered by ice sheets or glaciers. Glaciation creates distinctive landforms known as cirques, drumlins, and eskers. Cirque: a deep steep-walled basin high on a mountain, shaped like half a bowl and often containing a small lake caused especially by glacial erosion and usually forming the blunt end of a valley. Drumlin: an elongated or oval hill of glacial drift. Esker: a long, narrow, often sinuous ridge or mound of sand, gravel, and boulders deposited between ice walls by a stream flowing on, within, or beneath a stagnant glacier. The last Ice Age retreated only 20 millenia ago.

GLUTEUS MAXIMUS

The gluteal region of your body, commonly called the buttocks, overlies the posterior aspect of the pelvic bones and may be considered more properly as a transitional zone between the trunk and the lower limb. The gluteal muscles are three in number: gluteus maximus, gluteus medius, gluteus minimus. The gluteus maximus is the largest and most superficial of these muscles and forms much of the buttocks. It arises from the ilium, sacrum, and coccyx. It can extend the thigh or, if the lower limb is fixed, it can extend the trunk as one straightens up from a stooped position.

GODDARD, ROBERT

Twenty-seven years before he launched a liquid-fueled rocket from a jungle-gym gantry in his Aunt Effie's farm in Massachusetts, the American rocketry pioneer had climbed a cherry tree and experienced a kind of epiphanic vision that ignited his interest in rocket technology and space technology: He was then a seventeen-year-old high school sophomore. The United States ignored his experiments and achievements, but German scientists didn't, and they produced rockets in the closing months of World War II. As the *Apollo 11* astronauts prepared for their historic landing on the Moon, in the summer of 1969, *The New York Times* formally apologized for a 1920 editorial comment ridiculing Goddard's claim that rockets could fly through a vacuum to Earth's only natural satellite.

GOEBBELS, JOSEPH

Hitler's Jesuit-educated Minister for Propaganda and Enlightenment, "the only really interesting man in the Third Reich beside Hitler," he realized the full potentialities of mass media for political purposes in a dynamic totalitarian state. He created the "myth" of the Fuhrer. He gave him "the halo of infallibility." He believed that the fundamental principle of all propaganda is the repetition of effective arguments: "We can do without butter [1937], but, despite all our love of peace, not without arms. One cannot shoot with butter but with guns." He was a Rhinelander, the son of devout lower-middle-class Catholic parents. He was handicapped from childhood by a club foot. He blamed "the Jewish monopoly" for his failure to prosper in literature. Hitler's high priest joined the Nazi Party in 1925. Thanks to Goebbels, Nazi symbolism was full of analogies to Catholic symbolism, e.g., blood on the flag. "Whoever can conquer the streets will one day conquer the State," he said, "for every form of power politics and any dictatorially run state has its roots in the streets." A Goebbels assistant wrote, "Whenever Goebbels goes to Hitler's headquarters, he starts off full of distrust of the Führer's genius, full of irritation, criticism and hard words. Each time he is determined to tell Hitler what he thinks. What happens in their talks, I don't know; but every time that Goebbels returns from these visits, he is full of admiration for the Führer and exudes an optimism which infects us all." During the war, Goebbels produced a moral oxygen infusion, the large-scale propaganda movie *Kolberg,* and wrote a book, *The Law of War,* and an article, "History as Teacher." The Goebbelses poisoned their children, then committed suicide in Hitler's bunker.

GOLDEN HIND

Ferdinand Magellan, as every schoolboy knows, was the first man to sail around the world—or almost sail around the world. He was murdered in the Philippines but his ship and crew made it back to Europe. The first skipper to go all the way had no intention of doing it when he started out from England—Queen Elizabeth I's top sea dog, the piratical plunderer Francis Drake. Captaining the *Golden Hind* (its original name was the *Pelican*), he raided Spanish settlements on both coasts of South America, confiscated Spanish cargo, named New Albion (it's San Francisco today); when he realized that discretion would be the better part of valor, he continued westward across the Pacific, rather than return to England via the Horn and possible Spanish entrapment in the Atlantic. The marauder had been gone three years when his treasure-laden vessel anchored in Plymouth on September 26, 1580. Elizabeth responded to Spain's demand that *El Draque—The Dragon*—be punished by boarding the *Golden Hind* and knighting Drake. He was a vice-admiral in the English fleet that routed the "invincible Spanish armada" after he had raided Cadiz and destroyed thirty Spanish ships there: He was still singeing the king of Spain's beard, in the West Indies this time, when he died of dysentery, in 1596, and was buried at sea.

GOLDWATER, BARRY

Thomas Paine, who coined the name "the United States of America" and whose book *Common Sense* was an early best seller in the United States, declared in *Rights of Man,* in 1792, that "a thing moderately good is not so good as it ought to be. Moderation in temper is always a virtue; but moderation in principle is always a vice." In 1964, the Republican Presidential nominee said that "extremism in the defense of liberty is no vice. And . . . moderation in the pursuit of justice is no virtue." Senator Goldwater's campaign emblem was AuH_2O—the chemical symbols of gold and water. The hawkish champion of the right wing of the Republican party—the grandson of a Russian Jewish immigrant whose trading post burgeoned into a chain of department stores in Arizona—he offered the citizenry "a choice, not an echo": sharp cuts in social programs, sharp increases in the defense budget, the sale of the Tennessee Valley Authority, a voluntary Social Security, opposition to civil rights programs. Supported by big business interests and dedicated conservatives, he was able to net only 39 percent of the popular vote and 52 electoral votes (President Lyndon B. Johnson scored 486 electoral votes). Twenty years later, in 1984, ABC News used a Goldwater quote to stimulate TV viewership of the Republican National Convention in Dallas: "Our democratic way of life depends on a system of accountability. Government must be responsible to the people represented. And we the people are responsible for seeing to it that government represents us well. Let's all do our part. Let's continue to watch the conventions. And be sure to register and vote. It's more than political theory. It's a matter of conscience." Goldwater, a senator for more than three decades, has said it seems anyone can be President except him.

GONE WITH THE WIND—OSCARS

It reaped more Academy Awards than any other motion picture had. Ten —count 'em—ten on February 28, 1940: Vivien Leigh, best actress; Hattie McDaniel; best supporting actress, (the first Oscar for a black performer); Victor Fleming, best director; Sidney Howard, best screenplay; Ernest Haller and Ray Rennahan, best photography; Cameron Menzies, a specially worded award for achievements in design and color; Lyle Wheeler, best art direction; Hal Kern and James Newcom, best editing; Jack Cosgrove, special effects. David Selznick won the Irving Thalberg Memorial Award "for the most consistent high level of production achievement by an individual producer." Director Fleming did not attend the awards ceremony nor the sensational opening in Atlanta. He was alienated by the advance publicity in which Selznick was quoted as saying that Fleming had been "supervised" by Selznick. Even their personal relationship was gone with the wind.

THE GOOD EARTH

Pearl Comfort Sydenstricker Buck grew up in Chen-chiang, China, where her parents were Presbyterian missionaries, and spent two years at a boarding school in Shanghai. She was graduated in 1914 from Randolph-Macon Women's College, in Virginia, and was an instructor in psychology there. Her description of the cycle of birth, marriage, and death in a northern Chinese peasant family, *The Good Earth,* won the Pulitzer Prize in 1931 and was made into an Oscar-winning film. In 1938, she won the Nobel Prize in literature. She produced nearly 100 books, including *Dragon Seed.*

GOODYEAR, CHARLES

The American inventor was all but rubbed out by debt—he had even been imprisoned—and he needed a way to recoup his fortunes. Rubber wasn't a very useful material. Why not try to find a way to make it useful —to keep it from sticking and melting in hot water and becoming stiff and hard in cold weather. He experimented with sulphur. When he accidentally spilled the mixture on a stove, he found that when he picked up the hot rubber-sulfur mixture he had something dry and flexible at all temperatures. Goodyear had vulcanized rubber. But it was never a good year for him and he would never be rich. He had to market his patent rights for a fraction of their value, and many people infringed on the patent. When he died, in 1860, he was more in debt than ever, owing hundreds of thousands of dollars. (His discovery was the first big step toward what is now called polymer chemistry.)

GOOLAGONG-CAWLEY, EVONNE

Part Australian aborigine, and the third of eight children, she showed an aptitude for all sports. She played rugby, cricket, and soccer before developing her tennis talent. She won Wimbledon twice (1971, 1980), the Australian Open four times, and the French Open and the Italian once each. She was twice a finalist in the U.S. Open.

GORDON, CHARLES "CHINESE"

He was also known as "Gordon Pasha." The swashbuckler had a well-notched belt. He was graduated from Britain's Royal Military Academy, and he fought in the Crimean War, helped to capture Peking, led the Ever-Victorious Army protecting Shanghai from the Taipings ("great peace") rebelling against the Manchu dynasty and assured continued British trade privileges in China, campaigned vigorously against slave traders when governor of Equatoria and the Sudan, served in India, China again, Mauritius, and Cape Colony, and was killed in the last two days of a ten-month siege of the (oppressive) Egyptian military force in Khartoum by Islam's Muhammed Ahmad's Mahdi—"he who is divinely guided." Britain's failure to relieve the popular Gordon helped to bring to an end the Liberal ministry of William Gladstone.

GORILLA

Chest-beating seems to manifest "fight or flight" tensions for these largest of apes, native to the forests of western equatorial Africa. Chest-beating displays consist of nine more or less distinct acts. An expert on gorilla behavior, George B. Schaller, has observed that the entire sequence is given infrequently and then only by silverbacked males, fully adult, and at least ten years old. (Male gorillas reach a height of six feet, with a nine-foot arm spread, and weigh about 450 pounds in the wild.) The nine acts: ten to forty distinct hoots before blurring into a growl; symbolic feeding sometimes interrupts the hooting; rising on hind legs; throwing vegetation forward or sideways; kicking legs; diving both forward and afterward; slapping at vegetation afterward; running sideways; beating chest, hands held flat, the sound carrying as far as a mile. (The female may beat the back of her infants.) The gorilla kowtows to express submission. He is a late riser in the day and loves to sunbathe. The gorilla culture protects jungle flora. The mother teaches her infants to eat only twenty-nine kinds of the hundreds of edible plants. The gorilla's only enemies are the leopard and man.

THE GOSPELS

Four hundred and thirty-six years elapse between the last book of the Old Testament—known then as The Law and the Prophets—and Jesus' birth in the first book of the New Testament, the Gospel According to St. Matthew. The four Gospels were written in Greek, probably in the later decades of the first century A.D. (Gospel in Greek is "good news.") The earliest surviving manuscripts of any substance date from the fourth century. The Gospel According to St. Mark was probably the first to be composed. Only one of Jesus' miracles is recorded by all four evangelists: his feeding of a multitude on a few loaves and fishes. (There are many miracles in the Old Testament, including the feeding of many with few loaves.) Matthew, Luke, and Mark are the synoptic gospels, a comprehensive view agreeing in subject matter and order. The evangelist John identifies Jesus with the Word—"the Word was made flesh." Luke saw the evil hand of Satan in Judas' betrayal.

GOSSAMER ALBATROSS

It looked like a giant dragonfly with diaphanous wings spreading 96 feet across the skeletal workings of a bicycle: a seat, pedals, and a chain that powered a plastic propeller. In the translucent shell of the 75-pound machine he had named the *Gossamer Albatross* sat the 140-pound pilot and "engine," Bryan Allen, a bespectacled twenty-six-year-old beanpole, from Tulare, California, garbed in running shorts and leather cycling shoes, a plastic crash helmet, and a red life jacket around his bare chest. He had eaten a high-carbohydrate Chinese dinner; just before the scheduled 5:10 A.M. takeoff he wolfed down "the best possible fuel," large plain rolls and fruits. Below the chalky cliffs at Folkestone, England, that June morning in 1979, Allen pedaled furiously along a makeshift wooden runway laid on a concrete quay—he needed to generate one-half horsepower for takeoff. It was a no-go; one of two tiny plastic wheels had broken. (Wilbur Wright had won the coin toss to go first that windy December day in 1903, but his try wasn't successful. Brother Orville then tried it, and became the first man to fly in a heavier-than-air machine.) Allen rose into the sky on his second try, climbed to 20 feet, pedaled at a steady 12 miles per hour (seventy revolutions per minute), dipped to within 6 inches of the swells of the English Channel, and two hours and forty-nine minutes after takeoff touched down 23 miles away on a beach at Cap Gris-Nez, France. "Wow . . . wow . . . WOW!" the pedaler of the sky exclaimed, insisting that he couldn't have gone another 10 feet. The first muscle-powered flight across the Channel, designed by Paul MacCready, an aeronautical engineer and America's first international soaring champion, in 1956, earned the coveted $210,000 prize offered by British industrialist Henry Kremer.

GRAHAM, BILLY

The evangelist ("May the Lord bless you real good") was once "the fastest milker in Mecklenburg County" and the best brush salesman in all of North Carolina. He is well known for milking his campaigns for Christ for all they're worth. He gives critics of his sartorial splendor the brushoff: "There is nothing in the Bible that says I must wear rags." During a tent crusade in Los Angeles, he caught the eye of Super Publisher William Randolph Hearst, and the word went out from San Simeon: PUFF GRAHAM. And Graham puffed the New Testament: "Things Go Better with Jesus!" "You Have a Lot to Live and Jesus Has a Lot to Give." His "religious Woodstock" had joints jumpin' for Jesus! When the United States bombed North Vietnam unmercifully around Christmas 1972, Graham—tight with then President Richard M. Nixon—was implored by other religious leaders to urge the President to reconsider what he was doing; Graham was quoted as responding testily that he was a "New Testament evangelist, not an Old Testament prophet," again insisting that "all through this period, I have not been sure whether our involvement was right or wrong . . . I don't want to get involved on either side." He revisited Moscow in September 1984, to "proclaim the Gospel, the good news of the cross and the resurrection. Jesus was a sower of seeds, and this is exactly what I'm doing." The fiery preacher also insisted, "If I didn't have spiritual faith, I would be a pessimist. But I'm an optimist. I've read the last page in the Bible. It's all going to turn out all right."

GRAHAM CRACKER

The father of the graham cracker was called the "poet of bran bread and pumpkins" by Ralph Waldo Emerson. Sylvester Graham was a nineteenth-century reformer, Presbyterian minister, and temperance lecturer —a bug on health and personal hygiene. He advocated coarsely ground whole wheat (Graham) for bread, hard mattresses, open bedroom windows, cold showers, looser and lighter clothing, daily exercise, vegetables, fresh fruits, rough cereals, pure drinking water, and cheerfulness at meals. Among his many adherents was Horace Greeley, who was to die insane.

GRANADA—ALHAMBRA PALACE

Granada was the capital of Islam in the thirteenth and fourteenth centuries, and the towers of the Moors' fortress citadel-palace Alhambra (Arabic for "the red") crowned the Spanish city like a tiara of antique gold. Arcades in the Court of Lions rested on 124 white marble columns. Sultans and harems reposed amid perfumed air and splashing fountains —the Koran describes paradise as a garden flowing with streams. The plumbing system worked on the principle of gravity. The Moors were expelled from Spain in 1492—once done, the monarchs could turn to Columbus' *noodging*—but the incomparable, furbeloved Alhambra freezes forever the high tide of Arab advancement into Europe.

GRAND CANYON

Meanwhile, out in the West, in what is now northwestern Arizona, two Spanish priests, Francisco Garces and Silvestre Velez de Escalante, were rediscovering the "awesome abyss." The year was 1776 and it had been two hundred and thirty-six years since the world's most intricate and complex system of canyons, gorges, and ravines had first been seen by Europeans, Garcia Lopez de Cardenas and the Coronado expedition. Dug out by downcutting of the Colorado River, this really grand canyon is 217 miles long, up to 18 miles wide, and "up to" a mile deep. The time scale of Earth's history is revealed in the exposed red rocks of the walls. Rocks of the inner gorge are millions of years old. The North Rim is 2,000 feet higher than the South Rim and is usually snowbound in winter. It's been Grand Canyon National Park since 1919 and it attracts 2 million visitors every year.

GRAND CENTRAL STATION

The largest railroad station in the world, since 1913, was originally Grand Central Depot, built by Commodore Cornelius Vanderbilt when 42nd Street in New York was well north of the city's center. Proscription of steam locomotives below 42nd Street determined its location. Every day, half a million people circulate through the lobby and under the 140-foot-high ceiling painted with the constellations of the zodiac. On the south facade, at 42nd Street and Park Avenue, are three colossal figures in

Indiana limestone grouped around a clock 13 feet in diameter: Mercury, representing Commerce; Hercules, Physical Energy; and Minerva, Intellectual Energy. The statuary was created by the Frenchman Jules Coutan; his selection by the terminal's architect, Whitney Warren, was controversial. A foreigner? And Coutan had no desire to visit America: "From what I have learned pictorially of the characteristics of your country, especially with reference to the standards of art, I do not think it would interest me. In fact, I should wish rather to avoid it. I fear that the sight of some of your architecture would distress me."

GRAND HOTEL

The 1932 best-picture Oscar-winner starred Greta Garbo, John Barrymore, Lionel Barrymore, Wallace Beery, and Joan Crawford—a day in the life of guests in a Berlin hotel. The other nominees were *Shanghai Express, Bad Girl, Arrowsmith, The Champ, Five Star Final, One Hour with You,* and *Smiling Lieutenant.* None of the "guests" was nominated for an Oscar, but Beery was co-winner of an Oscar for his work in *The Champ. Grand Hotel* was based on the novel by the prodigiously popular German author Vicki Baum, who used a similar device—the interweaving of lives in a hotel setting—in *Shanghai '37,* which may be made into a television series; the working title is *Nanking Road,* which was the name of the "Fifth Avenue" of China's largest city and the title under which *Shanghai '37* has also been published: "*Maskee* is what we all say here [in Shanghai] in such eventualities. What must happen, happens."

GRANDMA MOSES

When farm work became too hard for her at the age of seventy-eight, Anna Mary Robertson Moses took to embroidering pictures in worsted in her white farmhouse in Eagle Bridge, New York. When arthritis forced her to give up the needle, she took up painting, copying Currier and Ives prints and pictures on postal cards. In 1939, when Mrs. Moses was in her eightieth year, an engineer–art collector discovered four of her paintings in a woman's exchange exhibit in a drugstore window in nearby Hoosick Falls. He bought the four, then drove to the Moses farm and acquired all fifteen landscapes that she had made. That fall, her primitives were on exhibit at the Museum of Modern Art. Twenty friends of lavish-gift-giving Cole Porter awoke one day to discover that paintings he had given them were Moseses. She painted three or four pictures at once: "It's the Scotch in me. Saves paint, saves time." She was still active a year before she died at the age of one hundred and one.

GRAZ AND LINZ

If you need the time of day in Graz, once the capital of all Inner Austria, make sure you remember that the big hands on the gigantic clockfaces on the Uhrturm tell the hours and that the little hands tell the minutes. The Uhrturm was saved from destruction during the Napoleonic wars when Grazians paid the French a bribe of 3,000 gilders. The astronomer Johannes Kepler taught at the state university at Graz. The capital today of Styria, on the Mur River, in southeast Austria, Graz was built eight centuries ago around the mountain peak Schlossberg. Linz, on the Danube, is the country's third largest city (after Vienna and Graz) and the capital of Upper Austria. Its name derives from Lentia, a Roman settlement of the fifth century, possibly earlier. Emperor Friedrich III lived in Linz from 1489 to 1493. Yes, you can enjoy a Linzertorte in Graz.

GREASE

Before *A Chorus Line,* Broadway's longest-running musical was "the new '50s rock 'n' roll musical" with book, music, lyrics by Jim Jacobs and Warren Casey, directed by Tom Moore. It was said that many of the boys of Rydell High's class of '59 looked as if they'd slouched out of *The Blackboard Jungle* while the girls looked like camp followers of *The Wild One,* and everyone used the kind of language that drove most benefit-matinee ladies right up the wall. So it only ran 3,388 performances on Broadway, after opening near the Lower East Side in New York. It was all very groovy.

GREAT BARRIER REEF

Its coral seaward side is the official state boundary of Queensland, in northeast Australia, from which it is separated by a shallow lagoon from 10 to 100 miles wide. The world's largest coral reef, it is 1,250 miles of atolls, keys, and underwater ledges (as vast in area as Kansas) made by tiny polyps extracting lime from seawater—the largest structure ever formed by living organisms. (Charles Darwin was the first to explain how coral reefs came to be.) It is home to the 300-pound giant clam, to lionfish and stonefish, and to the moray eel and the hammerhead shark.

THE GREAT ESCAPE

Tom, Dick, and Harry were the names of tunnels through which seventy-six prisoners of war escaped from the Nazis' Stalag Luft III, sixty miles northeast of Berlin, on March 25, 1944. Fifty of the seventy-three recaptured POWs were executed by the Gestapo. In the 1963 movie Charles Bronson was "the tunnel king" and Steve McQueen "the cooler king."

GREAT LAKES

They are five great lakes, together the largest surface of fresh water in the world, a combined 95,000 square miles, carved by retreating glaciers, 12,000 or so years ago, 1,600 miles from Duluth, Minnesota, at the western end, to the outlet of Lake Ontario at the eastern end. Lake Michigan lies entirely within the United States; the international boundary line between Canada and the United States crosses through the other four. Lake Superior, the largest, highest, deepest of the quintet, is a little larger in size than the state of South Carolina, a little smaller than Maine. The second largest, Lake Huron, is about as large as West Virginia. Lake Michigan is about equal to the combined areas of Maryland, Massachusetts, and Delaware. Lake Erie, the shallowest, is about the size of Vermont. Lake Ontario, the smallest, is not quite as large as New Jersey. Niagara Falls is between Lakes Erie and Ontario. With construction of the St. Lawrence Seaway, from Montreal to Lake Ontario, oceangoing vessels now reach Duluth. How best to remember the names of the Great Lakes? Try the acronym H.O.M.E.S.—Huron, Ontario, Michigan, Erie, Superior.

GREAT SALT LAKE

The erratic, largest salt lake in North America, saltier than sea water, shallow (the average depth has been 14 feet), a remnant of widespread, prehistoric Lake Bonneville, which was 1,000 feet deep, has risen and expanded by 30 percent to 2,250 square miles because of recent prodigious storms. Lying between the Wasatch Range on the west, the Great Salt Lake Desert on the east, the lake generates its own weather, the dreaded lake effect (DLE). A meteorologist, in 1984, said, "If you compared it to earthquakes, it would be as if you had a Richter scale from one to nine and the last two years were 15." Three-quarters of 400,000 acres of protected freshwater marshland was flooded with salt water. Only bone shrimp and colonial algae live in the bluetiful lake: no fish, not even frogs. Swimmers bob on the surface like corks; some discover they are allergic to salt in such concentrated solution. Horace Greeley, who took John Babsone Lane Soule's advice (1851) to go West, observed that "You can no more sink in it than in a claybank, but a very little of it in your lungs would suffice to strangle you."

GREAT WALL OF CHINA

It can't be seen by the Man in the Moon, much less by astronauts. The legend that it could be seen has flourished at least since William Edgar Geil wrote, in 1909, that "the . . . Wall of Ten Thousand Miles could be clearly defined by the mysterious Man-in-the-Moon, if such an individual exist . . ." A lecturer in history at Princeton University, Arthur N. Waldron, has hypothesized that "this fascinating piece of folklore originated during the widespread discussions of the 'canals of Mars' that took place in the years just before Geil wrote." Waldron has also noted that the walls tourists visit today were built in the sixteenth century by the Ming dynasty. The semi-legendary defenses said to have been built by Ch'in Shih-huang more than 2,000 years ago were well to the north of Peking, and nearly all traces have long since vanished. China does not have a vast and ancient "Great Wall"—which would be better translated "long wall" or "walls"—there is no "great" in the Chinese term.

THE GREAT WHITE HOPE

The first black to be the heavyweight boxing champion, Jack Johnson battered James J. Jeffries in fourteen rounds at Reno, Nevada, in 1910. In the wake of that bout: riots around the country that resulted in eight deaths and injuries to many and a search for "the great white hope." He admitted throwing his title match with Jess Willard in Havana, in 1915— it took Willard twenty-six rounds to "kayo" the champion—Johnson didn't collect the $50,000 promised for the tank job. He married two white women, fled the country for seven years when he was convicted on a charge of violation of the Mann Act, returned to serve a year in prison. He was old and fleshy when he emerged from Leavenworth, all but down for the count—he could barely flash his gold teeth. He was killed in an automobile crash in North Carolina in 1946. *The Great White Hope* was the name of Howard Sackler's Pulitzer Prize–winning drama (1969) based on the Johnson era in "the sweet science."

GREENLAND

It was a Danish colony until 1953. Now several agencies, including a Danish ministry, govern the world's largest island, 85 percent of which is ice-sheeted. (The extreme northern peninsula has no ice cap.) A Norse ad man named it Greenland as a come-on for settlers. There are no forests, and the world's largest cryolite mine, at Ivigtut, has been exhausted. (Cryolite is a rare sodium-aluminum fluoride.) About half the Eskimo population of the world lives there. Shrimping and sealing are important industries. The capital is Godthab. Technically, semiautonomous Greenland is really Kalaallit Nunaat.

GREYHOUND

The fastest dog has been chasing a mechanical rabbit since the turn of the century. It's been around for five millenia. It has no scenting ability; as a hunter, it must keep the game in sight. In England, the greyhound was bred and raised by the aristocracy; for hundreds of years, it was illegal under English law for a commoner to own a greyhound. The greyhound family includes the whippet, which is also used for parimutuel racing.

GREY, ZANE

"No kin of mine ain't goin' write none," Pearl Gray's Daddy Dearest shouted as he whipped the boy. He was partially right: His son's melodramatic tales of the West and the Southwest are improbable in character and situation, but they sure are popular, especially *Riders of the Purple Sage*. Yes, Pearl Gray changed his name, to Zane Grey—he had been born in Zanesville, Ohio. To bring vivid detail to his westerns, the novelist became an explorer, a hunter, and a fisherman. He was also a baseball star at the University of Pennsylvania and a dentist in New York City.

GROUNDHOG DAY

February 2, the day the woodchuck plays Willard Scott. If he comes out of his hole and sees his shadow, he will duck right back in and pull the blankets up tight—there're going to be six more weeks of severe winter weather. February 2 is also Candlemas—the Roman Catholic Church celebrates the purification of the Virgin Mary, the Eastern Church celebrates the presentation of the infant Christ in the temple. It is the day that all the candles that will be needed for church services throughout the year are blessed. In Scotland, Candlemas is also one of the four days in the year for the payment of debts.

GUESS WHO'S COMING TO DINNER

It was Spencer Tracy's last movie—he was manifestly dying—but he didn't win best-actor Oscar. Co-star Katharine Hepburn won for best actress—the second of four she's won—and *In the Heat of the Night* was named best picture. Stanley Kramer's "daring" film (1967) was "unique in cinematic history: an honest, realistic, and at times hilarious portrayal of interracial love and the complications surrounding it," *Ebony* declared. Sidney Poitier played a brilliant young physician (black) and Katharine Houghton, in her film debut, was the daughter (ofay) of a wealthy publisher (Tracy) and Hepburn. Poitier said he decided to do the film "because it's time the subject is dealt with straight, with no cop-outs. This subject certainly had to come up for theatrical exploration sooner or later." Said *Esquire*'s reviewer: "The liberal daddy thoughtfully gives his consent, and then has the gall to give a speech about love conquering all. . . . Stanley Kramer . . . also believes that Negroes can and should out-middle-class the white folks, and ever'thing gwine be okay. What audiences pinioned above One Hundred Twenty-fifth Street, or in one of our other great Folk Reservations, will make of this good news it's probably better not to think about." Coming to dinner were *his* parents. "These are such darlings," *Esquire* observed. "And such beautiful manners. (You can just tell they keep a spotless home.)" Tracy is the only player to win two consecutive best-actor Oscars, for *Captains Courageous* in 1937 (it was engraved "Dick Tracy") and for *Boys Town*: "I don't think anything an actor does is important," he used to say, "except maybe to himself." Hepburn: "He belonged in an era when men were men."

GUINNESS BOOK OF WORLD RECORDS

It was first published in the 1950s in the hope of providing a means for peaceful settlement of arguments about record performances in a record-breaking world—a means of turning heat into light. The publishers to this day do not list gratuitously dangerous categories, such as the lowest height for a handcuffed free-fall parachutist to dive from or the thinnest burning rope suspending a man in a straitjacket from a helicopter. The first memory of the twins who created the book is, not unnaturally, of each other. Ross and Norris McWhirter told me, "Since we suppose that it is the same for all identical twins, this is not a fact so startlingly unusual that it could be included in our own book. One of our mother's preoccupations was in endeavoring to prevent, or at least mitigate, physical injury due to our endeavors to emulate Houdini, as escapologists. We both have memories (though not our first) of the protective netting across the top of our respective cots, and the elaborate harness and straps in our joint pram (which was, as an additional precaution, put inside a locked tennis court with chain-link fencing as a second line of defense). However, the defenses were not so good on family holidays, and at Bognor Regis, on the south coast, we achieved final success at the age of two: We were found a half mile from home, inspecting some level-crossing bars on the local railway system. The puzzling mixture of anguish and relief at our discovery is jointly our first indelible memory." Ross McWhirter was killed in cold blood by Irish Republican Army terrorists in London in 1975 after he had offered a large reward for information on IRA bombers.

GULF OF BOTHNIA

Between Sweden and Finland, a 415-mile-long, 93- to 149-mile-wide sea with many islands, the northern arm of the Baltic Sea, which itself is a crooked arm of the Atlantic Ocean. This "Scandinavian lake" has low salinity; frozen for up to five months of the year, it then can be traversed by blade. It's shallow and getting shallower, despite repeated dredging. The gulf was named for its former riparian region of Bothnia—Botten in Swedish, a name that survives in two Swedish counties, Norbotten and Vasterbotten, on the northwestern shore.

GULF OF CALIFORNIA

Against the orders of Viceroy Antonio de Mendoza, Hernando Cortes directed Francisco de Ulloa to explore the Gulf of California, and he sailed to the head of the gulf, 1538–39, proving that lower California was a peninsula. Once called the Sea of Cortes (for the Spanish conquistador, conqueror of Mexico, *marques del Valle de Oaxaca*) and once the Vermilion Sea, the 700-mile-long arm of the Pacific Ocean separates the Lower California (Baja) peninsula and the Mexican mainland in part of a depression in the Earth's surface that extends inland to the Coachella Valley, in southern California. Imperial Valley was part of the northern end of the gulf until the Colorado River delta expanded. The southern end of the gulf is more than a mile deep. Aboriginal tribes live on Tiburon, one of numerous islands in the gulf, which can be stormy. Big-game sailfish and pearl, sponge, and oyster beds are come-ons.

GULF OF MEXICO

The world's largest—about 700,000 square miles. A gulf is usually defined as a body of water whose length is great compared with its width, a part of an ocean or a sea extending into the land, a partially landlocked sea that is usually larger than a bay. The Gulf of Mexico is about 1,100 miles wide and about 800 miles north to south and is bordered by five gringo states. The deepest part of the gulf is Sigsbee Deep, 12,714 feet, off the coast of Mexico. Most of the United States shrimp catch comes from the gulf. The *Ocean World Encyclopedia* states that seas may be classified as enclosed or partly enclosed. Those that are enclosed are also referred to as intercontinental seas, or mediterranean seas. Examples listed are the Mediterranean Sea, the Caribbean Sea, and the *Gulf* of Mexico.

GULF STREAM

The warm ocean current originates in the Gulf of Mexico, passes through the Straits of Florida, and flows northeast into the Atlantic Ocean, then becomes indistinguishable from the North Atlantic Drift. Gulf Stream waters are often much warmer than the surrounding waters. A ship entering the stream from the Labrador Current may momentarily be twenty degrees warmer in the bow than in the stern. The Gulf Stream was first charted by—who else?—Benjamin Franklin, after he had noted that eastbound ships took two weeks less to cross the Atlantic than did westbound ships. It was the polymath who named "the river in the ocean" the Gulf Stream.

GUMBO

There is gumbo—a rich, black, alkaline alluvial soil in the western United States which is soapy or sticky when wet—and there is gumbo—or okra, a plant native to Africa, whose mucilaginous pods are used as a vegetable and in soups and stews—and there is gumbo—a thick soup made with crabs, shrimp, ham, sometimes with chicken, beef, or sausage, and thickened with filé, the powdered leaves of the sassafras plant, or with okra. A 4,000-gallon pot is the centerpiece of the annual Gumbo Festival in Louisiana. Cajun Heaven is "gumbo, go-go, and do-do!"

GUTENBERG

In the good olde days, every booke had to be written by hand and copied by hand. (The Jewish copyists of the Bible counted every letter in an effort to guard against error.) About 1450, the German printer Johann Gutenberg figured out how to print with movable type cast in molds. It meant he could take the letters of, say, the word c h a n g e and use them again to make other words from them, such as h a g or c a n. What better way to show off his invention than to produce the most beautiful book that could ever be produced—which is what Gutenberg or, rather, others, including his erstwhile partner, did—Gutenberg had gone into debt, lost a lawsuit, and been forced to hand over to others his tools and presses and the distinction of being the publisher of about 200 copies of each of 1,282 forty-two-line pages of the first book in the Western world to be printed from movable type. The Gutenberg Bible remains the most valued book in the world—there are 47 known copies. By the 1500s, up to 9 million copies of 30,000 different books were in circulation—freedom and the Renaissance were in the air. By an extraordinary coincidence in time, movable type was invented in Tibet in the fourteenth century, but the word didn't get out.

GUTHRIE, JANET

The first woman to compete in the Indianapolis 500-mile car race. The year was 1977. The track's longtime owner, Tony Hulman, planned to start the race as usual, "Gentlemen, start your engines." When Kay Bignotti, a mechanic and the wife of the master mechanic, George Bignotti, volunteered to start Miss Guthrie's engine—mechanics, not the drivers, start the engines—Hulman announced, "In company with the first lady ever to start the Indianapolis 500, gentlemen, start your engines." Miss Guthrie's race was brief. Within ten laps, an intake valve seat cracked; a small piece disengaged from the cylinder head and vanished, and she had to quit the race after twenty-seven laps. Her favorite sport is swimming. Desire Wilson, once South African Sportswoman of the Year, has driven in many championship races but has not qualified for the Indianapolis 500; her activities there in 1984 were limited to a couple of unimpressive practice laps.

HABOOB

From the Arabic *habub*, "violent storm," which indeed is what it is. Intense heating of a desert area creates a strong dry wind that whirls up sand and dust into a wall as high as 5,000 feet—nearly a mile! They have haboobs in northern Africa, in the region of the Sudan around Khartoum, in India, and they've got them in the southwest United States. One near Tucson, Arizona, in mid-July 1971, was nothing to sneeze at.

HAGGARD, MERLE

The Nashville West exponent was mistakenly identified with the proud Okie from Muskogee, where even squares can have a ball, where Ol' Glory is still waved down at the courthouse, and the biggest thrill of all is white lightning. The "silent majority" raised its voice in praise. Haggard's an ex-con, having served twenty-seven months in San Quentin for burglary. He's been the Academy of Country and Western Music's top male vocalist many times. His father was one of Oklahoma's best fiddlers. It is said that his hedonism is best expressed when he sings that the good times are here today, let's not think about tomorrow.

HALLEY'S COMET

Edmund Halley (1656–1742) didn't know he was looking at *Halley's* comet in 1682 and he didn't live long enough to see his most famous prediction come true. The English astronomer established his scientific reputation in 1678 by publishing the first catalog of southern stars made with the aid of a telescope—*Catalogus Stellarum Australium:* 341 stars. He encouraged—and paid for—the publication of Isaac Newton's masterpiece, *Principia*. When Halley calculated the orbit of the giant comet of 1682, he noted that it was similar to those of the comets of 1531 and 1607—it appeared to be an elliptical seventy-six-year orbit. If the three comets were indeed one and the same—a mass of 50 trillion tons with a

20-million-mile tail at perihelion—it would be back again in 1758. And sure enough it was, swinging around the Sun and into view a week before the end of the year; its closest approach to Earth was on March 13, 1759. And there it was again, right on schedule, in 1835, and again, as predicted, in 1910. (Mark Twain was born in 1835 and said that he would die when Halley's comet came round again, and he did.) The comet has been identified at twenty-one returns prior to 1531. Its next return will be February 1986, but it will be badly placed for a spectacular show.

HAL 9000

"Open the pod bay door, HAL." HAL was not the original name of the computer in the far-out motion-picture saga *2001: A Space Odyssey* and Douglas Rain was not HAL's original voice. In the beginning, HAL's name was Athena, named for the goddess of war, wisdom, and fertility, and its voice was Martin Balsam's. The movie at first had a voice-over narration by Douglas Rain, the Winnipeg-born actor who has played a variety of roles in the Stratford (Ontario) Festival of Shakespearean plays. Rain became HAL when the narration was struck and the director, Stanley Kubrick, decided that Balsam's voice was too emotional, making the visuals redundant. Kubrick wanted an unctuous, patronizing, neuter quality—"Rain was great," Kubrick said. Rain: "I wrapped up my work in nine and one-half hours. I never saw the finished script and I never saw a foot of the shooting." Kubrick: "Maybe next time I'll show Rain in the flesh, but it would be a nonspeaking part, which would perfectly complete the circle." The cost of construction of the 200-inch Hale telescope at Palomar and the cost of production of *2001* were about the same: $10.5 million. And what became of Margaret Stackhouse, the seventeen-year-old North Plainfield (New Jersey) High School student whose speculations on *2001* were, for Kubrick, "perhaps the most intelligent that I've read anywhere, and I am, of course, including all the reviews and the articles that have appeared on the film and the many hundreds of letters that I have received. What a first-rate intelligence," as quoted by Jerome Agel in his book *The Making of Kubrick's 2001*? Miss Stackhouse went on to be graduated Phi Beta Kappa and summa cum laude in medieval studies/romance languages, from Princeton University, and to garner many honors in poetry, mathematics, and science, and to learn and speak seventeen languages. She died (causes still unknown at this writing) in October 1984 in Bangalore, India, where she had gone two months earlier to negotiate with her poetic muse. Her last letter to Mr. Agel ended, "The cauldron's been bubbling furiously and it now smells as though something is about ready to gel (or explode? or scorch?). Whatever the inscrutable gods decide as their next game with me . . . ."

HAMELIN

A port on the Weser River in Lower Saxony, in northcentral West Germany, Hameln (its German name) was the scene of the 1284 legend of the Pied Piper of Hamelin (its English name). The Pied Piper, in particolored clothes, rids the town of its plague of rats. When the town's officials don't make the agreed payment, the magician once more plays his pipes. This time, all of the town's children are enchanted. They follow him to Koppenberg hill, where they go through a doorway and are never seen again. Frescoes illustrating the tale adorn the town's so-called Ratcatcher's House (built 1602–03). Robert Browning—yes, *that* Robert Browning—told the story in his poem "The Pied Piper of Hamelin" (1842).

HAMLET

Adultery, fratricide, revenge, the hero's feigned madness, prototypes of Ophelia, Horatio, Polonius, Rosencrantz and Guildenstern, the journey to England, the exchange of letters—they are features in Belleforest's adaptation, in 1576, of Saxo Grammaticus' *Historia Danica* (c. 1200). Between Belleforest's story and Shakespeare's masterpiece stands a lost play. The author may have been Thomas Kyd. In it were the Ghost, probably the play within the play, and the fencing match in which Hamlet is slain. But no one else could have written the tragedy that begins, "Who's there?" Many people, when asked what events in history they would like to have witnessed, list rehearsals of *Hamlet*—Shakespeare's face, his voice, his stage directions, did he in fact play the Ghost. Hamlet has the most lines of any Shakespearean character: 1,422.

HANCOCK, JOHN

In 1755, the British offered amnesty to all colonists who would lay down their arms. The two exceptions: Samuel Adams and John Hancock. Hancock was twice president of the Continental Congress and the first signator (with a bold flourish) to the Declaration of Independence on August 2, 1776—"There, I guess King George can read that!" The wealthy Boston patriot (the mercantile business) was bitterly disappointed when he was not named commander-in-chief of the Continental Army. He was an inept treasurer of Harvard College for four years. He was elected to a term in Congress and nine times governor of Massachusetts, dying of gout in office.

HAND

A unit of measurement for a horse's height, it is four inches. A horse that is 14.1 hands high is five feet tall.

HANNIBAL

The Carthaginian general used fire and vinegar to smash a path through the Alps for thirty-seven or thirty-eight of his elephants and full baggage train. His engineers heated immovable rocks with blazing logs, then poured vinegar over the rocks. The rocks split into fragments that could be pushed aside. And where had Hannibal gotten his elephants? Probably from the Atlas Mountains of Morocco and Algeria or from south of the Sahara. "Not only did the elephants' appearance, their smell, and the noise of their trumpeting alarm both men and horses opposed to them," a director of the British Museum of Natural History has written, "but they were highly dangerous when charged, fighting with their tusks and their trunks and trampling down their opponents." Only Hannibal's elephant, named Surus, survived the war. Hannibal was an implacable enemy of Rome. He fought his way over the Pyrenees, over the Alps, and seized almost all of Italy—he bypassed Rome. Near Naples, he was reinforced—more elephants, horses, soldiers—by a convoy of ships from North Africa. He eventually withdrew into the mountains of Bruttium and was recalled to Carthage.

HANS BRINKER AND THE SILVER SKATES

The carefully researched classic of children's literature about Dutch kids and a pair of silver skates was written in 1865 by an American woman, Mary Elizabeth Mapes Dodge, who turned to her pen after her lawyer husband had died. Subsequent books, including *A Few Friends and How They Amused Themselves, Rhymes and Jingles,* and *The Land of Pluck,* and her magazine stories and editorship helped to make her the preeminent author in the field of children's literature in the United States.

THE HARDY BOYS

Edward L. Stratemeyer, under the pseudonym Franklin W. Dixon, created the teen-age detective-brothers Joe and Frank, who solve mysteries on their own or with their hardy detective father or with their hardy friends, particularly fat, good-natured Chet Morton. Stratemeyer, under a variety of pseudonyms, had other children: the Bobbsey Twins, the Boy Scouts, Nancy Drew, the Motor Boys, Tom Swift, and the Rover Boys. He greatly admired Horatio Alger, the homosexual former minister whose series of rags-to-riches stories were the most popular of the age, despite their consistently, outrageously inferior quality.

HARLEM GLOBETROTTERS

The perfectly named all-black basketball barnstormers have played in 120-degree heat in Formosa, in a sandstorm in Egypt, at one in the morning in Spain, in Attica prison, in drained swimming pools, on aircraft carrier flight decks, in bullrings, on dance floors, in opera houses, and for an audience of one at Castel Gandolfo, where their famous "Sweet Georgia Brown" theme reportedly set Pope Pius XII's toes tapping. The St. Louis Cardinals' winningest pitcher, Robert "Hoot" Gibson (two Cy Youngs), played a few months with the Trotters. Wilt Chamberlain, the second-highest scorer in the history of the National Basketball Association, donned a red-white-and-blue-striped uniform for a season. Goose Tatum's wingspan was eighty-four inches and he had the world's most successful hook shot. Marques Haynes drove everybody into hysterics with his dribbling. The team was formed in Chicago, in 1927, by Abe Saperstein, who had coached a black basketball team named the Savoy Big Five. With the Trotters, he hit the road in search of "the golden basket." Clowning acts developed after the players had proved they were among the best. (Saperstein introduced the three-point play in the American Basketball League, which folded in 1962, its second season.)

HARNESS RACING

A free-legged pacer is a pacer that races without hobbles, the leg harness that guides the horse's stride. A green horse is one that has never trotted or paced in a public race or against time. A maiden is a horse, mare or gelding, that has never won a heat or a race at the gait being raced. A standardbred is a purebred trotting or pacing horse. A nonstandard horse is a crossbred horse or one that can't be traced in breeding far enough to qualify for standard registration. A crab is a bit with prongs extending at the horse's nose—the purpose is to tip the horse's head up and help prevent it from ducking its head, bowing its neck, and pulling hard on the reins. Before it is raced, a harness horse is warmed up thoroughly, tuned to racing pitch. It might even have *six* warm-up miles under its harness before the parade to the post.

HARVARD UNIVERSITY

Galileo could have taught there, for the oldest American college was founded in 1636, five years before the blind Italian scientist died. John Harvard, grandson of a woman who was Shakespeare's neighbor, and an English clergyman in New Towne (now Cambridge, Massachusetts), was its first benefactor: 800 English pounds and 300 books; the institution was named for him in 1638. When it was incorporated and chartered in 1650, Harvard was intended to be an institution for the education of Puritan ministers. In the late 1820s it became a nucleus of theological teaching in New England. Two articles on "The New Education: Its Organization" led in 1869 to the election to the presidency of their author, Charles William Eliot, and to his expansion over forty years of a small college with attached professional schools into a great modern university.

HATHAWAY, ANNE

Shakespeare also had his "missing years." About all that we know of most of his twenties, from the early 1580s to his emergence as a playwright in London in 1592, is that there was a shotgun marriage with Ms. Hathaway, eight years his senior, and the birth of three daughters. What did the greatest playwright who has ever lived name his daughters? Susannah and the twins Hamnet and Judith. Mrs. Shakespeare was a rigid and enthusiastic Puritan; in those days, Puritans disapproved of her husband's stage activities, which may be why he moved bodkin and quill to London. After the Bard's death and funeral, in 1616—details are nonexistent—it is probable that the widow married again, Richard James, a shoemaker, a Puritan exhorter, or preacher. She would have been a catch. She died seven years later. As to the Shakespeares' children: Hamnet died young; Susannah gave birth to a daughter who married twice but had no children; Judith had three sons who had no children.

HAUPTMANN, BRUNO RICHARD

"Wanted: Information as to the whereabouts of Chas. A. Lindbergh, Jr., of Hopewell, N.J., son of Col. Chas. A. Lindbergh, world-famous aviator." The illustrated posters were omnipresent. Lucky Lindy's kid had been kidnapped in what H. L. Mencken termed "the biggest story since the Resurrection." The baby's battered body was found near his home. Two and a half years later, a carpenter, Bruno Richard Hauptmann, who had been born in Germany, was caught with the goods, part of the $50,000 ransom. Or so the authorities claimed, and still do. Anthony Scaduto's

1976 book, *Scapegoat,* based on his three-year investigation of the case and the "trial of the century," claims on the other hand that Hauptmann, who always claimed his innocence, was railroaded into the electric chair in 1936. "Every piece of physical evidence introduced at the trial was fabricated, distorted, or tampered with. Each of the key witnesses lied. All the evidence that would have helped Hauptmann prove his alibi was suppressed by the authorities. . . . When this poor guy Hauptmann came along, they came to the conclusion he was the man and they bent all the evidence to fit that preconception." Crowds shouted at the jurors, "Burn Hauptmann." Said *The New York Times* reviewer of *Scapegoat:* "Sifting out the hard data from the soft, I think that Hauptmann probably did not commit the kidnapping and very possibly had nothing to do with the extortion of the ransom, which may well have been separate crimes. *Scapegoat* should be compulsory reading for those who fear that postwar rulings by the Supreme Court protecting the rights of the accused have tied the hands of justice. By overriding the rights of Hauptmann, the authorities may well have let the real perpetrators get away." Hauptmann was offered a life sentence in exchange for a confession. He didn't confess. He may have had nothing to confess. The Lindberghs moved to England before The Bronx immigrant was fried.

HAVERSIAN CANALS

In a cross section of a long bone, a pattern of many groups of concentric circles is evident. At the center of each group of circles is a longitudinal hollow passage—that's a haversian canal, named for a seventeenth-century English physician, Clopton Havers. The canal has minute blood vessels that carry the blood supply to the osteocytes, or bone cells.

HAWAII

The last state to join the Union (1959), the only island state, the only state not on the North American continent, the southernmost state. Eight major islands, they are almost exclusively mountains of lava, which came roaring out of great fissures in the floor of the Pacific Ocean. Lava flows from Mauna Loa cover more than 2,000 square miles of Hawaii, the largest and the easternmost island of the chain. There are five volcanic cones on the island, and Mauna Loa and Kilauea are active. Mauna Loa, in fact, is believed to be the world's largest active volcano. It soars more than 30,000 feet above the bottom of the ocean, 13,680 feet above sea level. It last erupted in 1978. Kilauea has been blowing its top the last few years. Its most active vent is Halemaumau, the traditional home of Pele, Polynesian goddess of volcanoes. In its veritable lava lake geysers of lava shoot a third of a mile into the sky. The 141-square-mile island of Lanai—the pineapple island—has been owned since 1922 by Dole.

HAYDEN, TOM

The radical political activist has said he wanted to affect the politics of the President, "to make solar power versus nuclear power and economic democracy versus corporate power the issues in the United States." He was one of the Chicago Seven convicted on charges of conspiring to cause violence at the 1968 Democratic convention: "Our conviction was not for what we did but for the total crime of a disrespectful identity." The conviction was reversed. Hayden disagreed fundamentally with Weathermen politics, which emphasized violence and identification with the Third World as a substitute for organizing a mass movement among whites in the United States: "If anything, most white radicals were too soft, as the Weathermen charged, not too militant. Why should the Panthers or the Conspiracy put the clamps on the rising spirit of militancy among students and young people?" Hayden married an older woman— he met Jane Fonda on one antiwar tour, fell in love on a second, fathered a son on a third. They've been called the Mork and Mindy of the American Left, stalking horses for Presidential hopeful Jerry Brown, New Left opportunists in search of an issue. The Haydens direct the Campaign for Economic Democracy.

HAYES, GEORGE "GABBY"

What was the grizzled, gravel-voiced movie actor's name as Hopalong Cassidy's sidekick? What was the name of his trusty burro? "Windy Halliday" and "Hannibal," respectively. The comic character-actor, a headliner in vaudeville, had about a six-month lay off in pictures and decided to do away with his famous silver mop of a beard: "The barber said it would grow back in five weeks. When I looked at myself in the mirror, without the whiskers, I felt terrible. I thought I looked 20 years older. It was like walking down the street with my pants off. I went home and walked through the back door. Wouldn't dare to go in through the front door. Told my wife 'Let's get in the car and go to our house in Palm Springs until the whiskers grow back.' I stayed in the house until the whiskers came out again." He played in about 200 Westerns, with William Boyd, Roy Rogers, Gene Autry, John Wayne, Randolph Scott. A tenderfoot from Wellesville, New York, he typified the movies' notion of the Old Man of the Wild West: whiskey-sodden, cantankerous disposition, Buffalo Bill coiffure, rags, scratchy beard.

HAYES, HELEN

The octogenarian five-foot "first lady of the American stage" admits she's "bossy. I'm not imperious, I don't really want people to curtsy low before me and back out of rooms, but I do like to run things. My husband used to call me the Little Corporal, after Napoleon." The actress made her professional debut on Broadway as a shy eight-year-old in the role of Little Mimi in Victor Herbert's *Old Dutch*. She regrets that she had so many long-running plays, including her favorite, Laurence Housman's *Victoria Regina*, which was on the boards for five years: "There was an eleven-year period in which I did just five plays—a stultifying state of affairs for an actress, because the best way to become a better actress is to expand and stretch." She won a best-actress Oscar for *The Sin of Madelon Claudet* (1931), written by her husband, Charles MacArthur. She didn't dislike Hollywood "because I felt superior to the whole scene . . . it was because I didn't think I did it well. And I thought that the character of my face didn't seem to me expressive. . . . Everything about me was ordinary, ordinary. That was the word for me on the screen." At a celebrity-studded party in the late twenties, a young man approached her and asked, "Do you want a peanut?" Nearly speechless, she nodded, and with that he poured peanuts from a crumpled paper bag into her trembling hands as he said, "I wish they were emeralds." This was her introduction to Charles MacArthur. Years later, after World War II, Colonel MacArthur returned from India and poured emeralds from a brown paper bag into his wife's hand and said, "I wish they were peanuts."

"HEARTBREAK HOTEL"

It's down at the end of Lonely Street. It's a new place to dwell when your baby's left you: "We'll be so lonely that we could die." Elvis Presley popularized "the desk clerk draped in black."

HELIUM

It is the second most common atom—hydrogen is the most common element—and it forms no compounds. It makes up about 23 percent of the mass of the visible Universe. The Scottish chemist William Ramsay isolated helium from a sample of the uranium mineral clevite, in 1895. When tested spectroscopically, the gas showed lines first observed in the Sun during an eclipse in 1868, when the new element was named helium, from *helios,* Greek for "sun." It is a rare and costly gas; the United States is the major producer.

"HELTER SKELTER"

Charles "Tex" Manson, ex-reform school inmate, ex-prison inmate, said he had been inspired by the Beatles' rock song, on the White Album: "You may be a lover, but you ain't no dancer." Manson and three members of his "family" wrote the title in blood at the home of their murder victims Leno and Rosemary LaBianca, two days after they had shot, stabbed, and clubbed to death five others, including the pregnant actress Sharon Tate Polanski. To Manson, "helter skelter" meant that the black race was fated to rise up and destroy the entire white race with the exception of Manson and his cultists. The killers were sentenced to life imprisonment, rather than to death, only because the Supreme Court had outlawed capital punishment.

HEMOPHILIA

The hereditary "royal disease," "the bleeder's disease"—the families of Queen Victoria of England and King Alfonso XIII of Spain and Czar Nicholas of Russia were plagued with it. The victim experiences impaired clotting of the blood and excessive bleeding. Hemophilia is transmitted only through the female and invariably affects only male offspring. If blood taken from a vein is placed in a glass test tube, it clots in five to fifteen minutes. In a hemophiliac, the clotting time is usually thirty minutes to several hours, sometimes even longer. The word hemophilia literally means an affinity or liking for blood. Delineation of the disease first occurred in Philadelphia in 1802.

HENIE, SONJA

"All my life I have wanted to skate," the five-foot-two, dimpled, blond, Norwegian whirling dervish said, "and all my life I have skated." And all her life she was a winner—ten consecutive world titles, six European championships, and an unprecedented string of three women's Olympic championships, in Switzerland, the United States (Lake Placid), Germany, 1928, 1932, 1936—257 medals, cups, plates, bowls. She was only ten years old when she won Norway's figure-skating championship. At eleven, she copped third place in free-skating competition in the winter Olympic Games at Chamonix in the French Alps. She was inspired by the ballerina Anna Pavlova. She introduced the miniskirt; traditionally, women skaters had worn ankle-length dresses and hats. She was known as ''a good skate'' in Hollywood, where she made several movies and a lot of money. She died of cancer while flying to her home in Oslo, in 1969.

HENRY VIII

His first wife was the widow of his older brother, Arthur, who had died in his sixteenth year, a few months after he had wed, in an unconsummated marriage, Katharine of Aragon, the daughter of King Ferdinand and Queen Isabella—the same!—and set up court in Ludlow as the Prince of Wales. (Negotiations for Arthur's marriage had been initiated when he was two years old.) A year after Arthur's demise, Prince Henry was permitted by papal dispensation to marry Katharine. (Smart Papa [Henry VII] did not want to lose the Spanish dowry just because Arthur had died.) Prince Henry was handsome, hot-tempered, generous, sometimes mean-spirited, athletic, artistic, a multilinguist proficient in Latin. By marrying Katharine, the Tudors took the first step toward the English Reformation. He established the Church of England in 1534.

HEPBURN, KATHARINE

The four-time Oscar winner as best actress (from *Morning Glory*, 1933, to *On Golden Pond*, 1982) was Spencer Tracy's best friend for going on 30 years. They met in 1941 when Metro-Goldwyn-Mayer decided to star them in *Woman of the Year*. Miss Hepburn, five-foot-seven and willowy, surveyed Mr. Tracy at their first meeting and observed, ''You're not as tall as I thought you were.'' Tracy countered, ''That's all right. I'll cut you down to my size.'' No one could handle Tracy the way she could: A few simple, tactful words might do it. ''We're not going to worry about hurting other people's feelings because we don't have time,'' she said on the first day of rehearsals of her most recent Broadway success, *West Side Waltz*. She's still an independent lady: That was the madam herself who leaped off a running speedboat in *On Golden Pond*. ''If you're an actor,'' she once told Michiko Kakutani, ''it means you're automatically self-centered, and if you're self-centered, you should not burden a family. I had the most *wonderful* childhood of anyone in the world. I know how much time my parents took with us, and I thought, what would I do if I had a child and the child got sick and we had an opening night? Why, I'd be *furious* at the child. I can be terribly selfish.'' One of her directors has said, ''She's not really as strong and bossy as she appears.'' She adores calla lilies.

HERCULES

"Nothing without Hercules." The illegitimate son of Zeus, and the most popular of all Greek heroes, the courageous strongman performed ten labors to atone for having slain his wife and children in a fit of madness: Kill the Nemean Lion, which could not be wounded; kill the nine-headed Hydra of Lerna, which lived in the swamp of Lerna and roamed the countryside killing cattle and laying waste to the land; capture alive the golden-horned Cerynean Hind; capture alive the Erymanthian Boar, which was destroying the countryside; clean the stables of Augeas in a day; get rid of the Stymphalian birds; capture the Cretan Bull; capture the mares of Diomedes of Thrace; snatch the girdle of the warrior queen of the Amazons, Hippolyta; bring back the cattle of Geryon from Erythea, an island near the ocean. Hercules spent eight years doing the ten, then had to perform two more: fetch the Golden Apples of the Hesperides and bring up Cerberus, the three-headed dog, from Hades. Appropriately, a globular cluster of stars in the constellation Hercules (Heracles in Greek) is the brightest to be seen in the Northern Hemisphere.

HERSHEY

The town a candy bar made. The world's largest chocolate-manufacturing plant was built near the birthplace in Derry Township, in southeastern Pennsylvania, of Milton Snavely Hershey, who had sold his caramel-making company for a million dollars. Hershey's Milk Chocolate Bar and Hershey's vision combined to create a successful community. The economy there was stable even during the Depression. Early building activities included an amusement park, a golf course, a zoo, a football field, a dance pavilion, an outdoor theater. Subsequent construction included a hotel, a community building, a windowless office building, the senior hall of the Milton Hershey School (finished in 1934), a rose garden, a sports area, a stadium. The Hershey Museum displays American Indian and Pennsylvania Dutch artifacts and Stiegel glassware. During World War II, Hershey developed the Field Ration D bar which provided a soldier with 600 calories. The town is also headquarters of the Antique Automobile Club of America.

HESS, RUDOLPH

Hitler's devoted and fanatically loyal follower for two decades, his amanuensis on *Mein Kampf*, the nearest there was to "a friend"—the news that the beetle-browed "Brown Mouse," in May 1941, had parachuted into Scotland hit the Führer "as though a bomb had struck the Berghof." The Nazi cabinet member told the British that he was on a mission of humanity, the Führer did not want to defeat England and he wished to stop the fighting. Did a frustrated and jealous Hess believe he could restore his former position of prestige with his beloved leader by pulling off a brilliant and daring stroke of statesmanship, singlehandedly arranging peace between Germany and Britain? He was imprisoned in the Tower of London, then sentenced to life imprisonment by the International Tribunal at Nuremberg. For nearly twenty years he has been the only prisoner in Spandau, the Berlin prison run at huge cost by the British, Russians, French, and Americans.

"HE THAT IS WITHOUT SIN"

"Jesus went unto the mount of Olives. And early in the morning he came again into the temple, and all the people came unto him; and he sat down, and taught them. And the scribes and Pharisees brought unto him a woman taken in adultery; and when they had set her in the midst, They said unto him, Master, this woman was taken in adultery, in the very act. Now Moses in the law commanded us, that such should be stoned: but what sayest thou? This they said, tempting him, that they might have to accuse him, But Jesus stooped down, and with his finger wrote on the ground, as though he heard them not. So when they continued asking him, he lifted up himself, and said unto them, He that is without sin among you, let him first cast a stone at her."—The Gospel According to St. John 8: 1–12

HIAWATHA

The legendary chief of the Onondaga Indians and founder of the Iroquois Confederacy was immortalized by Henry Wadsworth Longfellow, who achieved fame with long narrative poems such as *The Courtship of Miles Standish* and *Paul Revere's Ride. The Song of Hiawatha* is in the meter of the Finnish epic *Kalevala,* a compilation of folk verses dealing with the deeds of three semidivine brothers of gigantic stature. "All your strength is in your union. All your danger is in discord; therefore be at peace henceforward, and as brothers live together. . . . By the shores of Gitche Gumee, by the shining Big-Sea-Water, stood the wigwam of Nokomis, daughter of the Moon, Nokomis. . . . As unto the bow the cord is, so unto the man is woman, though she bends him, she obeys him, though she draws him, yet she follows, useless each without the other!" Longfellow's was the first bust of an American in the Poet's Corner in Westminster Abbey.

237

HIBERNATION

Hibernation is a state of suspended animation, of reduced bodily function and activity, permitting survival by animals during periods of food shortage or water shortage. During a drought, crocodiles, alligators, and some turtles remain buried in mud until water returns. Estivation is the summer counterpart of hibernation. Fish that estivate include the lungfish and the dipnoans.

HICKOK, WILD BILL

There are two Abilenes—the one in Texas was named after the one in Kansas. Abilene, Kansas, was so rough and so tumble that it had to have the famous frontiersman James Butler "Wild Bill" Hickok as its marshal; in spite of his Prince Albert coat, checked trousers, embroidered waistcoat, and silk-lined cape—or maybe because of them—he was the fastest gun in the West. He was shot from behind by a drunken, cross-eyed gambler in Deadwood, South Dakota, during a "friendly" poker game, in 1876; Wild Bill was holding aces and eights—the "dead man's hand." Meanwhile, back at the terminus of the Chisholm cattle trail greyhound racing dogs have been bred, and President Dwight D. Eisenhower romped as a kid with his pacifist mother and is buried there. The new Abilene has a population of around 100,000, more than fifteen times its namesake. It is also the financial, commercial, and educational center of west Texas.

HILLARY, EDMUND

"Because it is there," George Leigh Mallory responded when he was asked why he wanted to scale Mount Everest. About fifty years later, in May 1953, the former beekeeper Edmund Hillary, of New Zealand, and the Sherpa guide Tenzing Norkay, of Nepal, did what no men before them, including Mallory, had done: They reached the very summit of the world's highest mountain, Chomo-lungma to Tibetans, soaring 29,141 feet at the Tibet-Nepal frontier. The mountaineers' biggest challenges: glaciers and howling winds. Hillary, who was knighted by Queen Elizabeth II, didn't get cold feet at the thought of an additional challenge. In 1958, he was part of the first expedition in 46 years to reach the South Pole by overland. Everest had been named for a British surveyor-general in India, Sir George Everest, who had determined the mountain's position and altitude, in 1841.

HIMMLER, HEINRICH

The bespectacled son of a secondary schoolmaster was a poultry farmer with a devout Roman Catholic background when he took part in Hitler's beer-hall putsch in Munich in 1923. He became head of the SS, or *Schutzstaffel*, the Nazis' blackshirted elite corps, in 1929, then head of police in Munich, then chief of the political police throughout Bavaria, then head of the Gestapo, the *Geheime Staatspolizei*, responsible for "the general welfare of the loyal subjects from the negative, as well as the positive, point of view"—a cold-blooded, bureaucratic "trustee for the consolidation of German nationhood." The Gestapo was above the law; it *was* the law. Himmler's goal was to establish the supremacy of the Aryan race by eliminating the racially unwanted and expendable. He established concentration camps and killing camps. When news reached Hitler that Himmler had tried, in April 1945, to approach the Allies for peace negotiations, he ordered his arrest. Himmler, trying to escape, was arrested by British troops; two weeks after V-E Day, he committed suicide—poison!

HINDENBURG

Thirty-two of the 97 passengers and crew were killed or later died of burns and injuries when the lighter-than-air German Zeppelin *Hindenburg,* approaching the mooring mast at Lakehurst, New Jersey, in May 1937, caught fire and in 34 seconds, in a soft-as-a-feather crash, became a white-hot, crumpled skeleton, its stern in flames, the fuselage "melting away like wax paper held to a bonfire." A thirty-third victim was a youth serving as a civilian member of the ground crew—he was unable to get out of the way when the gigantic bonfire hit the ground. The Lakehurst chief testified that the basic cause of the disaster was a hydrogen gas fire. Such a catastrophe, he claimed, would have been impossible if the transatlantic airship had been inflated with a noninflammable, nonexplosive helium gas, which was being used in American lighter-than-air craft.

HINES, DUNCAN

This guy really slept around. And ate around. And he was to make his living telling fellow travelers how it was. His goals: the satisfying meal, the good night's rest in the clean lodging. The notes he made on accommodations enjoyed and suffered as a salesman were shared with friends and acquaintances, then published in book form in *Adventures in Good*

Eating, in 1936, and in *Lodging for a Night,* a guide to inns and hotels. Additional publications included *Duncan Hines Vacation Guide,* first issued in 1948. He shaped up the culinary and sanitary practices of the American restaurant. "Recommended by Duncan Hines" meant that the inn was in.

HIPPOCRATES

He was not the first physician—his father was a physician—but he is known as the father of medicine for having founded a school of medicine on Cos in the fourth century B.C. that put medicine on a strictly scientific plane. Building the patient's strength through diet and hygienic measures should be the goal of medicine. The body's problems could be inherited. The Hippocratic oath, reflecting the Greek's ideals and principles and administered to this day to medical graduates in many universities, says in part, ". . . you will exercise your art solely for the cure of your patients and will give no drug, perform no operation, for a criminal purpose, even if solicited, far less suggest it; that whatsoever you shall see or hear of the lives of men which is not fitting to be spoken, you will keep inviolably secret."

HIROSHIMA

John Richard Hersey was born, the son of missionary parents, in Tientsin, China, in 1914, and spoke Chinese fluently before he knew a word of English. He was a war correspondent for Time, Inc., and commended for heroism for his assistance to wounded combatants on Guadalcanal. His novel *A Bell for Adano* (1944), the story of the American Army's occupation of a rural town in war-ripped Italy, was awarded the Pulitzer Prize. In 1946, *Hiroshima,* based on his interviews with six survivors of history's first atomic bombing, August 6, 1945, was published as the only article in an entire issue of *The New Yorker*—yes, advertisements ran as scheduled. The six, he wrote, "still wonder why they lived when so many others died. Each of them counts many small items of chance or volition —a step taken in time, a decision to go indoors, catching one streetcar instead of the next—that spared him. And now each knows that in the act of survival he lived a dozen lives and saw more death than he ever thought he would see. At the time, none of them knew anything." Mr. Hersey in conclusion reported that many citizens of Hiroshima felt a hatred for Americans which nothing could possibly erase, and that it would be impossible to say what horrors were embedded in the minds of the children who lived through the day of the bombing. On the surface, their recollections, months after the calamity, were of an exhilarating adventure. At "ground zero," the temperature at the moment of detonation had been several thousand degrees centigrade. Sixty-two thousand of the city's 90,000 buildings were destroyed. Of the estimated 320,000 people in the city, about 80,000 were killed instantly or wounded mortally. There are 55,000 nuclear weapons in the world today!

HITCHCOCK, ALFRED

The director of suspenseful motion pictures appeared in each of his films since assuming a bit part to "fill the screen" in *The Lodger.* He is seen twice in *The Lodger:* at a desk in a newsroom and among a crowd of people watching an arrest. *Blackmail:* reading a newspaper in a subway as he is pestered by a boy. *Murder* and *The Thirty-Nine Steps:* walking in a street. *Young and Innocent:* a clumsy photographer outside the courtroom. *The Lady Vanishes:* in a London railroad station. *Rebecca:* walking by a telephone booth. *Shadow of a Doubt:* a bridge player on a train. *Lifeboat:* in "before-and-after" photographs in a diet ad in a newspaper, "my favorite role . . . hard to think up." *Spellbound:* exiting a crowded elevator. *Notorious:* drinking champagne at a party. *The Paradine Case:* carrying a cello case. *Rope:* crossing a street after the main title. *Under Capricorn:* listening to a speech. *Stage Fright:* turning back in the street to look at the then Mrs. Ronald Reagan, who is talking to herself. *Strangers on a Train:* boarding a train carrying a double bass. *I Confess:* crossing the screen at the top of a staircase. *Dial M for Murder:* in a college photo album. *Rear Window:* winding a clock. *To Catch a Thief:* sitting next to Cary Grant in a bus. *The Trouble with Harry:* sharing the frame with the rich man poking around Wiggs's Emporium. *The Man Who Knew Too Much* (1956 version): seen from the back watching Arab acrobats. *Vertigo:* crossing a street. *North by Northwest:* being shut out of a bus. *Psycho:* wearing a wide Texas hat while standing on a sidewalk. *The Birds:* walking two small dogs. *Marnie:* strolling through a hotel corridor. *Frenzy:* in a crowd watching police retrieve a corpse (at first the cameo was to be a prop of Hitchcock's head attached to a dummy floating in the Thames). *Family Plot:* an imposing silhouette behind a door marked Registrar of Births and Deaths.

HITLER, ADOLF

Did he or didn't he? William Stevenson (*A Man Called Intrepid*) says Hitler's "little known sojourn" is authenticated. The protean biographer Robert Payne says Hitler arrived there a pale, haggard, shifty-eyed young man without any luggage who began agitatedly whispering in German to his half brother. John Toland, a World War II expert, says that reports of a visit by Hitler to Liverpool between November 1912 and April 1913 seem "to have been a tale fashioned by the Irish-actress wife of Hitler's half brother whose memoirs were never published." Hitler's sister, Paula, who died about 1960, never wrote about her brothers. Most Hitler students agree that the Austrian went abroad only once—to Germany —he never left the continent, never studied art in England. In the five months before he married Eva Braun (a day later both committed suicide), Hitler may have left his underground bunker in Berlin only once. He never had formal art training. He could render structures exquisitely but he had no natural talent for drawing the human form. He tried to peddle his drawings door to door and in beer halls. He became Germany's all-time best-selling author—a German family wouldn't be caught dead without a copy of *Mein Kampf—My Struggle*—composed in the old fortress-prison at Landsberg, high above the River Lech; he was jailed after the abortive putsch in Munich fifteen years to the day before Crystal Night. Hitler wanted to call his magnum *Four and a Half Years of Struggle Against Lies, Stupidity, and Cowardice,* but the publisher typically exercised his right to call it what he wanted to. Since Napoleon's invasion of Germany in the early nineteenth century, anti-Semitism there had been mild and innocuous. Eighty thousand German Jews fought under the Kaiser, and 12,000 were killed. Hitler's lawyers in America sued a former foreign correspondent, Alan Cranston (today a California senator), to keep him from continuing to publish an abridged, ten-cent translation of *Mein Kampf*—it included "all the outrageous, anti-Jewish parts that Hitler's Boston publisher left out," says Cranston, who wanted Americans to know exactly what the Führer was thinking. Hitler always said, "The victor will never be asked if he told the truth." (Vice-President George Bush's press secretary said in the 1984 reelection campaign, "You can say anything you want during a debate, and eighty million people hear it;" if the media report that the statement is inaccurate, "So what? Maybe two hundred people read it, or two thousand, or twenty thousand.") The Third Reich lasted little more than a decade, not the promised thousand years.

HOLIDAY, BILLIE

"When I was thirteen," the jazzy Lady Day said, "I got real evil one day and just plain decided I wasn't going to say anything or do anything unless I meant it. Not 'Please, Sir,' not 'Thank you, Ma'am,' nothing. Unless I meant it. You have to be poor and black to know how many times you can get knocked in the head just for trying to do something as simple as that. But I never gave up trying." It was said that truth was her habit, heroin only a part-time crutch. Why did she like being a jazz singer? "Nobody knows what you're going to sing before you get up there. Not even you." When Lady sang the blues, it sounded as if her shoes pinched. She was forty-four years old when she died in hospital, pure heroin hidden in a Kleenex box beside her bed.

THE HOLLYWOOD TEN

"Are you now or have you ever been a member of the Communist Party?" In the late 1940s, motion picture directors, producers, and writers refused to answer questions from the House Committee on Un-American Activities (HUAC) about Party membership. They basically based their stand on the First Amendment's guarantee against incursions on free speech rather than on the Fifth Amendment's protection against self-incrimination. They were imprisoned for terms up to one year. The ten were: Alvah Bessie, an active Party member and screenwriter *(Hotel Berlin, Objective Burma)*, who had fought in the Spanish Civil War; Herbert Biberman, a Party member who had directed *Meet Nero Wolfe* and *The Master Race;* Lester Cole, a hard-line Communist who had not gone to college and had written thirty-six films, and was running for reelection to the Screen Writers Guild executive board; Edward Dmytryk, who had directed twenty-four films, including *Crossfire;* Ring Lardner, Jr., son of the humorist and coauthor of the Oscarized screenplay for *Woman of the Year;* John Howard Lawson, founder and first president, Screen Writers Guild, and the screenwriter of *Action in the North Atlantic* and *Sahara;* Albert Maltz, an O. Henry Award winner and screenwriter: *This Gun for Hire, Destination Tokyo;* Sam Ornitz, screenwriter, twenty-five films; Robert Adrian Scott, writer-producer; Dalton Trumbo, the highest paid writer in Hollywood *(Kitty Foyle, Thirty Seconds Over Tokyo)*. An eleventh was called, answered the questions "No, no, no, no, no, never," and skipped the country: the playwright Bertolt Brecht.

HOLMES, SHERLOCK

The tall, thin, fictional sleuth with the close-fitting cap and smoking pipe made brilliant diagnoses through observation, and he was modeled by Sir Arthur Conan Doyle partly after Joseph Bell, a Scottish physician known for *his* brilliant diagnoses through observation. (Holmes was also an accomplished violinist and an expert on beekeeping.) Dr. John H. Watson —square jaw, thick neck, mustache, burly shoulders, indeterminate bullet wound—was drawn in general terms from a Major Wood, a Southsea friend. It was almost "Sherrinford Holmes"—Holmes for Doyle's revered sage of New England, Oliver Wendell Holmes—Sherrinford had a nice Irish ring to it. Dr. Watson was originally "Ormond Sacker," but the name smacked of dandyism. Doyle himself was a physician, having been educated at the Royal Infirmary in Edinburgh. After the first Holmes appeared, in *A Study in Scarlet* (originally *A Tangled Skein*), in 1887, Doyle gave up the microscope for the magnifying glass. There were four Holmes novels and fifty-six short stories. Doyle also wrote historical romances, a play, two political pamphlets justifying England's action in the Boer war, and a history of spiritualism when he became an ardent spiritualist.

HOLMES, SHERLOCK—BEEKEEPER

The fruit of his leisured ease, the *magnum opus* of his later years, the volume *Practical Handbook of Bee Culture, with Some Observations upon the Segregation of the Queen:* "Alone I did it. Behold the fruit of pensive nights and laborious days when I watched the little working gangs as once I watched the criminal world of London." Holmes was not yet fifty years of age when he quit Baker Street for a small farm on the Sussex Downs, five miles from Eastbourne, to divide his time between philosophy and apiculture. He was somewhat crippled by occasional attacks of rheumatism. He refused the most princely offers to take up various cases, but his retirement turned out not to be a permanent one. The approach of the German war caused Holmes, his trusted friend and roomie Dr. John H. Watson informs the devoted, to lay his remarkable combination of intellectual and practical activity at the disposal of the government. The historical results were recounted in *His Last Bow.*

HOLMES, SHERLOCK—COCAINE

The uncanny sleuth, smack on page one of *The Sign of Four,* "took his bottle from the corner of the mantelpiece, and his hypodermic syringe from its neat morocco case. With his long, white, nervous fingers he adjusted the delicate needle and rolled back his left shirtcuff. For some little time his eyes rested thoughtfully upon the sinewy forearm and wrist, all dotted and scarred with innumerable puncture-marks. Finally, he thrust the sharp point home, pressed down the tiny piston, and sank back into the velvet-lined armchair with a long sigh of satisfaction. . . . 'Which is it to-day,' I [Watson] asked, 'morphine or cocaine?' He raised his eyes languidly from the old black-letter volume which he had opened. 'It is cocaine,' he said, 'a seven-per-cent solution . . . I suppose that its influence is physically a bad one. I find it, however, so transcendently stimulating and clarifying to the mind that its secondary action is a matter of small moment.' 'But consider!' I said earnestly. 'Count the cost! Your brain may, as you say, be roused and excited, but it is a pathological and morbid process which involves increased tissue-change and may at least leave a permanent weakness. You know, too, what a black reaction comes upon you. Surely the game is hardly worth the candle. Why should you, for a mere passing pleasure, risk the loss of those great powers with which you have been endowed? Remember that I speak not only as one comrade to another but as a medical man to one for whose constitution he is to some extent answerable. . . .' 'My mind,' he said, 'rebels at stagnation. Give me problems, give me work, give me the most abstruse cryptogram, or the most intricate analysis, and I am in my own proper atmosphere. I can dispense then with artificial stimulants. But I abhor the dull routine of existence. I crave for mental exaltation. That is why I have chosen my own particular profession, or rather created it, for I am the only one in the world.' "

HOLMES, SHERLOCK—DIOGENES CLUB

The London club of Holmes' seven-years-older brother, Mycroft, who has an extraordinary faculty for figures and audits the books in some of the government departments—he may even be the government. When Dr. John H. Watson cannot recall the name of the club, Holmes enlightens him: "There are many men in London who, some from shyness, some from misanthropy, have no wish for the company of their fellows. Yet they are not averse to comfortable chairs and the latest periodicals. It is for the convenience of these that the Diogenes Club was started, and it now contains the most unsociable and unclubable men in town. No member is permitted to take the least notice of any other one. Save in the Stranger's Room, no talking is, under any circumstances, allowed, and three offences, if brought to the notice of the committee, render the talker liable to expulsion. My brother was one of the founders, and I have myself found it a very soothing atmosphere."

HOLMES, SHERLOCK—MORIARTY, PROFESSOR JAMES

Sherlock Holmes considered him to be the "Napoleon of crime," the most dangerous man in London, also "a genius, a philosopher, an abstract thinker." Holmes and Professor Moriarty met finally at the edge of the Reichenbach Falls, in Switzerland: ". . . a fearful place. The torrent, swollen by the melting snow, plunges into a tremendous abyss, from which the spray rolls up like the smoke from a burning house. The shaft into which the river hurls itself is an immense chasm, lined by glistening coal-black rock, and narrowing into a creaming, boiling pit of incalculable depth, which brims over and shoots the stream onward over its jagged lip. . . . An examination by experts leaves little doubt that a personal contest between the two men ended, as it could hardly fail to end in such a situation, in their reeling over, locked in each other's arms. Any attempt at recovering the bodies was absolutely hopeless, and there, deep down in that dreadful cauldron of swirling water and seething foam, will lie for all time the most dangerous criminal and the foremost champion of the law of their generation.'' But Holmes survived, confiding only in his brother, Mycroft, in order to obtain needed money; after three years, he returned to London to tell an electrified Watson: "We tottered together upon the brink of the fall. I have some knowledge, however, of baritsu, or the Japanese system of wrestling, which has more than once been very useful to me. I slipped through his grip, and he with a horrible scream kicked madly for a few seconds, and clawed the air with both his hands. But for all his efforts he could not get his balance, and over he went. With my face over the brink, I saw him fall for a long way. Then he struck a rock, bounded off, and splashed into the water.''

HOLMES, SHERLOCK—MRS. HUDSON

Sherlock Holmes's landlady—plus housekeeper, cook, office manager, curator, foil, admirer, and occasional assistant. In economic terms, it has been said that she did very well for herself. She charged a "princely" monthly rent, according to John H. Watson: "I have no doubt that the house might have been purchased at the price which Holmes paid for his rooms during the years that I was with him." She was also a devoted worrywart. In *The Sign of Four*, she was concerned for Holmes's health. She told Watson: "After you was gone he walked and he walked, up and down, and up and down, until I was weary of the sound of his footstep. Then I heard him talking to himself and muttering, and every time the bell rang out he came on the stairhead, with 'What is that, Mrs. Hudson?' And now he has slammed off to his room, but I can hear him walking away the same as ever. I hope he's not going to be ill, sir. I ventured to say something to him about a cooling medicine, but he turned on me, sir, with such a look that I don't know how ever I got out of the room." She accompanied Holmes into retirement on a small farm on the Sussex Downs, where he soon had another bee in his bonnet.

HOLMES, SHERLOCK—MYCROFT

Sherlock Holmes's smarter brother, "the most indispensable man in the country. Tall, portly, heavily built, massive, with a suggestion of uncouth physical inertia in his figure. Above this unwieldy frame there perched a head so masterful in its brow, so alert in its steel-gray, deep-set eyes, so firm in its lips, and so subtle in its play of expression, that after the first glance one forgot the gross body and remembered only the dominant mind. He had the tidiest and most orderly brain with the greatest capacity for storing facts of any man living. The same great powers that Sherlock Holmes had turned to the detection of crime he had used for his particular business. You would be right in thinking that Mycroft was under the British government. You would also be right in a sense if you said that occasionally he *is* the British government. The conclusions of every department were passed to him, and he was the central exchange, the clearinghouse, which made out the balance. All other men were specialists, but his specialism was omniscience. 'Why do you not solve it yourself, Mycroft? You can see as far as I?' 'Possibly, Sherlock. But it is a question of getting details. Give me your details, and from an armchair I will return you an excellent expert opinion. But to run here and run there, to cross-question railway guards, and lie on my face with a lens to my eye—it is not my metier. No, you are the one man who can clear the matter up. If you have a fancy to see your name in the next honours list—' ''

HOLMES, SHERLOCK—*A STUDY IN SCARLET*

Six pages into the reprint from the reminiscences of John H. Watson, M.D., late of the army medical department—Conan Doyle's first Holmes —we meet The Great Deducer: "His very person and appearance were such as to strike the attention of the most casual observer. In height he was rather over six feet, and so excessively lean that he seemed to be considerably taller. His eyes were sharp and piercing, save during those intervals of torpor; and his thin, hawk-like nose gave his whole expression an air of alertness and decision. His chin, too, had the prominence and squareness which mark the man of determination. His hands were invariably blotted with ink and stained with chemicals, yet he was possessed of extraordinary delicacy of touch, as I frequently had occasion to observe when I watched him manipulating his fragile philosophical instruments. . . . Nothing could exceed his energy when the working fit was upon him; but now and again a reaction would seize him, and for days on end he would lie upon the sofa in the sitting room, hardly uttering a word or moving a muscle from morning to night. On these occasions I have noticed such a dreamy, vacant expression in his eyes, that I might have suspected him of being addicted to the use of some narcotic, had not the temperance and cleanliness of his whole life forbidden such a notion. . . . His ignorance was as remarkable as his knowledge. Of contemporary literature, philosophy and politics he appeared to know next to nothing. . . . 'I consider that a man's brain originally is like a little empty attic, and you have to stock it with such furniture as you choose.

It is a mistake to think that the little room has elastic walls and can distend to any extent. Depend upon it, there comes a time when for every addition of knowledge you forget something that you knew before . . . [don't have] useless facts elbowing out the useful ones.' "

HOLY KAABA

The holy of holies for Muslims, the nearly cubic-in-shape stone sanctuary in a courtyard at the Great Mosque of Mecca, in western Saudi Arabia, which all Muslims face when praying. The south wall houses the most venerated Muslim object, the Black Stone, which legend says was sent from heaven by Allah and is today the object of ritual kissing. The Kaaba was a pagan holy place before the founder of Islam, the prophet Muhammad, was born in Mecca. On a road around the Kaaba pilgrims perform the seven-fold circuit, or *tawaf*. In the classic *New Yorker* drawing by Peter Arno, two Westerners driving in the Arabian desert hail a praying Muslim, "Hey, Jack, which way to Mecca?"

"HOLY TOLEDO"

The once common exclamation, ejaculation, the expression of surprise, awe, or mild vexation is now rare but still understood. Medieval Toledo was an important religious center for Moors and Spanish Catholics. A holy city to both, it was noted for its mosques, cathedrals, and solemn coronation pomps. (The exclamation "Holy Cow" was first broadcast nationally in the United States by a Chicago play-by-play baseball announcer, perhaps on first looking on a homer.)

HOMOSEXUALITY

About ten percent of the population of the United States, or about 23 million men and women, may be homosexual, that is, in the Kinsey definition, they have had more than six sexual experiences with a member of the same sex. The Institute for Sex Research, in 1978, reported that 20 percent of the gay men it had interviewed in San Francisco, by far the most permissive city in the nation, the "gay mecca" of America, had attempted suicide. More than half of the white males and one-third of the black males each said that he had had at least 500 sexual partners. ("Show me a happy homosexual," says a character in *The Boys in the Band*, "and I'll show you a gay corpse.") Many of the world's luminaries have been homosexuals: Socrates, Plato, Euripides, Sappho, Erasmus,

Michelangelo, Leonardo, Marlowe, Sir Francis Bacon, Tchaikovsky, Rimbaud, Verlaine, Proust, Gide, Maugham, Gertrude Stein, Willa Cather, Forster, Whitman, Crane, Colette, Laughton, T. E. Lawrence, Lorenz Hart, Benjamin Britten, Noel Coward, Santayana, Isherwood, Keynes, Auden, Cole Porter, Montgomery Clift, Diaghilev, James Baldwin, Allen Ginsberg, Truman Capote, Tennessee Williams—Oscar Wilde spent two years at hard labor in jail after a trial for the love that dared not speak its name (i.e., for his relationship with the son of the Marquess of Queensberry, whose name adorns boxing's rules). In his controversial book, *Overcoming Homosexuality,* Robert Kronemeyer, of New York, claimed from a quarter-century of clinical experience with gay men and women that homosexuality stems from a disabling psychological disorder that can, if therapeutically treated, be overcome: "With rare exceptions, homosexuality is neither inherited nor the result of some glandular disturbance or the scrambling of genes or chromosomes. Homosexuals are made, not born 'that way.' I firmly believe that homosexuality is a learned response to early painful experiences and that it can be unlearned. For those homosexuals who are unhappy with their life and find effective therapy, it is 'curable.' " President Ronald Reagan declared in 1984 that his administration would resist efforts to obtain any "government endorsement of homosexuality."

HONG KONG

The British comedian Derek Nimmo likens the crown colony to a psychiatrist—"it's the last refuge of the insane." The Chinese reckon it to be a three-legged stool—with one leg in London, one leg in Peking, the third leg in Hong Kong itself. Bordering 22 miles of southeast China, on the estuary of the Canton River, the colony comprises Hong Kong Island, ceded by China in 1842 after Britain's victory in the Opium War; Kowloon peninsula, and the mountainous New Territories—in all, 399 square miles, 4 million cramped people, mostly Chinese. The capital is officially named Victoria but is commonly called Hong Kong; it is at the foot of 1,805-foot-high Victoria Peak on the northwest shore of Hong Kong Island. When Britain's ninety-nine-year lease expires on June 30, 1997, the People's Republic of China plans to stuff troops into what was once known as a Victorian white elephant and is now the world's third-largest port.

HONOLULU

The kingdom of Hawaii had monarchs of course, from Kamehameha I, in 1810, to Queen Liliuokalani, 1891–93, or until the United States proclaimed the country a protectorate and established a republic, in 1894, with Sanford B. Dole as president. (Liliuokalani wrote two popular songs, "Aloha Oe" and "Farewell to Thee.") The capitol of the monarchs was Iolani Palace, in Honolulu, the only royal palace in the United States. It stands across the street from the state capital. The governor resides in Washington Place, a home of Queen Liliuokalani. Tourists visit a home of the wife of King Kamehameha IV that is known as Queen Emma's Summer Palace.

HOPE, BOB

His obituary will be published under the loving headline "Thanks for the Memory" and will mention that after graduation from high school in Cleveland he tried his hands at boxing under the name "Packy East." Packy East presently packed it in. The suave, great actor and comedian remembers that he got his first laugh when he hit a sour note at the end of a song in a family gathering. (If the family doesn't laugh, who will?) But Ski Nose was soon on the Road to Lucre with his extraordinary talent for the funny. He's entertained America's fighting men around the globe for more than four decades. Once when he showed up unannounced in Wyoming, the locals ducked for cover—"Where there's Hope, there's war." The English-born octogenarian has laughed all the way to the bank —he's one of the nation's richest men.

HOUSEFLIES

It's a fly-by-night old wives' tale, that there are no ordinary houseflies in Alaska. The housefly cannot breed in the cold climate there. Those trapped in packages shipped there soon die, without reproducing. So why are there so many houseflies in the forty-ninth state?

"THE HOUSE OF THE RISING SUN"

Many a poor country boy and many a poor country girl have been ruined in this bawdy house in New Orleans, popularized in several traditional songs. "Go tell my baby sister (or brother), never do like I have done, tell her (him) shun that house in New Orleans, they call the Rising Sun." Ambidextrously, that is, on the other hand, there are those who went back to New Orleans, the true capital of the South in antebellum days, more than willing to wear that ball and chain and spend the rest of their days Beneath the Rising Sun.

HOUSTON ASTRODOME

"If the Astrodome is the eighth wonder of the world," Houston Oilers' owner Bud Adams said, "the rent is the ninth." It is the world's largest air-conditioned room; an eighteen-story building could fit inside. The temperature is maintained at seventy-two degrees. It has baseball's longest dugouts (120 feet) because the planners realized that most people like to boast, "I sat behind the dugout." Baseball's first indoor game was an exhibition between the host Astros and the New York Yankees, on April 9, 1965. Baseball's longest single may have been hit there. Mike Schmidt, of the Philadelphia Phillies, struck a tape-measure blow—but the ball crashed into a public-address speaker 117 feet above the field, 329 feet from home plate. What might have been a 500-foot blast was "held" to a single.

HOWE, GORDIE

Professional hockey's best all-around player came out of retirement to play one season (1979–80) with the Hartford Whalers when he was in his late forties and the Whalers were a new franchise in the National Hockey League. He played in 1,767 games in five decades and 26 seasons (25 with the Detroit Red Wings, 1946–71) and posted these N.H.L. records: most games; most seasons; most goals—801; most assists—1,049; most points—1,850; most games including playoffs—1,924; most goals including playoffs—869; most assists including playoffs—1,141; most points including playoffs—2,010; most 20-or-more goal seasons—22; most consecutive 20-or-more goal seasons—22. He was penalized 1,685 minutes —that's more than 28 hours in the box. In 157 playoff games, he scored 68 goals, 42 assists, 160 total points.

HUCKLEBERRY FINN

"If Mr. Clemens cannot think of something better to tell our pure-minded lads and lasses, he had best stop writing for them." Which is how Louisa May Alcott greeted Mark Twain's classic, in 1885. When the Committee of the Public Library of Concord, Massachusetts, expelled *Huck* from their library as "trash and suitable only for the slums," Twain chortled, "That will sell 25,000 copies for us sure." There were actually 51,000 sales, hardcover, within the first couple of months of publication. The book had seemed to be jinxed. An engraver made a last-minute addition to the printing plate of a picture of old Silas Phelps. In a pleasant scene in which an appreciative Aunt Sally asks, "Who do you reckon it is?," the graffitist, whose identity was never discovered, sketched in the male sex organ, turning the illustration into a flagrant case of indecent exposure. The incident forced postponement of publication of the book.

HUDSON, HENRY

Not much is known about the English navigator and explorer. Nothing at all, in fact, except for the years (1607–11) in which he sailed four times west across the Atlantic in search of a sea route to the Orient. He sailed the Dutch East India Company's *Half Moon* into the Hudson River nearly a century after the King Francis of France-sponsored Italian navigator and pirate Giovanni da Verrazano had. This was during Hudson's third voyage, and he had already poked around what is now North Carolina and explored, briefly, Chesapeake Bay and Delaware Bay. He traveled along the "Hudson" River to Albany. His first two voyages to the New World, in the *Hopewell,* were sponsored by an English trading firm, the Muscovy Company; he got no farther than the ice east of Greenland, but his reports of whales in northern waters led to English and Dutch whaling expeditions near Spitzbergen. On his fourth, and last, odyssey, again sponsored by English merchants, he sailed the *Discovery* south of Greenland, through Hudson Strait, into Hudson Bay, and south to James Bay, where the ship became stuck in the ice. In the spring (1611), some members of the crew mutinied and set Hudson, his son John, and seven loyal sailors adrift in a small boat that was never seen again. European explorers were still at sea two centuries later as to how to cross the Arctic Ocean into the Pacific—the Northwest Passage.

HUDSON RIVER

The 315-mile-long Hudson River, navigable by ocean vessels to Albany, the capital of New York State, was discovered by the Florentine explorer Giovanni da Verrazano skippering the *Dauphin* on a French-sponsored expedition. On his return to the French seaport of Dieppe, on a July day in the year 1524, Verrazano wrote to his employer, "his most serene and Christian Majesty," Francis I, "We found a pleasant place below steep little hills. And from among those hills a mighty deep-mouthed river ran into the sea. . . . We rode at anchor in a spot well guarded from the wind, and we passed into the river with *Dauphin*'s little boat. . . ." Eighty-five years later, an 80-ton Dutch East India Company yacht, the shallow-bottomed, high-pooped *Half Moon,* commanded by the English sea captain Henry Hudson, nosed into the "Hudson" in Hudson's search for the Northwest Passage to China: "This is a very good land to fall with and a pleasant land to see. . . ."

HUMMINGBIRD

There's nothing ho-hum about these mighty mites, the smallest birds in the world—they're found only in the Western Hemisphere and only 19 varieties of the 400 species in the family *Trochilidae hum* zip around the United States. The smallest of the smallest is the fairy hummingbird of Cuba: 2¼". There is a "giant" hummer, *Patagonia gigas,* 8½", in the Andes of South America. The hummingbird beats its wings 50 to 70 times a second, making a hum, thus getting its name. It seems they don't sit still for a moment, diving, racing at speeds of up to 60 miles per hour. They can't stand on their own two feet—they're too weak to support the birds on a flat surface.

HUNDRED YEARS' WAR

Actually, an intermittent 116-year war, 1337–1453, ignited when Edward III of England married Philippa of Hainault and assumed the title King of France. Other immediate issues: establishment by England of trading markets in the Low Countries and France's support of Scotland against England. The Treaty of Bretigny was signed in 1360 after a series of English victories, including Crecy and Poitiers. In 1373, du Guesclin regained most of the lost French territory. In 1415, the English routed France's pride-and-joy knights at Agincourt. Joan of Arc rallied French forces. In 1453, England held only Calais, and made no further attempt to conquer France, which finally conquered Calais in the 1500s. Shakespeare dramatized the war in *Henry V* and *Henry VI:* "And gentlemen in England now a-bed Shall think themselves accurs'd they were not here, And hold their manhoods cheap whiles any speaks That fought with us upon Saint Crispin's day."

HURLING

It's an Irish game (two 30-minute halves) resembling field hockey or lacrosse. Two teams of fifteen players on a field 240 feet by 420 feet use a broad-bladed stick (a hurley) to catch, balance, and run with or hurl a nine- to ten-inch cork-centered ball (a slitter). The goal: hurling the slitter over or under the crossbar of the goalposts. For getting the slitter under the crossbar of the goal the team gets three points, but it nets only one point for getting it over the crossbar. A player may catch the ball in his hands or pick the ball off his hurley and hit it fungo-style. He may not use his hands to pick up or to hurl the slitter. Running with the ball in his hands is a no-no.

HYDROGEN

It is the major fuel in the fusion reactions from which stars derive their energy. Hydrogen makes up about three-quarters of the mass of the Universe, or over 90 percent of the molecules. Two hydrogen atoms and one oxygen atom (oxygen is the third most-common atom) make up the molecule of water, the most common compound in the Universe. Colorless, odorless, tasteless (under ordinary conditions), hydrogen was discovered as a substance distinct from other flammable gases in 1766 by the English chemist and physicist Henry Cavendish. The Greek notion of the elements received its death blow when Cavendish, in 1784, demonstrated that hydrogen, on burning, produced water. The German airship *Hindenburg* that exploded at Lakehurst, New Jersey, was filled with hydrogen—the fiery crash was the death knell for lighter-than-air mass transportation.

I

I AM CURIOUS (YELLOW)

"When I attended the Rendezvous in the early afternoon," Vincent Canby wrote in *The New York Times*, in 1969, "the crowds were large, mostly middle-aged, and ruly. This week's landmark film doesn't seem to be unhinging the populace." Watching sexual congress in a tree or on a balustrade in front of a royal palace or even more titillating stuff was like being softened to death by detergent commercials. But Rex Reed got his pecker up: "This genuinely vile and disgusting Swedish meatball is pseudo-pornography at its ugliest, and pseudo-sociology at its lowest point of technical ineptitude." At first, Vilgot Sjoman's Swedish film (1969) was confiscated by the U.S. Customs and found obscene by a federal court jury. Another court kept its head, and so there was another milestone in the fight against censorship. *I Am CURious (George)*—now *there's* an idea, Darryl.

ICE AGE

The fourth, or most recent, ice age melted off the Scandinavian peninsula only 8,000 years ago and off the northern Canadian mainland barely 6,000 years ago. Ice covering Greenland and Antarctica is still two miles thick. Ice has ruled the climate of the Earth. A mile or more thick, the last advance of ice (the Pleistocene glacial period) carved out the Great Lakes basin, covered virtually all of Canada, and stretched as far south on the American mainland on a line westward from Cape Cod across Long Island, New Jersey, and Pennsylvania, along the Ohio and Missouri rivers to North Dakota, across northern Montana, Idaho, and Washington to the Pacific. Ice sheets covered the British Isles and northern Germany and the northwest Soviet Union. In South America, Patagonia and the southern Andes lay under an extension of the Antarctic sheet. The Pleistocene made possible the first migration of man from Asia into North America. The "greenhouse effect" could melt enough ice to raise sea levels four to seven feet by the year 2100. The first National Scientific

Reserve in the United States is the Ice Age, 32,500 acres in Wisconsin containing features of continental glaciation.

ICEBERG

Since establishment in 1914 of an international ice patrol in the wake of the *Titanic* disaster in the North Atlantic south of Newfoundland, not a single ship has collided with an iceberg in regions guarded by cutters patrolling the steamer lanes. About 16,000 icebergs, which break off from glaciers, form annually in the Arctic; one has floated as far south as the latitude of northern Florida. Icebergs in the North Atlantic tend to be peak-shaped; those in the South Atlantic are more often flat-topped and block-shaped. Some bergs are as tall as a twenty-five story building, which means that they extend a quarter-mile or so under the waterline. It is not surprising that nine-tenths of a berg is under water. What is surprising is that as much as one-tenth of the "floating crystal castle" (the Irish monk St. Brendan's description in 500 A.D.) is above water. Ice floats because water expands when it freezes, but almost everything else contracts on freezing. Small flat icebergs have been fitted with sails and piloted from the Antarctic to Peru and Chile.

ICE SKATING

The axel is a jump from the forward outside edge of one ice skate with 1½ turns in the air and a return to the backward outside edge of the other skate. It's also known as Axel Paulsen. The Haines spin, or the Jackson Haines spin, was named for the American skater and instructor who made popular the sit spin: a spin on one skate made in a squatting position, usually with the free leg stretched out in front of the body.

I CHING

The Book of Changes is said to be the world's oldest and most revered system of fortune-telling—"the modern key to your true destiny." How did the system develop? Five millennia ago, Emperor Fu Hsi—"born after twelve years in gestation"—constructed from markings on the back of a tortoise the eight diagrams that are the basis for *I Ching*. It was first of all a book of divination, an attempt to resolve doubts of the mind or mysteries of the Universe. Would a particular day be the right day to make a pilgrimage? Would it be wise to plant certain crops? Would Ah Chang be gracious enough to grant deliverance from the menacing calamities of the day, whether they be threats from barbaric tribes or Halley's comet? Would the Supreme Being be interested in the creative effort? The bisexual occultist Aleister Crowley, labeled "the beast" and "the wickedest man in the world," who was expelled from Sicily by Mussolini in 1923, translated the Book of Changes. He believed passionately in the predictions of the *I Ching* as he spread his belief in the worship both of the Sun and of man's organ of creation—sexual union was the highest form of religious devotion. He read the hexameter to mean that he must create a community, the archetype of all future communities, whose only code of convention would be the law "Do What Thou Wilt." Every man and every woman was a star. The only sin was restriction.

IDES OF MARCH

Every month in the Julian calendar had an Ides. It was the fifteenth of March, May, July, and October, the thirteenth of the other months. Plutarch wrote, "Furthermore, there was a certain soothsayer that had given Caesar [idolized, deified, hated, whoring Caesar] warning long time afore, to take heed of the day of the Ides of March . . . for on that day he should be in great danger. That day being come, Caesar going into the Senate-house and speaking merrily unto the soothsayer, told him, 'The Ides of March be come.' 'So be they,' softly answered the soothsayer, 'but yet are they not past.' " He was right—for a change? In addition to the Ides, two other days in the month were used for counting the date in the Julian calendar: the Kalends, the first day of the month, and the Nones, the seventh day in March, May, July, and October, the fifth in the other months. The days were counted before, not after, the Kalends, Nones, and Ides. Because the Romans counted inclusively, January 10 was the fourth day before the Ides of January or the fourth day of the Ides of January.

IDIOT

The idiot savant, now called the savant syndrome—a mentally retarded individual possesses a remarkable, highly developed ability or talent in one area, such as rapid calculation, music, or feats of memory. Such cases, the *Longman Dictionary of Psychology and Psychiatry* has pointed out, are rare and usually occur in a person who is mildly or moderately retarded. The celebrated Leslie Lemke—he is retarded, blind (he has no eyes), and cerebral-palsied—one middle-of-the-night began to play from memory Tchaikovsky's *Piano Concerto #1*—perfectly. Soon, he was also playing Gershwin's *Rhapsody in Blue*. He can play from memory anything he hears only once. A sudden gift for mimicry had

257

Leslie singing like Luciano Pavoratti in two Italian operas, Jimmy Durante in "Inka Dinka Doo," Louis Armstrong in "Hello, Dolly," and doing both parts of the Jeanette MacDonald-Nelson Eddy duets in *Sweethearts*. Another youth, who has never spoken a word and has spent most of his life rocking in a chair, can perfectly align a scrambled Rubik's cube in less than forty seconds. An autistic young man, who has difficulty counting up to ten, sculpts horses from memory. There is in The Bronx a "calendar computer" who can't multiply 5 × 7, but George Finn has the ability to identify in a matter of seconds the day of the week of any given date, such as May 25, 1930. He can recall the weather on every day of his adult life. He scored perfectly when he was interviewed by Morley Safer on CBS' "60 Minutes." The film ended with the savant both effusively thanking Mr. Safer (whose name he could not recall) for visiting with him and saying, perhaps unthinkingly, "and I will remember this day as long as I live." It's all a wonderful mystery that isn't being solved —remarkable memories, islands of genius in brains otherwise retarded. Obviously, the brain doesn't know what it doesn't know.

INDIA—STATES OF MYSORE AND MADRAS

The southwest Indian state of Mysore, bordering on the Arabian Sea, changed its name to Karnataka in 1973. The linguistic uniformity of the state and its superlative educational system contribute to one of India's highest literacy rates. Before independence, in 1947, Mysore was a prosperous and progressive princely state ruled by a maharaja. It was a pioneer in hydroelectric power development. Today, Karnataka is governed by a chief minister and a cabinet responsible to a bicameral legislature (with one elected house). Madras is the capital of the state of Tamil Nadu on the Bay of Bengal. It was largely built, about 1640, around the British outpost of Fort St. George. Near the city is Mount St. Thomas, the traditional site of the martyrdom, in 68 A.D., of the apostle Thomas, who may be buried in Madras.

INHERIT THE WIND

"He that troubleth his own house shall inherit the wind: and the fool shall be servant to the wise of heart"—Proverbs 11:29. *Inherit the Wind*—the title of the long-running Broadway drama and movie about the "monkey trial" in Tennessee—evolution vs. fundamentalism. "The fruit of the righteous is a tree of life; and he that winneth souls is wise. Behold, the righteous shall be recompensed in the earth: much more the wicked and the sinner."

I.N.R.I.

The initial letters of the Latin *Iesus Nazarenus Rex Iudaeorum.* "And they took Jesus, and led him away. And he bearing his cross went forth into a place called the place of a skull, which is called in the Hebrew Golgotha: Where they crucified him, and two others with him, on either side one, and Jesus in the midst. And Pilate wrote a title, and put it on the cross. And the writing was, JESUS OF NAZARETH, THE KING OF THE JEWS. This title then read many of the Jews: for the place where Jesus was crucified was nigh to the city: and it was written in Hebrew, and Greek, and Latin. Then said the chief priests of the Jews to Pilate, Write not. The King of the Jews; but that he said, I am King of the Jews. Pilate answered, What I have written I have written."—The Gospel According to St. John 19: 16–22.

INSECT

There are three times as many insect species as all other animal species together, and thousands of new insects are added every year to the list of more than 1,100,023 species already described. The beetle is the largest of 27 orders; next, in order of size, are the moth, the butterfly, the wasp, the ant, the bee, the fly, the mosquito. The adult insect is the only flying invertebrate. Fossil records indicate that many species exist today in much the same form as they did 200,000,000 years ago. About 80 percent of all insect species go through the stages of egg, larva, pupa, and adult. The fruit fly has been the major experimental animal in genetics.

INTERPOL

*Inter*national Criminal *Pol*ice Organization, the international agency for exchanging police information among member nations. It cannot arrest anyone directly. Headquarters were established in Vienna in 1923 and reestablished in Saint-Cloud, a Paris suburb, after World War II. There are departments to develop and disseminate information on murder, burglary, assault, larceny, car theft, missing persons, bank fraud, embezzlement, drug traffic, moral offenses, forgery, and counterfeiting. Big cases have involved the narcotics trade and abductions for purposes of enforced prostitution. Interpol has itself been investigated. The London Sunday *Times* reported that "far from being the slick and sophisticated organization of popular mythology, Interpol . . . wracked by political conflict and short of money . . . [and is considered] an irrelevance by

259

many police forces" in the world. It has been described by one police official as "little more than a post office. It takes no initiatives of its own." Only a few days after Interpol boasted that the "French connection" was no longer operative, New York officials confiscated heroin valued at $12 million that had come through the French connection.

I.Q.

Intelligence quotient (I.Q.) test scores appear to be related to success in school but have surprisingly little to do with success in careers. Studies show that the majority of successful people in any field have I.Q. scores that fall within the normal range. Dr. Arthur Jensen, a psychologist at the University of California, Berkeley, generated headlines several years ago when he proposed that differences in I.Q. among races are mostly hereditary rather than environmental. Robert J. Sternberg, a psychologist at Yale University, contends that intelligence tests should measure mental skills like insight. An example: Water lilies double in area every twenty-four hours. At the beginning of the summer there is one water lily in the lake. It takes sixty days for the lake to become covered with water lilies. On what day is the lake half-covered? The fifty-ninth day. Alfred Binet, the French psychologist, devised the I.Q. test, a rating of intelligence based on psychological tests, calculated by dividing the mental age by the chronological age, and multiplying by 100 to eliminate decimals. He developed a variety of verbal and numerical test items that could be used to determine a child's mental age and to differentiate between learning-disabled children and others who had the ability to succeed. He was dismayed to have it applied to normal children. A normal intelligence quotient ranges from 85 to 115. Only one percent of the people in the United States have a genius I.Q. of 140 or over. Two hundred is tops. It has been figured that John Stuart Mill had an I.Q. of 190. Thomas Jefferson and Benjamin Franklin, 145; George Washington and Abraham Lincoln, 125.

IRISH FAMINE

The potato crop along the eastern seaboard of the United States and Canada was ravaged by a blight in 1842, but the population was not dependent on the recurring fruitfulness of the potato. Ireland's impoverished, growing population was. About half of the people there lived on small farms, many others had to pay high rents to landlords. When a strange disease attacked the potato crop, the country was in very bad shape. A scientific commission appointed by Prime Minister Robert Peel failed to discover that blight is actually a fungus growth and not a disease of the potato itself. It doesn't rain, it pours. Winter—with no food at hand—was the harshest and longest in memory. "Famine fever" was in fact typhus and relapsing fever. There was dysentery and scurvy. Starvation led to famine dropsy, or hunger edema. About three-quarters of a million people died in the Great Hunger, 1845–46, and hundreds of thousands emigrated. The potato had become the principal crop of Ireland because it grows so well there—when it is healthy. English explorers discovered the spud in the New World.

IRISH WOLFHOUND

The world's tallest dog—it's about thirty-four inches high at the shoulder, and weighs about 140 pounds—was a gift of great status for the all-time A list. Cardinal Richelieu and Henry VIII and Elizabeth I couldn't get enough of them. It was depicted in stories, legends, and paintings, and the Celts had some along on their invasion of Greece in 279 B.C. The Spanish poet Lope de Vega wrote a sonnet to the wolfhound. Muscular, strongly though gracefully built, rough, wiry coat usually gray in color, it was bred as a hunter. It almost became extinct by the middle 1800s as a result of the gradual disappearance of its natural quarry, the wolf and the elk, and the depletion of its native Irish stock by exportation. Thanks to G. A. Graham, it has its day again; the breed has been revived and now is kept primarily as a companion dog.

IRVING, WASHINGTON

The life-long bachelor, who had trained as a lawyer, was encouraged to stick to literature by Sir Walter Scott when they met when the New Yorker was in England to run the Liverpool branch of the family hardware business. He did, and he didn't. He was a diplomatic attaché at the American embassy in Madrid and at the American legation in London, and from 1842 to 1846 the American minister to Madrid. Still, he did keep his pen busy: He was the first native American to succeed as a professional writer, an essayist, a pioneer in humor and the modern short story: "Rip Van Winkle," "The Spectre Bridegroom," and "The Legend of Sleepy Hollow" were popular folktales. Other Irvings, often of uneven quality: *A History of New York,* his satire that introduced Father Knickerbocker; *The Life and Voyages of Christopher Columbus,* a five-volume biography of George Washington, *The Conquest of Granada,* and *Bracebridge Hall* (1822), which established him as the leading man of letters. Oxford University honored Irving with an honorary degree.

ISLETS OF LANGERHANS

The pancreas is the large glandular organ—it secretes digestive enzymes and hormones—that lies crosswise beneath the stomach and is connected to the small intestine at the duodenum. The islets of Langerhans, named for the man first to describe them, are endocrine cells scattered among the enzyme-producing cells of the pancreas. The islets secrete the hormones insulin and glycogen directly into the bloodstream, where they regulate the level of glucose. "Insulin" is from the Latin word for "island."

ISRAEL

It was admitted to the United Nations on May 11, 1949, a year after being founded, with Chaim Weizmann as president and David Ben-Gurion as prime minister. Albert Einstein had turned down the Presidency because, he said, he had no head for human problems.

ISTHMUS OF CORINTH

About twenty miles long and four to eight miles wide, between the Gulf of Corinth and the Saronic Gulf, it connects the Greek peninsula with what otherwise would have been the island of Peloponnese. The Corinth Canal, built at the end of the last century, crosses the windswept isthmus; parallel to it are the ruins of the ancient Isthmian Wall. The city of Corinth, on the gulf's southeastern shore, was one of the most important (large, wealthy, powerful) cities of ancient Greece. Homer said that it was the home of Medea and Sisyphus; things at times *were* uphill for Corinthians. Earthquakes have wracked the area, and Romans in 146 B.C. knocked it down. Julius Caesar ordered the city rebuilt and St. Paul founded a church there in A.D. 51.

IVORY

A semisolid vascular pulp that gathers phosphates and becomes hardened, it is not easily damaged or destroyed. It does not burn and it is little affected by immersion in water. Walrus tusks are ivory, as are the teeth of the hippopotamus, the narwhal, the sperm whale, and some types of wild boar and wart hog; because they are small, they have little commercial value. The best source of ivory are the good-sized tusks of male and female African elephants and male Asiatic (Indian) elephants. The tusks, or upper incisor teeth, grow during all of the elephant's life. Every tusk that comes to market represents a dead elephant. The solid (or close-grown) scrivello tusk is used for making billiard balls.

IWO JIMA

Formerly Sulphur Island, only 750 miles from Tokyo, the largest (but only 8 miles square) and most important of the three Volcano Islands, in the western Pacific. Seventy-four consecutive days of pounding by air and sea preceded the U.S. Marines' invasion in February 1945. The jagged "doorstep of Japan" was taken at great cost: 4,189 U.S. servicemen killed, more than 15,000 wounded. More than 21,000 Japanese soldiers were killed in interlocking underground strongholds, in thousands of blockhouses and pillboxes and fortified caves; only 200 were taken prisoner. Iwo Jima was needed as a base for fighter planes, a haven for crippled aircraft, a refueling depot for B-29 Superfortresses returning to bases in the Mariana Islands after raids on Japanese cities. The famous Joe Rosenthal photograph—"The Spirit of '45"—was made when the Stars and Stripes was planted on rocky, extinct volcano Mount Suribachi.

J

JACKSON, REGGIE

"Mr. October" is at his blisterin' best before crowds of 10,000 to 20,000 —which should make him "Mr. Second Week in April." Twice the most valuable player in the World Series, once the most valuable player in the American League, and four times the league's home-run leader, the much traveled (four teams) outfielder has struck 500 HRs and also holds the major leagues' strikeout record—he's whiffed more than 2,000 times. As a New York Yankee, he hit four home runs on four consecutive swings in the Yankees' World Series triumph of 1977, three in the last game. He had been benched in the third game of the Series, against the Los Angeles Dodgers, because "I'm fairly certain [principal owner George] Steinbrenner had already made up his mind to let me go, so he wanted to sweep the Dodgers without me." The Yankees lost that game. Jackson also says he never said he was "the straw that stirs the drink," it was Goose Gossage who said it. His self-picked memorable home runs include an inside-the-parker and the one he hit in his next at-bat after being hit in the face by a pitch. He doesn't list his famous home run in Tiger Stadium in the 1971 All-Star game: "It didn't mean a thing. It was an All-Star game. The game didn't count."

JACKSON, THOMAS

"There is Jackson, standing like a stone wall!," said Confederate General Barnard Bee about Confederate General Thomas Jonathan "Stonewall" Jackson at the First Battle of Bull Run, in Virginia, in the first year of the Civil War. Two years later, General Robert E. Lee's most trusted lieutenant—a brilliant tactician and a veteran of the Mexican War—was killed by friendly fire after turning the right wing of the Union army at Chancellorsville, Virginia. He probably never met or even *saw* Barbara Fritchie, celebrated in John Greenleaf Whittier's ballad for facing down Jackson as his troops marched through Frederick, Maryland, in 1862. She was ninety-five years old and bedridden when Whittier had her protesting the dragging of the United States flag in the dust: "Shoot if you must this old gray head, but spare your country's flag." The ballad was popular with Southerners, too, for Whittier had noted Jackson's chivalry: " 'Who touches a hair of yon gray head, dies like a dog! March on,' he said."

"JACK SPRATT"

He all but fasted. Mrs. Spratt always went whole hog. The nursery rhyme goes, "Jack Spratt could eat no fat, His wife could eat no lean, And so betwixt them both, They licked the platter clean." Jack has been a popular name in rhymes and poems and songs for children. The house that Jack built. Jack and Jill went up the hill. Little Jack Horner sat in a corner. Jack and the beanstalk. Jack Robinson. Jack be nimble, Jack be quick. Jacky shall have a new master. There was even a blackbird named Jack: "There were two blackbirds, sitting on a hill, the one named Jack, the other named Jill; fly away, Jack! fly away, Jill! Come again, Jack! Come again, Jill!" By the way, Jack finished building the house.

"JACK THE RIPPER"

The London butcher struck five times, twice in one night, between August 31 and November 9, 1888, and was never heard from again..Street-walkers, bag ladies good only with the bottle: a pretty mess when the Ripper did his dirty work. Kelly: her breasts, kidneys, heart, nose, and liver were found on a table by a bed in room 13 Miller's Court. Nichols, Stride, Eddowes, Chapman: slaughtered on the street. The case is still open at Scotland Yard.

JAI ALAI

"Faster than a speeding bullet"—not really, of course, but that's how fast this handball-like game seems to be played—speeds *do* exceed 150 miles per hour. In Spanish Basque, jai alai means "merry festival." To avoid collisions, left handers are not allowed to play. The player uses a wicker basket or scoop (cesta) attached to his right arm to heave the ball, or pelota, against the three walls of the court (concha). The ball is about three-fourths the size of a baseball and much harder and far more lively. It is made of hand-wound virgin de Para rubber, from Brazil, which is wrapped in a layer of linen thread and two coats of especially hardened goatskin. The outer cover is replaced frequently. The jai alai auditorium is called a fronton—the first one in the United States was in Miami—and betting is popular; spectators sit on the fourth, nonwall side of the playing area.

JAMES BOND

A billion tickets—that's been the ticket for the James Bond movies. Plus all those television showings for free; with only a couple of exceptions, every telecast has generated a viewership that puts the film near the top or at the tippy top of the weekly Nielsen chart. In Bondage seem to be men ages 18 to 49, no matter who's playing Bond, Sean Connery, Roger Moore, David Niven, or George Lazenby. Lazenby? He was Bond in *On Her Majesty's Secret Service* (1969). The only movies that rival 007 in TV staying power feature Clint Eastwood. Bond, with a license to kill, was the creation of Ian Fleming, who also wrote the children's book *Chitty-Chitty Bang-Bang*.

JARRY PARK

Major league baseball's first game outside of the United States was played in the first home park of the Montreal Expos when they joined the National League in 1969. Parc Jarry was a good-sized playing field—420 feet to center field and 340 feet down the foul lines. But the seating capacity was not major league—under 30,000. In 1977, the Expos moved to the stadium (capacity: 58,000) that had been built for the 1976 Olympic Games in Montreal.

JASON

If the son of the deposed king of Aeson of Ioleus, in Thessaly, could retrieve the golden fleece from King Aeëtes of Colchis, in Russian Georgia, he would be allowed to assume the throne usurped by Pelias. In the Greek myth, the golden fleece was the magical coat of the winged ram on which Phrixus had escaped from Thebes to Colchis. Phrixus sacrificed the ram to Zeus, hung its fleece in the grove of Ares, and installed a dragon to make sure it wasn't fleeced. Jason and the Argonauts sailed after the fleece on the *Argo*, a beam for which had been cut from the divine tree of Dodona, which could foretell the future. Jason retrieved the fleece with the help of the enchantress Medea. When he broke his oath of fidelity to Medea, he was made by the gods to wander for many years.

JEEVES

He was a valet—a gentleman's personal gentleman who first entered the literary world in a story by his creator, P. G. Wodehouse, in a volume entitled *The Man with Two Left Feet*. His very first spoken line was, "Mrs. Gregson to see you, sir." His second was, "Very good, sir. Which suit will you wear?" In scores of novels, the unflappable Jeeves leads his seigneur and employer, Bertie Wooster, out of his scrapes. "We must think, sir," Jeeves says. "You do it," Wooster replies. "I don't have the equipment." He was a clever talker, sophisticated, a mastermind, a defender of the simple. "Butlers have always fascinated me," Wodehouse once said. "As a child I was raised on the fringe of the butler belt. And all through the years these men have piqued my curiosity. Mystery hangs about them like a nimbus. How do they get that way? What do they think about?" Pelham Grenville Wodehouse, who had moved from England to the United States in 1910, was living in France when World War II erupted. He was interned in Poland by the Germans, then moved to the plush Adion Hotel in Berlin, where he made five broadcasts on prison camps for the Nazis. He was denounced in the West as a Hitlerite and a traitor. The Germans then moved him and his wife to the plush Bristol Hotel in Paris, where they stayed until the liberation. Wodehouse was knighted by Queen Elizabeth in 1975, shortly before he died.

JEFFERSON, THOMAS

"Here was buried Thomas Jefferson, Author of the Declaration of Independence, of the Statute of Virginia for Religious Freedom, and the Father of the University of Virginia." The third President, who died dead-broke on July 4, 1826, wrote his own epitaph, and chose not to list his two-term presidency. For years, he sent to friends copies of both the original Declaration and the final version and asked which version they preferred. He could not attend the Constitutional Convention of 1787—he was serving as the United States's minister to France. He did not attend ceremonies marking George Washington's death nor did he write a note of condolence to Martha Washington—he had been Washington's first Secretary of State, and was John Adams' Vice-President when the Father of His Country died—there was a chill between Jefferson and Washington in the late 1700s. In 1800, Jefferson and Aaron Burr tied in electoral votes for the Presidency. Jefferson won the election forced into the House of Representatives by only one vote and only after thirty-five ballots. (Burr became Vice-President and the deadlock prompted passage of the Twelfth Amendment.) He's been the only Vice-President to serve two full terms as President. He signed into law legislation prohibiting the importation of slaves legally into the United States after New Year's Day 1808. His book collection was the core of the Library of Congress. In drawing up the course of study for the University of Virginia, which he founded at Charlottesville after retirement from the White House, Jefferson made it a point to omit religious instruction.

JEREZ

The amber wine of varying sweetness known as sherry took its name from the city of Jerez de la Frontera in Cadiz province in southwest Spain, in Andalusia, celebrated for both its sherry and its cognac, which got *its* name from the French city of Cognac on the Charente River. Jerez is also celebrated for its horses of mixed Spanish, Arabian, and English blood.

JERUSALEM

Under the name of Zion, it has figured familiarly in Jewish and Christian literature as a symbol of the capital of the Messiah. Half a mile above sea level to the west of the Dead Sea and the Jordan River, it is today the capital of Israel and a holy city for Jews, Christians, and Muslims. The Sabbath is observed on three different days: on Sunday, by Christians; on Saturday by Jews, who dominate the modern section, or West Jerusalem; and on Friday, by Muslims, or Arabs, who dominate East Jerusalem, in which the Old City is located. The Old City is a quadrangular area built on two hills and surrounded by a wall more than four centuries old. In the second century, Hadrian rebuilt the city, which had been demolished by the Roman emperor Titus in A.D. 70, as a pagan shrine called Aelia Capitolina, and he forbade Jews to live there. West Jerusalem was made the capital of Israel in 1949, and the Old City was seized in the Arab-Israeli war of 1967.

JESSEL, GEORGE

Every time the "toastmaster general of the United States" saw half a grapefruit he automatically stood up and announced, "Ladies and gentlemen, we have here tonight. . . ." Jessel said he was a showman . . . a songwriter, a producer, a dramatist: "You might say I'm a comedian by necessity. Luck? I'm just about breaking even. . . . Success? I haven't even gotten anywhere yet"—he was forty-five years old at the time. Brooks Atkinson observed, "At his best, Jessel is a master entertainer. If there ever was a man born for the stage, it is Mrs. Jessel's comic and sentimental son Georgie, who can make an audience sit back and expand and enjoy itself." His "appallingly bad taste" autobiography, *So Help Me,* sold like French postcards. Burton Rascoe commented: "If it is bought by all the persons Mr. Jessel believes are out to do him dirt plus all the others whom he mentions by name, the book will be a fair success even if nobody else buys a single copy."

"JESUS WEPT"

The shortest verse in the Bible, John 11:35. Jesus saw that his friend Lazarus was dead and He wept. "Then said the Jews, Behold how he loved him! Could not this man, which opened the eyes of the blind, have caused that even this man should not have died? Jesus therefore again groaning in himself cometh to the grave. . . . And Jesus lifted up his eyes, and said, Father I thank thee that thou hast heard me. And I knew that thou hearest me always: but because of the people which stand by I said it, that they may believe that thou hast sent me. And when he thus had spoken, he cried with a loud voice, Lazarus, come forth. And he that was dead came forth, bound hand and foot with graveclothes: and his face was bound about with a napkin. Jesus saith unto them, Loose him, and let him go. Then many of the Jews which came to Mary, and had seen the things which Jesus did, believed on him. But some of them went their ways to the Pharisees, and told them what things Jesus had done. . . . Then from that day forth they took counsel together for to put him to death." The longest verse in the Bible is Esther 8:9. The shortest chapter is Psalms 117—two verses. The longest chapter: Psalms 119—176 verses.

JEW'S-HARP

That small lyre-shaped musical instrument with a thin metal tongue that you place between your teeth and strike with a finger—it's a Jew's-harp. From the Dutch *jeugd-tromp* for "youth's trumpet." It's been twanged for a millennium in China, nearly 700 years in Europe. In Germany, Jew's-harps have been made with as many as sixteen tongues.

JOAN OF ARC

After hearing "voices" of saints, the Domremy farmgirl convinced the dauphin to let her lead a French army in the Hundred Years' War. In the name of God, she raised the siege of Orleans, took English posts on the Loire, and set back the English at Patay. She stood beside the reluctant dauphin when he was crowned King Charles VII at Rheims, in 1429. He made no attempt to rescue her, however, when she fell into English hands. In 1431, the Maid of Orleans was burned at the stake in Rouen by French clerics who supported the English and demanded she both deny her claim of direct inspiration from God and accept the church hierarchy. In a rehabilitation trial, Charles made belated recognition of her services. Joan was beatified and canonized nearly five centuries later. Her feast day is May 30.

JOHANNESBURG

South Africa's largest city is "the city that was built on gold"—ductile, malleable gold, the world's most precious metal. (The chemical symbol for gold is Au—from the Latin *aurum*, "shining dawn.") Gold was discovered in the Transvaal, in northeastern South Africa, in 1886. By the turn of the century, about 100,000 called Johannesburg their burg and spread out more than a mile up the southern slopes of the Witwatersrand. Field Marshal Jan Christiaan Smuts became a hero. He was instrumental in the creation (in 1910) of the Union of South Africa and he was a power in government into the late 1940s; he was prime minister during World War II. Johannesburg's international airport is named for him. The city's hundreds of thousands of blacks, many of whom work in mines, live in Soweto, a ghetto of townships in the southwestern section.

JOHANSSON, INGEMAR

He was the first European since Max Schmeling to be named Fighter of the Year and the first European heavyweight boxing champion since Schmeling—and the first Scandinavian champion ever. He trained for his 1959 title bout with the champion Floyd Patterson by installing his fiancee in his Catskills camp and by dining and dancing up a storm with her at night in New York City. Ingo knocked down Patterson six times and the referee stopped the fight in the third round. One of Ingo's atomic punches instantly became part of boxing lore. In 1960, Patterson became the first fighter ever to regain the heavyweight title, knocking out the handsome Swede in the fifth round. The rubber match was in '61 in Miami Beach's Convention Hall. There was a first round like no other since Jack Dempsey and Luis Firpo murdered each other in 1923. Ingo jumped up at the ten count in the sixth round but it was too late. The battered Patterson said, "We both fought a confused fight, I think, we didn't know what we were doing at times." Johansson, who liked to watch American movies, became a movie actor while still a boxer. He was in *All the Young Men*, with Alan Ladd, Sidney Poitier, and Mort Sahl: racial prejudice among twelve Marines in the Korean War. Johansson is the last white to wear the heavyweight crown.

JOHN, ELTON

In green silk shirt, pink pants and floppy oversized cap, the "singer and pianist" was the first rock star to play Russia, in 1979: "I think people there were not used to the sort of concert we gave them." Captain Fantastic once said he'd like to be singles champ at Wimbledon. In 1971, he had four albums in the top ten. His hits in the '80s have included "I Guess That's Why They Call It the Blues" and "Sad Songs (Say So Much)." The bisexual John, who admits he got a lot of funny telegrams at his wedding in 1984, believes "sorry seems to be the hardest word." He's planning to give up marathon tours and to concentrate on making records and doing occasional concerts.

JOHNNY APPLESEED

The frontiersman's real name was John Chapman. Nothing is known about him until he was about twenty-five years old and began collecting seeds from apple orchards and cider presses in Pennsylvania. He headed west, fructifying the earth in Ohio, Indiana, and Illinois. Nineteenth-century migrants, the legend goes, followed his trail of seedling orchards. Marietta, Ohio, is today the center of one of the finest apple regions in the nation. Appleseed was said to have had a way with animals, even beasts. He was eccentric in dress; he would wear a tin plate on his head.

JOHNSON, ANDREW

The only southern senator loyal to the Union on the eve of the Civil War, he was dragged from a train by a mob in Virginia as he was returning to Tennessee from Abraham Lincoln's first presidential inauguration. A noose was placed around his neck, but he was let go when somebody suggested that Tennessee should have the privilege of the lynch. Later, Johnson convinced the President to exempt Tennessee from the Emancipation Proclamation. Johnson had been an indentured servant to a tailor. He couldn't write and could barely read until he was taught by his wife, who was only sixteen when they were married. As a state senator, he suggested that a new state, to be named Frankland, be carved from the mountain regions of four southern states, including the eastern part of his own state. He became Lincoln's running mate in 1864 when the Republicans dumped Vice-President Hannibal Hamlin, a Maine liberal.

On February 24, 1868, the House voted by a wide margin to impeach the seventeenth President for trying to force the Secretary of War out of office in the face of Congress' Tenure of Office Act. He was given only ten days to prepare for his Senate trial for "high crimes and misdemeanors during Reconstruction." He claimed he was obeying the Constitution as he understood it. He was acquitted of the Tenure charge by one vote. He was similarly acquitted of two other charges, and additional charges were dropped. In 1875, he became the only former President to sit in the Senate; he served a few months before dying. Near his burial site was a willow tree taken as a shoot from a tree grown at Napoleon's tomb on St. Helena.

JOHNSON, LYNDON B.

A couple of weeks after barely edging out the challenging Senator Eugene McCarthy in the New Hampshire presidential primary in March 1968, the thirty-sixth President announced on prime-time television that he would neither seek nor accept renomination, he would utilize the remainder of his term in a nonpartisan search for peace, and beginning immediately there would be a reduction, even a halt of the bombing of northern North Vietnam. Still, five months later, five thousand demonstrators clashed with police in the streets of Chicago when the Democrats met there to choose Vice President Hubert Humphrey to head the ticket against Richard M. Nixon. An eyewitness, Norman Mailer: "Children, and youths, and middle-aged men were being pounded and gassed and beaten, hunted and driven by teams of policemen who had exploded out of their restraints like the bursting of a boil. . . . It was as if war had finally begun, as if the gods of history had come together before the television cameras of the world and the eyes of the campaign workers and the delegates' wives and half the principals at the convention . . . as if the Democratic Party had broken in two before the eyes of the nation." Johnson had recognized that "many Americans live on the outskirts of hope—some because of their poverty, some because of their color, and all too many because of both. Our task is to help replace their despair with opportunity." ". . . The challenge of the next half century is whether we have the wisdom to use [our] wealth to enrich and elevate our national life—and to advance the quality of American civilization . . . we have the opportunity to move not only toward the rich society and the powerful society but upward to the Great Society . . . a place where the meaning of man's life matches the marvels of man's labor."

JOHNSON, LYNDON B.—THE GREAT SOCIETY

One afternoon in the White House swimming pool, while paddling around with Bill Moyers, Richard Goodwin, and others, President Lyndon B.

Johnson said he wanted to let the country know where he was going. Goodwin drafted the Good Society speech for the President's delivery at the first presentation of the Eleanor Roosevelt Memorial Award. It was discarded for a more woman-oriented one, then redrafted for a commencement address at the University of Michigan on May 22, 1964. L.B.J. promised to assemble the best thought and the broadest knowledge from all over the world to find answers for America. He challenged the graduates to join in the battle to build the Great Society: "There are those timid souls who say this battle cannot be won, that we are condemned to a soulless wealth . . . let us from this moment begin our work so that in the future men will look back and say: It was then, after a long and weary way, that man turned the exploits of his genius to the full enrichment of his life." On the plane back to Washington, L.B.J. was euphoric. He even had a drink, a Scotch highball. (Vietnam was still just a cloud no bigger than a man's hand.) Hugh Sidey, *Time* magazine's columnist on the presidency, has noted that he was amazed at some of the devices Johnson would use to get what he wanted: "He would lie, beg, cheat, steal a little, threaten, intimidate. But he never lost sight of that ultimate goal, his idea of the Great Society." He began with Medicare.

JOHNSON, LYNDON B.—POVERTY

Lyndon B. Johnson wanted to be the President who had eliminated poverty. In his State of the Union message less than two months after succeeding to the presidency, L.B.J. declared, "This administration today, here and now, declares unconditional war on poverty in America. I urge this Congress and all Americans to join with me in that effort. It will not be a short or easy struggle—no single weapon or strategy will suffice—but we shall not rest until that war is won. One thousand dollars invested in salvaging an unemployable youth can return forty thousand dollars or more in his lifetime." It was to be a "hand up" rather than a "handout." Congress appropriated $970 million—Barry Goldwater called the enterprise "a Madison Avenue stunt"—and Sargent Shriver was named to head the Office of Economic Opportunity.

JOHN THE BAPTIST

Long a puzzle to the Church has been Jesus' baptism by his cousin John in the River Jordan. If He was born sinless, why did He undergo the baptism of repentance for the remission of sins? ". . . And it came to pass in those days, that Jesus came from Nazareth of Galilee, and was baptized of John in Jordan. And straightway coming up out of the water, he saw the heavens opened, and the Spirit like a dove descending upon him: And there came a voice from heaven, saying, Thou art my beloved Son, in whom I am well pleased. . . . And when the daughter of the said Herodias came in, and danced, and pleased Herod and them that sat with him, the king said unto the damsel, Ask of me whatsoever thou wilt, and I will give it thee. And he sware unto her, Whatsoever thou shalt ask of me, I will give it thee, unto the half of my kingdom. And she went forth, and said unto her mother, What shall I ask? And she said, The head of John the Baptist. And she came in straightward with haste unto the king, and asked, saying, I will that thou give me by and by in a charger the head of John the Baptist. And the king was exceedingly sorry; yet for his oath's sake, and for their sakes which sat with him, he would not reject her. And immediately the king sent an executioner, and commanded his head to be brought: and he went and beheaded him in the prison. And brought his head in a charger, and gave it to the damsel: and the damsel gave it to her mother."—The Gospel According to St. Matthew 3, 14.

JONES, BOBBY

Woodrow Wilson, a frustrated golfer, defined the sport as "an attempt to place a small little sphere . . . in a slightly larger hole . . . with utensils totally unsuited to the task." Robert Tyre Jones, Jr., knew something. He won a junior golf tournament when he was only nine, and in the 1920s popularized the sport all by himself. He won the U.S. Open four times, the U.S. Amateur five times, the British Open three times. In 1930, he became the only player to make the grand slam—winning the National Open, the National Amateur, the British Open, the British Amateur. He quit tourney play at age twenty-eight. "Emperor Jones" became a practicing lawyer. He founded the prestigious Masters tournament at the Augusta National Golf Club, which he had helped to establish. In 1958, he was honored with the freedom of the burgh of St. Andrews, Scotland, site of the world's most famous golf course—the only other American so to be honored was Benjamin Franklin.

JONES, THE REVEREND JIM

A self-styled Messiah and the founder of the People's Temple cult, he insisted on complete obedience from his flock of religious fanatics at Jonestown. "We are committing an act of revolutionary suicide, protesting the conditions of an inhuman world," he told them in November 1978, in his commune in Guyana. He ordered fruit juice to be laced with cyanide and 913 of his 1,000 followers drank up. Jones himself didn't. He was found shot to death, but it isn't known if he killed himself or was killed by a follower who didn't want to follow him anymore. "Our Father Who Art in Hell."

JOPLIN, SCOTT

"The king of ragtime" played in honky-tonks, a euphemism in those days for whorehouses, the resident "professor," or pianist, setting the rhythm for stripping in many a bordello. He classicized two popular American dance forms, the cakewalk and the two-step. Joplin piano rags are hailed as "the precise American equivalent, in terms of a native style of dance music, of minuets by Mozart, mazurkas by Chopin, or waltzes by Brahms." His ragtime—the rhythm has strong syncopation in the melody with the accompaniment in 2/4 time—fused African-white–American-European elements—the first music to allow the black and white races to function on both the creative and the performing levels. Joplin studied music at George Smith College, an educational institution for blacks sponsored by the Methodist Church. "Maple Leaf Rag," in 1899, was an instant hit. A folk ballet and ragtime operas failed to gain recognition, but his ragtime music, highly innovative, lyric, supple, was indeed a serious art form. Joplin rags were used as background music for the motion picture *The Sting,* in 1973, and his popularity was rejuvenated, 2/4.

JORGENSON, CHRISTINE

"I feel very content with what I am and who I am. I just hope I can grow old gracefully." In 1953, the former Army private (two years) George W. Jorgenson, Jr., had come back from abroad Christine Jorgenson after elective surgery—the world's first publicized sex-change operation—several major operations, thousands of hormone injections. She recalls that "insanity reigned" when she landed from Copenhagen—"The press followed me everywhere as if they expected me to suddenly do something bizarre—strip off my clothes and run naked in the street. I guess I disappointed them." In nightclubs the blonde chanteuse has swept onstage wearing a floor-length fur coat over a strapless gold lame gown and purred her theme song, "I Enjoy Being a Girl." She has been engaged twice but never married. She delivers lectures on "gender identity" to college students. "I found that as long as I told them the truth, we get along great," she told a *Newsweek* reporter. "They want to know everything, and they aren't filled with a lot of prejudice." The best of times are now.

JOSEPH

"Israel loved Joseph more than all his children, because he was the son of his old age: and he made him a coat of many colors. And when his brethren saw that their father loved him more than all his brethren, they hated him, and could not speak peaceably unto him. . . . And it came to pass, when Joseph was come unto his brethren, that they stript Joseph out of his coat of many colors that was on him . . . And they took Joseph's coat, and killed a kid of the goats, and dipped the coat in the blood; And they sent the coat of many colors, and they brought it to their father, and said, This have we found: know now whether it be thy son's coat or no. And he knew it, and said, It is my son's coat, an evil beast hath devoured him; Joseph is without doubt rent in pieces. And Jacob rent his clothes, and put sackcloth upon his loins, and mourned for his son many days. [Much Later, in Egypt] And Joseph said unto his brethren, I am Joseph; doth my father yet live? And his brethren could not answer him; for they were troubled at his presence. And Joseph said unto his brethren, Come near to me, I pray you. And they came near. And he said, I am Joseph your brother, whom ye sold into Egypt. Now therefore be not grieved, nor angry with yourselves, that ye sold me hither; for God did not send me before you to preserve life. . . . Haste ye, and go up to my father, and say unto him, Thus saith thy son Joseph, God hath made me lord of all Egypt: come down unto me, tarry not: . . . And Jacob's heart fainted, for he believed them not. And they told him all the words of Joseph, which he had said unto them: and when he saw the wagons which Joseph had sent to carry him, the spirit of Jacob their father revived: And Israel said, It is enough: Joseph my son is yet alive: I will go and see him before I die.''—Genesis 37–45.

JOSEPHINE

Napoleon was probably never caught napping on any subject. Nor, as you will see, asleep at the switch. "Woman is given to man," he said, "that she may bear him children; . . . consequently, she is his property, just as the fruit of the tree is the property of the gardener." France's imperious emperor-general and number-one male chauvinist pig swinishly added, "We treat women too well, and in this way have spoiled everything. We have done every wrong in raising them to our level. Truly the Oriental nations have more mind and sense than we in declaring the wife to be the actual property of the husband. In fact, nature has made woman our slave." He really dug Josephine, the comely widow six years his senior who had had two children with the late Vicomte Alexandre de Beauharnais (the guillotine, the unkindest cut of all). When empress, she did not come through with an heir; the marriage was annulled and Napoleon married by proxy a woman he hadn't even laid eyes on—the daughter of Emperor Francis I of Austria, the Hapsburg Archduchess Marie-Louise, who had written, "I am sorry for the unfortunate princess whom [Napoleon] will choose." She did her duty and he did his thing when they finally got together and Napoleon got his son, Napoleon II, and the two nations lived happily ever after for a while. Josephine lived in retirement at Malmaison. Marie-Louise chose not to live in exile and eventually married twice more. Napoleon II died of tuberculosis in Austria at the age of twenty-one. In 1940, his remains were transferred from Vienna to Paris at Hitler's direction—a gift to France from the Führer—and laid to rest beside his father's in the Invalides.

JOUSTING

The Jousting Hall of Fame is located at Natural Chimney's State Park, Mount Salon, Virginia. Since 1962, the joust has been Maryland's official state sport, although the mounted combatants eager to be "well seene at armes" now spear dangling rings rather than "tourney one against one, or two against two." The joust was a military exercise, generally performed at a court of a prince or at the castle of a feudal lord, a single combat bout fought by two knights with weapons of war. "Charge, sir knight." There was the *joute à l'outrance,* or mortal combat, and the *joute à plaisance,* or joust of peace. The tournament is said to have been invented in the eleventh century by a French baron, Geoffre de Prulli. Henry II of France died of a wound incurred in a tournament. By the sixteenth century, "joust in time," the martial element in the game had yielded to gorgeous show; promoters may have run out of free lancers.

JOYCE, JAMES

The most famous date in all of English literature, in all of world literature —June 16, 1904—the day that everything happens in James Joyce's *Ulysses.* It was the date that Joyce had his first "appointment" with his future wife, the tall, auburn-haired Nora Barnacle. (Hearing her name, Joyce's witty father said, "She'll never leave him.") She had stood Joyce up two days earlier, and he sent around a note to the slightly exalted rooming house Finn's Hotel, where she worked: "I may be blind. I looked for a long time at a head of reddish brown hair and decided it was not yours. I went home quite dejected. I would like to make an appointment but it might not suit you. I hope you will be kind enough to make one with me —if you have not forgotten me." She showed up on the 16th, and Richard Ellmann has written, "On June 16 he entered into relation with the world around him and left behind him the loneliness he had felt since his mother's death. He would tell her later, 'You made me a man.' To set Ulysses on this date was Joyce's most eloquent if indirect tribute to Nora, a recognition of the determining effect upon his life of his attachment to her." The lawyer Morris Ernst persuaded the United States that the banned *Ulysses* was not obscene, and he received in payment from Random House a share of the royalties rather than a one-time fee.

JUDAS ISCARIOT

His name may have been a corruption of the Latin word for "murderer," *sicarius*. If so, Jesus' betrayer may have belonged to the Sicarri, the radical anti-Roman Jewish sect. This possibility supports the theory that the disciple, and probable treasurer of the dozen, might have betrayed the Son of God out of disappointment and anger. Judas was looking for a political Messiah and Jesus was not going to be he. He repented and killed himself even before Christ was crucified. "When the morning was come, all the chief priests and elders of the people took counsel against Jesus to put him to death: And when they had bound him, they led him away, and delivered him to Pontius Pilate the governor. Then Judas, which had betrayed him, when he saw that he was condemned, repented himself, and brought again the thirty pieces of silver to the chief priests and elders. Saying, I have sinned in that I have betrayed the innocent blood. And they said, What is that to us? see thou to that. And he cast down the pieces of silver in the temple, and departed, and went and hanged himself. And the chief priests took the silver pieces, and said, It is not lawful for to put them into the treasury, because it is the price of blood. And they took counsel, and bought with them the potter's field, to bury strangers in. Wherefore that field was called, The field of blood, unto this day."—The Gospel According to St. Matthew 27.

JUDGMENT AT NUREMBERG

The nine-months international war crimes trial staged at the scene of delirious annual Nazi party rallies was not the basis for the 1961 motion picture; Maximilian Schell, as a German defense lawyer, won the best-actor Oscar in the film about the relatively minor trial of Nazi judges several years after World War II. A dozen of the Nazi war criminals at the Nuremberg trial, which opened on November 20, 1945, were sentenced to death; they included Hermann Goering, Joachim von Ribbentrop, Wilhelm Keitel, Alfred Rosenberg, Julius Streicher, Alfred Jodl, and, in absentia, Martin Bormann. Among the acquitted were Franz von Papen and Hjalmar Schacht. Rudolph Hess and Eric Raeder were sentenced to life imprisonment, and Albert Speer was sentenced to twenty years. The Americans had wanted the trial from the first. The British were opposed to it as late as 1944. Stalin's view: "The grand criminals should be tried—before being shot." The defense lawyers at Nuremberg argued that the defendants could not be held liable for crimes that were not punishable when they committed them. Robert H. Jackson, an Associate Justice of the United States Supreme Court, and the chief American prosecutor, argued that punishment would be for acts regarded as criminal since the time of Cain. In Tokyo, the Allies tried twenty-eight Japanese war criminals. The Tokyo Military Tribunal sentenced seven of the defendants to death; they included Premier Hideki Tojo, whose suicide attempt was thwarted by an American doctor, who arranged a quick blood transfusion. Also executed were General Kenji Doihara, who had engineered the Mukden incident of 1931 that led to the capture of Manchuria; General Heitaro Kimura, commander of Manchuria; General Iwane Matsui, commander of troops in the rape of Nanking; General Akira Muto, chief of staff, the Philippines; Koki Hirota, the pre–Pacific-war premier, and Seishiro Itagaki, the war minister.

JUDO

An Olympic event since 1964, when the international games were staged in Japan, judo was developed in the 1880s by a Japanese, Jigoro Kano, a little man who wanted to defend himself against bullies; in 1909, he became the first Japanese to be on the International Olympic Committee. Judo makes use of the weaponless system of self-defense (*jujitsu*) developed over a period of two millennia by Buddhist monks in China, Japan, and Tibet eager for a way to turn away armed enemies without being in conflict with their religion. Jujitsu holds too dangerous to use in sport were modified or dropped. An experienced judo participant can use his opponent's weight to his own advantage. Dr. Kano introduced the belt system of indicating proficiency; white indicates a beginner, black an expert. A point is scored and a victory awarded when a contestant is choked into resigning, becomes unconscious, or resigns because of an endangered joint.

JULY 4

On July 4, 1776, George III wrote in his diary, "Nothing of importance happened today." He, of course, had no way of knowing what had occurred that day 3,000 miles away in the Colonies, in Pennsylvania, in Philadelphia, Pennsylvania, in particular. Other things have happened on July 4. In 1567, Mary, Queen of Scots, abdicated. In 1754, George Washington surrendered Fort Necessity to the French and Indians. In 1802, the United States Military Academy opened at West Point. In 1817, construction of the Erie Canal began. In 1821, slavery was abolished in New York State. In 1826, Stephen Foster was born and John Adams and Thomas Jefferson died, and in 1831 James Monroe died. In 1845, Texas voted for annexation to the United States. In 1848, the cornerstone of the Washington Monument was laid. In 1862, on a historic (literarily) cruise and picnic, Lewis Carroll made up the story of a little girl named Alice who falls down a rabbit hole and has wondrous adventures. In 1863, Vicksburg, Mississippi, surrendered to the Union army. In 1866, half of Portland, Maine, was destroyed by fire. 1872, Calvin Coolidge was born. 1884, the Statue of Liberty was presented to the United States by France. 1946, the Philippines were granted their independence by the United States. 1954, meat rationing ended in England (after 15 years). 1976, the U.S. bicentennial was observed.

JUPITER

Its mass is two and one-half times the mass of all other planets combined. Because its atmospheric composition is similar to that of the primitive Earth at the time of the origin of life, the most Jovian of the Jovian planets, the fifth from the Sun, may be the key to many questions on the origin and the evolution of all the planets as well as to questions of how life started on the third planet from the Sun. The first of the massive, low-density giants (Jupiter, Saturn, Uranus, Neptune) has a diameter nearly 11 times that of Earth and a volume more than 1,300 times greater than Earth's and a mass 318 times that of Earth's. Its satellite Ganymede is the largest moon in the solar system, larger even than the planet Mercury; at least a dozen moons orbit Jupiter. The Great Red Spot, in Jupiter's southern hemisphere, is about 30,000 miles long by 10,000 miles wide. Six Earths could be tucked into it. The GRS may be a prodigious storm system. (Dante wrote, "Dark and deep, And thick with clouds o'er-spread, Mine eye in vain explored its bottom, Nor could ought discern.") A day on Jupiter is nine hours, fifty-five minutes.

JUTLAND

It's that 250-mile-long digit that sticks into the North Sea, the Skagerrak, and the Kattegat—it's continental Denmark in the north and the West German state Schleswig-Holstein in the south. The peninsula is cut through in the north by the Limfjord strait, and a glacial ridge juxtaposes the western and eastern sections; the fertile eastern coast is much the more pleasant. Its elevation is only 568 feet, but Yding Skovhoj in east Jutland is Denmark's geographical high point. The Skagerrak separates Denmark from Norway; the Kattegat separates Denmark from Sweden. The battle of Jutland, as it is known among the allies, or the battle of the Skagerrak as it is known in Germany, was the only major contest between British and German fleets in World War I; it was fought to no-decision in 1916.

K

KAMIKAZE

Japanese for "divine wind." And divine the wind was in 1281—never was a typhoon more God-sent, if one were Japanese. The typhoon crushed the invasion fleet mounted by the ambitious Mongol emperor Kublai Khan (Marco Polo's Kublai) in the wake of his conquest of China's Sung dynasty. To take the wind out of the sails of the United States naval juggernaut, the retreating Japanese organized their own kamikaze in World War II—a suicide air force. Navy pilots slammed their bomb-laden planes—and themselves—into American ships in the Pacific. Twelve hundred pilots killed themselves taking out thirty-four U.S. ships. The Japanese army air force had its own suicide squadron, called Tokko Tai.

KATMANDU

The name of the picturesque capital and largest city of Nepal nearly a mile above sea level in the east Himalayas derives from "Kasthmandap," the name of a wooden, pagoda-shaped temple carved from the lumber of a single tree near Durbar Square, the heart of the city in olden days. Trade and pilgrim routes pass through Katmandu—India-Tibet-China-Mongolia. One reason: the Buddha, "the enlightened one," may have been born nearby, in the sixth century B.C. It is a city of temples and shrines. The three-tiered Telaju Temple, built in the sixteenth century, is today the royal chapel, and as such is closed to foreigners all the time and open to "ordinary" Nepalese only once a year. (Nepal, virtually closed to the outside world for centuries, officially abolished polygamy, child marriage, and the caste system in 1963.)

KEATS, JOHN

He wanted to be a surgeon, and he became one of the three great Romantic poets before dying at age twenty-five of tuberculosis, probably from nursing his brother. "Beauty is truth, truth beauty"—*that* is all Ye know on earth, and all Ye need to know. He believed that the mind should be a thoroughfare for all thought. On first looking into Keats has been compared to first looking into Chapman's Homer. His sonnet to one who has been long in city pent is still read with éclat: "To one who has been long in city pent, 'Tis very sweet to look into the fair And open face of heaven, —to breathe a prayer Full in the smile of the blue firmament. Who is more happy, when, with heart's content, Fatigued he sinks into some pleasant lair Of wavy grass, and reads a debonair And gentle tale of love and languishment? Returning home at evening, with an ear Catching the notes of Philomel,—an eye Watching the sailing cloudlet's bright career, He mourns that day so soon has glided by: E'en like the passage of an angel's fear That falls through the clear ether silently."

KELVIN SCALE

Named for the British mathematician and physicist William Thomson Kelvin, it is a temperature scale used by scientists that is based on the properties of gases. It is the absolute scale of temperature, and is convenient in thermodynamics. All gases, when their temperature is reduced, contract at such a rate that their volume is zero at a temperature of $-273.15°C.$ (degrees Celsius). The boiling point of water (100°C.) corresponds to 373.15°K. Lord Kelvin was an infant prodigy. He introduced the term kinetic energy, the energy of motion. He invented improvements in cables and galvanometers without which the new Atlantic cable would have been useless. He improved the mariner's compass and invented tide predictors. He introduced Bell's telephone into Great Britain, and for four years, 1890–94, was president of the Royal Society.

KENNEDY, JACQUELINE

"Is Jackie all right?" Marina Oswald asked instantly on learning that bullets had been fired at President John F. Kennedy's motorcade from the Texas School Book Depository where her husband, Lee, worked in Dallas. Marina "identified" with Mrs. Kennedy. She considered the First Lady to be a "goddess." Marina gobbled up all the news about Mrs. Kennedy that she could. "It occurred to Marina," the Oswalds' authorized biographer has written, "that perhaps Mrs. Kennedy was 'cold,' and that the President might need extra warmth in his life, warmth that a less perfect, more earthy woman such as she herself might provide." Three months before the assassination, the Kennedys' infant son had died; a month before the assassination, Mrs. Kennedy cruised the Mediterranean as a guest of Aristotle Onassis before being ordered off the yacht by the President. She was criticized by a congressman for "poor judgment and perhaps impropriety" for accepting the hospitality of a "clever—and some might say unscrupulous" man once fined $10 million by the United States. In Lee Oswald's troubled mind, was Jackie letting her husband down as Marina was letting him down? Mrs. Kennedy was accompanying her husband on a political trip for the first time in three years, and she was a tremendous, radiant hit. John K. Lattimer, of Columbia University's College of Physicians and Surgeons, in New York, tested Oswald's antiquated Mannlicher-Carcano rifle and concluded that if "the telescopic sight had not been incorrectly pointed, so as to cause the bullets to strike to the right of the aiming point, Mrs. Kennedy might very well have been hit by the fatal bullet that struck her husband in the head." She was lucky not to be blinded by the exploding fragments. (It was Dr. Lattimer who proved that a head struck from the rear by a high-powered bullet ineluctably jumps backward as heavy brain matter jets forward through the massive exit cavity—Mr. Kennedy was not struck by a shot from the grassy knoll in front.) Only one private person paid a call on Mrs. Kennedy in the Queen's Suite of the White House that fateful weekend—Mr. Onassis. She married him five years later. Marina Oswald told the Warren Commission that she believed that her distraught husband had been the lone gunman but had not shot at President Kennedy— Lee thought J.F.K. was doing a good job, with many fine ideas, as Lee himself had—was there someone else important in the limousine? Former President Gerald R. Ford, who was a Warren Commissioner, has said that we shall not know what really happened in Dallas until Mrs. Oswald tells all she knows.

KENNEDY, JOHN F.

A "most likely to succeed" in his Harvard class wrote two books, *Why England Slept,* a study of England's complacency on the eve of World War II, and *Profiles in Courage,* decisive moments in the lives of celebrated Americans: John Quincy Adams, Daniel Webster, Thomas Hart Benton, Sam Houston, Edmund G. Ross, Lucius Quintus Cincinnatus Lamar, George Norris, Robert A. Taft—courage, that most admirable of human virtues, grace under pressure. *Why England Slept* was based on J.F.K.'s magna cum laude political science thesis. *Profiles in Courage* was awarded a Pulitzer Prize. He had help with both books: Arthur Krock, *The New York Times* Washington bureau chief, had a hand in getting *Why England Slept* published, research associate Theodore C. Sorensen delivered "invaluable assistance in the assembly and preparation of the material upon which *Profiles* was based." The thirty-fifth President donated the English royalties from *Why England Slept* to the Nazi-bombed town of Plymouth, England. He wrote *Profiles in Courage* during a long period of hospitalization and courageous convalescence following a spinal operation in October 1954. He was the first Chief Executive born in this century and the youngest (43) elected and to date the only Catholic. J.F.K. is one of two Presidents buried in Arlington National Cemetery—William Howard Taft is the other. (The first Kennedy to arrive in the New World, J.F.K.'s paternal greatgrandfather, also died on a November 22, in 1859, shortly after the birth of his son, Patrick; J.F.K. was murdered shortly after the birth of *his* son Patrick.)

KENTUCKY

"D. Boon cilled a bar on this tree in 1760" is a popular sign in the Bluegrass State. Kentuckians fought on both sides in the Civil War. The state is 425 miles at its greatest length, 182 miles at its greatest breadth. Owing to a double bend in the Mississippi River, there is an area of about 10 square miles in the southwest corner that cannot be reached from the rest of the state without passing through a bit of Missouri or Tennessee. The state motto is, "United We Stand, Divided We Fall." The only lake of importance, Reelfoot, was created during an earthquake in the early nineteenth century. The United States Depository is at Fort Knox. When President Dwight D. Eisenhower ordered the gold there counted, in the late 1950s, it totaled $30,442,415,581. And seventy cents.

KENTUCKY DERBY

It's the first leg in thoroughbred horse racing's Triple Crown for three-year-olds but it was the third to be inaugurated. The Belmont Stakes was opened at 1½ miles in New York in 1867. The Preakness Stakes opened at 1¹³⁄₁₆ miles in Baltimore in 1873, and has been held at Pimlico there since 1909. The Derby was inaugurated at Churchill Downs, in Lexington, Kentucky, at 1½ miles in 1875; it was shortened to 1¼ miles in 1896. Only two fillies, Regret and Genuine Risk, have won the Derby. The Triple Crown has been won five times by two jockeys, Eddie Arcaro and Bill Hartack, and three times by three jocks, Isaac Murphy, Earle Sande, and Willie Shoemaker. Murphy was one of many black jockeys who won the Derby before racial prejudice threw them out of the saddle. The first winner, in '75, Oliver Lewis, was black.

KEY, FRANCIS SCOTT

"The Defence of Fort McHenry"—that's what the lawyer first called his eyewitness poem of an overnight British bombardment of Fort McHenry in Baltimore harbor, during the War of 1812, and it was so published in the Baltimore *Patriot* later that year, 1814. It was renamed "The Star-Spangled Banner" about a month later. Under a flag of truce, Key had been seeking the release of a captured friend from the British, and was detained overnight. By the dawn's early light, he was so inspired that he set down words that could be sung to the popular English drinking song *Anacreon in Heaven*. He was a devout lay reader in the Episcopal Church and wrote many songs on religious themes, some of which appear in a posthumous collection, *Poems* (1857). He wrote *The Power of Literature and Its Connection with Religion*. He was United States attorney for the District of Columbia for eight years. It wasn't until Herbert Hoover was President that "The Star-Spangled Banner" became the official national anthem of the United States.

KHYBER PASS

It's been said that the narrow, steep, shale-limestone-sided, twenty-eight-mile-long defile through the Safed Koh Mountains on the Pakistan-Afghanistan border has had too much history: "It has seen so much of slaughter that the very stones that speckle its arid hillsides might be the bones of dead men." From the time of Alexander the Great (327 B.C.) it has been the military and the trade gateway into India from the Asiatic countries to the west. Tamerlane, Babur, Mahmud of Ghazni, and Nadir Shah also stormed through the pass and invaded India. The Khyber was adopted by the British as the main road to Kabul. It was the scene of many skirmishes in the First Afghan War. The treaty that closed the Second Afghan War, in 1879, left the Khyber tribes under British control. Under British rule, traffic moved into landlocked Afghanistan in the morning, moved out in the afternoon, and nothing dared move at night. The cities of Kabul, Pakistan, and Peshawar are linked by the pass, and a railroad runs through thirty-four tunnels and over ninety-two bridges and culverts. The pass is today under the control of Pakistan. The temperature there can approach 120°F.

KILLEBREW, HARMON

He is major league baseball's fifth most-productive home run slugger and the American League's foremost right-handed home run hitter—he smashed 573 for the Washington Senators (in cavernous Griffith Stadium) and the Minnesota Twins—and he was inducted into major league baseball's Hall of Fame in 1984. "The Killer" was six times the league's HR leader, three times the runs-batted-in leader, and once, in 1969, the most valuable player. (There are now 226 men in the Hall of Fame.)

KILMER, JOYCE

He taught Latin in a high school in Morristown, New Jersey. He was on the staff of a dictionary publisher, the literary editor of the *Churchman* (an Episcopalian magazine), and on the staff of both the Magazine and the Book Review of *The New York Times*. In 1914 he wrote the popular poem "Trees." "Poems are made by fools like me, but only God can make a tree." When the United States declared war on Germany in 1917, he enlisted in the 7th Regiment, New York National Guard, then requested a transfer to the Fighting 69th, a unit of Irish Americans; Kilmer claimed to have been half Irish, though he was of German and English ancestry. A little more than three months before Armistice Day, he was killed on a reconnaissance patrol during the Second Battle of the Marne, near the village of Seringes, in France. He was remembered by his buddies for his readiness to volunteer for dangerous missions and for his poem "Prayer of a Soldier in France."

KILOGRAM

The only base unit of measure still defined by an artifact, the kilogram is not a natural phenomenon. It is represented by a platinum-iridium alloy cylinder kept in Sèvres, near Paris, at the International Bureau of Weights and Standards. There is a twin stored at the National Bureau of Standards in the United States. Seven base units have been defined by the International System of Units (SI). In addition to the kilogram (mass), they are: meter (length), kelvin (thermodynamic temperature), second (time), amphere (electric current), mole (amount of substance), and candela (luminous intensity). There are two supplementary units: radian (plane angle) and steradian (solid angle). With the exception of the kilogram, the base units are determined by natural phenomena that can be duplicated under laboratory conditions. Use of these phenomena eliminates the need for international models as reference. A kilogram is equal to 1,000 grams, or 2.2046 pounds. When the metric system was originally devised, in France, and adopted there in 1799, the kilogram was defined as the weight of 1,000 cubic centimeters (1 cubic decimeter) of pure water at 3 degrees Celsius.

KIMBERLEY

The city was founded in central South Africa in 1871 when diamonds were discovered on a farm there. Fifteen million carats of diamonds were unearthed from a 1,200-foot "big hole," now a tourist attraction. Kimberley was besieged for 126 days by Boer forces during the South African War at the turn of the century. The mines were closed during the Great War and the Depression. The site of the first major western Australian gold strike, in 1882, became known as the Kimberley Goldfield.

KIMBLE, DR. RICHARD

For 120 one-hour television episodes on ABC, 1963–67, David Janssen played "The Fugitive," who is sought by the law, which wrongly believes he has killed his wife, while he seeks the real killer, a one-armed robber (played by Bill Raisch). During his search, Kimble assumes various identities and assists troubled people. After four years, the killer is apprehended, then escapes. Kimble tracks him to a closed amusement park. There is a fight on the ledge of a water tower, the killer confesses.

KING, BILLIE JEAN

The first woman athlete to earn more than $100,000 in any one year, she captured Wimbledon's singles tennis title six times, the doubles title ten times, the mixed doubles four times—a record twenty crowns in all. She was the U.S. Open singles champion four times. She recently said, "With age, you appreciate things more." Mrs. King is not the holder of the record for most U.S. titles. Margaret Osborne duPont won twenty-five in all—three singles, thirteen doubles, nine mixed doubles.

KING, MARTIN LUTHER, JR.

The youngest recipient of the Nobel Peace Prize was thirty-five years old when he went to Oslo, where he said that "nonviolence is the answer to the crucial political and moral question of our time—the need for man to overcome oppression and violence without resorting to violence and oppression. Man must evolve for all human conflict a method that rejects revenge, aggression, and retaliation. The foundation of such a method is love. I accept this award with an abiding faith in America and an audacious faith in the future of mankind. I believe that unarmed truth and unconditional love will have the final word in reality." A month earlier, the director of the Federal Bureau of Investigation had labeled him "the most notorious liar in the country." In 1958, King traveled more than 700,000 miles around the world, 208 speeches insisting that black men and women were willing to risk martyrdom in order to move and stir the social conscience of their community and nation: Nonviolent action was the way for blacks to divest themselves of passivity without arraying

287

themselves in vindictive force. In 1968, the clergyman-civil rights leader was murdered in Memphis, Tennessee, during a strike of sanitation workers. His epitaph reads "Free at last, free at last. Thank God Almighty, I am free at last."

KINSEY, ALFRED C.

He was the world's foremost authority on the gall wasp, but he was known world-wide for what many considered his gall: asking thousands of Americans about their sex life and then blabbing. *Sexual Behavior in the Human Male*—the first Kinsey Report, in 1948—turned individual and social awareness upside down and sold like hotpants. Homosexual acts were found to be much more common than had been supposed. Come what may, the average man attained the peak of virility at about sixteen or seventeen years of age and petered out steadily—the midteens are the good old days. Men who began sexual activity early held their power longer. *Sexual Behavior in the Human Female* was promulgated five years later and didn't give as much bang for the buck; it did not sell as though it were going out of style. In the mid-60s, the sex therapists Masters and Johnson debunked myths about female orgasm and penis size in relation to sexual satisfaction.

"KITCHEN DEBATE"

A quarter-century after his famous joust of oneupmanship alongside the washing machine in a model American home on exhibition in Moscow, Richard M. Nixon remembered Soviet leader Nikita Khrushchev as a "man of great warmth, and totally belligerent." In the spontaneous verbal clash, Khrushchev had boasted about Soviet rocketry and the Vice President had retaliated with color television sets. Mr. Nixon's former White House counsel who first publicly tied him to the Watergate cover-up believes that Mr. Nixon is running today for "ex-President." Mr. Nixon himself often says, "Never look back. Remember Lot's wife. Never look back."

KIWI

It's the nickname for a New Zealander. It's the name of a shaggy, forest New Zealand bird about the size of a chicken. The bird is shy—it has tiny and useless wings, no tail, and can't fly. It is the only bird with nostrils in the tip of its (long) bill. The male kiwi bird takes seventy-five days to hatch the female's eggs. The kiwi is New Zealand's official symbol.

KLONDIKE GOLD RUSH

There was lots of gold in "them criks," came word to the United States a year after George Washington Carmack and two brothers, Skookum Jim and Tagish Charlie, found richer placer deposits of gold in Rabbit Creek, later renamed Bonanza Creek, which flowed into the Klondike River, a small-stream tributary of the Yukon, in northwest Canada, just east of the Alaskan border. Tens of thousands of Americans stampeded northward. The strike was a "goldmine" for Alaska, too; "very effective propaganda," said the railroad magnate Henry Villard. "The Klondike" was converted into optimism about riches everywhere—silver, copper, platinum, coal, furs, timber, not to mention gold. Entrepreneurs also struck it rich. In Dawson, they sold milk for $16 a gallon, eggs for $3 a dozen, onions for $1.50 apiece. (Down the line, in San Francisco, a good meal cost 25¢.) Jack London's popular novel *The Call of the Wild* (1903) is the story of a dog named Buck who becomes a sled dog and then the leader of a wolf pack in the Klondike.

KNOCK-KNEED

Or baker-kneed, or baker-legged, as far back as 1607: "Will women's tongues, like bakers' legs, never go straight?" In 1611: "Baker-legd, that goes in at the knees." In 1656: "He that is baker-legged rubs his knees against one another." Bakers become bowlegged because of the way they work. They also have swollen hands. In 1871, it was writ: Baker's knee, as it is called, or an inclining inwards of the right knee-joint until it closely resembles the right side of a letter K, is the almost certain penalty of habitually bearing any burden of bulk in the right hand. Like a baker's dozen.

KODAK

You pressed the button, George Eastman's company did the rest—making photography an enormously popular hobby. What to call the camera? The inventor-industrialist wanted a trademark that would "be short, vigorous, incapable of being misspelled to an extent that will destroy its identity and—in order to satisfy trademark laws—it must mean nothing. . . . The letter 'K' had been a favorite with me [this was before Kafka]—it seems a strong, incisive sort of letter. Therefore, the word I wanted had to start with 'K.' Then it became a question of trying out a great number of combinations of letters that made words starting and ending with 'K.' The word Kodak is the result. Instead of merely making cameras and camera supplies, we made Kodaks and Kodak supplies. It became the distinctive word for our products. Hence the slogan: 'If it isn't an Eastman, it isn't a Kodak.' '' The first Kodak—the Model T of cameradom—came loaded with enough film for one hundred exposures. When the last photo was made, the user sent the entire box to Eastman's company in Rochester, New York, for processing. The finished prints and the reloaded camera were then sent to the owner. Gilbert and Sullivan plugged the camera in their operetta *Utopia:* Two "modest maidens" sang, "Then all the crowd take down our looks In pocket memorandum books. To diagnose Our Modest pose The Kodaks do their best: If evidence you would possess Of what is a maiden bashfulness. You only need a button press—And we will do the rest." In 1931, Eastman began to suffer from a spinal ailment that threatened to make him a cripple. On March 14, 1932, he shot a bullet through his heart. "To my Friends," a note said, "my work is done. Why wait?" He had already given away nearly $75 million, which included generous benefactions to the black schools Hampton and Tuskegee—and also to dental clinics around the world, possibly because when people said "Cheese," their teeth would look nicer in the picture.

KON TIKI

To support his thesis that the first settlers of Polynesia were of South American origin, the Norwegian explorer and anthropologist Thor Heyerdahl drifted with five companions for 101 days on their primitive balsawood raft *Kon Tiki* from Peru to the Tuamotu Islands, in 1947. Twenty-three years after the Pacific odyssey, Heyerdahl sailed in a papyrus boat called the *Ra* from Morocco to Barbados to prove that ancient Mediterranean civilizations could have sailed in reed boats to America. The *Kon Tiki* and Heyerdahl's log books are on display in Oslo.

KOPECHNE, MARY JO

She drowned when the car in which she was riding with Senator Edward M. Kennedy spilled off a rail-less bridge on Chappaquiddick Island, Massachusetts, in the summer of 1969. She had been one of several "boiler room girls," former staff workers for the late Senator Robert F. Kennedy, at a party that was still going on when Edward Kennedy returned to report the accident. None of the aides has discussed the tragedy publicly. (There has been speculation that Mr. Kennedy and a second woman drove off from the party unaware that Miss Kopechne was asleep on the backseat of the automobile; they survived the accident; Mr. Kennedy, on learning back at the party that Miss Kopechne had been in the car, returned to the scene to try to rescue her.) The senator pleaded guilty to leaving the scene of the accident, and he wore a neck brace when he attended Miss Kopechne's funeral in Pennsylvania.

KOREAN WAR

It was a bitter civil war, thirty-seven months long, at the beginning of the 1950s, down and up the peninsula and back down again. The South Korean capital of Seoul was captured twice by the North Koreans, the North Korean capital of Pyongyang was captured once by Supreme Commander Douglas MacArthur's South Korean and United Nations forces, which included American land, sea, and air troops committed by President Harry S Truman less than a week after the Communists in June 1950 had crossed the 38th parallel that divided the country between the People's Democratic Republic of Korea (the north) and the Republic of Korea (the south). A letter from General MacArthur urging a full-scale war against Communism was read in Congress and led to his removal from command by President Truman at a meeting on Wake Island in the Pacific. More than a million people were killed in the war. Total U.S. casualties were 157,530, which included 54,246 dead: 37,133 Army; 4,501 Navy; 5,528 Marines, and 7,084 Air Force. Battle deaths were 33,629; other deaths, 20,617. Thirty-eight percent of Americans in captivity died. Nearly 6 million Americans were engaged in the war. (Eight million were involved in Vietnam.) At the end of the war, the boundary between the two Koreas was formed by the Demilitarized Zone (DMZ). It is a 4,000-meter-wide strip of land that runs along the line of ceasefire from the east coast to the west coast for a distance of 241 kilometers.

KOUFAX, SANDY

The Brooklyn-Los Angeles Dodgers righthanded batter holds the big leagues's strikeout record: He once fanned 12 straight times. The Dodgers lefthanded fireballing pitcher hurled four no-hit games, including a perfect game against the Chicago Cubs, in 1965, and for a time held the one-season K record with 382, also in '65. Lifetime, he fanned 2,396 enemy batsmen—"Pitching is the art of instilling fear"—and allowed only 1,754 hits. He won twenty-five games in 1963, twenty-six in 1965, and twenty-seven in 1966—and then had to quit because of a sore arm. His career was 165 W, 87 L, .655, and he was three times the majors' Cy

Young award winner. In the Dodgers' four-game sweep of the New York Yankees in the '63 World Series, Koufax set a strikeout record of fifteen in the first game and added eight more in the fourth game. He pitched two shutouts in the Dodgers' 4–3 World Series triumph over Minnesota in '65.

KREMLIN

Several Russian cities, such as Gorky, Pskov, Astrakhan, and Novgorod, have a kremlin, a citadel or walled center. The ninety-acre kremlin in the capital, Moscow, is *the* Kremlin; it was the residence of the czars until Peter the Great transferred the capital to St. Petersburg, in 1712. Since 1918, when the capital was moved back to Moscow, the Kremlin has been the political and administrative center of the Soviet Union. The architectural history of the Kremlin may be divided into three periods: the wooden Kremlin, founded in the thirteenth century, the Italian Renaissance Kremlin, and the modern Kremlin initiated by Catherine the Great in the eighteenth century. Italian craftsmen in the fifteenth century (as Columbus was crossing the Ocean Sea) worked on the Cathedral of the Assumption and the Granovitaya Palata, the Cathedral of the Archangel, and the crenellated red brick walls topped by twenty towers. "Russia for a number of years," said a President of the United States, "has treated the United States as badly as she has treated England. . . . Her diplomatists lied to us with brazen and contemptuous effrontery, and showed with cynical indifference their intention to organize China against our interests . . . I should have liked to be friendly with her; but she simply would not permit it, and those responsible for managing her foreign policy betrayed a brutality and ignorance, an arrogance and shortsightedness, which are not often combined." The President was Theodore Roosevelt.

KRUGER NATIONAL PARK

The several-times president of the South African Transvaal, Stephanas Johannes Paulus Kruger—known as Oom Paul—fought the British for years and established the wildlife sanctuary Sabi Game Reserve (1898) that was joined with Shingwedzi Game Reserve in 1926 and named the Kruger National Park. Nine rivers and hundreds of miles of roads lace its 8,000 square miles, home to lion, wildebeest, waterbuck, kudu, impala, sable, roan antelope, steenbok, giraffe, elephant, rhino, hippo, warthog, monkey, baboon, elephant, hippopotamus, rhinoceros, buffalo, leopard, wild dog, hyena, jackal, civet, cheetah, zebra, and bushbuck. The park attracts upward of half a million visitors annually.

KRYPTON

It's a gaseous element in the helium family as well as the name of the doomed fictional planet from which baby boy Superman (Kal-El) escaped. The element has the symbol Kr, the atomic number 36, and an atomic weight of 83.80 (carbon-12 scale). It is found in low concentrations in the atmosphere. Small concentrations have also been found in gases in some hot springs and volcanoes. The name was coined in 1898 by Sir William Ramsay and M. W. Travers, who discovered krypton in the residual liquid left after the nearly complete evaporation of liquid air. Its limited uses include lighting devices to obtain bright flashes of brief duration.

K2

The world's twenty highest mountains are in Nepal-Tibet-Kashmir-India. Everest is the tallest, at 29,028. Mount Godwin-Austen—or K2—is the second tallest, 28,250 feet, in Kashmir, 42 feet higher than Kanchenjunga, in India-Nepal. It is K for the first letter of the Karakorum range; 2 indicates that it was the second peak in the range to be measured. K2 was discovered and measured in 1856 by the Survey of India and named for Henry Godwin-Austen, an officer in the British army and topographer who explored and surveyed the region around the mountain. Ninety-eight years were to pass before the summit would be reached. It wasn't as easy as A B C.

L

LADY GODIVA

There really was a Lady Godiva. She was the wife of Leofric, earl of Mercia, one of Edward the Confessor's earls. The Mercias founded the monastery at Coventry, in 1043. But did she really ride naked through the streets of Coventry? The story goes, or so the bare facts tell us, that she had importuned her husband to roll back a heavy tax he had imposed on the townspeople. In jest, he said he would on the day that hell froze over or that she rode naked through the streets at noon, whichever came first. She took him at his word. She directed everyone to keep within doors and blind their windows. She took off all her clothes, mounted her steed, and did it.

LAETRILE

The president of Memorial Sloan-Kettering Cancer Center in New York once said, "These are bad times for reason all around. Suddenly, all of the major ills are being coped with by acupuncture. If not acupuncture, it is apricot pits." Exhaustive studies prove that Laetrile has no anticancer properties. It's made from apricot-pit extract, also known as vitamin B-17. It is illegal to transport the controversial drug over state borders.

La GUARDIA, FIORELLO

New York City's mayoral "Little Flower" was never at a loss for quotable quotes: "I think the reporter should get his facts straight before he distorts them. . . . I had a good secretary once. I married her and got a bad cook. . . . To the victor belongs the responsibility for good government. . . . This is a city of huge spaces that are too small—of millions of people that are really big. . . . It seems to be one of the rules of the game for a councilman to appear half-witted, even if he knows better. . . . When it comes to overstatement I am an expert—but that was too much for me. . . . I never have conflicts between my commissioners, though I may have a conflict with an ex-commissioner. . . . When I make a mistake, it's a beaut." He was a courageous, vigorous, liberal New York congressman and for four terms a courageous, vigorous, reform mayor. He served a year as director of the United Nations Relief and Rehabilitation Administration, and during World War I he led United States air forces on the Italian-Austrian front. Among the sites named for the Lou Costello lookalike was New York City's second airport—its first airport was Floyd Bennett Field, in Brooklyn. LaGuardia Airport was laid out in Jamaica Bay in the borough of Queens in conjunction with the New York World's Fair of 1939–40 nearby. The entire area had been a swamp, then garbage acreage known as Corona Dump during "sanitary landfill" operations there. On the northwestern edge of the airfield is Marine Terminal, built to service flying boats, including the famed *China Clipper*. It is an art deco extravaganza.

LAKE MARACAIBO

It is the largest lake of South America, it is one of the great oil-producing areas in the world, but you wouldn't want to live there without combat pay—the 5,100 square miles in northwest Venezuela are hot, humid, rainy, disease-ridden, and, maybe worst of all, some of the Indians, particularly the Motilones, are hostile. One of the world's longest bridges, the Lake Maracaibo Bridge, spans the lake's outlet at the Gulf of Venezuela, site also of Venezuela's second largest city and the continent's oil capital, also named Maracaibo. Home for many is a thatched hut built on stilts over the lake. The name "Venezuela" is Spanish for "little Venice."

LAKE OF LUCERNE

Forty-four square miles, irregularly shaped by retreating glaciers, it has a maximum depth of about 700 feet and borders on the central Swiss forest canton of Lucerne. It is breathtakingly beautiful there. The Lake of Kussnacht, the Lake of Alpnacht, and the Lake of Uri are three units of the Lake of Lucerne, and the river Reuss both feeds and drains it. On both banks of the Reuss where it flows out of the Lake of Lucerne is the city of Lucerne, the capital of the canton.

LAKE TITICACA

The legendary birthplace of the Incas are the islands of Coati and Titicaca in the world's highest lake (12,500 feet in the Andes, at the Bolivia-Peru border) and the largest fresh water lake in all of South America. Ruins of past civilizations can still be seen there. (Originally, the name "Inca" did not refer to a race or to a nation of people. When Francisco Pizarro landed in South America, in 1532, "the Inca" meant king or ruler, and by extension one of his ancestors or relatives.) The "lake of the clouds" is 110 miles long, 900 feet deep at its deepest, and covers about 3,200 square miles. A ferry boat was brought up the mountains and to the lake, piece by piece on the backs of mules, and reassembled on the shore.

LANDIS, KENESAW MOUNTAIN

Major league baseball had two strikes on it in 1920 when the long-time United States district judge in northern Illinois was engaged as the national pastime's first commissioner. He helped to restore public confidence in the sport after the "Black Sox" World Series scandal in 1919. Eight Sox players were banned for life—to this day it is not known who bribed whom, who threw what—and the czar subsequently issued other similarly arbitrary edicts to insure the game's integrity. He "freed" ninety-one St. Louis Cardinal farmhands in 1938 and a similar number from the Detroit chain in 1940. He blacklisted several players for wrongdoing and fined club owners for breaking rules. Landis is in baseball's Hall of Fame.

LANDON, ALF

"Deeds, not deficits"—the Republican presidential candidate's campaign theme in 1936 against the incumbent Franklin D. Roosevelt, whose New Deal was labeled as having "dishonored" American traditions. The crippled President, after falling to the floor as he prepared to accept the Democrats' bid to run for a second term, delivered his "rendezvous with destiny" speech at the party's convention. *Literary Digest* got on the telephone and learned that the popular Kansas governor would win by a landslide—forgetting that most of the people with a telephone were among the fortunate few in the Depression and likely to vote for the G.O.P. candidate. It was the year that blacks moved away from the party of Lincoln. F.D.R. won by a landslide—he copped 61 percent of the popular vote and lost only 2 of the 48 states's electoral votes: Maine's and Vermont's. In 1972, Richard M. Nixon did even better, winning the same percentage of the popular vote as F.D.R. did in '36 but holding his Democratic opponent to the electoral votes of only one state, Massachusetts, plus the District of Columbia. The Democrats' 1984 presidential contender, Walter Mondale, netted only his home state, Minnesota, and D.C. in his lackluster campaign against incumbent Ronald Reagan.

LANGUAGES

Byron loved Latin, "that soft bastard Latin, which melts like kisses from a female mouth." More people today speak Fon or Quechua or Tiv or Rundi or Yiddish or Madurese than speak Latin, once politically and literarily significant. It survives as the official tongue of Vatican City and as the official language of communication of the Roman Catholic Church. The world's major languages now are Chinese, English, Spanish, Russian, Hindi, Bengali, Portuguese, Arabic, Japanese, German, Indonesian, French, Punjabi, Italian, Korean, Telugu, Marathi, Tamil, Javanese, Turkish, Urdu, Vietnamese, Polish, Ukranian, Thai, and Persian. That's the word, anyway.

LA PAZ

Everything is "est" in Bolivia. It has the world's highest commercial airport (El Alto, on a plain at 13,300 feet), the world's highest administrative capital (La Paz, 12,000 feet and about one-quarter hour away from El Alto by taxi), the highest navigable lake (Titicaca), the highest golf course, the highest ski run, and the highest concentration of cosmic rays. (Bolivia's constitutional capital is Sucre, at "only" 8,500 feet on the eastern slopes of the Andes. (Bolivia once changed its president five times in a single day.) The full name of La Paz is La Paz de Ayacucho, after a Bolivian victory at Ayacucho, Peru, in the war for independence in the first quarter of the nineteenth century. The discomfort of soroche, or altitude sickness, is more than repaid by the majestic beauty of snow-capped mountains that surround the city. Snow is rare there, but it rains almost every day from December to February. Big fires are rare in the thin air.

LARSEN, DON

The six-foot-four, 215-pound New York Yankee righthander's first start in the 1956 World Series: He gave up a hit and he walked four Brooklyn Dodgers and he was out of there in less than two innings. The Yankees used seven pitchers to set a Series record as the Dodgers won a 13–8 slugfest in the longest nine-inning game in Series history. Larsen's next start was something else: Not a Dodger reached first base, a perfect game, the only one that's been twirled in a Series game. The Dodgers' Sal "the Barber" Maglie was pretty good, too; he gave up a home run to Mickey Mantle and only four other hits in the Yankees' thin 2–0 win. Larsen had a .471 winning percentage in his fourteen-year career, winning only 81 of 172 decisions. In 1962, he pitched the San Francisco Giants to a Series triumph over the Yankees.

LASSEN VOLCANIC NATIONAL PARK

Before Mount St. Helens, there was Lassen Peak, in northeastern California. On May 30, 1914, the southernmost great peak of the Cascades began a period of volcanic activity that lasted nearly seven years. In the first year alone, there were some 150 explosions, some quite violent, including what's come to be known as The Great Hot Blast. Lassen Volcanic National Park was established by Congress in 1916. (Lassen was the name of a Danish immigrant who came to the United States in 1830 and settled in California.) Lassen anchors a procession of volcanic cones studding the Cascades: Shasta in California; Three Sisters, Jefferson, and Hood in Oregon; St. Helens, Adams, Rainier, Glacier Peak, and Baker in Washington. Until Mount St. Helens erupted in 1980, Lassen Peak was the only active volcano in the continental United States below Alaska.

THE LAST SUPPER

There were thirteen at table, Jesus and the twelve apostles, whom He had chosen to be with Him during His ministry and to preach His doctrine. The apostles were working-class men, except for Matthew, a tax collector. (The term apostle is sometimes used for Paul and Barnabas, although they were not among the twelve. The term disciple refers only to close followers of Jesus.) "And the disciples did as Jesus had appointed them; and they made ready the passover. Now when the even was come, he sat down with the twelve. And as they did eat, he said, Verily I say unto you, that one of you shall betray me. And they were exceeding sorrowful, and began every one of them to say unto him, Lord, is it I? And he answered and said, He that dippeth his hand with me in the dish, the same shall betray me. The Son of man goeth as it is written of him: but woe unto that man by whom the Son of man is betrayed! It had been good for that man if he had not been born. Then Judas, which betrayed him, answered and said, Master, is it I? He said unto him, Thou hast said. . . Rise, let us be going: behold, he is at hand that doth betray me. And while he yet spake, lo, Judas, one of the twelve, came, and with him a great multitude with swords and staves, from the chief priests and elders of the people. Now he that betrayed him gave them a sign, saying, Whomsoever I shall kiss, that same is he: hold him fast. And forthwith he came to Jesus, and said, Hail, master; and kissed him. . . ."—The Gospel According to St. Matthew 26.

LATITUDE

The last state to become a United State, Hawaii shares a latitude with Mexico City, Puerto Rico, Mali, Mecca, Bombay, and Rangoon. The northern border of the United States is south of Paris, Saka Sakhalin, Odessa, Prague. Los Angeles is north of Atlanta, North Africa, Baghdad, Kaul, Tibet, Osaka. Anchorage is north of Stockholm, Oslo, and Helsinki. The Cape of Good Hope is on the same latitude as Montevideo, Valparaiso, and Sydney. South America extends about 20 degrees farther south than does South Africa; that is, Cape Horn is that much farther south than Cape of Good Hope. South Florida is on the same latitude as southern Algeria, Libya, Egypt, mid-Saudi Arabia, and is south of Pakistan, New Delhi, and at about the same latitude as Taiwan and Foochow.

"LAUGH-IN"

"Don't adjust your set," Chelsea Brown said. "I'm colored." Henry Gibson as a preacher: "I'm all for change, but a loose-leaf bible is going too far." Goldie Hawn: "I don't like Viet Cong. In the movie he nearly wrecked the Empire State Building." "If Shirley Temple Black had married Tyrone Power, she'd be Shirley Black Power." "Forest Fires Prevent Bears." "Truman Capote—Man or Myth?" Bartender: "Are you sure you're old enough to drink?" Girl: "Of course I am!" Bartender: "Okay, okay, what'll you have?" Girl: "A Scotch and wa-wa." For five years, quickies were socked to 'em by the television comedy forces of Dan Rowan and Dick Martin, but you can't look *that* up in your Funk and Wagnall's. No joke—Richard M. Nixon was once a guest. Talking about the Flying Fickle Finger of Fate!

LEADVILLE

It's the highest city in the United States—nearly two miles above sea level in the Rocky Mountains, in central Colorado, near the headwaters of the Arkansas River. Denver is the "mile-high" city—it's exactly 5,280 feet above sea level. Gold and silver and lead made Leadville anything but dullsville. Forty-thousand hopeful people picked their way to "cloud city." The most celebrated prospector was Horace Austin Warner "Silver Dollar" Tabor. He made a fortune from the Matchless Mine and became Leadville's first mayor, a lieutenant governor of Colorado, and a senator of the United States. The second Mrs. Silver Dollar Tabor was Baby Doe.

LEANING TOWER OF PISA

It's been leaning from the beginning. Construction, begun by Bonanno Pisano around 1173, had reached about 40 feet in height when a subsidence in the ground caused the first inclination. The tilt increases by about one millimeter every year and the 180-foot-high tower is now 16 feet out of whack. The interior is cylindrical in form, and the spiral staircase has 294 steps to the top. Galileo ("the Wrangler") Galilei conducted experiments there. He probably didn't drop two cannon balls, one ten times heavier than the other, from the tower and that were seen and heard to strike the ground simultaneously. He *did* conjecture that in a vacuum all objects would fall at the same rate, and centuries later he was proved to be right.

"LEAVE IT TO BEAVER"

Wally, Beaver's older brother on the "Leave It to Beaver" television sitcom series (1957–63), was played by Tony Dow. His oft-whined "Aww, Beav'!" expressed both genuine concern and total exasperation with ten-year-old Beav's frequent ineptitude in growing up. The amusing Wally was himself no wallflower, which often led to bemusement: He knew *they* were girls but he was still too young to rise to the occasion. Beav' and Wally have lived happily ever after. There's now an adult version of the program. The Cleaver family has grown up, finally, but Tony Dow is still Wally and Jerry Mathers is still Beav' in the new series

le CARRÉ, JOHN

The master English spy-espionage novelist (*The Spy Who Came In from the Cold, Tinker Tailor, Soldier Spy, Little Drummer Girl*) thinks all the time about God, "but I find the Christian faith inadequate to my needs, at least as it is incorporated on Earth." He believes that a great part of one's adult life is concerned with getting even for the slights one suffered as a child. His father was "just a guy who visited us at school." Le Carré (real name: David John Moore Cornwell) worked for the British Foreign Service in London, Bonn, and Hamburg. "All sorts of Foreign Service activities," he told the writer Mark Abley, "spill over into the secret side, inevitably, but not all of them are half as enchanting as we fiction writers would wish them to be." On the very first page of le Carré's very first book, *Call for the Dead* (1961), the quiet, bespectacled, corrosively perceptive spy George Smiley made his debut, as did David Cornwell's pseudonym, "the gentlemanly thing for a novelist to do as a member of the Foreign Service." When television commentators guessed wrong, le Carré revealed that Vivian Green, an Oxford historian, was his primary model for Smiley—"small, pudgy, and at best middle-aged, [Smiley] was by appearance one of London's meek who do not inherit the Earth." Le Carré's concerns are with moral behavior, what should people do. "If you have just come back from Beirut, knowing what real suffering is, and you go to a dinner party and listen to people talking about their fourth year of analysis, you do feel rather short-tempered with their self-indulgence."

LEE, GYPSY ROSE

The ecdysiast said that she didn't have any education, "but my editors say I have natural, instinctive punctuation and paragraphing." The queen of burlesque was the subject of the terrific Broadway show *Gypsy,* by Jule Styne and Stephen Sondheim, directed by Jerome Robbins, with Ethel Merman playing Rose's pushy mother. And she was indeed a published author: *The G-String Murders,* written in crowded dressing rooms, in planes, in the tub, was a best-seller, and was followed by *Mother Finds a Body* (1942). Zip, she was an intellectual. She exhibited some of her paintings at the Guggenheim Galleries in New York. Zip, could Walter Lippmann write a great play? She had an out-of-wedlock son, Erik Lee Preminger, with Otto Preminger, the movie director. One Christmas she gave Erik two hazel glass eyes with a card reading, "Remember, dear, Mother is *always* watching."

LEEK

The Welsh national flower is a vegetable that resembles the onion, but unlike the onion it grows thick along the entire stem. It has a mild flavor and the Welsh like to eat it. And on St. David's day, March 1, the Welsh like to wear a sprig. The rose is the emblem of Britain, the thistle of Scotland, the shamrock of Ireland.

LEIGH, VIVIEN

She was paid $30,000 to play Katie Scarlett O'Hara. She'd been sure that Katharine Hepburn would get the part: "Everyone said I was mad to try, but I wanted it and I knew I'd get it. The only thing I didn't want was the seven-year film contract that went with it." She was little known when she made the screen test for producer David Selznick; British movies were not widely seen in the United States at that time. And there already were two other British players cast for *Gone With the Wind,* Leslie Howard and Olivia de Havilland. *And* she was having an affair with Laurence Olivier and both of them were married to others. And so they all thought about it tomorrow and Miss Leigh was the year's best actress, as she would be again in *A Streetcar Named Desire* (1951). Miss Leigh suffered from the *Gilles de la Tourette* syndrome—vocal tics and an irresistible urge to utter obscenities.

LE MANS

A Ford Mark 2 was the first American car to win the 24-hour endurance race in the Sarthe district in northwest France. Chris Amon and Bruce McLaren whirled 3,009.5 miles at 129.91 miles per hour in 1966. Ken Miles and Denny Hulme covered virtually the same distance in a sister car, sharing the honor of being the first to cover more than 3,000 miles in the sports car classic. Seventeen years later, the winning m.p.h. was only about one mile faster. Le Mans was the first international road event run "twice round the clock," a tour de force for touring cars and speed freaks. The first Le Mans Grand Prix d'Endurance was staged in 1923 and won by a 3-liter Chenard et Walcker at 57.21 m.p.h. Some drivers have tried to burn rubber the entire race without a partner. The race used to be started with the cars parked side by side along one edge of the course facing the center of the track and the drivers lined up on the opposite edge, across from their cars. At a signal, the men dashed across the track, leaped into their cars, and were off in a blaze. An *auto-da-fé* from time to time put the brake on the chaos.

LESBOS

The rugged, earthquake-prone 630-square-mile island in the Aegean Sea, east of Greece and near Turkey and the trade route of the Hellespont, was a center of Bronze Age civilization, and for a century (700–600 B.C.) a brilliant cultural Aeolian mecca for the likes of Aristotle and Epicurus and Pittacus and Alcaeus and Sappho. Sappho, who was born there about 600 B.C., was noted for her beauty, poetical talents, and amorous disposition. Her sultry poems were highly erotic and dealt with the lesbianism of the women of good families there. The word "lesbian" has its root in the debauchery and extravagance of women of Lesbos. In what has been described as "three or four bursts of puritanical zeal," her lyric poetry was nearly destroyed in the twelfth century. The discovery of the Oxyrhynchus Papyri in the sands of Egypt in the Nile Valley between 1897 and 1906 yielded about one-twentieth of what Sappho apparently wrote.

LHASA

The second-highest capital city in the world may be the highest capital—it depends how capitals are figured. La Paz (12,000 feet) is the administrative capital of Bolivia, but Sucre (8,500 feet) is the constitutional capital. Lhasa is at 11,800 feet and the capital of Tibet Autonomous Region in southwest China—the Chinese occupied Tibet in 1951. Until 1904, Europeans weren't allowed to visit what had become known as the Forbidden City: Tibetan clergy had long been hostile toward foreigners. The Dalai Lama lived in the city's most famous landmark, the nine-story, 1,200-foot-long, myriad-roomed Potala. The nearby Drepung monastery is one of the largest in the world.

LIBERTY BELL

In 1828, the City of Brotherly Love tried to sell it as scrap but couldn't find a buyer: It wasn't worth the expense of removing the bell from its brick tower. "Proclaim Liberty throughout all the Land unto all the inhabitants Thereof"—Leviticus 25:10—the inscription on the bell when it was hung, in 1753, in the Philadelphia statehouse. It had been cast in England. But was it rung on the day that the American colonies' independence from Britain was proclaimed? Historians disagree, but it probably wasn't. The ringing tale seems to have been invented by a Philadelphia journalist, George Lippard—in 1847. It wasn't known as the Liberty Bell until 1839—in a pamphlet entitled "The Liberty Bell, by Friends of Freedom," distributed at the Massachusetts Anti-Slavery Fair, the bell symbolized the freedom of black slaves. The bell was cracked in 1835 tolling the death of John Marshall, the fourth Chief Justice. It was housed in Allentown, Pennsylvania, for two years during the British occupation of Philadelphia.

LIBRA

Latin for "scales," the root for the abbreviation lb. for pound weight and £ for British monetary pound. Sometimes, the southern constellation Libra is depicted as a pair of scales on the zodiac. The ancient Greeks represented Libra as the claws of the Scorpion. The Beta Librae star Zubenelschemal, between Arcturus and Antares, is the only star observable by the naked eye that has been reported to appear greenish.

LIBRARY OF CONGRESS

It has hundreds of miles of bookshelves. Thousands of books and items pour in every day from around the world. (". . . of making books there is no end."—Ecclesiastes 12:12.) The original library of 3,000 volumes was incinerated by the British in the War of 1812. Former President Thomas Jefferson, needing the money, sold the government nearly 6,500 volumes collected over a lifetime of humanistic study to start the library again: "There is, in fact, no subject to which a Member of Congress may not have occasion to refer," the old redhead averred. Fire in 1851 destroyed 35,000 volumes. The Copyright Act of 1870, requiring the deposit in the library of all copyrighted material, accelerated growth. The Congressional Research Service, the official *raison d'être* for the library, answers hundreds of thousands of congressional requests annually. The national library of the United States houses Jefferson's original draft of the Declaration of Independence, Abraham Lincoln's draft of the Gettysburg Address—it was written on Executive Mansion stationery, not on the back of an envelope—and a Gutenberg Bible.

THE LIDO

Fifty-million Italians can't be wrong—the Lido is the top, at least for the rich-rich who have the wherewithal to spend time in the swank, chic resort on fashionable stretches of sand, a 15-minute trip across the Venetian Lagoon in the glass-enclosed cabin of a speedboat. It was there that every doge had his day. Everyone who was anyone or had aspirations begged, borrowed, or stole invitations to the Cole Porters' parties there. Fat Elsa Maxwell, a hostess with the mostest, was Lido's number-one party-thrower. In 1925–26, she organized the International Motor Boat Races there. Rothschilds and Khans came flying when she crooked a finger, or so she said. Lido is the only Venetian island on which automobiles are allowed. Thomas Mann's *Death in Venice* is set there.

LIFE EXPECTANCY

Recent data on average life expectancy for Americans: If you have a child who is 0–1 years old, he or she can expect to live another 74.1 years. If the child is 1–5, another 74.0 years. If you are 5–10 years old, you can expect to live another 70.2 years. 10–15, 65.3 years. 15–20, 60.4. 20–25, 55.6. 25–30, 50.9. 30–35, 46.3. 35–40, 41.6. 40–45, 36.9. 45–50,

32.4. 50–55, 28.1. 55–60, 24.0. 60–65, 20.2. 65–70, 16.7. 70–75, 13.5. 75–80, 10.7. 80–85, 8.2. 85 and over, 6.2.

LIFE MAGAZINE

The front cover of Volume 1, issue Number 1, dated November 23, 1936, was a photograph of a dam at Fort Peck, Montana, made by Margaret Bourke-White. "Franklin Roosevelt's Wild West" was nine pages of photographs of multi-million dollar projects in the Columbia River Basin, "a human document of American frontier life," which to *Life* editors was a revelation. South America, the editors wrote in their Introduction, "was the continent Americans *ought* to be most interested in, and usually just plain won't be. But a month ago *Life* decided to do its duty and be interested—a duty which turned out to be surprisingly easy to take. This week, Brazil. Next week, The Argentine." Other articles in the maiden venture: "Chinatown School." "Curry of Kansas." " 'Greatest Living Actress' . . . and Helen Hayes' Child." "Cheerleader." "Fort Knox." "Robert Taylor . . . into 'Camille.' " "One-Legged Man on a Mountain." And what came to be a popular weekly feature, "*Life* Goes to a Party." The cover price was one thin dime. The last weekly number of the Time, Inc. publication was dated December 29, 1972.

LIGHTNING

Not even Superman is this fast: The speed of a lightning discharge can reach 1,000 miles per second. Lightning strikes the Earth about 100 times every second. Twenty-one people were killed when a lightning bolt struck a hut in Chinamasa Kraal near Umtali, Rhodesia, in late 1975. It was Benjamin Franklin who first demonstrated that lightning is electricity. He was lucky: Two men who tried to duplicate the polymath's experiment were killed. Franklin also invented the lightning rod. The most intellectual of the fathers of the American Revolution, James Otis—he inspired the Committees of Correspondence—said that he would like to die in a truly unexpected, heaven-sent way, and he did. He was killed by a bolt of lightning, in 1783. No building gets hit as often as New York City's 102-story-tall Empire State Building—more than fifty times a year, about nine times in every twenty minutes of a passing thunderstorm. Its lightning rod is a 60,000-ton steel cage that casually, like Superman in mufti, throws off a 200,000 amp strike. (A charge of a $\frac{1}{6000}$ amp through a person's heart is lethal.) No building within a mile of the Empire State Building gets hit by lightning. It's as though King Kong were vacuuming the sky.

"LIGHTNING WAR"

Blitzkrieg, in German, "lightning war," from *blitz* lightning + *krieg* war —it is war conducted with great speed and force, specifically a violent surprise offensive by massed air forces and mechanized ground forces in close coordination, and with objectives (isolation of bodies of troops, disruption of communications, capture of materiel) such that mobility may be exploited to the fullest.

LIGHT-YEAR

Light travels at the speed of 186,282 miles per second. In a year, it therefore travels 5,878,000,000,000 miles. The nearest star to Earth (other than the Sun) is 4.28 light-years away—Alpha Centauri C. It is the third brightest star in the sky, and the brightest star in the constellation Centaurus.

LILLIPUT

In his travels from the ruthless, satiric pen of Jonathan ("I am what I am") Swift, Lemuel Gulliver, surgeon, sea captain, washed ashore on Lilliput, whose inhabitants were no more than six inches tall—Lilliputians. Their most heated political controversy: Which end of an egg ought to be broken? Gulliver was exhibited as a great curiosity. Swift's attack on courts, statesmen, and political parties—understandably, it was denounced on all sides as wicked and obscene—has Gulliver also meeting Brobdingnags, giants with a magnanimity that contrasts with the pettiness of human beings; the intellectuals of the flying island of Laputa, who occupy themselves with obtaining sunbeams from cucumbers; the last of the Houyhnhnms, a race of supremely intelligent horses, served by Yahoos, reasonless and conscienceless beasts in the shape of men. On Glubbdubdrib, the island of sorcerers, famous men of old revealed how often history has credited cowards with courageous deeds, the wicked with virtue, the foolish with wisdom. The Stuldbruggs, a race of immortals, prove to be the most unhappy people of all. "Principally I hate and detest that animal called man," Swift wrote, "although I heartily love John, Peter, Thomas, and so forth." Before he wrote, privately printed, and published anonymously *Gulliver's Travels,* the Irish-English Swift issued—tongue in cheeky?—*A Modest Proposal* (1729), propounding that the children of the poor be sold as food for the tables of the rich. Three years before he died, in 1745, Swift was declared unsound of mind.

LINCOLN, ABRAHAM

His was an extraordinary personal history of failure: lost job, 1832; defeated for legislature, 1832; failed in business, 1833; suffered nervous breakdown, 1836; defeated for Speaker, 1838; defeated for nomination for Congress, 1843; lost renomination to Congress, 1848; rejected for land office, 1849; defeated for Senate, 1854; defeated for nomination for Vice-President, 1856; defeated for Senate, 1858. Five years before he became the sixteenth, and tallest, President and the Civil War exploded, Honest Abe declared that "the ballot is stronger than the bullet." He was a veritable Bartlett's. "No man is good enough to govern another man without that other man's consent. . . . Nobody has ever expected me to be President. In my poor, lean, lank face nobody has ever seen that any cabbages were sprouting out. . . . Truth is generally the best vindication against slander. . . . It may seem strange that any men should dare to ask a just God's assistance in wringing their bread from the sweat of other men's faces, but let us judge not, that we be not judged. . . . If you once forfeit the confidence of your fellow citizens, you can never regain their respect and esteem. . . . It is true that you may fool all the people some of the time; you can even fool some of the people all the time; but you can't fool all of the people all the time. . . . I shall try to correct errors when shown to be errors; and I shall adopt new views so fast as they shall appear to be true views. . . . I intend no modification of my oft-expressed personal wish that all men, everywhere, could be free. . . . I claim not to have controlled events, but confess plainly that events have controlled me." From his last public address, four days before he was shot in the back of the head: "Important principles may and must be inflexible." When the "Illinois Railsplitter" was assassinated on Good Friday, a week after Appomattox, he was carrying Confederate money.

LINCOLN—ASSASSINATION CONSPIRATORS

The Dixiephiles murdered President Abraham Lincoln and seriously wounded Secretary of State William H. Seward; the conspirator assigned to kill Vice-President Andrew Johnson lost his nerve. As Lincoln watched from a tier a performance of *Our American Cousin* in Ford's Theater, he was shot in the back of the head by John Wilkes Booth, the renowned Shakespearean actor, who had continued his theatrical career in the North during the war. Booth leaped to the stage and ran across it shouting *"Sic semper tyrannis!* The South is avenged!" A month earlier, they had plotted to abduct the President. Eight alleged accomplices were tried for having "incited, concerted, and procured" Lincoln's murder; six, including a widow who kept the boardinghouse where the assassination plan

307

was hatched, were hanged; the other two were given life sentences. (A member of the military tribunal was a general who presently would write *Ben-Hur,* the first novel to be blessed by a Pope.) The widow, Mary Eugenia Surratt, was probably not a party to the assassination. (President Andrew Johnson assured the nation that "the rights of the accused were watched and zealously guarded by able counsel of their own selection.") At the hanging, soldiers politely removed her bonnet and respectfully fixed the noose around Mrs. Surratt's neck. Booth, who had broken a leg in his flight from the D. C. theater, either was shot in a burning barn in Virginia or committed suicide there when he was surrounded two weeks after the assassination.

LINDBERGH, ANNE MORROW

She learned to fly following her marriage to Charles Lindbergh, and together they chartered routes for burgeoning airlines. Her father was an American diplomat in Mexico City, where she met "the Lone Eagle," who was flying into various Latin American countries as a symbol of American goodwill, in December 1927. The Lindberghs moved to Europe after their infant son was kidnapped and murdered in "the crime of the century." She is celebrated for her books *Gift from the Sea,* essays about the meaning of a woman's life, and *The Unicorn and Other Poems.*

LINDBERGH, CHARLES AUGUSTUS

"This is Charles Lindbergh," one of America's heroes said in a telephone call from his hospital room in New York to the village of Hana in Hawaii, in 1974. "I have had a conference with my doctors and they advise me that I have only a short time to live. Please find me a cottage or a cabin near the village. I am coming home." He supervised the building of his eucalyptus wood coffin and construction of his grave. He laid out a khaki shirt and cotton pants. He asked those attending his funeral to wear work clothes. He planned his funeral service and what would be sung and said. He said goodbye to his family. The Lone Eagle then took off on his last flight into the unknown. He was the only child of his congressman-father's second marriage. At the age of fourteen, he drove a six-cylinder Saxon 1,600 miles mostly over unpaved roads to California in a trip that took forty days. He loved to wing-walk, and could stand on the wing as the plane made loops in the air. He loved to parachute. He warmed up for his historic transatlantic solo (and $25,000 prize) by flying *The Spirit of St. Louis* in record time from California to Long Island. (He took a boat back from Paris.) He married the remarkable daughter of United States Ambassador Dwight W. Morrow. Their first son was kidnapped and murdered—the most sensational crime of the 1930s. Lindy helped to develop the artificial heart. He was an American Firster, urging that the United States remain out of the European war. (He had lived in Europe for four years after the murder of his son.) As a civilian, he accompanied fifty combat missions in the Pacific theater. He won the Pulitzer Prize for the story of his flight to Paris. Between birds and airplanes, he said that he would choose the birds.

LISBON

The capital of Portugal is farther west than either Dublin or Glasgow. Lisbon is at 9° west longitude. Dublin is at about 6°; Glasgow is at 5°. The westernmost point in Africa is at 18° west longitude. Lisbon is at about the same latitude as Washington, D.C. Dublin is at about the same latitude as Edmonton. Hawaii is at about the same latitude as Cuba and Mali. Practically all of South America, including its Pacific coastline, lies east of Washington, D.C.

LITTLE AMERICA

The United States camp on the Ross Ice Shelf, south of the Bay of Whales, in Antarctica, a base for exploring expeditions. The shelf, an area about equal to that of France, is ice in a layer hundreds of feet thick which was forced out over the Ross Sea. Little America was established and named in 1929 by Richard E. (for Evelyn) Byrd. In the three-engine Fokker *Josephine Ford,* Byrd and Floyd Bennett were the first to fly over the North Pole, in 1926, a 15½-hour round-trip from Spitsbergen. In 1929, Byrd and a crew of three were the first to fly over the South Pole—he dropped a Stars and Stripes there—a round-trip from Little America. Antarctica is nearly one and a half times as big as the United States. There are jagged mountains, an ice-covered lake whose depths register 80°F., and a smoking volcano; the Pole itself is flat, snow-covered ice. Rear Admiral Byrd returned to Little America twice more in the 1930s. He spent five months all alone making observations. It's cold comfort to know that the South Pole, like the North Pole, was at one time free of ice.

"LITTLE BLACK SAMBO"

"Once upon a time there was a little black boy, and his name was Little Black Sambo. And his Mother was called Black Mumbo. And his Father was called Black Jumbo. And Black Mumbo made him a beautiful little

Red Coat and a pair of beautiful little Blue Trousers. And Black Jumbo went to the Bazaar, and bought him a beautiful Green Umbrella, and a lovely little Pair of Purple Shoes with Crimson Soles and Crimson Linings. And then wasn't Little Black Sambo grand?" Or so the Scottish-born Helen Bannerman thought when she wrote "The Story of Little Black Sambo" for her two daughters to console them for having to go to the hills in India while she remained at home with her husband, a doctor in the Indian Medical Service. Even though the cruel tigers that take all of Sambo's clothes outfox themselves and turn themselves into a great pool of melted butter (or *ghi,* as it is called in India) which is put into Black Mumbo's cooking pot and Black Mumbo eats 27 pancakes and Black Jumbo eats 55 and Little Black Sambo eats 169, because he was so hungry, and the story has a clear literary form and congenial illustrations, it all seems unsuitable for the classroom while "the multi-racial societies of the world are still in the sensitive process of settling down," a commentator on children's books has written. "As a folk tale, it belongs in any case rather to the nursery, to be shared by mother and child in an atmosphere where, one could hope, misunderstanding and false impressions could be avoided, and where it could be enjoyed as a piece of comic fantasy. It is obvious that Mrs. Bannerman had no intention of drawing deliberately offensive stereotypes of black characters, verbal or visual; it is equally clear that she wrote from the point of view of her period and not ours." Hers was the late nineteenth century. She also wrote "Little Black Mingo," "Little Black Quibba," "Little Black Quasha," and "Little Black Bobtail."

"LITTLE JOHNNY GREEN"

The cat's in the well. Round up the usual suspects. Okay, where was everyone? Little Polly Flinders was sitting among the cinders. Taffy was stealing a piece of beef—make a note. Jack was breaking his crown. The Queen of Hearts was making some tarts. The cow was jumping over the moon. Little Tom Tucker was singing for his supper. The three wise men of Gotham were at sea in a bowl. The pieman and Simple Simon were talking to a fare-thee-well. The king of France was going up the hill with forty thousand men. Little Jack Horner was eating a Christmas pie. That leaves Little Johnny Green. Is he our man? "Ding dong bell, the cat is in the well. Who put her in? Little Johnny Green."

"LITTLE MISS MUFFET"

A phobia is an excessive fear reaction both persistent and unadaptive. A phobic person has a strong, usually overwhelming emotional reaction when exposed to the fear-evoking stimulus or situation. The common phobias are fears of heights, spaces, snakes, animals, travel, thunder and lightning, death-disease-injury, and sex. Mother Goose's Ms. Muffet was afraid of spiders, which made her an arachnaphobic. When one sat down beside her as she sat on a tuffet eating curds and whey, why, she was quite naturally frightened away. It has been proposed that phobic disorders can best be regarded as conditioned fear (anxiety) reactions. "The distinctive feature of a classical phobia is the presence of clearly ostensible sources of anxiety. . . . a behavioristic analysis aims at the liquidation of these sources in every case."

LOCH NESS MONSTER

A few years ago, some local people put a raft out on the loch carrying some ham, kippers, some herring, and a trout to see if they could lure "Nessie" to the surface. Next morning, the food was gone but there was a note on the raft: "This bait is no bloody good. Signed, The Monster." The largest fresh water lake by volume in the United Kingdom, Loch Ness runs twenty-three miles, south from Inverness, through the mountains of Great Glen, to the village of Fort Augustus. It's moody, calm one minute, choppy the next. The water is dark, almost black, because it is filled with suspended particles of peat. Nessie was first spotted in early 1933. An authenticated photograph clearly shows an animal with a long, curved neck and a small sheeplike head moving in rippled water. The whateveritis has been spotted by tens of people. "At my estimation," one woman reported, "the length of the body was thirty feet. I didn't see any bumps on its head, and I couldn't see any eyes or mouth; the distance was a bit too much. I would say the thing's skin was slate gray and very much like an elephant's. It was, to say the least, fantastic."

LOCKJAW

A form of tetanus, it is an acute disease of the nervous system that once was a major killer, especially in rural areas where the infection is spread by contaminated animal and human feces; germs may enter the body through any break in the skin. An early symptom is a paralyzing spasm of the muscles involved in opening the mouth—lockjaw. A doctor should be consulted promptly if there is even a remote possibility that a wound has been contaminated by the tetanus bacillus. Adults who have not had a booster shot of tetanus vaccine within a five-year period should be especially alert to the dangers of infection if they are on farms and in stables.

LOLITA

"To think that between a hamburger and a Humburger she invariably plumbed for the former"—Humbert Humbert's lament in Vladimir Nabokov's masterpiece about a nymphet. The late Russian-born novelist said that the flickering of the theme that was to become *Lolita* was a filler item in a French newspaper about an ape "who, after months of coaxing by a scientist, produced the first drawing ever charcoaled by an animal: This sketch showed the bars of the poor creature's cage." Man was an invisibly caged animal. Graham Greene's listing of the book in the London *Times* as one of the year's best launched international interest in the work. When no American publisher would promulgate—Promulgate-gate?—his book, Nabokov had the infamous Olympia Press in Paris (*White Thighs, Sexual Life of Robinson Crusoe*) put it out. Nabokov did not expect the controversy. His Russian culture clearly defined the difference between pornography and serious sexual literature. It took four more years before an American publisher, Putnam, decided to take a chance on making a bundle. Adolf Eichmann found the story of the promiscuous teenager "quite an offensive book." Stanley Kubrick made *Lolita* into a very funny movie starring Sue Lyon, Peter Sellers, James Mason, with Shelley Winters as Lolita's mother. Nabokov termed his student Mrs. John Updike "a genius."

LOMBARD, CAROLE

The cinemactress—high-strung, energetic, blond—went into Mack Sennett comedies after an auto crash had scarred her face. Later, she played romantic roles, bursting forth as a star of the first magnitude—*My Man Godfrey, Nothing Sacred, Mr. and Mrs. Smith*. She married William Powell, then Clark Gable, and she was nationally popular for disdain of bunk. In January 1942, she helped to sell more than $2 million worth of war bonds at the State House in Indianapolis in her native Indiana. Her mother, a believer in numerology, tried to persuade her not to fly back to California after learning the number of the airplane, the name of the pilot, and other data, and making some rapid calculations: "Carole, we must not take that plane!" The thirty-three-year-old daughter overruled her mother. The passengers were burned beyond recognition when their plane plowed into the pine woods of Table Rock Mountain in Nevada. Her last movie, posthumously released, was *To Be or Not to Be.* The Lombard-Gable romance itself became a movie in 1976, James Brolin playing Gable, Jill Clayburgh playing Miss Lombard. Gable won only one Oscar, for *It Happened One Night,* in 1934. A week after his wife was killed, he joined the Air Force; a $5,000 reward for his capture reportedly was announced by Hermann Goering, the Nazis' air force commander. The "king of Hollywood" died shortly after completing the movie *The Misfits* (1960) with Marilyn Monroe.

LOMBARDI, VINCE

He was already forty-five years old when he became a head coach in the pros, first with the Green Bay Packers, steering them to six Western Conference championships, five National Football League championships, and two Super Bowl championships, then for one year (1969) with the Washington Redskins (it was their first winning campaign in fourteen years). "Winning isn't everything," the Hall of Famer is said to have said, "it's the only thing." He never had a losing season, and he was pro football's Man of the Decade in the sixties. "Some people try to find things in this game that don't exist. Football is two things. It's blocking and tackling."

LONDON, JACK

The illegitimate son of an itinerant astrologer and a Welsh farmgirl-spiritualist, he was born into the working class. "Early I discovered enthusiasm, ambition, and ideals; and to satisfy these became the problem of my child-life. My environment was crude and rough and raw. I had no outlook, but an uplook rather. My place in society was at the bottom. Here life offered nothing but sordidness and wretchedness, both of the flesh and the spirit; for here flesh and spirit were alike starved and tormented. Above me towered the colossal edifice of society, and to my mind the only way out was up. Into this edifice I early resolved to climb. Up above, men wore black clothes and boiled shirts, and women dressed in beautiful gowns. Also, there were good things to eat, and there was plenty to eat." He was a seaman, an oyster pirate, a gold-seeker, a newspaper correspondent, a war correspondent, and then an enormously popular novelist (*The Call of the Wild, The Sea-Wolf, White Fang*). He was a Socialist, too, and considered his social tracts to be his most important work. At the age of forty, beset by alcoholism and financial difficulties, he committed suicide.

LONG, HUEY

The political-patronage powerful Kingfish was murdered in 1935 by a young ear, nose, and throat specialist also accomplished in music, painting, mathematics, and mechanics. It will never be known why Dr. Carl

313

Weiss, also a new father, stepped out from behind a pillar in a corridor near the Louisiana governor's office in Baton Rouge and fired his .32-caliber automatic pistol at the senator, party boss (he ran the state from Washington), and former governor and traveling salesman. Weiss in turn was mowed down by at least 30 bullets—his face was all but shot away, his white suit was cut to shreds, he lay drenched in blood. An uncle claimed that Weiss was disturbed by Long's ruthless dictatorship and may have considered himself a martyr who would liberate those suffering under Long's hand. Long had had his eye on the White House. He advocated a share-the-wealth plan, guaranteeing an annual income and a homestead allowance for every family. Weiss's widow said that her husband took living seriously.

LOOMIS, BERT

The dribble wasn't part of James Naismith's original guidelines for the game he'd just (in 1891) invented—basketball—but it was soon introduced by several players, including Bert Loomis, as a protective maneuver, and it appears in the basketball literature of 1894. Number three in Naismith's rules had declared that a player could not run with the ball. He must throw it from the spot at which he caught it, allowance being made for a running catch as he tries to stop. If a player was guarded so closely that he could not pass off, he was allowed to throw the ball into the air (higher than his head) and then recover it. That one toss evolved into a series of tosses and presently there was the dribble. At first, the new sport was played with a soccer ball and with two peach baskets. The limit of five players per team at a time was established in 1897, the same year that the free throw line was moved from twenty feet from the basket to fifteen, as it is today. From the beginning, the height of the hoop from the floor has been ten feet. It wasn't until 1937 that the center jump after each score was eliminated, speeding up the game and increasing scoring, and reducing some of the advantage enjoyed by teams with taller players. Basketball is the only major sport to be invented in the United States—Naismith was a Canadian.

"LORD HAW-HAW"

The name for the Brooklyn-born Nazi propagandist William Joyce was coined by a British professor who taught pronunciation to B.B.C. announcers. The lord was a fascist, and traveled on an improperly issued British passport. He broadcast in English from Berlin throughout World War II. He was adjudged subject to British jurisdiction because he held a British passport, and was hanged for treason.

"LOST GENERATION"

The phrase originated with a garage owner in the French Midi after the Great War. He was talking one day with Gertrude Stein—yes, that Gertrude Stein—and referred to his young mechanics as *"une génération perdue."* She always knew a good thing when she heard it or saw it, and mentioned the phrase to her friend Ernest Hemingway, who then used "You are all a lost generation" as an epigraph for his first major novel, *The Sun Also Rises,* in 1926. Stein also told her compatriot and com-author, "Remarks are not literature."

LOT

"The Lord rained upon Sodom and upon Gomorrah brimstone and fire from the Lord out of heaven; And he overthrew those cities, and all the plain, and all the inhabitants of the cities, and that which grew upon the ground. But his wife looked back from behind him, and she became a pillar of salt. And it came to pass, when God destroyed the cities of the plain, that God remembered Abraham, and sent Lot out of the midst of the overthrow, when he overthrew the cities in which Lot dwelt. And Lot went up out of Zoar, and dwelt in the mountain, and his two daughters with him; for he feared to dwell in Zoar: and he dwelt in a cave, he and his two daughters. And the firstborn said unto the younger, Our father is old, and there is not a man in the earth to come in unto us after the manner of all the earth: Come, let us make our father drink wine, and we will lie with him, that we may preserve seed of our father. And they made their father drink wine that night: and the firstborn went in, and lay with her father; and he perceived not when she lay down, nor when she arose. And it came to pass on the morrow, that the firstborn said unto the younger, Behold, I lay yesternight with my father: let us make him drink wine this night also; and go thou in, and lie with him, that we may preserve seed of our father. And they made their father drink wine that night also; and the younger arose, and lay with him; and he perceived not when she lay down, nor when she arose. Thus were both the daughters of Lot with child by their father." [They both bore sons.]—Genesis 19.

LOUISIANA PURCHASE

His agreement with Napoleon was unconstitutional, but President Thomas Jefferson urged that Congress ratify it nevertheless, casting the "metaphysical subtleties" behind them. Gentlemen, we are talking about an area larger than the combined areas of France, Germany, Italy, Spain, and Portugal, an area *seven* times larger than England, Scotland, and Ireland combined—565,166,080 acres, or 883,072 square miles. At only two and one-half cents an acre, that's only $15 million. France knew that it could not hang onto the vast lands and preferred that the United States, rather than bitter-enemy Great Britain, have them. Jefferson's ministers had approached Napoleon only on the purchase of the "Isle of Orleans," that is, New Orleans, and West Florida. In secret, Spain had retroceded Louisiana to France in 1800. Runner-up to Jefferson in adding territory to the new nation was President James K. Polk: Another $15 million went to Mexico in the treaty of Guadalupe Hidalgo, in 1848, for a vast area of the present southwest from Texas to California which included most of what is now Colorado, Utah, Nevada, New Mexico, and Arizona. The treaty was negotiated by Nicholas Trist, who had studied law with former President Jefferson.

LOUVRE

France's foremost museum of art, once the monarch's palace, has a collection of about a half-million items, including the world's most-looked-at-painting, Leonardo's *Mona Lisa,* and the world's most-looked-at-sculptures, *Venus de Milo* and *Victory of Samothrace.* The royal art collection of François I, who had invited Leonardo to spend his last years in France, was enlarged by subsequent rulers and was the basis for the Louvre. When the court moved to Versailles, in 1682, work on the Louvre ceased and the buildings fell into disarray. Work resumed under Napoleon I. Many famous works in the Musée Napoleon, its temporary new name, were returned after the emperor's downfall.

LOVE

Love is more than never having to say you're sorry. On the men-u and women-u of love are these appetizers and entrees: Familiar acts are beautiful through love. All love is sweet, given or returned. Love is a kind of warfare: Every lover is a warrior, and Cupid has his camps. All's fair in love and war. I love thee with the breath, Smiles, tears, of all my life!—and, if God choose, I shall but love thee better after death. The woman is increasingly aware that love alone can give her her full stature, just as the man begins to discern that spirit alone can endow his life with its highest meaning. And on her lover's arm she leant, And round her waist she felt it fold, And far across the hills they went In that new world which is the old.

"LOVELY RITA"

She was a meter maid. Beatle Paul McCartney says, "I was bopping about on the piano in Liverpool when someone told me that in America they call parking-meter women meter-maids. I thought that was great and it got to be Rita Meter Maid and then Lovely Rita Meter Maid and I was thinking that it should be a hate song . . . but then I thought it would be better to love her, and if she was very freaky, too, like a military man, with a bag on her shoulder. A foot stomper, but nice." "Nothing can come between us, when it gets dark I tow your heart away." Honey pie was a working girl North of England way. Sgt. Pepper taught the band to play twenty years ago. The paperback writer wrote a dirty story of a dirty man whose clinging wife didn't understand. Eleanor Rigby keeps her face in a jar by the door. The barber in Penny Lane showed photographs of ev'ry head he had the pleasure to know. Bungalow Bill went out tiger hunting with his elephant and gun. Sexy Sadie was the latest and the greatest of them all. And happiness was a warm gun.

"THE LOVE OF MONEY IS THE ROOT OF ALL EVIL"

In a letter to his companion, friend, and helper, in 1 Timothy, 6, the apostle Paul (released from Roman imprisonment) advises Timothy on the problems of his work, on theological matters, and on personal conduct: "Perverse disputings of men of corrupt minds, and destitute of the truth, supposing that gain is godliness: from such withdraw thyself. But godliness with contentment is great gain. For we brought nothing into this world, and it is certain we can carry nothing out. And having food and raiment let us be therewith content. But they that will be rich fall into temptation and a snare, and into many foolish and hurtful lusts, which drown men in destruction and perdition. For the love of money is the root of all evil: which while some coveted after, they have erred from the faith, and pierced themselves through with many sorrows. But thou, O man of God, flee these things; and follow after righteousness, godliness, faith, love, patience, meekness." In a second epistle to Timothy, Paul (probably after a second imprisonment) writes that he expects martyrdom. Many of his former friends had deserted him and Paul urges Timothy to remain firm and to hasten to his side. The epistles to Timothy, and to Titus, are usually referred to as the pastoral epistles.

LOVE STORY

Erich Segal's slim novel about wealthy Harvard prelaw Oliver Barrett IV and flip Radcliffe cool Jenny Cavilleri wasn't popular with the critics: "The banality of *Love Story* makes *Peyton Place* look like *Swann's Way* as it skips from cliché to cliché with an abandon that would chill the blood of a *True Romance* editor." It wasn't popular with some paperback publishers: "Nobody buys a novel that is only 131 pages." It wasn't popular with movie people: "Get with it, Segal baby, this is soap opera stuff." Ali McGraw liked it. So did millions of readers. The movie version was nominated for seven Oscars—the story had been written originally as a film script—and the novel was recommended for candidacy for a National Book Award, in 1971. To some, loving this book meant having to say you're sorry. Five judges on the N.B.A.'s fiction panel threatened to quit if "the blue meanie" were not removed from the list of nominations. Segal, the son of an orthodox rabbi, has written a new novel for publication in 1985: *The Class,* about five male graduates of the class of Harvard '58—Segal's group. World rights went for seven figures.

LUSITANIA

Until a German U-boat torpedoed and sank the British oceanliner off the Irish coast, on May 7, 1915, killing 1,195 persons, including 128 Americans, in 18 minutes, there was considerable sympathy in the United States for the Kaiser's cause in the Great War. Four days before the *Lusitania* sailed, President Woodrow Wilson was informed by Secretary of State William Jennings Bryan that the ship would carry munitions to England. On the morning of the sailing, a warning signed by the Imperial German Embassy appeared in American newspapers. The skipper of the *Lusitania* ignored wireless warnings from the British Admiralty and he failed also to steer a zigzag course. Alteration of course to starboard brought the liner within range of the U-20. David Lawrence, the columnist, later analyzed the American press and learned that while a few people on the eastern seaboard were clamoring for war, less than a halfdozen of a thousand editorials in the three days after the sinking indicated a belief that war should be declared. Secretly, Germany ordered its Uboat commanders to avoid passenger ships.

LUXEMBOURG

"We want to remain what we are"—the national anthem reflects the independent spirit of the small (less than a thousand square miles), industrialized, wealthy grand duchy nestled among West Germany, Belgium, and France. (It's smaller than Rhode Island.) About a third of the working force are employed by the steel industry and another third by agriculture. The Netherlands ruled the country for more than four centuries, or until Wilhelmina became the Dutch queen in 1890—the grand duchy's laws did not allow a woman to rule, and so the association was ended. (The rule was modernized in 1912.) The name of the capital city is also Luxembourg.

LUXEMBOURG GARDEN

The lush, formal setting is the most extensive green open space on the left bank of the Seine in Paris. Statues of queens and illustrious women of France line the terrace. Luxembourg palace was built by Queen Marie dei Medici—she did not enjoy living in the Louvre and wanted a little something to remind her of her native Tuscany. The site, near the Sorbonne, belonged to the duke of Piney-Luxembourg, hence its name. A large Renaissance building, it was expanded in the 1800s and served as a prison and the headquarters of the Directoire. It is now the seat of the Senate, the French Upper House.

M

MA BARKER

She died with one of her four gangster sons—her pet son—in a four-hour shootout with the Federal Bureau of Investigation in Florida, in 1935. Was she a master criminal or simply a simpleton who did what her bank-robbing-kidnapping offspring asked her to do? Arizona Clark "Ma" Barker may have killed only one person: her "loving man," who probably ratted on the family—no one will know for sure. What is known is that her son Herman, wounded by the police, turned a gun on himself; son Lloyd served twenty-five years in jail, then was killed by his wife; son Arthur was shot while trying to flee Alcatraz; son Freddie took fourteen bullets when the G-men also got his sixty-four-year-old, dumpy, Bible-reading "Bloody Mom."

MACARTHUR, GENERAL DOUGLAS

Lieutenant General Arthur MacArthur, Douglas' father, a Medal of Honor winner for gallantry in the Civil War, openly criticized civilian officials and foreign policy. He never made chief of staff, though he had risen to highest ranking officer and was military governor of the Philippines. After a policy dispute with President William Howard Taft, he retired at age sixty-four, a deeply hurt and bitter man. Douglas' mother used to send fawning letters to Douglas' army superiors suggesting that it was time for Douglas to be promoted to general. Douglas MacArthur scored an outstanding record at West Point, where he was for three years superintendent after rising to brigadier general in France during World War I. He was department commander in the Philippines and for five years chief of general staff. He led troop action that evicted "bonus marchers" from Washington in 1932. After four years in retirement and five months before Pearl Harbor, he took command of United States armed forces in the Far East. To him, the Allies' commitment to defeat Germany first was "the greatest shock and surprise of the whole war." In 1942, he escaped with his family from besieged Corregidor Island, vowing on the back of an envelope(!) in the Adelaide station in Australia

"I shall return." The Office of War Information asked him to change it to "We shall return." MacArthur refused. Philippines leader Carlos Romulo declared, "America has let us down and won't be trusted. But the people still have confidence in MacArthur. If he says *he* is coming back, *he* will be believed." In October 1944, with Leyte Beach secured, MacArthur waded ashore and said into a waiting microphone, "People of the Philippines: I have returned . . . the hour of your redemption is here. . . . Let no heart be faint. Let every arm be steeled. The guidance of divine God points the way. Follow in His name to the Holy Grail of righteous victory." He was a five-star general when he accepted the surrender of Japan on the U.S.S. *Missouri* in Tokyo Bay on September 2, 1945. Defeat in the Wisconsin primary in 1948 discouraged presidential aspirations. When he publicly criticized President Harry S Truman's conduct of the Korean War—MacArthur wanted to bomb Chinese bases in Manchuria—he was removed as commander of allied forces in a meeting with Truman on Wake Island in April 1951. (Truman reaffirmed the principle of the subordination of the military to civilian officials and the theory of limited power.) MacArthur returned to the States; before a cheering joint session of Congress he delivered his famous "Old soldiers never die; they just fade away" speech.

MACDONALD, JOHN D.

There's a color in the title of every one of John D. MacDonald's stories about the combination detective-thief more avenger than private eye Travis McGee: *The Deep Blue Good-By, Nightmare in Pink, A Purple Place for Dying, The Quick Red Fox, A Dead Shade of Gold, Bright Orange for the Shroud, Darker than Amber, One Fearful Yellow Eye, Pale Gray for Guilt, The Girl in the Plain Brown Wrapper, Dress Her in Indigo, The Long Lavender Look, A Tan and Sandy Silence, The Scarlet Ruse, The Turquoise Lament, The Dreadful Lemon Sky.* McGee keeps half of the stolen property he recovers—invariably his "victims" are criminals. A houseboat in Fort Lauderdale, *The Busted Flush*, is where McGee hangs his hat.

MACHIAVELLI, NICCOLO

The English author and physician Thomas Browne didn't say that "Every Country hath its Machiavel" nor did the English historian and author Thomas Babington Macaulay say that "Out of his surname they have coined an epithet for a knave, and out of his Christian name a synonym for the Devil" because the Florentine statesman and diplomat to several power centers and philosopher and author had written the lively and ribald comedy *Mandragola* in 1524 or discourses on the first ten books of *Livy,* in which he expounded a general theory of politics and government that stresses the importance of an uncorrupted political culture and a vigorous political morality. No—he became a major figure of the Renaissance and an adjective meaning "crafty, double-dealing" for *il Principe* —*The Prince,* in which he expounded politics realistically, based on his view of human nature within the framework of history. He wrote it in 1513 (the same year he was briefly imprisoned and tortured on suspicion of plotting against Medici rule) but it wasn't published until 1532 and he had been dead for five years. Machiavelli called it as he saw it: The leader must use any means necessary to preserve the state, resorting to cruelty, deception, and force if nothing else worked. "Since love and fear can hardly exist together, if we must choose between them, it is far safer to be feared than loved. The chief foundations of all states, new as well as old or composite, are good laws and good arms; and as there cannot be good laws where the state is not well armed, it follows that where they are well armed they have good laws. The prince who relies upon . . . words, without having otherwise provided for his security, is ruined; for friendships that are won by awards, and not by greatness and nobility of soul, although deserved, yet are not real, and cannot be depended upon in time of adversity. When neither their property nor their honor is touched, the majority of men live content. A prince being thus obliged to know well how to act as a beast must imitate the fox and the lion. . . . One must therefore be a fox to recognize traps, and a lion to frighten wolves." In sum: His "ideal" prince must be an amoral and calculating tyrant who would be able to establish a unified Italian state.

MADDOX, LESTER

White supremacist Lester Maddox, who chased black customers from his restaurant Pickrick, whipped Jimmy Carter in Georgia's Democratic gubernatorial primary in 1966. The future President, in fact, ran third, behind Maddox, who was to become governor (1967–71), and Ellis Arnall. When Carter ran again, in 1970, he had arch-segregationist Governor George Wallace of Alabama, campaign for him. But in his inaugural, Governor Carter declared "that the time for racial discrimination is over." Maddox, who was lieutenant governor under Carter, supported the Vietnam War and on April 5, 1971, proclaimed "American Fighting Man's Day," in response to the court-martial of Lieutenant William Calley for the My Lai massacre. Two years before he was elected President, Governor Carter stumped the panel on the television game show "What's My Line?"

MADEIRA ISLANDS

Once part of the vanished kingdom of Atlantis? Ilha da Madeira—"island of timber," in Portuguese. Prince Henry the Navigator's settlers set fire to the dense forests in order to clear the land for tilling and building—the woods burned for seven years. The autonomous, scenic 308-square-mile archipelago in the Atlantic Ocean off Morocco in northwest Africa and some 350 miles southwest of Lisbon was known to the Phoenicians and was once also called the Insulae Purpuriae, after the purple dye produced there. The island of Madeira itself is an extinct volcano and is one of the two inhabited islands; the other is Porto Santo. Two island groups are uninhabited. Delightful climate is marred only by the occasional *leste,* a hot Saharan wind. Madeira wine of course comes from the islands.

MAFIA

The name wasn't even breathed in the motion picture *The Godfather.* Nor was Cosa Nostra. Nor were any Italian words. The moment the movie's producer and Godfather Joseph Colombo, Sr., struck a bargain that the film would not be damaging to the Italian-American image, union work stoppages and Mafiosi demonstrations and boycotts were no longer threatened and movie-making proceeded. Earlier, Colombo had forced the Justice Department to order the Federal Bureau of Investigation to stop using the terms Mafia and Cosa Nostra in its press releases. Another bonus for the movie's producer: Mafiosi served as consultants to insure that clothes, gestures, language, and gunplay were right on the money. *The Godfather* was the Oscar-winning film of 1972, and Marlon Brando was best actor for his portrayal of Don Vito Corleone. *The Godfather, Part II* was the Oscar-winning film of 1974.

MAGALLANES

The capital of the southern Chile province, in Tierra del Fuego, is Punta Arenas, the only city on the scenic Strait of Magellan, the southernmost of all cities in the world. It was settled by Chile midway on, and south of, the Strait in 1847 in order to maintain its claim to the winding, almost semicircular 350-mile-long passage between the Pacific and the Atlantic Oceans. It was a coaling station until the Panama Canal was built. In spite of a long rainy season, Punta Arenas is popular with tourists, because it has one of the finest museums of South America.

MAGNA CARTA

The "great charter" of civil liberties changed and reissued by King Henry III in 1225—and not its prototype extorted by barons and sealed by King John "in the meadow called Ronimed between Windsor and Staines on the fifteenth day of June in the seventeenth year of our reign" (1215)—is the Magna Carta of English law and history, the symbol of the supremacy of the constitution over the king. John wanted to avoid civil war, he was agreeable to a statement of feudal law, he had a desire to give good government to his subjects. In 1217, the Magna Carta of 1215, the most famous document of British constitutional history, was reconsidered clause by clause, as it was again eight years later. Four hundred years after Runnymede, Sir Edward Coke in the Common proclaimed, "Magna Carta is such a fellow that he will have no sovereign." Four of the original copies of the charter of 1215 still exist: Two are in the British Museum (which seems to have regained its charm) and the two others are in the churches in which they were originally placed, Lincoln and Salisbury.

MAGNET

Any object that exhibits magnetic properties. The term magnetism is derived from Magnesia, the name of a region in Asia Minor where lodestone, a naturally magnetic iron ore, was found in ancient times. Einstein, himself a magnet, got hooked on science when he discovered the behavior of the magnetic compass: "A wonder of such nature I experienced as a child of four or five years, when my father showed me a compass. That this needle behaved in such a determined way did not at all fit into the nature of events, which could find a place in the unconscious world of concepts (effect connected with direct 'touch'). I can still remember—at least believe I can remember—that this experience made a deep and lasting impression upon me. Something deeply hidden had to be behind things. What man sees before him from infancy causes no reaction of this kind. . . ." Magnetism is a vital force in nature. The best known magnets are pieces of metal that attract some other kinds of metal. A magnetic field surrounds the Earth. The magnetic compass doesn't know which end is up at either the north magnetic Pole or at the south magnetic Pole. The magnetic force there is vertical, so a gyrocompass must be used. It was the chief founder of scientific experimentation, the sixteenth century English physician and physicist William Gilbert, who suggested that the planet is a huge spherical magnet; the compass needle points not to the heavens but to the magnetic poles. Earth's magnetic field has reversed its polarity many times in the geologic past, and the poles have shifted considerably, each by about five degrees in the last century and a half alone. What creates the planet's magnetic field and its magnetic poles? One good guess: the interaction of motion and electrical currents in the earth's liquid core.

MAJOR BOWES

Bell ringers, toothbrush and kazoo players, musical sawyers, tap dancers, jug players—they were paid $10 and given all the food they could eat that night for performing on radio's Major Bowes' "Original Amateur Hour": "Around and around she goes and where she stops nobody knows." The title major was an obsolete reserve commission of the Army for Edward Bowes, who got into radio through real estate. There were road units of "Amateur Hour" winners selected weekly by listeners in the "honor city." Bowes was heavy-jowled, he dressed stylishly without being Broadwayish, he had most of his finely spun orange-blond hair, and his skin seemed to have been massaged, steamed, and lotioned for days. He was an officer of the Shakespeare Association of America. His script was Spencerian.

MALCOLM X

Malcolm Little's earliest vivid memory was of "a frightening confusion of pistol shots and shouting and smoke and flame." Malcolm X the militant black separatist died in a fusillade of bullets as he prepared to deliver a speech in a Harlem auditorium, in February 1965. He had lived in a foster home, a reform home, in Boston, in Harlem, in prison (sentenced to seven years on several counts of robbery). He was a gifted orator and became the first "national minister" of the Black Muslims. He was suspended by the leader, Elijah Muhammad, when Malcolm suggested that President John F. Kennedy's assassination was a matter of the "chickens coming home to roost." He made a pilgrimage to Mecca, converted to orthodox Islam, and came to believe that there could be brotherhood between black and white and that a socialistic alternative to American capitalism was possible. His "autobiography" was written by Alex (Roots) Haley. Claude Brown believes that the murder of the Orthodox Malcolm by Black Muslims was a major tragedy for blacks eager to remove themselves from a life in the ghetto, from a life of "doing time" and an early death.

MALENKOV, GEORGI MAKSIMILIANOVICH

Quick, who succeeded Joseph Stalin as premier of the Soviet Union? Right, his Trusted Aide and Deputy Premier. Malenkov was also, for a moment, first secretary of the Communist Party. His two years in power were marked by a foreign policy that was conciliatory and by the curtailment of the power of the secret police. When Malenkov resigned, quick, who succeeded him for three years? Nikolai Bulganin, whom party boss Nikita Khrushchev supported for the position. (In 1961, Malenkov was expelled from the Communist Party.) Khrushchev's turn to be top dog came in 1958, and for six years he was both the Soviet Communist leader and premier. In 1964 he was in the doghouse and was removed from power in the wake of repeated failures in agricultural production and the Cuban missile debacle.

MALLON, "TYPHOID MARY"

Though herself immune, she was linked to at least seven typhoid epidemics in New York City. She was taken into custody a second time after an outbreak of typhoid in a hospital where she worked, in 1915; she was apprehended while preparing gelatin for a friend. She spent the last twenty-three years of her life in quarantine on an island off Manhattan.

MALTESE CROSS

An eight-pointed, white enamel badge of the Knights Hospitalers, or Knights of Malta. The design refers to the cardinal directions. (Mystics believe it typifies the design of the Great Pyramid and is symbolic of divine or heavenly illumination.) The Knights Hospitalers are members of the military and religious Order of the Hospital of St. John of Jerusalem, sometimes called the Knights of St. John and the Knights of Jerusalem. (A hospital for ill or infirm pilgrims was established in Jerusalem in the 1000s.) The Order of Malta is the oldest order of knighthood continually in existence; it was founded well over two hundred years before the venerable British Order of the Garter. In 1530, Hapsburg Charles V granted devoutly Roman Catholic Malta to the Knights Hospitalers—the 122-square mile Mediterranean island south of Sicily has no rivers, no lakes, no natural resources, and few trees.

MAMMOTH CAVE NATIONAL PARK

If his actor brother hadn't murdered Abraham Lincoln, the great Shakespearean actor Edwin Booth would be best remembered today for his famous *Hamlet,* which he delivered in part (his favorite "To be, or not to be" part) in what came to be called Booth's Theater—in Mammoth Cave, deep under southern Kentucky. Known passages of the cave extend for 150 miles through limestone formations and beside lakes and rivers. Echo River is about 360 feet below the surface, and is home to a translucent blind fish—best known of the *Amblyopsidae* family—it's mistakenly spoken of as "eyeless"—it has vestigial eyes but it can't see. The cave, one of the largest known, was formed millions of years ago by a shallow sea covering central Kentucky. It has a constant temperature of 54°F. The park, established in 1936, is 51,354 acres. Today, the cave (visited by half a million people every year) is in danger of being fouled by sewage from nearby towns. "Fair is foul, and foul is fair: Hover through the fog and filthy air."

MANATEE

Legends about creatures half-fish, half-human—mermaids—were no doubt inspired by aquatic herbivorous mammals, such as manatees or sea cows, with two flippers and a broad-rounded tail. The females nurse their young at mammaries on their chest. "The Mermaid" is a sailors' song: "One Friday morn when we set sail, and our ship not far from land, we there did espy a fair pretty maid, with a comb and a glass in her hand. While the raging seas did roar, and the stormy winds did blow, and we jolly sailor-boys were all up aloft and the land-lubbers lying down below." Shakespeare's Oberon once sat upon a promontory and "heard a mermaid on a dolphin's back uttering such dulcet and harmonious breath that the rude sea grew civil at her song and certain stars shot madly from their spheres, to hear the sea-maid's music."

MANDRILL

A large dark-brown monkey, related to baboons, a terrestrial primate, in the forests of tropical west Africa, gregarious, in a well-defined social system, characterized by its size and distinctly doglike looks and, in the powerful male, an extravagant color pattern: blue cheeks, red nose, yellow beard, bright blue, red, and purple rumps. A long time ago, it is said, mandrills were trained by Egyptians to stack firewood and do other menial chores, though they are retiring in habits and avoid contact with humans.

MANHATTAN

Whatever happened to Peter Minuit, the first director-general of New Netherlands—the supervisor of the Dutch West India Company's holdings in America who purchased Manhattan from Manhattan Indians in

1626 for trinkets valued at $24 and made New Amsterdam (later New York City) its center and was dismissed in 1631 for shady dealings with Dutch Reformed ministers and went on to settle New Sweden, near Trenton, New Jersey, and build Fort Christina, at Wilmington, Delaware, for a Swedish company? He drowned, in 1638, when a hurricane struck his trading expedition to the West Indies.

MANHATTAN PROJECT

A secret $2.2-billion investment that was a gamble on the theoretical calculations of a group of scientists. The result: more bang for the buck —the design and the construction of the first nuclear weapons. The far-flung enterprise was run by the U.S. Army under the entrepreneurship of General Leslie R. Groves. The project—thirty-seven installations in nineteen states and in Canada, with tens of thousands of contract employees—consumed slightly more of the gross national product than did the Apollo project, which put men on the Moon. (At no time during the war did the West suspect that the Soviets were trying to build an atomic bomb.) The design of The Bomb involved the most abstruse physics calculations and complex processes to obtain sufficient amounts of the two necessary isotopes, then channel them to make plutonium (Nagasaki) and uranium (Hiroshima) bombs of unprecedented destructiveness. The scientific giant Niels Bohr, who had been rescued from occupied Denmark in 1943, argued that the only chance of forestalling a nuclear arms race was to inform Russia about the bomb and to agree on control before there was any apparent threat of duress. Six nations have tested atomic weapons.

MANIFEST DESTINY

"Our manifest destiny," John Louis O'Sullivan wrote in 1845 justifying the annexation of Texas, "is to overspread the continent allotted by Providence for the free development of our yearly multiplying millions." Nineteenth-century expansionists believed that it was indeed God's will to spread democracy from the Atlantic to the Pacific, and then *into* the Pacific with the annexation of Hawaii. Manifest destiny, with its racist, imperialist, and mercenary overtones, echoed during the Mexican War, the quest for Oregon, the slavers' interest in landing Cuba at any cost (that is, up to $120 million), "Seward's icebox."

MANNEKE PIS

At the corner of rue de l'Étuve and rue du Chêne in Brussels squirts the fountain of "Petit Julien," the reconstructed bronze statuette designed in 1619 by Jerome Duquesnoy. The original figure was stolen in 1817 and found smashed. The fragments were assembled to form the mold for casting the little pisher whose stream of consciousness is more than just water over the dam.

"MAN OF THE YEAR"

In 1967, *Time* selected as its "Man of the Year" America's men and women twenty-five years old and under, they'd soon be running the country, like now. Their "tell it like it is" demands showed mistrust for adult deviousness. From acidheads to activists, they derided their elders as "sellouts" and "stickwalkers." They were alienated or uncommitted. Political protest had declined. Their ideology was idealism. "Yet it is by no means a faceless generation." Henry David Thoreau would have felt at home with the young of the '60s; "they are as appalled as he was at the thought of leading 'lives of quiet desperation.' Indeed, for the future, the generation now in command can take solace from its offspring's determination to do better." The "Man of the Year" suggested, that he would infuse the future with a new sense of morality, a transcendent and contemporary ethic that could infinitely enrich the "empty society. If he succeeds (and he is prepared to), the 'Man of the Year' will be a man indeed—and have a great deal of fun in the process." It has been observed by a current, cynical student at Princeton University (class of '86) that *Time*'s "Man of the Year"-1966 may have had more to do with expanding the magazine's audience than with delivering significant social commentary: "The 67ers have made little contribution to society. Drug use has become the cornerstone of social status. The 'best seller' and the 'most popular' are without substance; they insult and they bore." *Time*'s first "Man of the Year" was Charles A. Lindbergh, in 1927. The first woman cited was Wallis Warfield Simpson, 1937. Other honorees have included Harlow Curtice, Owen D. Young, King Faisal, Walter P. Chrysler, Pierre Laval, and Hugh S. Johnson.

MANTLE, MICKEY

He was paid $1,100 to sign a contract with the New York Yankees and had trouble getting started in the big leagues—the highly touted rookie was shipped back to the minors. But once in the swing of things, the switch-hitter was a powerhouse: 536 home runs, including many tape-measure blasts, and three times the American League's most valuable player. He holds the World Series roundtripper record with 18. Mantle had come up as an infielder. When Yankee manager Casey Stengel saw how raw and erratic the farmboy was, he switched him to the outfield and personally supervised the conversion—Casey had been a pretty good outfielder in his own heyday. No. 7 was taciturn. He was once told there would be no speeches at an elaborate dinner in his honor, then suddenly was called upon to say a few words. "When I was told there would be no speeches," he replied, "I tore mine up!" He's been in baseball's Hall of Fame since 1974.

MAORI WARS

In the beginning were the Polynesian Maoris. They arrived in New Zealand from islands to the northeast about A.D. 750. A millennium later came the white man, and in 1840 the Maoris signed the Treaty of Waitangi giving Great Britain sovereignty over New Zealand. The brown-skinned Maori waged—and lost—an on-again–off-again war between 1845 and 1872 with encroaching British colonizers on North Island—many Maoris refused to sell their land to the pakeha, the white man. Nearly ten percent of New Zealand's population today is Maori, the largest minority group.

THE MAN WHO KNEW TOO MUCH

But it doesn't happen. Jimmy Stewart and Doris Day (his songbird wife) save a visiting prime minister from a bullet fired when symphonic cymbals clash by night in a (10-minute) *Storm Cloud Cantata* performed by the London Symphony Orchestra and the Covent Garden Chorus in Royal Albert Hall. Alfred Hitchcock made the movie twice. He told François Truffaut, "The idea for the cymbals was inspired by a cartoon, or rather by a comic strip that appeared in a satirical magazine like *Punch*. The drawings showed a man who wakes up in the morning, gets out of bed, goes into the bathroom, gargles, shaves, takes a shower, gets dressed, and has his breakfast. Then he puts on his hat and coat, picks up a small leather instrument case, and goes out. On the street he gets on a bus that takes him into the city and in front of Albert Hall. He goes in, using the musicians' entrance, takes off his hat and his coat, opens up the case, takes out a small flute. Then, with other musicians, he traipses onto the large podium and sits down in his place. Eventually, the conductor comes in, gives the signal and the symphony begins. Our little man is sitting there, turning the pages and awaiting his turn. At last the conductor waves the baton in his direction and the little man blows out a single note 'Bloop!' When that's over, he puts the flute back into the case, tiptoes out, puts on his hat and coat, and goes home." The Oscar-winning song "Que Sera, Sera" was a key to the Hitchcockian climax. Graham Greene complained that Hitchcock films are filled with "inconsistencies, loose ends, psychological absurdities" that "mean nothing: lead to nothing." At least he didn't mention symbols.

MARATHON

The run was once 26 miles. It was increased 385 yards—1,085 feet—in the 1908 Olympics Games in London so that King Edward VII could see the finish without moving from the royal box. The distance from Windsor Castle, the starting line, to the royal box in the stadium was 26 miles 385 yards—as simple as all that. The winner was an American, John Hayes. First into the stadium, however, was an Italian confectioner, Dorando Pietri, wearing long, bright-red shorts. But he ran the wrong way around the track and was so exhausted by the time he turned around and ran in the correct direction that he had to be aided to the finish line. He was disqualified, but received a special award from the Queen.

MARCH OF DIMES (NATIONAL FOUNDATION)

Never has a disease had such bad luck as did the acute infectious virus disease known formally as poliomyelitis—*polio* meaning "gray," and *myel,* "marrow." How could it have known that day at Campobello, in Passamaquoddy Bay, New Brunswick, Canada, off the coast of Maine, that its latest victim would survive, tough it out, and become the thirty-second President of the United States! At first, Franklin Roosevelt and a few private friends supported a small polio rehab center in Warm Springs, Georgia. Beginning in 1934, the President's Birthday Ball (January 30) became a nationwide fund-raiser—"dance so that others may walk." In 1938, radio personalities (the Lone Ranger, Jack Benny, among them) asked that there be a march of dimes right into the White House—nearly 3 million dimes were presently Washington-bound. Polio was nowhere the killer that heart disease and cancer were, or are today, but with the Boss having it—well, the March of Dimes was a goldmine. Only seven cents of every dollar contributed went into research, but it was enough for the Salk vaccine to be developed and virtually eradicate polio. The National Foundation's principal concern is now the prevention of birth defects.

MARCIANO, ROCKY

The Brockton Bomber—real name: Rocco Francis Marchegiano—had wanted to be a professional baseball player. He retired undefeated in 1956 after forty-nine professional bouts, winning forty-three by knockout, including the heavyweight championship, blasting Jersey Joe Walcott in thirteen rounds, in 1952. Twenty-six of the knockouts were within three rounds. He retired after defending his crown six times. He was killed in the crash of an airplane.

MARIANAS TRENCH

The deepest known depression in the surface of the planet is nearly a mile deeper than the world's highest mountain, Everest, is high. The bottom of the trench, or trough, or deep, or valley, is nearly seven miles (36,198 feet to be exact) under the Pacific Ocean, 210 miles southwest of Guam. In 1960, Jacques Piccard, the son of the Swiss physicist who invented the structurally strong diving vehicle known as the bathyscaphe (*bathys,* Greek for "deep"; *skaphe,* "boat"), and Lieutenant Don Walsh of the U.S. Navy dove the bathyscaphe *Trieste* within about 400 feet of the bottom of the trench. Towering cliffs thousands of miles long and thousands of volcanoes are in the Pacific. In the Atlantic Ocean, there is a 10,000-mile-long mountain range, the Mid-Atlantic Ridge; a deep valley snakes through the middle of it.

MARIE ANTOINETTE

The queen of France was known for ten months derisively as the "Widow Capet"—Capet was King Louis XVI's family name. She then was executed for treason by the Revolutionary Tribunal. The daughter of Austrian Archduchess Maria Theresa and Holy Roman Emperor Francis I, she had married to strengthen France's alliance with Austria, a long-time enemy. The marriage was not consummated for seven years. It was the Swiss-French philosopher Jean Jacques Rousseau, and not Marie Antoinette, who said, *Qu'ils mangent de la brioche,* "Let them eat cake."

MARIS, ROGER

The other famous person from Hibbing, Minnesota, was the American League's most valuable player in 1960 and 1961. He led the league twice in runs batted in, and won the league's slugging title with .581 in 1960.

He played in five World Series with the New York Yankees before being traded to the St. Louis Cardinals, which he paced to a World Series championship against the Boston Red Sox in 1967. In 12 seasons he hit 275 home runs. In 1961, he belted a historic 61, bettering by one Babe Ruth's 1927 mark of 60. Maris' feat is still under a tiny cloud: He played in 161 games, the Babe in 151 games. (Ruth averaged 50.2 homers a season between 1920 and 1931, clouting 714 in all.) On either side of his 61-HR year, Maris hit 39 in 1960, and 33 in 1962. In 1926, Ruth hit 47 HRs and in 1928, 54. Maris retired in 1968, a year after being afflicted with Bell's palsy, which prevented facial nerves and muscles from functioning normally and which temporarily paralyzed the right side of his face. His last salary was $75,000. Maris also holds a high school sports record—in football. He returned four kickoffs more than 80 yards each for touchdowns in Shanley (Fargo, North Dakota) High's 33–27 victory over Devils Lake, in a 1951 game.

MARSEILLES

The French conquest of Algeria, in northern Africa, and the opening of the Suez Canal, linking the Mediterranean with Asia, really put on the map this southern French seaport on the Gulf of Lions. Not that it hadn't already been a newsy seaport. Thousands of French boys and girls sailed from there to the Holy Land in the Children's Crusade of 1212. Marseilles is France's oldest town (it was called Massilia by the founding Asia Minorites 2,500 years ago) and that nation's second largest city (1 million population). A stupendous engineering feat in the early 1920s, the 4.5-mile-long underground Rove Tunnel, linked Marseilles with the Rhone River and boosted commercial supremacy. The thoroughfare Canebière is one of the world's great avenues. On an island in the harbor is the Chateau d'If, the former state prison that Alexandre Dumas, the Elder, immortalized in *The Count of Monte Cristo*.

MARSHALL PLAN

Austria, Belgium, Denmark, France, West Germany, Great Britain, Greece, Iceland, Italy, Luxembourg, the Netherlands, Norway, Sweden, Switzerland, Turkey—the European countries that responded after World War II to Secretary of State George C. Marshall's proposal, in a speech at Harvard, that European countries assess their resources and needs so that United States aid could be integrated on a broad scale. The Soviet Union and various countries in Eastern Europe viewed the European Recovery Program as an attempt to contain Communist aspirations. The United States poured $12-billion into the program between 1948 and

1952. General Marshall was awarded the Nobel Peace Prize for his strategy of economic assistance that put Europe back on its feet.

MARSHALL, THURGOOD

Before he became the first black to sit on the Supreme Court, Mr. Justice Marshall had appeared before the Court fourteen times as special counsel for the National Association for the Advancement of Colored People. He won the right for blacks to vote in the Texas Democratic primary; he had racial restrictions banned on buses in Virginia; he had a student admitted to the University of Texas Law School; he had state restrictions on housing banned; he had racial segregation ended in public schools. Several years after arguing the landmark Brown vs. Board of Education desegregation-in-education case before the Court, he was appointed a judge of the U.S. Court of Appeals, then U.S. Solicitor General. He was appointed to the high court by President Lyndon B. Johnson in 1967. "America's outstanding civil rights lawyer" at one time had "the largest law practice in Baltimore and still couldn't pay his rent," he was handling so many cases for people who could not pay a fee.

MARTHA'S VINEYARD

One of the Englishmen to settle the 100-square-mile island in the Atlantic four miles off southeastern Massachusetts was Bartholomew Gosnold. He named the place—maybe for his daughter, maybe for his mother-in-law, a woman of influence who had aided his fortunes. In the margin of John Brereton's *True Relation,* the name is "Marthaes Vineyard," with an "e" instead of an apostrophe. Authenticated beyond a doubt is the name "Martha" in the Gosnold family.

MARTINI

The most popular cocktail! How it has changed from the "Martinez Cocktail" of 1862: "1 dash bitters, 2 dashes maraschino liqueur, 1 pony Old Tom gin, 1 wineglass vermouth, 2 small lumps of ice. Shake up thoroughly and strain into a large cocktail glass. Put a quarter of a slice of lemon in the glass and serve. If you prefer it very sweet, add two dashes of gum syrup." The millions who have gotten out of their wet clothes and into a dry martini must agree with Bernard de Voto, the stirred but not shaken historian, who noted, most popular cocktail in hand, that "one can no more keep a martini in the refrigerator than one can keep a kiss there. The proper union of gin and vermouth is a great and sudden glory; it is one of the happiest marriages on earth and one of the shortest-lived." Ogden Nash said there is indeed something about a martini—he thought perhaps it's the gin, mother's milk to so many of us. Splash!

MARX BROTHERS

Gummo wanted out of the act, and got out when he got the chance. He got into ladies' apparel—that was always good for a laugh. The talented Zeppo was hailed by James Agee as "a peerlessly cheesy improvement on the traditional straight man," but he got tired of being "the other Marx brother." He built up a talent agency—Gummo later joined him— and invested in an engineering plant that made airplane parts and safety devices and he invented a wrist watch that measures the heartbeat and triggers alarms when the heartbeat maladjusts. Zeppo loved practical jokes. He walked up to total strangers and yelled, "Hey, how are you? How've you been? How's the family? I've never seen you before in my life!" Gummo's real name was Milton. Zeppo's was Herbert.

MARX, GROUCHO

Comedy's King Leer elevated the insult into one of the seven deadly virtues during a sixty-five-year career. "When it's 9:30 in New York, it's 1937 in Los Angeles." "Either my watch has stopped or you're dead." "Three years ago I came to Florida and I didn't have a nickel. Now I have a nickel." "You're only as young as the woman you feel." "You can't have my autograph, but you can have my footprints. They're upstairs in my socks." "I do not care to belong to a club that accepts people like me as members." Julius Henry Marx, one of many sons of a stage-struck daughter of a German magician, had the slouch of a born shyster and the impudence of a parvenu insulter. George Bernard Shaw called him "the world's greatest living actor." His correspondence with the likes and the don't-likes of President Harry Truman, T. S. Eliot, James Thurber, and Fred Allen has been donated to the Library of Congress. He was indeed a man of letters.

MARX, KARL

The German-born social philosopher, the chief theorist of modern social-ism and communism, predicted in a series of articles in the New York *Tribune* that the United States would have a civil war over slavery. Marxism is the professed political philosophy governing approximately one-third of the world's population. The concluding words of his co-written *Communist Manifesto* (1848): "The communists disdain to conceal their views and aims. They openly declare that their ends can be attained only by the forcible overthrow of all existing social conditions. Let the ruling classes tremble at a communist revolution. The proletarians have nothing to lose but their chains. They have a world to win. Workers of all countries, unite!" To Marx, the history of all hitherto existing society was the history of class struggle. It pitted the propertied bourgeoisie against the propertyless proletariat. The "inevitable" historical progression would find the downtrodden proletariat overthrowing the ruling bourgeoisie and establishing a classless society. His theory of the surplus value of labor held that a commodity's value is determined solely by the labor that went into making it. In 1983, a British Tory council member, on the occasion of the centenary of Marx's death and burial in London, suggested that "We don't owe anything to Marx; we owe more to Harpo and his brothers than to Karl."

MARX, KARL—EPITAPHS

Over their dead bodies have been composed words of varying import. Karl Marx: "Workers of all lands, unite. The philosophers have only interpreted the world in various ways; the point is to change it." Carry Nation: "She hath done what she could." Edgar Allan Poe: "Quoth the Raven nevermore." William Shakespeare: "Good friend for Jesus sake forbeare, To digg the dust encloased heare! Blest be the man that spares thes stones, And curst be he that moves my bones." (On the headstone of the world's biggest prevaricator would be the epitaph "Here lies ——————.")

MARY, QUEEN OF SCOTS

What becomes of you if you're six days old and your father dies? If your father is James V, king of Scotland, you inherit the crown and become queen of Scotland. Mary grew up in the gay and elegant French court and, at the age of fifteen, married the sickly young dauphin, who a year later became King Francis II. When he died, she returned to Scotland. Her claim to the throne of England (and her Roman Catholicism) made her a threat to Elizabeth I. Even so, it was with great reluctance that Elizabeth had the eloquent, courageous, beautiful Mary beheaded after discovery of Mary's involvement in a plot to assassinate Elizabeth. But Mary's son, James VI of Scotland, was to succeed where Mary didn't—as James I, he followed Elizabeth on the English throne.

MASON-DIXON LINE

Charles Mason and Jeremiah Dixon were English astronomers appointed to settle by surveying tool in the 1760s the boundary dispute between the Calvert-family proprietors of Maryland and the Penn-family proprietors of Pennsylvania. Had all of Maryland's claims been recognized, it would be Philadelphia, Maryland, today. The Maryland western end of the line was extended during the Revolutionary War to mark the southern boundary of Pennsylvania with Virginia (present-day West Virginia). The Mason-Dixon Line (39°, 43', 26.3" north latitude) became the symbolic border line between north and south, politically and socially, dividing the free states from the slave states. Until the end of the Civil War, the United States was thought of geographically in terms of three large and ill-defined regions: the North (the area north of the Ohio River and the Mason-Dixon Line); the South (the region below that boundary), and the West (everything to the west of the Appalachian Mountains).

MATCHES

Man was matchless until the friction match was invented in 1834. The only "match" had been a slender sulfur splint that was ignited by being drawn quickly through a double fold of sandpaper. The friction match was invented by Daniel M. Chapin and Alonzo Dwight Phillips, of Chicopee, Massachusetts (then a part of Springfield). When they sold their business to a Boston firm, the Chapin-Phillips match became known as the Boston match. "Book matches" were not introduced until 1896, by the Diamond Match Company, in Ohio.

MATHIAS, BOB

The only man to win the Olympic decathlon twice has been hailed as the most versatile athlete the United States has had since the immortal Jim Thorpe. Unlike most decathloners, he had no strong event, but he also didn't have a weak event. The strapping 6-foot, 195-pounder was a "baby," only seventeen years old, when he first won the decathlon, in London in 1948. It was so dark during the javelin competition, in Wembley Stadium, that a flashlight had to be focused on the foul line. Four years later, in Helsinki, Mathias was hailed as a Grecian god from the California town of Tulare, where he was both an outstanding basketball and football player. The ten events in the decathlon are: 100 meters; 400 meters; high jump; shotput; broad jump; 110-meter hurdles; discus throw; pole vault; javelin throw; and 1,500 meters. Self-tutored Bruce Jenner, who set a decathlon scoring record in the Olympics in Montreal in 1976, found that "the hardest thing is not the actual competition but training for it," which was for an average of six hours a day every single day of the year. "It's almost impossible to train to be a very fast sprinter and also a distance man. They just don't mix. How do you train to be a good long jumper and also a shot putter? You have to be a 100 percent decathlon man and train accordingly." Points are awarded according to performance in relation to a predetermined standard for each event. Mathias, after graduation from Stanford University, where he played football, and after service in the Marine Corps, was elected several times to the House of Representatives.

MAURITANIA

The Islamic republic in northwest Africa is surrounded by the Atlantic Ocean, Spanish Sahara, Algeria, Mali, and Senegal. The Atlantic coast has a noticeable lack of gulfs and estuaries. The country's name is from the Greek for "land of Mauri," Mauri probably meaning "black men." Only 20 percent or so of livestock in the agriculturally based economy has survived a series of recent droughts. The country was not included in the Roman Empire, though lands to the south were. The capital is Nouakchott. Wood from the slopes of Mt. Atlas was used to make luxurious furniture.

MAYAGUEZ

It was the first sign of a new iron-fisted policy in the Oval Office, and the cost of the rescue operation was announced as one Marine killed, twenty-two wounded, thirteen missing. Secretary of State Henry Kissinger said, "There are limits beyond which America cannot be pushed." Senator Barry Goldwater said he thanked God "we have a President who has shown guts enough to do what he should have done." Presently, it was revealed that forty-one Marines had been slain and about fifty wounded. Monday, May 12, 1975: The American cargo ship *Mayaguez* radios a Mayday signal from the Gulf of Siam—"Have been fired upon and boarded by Cambodian armed forces. . . . Ship being towed to unknown Cambodian port." There was a crew of thirty-nine. President Gerald R. Ford declared it was an "act of piracy." There would be the most serious consequences if the Khmer Rouge did not release the ship and the crew. During a bitter battle on Tang Island—Cambodian forces there were perhaps ten times stronger than United States intelligence had indicated —the *Mayaguez* crew was released—they weren't even on Tang—an-

338

other intelligence failure. The *Mayaguez* was under way again before the Marine rescuers were helicoptered away from gunfire on Tang. (U.S. credibility had been widely questioned following the debacle in Vietnam.)

MAYFLOWER

The whaler-slaver-wineship, of 180-ton burden, set out for the New World in tandem with the *Speedwell*. When the latter proved unseaworthy, after 300 nautical miles, the pair returned to England and Captain Christopher Jones' *Mayflower* took on some of the *Speedwell*'s passengers and supplies. The original destination was Virginia. The non-Separatists among the Puritans were so upset with the decision to change course—the ship would not be welcomed in Virginia—they became mutinous. Most of the men signed the Mayflower Compact providing for a government under law and by the will of the majority. Cape Cod was sighted on November 19, 1620. A month was spent in selecting a suitable place for a colony. A landing was made at Plymouth, Massachusetts, on December 26.

MAYS, WILLIE

The contract was for "only" $15,000, but the glorious major league outfielder says it was his biggest moment in baseball. His first contract, with the New York Giants, gave him the money to buy an automobile, clothes, and a house for his family. Twice the National League's most valuable player, in 1954 and again in 1965, the "Say Hey" kid (he could not remember names, so he got someone's attention by saying "Say hey") says that baseball was "a fun game for me. I played baseball to do everything good, not to beat any records." He made one of the pastime's great catches, a back-to-the-plate basket catch of a 444-foot smash off the bat of Cleveland's Vic Wertz in the Polo Grounds in the 1954 World Series! "The catch wasn't too difficult, but the throw was. I had to get the ball into the infield fast," and he did, spinning and in the same motion pegging the ball back in. His hat flew off, of course. If Bobby Thomson had not hit the home run of all home runs—the "shot heard 'round the world" that gave the Giants a sudden-death, pennant-winning playoff triumph over the Brooklyn Dodgers in the Polo Grounds in 1951—Mays would have been the next batter. He was in the Giants's batter's circle when Thomson's high pop fly fell into the first row of the leftfield stands less than three hundred feet from the plate. Mays ended his career with 660 home runs, many of them out-of-sighters. He's been in the Hall of Fame since 1979.

McDONALD'S

Ray A. Kroc wisely called "two all-beef patties, special sauce, lettuce, cheese, pickles, onions, and a sesame seed bun" a Big Mac rather than a Big Kroc. In the beginning, there was a small restaurant in San Bernardino, California, where two brothers, Mac and Dick McDonald, turned out hamburgers, French fries, and milk shakes with assembly-line precision. Kroc started a chain of hamburger drive-in restaurants, bought out the McDonald brothers for nearly $3 million, and put the fast-food industry into orbit. McDonald's people take the hamburger business a little more seriously than anybody else. The owner-operator of a McDonald's franchise is trained at Hamburger University, in Elk Grove, Illinois, and awarded a Bachelor of Hamburgerology, with a minor in French fries. Kroc also owned the San Diego Padres baseball team. During one of the club's inept performances, he turned on the stadium's public address system and apologized to the fans. *He* knew where the beef was. Thirty-six years after burger No. 1 was cooked in San Bernardino, Dick McDonald relished No. 50 billion, two days before Thanksgiving 1984.

McGOVERN, GEORGE

The former bomber pilot and teacher of American history was the Democratic party's presidential nominee in 1972. He promised to end the war in Vietnam (he had been an early, outspoken opponent of American involvement there), cut defense spending by $30 billion, and provide a guaranteed annual income ($1,000) for all Americans. He was unable to persuade the media to dig into Watergate. He also had trouble getting a Vice-Presidential running mate: Senator Edward M. Kennedy, Senator Abraham Ribicoff (who would have been the first Jew to run for high office), and Governor Reubin Askew declined. He was pressured to drop the convention's nominee, Senator Thomas F. Eagleton, of Missouri, when it was learned that Eagleton had undergone electric shock therapy for mental depression. (Eagleton is still a senator, and will be until 1986, when he plans to retire.) McGovern then selected a Kennedy brother-in-law, R. Sargent Shriver, who had been director of the Peace Corps. The ticket won less than 40 percent of the popular vote and carried only one state, Massachusetts—McGovern's home state, South Dakota, even went for incumbent Richard M. Nixon—and the District of Columbia: 17 electoral votes in all, to the President's 520. John Hospers, the nominee of the Libertarian party, was only 16 electoral votes behind McGovern; he got one, from Virginia. A *Time*/Yankelovich poll had reported that two-thirds of the interviewees believed Mr. Nixon more "open and trustworthy" than the "radical leftist." Within a year, Mr. Nixon's running mate, Vice-President Spiro Agnew, would resign in a scandal, and within two years Mr. Nixon himself would quit.

McKINLEY, WILLIAM

The only clean-shaven President between Andrew Johnson and Woodrow Wilson was shot twice at point-blank range by an unemployed wiremillworker queued up with others waiting to shake the twenty-fifth Chief Executive's hand in the Temple of Music on the grounds of the Pan American Exposition in Buffalo, New York, on September 6, 1901. The self-avowed twenty-eight-year-old anarchist, Leon F. Czolgosz, murdered the President "because I done my duty. I don't believe one man should have so much service and another man should have none." Two months later, as he went to the electric chair, Czolgosz said, "I killed the President because he was the enemy of the people—the good working people. I am not sorry for my crime." McKinley had lived for eight days, and there were optimistic reports on the chances for his recovery. Vice-President Theodore Roosevelt had hurried to McKinley's bedside; he was assured that all would be well, and went on holiday in the Adirondacks. President James Garfield was assassinated by a man who told the court that he had been ordered by God to kill the President. "The President's tragic death," Charles J. Guiteau, a thirty-nine-year-old disappointed office seeker, had written on the morning of Garfield's murder, in 1881, "was a sad necessity, but it will unite the Republic party and save the Republic. . . . His death was a political necessity." Guiteau pleaded not guilty by reason of insanity, but was hanged. President-elect Franklin D. Roosevelt was shot at five times by a thirty-two-year-old bricklayer shouting "Too many people are starving to death;" Giuseppe Zangara was found guilty of the murder of the mayor of Chicago, who was seated with the unharmed F.D.R. in a touring car in Miami, and electrocuted. John Wilkes Booth made no bones why he extinguished Abraham Lincoln: "The South is avenged!" Lee Harvey Oswald denied firing his misaligned rifle at John F. Kennedy.

McLUHAN, MARSHALL

The gospel according to the Canadian high pressure system: The medium is the massage? And how! The medium, or process, of our time—electric technology—has reshaped and restructured patterns of social interdependence and every aspect of personal life. Any understanding of social and cultural change is impossible without a knowledge of the way media work as environments. . . . Unhappily, we confront this new situation with an enormous backlog of outdated mental and psychological responses. Our most impressive words and thoughts betray us—they refer us only to the past, not to the present. Unlike animals, man has no nature but his own history—his total history. Electronically, this total history is now potentially present in a kind of simultaneous transparency that carries us into a world of what James Joyce called "heliotropic noughttime." We have been rapt in "the artifice of eternity" by the placing of our own nervous system around the entire globe. We now see the visual world very plainly and begin to realize that other cultures, native and Oriental, have been developed on quite different sensory plans, for not only is each sense a unique world, but it offers unique pleasures and pains. Perhaps our survival (certainly our comfort and happiness) depends upon our recognizing the nature of our new environment. It is sometimes blamed on the computer, which we have the habit of calling a "machine." Ours is a brand-new world of allatonceness. "Time" has ceased, "space" has vanished. We now live in a global village. (The hip culture maven Tom Wolfe once asked, "What if McLuhan is right?")

MEAD, MARGARET

The anthropologist Ruth Benedict (with whom she apparently had a lasting lesbian relationship) once observed that Margaret Mead "isn't planning to be the best anthropologist, but she *is* planning to be the most famous." Four years after gaining national celebrity in her mid-twenties for *Coming of Age in Samoa,* she anonymously submitted a poem, "Absolute Benison," to the *National Republic,* which turned it down, then published it when Miss Mead made known her authorship; she never wrote another poem. Biographer Jane Howard spent five years studying Miss Mead and concluded that she was loving, scolding, ebullient, irksome, heroic, and at times vindictive: "As a young girl, she acted like an old lady, and as one of the fabled elders of this century she could be a coquette and even, as one of her friends said, 'a brat'. . . . Because she was so chronically excited, she was exciting, and the excitement was contagious." She began observing human behavior when still a child: She recorded the patterns of speech of her younger sisters. Her mind "was the least empty one" a psychologist had ever seen. She said that homosexuals "make the best companions in the world." An ideal society would consist of "people who were homosexual in their youth and again in old age, and heterosexual in the middle of their lives."

MEDITERRANEAN SEA

The chief existing fragment of the Tethys Sea, which once girdled the Eastern Hemisphere, the world's largest sea—*Mare Nostrum,* "Our

Sea," the Romans called it—is approximately 2,500 miles long and averages about 500 miles in width, lapping up on the shores of northern Africa, southern Europe, and the Middle East, "the sea between the lands," the cradle of Western civilization. If the Sea of Marmara and the Black Sea are included, it has a square mileage of 1,145,000. Its greatest depth is about 14,450 feet, off Cape Matapan, Greece. It was first thoroughly explored only in the early years of this century, by a Danish expedition in the *Thor*. Fish (about 400 species—the bluefin tuna is one of the large fish), sponges (from the Dodecanese, the Gulf of Gabes, the western coasts of Egypt), and corals (Naples) are plentiful. The Po, the Rhone, the Ebro, and the Nile empty into the Mediterranean, and there is a continuous inflow of surface water from the Atlantic Ocean through the Strait of Gibraltar.

MEDULLA OBLONGATA

Laughing, vomiting, breathing, salivation, artery dilation, heart contraction—they are some of the involuntary muscular and glandular activities controlled by the medulla oblongata in your brainstem, the lower part of the brain, adjoining and structurally continuous with the spinal cord. The medulla also transmits ascending and descending nerve fibers between the spinal cord and the brain. Don't mess with your medulla oblongata, it could prove fatal.

MELVILLE, HERMAN

He was so disillusioned by the commercial failure of *Moby Dick* and his other novels that he put down his pen and became a district inspector of customs in the customhouse in New York City. *Billy Budd* wasn't published until he'd been dead for thirty-three years. Alfred Kazin has observed that *Moby Dick* "is the product of a powerfully crossed mind—imitating the bursting century, expanding America, the manifest destiny out of which it came . . . it is the most memorable confrontation we have had in America between Nature—as it was in the beginning, without man, God's world alone—and man, forever and uselessly dashing himself against it. . . . it is the greatest epic we have of the predatory thrill . . . *the* book of nineteenth-century American capitalism carried to the uttermost." In *The Bell-Tower*, Melville wrote, "Seeking to conquer a larger liberty, man but extends the empire of necessity." Melville's death went unnoticed by the leading literary journal of the day.

MENDELSSOHN, FELIX

All cultural forms in Nazi Germany were subjected to Gleichschaltung, or coordination, which meant that the works of Richard Wagner were encouraged because of Hitler's fanatical devotion to the composer and the works of the grandson of the Jewish philosopher Moses Mendelssohn and a major figure in nineteenth-century music (though he lived only thirty-eight years) were banned. Carl Orff and Wagner-Regency were commissioned to compose scores to replace the child prodigy's incidental music to *A Midsummer Night's Dream*—the "Wedding March." In 1936, a statue of the composer was removed from its place in front of the Gewandhaus, the hall in Leipzig where he had been a conductor. Mendelssohn had helped to found the Leipzig Conservatory and he was director of the music section of the Academy of Arts, Berlin. Hitler purged Jewish artists from all symphony orchestras and opera companies.

MENSA

This self-described roundtable society—Mensa in Latin is "table"—was founded in 1945 to bring together people of exceptionally high intelligence. Membership is limited to those who achieve a score, on an I.Q. test, that is in the upper two percent of the general population. There are about 70,000 members worldwide. Match wits with Mensa. You are in a country where there are only liars and truthtellers, and they cannot be told apart by sight. You set out on a dangerous trip. There is a fork in the road that can lead either to a crocodile swamp or to safety. When you reach the fork, the signpost is gone, but there are two men standing there. They will answer only one question between them. What question can you ask either of them that will tell you which is the road to safety? The answer: You ask either man, "Which road would the other man tell me was safe?" If you ask the liar, he will tell you to take the unsafe road because the truthteller would have pointed out the safe road. If you ask the truthteller, he will tell you the truth, that the liar would have named the unsafe road. In either instance, the man you ask will point out the unsafe road.

MERCATOR PROJECTION

There was indeed a man named Mercator, Geradus Mercator, the Latinized pen name of the sixteenth-century Flemish geographer whose real name was Gerhard Kremer. It was the Age of Exploration and mariners needed to know how to get where they were going. The Mercator projection is a map in which the "meridians are drawn parallel to each other and the parallels of latitude are straight lines whose distance from each other increases with their distance from the equator so that at all places the degrees of latitude and longitude have to each other the same ratio as on the sphere itself with resultant apparent enlargement of the polar regions but with great value in navigation because a rhumb line on a Mercator map is always a straight line." Know where you are? When Mercator's book of maps of various portions of Europe were published after his death, there was on the cover an illustration of Atlas holding the world on his shoulders. Ever since, a book of maps has been called an atlas.

THE MERCHANT OF VENICE

Not until the middle of the seventeenth century were Jews allowed to enter England in any number. One who was there in 1594 was Dr. Roderigo Lopez, a prominent physician who had gained the distinction of serving Queen Elizabeth herself. He was arrested on a charge of treason and conspiracy to murder the monarch and the Portuguese pretender, Antonio Perez, and was hanged. Shakespeare's romantic comedy—but love is not the central interest—seems to have been born out of the Lopez Incident. In *The Merchant of Venice* (Antonio is the merchant), the moneylender Shylock is one of the Bard's masterful creations. At many points he is affectingly human, eloquent upon the sufferings of his race and the common humanity of Jew and Gentile. How many times over the centuries have the children of Abraham and Sarah—the chosen people? *chosen for what?*—called up Shylock's magnificent speech: "I am a Jew. Hath not a Jew eyes? Hath not a Jew hands, organs, dimensions, senses, affections, passions; fed with the same food, hurt with the same weapons, subject to the same diseases, heal'd by the same means, warm'd and cool'd by the same winter and summer, as a Christian is? If you prick us, do we not bleed? If you tickle us, do we not laugh? If you poison us, do we not die? And if you wrong us, shall we not revenge? If we are like you in the rest, we will resemble you in that. If a Jew wrong a Christian, what is his humility? Revenge. If a Christian wrong a Jew, what should his sufferance be by Christian example? Why, revenge. The villainy you teach me, I will execute, and it shall go hard but I will better the instruction. . . ."

MERCURY

The smallest planet (about 3,000 miles diameter) is also the closest to the Sun—the mean distance is 36 million miles. (Earth's mean distance from the Sun is about 93 million miles.) It takes 59 Earth days for Mercury to revolve once and 88 Earth days for one Mercury year. It is a world without air or water. Like the Moon, it sports the scars of billions of years of impact of space debris. It wasn't until 1835 that its mass was determined from the effect of Mercury's gravity upon the orbit of the close-passing Encke's comet, the first short-period comet to be discovered (and the comet with the shortest period, as it turns out).

MERLIN

His parents were an incubus and the daughter of the king of South Wales. King Arthur's legendary magician and seer made the Round Table, led Arthur to the sword Excalibur that he took from the marvelous hand and arm that rose out of the lake, and helped win Guinevere for Arthur. He fell fatally in love with the Lady of the Lake; Vivien beguiled him into teaching her the charms and spells whereby she "detained him forever more" in a tower that he himself could not unmake—he was lost to the world forever; not even Arthur's knights could find him.

METHUSELAH

Living to a very ripe old age was old hat in the beginning. Methuselah lived to be 969 years old. His grandfather Jared is the second longest-lived man: "And Jared lived an hundred sixty and two years, and he begat Enoch: And Jared lived after he begat Enoch eight hundred years, and begat sons and daughters: And all the days of Jared were nine hundred sixty and two years: and he died. . . . And Methuselah lived an hundred eighty and seven years, and begat Lamech. And Methuselah lived after he begat Lamech seven hundred eighty and two years, and begat sons and daughters: and all the days of Methuselah were nine hundred sixty and nine years; and he died. And Lamech lived an hundred eighty and two years, and begat a son: And he called his name Noah, saying, This same shall comfort us concerning our work and toil of our hands, because of the ground which the Lord hath cursed. And Lamech lived after he begat Noah five hundred ninety and five years, and begat sons and daughters: and all the days of Lamech were seven hundred seventy and seven years; and he died. And Noah was five hundred years old: and Noah begat Shem, Ham, and Japheth."—Genesis 5.

MEXICO CITY

Montezuma's revenge on the world! Soon to pass Tokyo as the largest city in the world—26 million people at century's end? (The Mexican novelist Carlos Fuentes titled one of his books *Where the Air Is Most Clear.*) The heart of the megalopolis was the Aztec capital of Tenochtitlan, on an island in now-drained Lake Texcoco. The heavier buildings are sinking up to a foot a year. Winfield Scott's American army captured the city in 1847 and a French army captured the city in 1863. It was recaptured by Benito Juarez. An earthquake hurt Mexico's capital in 1957, and the Olympics were held in the thin air there in 1968—the world's broad jump record was set. Fiery murals blanket the city's public walls. Hernando Cortes wrote in the sixteenth century, "The magnificence, the strange and marvelous things of this great city are so remarkable as not to be believed." Today, more than 2 million residents have no running water in their homes. More than 3 million have no sewage facilities. Breathing the polluted air is estimated to be equivalent to smoking two packs of cigarettes a day; pollution may account for the deaths of nearly 100,000 people a year. Rats are legion.

MIAMI

"We speak English, too" has become a familiar sign in the city now one-third Cuban. Spanish-speaking influence has burgeoned since Fidel Castro led his band of guerrillas into Havana and Cubans by the thousands left for Florida in droves in practically anything that could navigate the 200 miles. Calle Ocho (S.W. 8th St.) is a kaleidoscope of *farmacias, bodegas, meublerias,* and *panaderias.* Sandwich Cubano is popular: meat and cheese stuffed into a crusty loaf. Miami was first settled in the 1870s, was built up by Henry M. Flagler (he developed Florida's Atlantic coast into a gigantic resort area), and was land-boomed in the 1920s. Tourism is the major industry. (The Miami Indians were middle Americans, not Floridians.)

MICE—SHOW BIZ

If the movies were good enough for Mickey, they'd be good enough for other mice and men. And they were, for Topo Gigio and the animated Speedy Gonzales, two stars who really knew how to put on the dog and say cheese. The quick-witted, gregarious, lovable Topo (Joan Rivers once put words in his mouth) was in the good hands of the puppeteer Mario Perego. He was the toast of the town for years on Ed Sullivan's Sunday night television program on the CBS network. In 1965, Topo put on the shades and, red-eyed, went bi-coastal, appearing in the feature film *The Magic World of Topo Gigio.* A decade earlier, Speedy Gonzales —"the fastest mouse in all of Mexico"—sped off with an Oscar for the short-subject cartoon appropriately named *Speedy Gonzales.* The disappointed competition that night had only one word to say: "Rats!" *Tom and Jerry* cartoons trapped seven Oscars in the 1940s.

MICHENER, JAMES

Paul Dudley White pointed directly at the novelist and said, "You're the archetype of the mesomorph—barrel-chested, heavy across the heart and rump, elbows out, sloping shoulders. You're the type who gets heart attacks." Not long afterward, Michener suffered a massive myocardial infarction. Dr. White flew to his side, and Michener credits the relatively good life he's enjoyed for the past two decades to Dr. White's subsequent wisdom, which included, "Don't ever again drink whole milk. Cut out eggs. Go light on cheese. Learn to walk away from tense situations. Take a deep breath and turn to something more pleasant. Exercise to the limit of your endurance, but also take a nap every day." Michener says he is a freak in the field of writing "because of the fact that I didn't do any creative writing until I was almost forty." His first book, written on a little island virtually in the middle of the South Pacific, was *Tales of the South Pacific,* and it won the Pulitzer Prize for fiction (1948). The author of *Hawaii, Iberia, Sports in America, Chesapeake, Centennial, Space,* and *Poland* says he has a responsibility to "lure people into a manuscript which they might not normally read, and to make it so proficient that they will be carried along by it and introduced to new ideas, new concepts, perhaps new experiences they might not obtain otherwise. . . . To the young writer I can only say, train yourself extensively and intensively, learn to write, travel, study, read. Write a big [artistic] novel about [one subject] and it would make anything that skirts the subject seem trivial." His next tomes will be on Texas and on Alaska. He has made an unrestricted gift of $2 million to his alma mater, Swarthmore, which gave him a $2,500 scholarship in the spring of 1925.

MICKEY MOUSE

Once upon a train, from New York to California, Mr. and Mrs. Walt Disney discussed "every possible idea" for a movie cartoon series with a new central character. They decided the new star would be a mouse named Mortimer; later, he was renamed Mickey. The first two Mickey Mouse cartoons were silent and met with no response. *Steamboat Willie,* in 1928, was in sound, Disney was the voice of Mickey, and it was a sensation. The Mick was honored with an Oscar in 1932. Disney—Father Goose—loved happy endings. Disneyland amusement parks will live happily ever after.

MIDAS

"The Midas touch" isn't all it's cracked up to be. The king of Phrygia in Greek mythology got his wish from Dionysus: Everything he touched turned to gold. But there was a catch—even the food and the drink that he touched would turn to gold. He chose to wash away his power in the Pactolus River, whose sands then turned to gold.

MIDNIGHT COWBOY

You had to be at least sixteen years old—or a liar—to see the best motion picture released in 1969, *Midnight Cowboy,* starring Dustin Hoffman (Ratso) and Jon Voight (Joe Buck), screenplay by Waldo Salt, based on the novel by James Leo Herlihy, directed by John Schlesinger. One reason it was X-rated: male hustler Buck is reamed over the hood of a car by some Texas hoods. ". . . so rough and vivid that it's almost unbearable," said a reviewer. When a cleavaged, diamonded, furious (her husband hadn't won the best-actor Oscar for *Anne of the Thousand Days*) Elizabeth Taylor announced *Midnight Cowboy*'s selection, the audience roared its approval.

MILLENNIUM

Events a millennium ago indeed seem a bit dated: in A.D. 885, Northmen were besieging Paris; Ashot I assumed the title of king of Armenia; King Alfred translated Gregory's *Cura pastoralis* into English; Stephen VI became Pope (for six years); Ibn Khordadhbeg wrote *The Book of the Roads and Countries*. Two millennia ago (900 to 801 B.C.): the Phoenicians settled in Cyprus; Assurnasirpal II became king of Assyria; Samaria (formerly Sichem) was rebuilt as the capital of Israel; Shalmaneser III became king of Assyria; Dorians conquered the city of Corinth; Queen Samuramat, the legendary Queen of Semiramis, became queen of Assyria; the twenty-third dynasty of Egypt reigned in tandem with the twenty-second; there was iron and steel production in the Indo-Caucasian culture; Chinese historical chronology began; the favorite royal sport in Kalach was hunting from chariots (the Nimrod legend of the royal hunter); Carthage was founded as a trading center with Tyre; the prophet Elijah argued against the worship of Baal and had Queen Athalia, who supported Baal, killed; Samaria became the religious center of Israel; the *Iliad* and the *Odyssey,* Greek epics traditionally ascribed to the blind Homer, were composed; the royal palace and Ishtar Temple were rebuilt at Nineveh; the bronze doors and black obelisk at the palace in Balawat were evidence of a highly developed metal and stone culture.

MILLER, ROGER

The abashed, pixieish king of the road says that you cain't roller-skate in a buffalo herd, but you can be happy if you've a mind to. He claims that his parents were so poor that he was made in Japan. He describes his college education as "Korea, Clash of '52." "I guess the reason a person writes," the multi-Grammy Award winner has said, "is he's not satisfied with what the world has and figures he can do better." Dang me.

"THE MILLIONAIRE"

What would you do if someone unexpectedly handed you a million tax-free dollars? How would your life change? Every week, for several years in the CBS television story, the eccentric multibillionaire John Beresford Tipton tried to find out. He would call his secretary, Michael Antony (played by Marvin Miller), into the study of his estate, Silverstone, deliver a few words of wisdom, and hand over the name of the next unsuspecting individual who was to receive a cashier's check for a million dollars. The money had to be forfeited if the recipient attempted to learn the identity of his mysterious benefactor. Only the back of Tipton's head and a hand on the arm of his chair were seen in the series—but like Charlie of "Charlie's Angels," his voice was heard. The deep, authoritative voice of John Beresford Tipton was that of the well-known Hollywood announcer Paul Frees.

MILTON, JOHN

The great English poet's goal was to use poetry to reform politics. When it didn't work, he wrote his revolutionary manifestoes in prose. He became totally blind and had to work through secretaries, one of whom was the poet Andrew Marvell. After the Restoration, he returned to poetry and dictated *Paradise Lost,* about the fall of man, to his three daughters —it is one of the great epic poems, and places him second only to Shakespeare among English poets. Six years later, he published *Paradise Regained*. His *Areopagitica* is the greatest plea for liberty of speech. And his sonnet on his blindness is one of the finest inspirational poems in the English language: "When I consider how my light is spent/Ere half my days, in this dark world and wide,/And that one talent, which is death to hide,/Lodged with me useless, though my soul more bent/To serve there-

with my Maker, and present/My true account, lest he returning chide;/
'Doth God exact day-labor, light denied?'/I fondly ask. But Patience, to
prevent/That murmur, soon replies, 'God doth not need/Either man's
work or his own gifts; who best/Bear his mild yoke, they serve him best:
his state/Is kingly; thousands at his bidding speed,/And post o'er land
and ocean without rest;/They also serve who only stand and wait.' "
Which is where *that* came from!

MILWAUKEE

Beer was the central pillar—if beer can be a pillar—in the city's temple
of progress. Many of the brewers were schooled in the European tradition. The product was zealously promoted. Fred Pabst employed matinee
idols to visit bars, buy beer "for the house," and drink to the health of
"Milwaukee's greatest beer brewer, Fred Pabst." Robert E. Peary reportedly found a Pabst bottle near the North Pole—the beer capital of
the United States drank to that. Milwaukee's American League baseball
team is called the Brewers. Its National League franchise, formerly the
Boston Braves, won two pennants, then moved on to Atlanta in 1966.

MINNEAPOLIS

Minne from the Sioux word for "water." The Greek suffix *polis*, "city."
The editor of the neighboring St. Anthony *Express* added an *a* for eu-
phony and Minneapolis it became, a hamlet once part of a military reservation between St. Anthony and St. Paul—Fort Snelling had been
established there in 1819—eventually, Minnesota's largest city. It also
became "the sawdust city," the foremost lumber center in the country.
Lakes (22 of them) and parks (153) and wide streets were incorporated
into its growth. Minneapolis—four of the world's largest milling companies are headquartered there—is an industrial might. Its twin city on the
Mississippi, St. Paul, is a trade and commercial center and the state's
capital. Minneapolis (and St. Paul even more so) is farther north than
Milwaukee and Toronto. Minneapolis is 45°00' N, 93°15' W. Milwaukee
is 43°03' N, 87°56' W. Toronto is 43°42' N, 79°25' W. Minnesota is the
most northerly of all the lower forty-eight states. Summers can be brutally hot, winters brutally cold.

MINNESOTA

The North Star, or Gopher, State is the land of 11,000 lakes. It has the
greatest water area of any of the states, if Hawaii doesn't count the

Pacific Ocean. About 4,800 square miles of the state's total of 84,068 is wet. Its watersheds are in a sense "the mother of three seas." Channels run to Hudson Bay and the Arctic, to the Atlantic, and to the Gulf of Mexico.

"MIRACLE METS"

It was indeed miraculous. After languishing in ninth or tenth place in the National League East for eight years, the New York franchise not only won the National League pennant in 1969, it copped the World Series with four straight wins after fair-haired Tom Seaver had lost the opener to the Baltimore Orioles, which had notched 109 regular season wins. The Mets's wins were by scores of 2–1, 5–0, 2–1, and 5–3. Tommie Agee made fingertip catches. Weak-hitting Al Weiss swatted a home run and batted .455. Cleon Jones proved he was struck on a foot by a pitched ball and Donn Clendenon followed with a game-winning two-run homer. The shoe fit this Cinderella team. Baltimore's last out was a fly ball to left field off the bat of secondbaseman Davie Johnson—now manager of the Mets.

MISSISSIPPI RIVER

The Spanish explorer Hernando de Soto discovered the lower Mississippi in 1541. The source of the river wasn't discovered until nearly 300 years later, by Henry Schoolcraft, at the head of a government research party. Small streams feed Lake Itasca in northern Minnesota. The United States acquired Old Man River as part of the Louisiana Purchase. It is 2,350 miles long, the world's third-longest river system—the Nile and the Amazon are larger. With its tributaries, "the father of waters" drains more than 1,240,000 square miles of the central United States (all or part of thirty-one states) and Canada.

MITCHELL, "BILLY"

The American career soldier believed in victory through air power. During World War I, he led mass bombing attacks on the Germans—once with nearly 1,500 planes. In the face of vehement protests of the Navy Department, he twice in the early 1920s demonstrated his view that the airplane had rendered the battleship obsolete. He sent to Davy Jones's locker with aerial bombs several captured and over-age battleships. Mitchell was transferred to an obscure post in Texas and demoted from the rank of brigadier general to colonel. A court-martial convicted him of insubordination for charging "incompetency, criminal negligence, and almost treasonable administration of the national defense" by the War and Navy departments when a navy dirigible was lost in a storm. After resigning, he continued to call for an air force as the keystone of national defense. He hypothesized an attack by enemy aircraft launched from carriers and aimed at the Hawaiian Islands. Ten years after his death, and five after Pearl Harbor, Congress authorized a special medal in Mitchell's honor.

MITCHELL, MARGARET

She wrote only one book—but what a book! (President Franklin Roosevelt didn't think too much of *Gone With the Wind:* "No book needs to be that long.") The original manuscript included sixty versions of the first chapter. She was obsessed with the Confederacy. Her model for Katie Scarlett O'Hara was none other than Mitchell herself. (Hers was a match for Scarlett's "smallest waist in three counties.") She had been a newspaper reporter, and she spent years studying the history of Atlanta and the Civil War. She died, in 1949, five days after being struck down in Atlanta by a speeding automobile. Whenever she was asked, which was constantly, what happened after Rhett walked out on Scarlett, she would say, "I don't know." And apparently didn't give a damn.

WALTER MITTY

As a fearless Navy commander, "The Old Man ain't afraid of Hell!" As a Royal Air Force wing commander, he was the scourge of the Luftwaffe in North Africa. "Somebody's got to get that ammunition dump," said Mitty. "I'm going over. Spot of brandy?" As an eminent surgeon, he operated with the aid of instruments that looked pretty much like a can opener, a sock stretcher, a sprinkling can, and oversized knitting needles. Daydreaming himself into wonderfully heroic stature made worthwhile the life of the meek little suburbanite nebbish burdened with domestic attachments and to whom in the movie version of James Thurber's short story "The Secret Life of Walter Mitty" the knockout-looking Virginia Mayo appears one morning on the train from Greater Perth Amboy. " 'To hell with the handkerchief,' said Walter Mitty scornfully. He took one last drag on his cigarette and snapped it away. Then, with that faint, fleeting smile playing about his lips, he faced the firing squad; erect and motionless, proud and disdainful, Walter Mitty the Undefeated, inscrutable to the last." Presently, Mrs. Walter brings her henpeckee back to Earth—again.

MIX, TOM

The cowboy star—a top box-office attraction in the silent 1920s—was born in Pennsylvania, but grew up in Iowa, where he learned to handle horses. He served in the Army in the Spanish-American War and may have served in China as well. His skills as a rider and with a rope led to an offer to make movie westerns. He and Tony the Wonder Horse starred in about 100 oaters before riding off into the sunset.

MOBY DICK

From Herman Melville's whale of a saga: "His three boats stove around him, and oars and men both whirling in the eddies; one captain, seizing the line-knife from his broken prow, had dashed at the whale, as an Arkansas duellist at his foe, blindly seeking with a six-inch blade to reach the fathom-deep life of the whale. That captain was Ahab. And then it was, that suddenly sweeping his sickle-shaped lower jaw beneath him, Moby Dick had reaped away Ahab's leg, as a mower a blade of grass in the field. No turbaned Turk, no hired Venetian or Malay, could have smote him with more seeming malice. Small reason was there to doubt, then, that ever since that almost fatal encounter, Ahab had cherished a wild vindictiveness against the whale, all the more fell for that in his frantic morbidness he at least came to identify with him, not only all his bodily woes, but all his intellectual and spiritual exasperations. The White Whale swam before him as the monomaniac incarnation of all those malicious agencies which some deep men feel eating in them, till they are left living on with half a heart and half a lung. . . . He piled upon the whale's white hump the sum of all the general rage and hate felt by his whole race from Adam down; and then, as if his chest had been a mortar, he burst his hot heart's shell upon it.''

MONACO

Want a job? Don't want to pay taxes? Move to Monaco. Unemployment is nonexistent there and there are no income or corporation taxes. But there's a catch if you become a resident: Monegasques are not admitted to the gambling tables. Ruled since the late thirteenth century by the House of Grimaldi, it has been an independent principality since 1414. Should the throne become vacant for any reason, it would become an autonomous state under French protection. Monaco is the best-known resort on the Riviera. At about 370 acres, it is less than half the size of New York City's Central Park, and it has a population density of about

46,000 people per square mile. Monte Carlo, named in 1866 for Charles III, is the site of casinos. Only about three percent of the state's budget is derived from gambling concessions. In 1967, the government under Prince Ranier III bought out Aristotle Onassis, who had owned a majority interest in most businesses in the principality.

MONA LISA

For two years early in this century, 1911–13, the world's most famous portrait—the Renaissance-type portrait par excellence—lay hidden under a bed in Italy. A patriotic waiter, Vincenzo Peruggia by name, posing as an official photographer, had stripped *La Gioconda* off the wall of Salon Carré, and walked out of the Louvre with it under an arm. Peruggia swore that all he wanted to do was to return the masterpiece to its "rightful home"—to Italy, that is, not to his bedroom. *Mona Lisa* was probably Lisa Gherardini, who at sixteen was married to the twice-widowed, rich Francesco del Giocondo, who commissioned Leonardo da Vinci to paint the portrait after Lisa at twenty-four had suffered the loss of her only child, a girl. Late in the day for three years, when the soft light "gives most grace to faces," Lisa sat amid musicians and readers providing melody and poetry. Leonardo wouldn't let *La Gioconda* out of his sight: Milan, Rome, then across the Alps to France, where he settled, in 1516, at the invitation of King Francis I, in the Chateau de Cloux, near the palace at Amboise. The monarch is reported to have paid Leonardo 4,000 gold crowns for the portrait, but he didn't gain possession until Leonardo died, in 1519, following a stroke. *Mona Lisa* then belonged to a series of kings and emperors, including Napoleon, who hung it on a bedroom wall in the Tuileries. It traveled to the United States in an airtight aluminum box aboard the liner *France* and was exhibited in the nation's capital from December 14, 1962, to March 12, 1963.

MONGOOSE

Because of its destructiveness, the small (up to 3½ feet in length), carnivorous terrestrial mammal cannot be imported into the United States. Indigenous to Africa and to southern Asia, it is a fierce, active hunter which lives in a variety of habitats—burrows, rock crevices, roots of trees. It swims well when forced to do so. It eats insects and spiders and snails, slugs, frogs, toads, lizards, birds, eggs of reptiles and birds, mice, rats, and mammals up to the size of a hare. Some species will eat fruits, berries, nuts, roots, tubers, and young leaves. The Indian gray mongoose is celebrated for its ability to kill snakes, even cobras. A researcher's pet

"Rikki-Tikki-Tavi" liked salad if it was liberally mixed with French dressing.

MONITOR AND VIRGINIA

History's first naval battle between steampowered ironclad vessels, the Union's *Monitor,* built by the Swedish immigrant John Ericsson, and the C.S.S. *Virginia,* formerly the steam frigate *Merrimack,* which retreating Union forces had scuttled at Portsmouth, Virginia, and Confederates raised and rebuilt. The day after the *Virginia* had rammed and destroyed and scattered wooden ships of the Union fleet blockading Hampton Roads, the twin-gunned armor-plated raft *Monitor* showed up from New York. A four-hour duel to a draw was fought that March day in 1862. In April, the *Monitor* chose not to fight again. In May, the *Virginia* was scuttled. In December, the *Monitor* sank in a hurricane off Cape Hatteras.

MONOPOLY

After testing for several weeks the board game that Charles Darrow, of Germantown, Pennsylvania, had patented as his own invention in 1935, Parker Brothers decided not to go with it. There were "fifty-two fundamental errors" and, besides, a game of real estate would never be accepted by the public. One error: A "family game" should last approximately 45 minutes; Monopoly could go on for hours; there was no specific goal. Too, the players would not be able to handle mortgages, rents, and interest. Darrow continued to produce the game himself, it caught on nationally, and Parker changed its corporate mind. According to a Parker Brothers brochure, Darrow had been hard hit by the Depression and "decided to devise a game dealing with imaginary real estate investments." He "placed a piece of oilcloth on the kitchen table and began to sketch out street names from Atlantic City, a favorite holiday place." There is today on the Boardwalk in Atlantic City, near the juncture of Park Place, a commemorative plaque in Darrow's honor. It turns out that the abiding inspirational tale of American commerce is not true. The social commentator Calvin Trillin has reported that one version or another of Monopoly had been played for years—largely by people who thought of it as a game that was, to quote from rules typed out several years before Darrow's involvement, "designed to show the evils resulting from the institution of private property." There is now no disagreement: Monopoly was not derived from a game thought up by a plucky and ingenious Darrow but by Lizzie J. Magie "around the turn of the century as a way to popularize the theories of Henry George, the late-nineteenth-century reformer who believed that capitalism could work only if no one were permitted to profit from the ownership of land''—the Landlord's Game. Because it doesn't really matter who invented Monopoly, Monopoly fans stormed a meeting of Atlantic City commissioners hearing a proposal, in 1973, that part of a city beautification program include changing the names of the less than picturesque Baltic and Mediterranean Avenues, the cheapest properties on the Monopoly board. A poem was read: "To this ordinance vote no. To our residents it presents a great woe. Baltic and Mediterranean are the streets we know. Without them we could never pass GO.''

MONOPOLY—LANDING PROBABILITIES

Illinois Avenue. A computer analysis reports that it's the most landed-upon space in the board game Monopoly. Go is the second-most landed-upon space. The next eight: B & O Railroad, Free Parking, Tennessee Avenue, New York Avenue, Reading Railroad, St. James Place, Water Works, Pennsylvania Railroad. Orange is said to be the color most often landed on. Marvin Gardens is the one color-block Monopoly property that is not in Atlantic City.

MONROE, MARILYN

Wrapped in skin and beads, she sang "Happy Birthday" as it's never been sung: "Happy Birthday, *Dear* President Kennedy." Adlai Stevenson said of the celebration in Madison Square Garden, in 1962, "I do not think I have seen anyone so beautiful . . . my encounters, however, were only after breaking through the strong defenses established by Robert Kennedy, who was dodging around her like a moth around the flame." Ralph G. Martin reports MMmmmm was the last to arrive at the President's intimate party later at the Carlyle on Madison Avenue after the Garden fete, and "the last to leave," and that the forty-five-year-old J.F.K. may have satisfied "his curiosity about Marilyn Monroe that night." Norma Jean Mortenson had become Norma Jean (sometimes Jeane) Baker; Baker was her mother's name—Gladys Monroe Baker. Should she become Jean Norman? She had sentimental ties to Jean Harlow and Norma Talmadge. Hollywood bigwigs talked about changing her name when the screen test showed flesh that photographed like flesh. Biodocumentarian Norman Mailer says, yes, she could develop sentimental ties to Marlene Dietrich and President James Monroe; she had a grandfather Monroe. One of Marilyn's grandmothers had been committed to a mental hospital, and Marilyn's schizophrenic mother was in an asylum for most of Marilyn's life. Marilyn's mother's brother killed himself. Three years passed between Marilyn's screen test and her first movie, *The Asphalt Jungle*, six years before *Gentlemen Prefer Blondes*, nine before *The Seven-Year Itch*. She would have been fifty-nine years old in 1985.

MONROVIA

The American Colonization Society, founded in 1816 by the Reverend Robert Finley, of New Jersey, stimulated Congress to help establish a haven in Africa for slaves freed or born to free parents. Among the prominent slaveholders supporting the scheme were John C. Calhoun, Henry Clay, and future President Andrew Jackson. Land fronting the Atlantic Ocean at Cape Mesurado was secured from local De chiefs, Liberia was founded in 1821, and the first of 15,000 settlers from the United States and the West Indies began relocating there the next year. One of the society's agents, Jehudi Ashmun, was instrumental in keeping the colony alive. The capital was named Monrovia for the United States President at the time, James Monroe.

MONSOON

Every continent except Antarctica experiences monsoonal winds, but they are lesser in intensity away from various latitudes in the Indian Ocean and southern Asia. There, the winds blow from the southwest from the latter part of April to the middle of October, from the northeast from about the middle of October to April. The season of the southwest monsoon is a time of monstrous rainfall.

MONT BLANC TUNNEL

The world's longest highway tunnel (7.2 miles), it was the first large rock tunnel (29½ feet high, two 12-foot-wide lanes) to be excavated full-face —the diameter was bore-drilled and blasted. The Italian work force started out from Entreves, near Courmayeur in Valle d'Aosta, and the French from Pelerins, near Chamonix, and they reached the mid-point after 3½ years, only 11 days apart—and only nine inches off a perfect junction. There were twenty-three deaths during 6½ years of construction and the tunnel opened to traffic in 1965. The pair of nearly thirteen-mile-long Simplon railroad tunnels under western Europe's highest mountain link Switzerland and Italy; they were opened in 1906 and 1922. Mont Blanc is Europe's second highest peak (15,771 feet).

MONTHS

From the Anglo-Saxon word *mona* for "moon." April, T. S. Eliot noted, is "the cruelest month, breeding lilacs out of the dead land, mixing memory and desire, stirring dull roots with spring rain." May, Thomas Hardy observed, "flaps its glad green leaves like wings, delicate-filmed as newspun silk." Thomas Hood: "No warmth, no cheerfulness, no healthful ease, no comfortable feel in any member—no shade, no shine, no butterflies, no bees, no fruits, no flowers, no leaves, no birds, November!" January, from the two-faced god, Janus. February: from the Latin for purification. March, from the god Mars. April, from Aphrodite, or the month of Venus. May, for Maia, the Roman goddess of growth. June, for Juno, the wife of Jupiter, the Romans' top god. July, for Julius Caesar, by order of Marc Antony immediately after the assassination. August, for Augustus Caesar. September, from the Latin for seven—it was once the seventh month. October, for eight—it was once the eighth month. November, nine. December, ten. (*Octo, novem, decem.*)

MOON

It weighs 81,000,000,000,000,000,000 tons and circles Earth once every 27⅓ days at an average distance of 238,857 miles. There are still some people who believe it has absolutely no effect on their lives. In the racial memory, *The New Yorker* magazine has noted, "the Moon is bad news, and the lunatic is simply a fellow who happens to remember better." The personal, empirical observations of emergency-room and psychiatric-ward personnel emphatically suggest that Earth's only natural satellite plays a key role in the behavior of normal and mentally aberrant people. Arson cases in New York have increased 100 percent at full moon. Shakespeare, who knew everything, wrote, "It is the very error of the moon; She comes more near the earth than she was wont, and makes men mad." Dr. Arnold L. Lieber, who has long studied the lunar effect on biological tides and human emotions, believes that the Moon represents one of the many subtle cosmic forces that, by their configuration, give man a pattern in which to synchronize his life with the Universe: Life has biological high and low tides governed by the Moon. Where did it come from? It may have been torn out of the Pacific Ocean. It may have been captured by the Earth. Why is it where it is and not much closer or much farther away?

MOON—FEATURES

As long ago as 150 years, Wilhelm Beer was able to measure accurately the heights of myriad mountains 240,000 miles away—even though he was in his observatory in Germany and the mountains were on the Moon. Naming sites on Earth's only natural satellite goes back to the gaze of naked-eye observations. In the 1600s, the Italian astronomer Giovanni Battista Riccioli named lunar craters in honor of astronomers of the past. A contemporary, the German astronomer Johannes Hevelius, dubbed "seas" the dark, relatively flat, dry stretches of dust (*maria* in Latin); there is a Pacific Ocean—*Mare Serenitatis*—out there as well as in here. Man first walked in the Sea of Tranquillity. On the near side, the side of the Moon always facing Earth, are the Sea of Showers, the Sea of Serenity, the Lake of Dreams, the Sea of Crises, the Ocean of Storms, the Sea of Cold, the Sea of Nectar, the Sea of Clouds, the Sea of Rains, Clavius, Tycho, Pythagoras, Plato, Copernicus, Humboldt, Fra Mauro. It's only been within the last two decades, as unmanned and manned vehicles have sent back the first photographs, that man has seen the dark, or far, scape: Borman, Lovell, Anders, Moscow Sea, Joliot-Curie, Jules Verne, Korolev, Kibalchich, and Tsiolokovsky.

MOON WALK

"The surface is fine and powdery," Neil A. Armstrong radioed to Earth and the mission-control center in Houston as he became, in July 1969, the first man to step on the Moon. "I can pick it up loosely with my toe. It does adhere in fine layers like powdered charcoal to the sole and sides of my boots. I only go in a small fraction of an inch. Maybe an eighth of an inch, but I can see the footprints of my boots and the treads in the fine, sandy particles." The civilian commander of the lunar module *Eagle* was joined by co-pilot Col. Edwin E. Aldrin, Jr., of the Air Force. He could see "literally thousands of small craters" and was impressed by the "variety of shapes, angularities, granularities" of the rock and the soil. President Richard M. Nixon congratulated Armstrong and Aldrin in what he said "certainly has to be the most historic telephone call ever made." Another astronaut who followed radioed back, "There's just hardly any place that hasn't got craters around it. . . . I'll tell you, this place is full of holes." Thomas More, before he became Sir Thomas More, declared that the Moon was made of green cheese.

MOORE, ARCHIE

Real name: Archibald Lee Wright. Real age: It's anybody's guess. "Old Man River," or the "Ol' Mongoose," was at least forty-four years old—he was definitely the oldest man ever to hold a world boxing title—when he was stripped of his light heavyweight crown by the National Boxing Association in 1960. Two years later, other boxing units also withdrew recognition of his championship. Moore had copped the title in 1952 in a 15-round bout with Joey Maxim. He sometimes fought out of his weight class, and was outclassed by heavyweights Rocky Marciano, in 1955, Floyd Patterson, in 1956, and Cassius Clay, in 1962. Moore's 234th, and last, bout was a knockout of Mike DiBiase, in 1963—in all, he punched out a record 145 KOs among his 199 triumphs. (He fought eight draws, one no-contest, and he lost 26 times.) He was elected to boxing's Hall of Fame in 1966.

MOORE, CLEMENT CLARKE

The son of a president of Columbia University who became the second Episcopal bishop of New York compiled a two-volume compendious lexicon of the Hebrew language and later was a professor of Oriental and Greek literature at Episcopal General Theological Seminary, built on land in New York that he had donated. He also casually but felicitously wrote a little poem to amuse his children at Christmastime in 1822. A house guest copied it surreptitiously and a year later "Visit from St. Nicholas" was published without byline and without Moore's prior knowledge in the Troy, New York, *Sentinel*. Not a creature was stirring? "Happy Christmas to all, and to all a good night!"

MOORE, MARY TYLER

She was seen and she was heard, but because they loved her for her dancer's legs she was seen only from the waist down. Actresses have been known to do almost anything—well, anything—to get a leg up, but this was ridiculous, and there wasn't even a screen credit, to boot. So she asked out after thirteen episodes in her first role in a television series, as Sam, the answering-service girl in "Richard Diamond, Private Eye." (She was always warning him of danger.) Her successor was another unbilled leggy actress, Roxanne Brooks. Miss Moore's Sam was revealed when she modeled the latest in women's hosiery for *TV Guide*. For five years, in the 1960s, she was seen body and soul as the wife in "The Dick Van Dyke Show"; then as Mary Richards, she went into her own enormously popular series.

MORPHINE

The crystalline alkaloid extracted from opium and used in medicine to produce sleep and insensibility to pain—morphine—got its name from Morpheus, the Roman and Greek god of dreams. Morpheus was the son of the god of sleep, Somnus or Hypnos. He summoned human shapes for dreamers. Morpheus' two brothers were also in the dream world. Phobetor induced dreams of animals. Phantasos induced dreams of inanimate objects. Morpheus is often depicted as a chubby child wearing wings. Sounds like a dream.

MORSE CODE

"If the presence of electricity can be made visible in any desired part of the circuit," Samuel F. B. Morse reasoned, "I see no reason why intelligence might not be instantaneously transmitted by electricity to any distance." ·— —· —·· ··· ———— ·· — —·—· ·— ——— · — ———— —··· ·
And so it came to be: a code in which letters of the alphabet, numbers, and other symbols are represented by dots and dashes or long and short sounds and used for transmitting messages by audible or visual signs, as by telegraphy, wigwag, or light flashes. The American Morse code differs from the international code in eleven letters (c, f, j, l, o, p, q, r, x, y, z), the numbers 0–9, the period, the comma. With reluctant congressional support, Morse built a poled line between Washington and Baltimore, thirty-seven miles, and on May 24, 1844, tapped out, "What hath God wrought?" The Leyland liner *California* was close enough to receive wireless messages from the *Titanic* foundering in the North Atlantic that foggy fateful April night in 1912 and to effect a rescue. But the *California*'s radio operator was not on duty—he had had no relief, and had to sleep sometime.

MORSE, SAMUEL F. (FINLEY) B. (BREESE)

"What hath God wrought?"—practical telegraphy's first long-distance message, in 1844, from the Supreme Court chamber in the Capitol to Baltimore, on a $30,000 line paid for by the Congress, which then decided not to buy all rights to the telegraph for $100,000. Morse was for nineteen years president of the National Academy of Design—he was a painter—and he ran unsuccessfully for mayor of New York City—he was a nativist, bitterly anti-Catholic. He helped Cyrus Field in laying a transatlantic telegraph cable and he helped found Vassar College. In old age, he hated Abraham Lincoln, believing slavery "divinely ordained." (In 1831, Joseph Henry, a physicist, published a detailed proposal for a telegraph; in a court trial, he proved that he, and not Morse, had invented the electromagnetic telegraph. Henry was first director of "America's attic"—the Smithsonian Institution.)

MOSES—STRANGER IN A STRANGE LAND

"And it came to pass in those days, when Moses was grown, that he went out unto his brethren, and looked on their burdens: and he spied an Egyptian smiting an Hebrew, one of his brethren. And he looked this way and that way, and when he saw that there was no man, he slew the Egyptian, and hid him in the sand. And when he went out the second day, behold, two men of the Hebrews strove together: and he said to him that did the wrong, Wherefore smitest thou thy fellow. And he said, Who made thee a prince and a judge over us? intendest thou to kill me, as thou killedst the Egyptian? And Moses feared, and said, Surely this thing is known. Now when Pharaoh heard this thing, he sought to slay Moses. But Moses fled from the face of Pharaoh, and dwelt in the land of Midian: and he sat down by a well. Now the priest of Midian had seven daughters: and they came and drew water, and filled the troughs to water their father's flock. And the shepherds came and drove them away: but Moses stood up and helped them, and watered their flock. And when they came to Reuel their father, he said, How is it that ye are come so soon today? And they said, An Egyptian delivered us out of the hand of the shepherds, and also drew water enough for us, and watered the flock. And he said unto his daughters, And where is he? why is it that ye have left the man? call him, that he may eat bread. And Moses was content to dwell with the man: and he gave Moses Zipporah his daughter. And she bare him a son, and he called his name Gershom: for he said, I have been a stranger in a strange land. And it came to pass in process of time, that the king of Egypt died: and the children of Israel sighed by reason of the bondage, and they cried, and their cry came up unto God by reason of the bondage. And God heard their groaning, and God remembered his covenant with Abraham, with Isaac, and with Jacob. And God looked upon the children of Israel, and God had respect unto them." —Exodus 2. The creator of Judaism and the father of monotheism was born in Egypt. He was hidden on the banks of the Nile when the Pharaoh ordered that all male babes be slain. He was rescued in the bulrushes by Pharaoh's daughter and returned to his mother's breast. The Lord spoke to him from the burning bush that miraculously was not consumed. He led the exodus across the Red Sea, and he received the Ten Commandments on Mt. Sinai—twice. He led the Israelites through the wilderness for 40 years. Upon his death, on Mount Nebo at the age of 120, leadership of the Israelites passed to Joshua. The Gospel according to St. Mark reports that high on a mountain the disciples Peter, James, and John saw Jesus talking with Moses.

MOSQUITO

It has forty-seven "teeth." It is a bloodsucker. The female must feed at least once upon mammalian blood before her eggs can develop properly. Both male and female mosquitos feed on flowers, for nectar is their principal source of energy. Mosquitos are a worldwide nuisance. They've bugged humans way up the Andes, and mosquito larvae have been found at 12,000 feet in the Himalayas and in the frozen north of the Arctic Circle. The Anopheles mosquito carries the protozoan parasite that causes malaria.

MOTHER'S DAY

It was first observed in 1908, a year after Miss Anna M. Jarvis, of Philadelphia, urged that a carnation be worn in honor of one's mother on the second Sunday in May. England began observing Mother's Day in 1913; there had been a rural custom there of visiting one's parents on Mothering Sunday, in mid-Lent.

MOTHER TERESA

On a train ride to Darjeeling, she felt the touch of a divine command. Its message: She must quit her cloistered existence—she was a Roman Catholic teaching nun in India—and plunge into Calcutta's clamorous, desolate slums to care for the poorest of the poor. Plunge she did, collecting abandoned babies from gutters and garbage heaps and creating The Missionaries of Charity, in 1948. Born, in 1910, in Yugoslavia, to Albanian parents and baptized Agnes Gonxha Bojaxhiu, she wanted even at the age of twelve to "go out and give the love of Christ." Her worldwide unit based in Calcutta serves the sick, the lonely, the destitute, and the dying. "For me, each one is an individual. I can give my whole heart to that person for that moment in an exchange of love. It is not social work. We must love each other. It involves emotional involvement, making people feel they are wanted." In 1979, she was awarded the Nobel Peace Prize: "Personally, I am unworthy," she said. "I accept in the name of the poor, because I believe that by giving me the prize they've recognized the presence of the poor in the world." She planned to use the award, $190,000, to build more hospices, especially for the lepers.

MOUNT ETNA

Dominating the eastern coast of the island of Sicily, in the Mediterranean, the highest (10,958 feet, but dwindling) active volcano in Europe has erupted about 80 times, sometimes violently and as recently as thrice in the 1970s and again in 1981. The southeastern slope has been slashed by a deep (2,000–4,000 foot) precipitous cleft, the Valle del Bove. The wide base of the mountain is nearly 100 miles in circumference and is encircled by a railroad. Up to 1,600 feet, the vegetation (citrus fruits) is subtropical. Between 1,600 and 4,300 feet, there are vineyards and various fruit trees in a temperate zone. Farther up, chestnut, birch, and pine woods, then a desolate waste of lava and ash. Most of the year there's snow on the peaks.

MOUNT EVEREST

Chomo-Lungma—Mother Goddess of the Land—to Tibetans, Sagarmatha to Nepalese, the world's tallest mountain was measured at 29,002 feet in the middle 1800s, at 29,028 feet in 1954, and at 29,141 feet recently, give or take a millimeter. It was first scaled in 1953, Edmund Hillary and the Nepalese Sherpa tribesman Tenzing Norgay taking photographs at the tip on May 29. They had started out in a British expedition on March 10. The first American reached the top in 1963—James W. Whittaker.

MOUNT FUJI

An up-to-30,000-foot-high mountain chain that projects above the Pacific Ocean—that's Japan. Sticking out the highest, from a lake-covered plain, is the sacred cone-shaped Fuji, in Honshu National Park—it is 12,389 feet above sea level. Its snow-capped, symmetrical cone has been worshipped by poets and balladeers and lovers for centuries. It is said to be the most photographed, painted, and climbed mountain in the world. Japan has about 50 active volcanoes. Fujiama last blew its top in 1707. But 300,000 tons of mountainside are torn away by cascades every year, and government officials believe that the mountain may well split in the next 100 years from its foot to its summit. A seventeenth-century poet wrote, "Rain obscures the scene; but Fuji still exerts a charm even when unseen."

MOUNT HOOD

It's the highest point in Oregon—11,235 feet tall, in the Cascade Range, east of Portland. Like many of Cascade's highest peaks—Lassen Peak, Mt. Rainier (14,410 feet), and Mt. Shasta—Hood is a volcanic cone with glaciers; but unlike Lassen, Hood is extinct.

MOUNTIE

Originally (1873) the North West Mounted Rifles, the name of Canada's federal police force was changed at the insistence of the United States, which did not like the idea of an armed force patrolling the border. The new-name North West Mounted Police became in 1920 the Royal Canadian Mounted Police—the Mounties—also the provincial and criminal police in all provinces except Quebec, Ontario; also the only police force in the Yukon and Northwest Territories. An early assignment: Get rid of the American traders creating havoc among the Indians by trading cheap whiskey for buffalo hides. Service in the far north is voluntary and horses have been supplanted by motorized vehicles.

MOUNT KENNEDY

The 13,095-foot-high Canadian mountain was named for the late United States President. It was scaled for the first time, in 1965, by a force that included Robert Kennedy. It's in the Saint Elias Mountains in the southwest, triangularly shaped Yukon Territory; the territory's tallest mountain, at 19,850 feet, is Logan. (The Yukon is thinly populated. Each resident could have about 11 square miles all to himself.)

MOUNT KILIMANJARO

Africa's highest mountain is an extinct volcano rising in two snow-capped peaks—Kibo is the highest point on the continent (19,340 feet) and always covered with snow and ice about 200 feet deep; Mawenzi (17,564 feet) does not have glaciers but is called "the mountain of the cold devils." Plantains (a fruit larger and less sweet than the banana) and coffee are grown on the lower southern slopes. Kilimanjaro is near the equator in the United Republic of Tanzania in East Africa. Not too far off, at Lake Tanganyika, is the lowest point on the continent.

MOUNT KOSCIUSKO

Named for the Polish general who fought with American Revolutionary armies and championed Polish independence from both Russia and Prussia, the highest mountain in Australia rises 7,305 feet in the Australian Alps, in southeast New South Wales, 200 miles east-northeast of Melbourne. It was discovered in 1840 by Sir Paul Strzelecki. Australia is the least mountainous of the continents and the only one on which there are no peaks high enough to carry glaciers. A chain of miniature snowfields —each about 200 yards long and five feet thick—remains on Kosciusko even in midsummer, on the sheltered eastern slopes. The summit is accessible only to skiers in winter and hikers in summer—motor vehicles have been banned in order to preserve wilderness values. Kosciusko isn't among the eight highest mountains in Oceania. Seven of the eight are in Indonesia: Sudirman is 16,500 feet high, Kubor is 14,300 feet. The exception among the eight is Cook in the Southern Alps, in South Island, New Zealand (12,350 feet).

MOUNT McKINLEY

Mount McKinley National Park in southcentral Alaska luxuriates in wildlife: timber wolves, grizzly bears, Dall sheep, caribou, moose. But the site for soaring eyes is North America's tallest mountain, Mount McKinley, still known locally as Denali, 20,320 feet high in the Alaska range. It took three months of climbing for Harry P. Karstens and Hudson Stuck to become the first to ascend McKinley, in 1913. The United States's second- and third-highest mountains are Mount Whitney (14,494 feet) in California and Mount Elbert (14,433 feet) in Colorado.

MOUNT OLYMPUS

"Olympus, the reputed seat eternal of the gods, which never storms," Homer wrote. Olympus—it made the world go round for the Greeks, who believed the world was flat and circular, their own country in the middle of it, the central site being their mountain, Olympus, whose cloud-shrouded summit was out of sight. The gate of clouds, manned by goddesses called the Seasons, opened only to permit the passage of the Celestials to Earth and on their return. The mythologist Thomas Bulfinch noted: "The gods had their separate dwellings; but all, when summoned, repaired to the palace of Zeus, as did also those deities whose usual abode was the earth, the waters, or the underworld. [Zeus' brothers, Poseidon and Hades, ruled the sea and the underworld, respectively.] It was also in the great hall of the palace of the Olympian king that the gods feasted each day on ambrosia and nectar, their food and drink, the latter being handed round by the lovely goddess Hebe. Here they conversed of the affairs of heaven and earth; and as they quaffed their nectar, Apollo, the god of music, delighted them with the tones of his lyre, to which the Muses sang in responsive strains. When the sun was set, the gods retired to sleep in their respective dwellings.'' The 9,570-foot-high summit in northern Greece was first scaled only in 1913, although the Olympian gods had begun about the sixth century B.C. to fade in importance to the mystery cults. The religion of ancient Greece is extinct. There isn't a single known worshipper of the divinities of Olympus today in the world, round or flat.

MOUNT RUSHMORE

If you're seeing five-story-tall busts, carved out of a granite cliff, of Presidents George Washington, Thomas Jefferson, bespectacled Theodore Roosevelt, and Abraham Lincoln, you're in the Black Hills of southwest South Dakota, twenty-five miles from Rapid City. A superintendent of the South Dakota State Historical Society, Jonah Leroy "Doane" Robinson, conceived of the memorial as "a shrine of democracy," the Presidents representing the founding, the expansion, the preservation, and the unification of the United States. The sculptor was Gutzon Borglum, whose statue of Lincoln stands in the rotunda of the Capitol and whose figures of the apostles are in the Cathedral of St. John the Divine, New York City. In 1916, he designed and began carving a Confederate memorial on Stone Mountain, Georgia. He ceased working and destroyed his models after a controversy with the memorial association. He designed the Mount Rushmore memorial, and supervised the drilling and the dynamiting and the sculpting over fourteen years, dying in 1941 just before it was completed; his son Lincoln tidied up.

THE MOUSETRAP

The longest-running play in the English language—that is, in English English, not in American English. Agatha Christie made a better play than her neighbor, and the world has made a beaten path to her London door for more than three decades—but not here. Her drama of a group of people trapped with an unknown murderer in a remote lodge was panned by the New York critics—no gold. The British actor Ian McKellen infuriated viewers of his recent one-man television performance of Shakespearean roles by gratuitously spilling the beans as to the identity of the murderer.

MR. CHIPS

Robert Donat won the best-actor Oscar in 1939 for his kindly British schoolmaster of Latin, Mr. Chipping, in *Goodbye, Mr. Chips*. Greer Garson as Kathy Bridges, Mrs. Chipping, became a star overnight. (Brits swept the two actor Oscars that year: Vivien Leigh was best actress for *Gone With the Wind*.) James Hilton wrote the sentimental romance in the early 1930s when he was asked to produce a Christmas story for an English newspaper. "Chips"—eighty-five years old and with a stormy chest—reminisces happily and sadly one gray November day of the many years he had spent at the boys' school Brookfield. That night, he dies quietly in his sleep. Mr. Hilton also wrote *Lost Horizon*.

MR. SPOCK (S179–276SP)

The first officer and chief science officer on the starship U.S.S. *Enterprise,* in the television series "Star Trek," was born in the city of Shi-Kahr on the planet Vulcan. His heart is in his lower abdomen, his skin is greenish, he sleeps with his eyes open, his pulse throbs hundreds of times per minute, he has sharply pointed ears, and he can communicate telepathically by touching someone. His skin is green because his blood is green. Says Gene Roddenberry, *Star Trek*'s creator and producer: "It is green because of traces of copper and nickel which our blood does not have. There is actually no inconsistency in having a pulse rate of hundreds of beats per minute and practically no blood pressure by our standards. The average diameter of Spock's arteries is larger than Terrans', more efficient, and the faster, lower-pressured hydraulic action of his 'slightly different' heart results in about the same volume delivered as our slower, higher-pressured system."

MUHAMMAD

"The Praised One"—the founder in the 600s of the Islamic religion. *Islam* means submission—Muhammad taught that the one God requires people to make Islam. He was a wealthy merchant when he felt himself, at age forty, selected by God to be the Arab prophet of true religion— Arabs had had no prophet. Many of his revelations were recorded in the Koran. Islam counts its date from Muhammad's flight, or hegira, to Medina from a murder plot. When the Jews there broke their alliance with him, Muhammad ordered Muslims to face Mecca, instead of Jerusalem, when praying.

MUNICH

Once (1632) occupied by Gustavus II of Sweden, now the capital of Bavaria, in southwest Germany, the "place of the monks" was where the Austrian Adolf Hitler settled in 1913 and where, in 1920, the German Workers' party was renamed the National Socialist German Workers', or Nazi, party. On November 8, 1923—fifteen years to the day before Crystal Night—Hitler and storm troopers tried to overthrow Munich's republican government, surrounding and making Bavarian officials meeting in a beer hall swear loyalty to "revolution." The day after the "putsch," sixteen Nazis and three police were killed in a street confrontation—Hitler clutched the pavement to save his life—Hermann Goering went down with a serious wound in a thigh and was given first aid by the Jewish proprietor of a nearby bank. But the fiasco made Hitler a national figure, a patriot and a hero to many; he was sentenced to five years in the old Landsberg fortress but served only nine months—he was treated in jail as an honored guest, with a room of his own, a splendid view high above the River Lech, and he began to dictate to Rudolf Hess chapter after chapter of *Mein Kampf.* The Munich Pact was signed in 1938—it "guaranteed" peace for our time—and in 1972 the Munich Olympics saw the kidnapping and slaughter of eleven Israeli athletes.

MURPHY, AUDIE

The nation's most-decorated hero of World War II and five other men were killed in the crash of a twin-engine Aero Commander near the summit of a craggy, heavily wooded mountain twelve miles northwest of Roanoke, Virginia, in 1971. According to the Defense Department, Murphy killed or captured 240 German soldiers; he said he wasn't sure what the count was. His company had marched north through Italy and was in the invasion of southern France. In eastern France, the baby-faced second lieutenant leaped to the top of a burning tank, grabbed its .50-caliber machine gun, and fired into the German lines for more than an hour. It was to hell and back. When the enemy fled, Murphy rejoined his men, organized an attack, and secured the area. He was awarded the Congressional Medal of Honor, nearly thirty medals in all, including the Croix de Guerre with palm, and gave most of them away to children. For years, he couldn't go to sleep unless he had a loaded German Walther automatic pistol under his pillow. James Cagney saw Murphy's picture on the cover of *Life* magazine and persuaded him to become an actor.

MURPHY, BRIDEY

Interest in reincarnation—rebirth of the soul in a new body—got a new life in the early 1950s when a Colorado housewife named Virginia Tighe said under hypnosis that she had lived in Ireland a century earlier, and her name was Bridey Murphy. She had died in a fall, when she was sixty-six years old, then lived in a sort of limbo until she was born again as Virginia Tighe. The hypnotist said that he found points of congruence between Bridey's story and Irish life at the time. He wrote a book, *The Search for Bridey Murphy,* an immediate best-seller, and he peddled a long-playing record of his first session with Mrs. Tighe. "Come as you were" parties became the rage, as did debunking articles. Henry Ford believed in re-in-car-nation. Shirley MacLaine does. The comedian Morey Amsterdam is so hepped on reincarnation that he changed his will: He's leaving everything to himself.

MURROW, EDWARD R.

Broadcasting's most distinguished newsman was addicted to smoking—60 to 70 cigarettes a day. He doubted that he could spend a half hour without a cigarette, "with any comfort or ease." He even smoked during his television interview with government officials announcing a definite connection between cigarette smoking and cancer. Murrow died of lung cancer, in 1965. "He was a shooting star and we will live in his afterglow a very long time," his long-time friend and colleague Eric Sevareid said. "I never knew any person among those who worked in his realm to feel jealousy toward him: not only because he made himself a refuge for those in trouble, a source of strength for those who were weak, but because there was no basis for comparison. He was an original and we shall not see his like again." He was a compassman and a topographer for timber cruisers in Washington for two years before entering college—and he knew his way around the world thereafter. His reports from a blitzed London during World War II were memorable—"This is London" was his signature, convincing Americans that there'd always be an England. He flew twenty missions over Europe, and lay down in a gutter to get the right sound of an air raid for his listeners. His "See It Now" television series ruined Senator Joseph McCarthy by showing the man in his full flavor. "My father," Murrow once said, "does not go so far as to say that there's something dishonest about a man making a living by merely talking, but he does think there's something doubtful about it." First conversationalists on Murrow's "Small World" TV culture series were Jawaharlal Nehru, Thomas E. Dewey, and Aldous Huxley, in 1958.

MUSIAL, STAN

"Stan the Man" went to bat 10,972 official times—he also walked 1,599 times—in his twenty-two star-spangled years with the St. Louis Cardinals. His 3,630 hits included 1,377 extra-base wallops, which included 475 home runs. He won the National League batting championship seven times and the most valuable player honor three times. No. 6 played in four World Series and was elected to major league baseball's Hall of Fame in 1969.

THE MUSIC MAN

Meredith Willson was the music man and his home town of Mason City, Iowa, was a town not unlike the setting of his incomparable Broadway musical, River City, Iowa. He spent six years writing and rewriting and rewriting his most successful work, which won the New York Drama Critics Circle and Antoinette Perry—the Tony—awards for outstanding musical of the 1957–58 season. An accomplished pianist and flutist, Willson had toured with March King John Philip Sousa's band; in 1924, he became the first flutist with the New York Philharmonic, under Arturo Toscanini. He composed and arranged the film scores for Charlie Chaplin's *The Great Dictator,* a satire of Nazism, and for Lillian Hellman's *The Little Foxes*. Like *The Music Man*, his musical *The Unsinkable Molly Brown* also made the upstream struggle from Broadway to Hollywood.

MUSKIE, EDMUND SIXTUS

Governor of Maine, the state's first Democratic senator, the Democratic Party's vice-presidential nominee in 1968, Secretary of State in the Carter administration—he edged Senator George McGovern in the New Hampshire presidential primary in 1972 but was effectively taken out of the campaign when the news media shamelessly drubbed him for weeping during a noble attack on malicious, gossipy reports about Mrs. Muskie. In 1980, the news media shamelessly slashed President Jimmy Carter for his "self-serving, insincere" remark in a debate with Republican contender Ronald Reagan about his daughter Amy's honest concern about nuclear weapons.

MUSSOLINI, BENITO

Italy's fascist leader and dictator did his best to make train service a symbol of fascist efficiency: An effort was made to conceal the fact that railway beds and rolling stock, run down during World War I, had been upgraded *before* Il Duce took power. He said Italy had nothing to learn from anyone else! Her ships were faster and bigger than anyone else's, too. Mussolini could turn his leadership to Rome's "universal mission": the defense of Western civilization against the colored races. He didn't stand on ceremony nor did he mince his words: "The Italian proletariat needs a blood bath for its force to be renewed. . . . Fortunately, the Italian people is not yet accustomed to eating several times per day. . . . We have buried the putrid corpse of liberty. . . . The Italian race is a race of sheep. . . . War alone brings up to its highest tension all human energy and puts the stamp of nobility upon the peoples who have the courage to face it. . . . To make a people great," he said in 1940, "it is necessary to send them to battle even if you have to kick them in the pants." For a time, he was a British Knight of the Bath. On June 2, 1941, in a meeting at Brenner Pass, Mussolini was told by Hitler that after the war every Jew must get out of Europe and settle, perhaps, on Madagascar; the Führer did not mention preparation for Barbarossa—his surprise invasion of the Soviet Union—less than three weeks off. Duce and his mistress, Clara Petacci, were captured escaping to Switzerland at the end of World War II and shot by the Italian communist partisan Walter Audisio. Their corpses were taken to Milan and hanged in a public square.

N

"N"

All Japanese words end in either the letter "n" or in a vowel. There are eight vowel sounds in the language: *ah, eh, ee, o, oo, i, oi, ay*. The verb at the end of the sentence comes. There is no single word in Japanese for "yes" or for "no." The social situation dictates which style of Japanese is spoken. For everyday conversation, the intimate is used. With cultivated company, the polite. When respect and honor should be conferred, the honorific style, used for older people and superiors, the subject always of respect and honor, is employed. In speeches and in writing, the impersonal style. A fifth style is modern literary. More than a millennium ago, the Japanese borrowed and adapted Chinese ideographs—although Japanese and Chinese are totally different languages—so that the spoken language of the Japanese could be written.

NAMATH, JOE WILLIE

"I know they'll be laying for me, it's just natural. But I am not scared. I don't run scared any more, I've had all the scare knocked out of me. I know pro football is tough, but ability doesn't change. The difference in pro and college football is that the pros are smarter. They are big and good at every position but I figure I can learn, too." And with that, the 194-pound, 6-foot-2 quarterback with the rifle arm from Coach Bear Bryant's University of Alabama eleven signed a contract with the New York Jets worth at least $427,000, the largest financial package for a player to that date, 1965. Probably his greatest achievement in the pros: Quarterbacking the Jets of the American Football League to a 16–7 upset victory over the heavily favored Baltimore Colts of the National Football League in Super Bowl III, in 1969. (The two leagues merged before the next season.) Broadway Joe was never among the game's passing leaders, but he had a flair that helped to make the sport even more popular. Not to mention himself. His last pass was caught in late 1984 by Deborah Lynn Mays, age twenty-two, who made the ultimate score: She married him. New York headlines: "Say It Ain't So, Joe."

NAMES

Woody Allen's given name was Allen Stewart Konigsberg. Twiggy—
Leslie Hornby. Natalie Wood—Natasha Zacharenko. Hedy Lamarr—
Hedwig Fua Maria Kiesler. Peggy Lee—Norma Engstrom. Fred Astaire
—Frederic Austerlitz. Lauren Bacall—Betty Joan Perske. Bruce Lee—
Li Juan Fan. Dean Martin—Dino Paul Crocetti. Karl Malden—Malden
Sekulovich. Judy Garland—Frances Ethel Gumm. Rose is not always a
Rose.

NAPOLEON

The emperor of France and the dictators of Germany and the Soviet
Union—three of the men who shaped the world of the last two centuries
—were all outsiders. Napoleon was born in Corsica. Hitler was born in
Austria. Stalin was born in Georgia. Hitler and Stalin spoke their native
language with a pronounced accent. Both men managed to slaughter
millions of their adopted compatriots while being accorded all kinds of
adulation, amounting almost to worship, by their besotted subjects. Sir
Karl Popper exhorted citizens: Rather than preoccupy themselves with
the selection of the ideal ruler, they should devise means of ridding themselves quickly and effectively of unsatisfactory rulers. (But what if the
citizens adore their philosopher-king, führer, or vozdh?) The Little Corporal, by the way, *was* educated in French military schools, at Brienne
and Paris, before he spread the French Revolution throughout Europe
(and developed canned foods to feed his troops). He was hoping the
British warship the *Bellerophon* was taking him to asylum in England.
The lonely island of St. Helena in the South Atlantic was not what he had
had in mind when he abdicated and surrendered after Waterloo.

NARCISSUS

The gorgeous youth in Greek mythology, a son of the river god Cephissus
and the river nymph Liriope, was told he would live to old age if he never
saw his own features. But he was narcissistic, of course, exclusively self-
absorbed. Out of pride in his own beauty, the heart-throbber scorned all
suitors, both maidens and young men. When the mountain nymph Echo's
hopeless less less less less and unrequited love love love love for Narcissus caused her to become only a voice voice voice voice, the gods
wrought vengeance. Narcissus was made to fall in love with his own
reflection in a pool deep in a forest—each time he stretched his arms into
the waters to clasp his image, it disappeared. He pined away, he wasted

away. He finally disappeared, and a flower with a golden center surrounded by white petals bloomed by the pool in his stead—the lovely narcissus.

NASSER, GAMAL ABDEL

An estimated 4,000,000 grieving people jammed the streets of Cairo during the funeral in 1970 for the first president (for fourteen years) of the republic of Egypt. A life-long revolutionary, he had directed the Free Officers' army coup that got rid of King Farouk in 1952. When western financial support for construction of the Aswan High Dam petered out, he nationalized the Suez Canal, in 1956, and turned back an angry Anglo-French invasion. He served three years as president of the United Arab Republic, the short-lived merger of Egypt and Syria. He resigned his Egyptian leadership following a disastrous war with Israel in 1967, but was swept back into office by massive demonstrations of support. The most important Arab leader of the century then turned to the Soviet Union for aid. He was only fifty-two when he died of a heart attack.

NASTASE, ILIE

Jimmy Connors, who knows from obstreperous, has said that "Nastie" is the only tennis player he'd pay to see play. The six-foot-tall clown prince of the professional circuit—the Romanian's been known to change his pants near center court—has won the United States, French, and Italian championships once each and the Grand Prix Masters four times. He lost twice in the finals of Wimbledon, in 1972 to Stan Smith and in 1976 to Bjorn Borg.

NATCHEZ TRACE

A series of Indian trails expanded in turn by the French, the English, and the Spanish, not to mention Andrew Jackson and his men in 1814–15, made even more famous, at least these days, by passing through the northeast Mississippi hometown of Elvis Presley—Natchez, Mississippi–Nashville, Tennessee, via the shrine in Tupelo. It was at first a one-way street—one could more easily return to Natchez by floating south on the Mississippi River. The French established a permanent settlement and military base in Natchez in 1716. The Natchez Indians, resenting the encroachment, massacred nearly 300 of the French, only to be nearly wiped out by a French-Choctaw coalition. The British took over Natchez at the end of the French and Indian wars, then, distracted by the American Revolution, ceded it to Spain. Spain turned it over to the United

States in 1795. As the War of 1812 was drawing to a close in 1814–15, Andrew Jackson marched south on the Trace to New Orleans, arriving there two weeks after the war was officially over, but who knew? Steamboat transportation put a detour in the commercial and even the military importance of the road.

NATION, CARRY

Once married to a hopeless alcoholic, she became convinced of divine appointment to destroy The Saloon. The six-foot-tall, hatchet-wielding advocate of both temperance and woman suffrage smashed saloon liquor and property in Kansas at the turn of the century, and is credited with creating a public mood favorable to passage of the Eighteenth Amendment to the Constitution—Prohibition. She also protested the "evils" of tobacco, foreign foods, and corsets. She was beaten up often and arrested at least thirty times, and she died at the edge of madness. Her mother was rebellious and mad. She believed she was Queen Victoria. Decked out in purple robes, she would ride around in a plush-upholstered carriage pulled by horses with silver-mounted harnesses. A tall Negro in a scarlet hunting jacket blowing a trumpet heralded the queen's approach.

NATIONAL AUDUBON SOCIETY

His middle name was Bird—George Bird Grinnel—and in 1886 he formed the first Audubon Society, named for the bird painter. Egrets, herons, roseate spoonbills, gulls, and terns were being murdered mercilessly to satisfy a craze for wild-bird feathers for women's hats. In 1905, the National Association of Audubon Societies for the Protection of Wild Birds and Animals was founded to advance public understanding of the value and the need for conservation of soil, water, plants, and wildlife and the relation of their intelligent treatment and wise use to human welfare. (In 1910, the Audubon Plumage Bill was signed—the "feather fight" had been won.) The name of the organization was shortened in 1940 to the National Audubon Society. Education is its lifeblood. Why doesn't a bird fall off its perch when it sleeps? When a bird "falls" asleep, it relaxes and slumps down until its body rests against the perch. This pulls a tendon in its legs that causes its toes to clamp around the perch. The bird must straighten its legs to release this clamp.

NAVEL ORANGE

It originated in Brazil and is seedless, or nearly so. The navel orange (sometimes spelled naval) encloses a small secondary fruit. The rind shows on the exterior and there is a pit at the apex. (A naval orangeworm is a caterpillar.)

NEHRU, JAWAHARLAL

The Indian statesman is credited with coining the term "Third World" to distinguish technologically less-advanced nations of Asia, Africa, and Latin America from the technologically advanced nations influenced by the United States and by the Soviet Union. All of his major works were written in prison. He told Edward R. Murrow that he would recommend prison not only to aspiring writers but to aspiring politicians, not that prison is too good a thing but in the sense that it helps one to live quietly and think: "I think the years I have spent in prison have been the most formative and important in my life because of the discipline, the sensations, but chiefly the opportunity to think clearly, to try to understand things." He believed that the forces of a capitalist society, if left unchecked, tend to make the rich richer and the poor poorer. He told Edgar Snow, "I want nothing to do with any religion concerned with keeping the masses satisfied to live in hunger, filth, and ignorance. I want nothing to do with any order, religious or otherwise, which does not teach people that they are capable of becoming happier and more civilized, on this earth, capable of becoming true man, master of his fate and captain of his soul." The nationalist was the leader of 360-million Indians—and enormously popular. His daughter Indira Gandhi became the nation's first woman prime minister and ruled over *750-million* Indians.

NELSON, HORATIO NELSON, VISCOUNT

The British naval hero lost the sight of an eye at Calvi and later, in 1797, in the unsuccessful British attempt to capture Santa Cruz de Tenerife, he lost his right arm. He made Emma, Lady Hamilton, the wife of the British ambassador to the Two Sicilies, his mistress, and presently they had a daughter, Horatia. He moved in with the Hamiltons in the English countryside, 1802–03. In 1805, from the flagship *Victory* off Cape Trafalgar, he issued the famous cheer "England expects that every man will do his duty" and directed a spectacular victory over Franco-Spanish fleets. He abandoned the traditionally rigid tactics of fighting in line of battle, advancing on the enemy in two divisions to break their line and destroy them piecemeal—"the Nelson touch." Small-arms fire was exchanged at point-blank range, and the admiral was shot through the shoulder and chest by a French sniper. As he lay dying in surgery, Nelson was told that fifteen enemy ships had been taken: "That is well," he said, "but I had bargained for twenty." His last words were "Now I am satisfied.

Thank God, I have done my duty." Nelson's popularity was recorded in countless monuments, streets, and inns named after him, paintings and prints, busts and plaques. Emma Hamilton died raddled and almost destitute; Horatia mothered a large family.

NEWFOUNDLAND

The butt of mean-spirited, Polish-type ethnic jokes from one end of the nation to the other became Canada's tenth province in 1949. Have you heard about the "Newfie" on his way to Ottawa who spots a sign "Clean Washrooms Ahead" and cleans nearly 100 before reaching the capital? So that it would not fall on April Fool's Day, the admission of Newfoundland and Labrador, as the 156,185-square-mile island and peninsula are collectively called, was pushed back by 24 hours. The earliest known European, or Norse, structures in North America are in the rocky island's northern region, the northeastern tip of the Canadian mainland. The capital, St. John's, experienced a disastrous fire in 1895. Nearly half of the population of 550,000 lives today in St. John's or in the surrounding Avalon Peninsula. Heart's Content was the western terminal of the transatlantic cable in 1866. The Labrador current keeps temperatures in Labrador below freezing eight months of the year. The Strait of Belle Isle separates Newfoundland and Labrador. Cod-fishing in the Grand Banks to the east may be the best in the world.

NEW ORLEANS

The original Dixie. The oldest major city in the South. It was founded in 1718 by Jean Baptiste le Moyne, sieur de Bienville, France's governor of the Louisiana colony. It was named by Bienville for Philippe, duke of Orleans, who was ruling France for King Louis XV, then a youth. There are several explanations for the derivation of Dixie. A bank in Louisiana printed ten-dollar bills bearing the French word "dix," or ten. Louisiana was once called "Dix's land." There were Mason and Dixon and everything south of their line may have been heard as Dixie. There was Thomas Dixon, whose best-selling racist novel, *The Clansman,* was about the Reconstruction period in the South and served as the basis for the film *The Birth of a Nation.*

NEWS

It would be nice news if it were an acronym for north-east-west-south—but it isn't. Older forms of its etymology may be Middle English *newe,*

Old English *noewe*—just *akin* to Latin *novus,* whence also French *nouveau, nouvelle.* Or it may be merely a loan translation from the French plural *nouvelles.* Not all news people dig news. The Ohio newspaper publisher who became the twenty-ninth President had secrets he didn't want leaked and certainly not printed. He told the Republican National Party's smoke-filled-room selection committee in 1920 that he was as clean as a hound's tooth, there was nothing in his history that was scandalous, of course they could nominate him to be their presidential standardbearer. And they did, and he ran, on the post-World War I theme "return to normalcy," and he was elected by a large margin—61 percent of the popular vote and 404 electoral votes. Among his social secrets: A year earlier, Warren G. Harding's long-time mistress, his thirty-years-younger blonde "niece," Nan Britton, had given birth to their daughter. In the White House, Harding and Miss Britton snatched quickies in a twenty-five-square-foot closet. (One of publisher Harding's newsboys in Marion was a future presidential candidate himself, the Socialist Norman Thomas.)

NEW YORK CITY

Four of the five boroughs of the largest city in the United States are on islands: Brooklyn, Staten Island, Queens, and Manhattan. The Bronx is a peninsula. It was held by the British for two years after Yorktown, and was the nation's first capital. In 1824, the Marquis de Lafayette, on his triumphal return to America, was the honored guest at the hanging of twenty highwaymen in Washington Square, now the downtown campus of New York University. There are today more blacks in the Big Apple (about 1,800,000) than in any other city in the world.

THE NEW YORKER

The periodical has "devoted itself for fifty-nine years not only to facts and literal accuracy but to truth. And truth begins, journalistically, with the facts," William Shawn, the editor, who has been associated with America's leading magazine for nearly half a century, said in mid-1984, "We have eight people in our Checking Department who spend their days and, if need be, their nights rigorously verifying every checkable fact before it goes into the magazine. Every writer is held to the same severe standards of factuality. Errors still occur, but they are inadvertent and rare. We do not permit composites. We do not rearrange events. We do not create conversations. The only exceptions are characters invented in the spirit of fun for 'The Talk of the Town' (Mr. Stanley, Mr. Frimbo, the Long-Winded Lady, various 'friends'), and when this is done it is well understood by our readers. Anything that purports to be a fact in 'The Talk of the Town' is a fact.'' *The New Yorker* receives upwards of a quarter-million unsolicited items every year—and each is looked at by at least two people.

NEW YORK METS

Major league baseball's all-time losingest team for one season. The new New York franchise in the National League won only 42 of its 162 games in its premier season, 1962, under Casey Stengel, who had piloted the New York Yankees to 10 titles. The Cleveland team, of the National League, won only 20 of its 154 games in 1899 and Philadelphia (American League) won only 27 games in 1916. The Chicago team in the National League in 1906 won 116 games in a 154-game schedule, posting the National League's highest winning percentage ever, .763; Cleveland in 1954 posted the American League's best winning percentage, .721. The New York Yankees of Joe DiMaggio's 56-consecutive-game hitting streak in 1941 clinched the league pennant at the earliest date, September 4. Cincinnati won its N.L. Western division in 1975 on September 7.

THE NEW YORK TIMES

For six months in 1906, the world's greatest newspaper (''All the news that's fit to print'') found it fit to print a comic-strip poem about the adventures of two grizzly bears. It's the only time that ''the newspaper of record'' has published a comic; the exception was made to please the daughter of the publisher, Adolph S. Ochs. The *Times* made its name by printing records that exposed the Tweed ring defrauding New York City, in 1871. Recent documentary scoops have included Nikita Khrushchev's ''secret speech'' revealing the crimes of Joseph Stalin and the Pentagon Papers. Harrison E. Salisbury, the veteran *Times* reporter and executive, has written that it was hard to find anyone on the *Times* except then managing editor Abe Rosenthal who had a real concept of the historic consequences of the *Times*'s publication of the Vietnam Archive. Rosenthal: ''Seeing all those documents from the government files! You can't imagine the feeling it gave you. It was strange. I just walked around looking at them. I could hardly believe it. This hadn't been done before. The *Times* wasn't used to publishing secret documents.'' The very first issue of the *Times* was printed on September 18, 1851, and the lead paragraph of the city story on the front page said: ''The weather was the theme upon which we hinged an item for this morning's edition, but we have been forced to forgo the infliction of it upon the public by the proceedings of the Boston Jubilee, which our special correspondent has forwarded us. Never mind, the President cannot always be lionizing through the country, and as soon as he returns home, we shall endeavor to do this important subject full justice." The strongest belief that publisher Ochs held from boyhood was "Honor thy father and thy mother."

NEW YORK YANKEES

Major league baseball's most successful franchise—its exploits fill book after book—was known as the Highlanders before 1913. In eighty-one campaigns through 1984, the team raised the American League championship pennant thirty-three times and went on to cop the World Series twenty-two times. In 1920, with Babe Ruth in the lineup for the first time, it became the first professional sports team to attract a million customers. Two years later, the club moved from the Polo Grounds (it was a time when base hits that bounced into the stands counted as home runs, not as two-baggers as they do today), across the Harlem River, and into the House that Ruth Built—Yankee Stadium. In 1927, the team was a Murderer's Row—Koenig, Meusel, Combs, Dugan, Lazzeri, Gehrig, Ruth—the Bronx Bombers. In 1929, it became the first team to make numbers a permanent part of the uniform. In 1941, the year of Joe DiMaggio's historic fifty-six-consecutive-game hitting spree, the Yanks clinched the pennant around Labor Day, the earliest any team has. They finished last in 1966, the first time in 54 seasons. Bill Virdon managed the Yanks for two years in the 1970s and never won a game in Yankee Stadium—it was being rehabilitated and the team played its home games in Shea Stadium, in Queens.

NEW ZEALAND

If you are afraid of snakes, you might want to move to New Zealand. There are no land snakes in the South Pacific several-island country. Native to the land are the kiwi and the albatross. The two principal islands, North Island and South Island, are separated by a strait twenty miles wide at the narrowest point. The massive Southern Alps extend almost the entire length of South Island; active volcanic mountains, hot springs, and mineral deposits are dominant features of North Island. There's as great an earthquake frequency in New Zealand as there is in California. New Zealand and its Polynesian Maoris were first seen by a European in 1642, a Dutch navigator, Abel Tasman, who circumnavigated Australia and demonstrated that it was not attached to the polar continent in the South. New Zealand was rediscovered by Captain James Cook more than a century later, in 1769. Discovery of gold in the 1860s quickened the pace of development. In the middle of World War II, thousands of New Zealanders were released from the armed services to help increase food and factory production, badly needed by the United States military in its overall Pacific operation.

NIAGARA FALLS

The international line between the cities of Niagara Falls, Ontario (population about 70,000 and formerly named Elgin, then Clifton), and Niagara Falls, New York (population about 90,000 and formerly named Manchester, for the English industrial center). Goat Island on the lip of the Falls splits the cataract into the American Falls (167 feet high) and the Horseshoe, or Canadian, Falls (158 feet high). Less than a mile in length, Goat Island (New York) is the largest of several islands at the approach to the Falls. The two cities are linked by the Rainbow and the Whirlpool Rapids bridges. John Augustus Roebling (Brooklyn Bridge) put a railroad bridge across the gorge in 1855. Waters from four of the Great Lakes flow north from Lake Erie and over the Niagara scarp and into Lake Ontario, the easternmost of the five Lakes. Three of eight men who are known to have gone over the Falls in a barrel were killed. A French acrobat, Charles Blondin, twice performed on a tightrope stretched across the gorge, the second time in 1860 on the occasion of the visit of the Prince of Wales, who became Edward VII. The Robert Moses Niagara Power Plant is one of the largest in the world.

NICTITATING MEMBRANE

Why do nictitating women wink at men? Why do nictitating women wink at other women? Why do nictitating men wink at women and at other men? "To nictitate" is "to wink." But there's more here than meets the eye. A nictitating membrane is a thin membrane found at the inner angle or beneath the lower lid of the eye and capable of extending across the eyeball. A nictitating spasm is a clonic spasm of the eyelid. If you have a nictitating spasm—well, it's nothing to wink at. You have an eye that can't help itself.

NIGHTINGALE, FLORENCE

Care of the sick and of the war-wounded: This was the lifetime goal of the Italian-born "Lady with a Lamp" who headed a unit of thirty-eight British women nurses in the Crimean War: "Nursing is a noble profession for women." She founded modern nursing and was a pioneer in preventive state medicine and was described as being paradoxical, vacillating, opinionated, autocratic, intolerant, prejudiced, self-willed, masterful, and in discipline a martinet. She was the first woman to receive Britain's Order of Merit and she lived to be ninety years of age.

NINETEEN EIGHTY-FOUR

"It was a bright cold day in April, and the clocks were striking thirteen." Newspeak, Doublethink, Big Brother, proles, Ministry of Love—no other book has preempted for itself a calendar year in the history of man. "It isn't a book I would gamble on for a big sale," George Orwell wrote to his publisher shortly before publication, in late spring 1949; the author himself was dead within the year. The brilliant literary critic George Steiner has observed that with one exception—Newspeak!—every major theme and most of the actual narrative situations in Orwell's text derive from Eugene Zamiatin's *We:* "Without *We, Nineteen Eighty-Four,* in the guise in which we have it, would simply not exist." Newspeak was inspired by Jonathan Swift. But would we still be reading about 6079 Smith W (and the thinly veiled allegory of Stalinism) if Orwell had stuck to his original title: *The Last Man in Europe?* By reversing the last two digits in the year in which he wrote the book, Orwell, in Steiner's words, "put his signature and claim on a piece of time."

NIPPON

The native name of Japan. From the phrase for Great Japan—*Dai Nippon,* "from the place where the Sun comes from," the Land of the Rising Sun. When a Japanese citizen is fervently devoted to the interests or glory of the floating kingdom, he is being Nipponistic. A Japanese businessman who brings his daughter into his company is still a nepotist.

NIXON, RICHARD M.

He was born in a house that his father had built. He weighed eleven pounds. He was a seventh cousin twice removed of President William Howard Taft and an eighth cousin once removed of President Herbert Hoover—Hoover and Nixon have been the only Quaker Presidents. He cannot tell a lie: His great-grandfather George Nixon crossed the Delaware with General George Washington during the American Revolution. He was graduated first in his class from Whittier (California) High School and the president of his graduation class at Duke University Law School, where he had the nickname "Gloomy Gus." He proposed marriage the same night he met Thelma Catherine "Pat" Ryan in a local theater group

384

playing *The Dark Tower:* "I thought he was nuts or something," Mrs. Nixon has since been quoted. "I guess I just looked at him. I couldn't imagine anyone ever saying anything like that so suddenly." Nixon is one of two men who have run five times for the presidency or the vice-presidency. (Franklin Roosevelt is the other.) He became President in 1968 with only 43.4 percent of the popular vote. In 1972, when eighteen-year-olds were allowed to vote for the first time, Mr. Nixon won 61 percent of the popular vote. Harry S Truman once said that "Richard Nixon is a no-good lying bastard. He can lie out of both sides of his mouth at the same time, and if he ever caught himself telling the truth, he'd lie just to keep his hand in." Jimmy Carter, when he was governor of Georgia, in 1974, said, "In two hundred years of history, he's the most dishonest President we've ever had. I think he's disgraced the presidency." Mr. Nixon is the only President to resign the office. During the Watergate furor, he swore, "I am not a crook!"

NIXON, RICHARD M.—*THE FINAL DAYS*

President Richard M. Nixon has said that the book about the downfall of his administration by Carl Bernstein and Bob Woodward so upset his wife that he will never forgive them. "As far as I am concerned, I have nothing but contempt for them." "Woodstein" had reported: " 'Will history treat me more kindly than my contemporaries?' Nixon asked Henry Kissinger, tears flooding his eyes, on the eve of his resignation. Certainly, definitely, Kissinger said. When this was all over, the President would be remembered for the peace he had achieved. The President broke down and sobbed. . . . The President was slurring his words. He was drunk. He was out of control. . . . [He] had one last request: 'Henry, please don't ever tell anyone that I cried and that I was not strong.' " Perhaps Mark Twain was right: "Only dead men tell the truth."

NIXON, PRESIDENT RICHARD M.—RESIGNATION

Friday, August 9, 1974. Alexander Haig, White House Chief of Staff, arrived in the Lincoln Sitting Room of the White House with the last piece of business—a letter to the Secretary of State, Henry Kissinger, for Mr. Nixon to sign. One sentence: "Dear Mr. Secretary: I hereby resign the Office of the President of the United States." R. M. N. took his pen and scrawled "Richard Nixon" at the bottom. When Kissinger received the letter, Nixon by law ceased to be President; his successor, Gerald R. Ford, could take the oath of office, and he did, becoming the first President never to have been elected to either of the nation's two top political positions.

NOAH

Records found in all parts of the world tell of a great flood meant to destroy mankind. Traditionally, it has been ascribed to man's rampant wickedness augmented by a race of giants born to mortal women who had mated with "the sons of God." Regretting that he had created man —the wickedness of man was great—Yahweh determined to exterminate all flesh except for Noah and his immediate family and two (or seven) of every kind of animal, bird, and reptile. Genesis 6, 7, 8: "And the waters prevailed, and were increased greatly upon the earth; . . . And it came to pass at the end of forty days, that Noah opened the window of the ark which he had made: And he sent forth a raven, which went forth to and fro, until the waters were dried up from off the earth. Also he sent forth a dove from him, to see if the waters were abated from off the face of the ground; But the dove found no rest for the sole of her foot, and she returned unto him into the ark, for the waters were on the face of the whole earth: then he put forth his hand, and took her, and pulled her in unto him into the ark. And he stayed yet other seven days; and again he sent forth the dove out of the ark; And the dove came in to him in the evening; and, lo, in her mouth was an olive leaf pluckt off: so Noah knew that the waters were abated from off the earth. And he stayed yet other seven days; and sent forth the dove; which returned not again unto him any more." The wooden ark is said to have come to rest on a mountain in Turkey. The races of mankind are said to be descended from the three sons of Noah.

NOBEL PRIZE

The Swedish inventor of dynamite and blasting gelatin, Alfred Bernhard Nobel, believed that the explosives would induce the nations of the world to outlaw war, because war had been made even more horrible by the explosives. (His brother was killed when Alfred's nitroglycerine factory blew up, in 1864, and Alfred came to be looked upon as a mad scientist manufacturing destruction.) He willed a fund of $9.2-million for the establishment of supreme honors—the annual Nobel prizes—in peace, literature, physics, chemistry, physiology, and medicine. Sinclair Lewis, in 1930, was the first American to win the Nobel Prize in literature—he had turned down the Pulitzer Prize, declaring such prizes make writers "safe, obedient, and sterile." The first American to win the Nobel Prize in physics was the German-born, Naval Academy instructor-researcher Albert A. Michelson, in 1907, for precision instruments for spectroscopic and meteorological studies—he discovered that light travels at exactly 186,508 miles per second, a foundation of Einstein's theory of relativity.

The youngest Nobel winner has been twenty-five-year-old William Lawrence Bragg, who, with his father, shared the award in physics in 1915 for work they had done on the determination of crystal structure by X-ray diffraction. Social reformer Jane Addams, of Chicago, was co-winner of the Peace Prize in 1931; she had been denounced as a traitor and "the most dangerous woman in America" when pacifists became synonymous with Reds—every criticism of World War I was interpreted by isolationist superpatriots as un-American and disloyal. A military man, George Marshall, Chief of Staff of the United States Army in World War II, was awarded the peace prize in 1953, for formulating the plan that helped to rescue shattered European countries after the war. The physicist Linus Pauling is the only individual who has been a Nobel winner in two different categories, in chemistry and in peace. The first black winner was Ralph Bunche, peace, 1950, for his role as mediator in the 1949 armistice negotiations between Israel and the Arab states.

NOBEL PRIZE—BEGIN, SADAT

In Oslo's high-walled medieval Akershus, which had served during World War II as headquarters for the quintessential Nazi collaborator and anti-Semite Vidkun Quisling, there was Israeli Premier Menachem Begin, picking up his half of 1978's Nobel Peace Prize. The other half belonged to Egyptian President Anwar Sadat, who didn't show; he sent a confidant. Why pick up a peace prize? Sadat asked, there was no peace in the Middle East. Negotiations begun at Camp David were stalled. Begin's own Likud coalition didn't want Begin to go, either: "It's like celebrating the circumcision ritual before the baby is born." As he had when the Camp David accords were signed on the White House lawn, the Israeli premier, in Oslo, quoted the prophet Isaiah: "And they shall beat their swords into plowshares, and their spears into pruning hooks," and he quoted the redshirted Italian revolutionary hero Giuseppe Garibaldi: "Peace means—to fight for human dignity, survival, and liberty."

NOB HILL

Nob from nabob, from Hindi for "governor." Nabobs—rich or prominent men or rich *and* prominent men. Nob Hill for nabobs, on a peak in San Francisco, for those who had reached their peak. Robert Louis Stevenson described it as a "great net of straight thoroughfares lying at right angles, east and west and north and south over the shoulders of Nob Hill, the hill of palaces, must be counted the best part of San Francisco. It is there that the millionaires who gathered together, vying with each other in display, looked down upon the business wards of the city." Vainglorious display dazzled all beholders in the last decades of the nineteenth century—wood treated to resemble stone was used to build palaces and a parade of objects d'art marched into place. Ostentation was not discreet. West of Chinatown, the most congested site in the nation, Nob Hill came tumbling down in the quake of '06.

NOGGIN

It's a small quantity of drink, usually equivalent to a gill, which in the United States is a liquid unit equal to ¼ U.S. liquid pint. There are four noggins or gills in a pint.

NORDIC SKIING

A class of skiing competition—the undisputed king of winter athletic events—cross-country skiing (the most grueling event) and ski jumping (the most spectacular). Alpine skiing is the twisting slalom (the most graceful) and the fast downhill (the most dangerous).

NORTH CAROLINA

North Carolinians became Tar Heels during the American Revolution. Never known as sticks in the mud, they imaginatively impeded the retreat of General Charles Cornwallis' British troops in the fateful Carolina campaign by pouring tar into a stream—the Redcoats emerged with the substance sticking to their boots and couldn't get a move-on. On the heels of the Carolina campaign was the Yorktown confrontation—the American triumph there sealed the war's end.

NORTH DAKOTA

Dakota is from an Indian word meaning "allies." Progressivism was a vigorous force at the turn of the century, especially among Norwegians in the eastern lowlands. Predominantly rural (there are 9.7 people per square mile), the state is a leader in producing cattle, cattle products, oats, rye, barley, flaxseed, and King Wheat. The northwestern half was part of the Louisiana Purchase; the southeastern half was acquired from Great Britain in 1818 when the boundary with Canada was set at the forty-ninth parallel. A 2,200-acre "peace garden" extends across the border into Manitoba. North Dakota is known as the Sioux State or the Flickertail State. Motto: Liberty and Union, Now and Forever, One and

Inseparable. North Dakotans have included Maxwell Anderson, Eric Sevareid, Louis L'Amour, Peggy Lee, Lawrence Welk, and Angie Dickinson.

NORTHERN IRELAND

Six of the nine counties of the historic province of Ulster, or Northern Ireland (a division of Great Britain and Northern Ireland), are Armagh, Down, Antrim, Londonderry, Tyrone, and Fermanagh. (The capital of the country is Belfast, where some of the world's largest ocean liners have been built.) Armagh: Ireland's primatial city and once the home of the country's prehistoric Red Branch Knights. Down: hummocky drumlin countryside. Antrim: in the deeps of Lagan valley. Fermanagh: of the lakes, a county laid northwest by southeast, which at Belleek barely fails to reach the sea at Ballyshannon. Londonderry: called Derry before it was turned over, in 1613, to the corporations of the City of London. Tyrone: the largest county, uplands in the north and center, organized as a shire nearly three centuries ago after the English had defeated the O'Neills.

NORTON, KEN

The five–one underdog heavyweight boxer scored with only one of every dozen punches, but one of those punches broke Muhammad Ali's jaw, a clean break, all the way through the lower left side, and the former All-Marine champion went on to win a twelve-round, nontitle split decision in San Diego, California, in 1973. Ali was fat and unconditioned, and he had sprained an ankle the week before. Norton's style: peek-a-boo with his arms across his face; his best punch: a left hook to the body and the head; he slapped with an open glove—all in all, a "stutter-style." Only Joe Frazier, two years earlier, had silenced the Louisville Lip in the "fight of the century." Ali won the rematch with Norton six months later, but barely: "I feel I won the fight but lost to the name," Norton said. "When I had a chance to mull it around, I was convinced I'd won—the decision then depressed me." Norton boasted that anything the mind could see, the body could do.

NORWAY

For four centuries, Danish governors ruled the northernmost Scandinavian nation—one-third lies above the Arctic Circle. In the Treaty of Kiel in 1814, they ceded the western part of the peninsula to the Swedish crown in exchange for West Pomerania. Norway was an independent kingdom but accepted the Swedish monarchy. The Norway-Sweden union, after nearly a century of friction, was dissolved in 1905 when a plebiscite demonstrated that almost all Norwegians favored separation. Today, Norway is a constitutional monarchy, with legislative power vested in the Storting, or parliament.

NOSE

Want to make a hurricane, a very strong air current up to 100 miles per hour? Sneeze! There's a special area in your brain that perceives different smells as distinct from one another. In addition to serving your respiratory system by warming, cleaning, and moistening the air you breathe, your nose helps you to speak. The soft sounds coming through the vocal cords are amplified in part by your nasal cavity. Many animals have a heightened sense of smell, and can locate, by smell alone, mates many miles away.

NOVEMBER 11, 1918

When the armistice ending the Great War was signed at Compiègne, in France, at 11 A.M. on November 11, 1918—11/11/18—German troops were still occupying territory from the Crimea to France. No enemy soldier had set a boot in the Fatherland, there hadn't been a decisive battle in the four years, and at Brest-Litovsk the Russians had been forced by the Kaiser to sign over 5,000 factories and industrial plants. German morale collapsed, however, when the navy in Kiel revolted against Wilhelm. (Only twenty-two years later, France surrendered to Hitler in the same railroad car at Compiègne.) About 10 million people were killed and about 20 million were wounded during World War I, which was followed by starvation and worldwide epidemics that took more lives than did the War.

NURMI, PAAVO

The Flying Finn set twenty long-distance world running records and won nine Olympic gold medals plus three more golds in team events, between 1920 and 1930. He was disqualified from the 1932 Olympic games in Los Angeles because he had violated the amateur athletic code.

O

OAKLEY, ANNIE

Peerless Lady Wing-Shot, an incredible marksperson, could split a play-ing card held edge-on and hit coins tossed into the air. As a teenager, she bested vaudeville marksman Frank E. Butler, then married him; together, they shot the lights out on vaudeville and circus circuits. Anything he could do, she could do better. She shot a cigarette from the lips of the future Kaiser Wilhelm of Germany. Songsmith Irving Berlin hit the bull's-eye with his Broadway musical about Little Miss Dead Shot, *Annie Get Your Gun.*

THE OCCIDENT

The opposite of Orient: Western lands, Europe, as opposed to Asia and the Orient. Occident, from the present participle of *occidere,* "to fall down, set (of the Sun)." Also, the Western Hemisphere. "I may wander from east to occident." Orient, from the Latin *oriens,* "the rising of the sun," in the Eastern lands.

OCEANS

The third planet from the Sun is mostly water. Oceans cover 71 percent of the globe. Slightly more than four-fifths of the Southern Hemisphere is ocean. Ocean from Oceanus, the son of Heaven and Earth, the name given by the Greeks to an ever-flowing river that they supposed flowed around the Earth they thought was flat. The name was applied later to those waters that were far outside the range of land, such as the waters that lay beyond the Pillars of Hercules. The Atlantic was thought to be the grave of the mythical Atlantis. El Mar Pacifico was named by Magel-lan. The Indian Ocean was named for the large country to its north. The two other oceans are the Arctic and the Antarctic.

OCTOBER REVOLUTION ISLAND

It is the largest of four major Russian, glacial islands in the 14,300-square-mile archipelago Severnaya Zemlya (Russian, meaning "northern land") in the Arctic Ocean north of the Taymyr Peninsula. The Kara Sea is to the west, Laptev Sea is to the east, the Pole is less than ten degrees of latitude to the north. The three other major islands are, from south to north, Bol'shevik, Pioner, and Komsomoleta. There are several smaller islands, too, all separated from the mainland by the Boris Vil'kitskiy Strait. The archipelago wasn't discovered until 1913. It was called Nicholas II Land until the Bolsheviks' October Revolution. It was explored and mapped by a 1930–32 expedition. Approximately half of October Revolution is covered by glaciers (14,170 square miles), which in places extend to the sea. On the ice-free sections there is scanty vegetation of the polar desert and arctic tundra types.

OF HUMAN BONDAGE

Bette Davis says she won her first Oscar, in 1935, "for what had been denied to me the year before, when I played the extremely unsympathetic Cockney waitress Mildred in *Of Human Bondage*. Mildred was a marvelous opportunity for me. Playing 'a bad woman' was unheard of for a star of that era. Frankly, I could have won in '35 for reciting 'Little Miss Muffet.' When I lost in the Mildred part, Jack Warner said to me, 'Well, you were very good playing a bitch-heroine. But you shouldn't win an award for playing yourself.' " Somerset Maugham's classic autobiographical novel of the torments of young manhood were filmed twice more: Eleanor Parker played the viciously vulgar strumpet in 1946 and Kim Novak gave it a quick lick in 1964. In the original, Leslie Howard was the sensitive, clubfooted, medical student (and erstwhile painter) whom Mildred meets, seduces, and betrays with monotonous regularity. As Mildred dies of a euphemism in Philip's arms, she whispers her plea for "a proper funeral . . . like a lady."

OH, SADAHARU

Japan's "Hank Aaron" clouted 868 home runs in twenty-one seasons but never hit as many as sixty home runs in any one season. He did hit fifty-five. (The Japanese baseball season is twenty-two games less than the United States big leagues'.) The lefthanded first baseman played for the Yomiuri Giants, of Tokyo, and appropriately wore uniform number one. He lifted his right foot and leg slightly off the ground, leaned into a pitch, and snapped the bat with his wrists and shoulders, then would watch the ball sail beyond the fence. "But I am not Babe Ruth or Hank Aaron," Oh has said. "I cannot compare myself with them anymore than they might have compared themselves with me. I am the Japanese Oh Sadaharu. . . . Baseball was for me a form of spirit-discipline, a way to make myself a better person. It became my Way, as the tea ceremony or flower arranging or the making of poems were the Ways of others. . . . The opinions of someone who has spent his life chasing a little white ball around a field really ought not be offered as oracles from the Buddha."

OKLAHOMA

The forty-sixth state to join the Union (1907) got its name from two Choctaw Indian words, *okla,* "people," and *homa,* "red." Part of the Louisiana Purchase, it was known as Indian Territory when it was the home of the Five Civilized Tribes—the Seminole, Choctaw, Cherokee, Creek, Chickasaw. The only two large cities, Oklahoma City, the capital, and Tulsa, are among the great natural gas and petroleum centers of the world. Oklahoma City was settled overnight by "Sooners" in a land rush in 1889, and today is the second-largest city in land area in the country (650 square miles over three counties). No Republican was governor until 1962; during the 1920s, two governors were impeached. Prominent citizens have included Woody Guthrie, Mickey Mantle, Will Rogers, Wiley Post, Maria Tallchief, Jim Thorpe, General Patrick J. Hurley, Carl Albert, and the Dust Bowl Okies. You couldn't buy a drink legally in the Sooner State until 1959. The state motto is "Love conquers all things."

OLD IRONSIDES

Talking about having a strong constitution! The most-famous wooden vessel in the history of the U.S. Navy is still with us nearly two centuries after being launched. In 1798, the 44-gun frigate was in the undeclared naval war with the French; at the turn of the century, she fought in the Tripolitan War; in the War of 1812, she was the flagship for Isaac Hull. Condemned in 1830 as unseaworthy, she was saved by the power of Oliver Wendell Holmes's poetic pen—"Old Ironsides" was published in the Boston *Daily Advertiser*. The *Constitution*—her official name—was rebuilt in the wake of "Ay, tear her tattered ensign down! Long has it waved on high, And many an eye has danced to see That banner in the sky; Beneath it rung the battle shout, And burst the cannon's roar—The meteor of the ocean air Shall sweep the clouds no more." (A word is the skin of a living thought.) In 1925, public subscription led to another fitting out. "Old Ironsides" is a tourist attraction in the Boston Navy Yard.

OLIVER TWIST

The orphan-bastard was born on the first page of Charles Dickens' novel and almost dies on the second. His mother had crept into the workhouse wearing no wedding ring and quietly expired as her newborn son emitted his first cry. The infant was placed in a baby farm where "twenty or thirty other juvenile offenders against the poor-laws rolled about the floor all day, without the inconvenience of too much food or too much clothing, under the parental supervision of an elderly female, who received the culprits at and for the consideration of sevenpence-halfpenny per small head per week." Oliver celebrates his ninth birthday in a coal cellar, a pale, thin child, somewhat diminutive in stature, and decidedly small in circumference. At an undertaker's, Oliver's bed is in a showroom among the coffins! "Please, sir, I want some more." The master was a fat, healthy man; but he turned very pale. He gazed in stupefied astonishment on the small rebel for some seconds, then clung for support to the copper. The assistants were paralyzed with wonder; the boys with fear. " 'What!' said the master at length, in a faint voice. 'Please, sir,' replied Oliver, 'I want some more.' The master aimed a blow at Oliver's head with the ladle, pinioned him in his arms, and shrieked aloud for the beadle." Fortunately, the lad had a sturdy spirit in that breast of his.

OLYMPICS

The French educator Baron Pierre de Coubestin was inspired by discovery of ruins of the original Olympic stadium in Greece to organize the first modern Olympiad, in Athens, in 1896. He wrote the Olympic creed: "The important thing in life is not the triumph but the struggle. The essential thing is not to have conquered but to have fought well." An American, James B. Connolly, got the games off on the right foot when he won the first gold medal, for the hop, step, and jump (nearly forty-five feet), and Americans won nine of the twelve track and field events. The original games, which began in 776 B.C., when there was only one event, a sprint of about 200 yards, were a combination of a patriotic, religious, and athletic festival. Emperor Theodosius in 393 B.C. held that the games were pagan and abolished them. The first winter Olympiad was staged in Chamonix, France, in 1924, and women participated for the first time in the Olympics in Amsterdam, in 1928. African nations boycotted the games in 1972 and in 1976. Many Americans had sought to boycott the 1936 games in Berlin, but Nazi anti-Semitism was explained away as a "religious dispute." At Munich, in 1972, eleven Israeli athletes were killed in events surrounding the invasion of Olympic Village by eight Palestinian terrorists carrying machine guns and hand grenades in athletic equipment bags and demanding the release of 200 Arab political prisoners held in Israel; five of the terrorists and one West German policeman were also slain. An American Jew, Mark Spitz, swam to seven golds in Munich.

OLYMPICS—CANCELLED

The games of 1912 had brought the host Swedes such favorable publicity internationally that the Olympic Committee set the 1916 games for Berlin with the hope that the Kaiser would defuse his belligerent aspirations. And so the Olympic Committee came in dead-last that year in hope. The VI Olympiad was never held. The games in Antwerp in 1920 were numbered VII. The 1940 games were first scheduled for Tokyo, then rescheduled for Helsinki but they were not staged, nor of course were the 1944 games scheduled for London. Sixteen sites had been built or reserved in Tokyo for a program of eighteen sports and art competitions even though Japan was invading Indo-China. Finland's preparations were overtaken by Hitler's Baltic bloodbath. The first games after World War II were held in the British capital, in 1948. Winter Games—Garmisch-Partenkirchen, 1940, cancelled; 1944, not scheduled. Denver, Colorado, was awarded the Winter games of 1976, but the voters did not approve the necessary bond issue—the environmentalists went to the polls in force—the games were awarded to Innsbruck, capital of the Austrian province of Tyrol, which had been host in 1964. Sheila Young of the United States won the gold in the 500-, the silver in the 1,500-, and the bronze in the 1,000-meter speed-skating events. Peter Mueller of the United States copped the gold in the 1,000-meter speed-skating. Dorothy Hamill won the figure-skating gold. Bill Koch won the first medal in a Nordic event for the United States since 1924 when he placed second in the thirty-kilometer cross-country event.

OLYMPICS—U.S. HOCKEY TEAM

"The impossible dream," "the miracle on ice"—a 4–3 U.S. victory over the heavily favored Soviet Union hockey team in the semifinals in the 1980 Winter Olympics in Lake Placid, New York, was followed two days later by the gold medal 4–2 triumph over Finland, with Vice-President Walter Mondale in the rooting section. The program director of a television station in Memphis, Tennessee, later confessed that he might have made an error in judgment by airing a local church service instead of the championship game—he was inundated with hundreds of protests. The Yanks' goalie, Jim Craig, signed with the Atlanta Flames of the National

Hockey League, and won his first outing, 4–1, but didn't last long in the pros, quitting at the age of twenty-seven after splitting the 1983–84 season between the Minnesota North Stars and its Salt Lake City farm club. The U.S. hockey team had won the gold medal in the 1960 Winter Olympics in Squaw Valley, California, whipping Czechoslovakia, 9–4, in the final game. The 1988 winter games are scheduled for Calgary, Canada.

OMAR KHAYYAM

The Persian was the son of a tentmaker—Khayyam means "tentmaker" —and he himself was a tentmaker in early life. He also wrote a book on algebra that was the best of its time, prepared improved astronomical tables, and in his most spectacular feat reformed the Muslim calendar in 1074. He also wrote clever quatrains, or so his discoverer and adapter the poet Edward FitzGerald averred: "Wake! For the Sun who scatter'd into flight The Stars before him from the Field of night, Drives Night along with them from Heav'n and strikes The Sultan's Turret with a Shaft of Light. . . . The Leaves of Life keep falling one by one. . . . A Book of Verses underneath the Bough, A Jug of Wine, a Loaf of Bread—and Thou Beside me singing in the Wilderness—Ah, Wilderness were Paradise enow! . . . There was the Door to which I found no Key; There was the Veil through which I might not see. Some little talk awhile of Me and Thee There was—and then no more of Thee and Me. . . . 'While you live, Drink!—for, once dead, you never shall return.' " FitzGerald's work had no sales to speak of until it was discovered by Rossetti, who showed it to Swinburne and others; by century's end (the nineteenth), the Epicurean facile *Rubaiyat of Omar Khayyam* was the most quoted poem in English among Englishmen weary of Victorian moralizing. "Who *is* the Potter, pray, and who the Pot?"

OMNIVOROUS

It describes one who eats both plants and animals, or anything, or takes in everything. A reader can be omnivorous. An insectivorous is an animal (e.g., a frog) that feeds on insects. Frugivorous: an animal that feeds on fruit. Herbivorous: an animal that feeds on plants. Microphagous: an animal that feeds on small particles suspended in water. Granivorous: an animal that feeds on grains and seeds. Phytophagous: an animal that feeds on plants, including shrubs and trees. Graminivorous: an animal that feeds on grasses, grain, or seeds. Ichthyophagous: an animal that feeds on fish. Xylophagous: an animal that feeds on wood.

O'NEAL, TATUM

She was ten years old when she won the best-supporting-actress Oscar in 1973 for playing the leader of a juvenile ring of bicycle thieves in the movie *Paper Moon*. No one younger has won an Oscar. (Shirley Temple was given a miniature Oscar when she was six.) It was the year that a Hollywood advertising executive stripped off his clothes and streaked nude across the ceremony—and nationwide television—earning from David Niven the observation that "the only way he could get a laugh was by showing his shortcomings." Terrence O'Flaherty, the San Francisco newspaper columnist, suggested that "there's only one trouble with streaking—the wrong people usually do it. The ones who should have removed their clothes were Cher Bono, Twiggy, and Elizabeth Taylor."

ONISHCHENKO, BORIS

The Russian fencer was caught cheating at the Montreal Olympics in 1976 and sent home in disgrace. His épée was illegally wired—it would score a winning hit without making contact. The tip of the thin blade is wired through the contestant's sleeve to record any "touch" electrically. Onishchenko lunged at Britain's Jeremy Fox, who leaped back. There was no touch but the Russian's blade registered a score—lights flashed on the scoreboard, a buzzer sounded—Fox protested immediately. A subsequent investigation revealed that Onishchenko had won medals in the 1968 and the 1972 Olympics and in the Soviet championships in 1969 and 1970 in the same illegal manner. Touché!

ONTARIO

Canada's second largest province is the only one of the ten provinces that borders a Great Lake—and it borders all five, the largest body of fresh water on the globe. (Glacier-carved basins filled with meltwater when the most recent Ice Age gave up the ghost—the Great Lakes.) The largest of Canada's provinces is Quebec. The other provinces are British Columbia, Alberta, Saskatchewan, Manitoba, Prince Edward Island, New Brunswick, Nova Scotia, and Newfoundland. There are two territories as well: the Yukon and the Northwest. All of the North American continent north of the United States and east of Alaska is Canada (3,851,787-square-mile Canada), except for small islands in the Gulf of St. Lawrence south of Newfoundland: St. Pierre and Miquelon are owned by France.

"OPEN SESAME"

Ali Baba, Sinbad the Sailor, and Aladdin are three of the 1,001 stories—one a day—that Scheherezade told her husband, Schariar, the legendary king of Samarkand, to blunt his threat to have her executed. As an entity, *Thousand and One Nights,* or *Arabian Nights,* is a classical series of anonymous Oriental stories in Arabic. Many are set in India, and in their present form are completely Muslim in spirit. In Sir Richard Burton's sixteen volumes, "Open Sesame," or "Open, O Simsim" appears as follows in Ali Baba: "Ali Baba saw the robbers, as soon as they came under the tree, each unbridle his horse and hobble it; then all took off their saddle-bags which proved to be full of gold and silver. The man who seemed to be the captain presently pushed forwards, load on shoulder, through thorns and thickets, till he came up to a certain spot where he uttered these strange words, 'Open, O Simsim!' and forthwith appeared a wide doorway in the face of the rock. The robbers went in. . . . Then [Ali Baba] thought within himself, 'I too will try the virtue of those magical words and see if at my bidding the door will open and close.' So he called out aloud, 'Open, O Simsim!' And no sooner had he spoken than straightway the portal flew open and he entered within. He saw a large cavern and a vault, in height equalling the stature of a full-grown man and it was hewn in the live stone. . . .''

OPOSSUM

It's the only marsupial in North America, and is the only marsupial not found Down Under. A marsupial is an animal with a marsupium—an abdominal pouch in which the mother can carry her young. The young crawl into the pouch and from there suck the mother's nipples. Kangaroos, wallabies, koalas, and bandicoots are also marsupials. The adult red kangaroo stands about five feet tall; the baby measures only ¾ inch. The opossum sometimes plays possum, faking death to survive a possible attack. The gestation period of an opossum is only twelve days. Each newborn is smaller than a bee and weighs only two grams, and the mother delivers up to twenty at a time. The kangaroo has only one newborn at a time but conceives soon again. The new fetus develops a little, then stops, and is kept in reserve, that is, not born, until the pouch has been vacated. The marsupial reproductive system is not common. The females have two uteri and a double vagina. The males have a forked penis and their testes are situated in front of the penis, not behind it. These mammals are small-brained and of comparatively low intelligence.

OREGON

Emigration to the territories in the Northwest was stimulated when two women reached Oregon in 1836—Narcissa Prentiss Whitman and Eliza Hart Spalding. They were in a party organized by the American Board of Commissioners for Foreign Missionaries. Seven years later, the first large wave of settlers arrived via the Oregon Trail. Early in this century, Oregon adopted reforms that included the initiative, referendum, recall, direct primary, and woman suffrage—the "Oregon System." Linus Pauling, John Reed, Wayne Morris, Alberto Salazar, and Mary Decker are famous Oregonians. The motto of the Beaver State is The Union. Flower: Oregon grape. Bird: Western meadowlark. Tree: Douglas fir. Song: "Oregon, My Oregon." About one-half of the state's 31-million acres is rich forestland. When Oregon became the thirty-third state to join the Union, in 1859, its constitution both prohibited slaveholding and forbade free blacks from entering the state. The state was named for a river called Oregon, probably an Indian word.

ORIENTEERING

This rugged map-and-compass cross-country sport was instituted in 1918 by a Swedish youth leader, Major Ernst Killander. To rekindle interest in track and field events, he moved track and field into the great outdoors and challenged runners and skiers to find their way through the countryside. Orienteering techniques were already being used to teach messengers how to get across unfamiliar terrain with military intelligence information. Both ski and foot orienteering became popular in Scandinavia in the 1920s. There is no designated route to be followed; participants must find their way to various checkpoints and to the finish line in the shortest possible time. The National Canadian Orienteering Federation suggests that competitors—in order to save time—attach a cord of some kind to their compass so they can fasten it to their wrist while running. In that way, it will be easier to take bearings and check the course while moving from control point to control point. An easier form of the sport is called line orienteering—the participant must follow a designated course and mark the control points on his map as accurately as possible. The course is between two and four miles long and involves up to twelve control points. By examining how accurately the control points have been placed on the map, officials can determine how accurate the participant was in using his map and compass to know his way around.

ORKHAN

The language of Mork's home planet, Ork—"goodbye" in Orkan is "Nanoo-Nanoo." Orkhan has no connection with orkhon, a runic alphabet derived from Aramic by a Turkish tribe that occupied the drainage of the Orkhon River in northcentral Mongolia in the eighth century and practiced intensive irrigation agriculture. The Russian explorer N. M. Yadrinstev discovered the "Orkhon Inscriptions"—minor Chinese texts and the oldest known material in a Turkic language—a Russian turkologist studied them, and five years later, in 1896, the Danish philologist Vilhelm Thomsen deciphered them.

ORR, BOBBY

His ice escapades were without parallel in the firmament of the National Hockey League. The shooting star—his was a meteoric rise into the constellation of greats—was the first defenseman in the history of the league to win a scoring crown—and then he went out and won it a second time. In 657 games, he fired the one-inch-thick puck 270 times past the goaltender and assisted on 645 other goals, remarkable stats for a skater who was supposed to "stay back." He was rookie of the year at eighteen and a league All-Star eight consecutive years, the league's most valuable player three times—he played only nine full seasons—and he guided the Boston Bruins to two Stanley Cup championships (1969–70 and 1971–72). A sixth knee operation put him permanently on ice in late 1978, after he had joined the Chicago Blackhawks.

OSCAR

"Why, it looks just like my Uncle Oscar," the librarian of the Academy of Motion Picture Arts and Sciences is said to have said when she first saw the statuette to be given annually for distinguished achievement in the movie biz. A reporter overheard the blurt, printed it, and the rest is histrionics. Bette Davis, never one to look a gift horse in the mouth, thought at one time that she had coined the name: The backside of the statuette reminded her of her then husband's, Harmon Oscar Nelson's, and she began calling it Oscar. She now says, "The Academy has insisted that it was responsible for naming the statuette Oscar. I have willingly allowed it this dubious claim to fame." Miss Davis sweated through ten nominations, winning the best actress award only for *Dangerous* in 1935 and for *Jezebel* in 1938. "Warner Brothers had reluctantly loaned me to RKO to do this picture [she played the bad woman, Mildred, in *Of*

400

Human Bondage], then led a campaign against my Academy Award nomination to prevent one of their contract players from winning glory for another studio. Jack Warner personally pressured his employees not to vote for me. 'If Bette is nominated,' he said, 'she'll demand a higher salary.' '' The Academy reformed the nominating and voting procedures. Oscar was designed in 1928 by Cedric Gibbons, an M-G-M art director, and weighs in at 8 lbs. 13 oz. It has a 24kt gold exterior and an interior of a mixture of metals, the formula for which is known only to Dodge Trophy, its manufacturer in Crystal Lake, Illinois. During World War II, when precious metals were shy, Oscar was made of plaster. Real Oscars were given later to recipients of the simulacrum.

OSCAR—ONE OF A KIND

An Academy Award for title writing was awarded only once, in the very first awards ceremony: Within the year, sound was introduced to the movies. The sole winner (1927–28) for his titles was Joseph Farnham, for *three* movies: *The Fair Coed, Telling the World,* and *Laugh, Clown, Laugh.* With sound came new categories: best original musical score, best song, best sound. In that very first awards ceremony *Wings* won the best-picture Oscar, and all winners were announced three months before the event, held on May 16, 1929, at the Hollywood Roosevelt Hotel. A comedy-direction award was also given only that first year, Lewis Milestone (for *Two Arabian Knights*) edging Charlie Chaplin *(The Circus),* but Chaplin was honored with a special award for "versatility and genius in writing, acting, directing, and producing" the film. Also honored only that first year were artistic quality of production *(Sunrise)* and engineering effects *(Wings).* A special award was also presented to Warner Brothers, "for producing *The Jazz Singer,* the pioneer outstanding talking picture, which has revolutionized the industry." Best sound recording came in 1929–30; best score and song came in 1934. The policy of using sealed envelopes to announce the winners was initiated in 1941.

OSTRICH

The world's largest bird—the male is up to eight feet tall and weighs up to 300 pounds. Ostrich eggs are the world's largest—each weighs about three pounds. The male ostrich is polygamous. He mates with two to six females, which lay their eggs in a common nest, a hollow scooped out of the ground by the cock. Chicks hatch after forty days and become fully grown in a year and a half. The ostrich can run at great speed with wings outspread—up to forty miles per hour. It has only two toes on each foot.

It can drink salt water. Like the seabird, it has a large nasal gland that excretes excess salt.

OSWALD, LEE HARVEY (MUG SHOT 54018)

Informed opinion, based on documentation and previously suppressed and overlooked data, leans toward the view that the lumpen, misanthropic "silly little runt" (Jacqueline Lee B. Kennedy's description) indeed acted alone in the assassination of President John F. Kennedy, in Dallas, Texas, in 1963—and that the assassination was a mistake. Oswald was shooting at someone else. The loner was a woman-hater, the natural orientation of a youth who had been raised and taunted by voracious women. When he felt humiliated and emasculated, he resorted to violence. Oswald's widow, Marina, testified before the Warren Commission that her husband was the gunman but that he must have had someone other than the President in mind. Later, in day-long secret testimony before the Warreners, a psychiatrist asserted that shooting the President would have been the furthest thing from Oswald's sick mind: His anger was directed at women, not at men. . . . in the cross hairs of his telescope, Oswald must have perceived his wife and his mother. (Though they lived in the same community, Oswald had not spoken with his mother for fourteen months.) Government experts determined that Oswald's rifle and its cheap telescopic sights could not be aligned properly on the target. The scope was mounted off-center; it was a deficiency that could not be corrected. Bullets flew high and to the right of the aiming point. In his deranged vision, Oswald must have seen the chance at one stroke to avenge both his personal and the collective suffering of male-kind, and give the world proof of his own manhood. Shooting Marina or his mother would not gain notoriety, which Oswald desperately sought. But bullets aimed at his wife's idol, the First Lady—no one had shot a First Lady; *that* would make headlines—flew inexorably from the skewed rifle to the right and struck the President. (Oswald's favorite opera, which he played constantly on a phonograph, was the *Queen of Spades,* which is about the murder of the visiting queen.) Oswald in police custody repeatedly said that he knew nothing about the shooting of the President—not the position of a man so eager for attention—he needed time to figure out what had gone wrong. (All other presidential assassins confessed enthusiastically.) Believing that because Mr. Kennedy was shot the assassin was shooting at Mr. Kennedy is an example of psychological set theory. Once it is realized that the incipient schizophrenic was not shooting at the man he admired and that the assassination was, ergo, a horrendous misfiring, everything falls into place. Sherlock Holmes observed that when the impossible is eliminated, whatever remains, however improbable, must be the truth.

OSWALD, MARINA

The Lee Oswalds had an acquaintance in common with Jacqueline Kennedy—the polymath, mysterious George deMohrenschildt. He had known Jacqueline Lee Bouvier as a child—"very high strung, attractive, strong willed"—and he told the Warren Commission that he had persuaded J.B.K. as First Lady to be honorary chairman of his national cystic fibrosis organization. He made himself available to the Oswalds in Texas—"it's a mistake to picture all Russian women as commandoes, big fat horses working in brick factories"—and tried to satisfy Marina's interest in her idol, her "goddess," Mrs. Kennedy. Eventually, deMohrenschildt said, he and his wife were "acutely embarrassed and appalled at the nature of Mrs. Oswald's confidences and the way she expressed herself." He told investigators of the assassination of John F. Kennedy that "the only person I ever heard Oswald say he wanted to kill was Marina. And, gentlemen, I can't say I blamed him." On the eve of the assassination, Marina seems to have rejected Lee once and for all, declaring in so many words that he wasn't needed any more, he wasn't the American he had advertised, he should clear out and take his stuff with him—all he still had in the Paine house where Marina was staying, in Irving, Texas, a Dallas suburb, was his old rifle—her friend Ruth Paine was taking warm and loving care of her and the two baby girls. Two days after the assassination, Marina Oswald picked up and moved away from the Quaker Ruth Paine, who then pleaded for months to hear why her friend "has turned her face from me." (Mrs. Paine is said to have moved to a marina in Florida.) For a time after her husband's murder, the widow, Marina Oswald, was in the charge of *Life* magazine.

OUR AMERICAN COUSIN

Yankees were the rage during the World's Fair in London in 1850–51. The dramatist Tom Taylor saw the humorous side of the craze and wrote a play about it and called it *Our American Cousin*. It was a play of perverted parables: "Birds of a feather gather no moss." It was amid the laughter in Ford's Theater in Washington, D.C., that John Wilkes Booth —who knew the play by heart—murdered President Abraham Lincoln. It was Good Friday, April 14, 1865. The Civil War had been over less than a week. Miss Laura Keene was giving her nearly one-thousandth performance as Florence Trenchard, and it was a benefit—for herself. Late in the first act, she was trying to tell a joke to Dundreary, who typically did not get it. "Can't you see it?" Florence asked. "No, I can't see it," Dundreary insisted. At that moment, the President entered the state box on the upper righthand side. Miss Keene caught sight of him and announced, "Well, everybody can see *that!*" The orchestra struck up "Hail to the Chief," the capacity audience rose as one, and the play was at a standstill for a minute. During the second scene of the third act, the Confederate sympathizing, egomaniacal Booth mortally shot the sixteenth President, leaped to the stage, shouted *"Sic semper tyrannis! The South is avenged!,"* and bolted out through the "prompt entrance" and the stage door. The play was not presented again in Washington for more than four decades, until December 12, 1907. The theater was the Belasco, which coincidentally was on the site of the house where Lincoln's Secretary of State, William H. Seward, was nearly killed that same night by one of Booth's accomplices. Originally, Booth and six fellow conspirators planned to abduct Lincoln and carry him to Richmond, but the President failed to appear (March 20, 1865) at the place where they lay in wait.

"THE OUTSIDER"

"The Outsider" was the Marine second from the left in the Pulitzer Prize-winning photograph of five Marines and a sailor replanting the Stars and Stripes on Mount Suribachi, Iwo Jima, in 1945. (Three of the Marines soon died in the bloody clash with Japanese defenders.) The photograph made page one of newspapers across the United States and President Franklin Roosevelt ordered the copper-colored native American home as a hero. Hayes went on a war bond tour: "It was supposed to be soft duty, but I couldn't take it. Everywhere we went, people shoved a drink in our hands and said we were heroes. We knew we hadn't done much, but you couldn't tell them that. And I guess I was sort of a freak because I was an Indian." He left the Gila River Indian Reservation, in Arizona, and wandered from odd job to odd job. He was plied with liquor and couldn't hold it. He was bailed out of a jail in Chicago after being picked up barefooted, in tatters, drunk. "The trouble with me is that people are too nice to me. When I think of all the opportunities I've had and all the people I've let down, I want to get drunk all over again. But this time I'm not going to do it." Hayes died in 1953.

OUZO

It's an anise-flavored Greek liqueur—anise: plant of the parsley family, native in the east Mediterranean region, yielding aniseed. When mixed with water, it turns milky. An aperitif or a refresher, anise drinks are popular in countries bordering the Mediterranean. In Spain it's known as ojen; in France, pastis; in Italy, anesone; Israel, arak; Turkey, raki. In the United States, it's herbsaint. They vary one from another, but none is absinthe, because the formulas do not contain wormwood. Absinthe is prohibited in the United States and many other western countries because of the harmful effect it has on the nerves. Spain is an exception. Because an absinthe drink is an excellent restorative in cases of seasickness, airsickness, and nausea, myriad people have drunk to it.

"OVER THERE"

The popular American morale booster in World Wars I and II was composed by "Yankee Doodle Dandy" himself, George M. Cohan, who claimed to have been born on the Fourth of July—actually, he was born a day earlier. The exuberant song and dance man was awarded a special Medal of Honor by Congress in 1940 for both "Over There" and "You're a Grand Old Flag." The latter was composed in 1906 for the musical *George Washington, Jr.,* and "Over There" was composed in honor of the American Expeditionary Force (A.E.F.) heading for Europe in 1917. Cohan's other popular songs included "Mary's a Grand Old Name," "Give My Regards to Broadway," and "I Guess I'll Have to Telegraph My Baby." His first popular song, composed in 1895, was "Hot Tamale Alley." Cohan was also an actor, and in 1937 he impersonated President Franklin D. Roosevelt in the Kaufman-Hart drama *I'd Rather Be Right.*

OWENS, JESSE

Real name: J. C. Owens? James Cleveland Owens? John Cleveland Owens? After winning worldwide headlines for copping four gold medals and setting records in the Berlin Olympics, in 1936, and for being snubbed as a black man by master-race theorist Adolf Hitler, the café-au-lait cyclone left the sporting life. He was graduated from Ohio State University, where his career in track and field events had been little short of phenomenal, and went into the business whirl. He maintained that "There is no difference between the races. If the black athlete has been better than his white counterpart, it's because he is hungrier—he wants it more." There's now a Jesse Owens Avenue in West Berlin. It leads to the Olympic Stadium there, and was recently so named by the West Berlin senate, in part to stress the city's sports links to the United States.

P

PAAR, JACK

W. C. Fields was no problem, but w.c. meaning *w.c.*—welllllll! NBC censors thought the M.C. of "The Jack Paar Tonight Show" had gone to the well once too often, and in February 1960 deleted the broadcast videotape of his shaggy-dog story about an Englishwoman who planned to travel abroad and by post asked her host if the accommodations included a w.c. The host, who didn't understand English very well, wrote back extolling in detail the sumptuousness of the nearby w.c., cautioning that it most likely would be crowded on the two days a week that it was open—the host had deciphered w.c. as Wayside Chapel. NBC scissored the story without notice. *Welllllll!* All well broke out, which was Paar for the course—the controversial M.C. had more than a propensity to be irascible, pixieish, mercurial, petulant, emotional, not to mention controversial. "I kid you not." Paar (a high-school dropout and a protegé of Jack "Welllllll" Benny) quit the show the next night in a huff, not to mention a Maxwell and a chauffeur-driven limo, came back, then stuck to his word that he'd quit for good two years hence. Which paved the way for Johnny—as in mop. *Tempus fugit.* On "The Tonight Show" on Thanksgiving 1984 the comedian David Steinberg was able to say, without bleeps, that the hookers in his native Canada are so conservative, so laid back, that they "don't put out on their first date."

PACIFIC OCEAN

The world's largest ocean is so large that it covers 32 percent of the surface of the planet and occupies an area larger than that of all the land areas of the world combined! That 32 percent is an area of 69,364,200 miles. The mean depth of the Pacific is 13,211 feet; the depth is 37,720 feet, in the Marianas Trench. The distance across the Pacific from Panama to the Gulf of Thailand is 10,500 miles. The distance from Bering Strait to Cape Adare in Antarctica is 9,300 miles. Five states of the United States are bordered on the west by the Pacific, which was named by Ferdinand Magellan after a stormy unpacific Atlantic sail. It receives water from the Atlantic by way of the Drake Passage and the Arctic Ocean. Some years before he sailed through the "Strait of Magellan" at the southern tip of South America and into the Pacific on history's first circumnavigation of the Earth, Magellan had sailed around the southern tip of South Africa and into the Pacific as far east as Ternate in the East Indies. The English skipper James Cook was the first to cross both the Arctic and the Antarctic Circles in the Pacific. The rim of the Pacific basin is known as the "ring of fire"—it contains more volcanoes (active and dormant) and has more earthquakes than any other area. Immanuel Velikovsky speculated that the ocean was created when the Moon was ripped out of the land there by the close passage of a large gravitational body.

PAIGE, LEROY "SATCHEL"

"The World's Greatest Pitcher, Guaranteed to Strike Out the First Nine Men"—that's how the world's greatest pitcher was billed when the six-foot-three black righthander took the mound for the Kansas City Monarchs and the Black Barons. He was known for his "hesitation pitch." His motto was "Avoid running at all times," which may be why he was able to pitch (by one estimate) 2,500 games and tens of no-hitters. He was signed by the integrating major leagues in 1948, the oldest rookie ever (about forty-two), winning six of seven decisions and contributing to Cleveland's pennant chase. In 1952, with the St. Louis Browns, he won a dozen games and made the American League All-Star team. He pitched one more year for the Browns, then took a twelve-year vacation. He returned for one appearance, when he was fifty-nine or so, with the Kansas City Royals, in 1965. He was elected to the Hall of Fame in 1971.

PALACE OF VERSAILLES

Louis XIV didn't like Paris—he had unhappy memories of his childhood there—so he commandeered the services of three creative geniuses—the architect, the decorative arts impresario, the landscape gardener responsible for the sumptuous Chateau of Vaux-le-Vicomte. The Sun King wanted a palace large enough to be both the seat of the royal government and the living quarters for the thousand nobles of the court with their families and myriad retainers. Marshlands and woods were turned into a $100 million extravaganza. When Louis XVI and Marie Antoinette were guillotined a century later, the Palace was stripped of its furnishings and abandoned. In the mid-1800s, Louis Philippe saved Versailles from demolition by turning it into a museum dedicated to *Toutes les Gloires de la France*. Restoration and rehabilitation took place after the Treaty of

Versailles ending World War I was signed in the palace's half-mile-long Hall of Mirrors.

PALEONTOLOGY

A paleontologist studies the life of past geological periods through fossil remains of plants and animals. He learns about the phylogeny and relationships of modern animals and plants and about the chronology of the history of the Earth. The French anatomist Georges Cuvier was a firm anti-evolutionist but he worked with fossils and became the founder of paleontology. Let's make no bones about it: He missed identifying the dinosaurs, saying that the first teeth of such creatures to be discovered were mammalian rather than reptilian. The English zoologist Sir Richard Owen coined the word dinosaur—"terrible lizard"—in 1842. Owen's reconstruction of full-sized dinosaurs turned London upside down in 1854.

PALMER, ARNOLD

The superstar wasn't in the army of golfers who teed off for the U.S. Open golf championship in 1984. It was the first time he had not made the qualifying cut since he was an amateur in the 1953 Open at Oakmont, not far from his home in Latrobe, Pennsylvania; he had failed by two strokes to qualify. And so he and Gene Sarazen jointly hold the record of teeing off in thirty-one consecutive Opens. Palmer has been a storied Open golfer. He has won the Open only once, at Cherry Hills, in 1960. He lost an 18-hole playoff in three other Opens—in 1962 to Jack Nicklaus at Oakmont, the next year to Julius Boros at the Country Club, outside Boston, and in 1966 to Billy Casper at Olympic. Golf's first folk hero, the winner of four Masters, including the 1960, thrust the sport into the multi-million-dollar atmosphere. The son of a professional golfer, he got his first club at the age of three; six years later, he shot nine holes in 45. "Ever since I was able to walk," Palmer said in 1960, "I have been swinging a golf club, and ever since I was big enough to dream I have wanted to be the best golfer that ever lived."

PALMISTRY

One has to hand it to this form of divination, it has been practiced from the ancient world to today. Your palm is read as a map to your character and your future. The three long lines are the lines of life, head, and heart. Look at your palm. Your life line starts between the base of the first finger and the thumb and runs down your hand in a wide curve encircling the Mount of Venus at the base of the thumb. (There are seven mounts.) Your heart line is the upper of the two big lines that cross the top half of your palm more or less horizontally. The line of head is the lower of the two horizontal lines running across the upper part of your palm and below the heart line. On the line of life is read your general health and constitution and certain of the important events of your life. The line of heart deals with affairs of the heart and with every kind of emotion. The head line is the guide to the kind of mind you possess, your general abilities, the amount of concentration and self-control. A trick of the trade: The palm reader checks for bitten nails—ah ha, he's nervous.

PAMPAS

About 300,000 square miles of wide, flat, grassy plains in southern South America, from the Atlantic Ocean to the Andean foothills in Uruguay, bounded in the north by Gran Chaco and in the south by Patagonia. Pampas is a Quechua Indian word meaning flat surface, or prairie-like. Trees are rare and the soil is fertile. And there's the Pampa, about 250,000 square miles in central and northern Argentina. The principal cities are Buenos Aires, La Plata, Bahia Blanca, Rosario, and Santa Fe. The gaucho, the Argentine cowboy, was once the dominant figure in the Pampa. Cattle were introduced into the region by the Portuguese in the 1550s.

PAN

The son of Hermes—but no relation to the choreographer Hermes Pan— the Greek god of woods and shepherds in human shape with the feet and the horns of a goat was regarded both as the cause of the panic among the Persians at Marathon and of any sudden and groundless fear. He invented the panpipe, or shepherd's pipe, a musical instrument made of reeds, which he named "syrinx" for the nymph who fled his love, leaving him "nought but a lovely sighing of the wind." Elizabeth Barrett Browning once asked, "What was he doing, the great god Pan, Down in the reeds by the river? Spreading ruin and scattering ban, Splashing and paddling with hoofs of a goat, And breaking the golden lilies afloat With the dragonfly on the river." The rural, amorous deity of Arcadia often leaped from the—well, from the frying pan into the fire in his pursuit of Syrinx and Echo and his seduction of Selene, the mother of Pandia by Zeus. (Pandaemonium was the capital of Hell in John Milton's *Paradise Lost,* but that's another story—*pan,* all, all demons.)

PANTHER

It's a black leopard. Locally, "panther" is used sometimes to designate the jaguar and the puma. A large variation occurs within the leopard species, *Panthera pardus*. Male leopards are about seven feet long; the tail alone is three feet long. The cats roam Africa and Asia from the southwest to Korea and Java. They are not fussy eaters—a baboon, an antelope, a hunter, it's all the same. It was the dried and frozen carcass of a leopard, probably the remains of a *P. Quancia*, that Ernest Hemingway said was found close to the western summit of the extinct snow-covered volcano Kilimanjaro, the highest mountain in Africa: "No one has explained what the leopard was seeking at that altitude." Or had it been dropped from an airplane?

"PAPILLON"

Henry Charrière's nickname—he had a butterfly, a *papillon*, tattooed on his chest—and the title of his memoirs. He was a safecracker in Paris and a Parisite—he was condemned in 1931 to hard labor for life for the murder of a pimp—he claimed he was framed. He did fourteen years in penal colonies in French Guiana. He escaped from Devils Island for good on his ninth try by first throwing himself into the battering sea with two bags of coconuts.

PAPUA NEW GUINEA

The wild, rugged eastern half of stone-age New Guinea in the southwest Pacific sports some 500 different languages—but the *lingua franca* is English. The most widely used trade languages among the Territorians are Police Motu and New Guinea pidgin. Police Motu spread as government patrols moved out from the capital, Port Moresby, and along the Papuan coast. New Guinea pidgin developed from the visits of recruiters for the Queensland canefields to the Bismarck archipelago, where, as early as the 1870s, travelers heard people speaking a form of English. The southern section of the country, Papua, was annexed by Queensland in 1883 and became the British protectorate British New Guinea; it passed to Australia in 1905 as the Territory of Papua. The northern section of the country formed part of German New Guinea and was called Kaiser-Wilhelmsland; it was mandated to Australia by the League of Nations in 1920. English was made compulsory in all school classes beyond the second grade with the hope that communication throughout the territory would be made easier and a sense of national unity would develop.

PAR

Par on the golf course is determined strictly by length from tee to hole. Par is from the Latin for "an equal." Par is the point where a first-class golfer and the course or links are equal. If the total of the pars for 18 holes is 63, the first-class golfer will take 63 strokes to complete the round —it'll be par for the course. For men, par 3 is for a hole up to 250 yards from the tee; par 4: 251 to 470 yards; par 5: 471 yards and over. For women, par 3 is for a hole up to 210 yards from the tee; par 4: 211 to 400 yards; par 5: 401 to 575 yards; par 6: 576 and over. It is assumed that it takes two putts to hole out.

PARACHUTE

High-flying French aeronauts made no bones about it: Something was needed to make sure that if they had to bail out of a disabled balloon they could return to earth safely. Jean Pierre Blanchard jumped at the challenge and came up with an umbrella-shaped parachute. The year was 1785, the same year he really might have needed one for himself: He and Dr. John Jeffries, of Boston, Massachusetts, did the never-done-before, crossing the English Channel by *air*. He apparently never gave the chute a try, at least not from a great height, or he would be in the books as the first parachutist from on-high. (Blanchard did some ballooning before George Washington in the 1790s.) *That* giant leap for mankind was made by Jacques Garnerin. He dropped 3,000 feet from a balloon in 1797 and lived to tell about it. Charles Guille? He jumped over New York City, in 1819, from a wicker basket, decorated with flowers, suspended from a 25,000-cubic-foot silk balloon. He fell 300 feet before his chute expanded and he landed four miles away from his goal. The first parachute jump from an airplane seems to have been made on March 1, 1912, by Captain Albert Berry from a Benoist Pusher plane piloted by Anthony Jannus, at Jefferson Barracks, St. Louis, Missouri. Berry took the plunge from an altitude of 1,500 feet while the plane was traveling 50 miles per hour. In *The Real Stuff*, Tom Wolfe tells what it's like when the chute doesn't open: "Except that it was not an explosion; it was the tremendous *crack* of Ted Whelan, his helmet, his pressure suit, and his seat-parachute rig smashing into the center of the runway, precisely on target, right in front of the crowd; an absolute bull's-eye. Ted Whelan had no doubt been alive until the instant of impact. He had had about thirty seconds to watch the

411

Pax River base and the peninsula and Baltimore County and continental America and the entire comprehensible world rise up to smash him. When they lifted his body up off the concrete, it was like a sack of fertilizer.''

PARASITE

Sycophant, favorite, toady, lickspit, lickspittle, bootlick, bootlicker, hanger-on, leech, sponge, sponger—an organism living in or on another living organism, obtaining from it part or all of its organic nutriment, and commonly exhibiting some degree of adaptive structural modification. In ancient Greek religious rites, a parasite was one of a class of assistants who dined with the priests after a sacrifice. Havelock Ellis: ''. . . new friends who had faith in her ideas, as well as new parasites who hoped to profit by them.''

PARI-MUTUEL

It's French for mutual wager, ''betting among ourselves.'' It's a system of betting, as on a horse race, a greyhound race, jai alai games, in which those who bet on the winner share the total stakes minus a small percentage held out for management. The system was invented in 1872 by a French shopkeeper and bookmaker, Pierre Oller, as a method of guaranteeing the bookmaker (himself) a set commission regardless of the winner of the race. High-speed electronic calculating machines known as totalizators record and display up-to-the minute betting patterns. The gambling public makes the payoff odds.

PARIS LIBERATION

Caught up in the hysteria of his mounting rage, Hitler began to scream: *''Brennt Paris?''* Is Paris burning? The Allies were sweeping across France in the summer of 1944, two months after D-Day, and the Führer was faced with the loss of the last prize left in an empire that was to have lived a thousand years. Paris must be reduced to a pile of ruins. V-1 and V-2 bombs and every available Luftwaffe plane must blacken the City of Light. The Karl. Send in the Karl, the Karl—the most powerful single artillery piece developed by preatomic man, a tractor-mounted 600-millimeter mortar that could lob a two-and-a-half-ton shell two feet thick more than three miles. It had been used to batter Brest-Litovsk and Sebastopol. But Hitler's Paris commander, General Dietrich von Choltitz, did not want to go down in history as the man who destroyed Paris. He dragged his feet, he alibied, he ignored orders. He let it be known to the Allies that they should move rapidly on the city. A month earlier, Supreme Allied Commander Dwight D. Eisenhower had told the Free French that taking Paris was not an immediate mission, it could wait for two to three months. When inspired Resistance insurrection mounted, Ike was persuaded to let French General Philippe Leclerc's Second Armored Division do what it could—what it could do with the help of two American battalions of field artillery was to push from the southern outskirts of the city, over the Austerlitz Bridge to the right bank of the Seine, and up to the City Hall. Von Choltitz surrendered to Leclerc, and General Charles de Gaulle declared that radiant France was a great nation: "Here we are once again on our feet as victors."

PARIS SEWERS

On specific days—but not if it's raining or if the Seine is high—a tour of sewers in Paris is conducted from the entrance near the Lille statue on the square at Place de la Concorde. The engineer Belgrand directed construction of the city's sewer system. Secondary sullage pipes, into which smaller drains lead, empty into four main sewers. Ducts contain the pipes for drinking and industrial water, telephone and telegraph cables, the *pneumatique* and compressed air tubes.

PARROT

It's the common name for members of the order *Psittaciformes,* and there are 315 species of these colorful birds. They have four toes—the first and the fourth face backward, making two pairs of pincers that facilitate climbing and grasping. Only the kea, of New Zealand, is a scavenger (and that's in the winter) and not monogamous. The parrot is among the oldest domesticated animals. A helmsman in the fleet of Alexander the Great returned to Europe with ring parrots or rose-ringed parakeets, now known of course as Alexander parrots. Pliny the Elder had advice on getting the parrot to imitate words: "Take a stick as hard as the parrot's bill and hit it on the head." A parroteer has written that parrots have "absolute pitch" and can change from one scale to another (transpose). When someone sang or whistled the first few bars of a song that his gray parrot knew, the parrot would continue at the same pitch and rhythm from exactly where the tune had been broken off. Other birds also have the capacity for imitation. A human parrot repeats words without understanding their meaning.

PASCAL, BLAISE

The French mathematician and physicist with a deformed skull has been remembered for more than three centuries for saying, "Cleopatra's nose, had it been shorter, the whole face of the world would have been changed." He was full of observations: "What a chimera then is man! What a novelty! What a monster, what a chaos, what a contradiction, what a prodigy! Judge of all things, feeble earthworm, depository of truth, a sink of uncertainty and error, the glory and the shame of the universe. . . . Men never do evil so completely and cheerfully as when they do it from religious conviction. . . . Justice without strength is helpless, strength without justice is tyrannical. . . . Unable to make what is just strong, we have made what is strong just. . . . The state of man: inconstancy, boredom, anxiety. . . . I have discovered that all human evil comes from this, man's being unable to sit still in a room. . . . Man is neither angel nor beast; and the misfortune is that he who would act the angel acts the beast." In his short life—Pascal was chronically sick, and died just after his thirty-ninth birthday—he: made the first advance in nearly nineteen centuries on the geometry of the conic sections; invented a calculating machine that, by means of cogged wheels, could add and subtract (it was the ancestor of the modern cash register); co-founded the modern theory of probability; defined the basis of the hydraulic press. When he came under the influence of the Catholic sect Jansenism, he abandoned work on science and mathematics and devoted himself to meditation, asceticism, and religious writings: "To ridicule philosophy is really to philosophize."

THE PASSION PLAY

To take part in *The Passion Play,* which has been performed every tenth year for 350 years, one must be a Roman Catholic to play a major role in the elaboration on the New Testament accounts of Jesus' last days and to have lived in the Bavarian Alps village of Oberammergau, near Munich, for twenty years or have married a citizen and then lived there for a decade. The play requires a cast and crew of 1,400 villagers. Productions date to the 1600s, when inhabitants first pledged to present the drama in gratitude for being spared the ravages of the plague then sweeping Europe. Before recent editing, the florid script blamed the Jews for Jesus' death and turned them into a snarling mob. A study by the American Jewish Committee in 1970 concluded that the Oberammergau pageant was "pervaded by an anti-Jewish bias which not only distorts the facts of Jesus' history but also obscures those passages of the New Testament that offer a basis for balanced and positive images of Jews and

Judaism . . . a negative picture of first-century Judaism presents an invidious portrayal of the Jewish people as Jesus' opponents and shifts the responsibility for deciding on the crucifixion from Pontius Pilate to the Jewish people. In doing so, the play resists any serious accommodation to the scholarly findings of contemporary authoritative Biblical and historical research.'' Villagers who play in the mob scenes have complained that the closely scripted new eight-hour version has denied them the opportunity for ad-lib ravings.

PASTERNAK, BORIS

The distinguished poet, novelist, and translator, the son of a celebrated painter and a concert pianist, both Jewish, joyfully announced acceptance of the 1958 Nobel Prize in Literature for his epic *Doctor Zhivago*. But an unparalleled explosion of vilification by the Soviet government forced him to inform the Swedish Academy of his "voluntary" refusal of the award. Threatened with deportation, he wrote Premier Nikita Khrushchev, "Leaving my motherland would be equal to death for me. And that is why I ask that you do not take this final measure in relation to me. I can honestly say that I have truly done something for Soviet literature and can be useful to it in the future." *Doctor Zhivago* has never been published in the Soviet Union, nor has the prodigious success of the novel, notable for its harrowing description of the privations and sufferings endured by Russians in the tumultuous first thirty years of this century, ever been mentioned in the Soviet press. Pasternak was allowed to live in a Moscow suburb and to have visitors. He died in 1960.

PATAGONIA

Amerigo Vespucci—for whom America was named—dropped by in 1501, but it was Ferdinand Magellan on his historic circumnavigating feat who dubbed the natives Patagones, or "people with big feet," and so their land came to be called Patagonia. Jorge Luis Borges, the blind Argentine novelist, has said, "There is nothing in Patagonia. It's not the Sahara, but it's as close as you can get to it in Argentina. No, there is nothing in Patagonia." To be in Patagonia, the world traveler Paul Theroux observed, "it helped to be a miniaturist, or else interested in enormous empty spaces. There was no intermediate zone of study. Either the enormity of the desert space, or the sight of a tiny flower. You had to choose between the tiny or the vast." Primarily in southern Argentina, south of the Rio Colorado and east of the Andes, but including extreme southeast Chile and northern Tierra del Fuego, Patagonia is a collidescope of plains, Andes, wind-swept semi-arid plateaus, cliffs, transverse valleys, cradling rivers, dry river beds, lakes, glaciers, deep, fertile valleys, subantarctic conditions, sheep raising, oil production, coal mining, cattle raising, irrigated oases, guanaco, rhea, puma, deer—a rich field for the pioneer and the paleontologist and the hermit.

PATTON, GEORGE S.

Slapping a soldier cost "Old Blood and Guts" his command during World War II and leniency to Nazis cost him the military governorship of Bavaria in late 1945—"unser Patton, unser Freund" is how many Germans saw their conqueror, who also despised the Russians. His Third Army had ripped through Normandy, Brittany, Northern France—"Your army has written a great page in history of which the American people will always be very proud," General George C. Marshall wrote to Patton in December 1944—relieved Bastogne in the Battle of the Bulge, leaped the Rhine, and dashed across southern Germany into Czechoslovakia. On Armistice Day 1944, he "celebrated" his birthday "by getting up where the dead were still warm." He died in the early darkness of a winter afternoon, just before Christmas 1945, eleven days after a highway accident near Mannheim—his Cadillac and a truck collided as Patton was on the way to a pheasant hunt in Germany before returning to the States. He had told his son on D-Day, "To be a successful soldier you must know history. . . . What you must know is how man reacts. Weapons change but man who uses them changes not at all. To win battles you do not beat weapons—you beat the soul of man, of the enemy man."

PAUL BUNYAN

The legendary "mightiest of loggers" in the American northwest—"Tom Beaver" was the Paul Bunyan of southern lumber camps. Two cuts—one on the forward swing of Paul's ax, one on the backward swing—and the tree would crash to earth. He peeled logs by hitching his prized possession—Babe the Blue Ox—to one end of a log and holding onto the bark at the other; when Babe pulled, the log came out slick and clean. The distance between Babe's horns measured 42 ax handles and a plug of Star tobacco. Bunyan walked from Maine to Oregon because the trains were too slow. The Colorado Canyon? That's the scratch in the ground where the mighty lumberjack had dragged his pick on his way west.

PAVLOV, IVAN PETROVICH

Russia's Nobel Prize winner (1904) was on the road to the priesthood when he was detoured by reading Charles Darwin's *Origin of Species*. He will be celebrated always for his delicate work on the conditioned and the unconditioned reflex: "We introduce into the mouth of a dog a moderate solution of some acid; the acid produces a usual defensive reaction in the animal: by vigorous movements of the mouth it ejects the solution, and at the same time an abundant quantity of saliva begins to flow first into the mouth and then overflows, diluting the acid and cleansing the mucous membrane of the oral cavity. Now let us turn to the second experiment. Just prior to introducing the same solution into the dog's mouth we repeatedly act on the animal by a certain external agent, say, a definite sound. What happens then? It suffices simply to repeat the sound, and the same reaction is fully reproduced—the same movements of the mouth and the same secretion of saliva. Both of the above-mentioned facts are equally exact and constant. And both must be designated by one and the same physiological term—'reflex.' " Because Pavlov would become excited when the dog responded to the stimulus, it has been suggested that the animal may have been conditioning the scientist. There is today a theory that a good part of learning and of the development of behavior is the result of conditioned reflexes of all sorts picked up in the course of life. Pavlov was an ardent anti-Communist tolerated by the Red regime.

PEACE CORPS

It became in time—at least in the developing nations—the most stirring symbol of President John Kennedy's hope and promise. Theodore Sorensen, a close presidential aide, has recalled that the Peace Corps proposal was based on the Mormon and other voluntary religious service efforts, on an editorial Kennedy had read years earlier, on a speech by General James Gavin, on a luncheon Sorensen had with a Philadelphia businessman, on the suggestions of J.F.K.'s academic advisers, on legislation previously introduced, and on the written response to a spontaneous late-night challenge the candidate had issued to Michigan students during the 1960 election campaign. Liberals demeaned it as a gimmick. Conservatives dismissed it as a nonsensical haven for beatniks and visionaries. Communist nations denounced it as an espionage front. The first director was Kennedy's energetic, idealistic brother-in-law, Sargent Shriver. The volunteers have been called "Kennedy's children" and have served in more than sixty countries, working to improve food production, health education, and other basic needs. Applications are still being accepted: Peace Corps/ACTION, Washington, D.C. 20525.

PEACH MELBA

Helen Porter Mitchell wanted to change her name? Who wanted to hear a soprano named Helen Porter Mitchell sing lyric and coloratura roles? (Would anyone want to see Roberta Sue Ficker dance? They *would* if she were also, let's say, Suzanne Farrell. She is!) Should Ms. Mitchell rename herself after the city of Geelong in her native Australia? Or after Perth? Or Darwin? Or Bundaberg? How about Wollongong? She became Nellie Melba, for Melbourne, and presently was a star in London's Covent Garden ("Mary Garden" was already taken), where she sang for thirty-eight years, until 1926, and in the Metropolitan Opera, in New York, and she became Dame Nellie Melba, and got her just deserts, for which she will be famous always: The dessert peach melba was named for her—fruit, usually a half peach, served with ice cream, raspberry sauce, and whipped cream. Indulging in such a rich dessert prompts one to retreat to Melba toast—very thin-sliced toast—also named for the, well, the apple of many ayes.

PEACOCK

When the description "peafowl" is used, peacock refers to the male of the species and peahen to the female. But peacock may be used irrespective of gender. Until 1936, it was believed that the peacock, a large bird in the pheasant family, was native to East Asia. And then came the sensational discovery—large pheasants were found in Africa, in deep forests. The Congo Peacock *Afropavo congensis* is blue and green, with a fairly short, broad tail, a curious double crest of white and black, and a bare patch of red skin showing on the foreneck. The female is chestnut and coppery green. For over 2,000 years, the blue (or Indian), found in India and Ceylon, has been reared in captivity, without effecting changes in shape or size; two or three mutations (white, pied, black-shouldered) have developed, however. The green peafowl is found in Burma, Thailand, Vietnam, Malaya, and Indonesia.

"PEANUTS"

Somewhere on the West Coast at this very moment, a sixtyish-year-old man may be drawing a circle, a dash, a loop, and two black eyes. Soon, that figure will be a puzzled, victimized boy—Charlie Brown—who will be seeing a ducky and a horse in cloud formations while his playmates see the profile of Thomas Eakins, the famous painter and sculptor, or an impression of the stoning of Stephen, "I can see the apostle Paul standing there to one side." The creator is Charles M. Schulz, who wanted to call his new comic strip "Li'l Folks," but the title was already taken. "Peanuts" was christened in 1950 by United Feature Syndicate, and Schulz had some misgivings: The name sounded insignificant, there wasn't going to be any character named Peanuts, wouldn't the readers be confused? In high school in Minneapolis, "Sparky" Schulz flunked physics, algebra, Latin, and English. He must have gotten A plus in droll philosophy. Right, Charlie Brown?

PEARL HARBOR

Japan's military sneak attack on the land-locked harbor on the southern coast of Oahu Island, Hawaii, on December 7, 1941, while peace negotiations were going on in Washington, damaged or destroyed 19 U.S. naval vessels, including 8 battleships, destroyed 188 aircraft, and killed 2,280 military personnel and 68 civilians. It was a day that will live in infamy. Hirohito's Axis ally was bugeyed when he was informed of the raid: Hitler had been trying to keep the United States out of the war. British Prime Minister Winston Churchill's greatest fear: "We know that all the great Americans round the President and in his confidence felt, exactly as I did, the awful danger that Japan would attack British or Dutch possessions in the Far East, and would carefully avoid the United States, and that in consequence Congress would not sanction an American declaration of war." Japan's conquest of French Indochina, Manchuria, and most of eastern China had led to diplomatic recriminations and economic reprisals. Neither the evidence nor common sense justifies the thesis that Franklin Roosevelt "either permitted the attack on Pearl Harbor to take place or deliberately engineered it to bring the United States into the War." The lawyer and Nuremberg-prosecutor Telford Taylor has also observed, "An important part of prudence is taking precautions against seemingly improbable contingencies. The gross failure of foresight at the time of Pearl Harbor appears to have been largely due to the fact that few, if any, thought the probability sufficient to warrant preparing for the possibility. In retrospect, it is hard to understand how they could have bungled so badly. . . ." Harvard-educated Isoruku Yamamoto planned the preemptive strike at Pearl Harbor, though he had said he was opposed to war with the United States; he then argued that Japan should immediately negotiate peace with the crippled Americans. With the approval of President Roosevelt himself, P–38 Lightnings over Bougainville ambushed and shot down Yamamoto, in 1943. His was only the second State

419

funeral for a commoner in the history of Japan. He called himself "the sword of my emperor."

PEDOMETER

Usually in watch form, it is an instrument that records the distance a walker covers by responding to his body motion at each step. A passometer, on the other hand, is an instrument, also shaped like a watch, that is used to count the number of a person's steps.

PEEPING TOM

The story of Peeping Tom did not enter the legend of Lady Godiva's alleged nude ride through Coventry until 600 years after she had made the deal with her husband, Leofric, earl of Mercia, to trade the ride for a rollback of the heavy taxation he had laid on his people. It is said that Tom bored a hole in the shutter of his tailor shop so that he might see for himself if the "empress" wore no clothes. She literally had let her hair down, so no one could have seen her *apparentibus cruribus tamen candidissimis*. Still, Tom was struck blind for disobeying the proclamation to keep his shutter shut.

PEGASUS

A winged horse in Greek mythology. Zeus' son Perseus cut off the head of the Gorgon Medusa—winged, snakes for hair, protruding teeth—and Pegasus sprang from the blood of her neck or trunk. He flew up to join the gods and was tamed by Athena and Bellerophon, a grandson of Sisyphus. Bellerophon rode out on Pegasus to kill the monstrous, fire-breathing Chimera. Striking its hoof, the horse both stopped the growth of Mount Helicon toward the heavens and created the Hippocrene, a sacred spring of the Muses; its water inspired poets. Pegasus, in the northern constellation, southwest of Andromeda, southeast of Cygnus, is named for the horse.

PEKINGESE

The royal dog of China. Its origin goes back about four thousand years. It was unique to both the United States and to England until this century; it is now the most favored of the toy dogs. It stands from six to nine inches high at the shoulder and weighs up to fourteen pounds. The official standard for the Pekingese approved by The American Kennel Club: the Pekingese's expression must suggest the Chinese origin in its quaintness and individuality, resemblance to the lion in directions and independence, and should imply courage, boldness, self-esteem, and combativeness rather than prettiness, daintiness, or delicacy. It must be fearless, free and strong, with slight roll. Its adaptability is a quality that makes the dog a good family pet.

PELE

The real monicker of the "Black Pearl": Edson Arantes do Nascimento. Thrice, his outstanding ball control and tactical ability led Brazil to the world championship in soccer, in 1958, 1962, 1970. In the 1970s, he was engaged by the New York Cosmos in an effort to make the North American Soccer League more popular. Pele has been the world's highest-paid athlete, one reason he gets such a kick out of the game.

PENGUIN

A bird that can swim but can't fly. It is the most highly specialized of all birds for marine life—wings resemble flippers. It can go as fast as 25 miles per hour underwater in pursuit of its diet: fish, squid, shrimp. When on land, it fasts. During a two-month incubation period, it subsists on a layer of fat under the skin but loses about 75 pounds. The largest penguins, which stand up to four feet in height, are known as the emperor and the king. There is a penguin known as the jackass because of his braying cry. At one time, the great auk of the North Atlantic was known commonly as a penguin; the auk is extinct. There is no relationship between the auk and the diving bird of Antarctica.

PENNEY, JAMES CASH

If it is indeed true that many people are shaped by their names—a man named Cross writes about Jesus' crucifixion, a woman named Concepcion directs Manila's population control organization—this devout Christian from a long line of fundamental Baptist preachers could only have headed into the world of business. (Or become Secretary of the Treasury.) J. C. Penney became the second largest nonfood retailer in the United States. When he died, in the middle of his tenth decade, in 1971, there were 1,660 stores bearing his name with a gross of $4 billion, and every one of the tens of thousands of employees shared in the profit. In his latter years, he was a student of the breeding of Guernsey cattle.

421

PENTAGON

A Western Union boy went into the largest office building in the world to deliver a message, got lost, and emerged a quarter of a century later as a full colonel. Or so the story goes. The Empire State Building in New York City would have to be nearly three-quarters of a mile high to contain the same amount of space as the 34 acres of the five-sided nerve center and command post of the United States military, which is in Arlington, Virginia, across the Potomac River from the nation's capital. It was built in the first years of the country's active involvement in World War II at a cost overrun of $52 million—$83 million in all. Five stories high, reinforced concrete faced with Indiana limestone, five rings of buildings connected by ten corridors totaling 17½ miles in length.

"PENTAGON PAPERS"

A 47-volume, once top-secret history of the United States role in the war in Indochina, where 45,000 Americans had already died in the fighting. The Vietnam Archive was commissioned in 1967 (pre-Nixon administration) by Defense Secretary Robert S. McNamara and leaked to the press by a think-tanker, Daniel Ellsberg. The Supreme Court, by a 6–3 decision, ruled that newspapers could publish articles on the history—the right to a free press under the First Amendment to the Constitution overrode any subsidiary legal considerations that would block publication by the news media. Some of the historians' findings as summarized by *The New York Times:* United States involvement in Vietnam and the course of American policy there were set by the Truman administration's decision to help France militarily in her colonial war against the Communist-led Vietminh. The Eisenhower administration played a "direct role in the ultimate breakdown of the Geneva settlement" for Indochina in 1954 when it decided to help a fledgling South Vietnam and disrupt the new Communist regime of North Vietnam. An inherited policy of "limited-risk gamble" was transformed by the Kennedy administration into a "broad commitment." The Johnson administration, a year before it publicly revealed the depth of its involvement and its fear of defeat, planned overt war: Military pressure, which included bombing North Vietnam, was applied despite the judgment of the government's intelligence community that the measures would not cause Hanoi to cease its support of the Vietcong insurgency in the South. Neil Sheehan concluded in the *Times* that "the history as a whole demonstrates that the four administrations progressively developed a sense of commitment to a non-Communist Vietnam, a readiness to fight the North to protect the South, and an ultimate frustration with this effort—to a much greater extent than their public statements acknowledged at the time.''

PEPYS, SAMUEL

''Music and women I cannot but give way to, whatever my business is.'' —9 March 1666. ''And so to Mrs. Martin and there did what *je voudrais avec* her, both devante and backward, which is also *muy bon plazer*.''— 3 June 1666. ''To church; and with my mourning, very handsome, and new periweg, make a great show.''—31 March 1667: deciphered entries from the most famous diary in the English language, Samuel Pepys's, kept from January 1, New Year's Day, 1660 (he was twenty-six years old), to May 31, 1669, when failing eyesight forced the English public official to put down his quill. (Later, he was briefly imprisoned in the Tower, falsely charged with betraying naval secrets to the French.) He wrote about his haircuts, his bowel movements, his celebrated, unanesthetized gallstone operation, his peccadillos, the ''lewd'' book he bought in a plain cover, but never even hints at what he called his wife. (When she caught him with the maid, she pinched his nose with red-hot tongs.) The 3,000 pages are contained in six leather-bound octavo volumes on the shelves of the Pepys Library at Magdalene College; they had remained undeciphered for a hundred years after his death.

PERONI BEER

It's been made since 1846 by the best known of the Italian breweries, Birra Peroni. The malt comes from barley grown in central and southern Italy. The rice is also Italian, the hops are German and Czechoslovakian. Brewing is the classic Bavarian two-mash method. It's a somewhat cloudy beer due to the yeast—cloudy is good—sharp but not bitter. Peroni pleases both patron and producer—it has the distinction of satisfying thirst while stimulating the desire for still another one. A miracle.

PERPETUAL CALENDAR

It tells you the day of the week in any year desired. The letters after each year in the Table of Years refer to the first column of the Table of Months. The figures given for each month in the Table of Months refer to one of the seven columns in the Table of Days. For example, to find on what day of the week September 3 fell in 1939, look for 1939 in the Table of Years. The letter *g* follows. Look for *g* in the Table of Months, and, under September, you will find the number *5*. In the Table of Days, column *5* shows that the third day of the month fell on Sunday in 1939. To learn on what day of the week the first day of the next century falls, look for 2001 in the Table of Years. The letter *a* follows. Look for *a* in the Table of Months, and, under January, you will find the number *1*. In the Table of Days, column *1* shows that the first day of the next century will fall on a Monday.

PERPETUAL MOTION MACHINE

The law of conservation of energy makes one impossible. It is one of the great generalizations of physics that energy cannot be created or destroyed; it may be transformed from one form into another, but the total amount of energy never changes. There are few attempts any more to make a device that would be able to operate continuously and supply useful work in violation of the laws of thermodynamics.

PERRY, FRED

The first player to win three consecutive Wimbledon singles titles didn't take up tennis until he was eighteen years old. It then took him some time to learn to take the ball early on his continental forehand, the racket having to make impact instantly as the ball rose from the court. He swept Wimbledon without loss of a set in 1934 (John Crawford was the final victim) and in 1935–36 (Gottfried von Cramm, both times). He won the United States title in 1933, 1934, and 1936—the skein was interrupted in 1935 when Perry suffered a painful injury and lost in the semis. The Australian title and the French title were also his in 1934 and 1935, respectively. Perry was enshrined in the International Tennis Hall of Fame, in Newport, Rhode Island, in 1975, forty-two years after he had helped to bring the Davis Cup back to Britain after a 21-year absence.

PERU

South America's third-largest country is five-sixths the size of Alaska. It was the center of both the Inca empire and then the Spanish empire—the conquistador Francisco Pizarro, with his horses and firearms, proved that the medium is the message. In recent decades, Peru has been governed by foreign business enterprises and "40 families" and now the military. In 1942, it grabbed Amazon lands rich in oil and half of Ecuador. Splitting the country in two from north to south are the towering Andes, 27 percent of all Peru, which is at the southern portion of the protuberance on the west coast of the continent. The Pacific coastline is desert. From west to east on the map, it's desert, Andes, and montana sweeping into the Amazon lowland.

"PETER PRINCIPLE"

The employee who in a hierarchy tends to rise to the level of his incompetence is the Peter Principle at work. The concept was promulgated by Dr. Laurence J. Peter, who has listed ten famous historical persons who personify the principle: Socrates, Julius Caesar, Nero, Alexander Hamilton, Benedict Arnold, Ulysses S. Grant, George Armstrong Custer, Warren G. Harding, Adolf Hitler, and Richard M. Nixon.

PETRIFIED FOREST NATIONAL PARK

Virtually unknown until the late 1870s, the 135-million-year-old "stone trees" had been killed by natural processes and deeply buried in mud and sand that contained silica-rich volcanic ash. The logs became petrified as the mineral, carried into the wood by ground water, replaced the wood cells. Eventually, the surrounding material eroded away, and the petrified logs and fragments and chips of varied colors became exposed. The stone is of such hardness that it will scratch all but the hardest alloy steels. There are six great "forests" in the 94,189-square-mile Petrified Forest National Park within the Painted Desert of northern Arizona.

PEYTON PLACE

It's baby stuff compared with today's television soap operas and made-for-TV movies, where everyone is making a clean breast of absolutely everything, but in those days, the good old days of the late '50s, Grace Metalious' novel and its sequel, *Return to Peyton Place* ($3.95, *hardcover*), were scandalous. Teenage Allison MacKenzie, through whose lips the stories issue, well, Allison has an amorous education at the hands of her agent, the cad. And then—big thrill—she has the grand amour—with her publisher, a heavyhitter, no bantamweight. Selena Cross is raped. In volume two, the rape is recalled with an exuberance of detail and provocative circumstance that go far beyond the original account. So *that's* what they do in small towns, in hamlets! To tell or not to tell? There was no question. O, that this too too solid flesh would melt. Frailty, thy name is Metalious.

PHILADELPHIA

The name of several ancient cities, it is Greek for "brotherly love." In 1681, William Penn founded a colony in Pennsylvania on the former site of a Swedish settlement and made it an expression of the ideal for which the Quaker City was to strive. (The biblical city of Philadelphia was built by Attalus II, king of Pergamus, and had both a Christian Church and a synagogue of Hellenizing Jews. The locality was subject to constant earthquakes.)

PHOBIAS

"Unreasonable" fears include autophobia: fear of self—gynephobia: fear of women—xenophobia: fear of strangers or foreigners—basophobia: fear of standing—panophobia: fear of everything—triskadekaphobia: fear of the number 13. The novelist Sholom Aleichem (Solomon Rabinovitch) suffered so from triskadekaphobia that his manuscripts never had a page thirteen. He died on the 13th of May 1916, but the date on his grave stone in Mount Carmel Cemetery, Glendale, New York, reads May 12a, 1916.

PHOTO FINISH

It wasn't until Franklin D. Roosevelt was completing his first term as President—to posit the time—in other words, in 1936—that a photograph was used to determine the winner of a horse race, especially a race in which at least two horses are nose-to-nose at the finish line. The track was Hialeah, in Florida. Much earlier, photo-finish equipment was set up by Ernest Marks at Plainfield Track, in New Jersey, but it wasn't a winning ticket.

PHRENOLOGY

For character reading, this form of quackery divides the head into seven sections: Group One (front section, upper row), the Sympathetic Group; Group Two (middle section, upper row), the Religious or Devotional Group; Group Three (back section, upper row), the Governing Group; Group Four (front section, lower row), the Intellectual Group; Group Five (middle section, lower row), Self-Preservation Group; Group Six (back section, lower row), Social Group; and Group Seven (the lowest section behind the ear), the Vitality Group, which covers love of life, ability to protect oneself, sex and parental love, and nervous energy. Phrenology was developed about 1800 by Franz Joseph Gall, a German physiologist, and popularized in the States by Orson Fowler and Lorenzo Fowler.

PI—3.141592

There is no terminating or repeating decimal number that exactly represents the irrational pi, that constant ratio of the circumference of a circle to the diameter. The ratio of the circumference of a circle to the diameter is a little more than three. But how much more? In 1873, an Englishman, William Shanks by name, completed fifteen years of work of computing pi to 707 decimal places. His calculation was incorrect from the 527th place on. These are said to be the first hundreds of correct decimal places:

3.141,592,653,589,793,238,462,643,383,279,502,884,197,169,
399,375,105,820,974,944,592,307,816,406,286,208,998,628,
034,825,342,117,067,982,148,086,513,282,306,647,093,844,
609,550,582,231,725,359,408,128,481,117,450,284,102,701,
938,521,105,559,644,622,948,954,930,381,964,428,810,975,
665,933,446,128,475,648,233,786,783,165,271,201,909,145,
648,566,923,460,348,610,454,326,648,213,393,607,260,249,
141,273,724,587,006,606,315,588,174,881,520,920,962,829,
254,091,715,364,367,892,590,360,011,330,530,548,820,466,
521,384,146,951,941,511,609,433,057,270,365,759,591,953,
092,186,117,381,932,611,793,105,118,548,074,462,379,962,
749,567,351,885,752,724,891,227,938,183,011,949,129,833,
673,362,440,656,643,086,021,39.

Two Japanese computer-mathematicians calculated pi to 2-million decimal places.

PICASSO

He was almost dumped into a garbage pail at birth. He *was* abandoned on a table by the midwife, who thought the infant stillborn. An uncle was a physician and revived him with a blast of air into his lungs. In his early days as an artist, the genius kept warm by burning some of his drawings. Toward the end of his life, he was so rich that he could say that he had just wiped out a hundred thousand francs when he destroyed a new picture he didn't like. Picasso's estate was worth—at the official appraisal in 1973—approximately $250 million. Four repositories in the south of France held 1,876 paintings, 1,355 sculptures, 2,880 ceramics, more than 11,000 drawings and sketches, and some 27,000 etchings, engravings, and lithographs in various states. Why did Picasso stay in Nazi-occupied Paris through World War II? "Oh, I'm not looking for risks to take, but in a sort of passive way I don't care to yield to either force or terror. I want to stay here because I'm here. The only kind of force that could make me leave would be the desire to leave. Staying on isn't really a manifestation of courage; it's just a form of inertia. I suppose it's simply that I prefer to be here. So I'll stay, whatever the cost." In Nazi eyes, he was a "degenerate." What he feared most was that a visitor to his studio would plant incriminating papers, so that the next time the Gestapo came to search they *would* find something. He had returned from his seaside villa to his Paris studio on the Quai Saint-Augustin. In the Catalan, rue des Grands-Augustins, juicy chateaubriand steaks were grilled to perfection. At Picasso's table were sometimes grouped Eluard, Desnos, Braque, Leiris, Sartre, Auric, Simone de Beauvoir, and Albert Camus. He turned down the offer to do the sets for Paul Claudel's costume drama *Le Soulier de satin,* refusing to have anything to do with the Catholic Claudel. There was a reading of his play *Le Désir attrapé par la queue:* Had Picasso not been the author, this most indifferent relic from surrealist days would have stayed in a bottom drawer. Yes, this was all in Nazi-held Paris during World War II. David Pryce-Jones, in *Paris in the Third Reich,* also notes that on July 22, 1942, Picasso said to a visitor to his studio, "The two of us sitting here, as we are, could negotiate peace this afternoon. This very evening, everybody could light up."

PILGRIMS

It wasn't until forty-nine years after the religious reformers had landed in the New World that they were first referred to as Pilgrims: "They knew they were pilgrims" was a phrase in William Bradford's account, in 1669, of the Plymouth plantation.

THE PILGRIM'S PROGRESS

"We are never too old for this. . . ." Marmee says in Louisa May Alcott's *Little Women.* "Our burdens are here, our road is before us, and our longing for goodness and happiness is the guide that leads us through many troubles and mistakes to the peace which is the true Celestial City." John Bunyan's two-part allegory recounts in turn Christian's and his wife Christiana's pilgrimage from the City of Destruction to the Celestial City. The journey is through "the wilderness of this world" to Zion, threatened by the Slough of Despond, the Valley of the Shadow of Death, Vanity Fair, and Doubting Castle, refreshed in the Palace Beautiful and the Delectable Mountains. When he passes through the Waters of Death into the Golden City, "they shut up the gates, which when I had seen I wished myself among them." The seventeenth-century Puritan wrote the first part of his masterpiece—full title: *The Pilgrim's Progress from This World to That Which Is to Come*—during a second prison term; he had already been in prison for twelve years for unlicensed preaching and written nine books there. Bunyan died as a result of exposure while performing an act of charity. *The Pilgrim's Progress* has been rated next to the Bible in importance as a Christian document.

PILLSBURY BAKE-OFF®

Judging criteria sometimes change for the contest. They have most recently included taste and appearance, ease of preparation, general availability of ingredients, and appropriateness for the category and group entered. The only eligible product for the first eighteen contests was Pillsbury's Best Flour. In 1968, eligible products were any Pillsbury mix and refrigerated dough, in addition to flour. It marked the first creative use of refrigerated crescent dough instead of yeast dough for a variety of products. When the Tunnel of Fudge Cake was one of the money winners in 1966, Pillsbury received 200,000 requests for help in finding the Bundt cake pan needed in the recipe. For entry blanks or information about the contest: Bake-Off® Contest, Consumer Affairs, The Pillsbury Company, P.O. Box 550, Minneapolis, MN 55440.

PINEAPPLE

Columbus and Sir Walter Raleigh were the first to write about this shrub native to the American tropics and subtropics. The pineapple plant, with sharp spines, grows up to three feet tall and the fruit weighs from four to eight pounds. The climate must be warm, the soil well drained; too much water can be harmful. It got its name, probably, because the fruit looks like a big pine cone. Hawaii supplies the major portion of the world's canned pineapple.

PLACEBO

It's Latin for "I shall please," and is defined as "an inert substance, such as a bread or sugar pill, which superficially resembles an active drug but is administered either as a control in testing new drugs or as a psychotherapeutic agent, as in relieving pain or inducing sleep by suggestion." *Longman Dictionary of Psychology and Psychiatry,* a Walter D. Glanze book, goes on to describe the placebo effect as a "clinically significant response to a therapeutically inert substance or nonspecific treatment. Appearance of a placebo effect suggests the absence of an organic basis for the symptoms. It also must be assumed that remission of symptoms does not occur at the same time, as could occur in conditions such as rheumatoid arthritis marked by symptoms that may peak and wane regardless of therapy." A person who tends to react to a placebo as if the inert substance actually had a pharmacologic effect is known as a placebo reactor. Various studies, according to *Longman,* indicate that placebo reactor individuals are suggestible, or chronic liars, or possess other traits that account for their responses. However, a placebo reactor generally does not react to all placebos.

PLAGUE

Estimates have ranged between 25 percent and 70 percent—Europe's population killed by The Black Death in the Middle Ages—at least 60 million people. Plague and smallpox entered Europe through trade with the East. In 1348, under the Doge Andrea Dandolo, Venice was the first state to pass sanitary regulations for protection against the introduction of "quarantinable disease"—the word "quarantine" (from the Italian *quaranta,* "forty") related to the requirement that ships coming from areas suspected to be a source of the disease spend forty days in isolation. A WHO public-health specialist has noted that in the absence of epidemological knowledge, it was an empiric way to learn whether cases or carriers of the scourge were on board. Similar legislation was soon instituted by the Republic of Genoa and by Marseilles. A bubonic plague had swept much of the civilized world in A.D. 542–43, killing 10,000 a day in Byzantium alone. During the Thirty Years' War in Europe, 1618–48, about 60 million people died from smallpox. After World War I, at least a billion people were ill and at least 20 million died in a year-long influenza pandemic.

PLAINS OF ABRAHAM

They're not in the Middle East and they're not named for the progenitor of the Hebrews, a man devoted to God. They are beyond the walls of Quebec City and they were named for Abraham Martin, to whom they had been granted in 1645. One hundred and fourteen years later, during the Seven Years' War, British forces commanded by General James Wolfe defeated the French under the Marquis de Montcalm on the Plains of Abraham and captured Quebec. Both Wolfe and Montcalm died in battle. Wolfe: "What, do they run already? Then I die happy." The next year (1760), French forces under the Duc de Levin rallied, set back the

British commanded by General James Murray, and for a time regained the shelter of the city above the St. Lawrence River. Voltaire's "few acres of snow," as he called Canada, became a British possession by treaty in 1763 because William Pitt's hatred of France was so compulsive that he demanded every possible concession from his country's erstwhile enemy. (The choice was Canada or the West Indian sugar island of Guadeloupe.) When France surrendered Fort Chartres on the Mississippi River in 1765, its North American empire was no more.

PLANETS

Which planet's year is shorter than its day? Right! Venus'! A planetary day is the length of time it takes the body to make one complete revolution on its axis. The Jupiter day is the shortest: 9 hours 50 minutes 30 seconds. Saturn: 10 hrs. 14 mins. Uranus: 10 hrs. 49 mins. Neptune: 15 hrs. 48 mins. Earth: 24 hrs. Mars: 24 hrs. 37 mins. 23 secs. Pluto: the equivalent of 6.39 Earth days. Mercury: 58.65 Earth days. Venus: 243 Earth days. A planet's year is the length of time it takes the body to make one complete revolution around the Sun, the center of the Universe. It takes Venus "only" 224.7 days. Jupiter orbits the Sun every 11.9 years. Saturn: 29½ years. Uranus: 84.01 years. Neptune: about 165 years. Earth: 365 days, sometimes 366. Mars: 687 days. Pluto: 247.7 years. Mercury: 87.97 days. Venus and Uranus rotate on their axis in a retrograde direction. Uranus' axis is nearly in the plane of its orbit; the North Pole is inclined at 98° to the vertical, so that the planet appears to rotate about its axis in a retrograde direction, (i.e., rotation opposite to the direction of revolution. All of Uranus' five known natural satellites revolve in this retrograde direction.) The orbital motion is, of course, direct. A peculiar result of its highly tilted axis is that Uranus has extreme seasons: Each pole experiences a 42-year "summer" and a 42-year "winter."

PLATO

The Greek philosopher, the "father of western philosophy," had the opportunity to put his idea of a philosopher-king into practice. Engaged as a royal adviser, the Athenian encouraged Dionysius II, of Syracuse, to govern according to constitutional principles. The monarch soon wearied of restraints and philosophy—"Wealth is the parent of luxury and indolence, poverty of meanness and viciousness, both of discontent"— and sent Plato packing. His original name was Aristocles, but he received the nickname Plato—meaning "broad"—because of his broad shoulders. He was once held for ransom by pirates. To Plato, knowledge had no practical use; it existed for the abstract good of the soul. He had wise words for the wise: The life that is unexamined is not worth living. No evil can happen to a good man, either in life or after death. I have hardly ever known a mathematician who was capable of reasoning. When there is an income tax, the just man will pay more and the unjust less on the same amount of income.

PLAYBOY

The contents of the very first issue of the "men's entertainment magazine" (November 1953): Miss Gold-Digger of 1953, article; Strip Quiz, games; "Tales from The Decameron," fiction; Playboy's Party Jokes, humor; VIP on Sex, humor; "Introducing Sherlock Holmes," fiction; An Open Letter from California, pictorial; The Dorsey Brothers, jazz; Matanzas Love Affair, food and drink; "A Horseman in the Sky," fiction; The Return of the All-Purpose Back, sports; Desk Designs for the Modern Office, modern living. And Sweetheart of the Month, a nude Marilyn Monroe, who said that when the centerfold photograph was made she had nothing on except the radio.

PLAYER, GARY

The first non-American to win the Masters' golf championship, in Augusta, Georgia, the South African was also the first non-American in 45 years to win the United States Open. He first won the Masters in 1961, by one stroke under Arnold Palmer, and repeated in 1974 and 1978. He won the Open in 1965. His best shot in the 1961 Masters: a wedge on the par 3 fourth hole. A four-wood tee shot had drifted dangerously close to a trap at the left of the green and ended up in high grass and sand about 75 feet from the pin: "I didn't know whether to chip or explode from the lie. I finally decided to explode and play for a bogey. The shot wound up no more than five inches from the pin for a tap-in par."

PLIMPTON, GEORGE

No joke—he's been a stand-up comic in Vegas, a trapeze performer in a circus, a bit-part actor in a Hollywood movie, a percussionist with the New York Philharmonic under the baton of Leonard Bernstein, a golfer on the P.G.A. tour, a quarterback with the Detroit Lions, a pitcher against some of the top players in the American and the National Leagues, a bridge player against the late Oswald Jacoby (Plimp was rubbed out), a tennis player against Pancho Gonzales (0–6), and a boxer, for three rounds, against the world's lightheavyweight champ, Archie Moore. For the same reason that the venturesome climb Mount Everest —it's there to be done—he wants to show that he can do it, and he wants to write about it and talk about it. Plimpton was a founder of *The Paris Review*.

PLOCK

A thousand-year-old city of about 75,000 people on the north bank of the Vistula in east-central Poland, 60 miles northwest of Warsaw, it was the capital of the duchy of Masovia for more than two centuries. It passed in 1793 to Prussia and in 1815 to Russia and in 1921 to Poland. The city's cathedral was built in the twelfth century, remodeled several times, and was badly damaged during World War II. It houses the tombs of the two medieval Polish kings who had resided in Plock.

PLUTO

The most distant (usually) known planet from the Sun, it was spotted in 1930 by the astronomer Clyde W. Tombaugh at the Lowell Observatory. By means of a blink microscope, he was able to pick out on photographic plates containing as many as four hundred thousand stars the one star beyond Neptune that was moving, and that was Pluto, which circles the Sun every 247.7 years. Percival Lowell had first proposed the existence of Pluto: An unseen planet must be causing the perturbations of Neptune. (Lowell was sure he saw canals on Mars.) Pluto crossed Neptune's orbit in December 1978, and until March 1999 it will be the eighth planet from the Sun. Early in the twenty-first century, Pluto resumes its more familiar position and journeys to its farthest point in the Universe, over 4.5 billion miles from the solar oven. Pluto is one-eighth the weight of Earth's lone moon, and *its* lone moon, discovered in 1978, is about 12,000 miles above the planet and in synchronous orbit. (Seven of the planets have a total of 33 moons—Mercury and Venus, the two closest to the Sun, seemingly have none.)

POE, EDGAR ALLAN

The witty, intense, neurotic, affectionate, macabre alcoholic was the father of the detective story. He first published *The Murders in the Rue Morgue* in the magazine he was editing at the time, *Graham's*, in 1841. Right then and there the genre had a fascinating problem: An errant orangutan stuffs a young girl up a chimney, in Paris. Right then and there:

a solution that could be resolved, through ratiocination, by dick C. Auguste Dupin. Come to think of it, the locked-room mystery was invented right then and there. Drinking himself to death—to him there was no mystery why he was hitting the bottle so hard: His wife, a cousin only thirteen years old when they married, had died, and he was always miserably dead broke (the chicken or the egg?)—Poe still managed to compose some of his best verse. He was the first American author to be widely read and admired in France.

POITIER, SIDNEY

He was the first black to win the best-actor Oscar. He played a lighthearted itinerant construction worker who builds a chapel in the southwest desert for refugee nuns in *Lilies of the Field,* in 1963. "It has been a long journey to this moment," he said with a broad smile while accepting the Oscar. The only black to win an Oscar before Poitier was Hattie McDaniel, best-supporting actress, *Gone With the Wind* (she was Scarlett O'Hara's mammy). Poitier was the first black man nominated for the best-actor award, for *The Defiant Ones,* in 1958. In 1968, he was costar of best-picture *In the Heat of the Night,* for which costar Rod Steiger *was* voted best actor; Poitier was not nominated that year for either *In the Heat of the Night* or for *Guess Who's Coming to Dinner.* Another black man, James Haskett, was awarded an honorary Oscar for portraying Uncle Remus in *Song of the South* (1946). Other black women nominated for Oscars: Dorothy Dandridge in *Carmen Jones,* Ethel Waters in *Pinky,* Cicely Tyson in *Sounder.* Poitier had training as a physiotherapist at a mental hospital.

POLAR BEAR

"Nanook" in Eskimo, the white bear is at home on drifting pack ice at the coasts of arctic North America. It is impressive physically, standing about eight feet high and weighing about half a ton. It is also impressive in the frigid polar waters, swimming up to thirty miles at a clip. *Thalarctos maritimus* tends to be a solitary animal. But beware of the bear. It can be extremely dangerous. Hairy soles allow it to grip the ice and come after you at a speed of twenty-five miles per hourrrrrrrrrrrrrrrrrrrrrrrrrrrrr.

POLLOCK, JACKSON

"I can do anything and call it art," Jack the Dripper said. "Art can be anything I intend." He was an action painter. He nailed his canvases to the floor and charged over them with paint and brush. Out of the intricate net of drips, swirls, and spatters usually came works pulsating with life and vigor. In 1945, the poet-critic Clement Greenberg hailed the abstract expressionist as "the strongest painter of his generation." He went through alcoholism and psychological depression when there was harsh critical reaction to his show of wall-sized works in 1950. Pollock, who was killed in an automobile accident in 1956, at the age of forty-four, may have been the first artist to thrill the public.

POLO

As with jai alai, only righthanded players may compete in this rich man's sport. The United States Polo Association, in 1974, laid down the law to cut down on collisions between lefthanded and righthanded players charging on horses to hit a wooden ball with mallet-headed long sticks. An outdoor match is made up of eight periods, or chukkers, of 7½ minutes each. There are four chukkers in an indoor match. Because of the vigorous play, a player usually changes mounts several times during a match. America's greatest polo player was also the world's best, Tommy Hitchock. He flew with the Lafayette Escadrille in World War I, was shot down, and spent months as a German prisoner. While being transferred to another camp, he jumped off a moving train and walked 100 miles to the safety of the Swiss border. He was killed in an airplane crash in England during World War II.

POLYORCHID

A polyorchid man has a condition called polyorchidism—that is, he has a condition of having more than two testes, that is, he is a male with one or more supernumerary testes, that is, he has at least three testicles.

PONCE DE LEON, JUAN

The Caribbean-trotting explorer was no ponce; a Spanish nobleman, he did his own dirty work. He helped to drive the Moors out of Spain, paving the way for the monarchs' sponsorship of Columbus' historic voyages; he sailed on Columbus' second odyssey to the new lands; he helped to conquer and rule the Dominican Republic; he helped to conquer and rule Puerto Rico, personally cleaning up in the gold, slave, and land markets; he sought the Indians' fabled Fountain of Youth, poking through the Bahamas and along the east and west coasts of Florida, which he named Florida either because Florida in Spanish means "full of flowers," which

Florida is full of, or because he first stepped ashore at the time of the Easter feast—Pascua Florida; he landed on the Yucatan, returned to Spain, returned to the Caribbean to get rid of the Carib Indians at King Ferdinand's command, and tried to colonize Florida. Near either Charlotte Harbor or Tampa Bay, he was fatally wounded by a Seminole Indian's arrow. (There was also a "fountain of youth" in Asia. Alexander the Great and his troops are said to have bathed in it and been restored to youth and vigor.)

PONY EXPRESS

To this day, a century and a quarter later, the horseback relay mail service gallops in legend and westerns, defying weather and Indians, especially Indians. In reality, the postmen hoofed it for less than two years, 1860–61, between St. Joseph, Missouri, and Sacramento, California, nearly 2,000 miles, eight days. They were done in by the Civil War and the need for the speed of the telegraph, which transmitted its first coast-to-coast message at the speed of light to San Francisco on October 24, 1861, less than a score of years after Samuel F. B. Morse sent the first long-distance message, a question, all of 40 miles, from the nation's capital to Baltimore.

POOR RICHARD'S ALMANACK

The author was nagged by his wife, he was short of money, and he was a bumbler. He was also early to bed and early to rise, and he signed his name "Richard Saunders." He, of course, was the protean Benjamin Franklin and he published the *Almanack* for twenty-five years. Many sayings of Poor Richard have become standard proverbs. Time is money. Make haste slowly. Men and melons are hard to know. The tongue offends, the ears get the cuffing. Cut the wings of your hopes, lest they lead you a weary dance after them. Don't go to the doctor with every distemper, nor to the lawyer with every quarrel, nor to the pot for every thirst. Nothing humbler than ambition, when it is about to climb. Men take more pains to mask than mend. The good paymaster is lord of another man's purse.

POPE JOHN PAUL I

"I am in a place where everyone comes to complain about something. I don't know who I can have a friendly conversation with." Sixty-five-year-old Albino Luciani was in good health when he was elected Pope, but he was dead thirty-three days later, in 1978, a heart attack. He had been the first Pope in history to choose a double name, and he was the first to come from the working class. He refused to wear a papal crown. He saw himself as "only a poor man, accustomed to small things and silence." He would say the simple "I" instead of the formal "we" used for centuries, from Sylvester I (314–34) to Paul. His was the shortest papal reign in 373 years.

POPE JOHN XXIII

One of the most beloved, if not *the* most beloved, of recent Popes, Angelo Giuseppe Roncalli served in the Italian army in World War I, first in the medical corps, later as a chaplain. In World War II, he was papal nuncio to Nazi-held France. In 1953, he was made cardinal and the patriarch of Venice; five years later, white smoke signaled that he had succeeded the late Pius XII. The apex of his tenure was the convening of an ecumenical council to consider ways that the Church could be renewed in the modern world.

POPE PIUS XII

Eugenio Pacelli was the head of the Catholic Church through World War II and the years of postwar reconstruction. The first papal secretary of state to be elected in hundreds of years and the first Roman pope in more than two centuries, he was bishop nuncio in Germany during Hitler's rise to power; as a cardinal and the secretary, he negotiated the concordat with Nazi Germany in 1933. His brother was the lawyer who had fashioned the concordat with Italy's dictator, Benito Mussolini, that created the Vatican City state in 1929. Pius' encyclical *Divino Afflante Spiritu* ("With the Help of the Divine Spirit"), promulgated in 1943, was a fresh stimulant to Catholic biblical studies. He excommunicated Italian Catholics who joined the Communist party and he defined the dogma of the Assumption of the Virgin Mary. He has been universally berated for his "anti-Semitic" stance during World War II. Proceedings for his beatification have begun.

POPULATIONS

The United States is both fourth among world countries in population and fourth among world countries in land area. China has 20.8 percent of the world's population, the United States 5.3 percent. The ten most populated countries (in order) are China, India, U.S.S.R., the United States,

Indonesia, Japan, Brazil, Nigeria, Bangladesh, Pakistan. Russia has 14.9 percent of the world's land area, the United States 6.3 percent. The ten largest countries (in order): U.S.S.R., Canada, China, United States, Brazil, Australia, India, Argentina, Sudan, Zaire. The most densely populated countries are Macao, Monaco, Gibraltar, Melilla (in Africa), Hong Kong, Singapore, Ceuta, Vatican City, the Gaza Strip, and Bermuda. Puerto Rico is twenty-second, Grenada is twenty-third.

PORGY AND BESS

Al Jolson wanted to have a musical play made out of Du Bose Heyward's novel about the denizens of Catfish Row, and he of course would play Porgy in blackface. Pass. George Gershwin read *Porgy* in the mid-twenties, was exhilarated, and suggested an opera to Heyward. In the early thirties, Gershwin and Heyward agreed to go forward and Gershwin spent a fortnight in Charleston, where Heyward lived, to discuss the possibilities. Later, Gershwin lived for two months in a rough shack on Folly Island off the coast of South Carolina so that he could steep himself in the life of Gullah Negroes. He wrote the score in eleven months and spent eight more orchestrating it, 700 pages of music in all. "I think the music is so marvelous," Gershwin said, "I really don't believe that I wrote it." Heyward (who had been invalided for three of his teen years —infantile paralysis) and Ira Gershwin wrote the lyrics: "A Woman Is a Sometime Thing," "There's a Boat Dat's Leavin' Soon for New York," "I Got Plenty o'Nuttin," "I Loves You, Porgy." Said one critic, when *Porgy and Bess* opened in late 1935: "Fake folklore music." Said another: "It should be played in every country of the world—except Hitler's Germany, which doesn't deserve it." It had 124 performances on Broadway, and lost the entire production nut, $70,000. "With no new project around proving of interest, George felt Hollywood should be our next step," Ira remembered, "and he got in touch with an agent. After a couple of weeks, the agent wired that, so far, there were no takers, that since George had just written an opera he was now considered a highbrow." *Porgy and Bess* was George Gershwin's last Broadway show. He died two years later.

PORTUGUESE

The Pope gave Brazil to Portugal (he gave the rest of America and the Philippines to Spain), which is why so many Portuguese sailed to South America's largest country and Portuguese became its official language. It is also the official language of the People's Republic of Angola and the People's Republic of Mozambique. Portuguese is also spoken in Goa, Damão and Diu, on the western coast of India; in Macao in southeastern

China; in Portuguese Guinea, Cape Verde and Madeira Islands, São Tomé and Príncipe in Africa; and in Portuguese Timor in Oceania. Galician, a dialect of northwestern Spain, spoken by some 3 million people, is closer to Portuguese than it is to Spanish.

POSTCARDS

You're a deltiologist if you collect picture postcards. In 1907, a card showed a teddy bear whispering plaintively to President Theodore Roosevelt: "Mr. President, I feel blue, and I scarce know what to do, for I have been told to-day, that a third term you won't stay. Tell me quickly it's absurd, this rumor that I just have heard, for if to run you don't agree, my finish I can plainly see." Deltiologists are particularly eager for the world's first postcards, issued in Vienna in 1869, and for those made of ivory for an Indian prince, for which sixty elephants had to be slain. Postcards as souvenirs became popular at the World's Columbia Exposition, in Chicago, in 1893. Postcard collecting was a craze in Europe at the turn of the century. San Francisco-earthquake cards had widespread appeal in 1906. (They were the "T-shirt" of the day.) Picture postcards have been made of wood—one carried an illustration of the S.S. *President McKinley*. The top-selling postal card (over 350 million copies) is said to be a drawing of a couple with this caption: He: "How do you like Kipling?" She: "I don't know, you naughty boy, I've never Kippled."

POTATO CHIPS

The year was 1853 and the avid fisherman Franklin Pierce was President when an Adirondack Indian chef, George Crum, chipped the first potato, in a swank, smart, chic place in Saratoga Springs, New York, called Moon Lake Lodge. A lot happened during the Pierce administration: Gauss had an idea for informing extraterrestrials that we're here, *Walden* and *Leaves of Grass* and *The Song of Hiawatha* and *Ten Nights in a Barroom and What I Saw There* were published. The Republican Party was founded, and the dogma of the Immaculate Conception was promulgated, and the hypodermic needle and the accordion and the Bunsen burner were invented. Today, potato chips are the most popular snack food in the United States, far better known than President Pierce.

PRADO MUSEUM

Spain's national museum of painting and sculpture on the Paseo del Prado, in Madrid—1985 marks the 200th anniversary of its startup as a museum of natural history. At one time it housed only Spanish paintings.

Masterpieces there today include the Flemish and the Venetian schools (Bosch, Titian, Rubens, Van Dyke). The Royal Museum became national property in 1868.

PRAYING MANTIS

The large, slender, slow-moving winged insect is the only predatory member of the family *Mantidae* in the order *Orthoptera*. It practices cannibalism. During mating, the female often eats the head of the male while his hind end staunchly continues with copulation—conjugal murder, not at all irrelevant for preservation of the species. "The blood-thirstiness of the female," it has been writ, "is associated with the fact that she has a very high protein requirement because of the rapid production of eggs . . . as far as the male is concerned, this is simply a confirmation of the old law that nature is concerned only with the species and not with the individual. Once the male has unloaded his supply of sperm at the right place, he has finished his duty to the species." Over and out.

PRESIDENT OF THE UNITED STATES

If you were born after 1953, forget about running for President until at least 1992. If you were born after 1957, forget 1992, too. To be eligible to be President, you must be at least thirty-five years of age. There are other requirements. Article 11, section 1 of the Constitution: "No person except a natural-born citizen, or citizen of the United States at the time of the adoption of this Constitution, shall be eligible to the office of President; neither shall any person be eligible to that office who shall not have attained to the age of thirty-five years, and been fourteen years a resident within the United States." Not until 1824 was the Chief Executive elected by popular vote. Previously, the electoral college, selected by party caucus, selected the President; in the 1824 election, won by John Quincy Adams, the state legislatures nominated the candidates. George Washington has been the only unanimously elected President; James Monroe's second election (1820) would have been unanimous except for a single dissenting ballot, intentionally cast to keep Washington the only unanimously elected President. The second President, John Adams, was the father of the sixth President, John Quincy Adams; he died in 1826 while John Quincy was President. The ninth President, the one-month President, William Henry Harrison, was the grandfather of the twenty-third President, Benjamin Harrison. William Harrison's son John Scott Harrison is the only man to be both the son of one President and, with his second wife, the father of another. Franklin D. Roosevelt, the thirty-second President, was related to eleven Presidents, six by marriage, five by blood. He was a fourth cousin once removed of President Ulysses S. Grant, a fourth cousin three times removed of President Zachary Taylor, a fifth cousin of President Theodore Roosevelt, a fifth cousin once removed of his wife, Eleanor Roosevelt—and a seventh cousin once removed of Winston Churchill. Theodore Roosevelt was the youngest man to become President; he was forty-two years old, and Vice-President, when he succeeded the slain William McKinley. John F. Kennedy, the first President to be born in this century, was the youngest man to be elected President; he was forty-three when he was sworn in January 1961. Ronald Reagan, sixty-nine, was the oldest elected. Martin Van Buren was the first President to be born in the United States—his seven predecessors had been born in British colonies. Jimmy Carter was the first President to be born in a hospital. No President has been an only child. James Buchanan was the lone bachelor. Nine Presidents did not attend college, and only one, Woodrow Wilson, the only President buried in the nation's capital, held a Ph.D. degree. No President between John Adams and Wilson made an appearance before Congress. Wilson said that if he had been defeated for reelection, in 1916, he would have turned the government over immediately to his successful opponent, Charles Evans Hughes, rather than spend five months as a lame duck. Not until Herbert Hoover was President, in 1929, did the Chief Executive have a private telephone in his office. The most common Christian name among the Presidents: James—Carter, Garfield, Buchanan, Polk, Monroe, Madison. The capital city of four states was named for Presidents: Jackson, Mississippi; Jefferson City, Missouri; Lincoln, Nebraska; Madison, Wisconsin. A capital idea was naming the U.S. capital city for the Father of His Country. A state, several colleges and universities, and scores of counties, towns, and villages are also named for Washington.

PRESIDENTS—ASSASSINATIONS

Nine of the United States's 40 Presidents (nearly 25 percent) have been shot at, and four murdered: Abraham Lincoln, James Garfield, William McKinley, and John F. Kennedy. Andrew Jackson, Franklin D. Roosevelt (see page 471), and Gerald R. Ford were not hit. Theodore Roosevelt survived an assassin's bullet while campaigning in 1912 after being out of the Oval Office for four years, and Ronald Reagan survived an assassination attempt shortly after taking office, in 1981. (Lincoln's killer died of a gunshot wound in a burning barn. Garfield's and McKinley's assassins were put to death. Handcuffed, Kennedy's murderer was shot down in cold blood by a deranged thug.) Reagan was shot by a lovesick twenty-five-year-old psychopath who was trying to get the attention and the affection of the actress Jodie Foster: "The reason I'm going ahead with this attempt now is because I just cannot wait any longer to impress you," John Hinckley, Jr. wrote her. "I've got to do something now to make you understand in no uncertain terms that I am doing all of this for your sake." Hinckley was found innocent by reason of insanity.

PRESIDENTS—FOURTH OF JULY

Three of our first five Presidents died on Independence Day; two of them, John Adams and Thomas Jefferson, also our first two Vice-Presidents, died on the very same date, the fiftieth anniversary of the signing of the Declaration of Independence, while Adams' son, John Quincy, was the White House resident. Since 1813, and after a decade-long silence, Adams, in Quincy, Massachusetts, and Jefferson, in Monticello, Virginia, had engaged in a voluminous correspondence. Adams' last words were, "Jefferson still lives," but Jefferson had died a few hours earlier. Word of Jefferson's death did not reach the capital until July 6; news of Adams' demise took another two days. James Monroe, our fifth President, also died on a July 4, in 1831. George Washington died on December 14, 1799, and James Madison nearly died on the Fourth, expiring on June 28, 1836. Only one President, Calvin Coolidge, has been born on a Fourth—1872.

PRESLEY, ELVIS

First prize in the music contest in the Mississippi-Alabama fair went to Ring Childress, a banjo player, from Mobile. Second prize went to the Green Sisters, who had sung a duet. "Third honor goes to the pupil from East Tupelo who broke our hearts with 'Old Shep.' " That Mississippi pupil was a fifth-grader with the name of Elvis—Elvis Presley—and Old Shep was a faithful dog who'd saved a boy from drowning but the doctor said he'd have to be put to sleep. Elvis' prize was five dollars and a pass to all the rides at the fair. Life soon enough became a merry-go-round at Heartbreak Hotel for the rock-'n'-roll hound dog.

PRIESTLEY, JOSEPH

The English theologian and scientist had certain airs about him. He suggested the idea of "the greatest happiness of the greatest number" to Jeremy Bentham, the English philosopher and founder of utilitarianism. He discovered new gases, including what he called "dephlogisticated air," which A. L. Lavoisier would later name oxygen and make the basis of experiments that were the foundation of modern chemistry. (Oxygen is an abundant element, but its nature had eluded investigations of the early chemists.) Priestley adopted Unitarian views and rejected orthodox Calvinism. His *History of the Corruptions of Christianity* was published in 1782 and officially burned three years later. After his house was wrecked and his library and scientific apparatus destroyed by Englishmen not in sympathy with his support of the French Revolution, he emigrated to Pennsylvania.

PRINCESS ANNE

When she was a member of Britain's equestrian team at the Olympics in Montreal, in 1976, she may have been the only athlete to be excused from a urine test. She lived in Olympic Village, 45 miles from Montreal, in a three-bedroom apartment with six other athletes, including her husband, Captain Mark Phillips, an alternate member of the team. She stood on line for meals in the cafeteria. She rode in the bumpy shuttle bus from the village to the stables two miles away. In her event she fell from her horse and was slightly concussed. Mom was on hand for the debacle— she had opened the Olympics, which is still a billion dollars in debt nine years later.

PRINCESS ELIZABETH

Drawn by two gray horses and flanked by a Sovereign's escort of the Royal Household Troops in full dress, their polished cuirasses flashing, the Irish State Coach carried the bride to Westminster Abbey. Her dress was of ivory satin, woven in Scotland, with fitted bodice, long, tight sleeves, and a full skirt. Appliquéd in white satin was her gossamer fifteen-foot train. On her head, a sunray diamond tiara of her mum's. The King and Queen's dearly beloved twenty-one-year-old daughter, the Princess Elizabeth, was getting married that November day in 1947 to twenty-six-year-old Lieutenant Philip Mountbatten, R.N., formerly Prince Philip of Greece and Denmark, who had been entitled to British nationality after serving in the Navy during World War II. It was the first celebration in English history of the marriage of an Heiress Presumptive who was later to become Queen. King George was to write Elizabeth, "Our family, we four, the Royal family, must remain together, with additions of course at suitable moments!! I have watched you grow up all these years with pride under the skilful direction of Mummy who, as you know, is the most marvellous person in the world in my eyes, and I can, I know, always count on you, and now Philip, to help us in our work."

443

PRINCIP, GAVRILO

The teen-aged Serbian political agitator and member of the nationalist secret society Union of Death (known as the Black Hand) told the court that he drew the revolver, instead of the bomb that he had in his belt on the left side, and raised it against the automobile without aiming: "I even turned my head as I shot. I let go two shots one after the other, but I am not certain whether I shot twice or more often, because I was very excited. . . . Thereupon the people began to lynch me." The scene was Sarajevo, St. Vitus Day 1914, and Princip's shots killed Archduke Francis Ferdinand of Austria and the Duchess and precipitated World War I: Austria went to war against Serbia; two days later, Russia mobilized against Austria and her ally, Germany; Germany went to war against Russia and threatened France; on August 4, Britain declared that she was at war with Germany, an obligation that followed from the logic of her commitments to France but had to be justified by the Kaiser's invasion of Belgium that day. When he was shot, the extremely vain Ferdinand was wearing a uniform into which he had been sewn so there would not be a single crease to mar his appearance. By the time scissors were found, he had bled to death. Earlier that same day, a grenade had been hurled at the Archduke's car. Greeted by the Lord Mayor of Sarajevo at City Hall, Ferdinand harshly said, "Herr Burgermeister, what is the good of your speeches? I come to Sarajevo on a friendly visit and someone throws a bomb at me. This is outrageous." Princip was indeed nearly lynched. One arm was so badly damaged that it had to be amputated. The assassin died in 1918 of a rapidly advancing tuberculosis.

PROHIBITION

The United States was not the only nation after World War I to enact extreme regulatory liquor laws. The Scandinavian countries, Finland, and most of Canada passed prohibition laws. In the United States, the Anti-Saloon League and its allies had shifted from the advocacy of temperance to outright demands for government prohibition. They denounced the brewery business as being unpatriotic—it was dominated by German-Americans—there was a war on, you know, and liquor damaged soldiers' morale, you know. The Lever Act of 1917 prohibited the use of grain to make distilled liquors and empowered the President to extend the ban to beer, ale, and wine. On December 18, 1917, Congress passed and sent to the states the proposed Eighteenth Amendment by which "the manufacture, sale, or transportation of intoxicating liquors within, the transportation thereof into, or the exportation thereof from the United States and all territory subject to the jurisdiction thereof for beverage purposes" was prohibited. In only fourteen months, the necessary thirty-six states approved the amendment—only Connecticut and Rhode Island did not join in unanimous ratification. The War Prohibition Act—passed after Armistice Day!—had already made it unlawful to sell intoxicants after June 30, 1919—it turned out to be the last day for more than fourteen years on which such beverages could be sold legally. An unprecedented period of illegal drinking and lawbreaking ended in 1933 with acceptance by the states of the Twenty-first Amendment repealing the Eighteenth; it was unique in that it stipulated that it must be ratified by special state convention, and it marked repeal of the only amendment to date. The Democratic Convention of 1932 had called for repeal. The last statewide prohibition law fell in the 1960s.

PROXMIRE, WILLIAM

There will always be something to warrant Senator William Proxmire's Golden Fleece of the Month award to federal agencies wasting public money. Twenty-one prostitutes are interviewed "formally" in a sociological study of ethnic and class relationships in a Peruvian mountain society. The postal service spends millions of dollars to get people to write more letters, which then don't get delivered when people would like them delivered. The Federal Aviation Administration studies the physiques of airline stewardesses. The Department of Agriculture investigates how long it takes to cook eggs for breakfast. The Department of Labor takes a census of Samoans in Orange County, California. The Wisconsin maverick's presence is no boon to the dogglers in the nation's capital, home to 1,500 psychiatrists. He succeeded the late Joseph R. McCarthy and is the author of *Uncle Sam—the Last of the Bigtime Spenders*.

PSALM 23

The Book of Psalms in the Old Testament is a collection of 150 sacred poems expressing virtually the full range of Israel's religious faith. Psalm 23 is a psalm of David. "The Lord *is* my shepherd; I shall not want. He maketh me to lie down in green pastures; he leadeth me beside the still waters. He restoreth my soul: he leadeth me in the paths of righteousness for his name's sake. Yea, though I walk through the valley of the shadow of death, I will fear no evil; for thou *art* with me; thy rod and thy staff they comfort me. Thou preparest a table before me in the presence of mine enemies: thou anointest my head with oil; my cup runneth over. Surely goodness and mercy shall follow me all the days of my life: and I will dwell in the house of the Lord for ever." The poems are of varying date and authorship; many are ascribed to David.

PT-109

The plywood torpedo boat used by the U.S. Navy in World War II was designed by a British engineer to be lightly armed and to depend exclusively on speed for defense. Its insignia—a mosquito astride a torpedo—was designed by Walt Disney. John F. Kennedy, through his ambassador-father's influence, was able to get a sea command as skipper of *PT-101* and then *PT-109; 109* was rammed and sliced in two by the Japanese destroyer *Amagiri* in Blackett Strait off the Solomon Islands on August 2, 1943. Two of Lieutenant Kennedy's men were killed. Kennedy and the other survivors swam for hours to safety, and were discovered on Olasana Island by two natives. With a knife Kennedy scratched a message on a coconut shell: "Native knows posit. He can pilot. 11 alive need small boat." The native got the shell to Allied troops. Kennedy was awarded a medal and a Purple Heart: "His courage, endurance, and excellent leadership contributed to the saving of several lives and was in keeping with the highest traditions of the United States Naval Service." Kennedy then commanded *PT-59*. His ordeals, however, had further strained a damaged back and he was presently rotated home.

PUNS

Yes, a son of a gun is what someone born between two cannon is called. Well, James Boswell said, "I think no innocent species of wit or pleasantry should be suppressed; and that a good pun may be admitted among the smaller excellencies of lively conversation." Charles Lamb, whose periodically crazy sister (she no doubt loved magazines) drove him to drink, literally, believed that a pun is a pistol let off at the ear, not a feather to tickle the intellect. Or, as someone else said, Sikh and ye shall find. On the other hand (ambidextrously?), every doge has his day. Promiscuity but give her Arpège. For whom the belle toils. Champagne to your real friends—real pain to your sham friends. Though he might be more humble, there's no police like Holmes. A cat has its claws at the end of its paws, and a woman has her pause at the end of a clause. And to think it was all done in the wee wee hours of the morning, at the crackup of Dawn.

THE PURPLE HEART

Every American soldier killed in combat is awarded a Purple Heart. Every soldier wounded not fatally is awarded a Purple Heart. Members of another country's military forces, under certain conditions, have been awarded the Purple Heart. There are no data on the total number that have been awarded, nor is there, ergo, a definitive list of recipients. A realistic figure seems to be 1.2 million. George Washington himself created and planned the Purple Heart, naming this country's first decoration the Badge of Military Merit. August 1782: "The General ever desirous to cherish virtuous ambition in his soldiers, as well as to foster and encourage every species of Military merit, directs that whenever any singularly meritorious action is performed, the author of it shall be permitted to wear on his facings over the left breast, the figure of a heart in purple cloth or silk, edged with narrow lace or binding. Not only instances of unusual gallantry, but also of extraordinary fidelity and essential service in any way shall meet with a due reward. . . . The road to glory in a patriot army and a free country is thus open to all. This order is also to have retrospect to the earliest stages of the war, and to be considered as a permanent one." The award was revived in 1932 by President Herbert Hoover and General Douglas MacArthur. It is today an award of the Defense Department.

PYRENEES

More than 2 million pilgrims annually visit Lourdes on the French side of the 237-mile-long mountain chain, from the Bay of Biscay to the Mediterranean Sea, dividing the Iberian Peninsula and the European mainland. About two-thirds of the formidable barrier lies in Spain. The border between Spain and France has been unchanged since the Peace of the Pyrenees treaty of 1659. The Virgin Mary is said to have appeared in eighteen visions to a frail fourteen-year-old, Marie Bernarde Soubirous, in a grotto in Lourdes in 1858. (Saint Bernadette was canonized in 1933.) On the 100th anniversary of the apparitions, the world's largest underground church, the Basilica of Pope Pius X, was constructed in Lourdes. The Caverne Merveilleuse, formed by the Arize River, extends for more than two miles and contains impressive Magdalenian, or Paleolithic, period rock-drawings of bison, reindeer, horses, cats, as well as bones of prehistoric cave bear and mammoth. It is so vast that aircraft factories were installed there during World War II. Jai alai was developed in the Pyrenees.

PYTHON

It is the world's longest snake. The reticulated, or royal, python of southeast Asia, Indonesia, and the Philippines may reach a length of over thirty feet. It is a constrictor, squeezing its victim to death, then swallowing it whole. It can take several days for a python to digest what it eats. It is nonvenomous and does not attack human beings. (Python was the name of a frightful serpent in Greek mythology. *It* attacked people and cattle at Delphi, and was finally killed by an unerring Apollo arrow.)

Q

Q

The seventeenth letter of the English alphabet is not always followed by the letter u. There's a qadarite, a member of an early Muslim philosophical school asserting the doctrine of free will in opposition to the Jabarites. A qoph is the nineteenth letter of the Hebrew alphabet. A qintar is a monetary unit of Albania. And there's Qantas, the oldest airline in the English-speaking world. It was founded in Australia in 1920 to provide a scheduled air service and joy-riding facility for residents of a small part of North Australia. Its name was **Queensland** **and Northern Territory** **A**erial **S**ervices, Ltd., and its initials caught on: Q.A.N.T.A.S.—pronounced Kwontas.

QB VII

The title in Leon Uris' 1970 novel refers to the courtroom—Queen's Bench VII—QB VII. Dr. Adam Kelno, a Polish nationalist with a reputation for saving the lives of fellow prisoners of the Nazis in World War II, sues for libel the American-Jewish writer who accused him of performing experimental surgery on Jewish inmates at the Jadwiga concentration camp. The jury holds for Kelno, now a national health doctor in England, but awards him only one half-penny in damages. There was conflicting evidence from witnesses.

QUAKERS

Children of Light, Friends in the Truth, Friends—members of the new Christian sect eventually agreed upon the name Religious Society of Friends. They are also still called Quakers, which originally was a term of derision—the followers of the spiritually enlightened (and eight times imprisoned) George Fox, who founded the "purer" religious body in England in the mid-1600s, trembled, or quaked, when they prayed. Quakers believe that all men possess the "inner light" that enables them to hear God's voice. Fox visited the New World in the 1670s. Quakers were persecuted by Puritans in Massachusetts Bay colony but welcomed both in Rhode Island, where the first "Yearly Meeting" was held, in Newport, in 1661, and in Pennsylvania—William Penn was a convert. Quakers were prime figures in the abolition movement. Two Presidents have been Quakers: Herbert Hoover and Richard M. Nixon. Friends no longer address one another as "thee"—it was a mark of equality—nor do the women wear plain gray dresses and bonnets and men broad-brimmed hats. In 1947, the American Friends Service Committee shared the Nobel Peace Prize.

QUASAR

Short for *quas*i-stell*ar* radio source. Quasars were explained in the early 1960s by the Dutch-American astronomer Maarten Schmidt, at the California Institute of Technology. The spectra of radio-emitting stars was indeed strange. As Isaac Asimov has reported, "it suddenly occurred to Schmidt that the unfamiliarity of the spectra was the result of an enormous red shift and that the lines were familiar ones that ought to be in the ultraviolet section of the spectrum. This turned out to be correct and the enormous red shift indicated the objects to be very distant, a billion light-years away and more. In that case, they could not be stars but must be objects far more luminous than ordinary galaxies. They were called 'quasi-stellar objects'; that is, objects which had a starlike appearance; and the phrase was quickly abbreviated to 'quasars.' " Astronomers still have no easy way of accounting for the nature of quasars.

QUEEN ELIZABETH (THE SHIP)

The world's most luxurious (a crew of 1,296) and largest (83,000 tons) passenger liner (named for Britain's Queen Mother) when she was christened (in 1938) was so long—nearly a fifth of a mile—that the actress Bea Lillie quipped, "Say, what time does this place get to England?" The ship sailed 896 times between Southampton and New York, and during World War II did yeoman's duty as a troopship, carrying as many as 15,000 jam-packed G.I.s at a time. The jet age did the Queen in. In 1970, she was sold for $3.2-million to the Hong Kong shipping magnate C. Y. Tung, who renamed her Seawise University (Seawise was a play on Tung's initials) and ordered her refitted as a combination luxury cruise ship and school. When refurbishing was all but ten percent completed, the erstwhile last word in gracious living afloat burned and sank in Hong Kong harbor.

QUEEN OF SPADES

It's the crucial playing card in the game of hearts. It's also the name of a Pushkin short story on which Tchaikovsky based his opera *The Queen of Spades*—the opera that was the favorite of Lee Harvey Oswald—yes, *that* L. H. Oswald. He listened to a recording frequently. On the eve of Oswald's assassination of President John F. Kennedy, in Dallas, on November 22, 1963, Marina Oswald felt toward her husband "twenty-two fires" (a Russian proverb), that is, volcanic fury, out-of-control anger. The overwrought and obsessive Oswald again became "seized by the fantasy" that *he* was the hero of *The Queen of Spades*, who slays the visiting queen. *Vot on, smotri, Kak demon ada, mrachen . . . bleden. . . . His face is full of sorrow and gloom, ashen, a strange man. . . . No days of joy will ever smile on me. . . . At Paris was a Queen of Beauty, turning men's heads. . . . Her Majesty's arrival: how gracious that she shows herself. . . . Woman's presence presages danger. . . . Madness or illusion? Demons, I am pursued by demons. . . . You will receive a fatal stroke. . . . Poor girl! And I had to sacrifice her to my madness. No choice, no aim has life for me in store. Farewell, Proschai. . . . Lord, please forgive me.* After the assassination, Marina mysteriously declared that her woman-hating husband "must have staked everything on one card." Hating women was the natural orientation of a youth who had been raised and taunted by voracious women. When he felt humiliated and emasculated, Oswald resorted to violence. It has been convincingly argued that the First Lady, the visiting queen, was the apotheosis of the gender that was his tormentor, his wife's "goddess," the most glamorous and unattainable woman in the world.

QUEEN VICTORIA

England's longest reigning monarch by nearly four years—George III was king for sixty years—set the stuffy and hypocritical moral standards and conduct of an era. The low four-wheel pleasure carriage for two with a calash top and a raised seat in front for the driver—a fungus disease that is peculiar to oats that have Victoria variety in their parentage—a dye made from Michler's ketone and N-phenyl-alpha-naphthylamine—malachite green—a lily—a lake in east central Africa—cities in British Columbia and Australia—and so on and so forth—they were all named after the Queen and, from 1876, Empress of India. Nobody ever knocked at her door—a gentle scratching was all that she permitted. She was a widow at forty-two, with nine children, when her beloved Albert, a cousin to whom she had proposed, died. Every night at Windsor Castle, Albert's clothes were laid out, every morning fresh water was placed in the basin in his room, and the Queen slept with a photograph taken of Albert's head and shoulders. Only Prime Minister Benjamin Disraeli was able to flatter and comfort her, to make the lonely crown an easier burden. (Victoria's contemporary Austrian Emperor Franz Josef reigned even longer, 1848–1916—sixty-eight years.)

QUISLING, VIDKUN

Quisling—one who traitorously assists an enemy power to invade his country. The Norwegian fascist leader found Hitler's emphasis on Nordic superiority appealing. When the Norwegian government fell in 1933— Quisling had been an army attaché in Finland and Russia and assisted in relief work in Russia—he founded and modeled his own party, Nasjonal Samling (National Unity), on Hitler's Nazi party. It never won a seat in the parliament. In 1940, Quisling helped Germany prepare for the conquest of Norway. His reward: His party was the only one permitted by the conquerors and he was made premier. The puppet was unpopular with both the Germans and the Norwegians. He was arrested after the Germans surrendered in 1945 and hanged in Oslo.

QUITO

Ecuador's earthquaked, balmy capital, and largest city, just south of the equator and once the capital of the Inca Kingdom of Quito—it's pronounced Kē'tō. The unaccustomed get high there—Quito is nearly two miles up the Andes, at the foot of the Pichincha volcano. The great Church of San Francisco and the oldest art school in Latin America are there. Indians are more than half of the population of 600,000.

"QUO VADIS?"

And so Jesus said to his disciples, in the Gospel according to St. John, "But now I go my way to him that sent me; and none of you asketh me, Whither goest thou? But because I have said these things unto you, sorrow hath filled your heart. Nevertheless I tell you the truth; It is expedient for you that I go away: for if I go not away, the Comforter will not come unto you; but if I depart, I will send him unto you. And when he is come, he will reprove the world of sin, and of righteousness, and of judgment. Of sin, because they believe not on me; Of righteousness, because I go to my Father, and ye see me no more; Of judgment, because the prince of this world is judged. I have yet many things to say unto you, but ye cannot bear them now."—John 16.

R

RADIO CITY MUSIC HALL

It opened in Rockefeller Center on December 27, 1932. Sixty thousand people tried to get into the 6,200-seat hall to see Martha Graham, the Wallenda aerialists, the Kikuta acrobats from Japan, the soloists Titta Ruffo and Jan Peerce, and the choir of Tuskegee Institute. The evening was a spectacular success. But in a couple of weeks the Hall changed its entertainment policy. Henceforth, there would be a combination of films and live stage entertainment, otherwise there would be a box-office disaster. In 1937, the Rockettes won a Grand Prix for their 16-minute performance at the Paris Exposition. A quarter of a billion people have paid to see shows in the world's largest theater.

RADIO CODE, INTERNATIONAL

Words have been used to "spell" letters in situations such as military action to enhance and clarify communication. Alpha for A. Bravo, B. Charlie, C. Delta, D. Echo, E. Foxtrot, F. Golf, G. Hotel, H. India, I. Juliet, J. Kilo, K. Lima, L. Mike, M. November, N. Oscar, O. Papa, P. Quebec, Q. Romeo, R. Sierra, S. Tango, T. Uniform, U. Victor, V. Whiskey, W. X-ray, X. Yankee, Y. Zulu, Z. Another system begins Able for A, Baker for B, Charlie for C, Delta for D, Easy for E, Foxtrot for F.

RAILROAD

The world's highest standard gauge railway cuts through the Andes in Peru. The Central Railway climbs to over 15,800 feet (three miles) above sea level. Four railroads in all run up the west slope of the central Andes to rich mineral beds in the plateaus of Peru and Bolivia. Nowhere else in the world is there a mountain pass so high as the passes through which these railroads struggle. The Andes (a Quechuan word, "copper") is the longest chain of mountains anywhere, 4,500 miles stretching along the entire west coast of South America from Cape Horn to Panama. Several peaks rise over 20,000 feet. Some of the highest mountains are volcanic, a few actively.

RAINBOW

"I do set my bow in the cloud, and it shall be for a token of a covenant between me and the earth. And it shall come to pass, when I bring a cloud over the earth, that the bow shall be seen in the cloud. . . . And the bow shall be in the cloud; and I will look upon it, that I may remember the everlasting covenant between God and every living creature of all flesh that is upon the earth.''—Genesis 9. The Greeks and the Romans saw the rainbow as the sign of Iris, messenger of the gods. The Inca and other Indians saw it as a gift from the sun god. If the Sun is at the horizon, the rainbow is an arc of 180°. If the Sun is high in the sky, there can be no rainbow. Aristotle studied the phenomenon seriously, but an understanding of how the seven colors of the spectrum, violet inside and red outside, that appear when the Sun shines through water droplets had to wait until light and its reflection and refraction were understood. "My heart leaps up when I behold a rainbow in the sky: So was it when my life began; So is it now I am a man; So be it when I shall grow old. Or let me die!''—Wordsworth. The largest natural bridge in the world—it has a 278-foot span—is the symmetrical, pink sandstone arch Rainbow Bridge in southern Utah, in one of the most rugged and remote regions of the United States. Since 1942, there has been a Rainbow Bridge crossing Niagara River and connecting Niagara Falls, New York, and Niagara Falls, Canada; it superseded Honeymoon Bridge, which ice had destroyed in the late 1930s.

READER'S DIGEST

"Among our literary scenes, Saddest this sight to me, The graves of little magazines That died to make verse free." The *Reader's Digest, TV Guide, National Geographic, Modern Maturity, Better Homes & Gardens* are the leading general-interest magazines in circulation in the United States. The monthly *Digest* has a circulation of 18,299,091, nearly a million more copies than the weekly *TV Guide*. Other magazines with circulation above 5 million copies: *AARP News Bulletin* (8,163,151), *Family Circle, Woman's Day, McCall's, Good Housekeeping, Ladies' Home Journal*, and the *National Enquirer*. (AARP is American Association of Retired Persons.) "Individual man, supported by faith and determination, can make an imprint on society as clearly as a skier leaves his tracks on driven snow"—that was a favorite theme of the co-founder (with his wife, Lila Acheson) of the *Reader's Digest*, DeWitt Wallace.

More than 30 million copies are circulated every month, thirty-six international editions. At Macalester College, in St. Paul, Minnesota, in the early 1900s, Wallace noted down and filed highlights from magazine articles that he considered of more than just passing interest and value. He put out a 124-page booklet, "Getting the Most Out of Farming," which listed titles of free pamphlets and summarized their contents. During World War I, he was seriously wounded in the Meuse-Argonne offensive, in 1918, and spent his four months' convalescence mainly in reading and condensing general-interest magazine articles. The Wallaces launched the first issue of the *Digest* in February 1922: 1,500 copies. There was a no-ads policy until 1955. In 1961, Wallace told an interviewer, "My wife and I discovered many years ago that there are more satisfying uses for money than the accumulation of it."

RED CROSS

"Would it not be possible to found and organize in all civilized countries permanent societies of volunteers who in time of war would give help to the wounded without regard for their nationality?" So asked the Swiss philanthropist-humanitarian Jean Henri Dunant, who was in the field at Solferino the day after tens of thousands of men had been killed or wounded in a clash in the Austro-Sardinian War (1859). Formation of the Red Cross was the international response. Today, more than 120 nations have Red Cross societies, the name deriving from the organization's flag, a red cross on a white background, the reverse of Dunant's native Swiss flag. Fearing foreign entanglements, Congress did not authorize the United States's participation for eighteen years. The American Red Cross was organized in 1881 by Clara Barton, a former schoolteacher and patent office clerk who became the "angel of the battlefield" in the U.S. Civil War and worked for the International Red Cross behind German lines in the Franco-Prussian War.

RED GRANGE

'The "Galloping Ghost" owed a lot to Earl Britton. The blocking back opened up canyonwide holes for Grange's runs to glory for the University of Illinois football team in the 1920s. The whirling dervish was All-American for three straight years. He racked up hundreds of yards running a game. He ran back kickoffs 100 yards. He passed for touchdowns. When Grange joined the Chicago Bears after the 1925 college football season, he attracted unprecedented crowds and helped to put the National Football League on the map. He played two years for the New York Yankees football team and 1929–34 for the Bears again. In his latter campaigns, he excelled on defense. Grange was a charter enshrinee, in 1963, of the Pro Football Hall of Fame.

"RED RIVER VALLEY"

The theme song by Alfred Newman for the movie *The Grapes of Wrath* (1940) was not nominated for an Oscar, but director John Ford and supporting actress Jane Darwell won Oscars. The epic was based on John Steinbeck's Pulitzer Prize story of displaced Dust Bowlers' migration to California during the Depression. *Red River,* a classic Western film, was directed by Howard Hawks and starred Montgomery Clift and John Wayne. A Red River is the southernmost of the large tributaries of the Mississippi River, rising in two branches in the Texas Panhandle. A Red River flows north between Minnesota and North Dakota and empties into Lake Winnipeg in Manitoba. The chief river of North Vietnam is called Red River.

REFORMATION

The Protestant revolt against the supremacy of the Pope! It began in 1517 when Martin Luther, a German monk and a professor of theology, wrote his "Ninety-five Theses"—a series of statements attacking the sale of indulgences, pardons from some of the penalties for sins. He sent them to a church official, who leaked them after a time. Luther's doctrine of justification by faith in Christ alone contradicted the Church's teaching of grace and good works as a way to salvation. He was excommunicated by Pope Leo X in 1521 and declared a heretic. Emperor Charles V signed the Edict of Worms declaring Luther to be an outlaw—anyone could kill him without punishment. Luther was protected by the Prince of Saxony. Within half a century Protestantism was established in nearly half of Europe. Luther translated the Bible into German. He unexpectedly opposed the Peasants' War that his own spirit of independence had helped to nurture. He married, and fathered six children.

REVERE, PAUL

"Listen, my children, and you shall hear, of the midnight ride of Paul Revere, on the eighteenth of April, in Seventy-five; hardly a man is now alive who remembers that famous day and year." Henry Wadsworth Longfellow wasn't among them. "One if by land, and two if by sea; and I on the opposite shore will be, ready to ride and spread the alarm through every Middlesex village and farm." All right so far, but the Son of Liberty didn't spread the word that night in '75. He was captured by the British, who took his horse away from him and made him walk back to Boston. Four years later, Revere led a disastrous raid on the British at Penobscot, Maine, and twice stood court-martial. His silverware *was* highly prized. For years until his death, in 1818, he daily wore a uniform of the Revolution.

REYKJAVIK

The world's northernmost capital is Iceland's capital, the smokeless city. All of the westernmost state of Europe, which is in the northern Atlantic, 600 miles west of Norway, is unique. Everyone can read and write. There are no prisons. (More than 17 percent of America's convicts are illiterate.) About 80 percent of the 40,000-square-mile island is uninhabited. Many of the 200 volcanoes are still active. No tree may be cut legally. Almost every building in the capital of nearly 100,000 people is heated by waters channeled from subterranean thermal springs. The word "geyser" was coined in Iceland; the Great Geysir, or Stori Geysir, at Haukadalur is celebrated. But there's trouble in paradise. In 1984, Reykjavik experienced its first armed robbery.

RHODE ISLAND

It may not be named for the largest of the Dodecanese in the Aegean Sea near Turkey. Its official name is the State of Rhode Island and Providence Plantations, and its familiar name, as the smallest of the fifty, is taken from the nearby island Rhode Island, once known as Aquidneck, home of the Narragansett Indians. (The Portsmouth-Newport General Court on March 13, 1644, had changed the name of the island from Aquidneck to the Isle of Rhodes or Rhode Island.) It was founded by refugees from Massachusetts, seeking religious and political freedom. The first settlements were made at Providence by Roger Williams, and two years later, in 1638, by Anne Hutchinson and her numerous followers. The oldest synagogue in the nation is in Newport. About sixty species of trees are native to Little Rhodey (1,214 square miles), and there are nearly twenty species of snakes.

RHONE RIVER

"The blue rushing of the arrowy Rhone" is how Lord Byron in *Childe Harold's Pilgrimage* described part of the 500-mile river which rises in the Rhone glacier of Switzerland, passes through Lake Geneva, enters France and flows southwestward to Lyon, where it becomes navigable, then plunges south into the Gulf of Lions and the Mediterranean. A canal connects the Rhone with Marseilles. The river has been called the cradle of Provençal culture.

RHUBARB

There's no argument on this point: Rhubarb and asparagus are the only two perennial vegetables. A perennial is any plant that under natural conditions lives for several to many growing seasons. All other vegetables must be replanted every year. Rhubarb: any of a genus of plants of the buckwheat family with long, fleshy acid leafstalks, used in cookery. Asparagus: any of a large genus of Old World perennial plants of the lily family, esp. *A. officinalis,* which has tender edible stalks. Asparagus was under cultivation in Asia in antiquity.

RICHARD, MAURICE

The Rocket meant business. There was liftoff the moment he hit the ice. He joined the Canadiens in 1942–43, and in 1945 became the National Hockey League's first 50-goal scorer, a goal a game! He was an All-Star fourteen times in his eighteen-year career, scoring 544 goals in 978 league games, including 83 winning goals and 28 tying goals. In 133 playoff games, he scored 82 goals and notched 44 assists. On December 28, 1944, he spent the day moving into a new home, then scored a record eight points that night. He was once suspended from the playoffs for striking an official—there was a riot in the Montreal Forum and the Canadiens had to forfeit the game. The president of the N.H.L. once said, "Never . . . have I met a man with such singleness of purpose and so completely devoted to his profession."

RICHTER SCALE

Scale numbers on the logarithmic Richter scale—devised in 1935 by the American seismologist C. F. Richter, at the California Institute of Technology—range from 0 to 9, but no theoretical upper limit exists. The energy released in an earthquake of magnitude 8 is about ten times the energy released in an earthquake of magnitude 7, as an earthquake of magnitude 2 releases about ten times the energy released in an earthquake of magnitude 1. Magnitude 8.9 has been recorded at least three times. Each year, there are nearly 1,000 quakes above magnitude 5.0 and nearly 50,000 above magnitude 3.0. The region with the lowest percentage of total seismic energy release has been the Atlantic Ocean. More than three-quarters of total seismic energy release has been in Pacific areas.

RICHTHOFEN, MANFRED BARON VON

The "Red Baron" was Germany's most spectacular fighter pilot in World War I, shooting down 80 Allied aircraft before he was shot down in his red Fokker triplane over the Somme Canal near Amiens, France, probably by a Canadian, Captain Roy Brown, of the Royal Flying Corps, on April 21, 1918. He crashed two miles behind a line in a sector held by Australian troops, and was buried at Bertangles by the Allies with a wreath, "To our gallant and worthy foe." In 1925, his remains were reburied in Berlin. Richthofen had served in the cavalry, leading a troop of Ulanen, their flat-topped czapkas covered in drab cloth, across the border into Russian Poland, then in the infantry before transferring in 1915 to the flying service. He crashed on his first solo flight as an observer. His kills included the leading ace of the Royal Flying Corps.

RICKLES, DON

Mr. Warmth, the insulting little boychick against authority. He claims he's never met a man he didn't dislike. Admittedly, the Picasso of Putdown is an acquired taste, if one can ever dig venom. To the chairman of the board: "Come right in, Frankie. Make yourself at home. Hit somebody." To Sammy Davis: "Look at him! You can always tell a Negro. Throw a broom on the floor and see him grab it." To Bob Hope: "Why is he here? Is the war over?" To Italians: "What the hell do we need Italians for? Oh yeah, to keep the cops busy." To a guy's date: "Was anyone else hurt in the accident?" To Pat Boone: "You still think pimples come from Hersheys!" To Dean Martin: "What do we need Italians for—all they do is keep the flies off our fish." To Eddie Fisher: "Being married to Elizabeth Taylor is like me trying to wash the Empire State Building with a bar of soap." Is *he* here?

RIDDLE OF THE SPHINX

"What is it which, having but one voice, is first four-footed, then two-footed, and is at the last three-footed?" Greek mythology's Sphinx, another of the horrible issue of Typhon and Echidna: the face and breasts of a woman, the body and feet and tail of a lion, the wings of a bird. Passers-by who did not know the answer were devoured. Many perished, until Oidipous ("swollen foot") replied, "The answer is Man. In infancy, he crawls on all fours. In mature years, he walks upright on two feet. In old age, he goes as it were on three by the aid of a cane." The Sphinx cast herself down from a cliff.

"THE RIME OF THE ANCIENT MARINER"

"At length did cross an Albatross: Thorough the fog it came; As if it had been a Christian soul, We hailed it in God's name. It ate the food it ne'er had eat, And round and round it flew. The ice did split with a thunder-fit; The helmsman steered us through! And a good south wind sprung up behind; The Albatross did follow, And every day, for food or play, Came to the mariner's hollo! In mist or cloud, on mast or shroud, It perched for vespers nine; Whiles all the night, through fog-smoke white, Glimmered the white moonshine." The ancient mariner inhospitably kills the pious bird of good omen with his cross-bow. His shipmates cry out. But the fog clears off, they justify the crime, and make themselves accomplices. The fair breeze continues; the ship enters the Pacific Ocean and sails northward. "Down dropt the breeze, the sails dropt down, Twas sad as sad could be; And we did speak only to break The silence of the sea. . . . Day after day, day after day, We stuck, nor breath nor motion; as idle as a painted ship Upon a painted ocean." The Albatross begins to be avenged. "Water, water, every where, and all the boards did shrink; water, water, every where, nor any drop to drink." Instead of the cross, "the Albatross about my neck was hung." At the rising of the Moon, one after another, "Four times fifty living men, (And I heard nor sigh nor groan) With heavy thump, a lifeless lump, They dropped down one by one. The souls did from their bodies fly,—They fled to bliss or woe! And every soul, it passed me by, like the whizz of my cross-bow!"—Samuel Taylor Coleridge.

RINGO (BEATLE)

He replaced Pete Best on drums because the Beatles' manager, who had groomed the quartet into a worldwide phenomenon, thought Ringo had a better personality. The oldest of the Beatles—he'll be forty-five in 1985 —Ringo sat at his drums like a Buddha idol and wore a worried frown more often than a smile: "I'm not really miserable," he said, "it's just me face."

RIN TIN TIN

The German shepherd certainly didn't lead a dog's life in Hollywood. In fact, he was top dog for years at Warner Brothers, his silver screen productions Big Box Office. According to studio flacks, he was born to a war-dog mother in a German trench in France during the Great War and abandoned when the Huns retreated. He was rescued by an American army officer who happened to be a police-dog trainer in California: He trained the intelligent, bicontinental star when they got to the Coast. Hollywood in the 1920s: Griffith, Sennett, Chaplin, Keaton, Pickford, Mayer, Zukor, Lasky, Garbo, von Stroheim, Lubitsch—and Rin Tin Tin.

RIO DE JANEIRO

The eighty-two-foot-tall statue Christ the Redeemer on Corcovado peak looks down on South America's second-largest city and Brazil's former capital. Most of the city's 5 million residents (Cariocas) are Roman Catholic, hundreds of thousands of residents live in wooden and metal shacks in hillsides, there are about 81,000 persons per square mile. Historians believe that the Portuguese explorer Goncalo Coelho named the area for the month in 1504 that he arrived—the river of January. Rio gained celebrity as the shipping point for all gold from the interior. It replaced Bahia (now Salvador) as the country's capital in 1763; it was the capital of the exiled royal court of Portugal 1808–21. (Inland Brasilia became the Brazilian capital in 1960.) The crescent-shaped beach Copacabana, with its famous mosaic sidewalks, is a Rio tourist attraction.

RIO GRANDE

The two North American nations of the United States and Mexico share an unfortified transcontinental boundary of 1,500 miles, about 60 percent of which is the Rio Grande. Texas, California, Arizona, and New Mexico border their friendly neighbor to the south. Much of the southwest and most of the west of the United States was formerly and indisputably Mexican territory. They were taken away and incorporated into the United States as part of its manifest destiny by war, annexation, and purchase. The border was established between 1836 and 1855. All of what is now the United States was once ruled from Mexico City by Spain, which had been given exclusive grants by the Pope in 1493. The Rio Grande—known to Mexicans as Rio Bravo del Norte—sometimes changes its course, causing border disputes. The river is navigable only near its mouth at the Gulf of Mexico at Brownsville, Texas, and Matamoros, Mexico.

RIP VAN WINKLE

Washington Irving's simple, good-natured fellow took more than a few winks in the Kaatskill—he slept through twenty years! He was one of those happy mortals, of foolish, well-oiled dispositions, who take the world easy, eat white bread or brown, whichever can be got with least thought or trouble and would rather starve on a penny than work for a pound. The great error in his composition was an insuperable aversion to all kinds of profitable labor, and his wife kept continually dinning in his ears about his idleness, his carelessness, and the ruin he was bringing on his family. Poor Rip was at last reduced almost to despair; and his only alternative, to escape from the labor of the farm and clamor of his wife, was to take gun in hand and stroll away into the woods. . . . On waking, he found to his astonishment that his beard had grown a foot long! "Surely," thought Rip, "I have not slept here all night. Oh! that flagon! that wicked flagon!" thought Rip. "What excuse shall I make to Dame Van Winkle?" . . . When he learned that she had broken a blood vessel in a fit of passion at a New England peddler, Rip realized that one species of despotism had ended for him: petticoat government. He had got his neck out of the yoke of matrimony, and could go in and out whenever he pleased. His married daughter, Judith Gardenier, took him home to live with her in a snug, well-furnished home, and he was idle with impunity on the bench at the inn door.

RIVE GAUCHE

"Left bank" in French. When you face down the Seine, rive gauche is at your left. Paris is famed for its rive gauche. Its spirit lives on the left bank. The Latin Quarter is there—Latin, because professors and students there were at one time obliged to speak and write it for even the necessities of daily life. The Luxembourg Gardens and the Boulevard Montparnasse and the Sorbonne, the Collège de France, the Bibliothèque Sainte-Genevieve, Boulevard St.-Michel—left bankers all. Rive gauche is the powerhouse for the City of Light. On the right (northern) bank of Paris are the Bois de Boulogne, Arc de Triomphe, Élysée Palace, the Louvre, the Place de la Bastille, and Place de la Concorde.

ROB AND LAURA (THE PETRIES)

They lived at 148 Bonnie Meadow Road, in New Rochelle, New York, in the 1960s, the brainchildren of Carl Reiner. Rob (Dick Van Dyke) was the head writer for the comedy-variety "Alan Brady Show" (within "The Dick Van Dyke Show" television show) and Laura (Mary Tyler Moore, a former dancer) was a former dancer and Mrs. Housewife—a behind-the-scenes sit-com within a show. Episodes generally revolved around the problems of the writer and the home life of the Petries. "Brady," played by Reiner himself, was heard but not seen for several seasons. He played Rob and Barbara Britton was Laura in the pilot for network acceptance.

ROBERTSON, OSCAR

"Never turn your head on Oscar, there is no telling what he might do next. His body control is even more amazing than his shooting touch." Or as professional basketball's most victorious coach, Red Auerbach, has said about the Big O, who never played for him, "There is nothing he can't do." An All-American at the University of Cincinnati, he was three times the most valuable player in the National Basketball Association. Mr. Outside to Lew Alcindor's Mr. Inside, he spearheaded the Milwaukee Bucks to the league championship in the franchise's third season, 1970–71. He averaged a career 25.7 points a game (he played 1,040 games), made 7,694 free throws of 9,185 attempted, and set the league record for career assists (9,887, which led to at least 19,774 points).

ROBINSON, FRANK

The only baseballer to win the most valuable player honor in both major leagues and the first black manager. Battering the leather off the ball in the Pioneer League and the Sally League, he went up to the majors in 1956 and slugged 38 home runs and was rookie of the year. Five years later, he was the National League's MVP while pacing Cincinnati to the pennant; five years later, and now a Baltimore Oriole, he was the American League's MVP while copping the elusive triple crown in batting. In his debut in 1975 as manager of the Cleveland Indians, he characteristically crashed a home run in an opening-day triumph over the New York Yankees. His 18-season career HR total was 575. He played sports at McClymonds High School, in Oakland, California, which also produced

Bill Russell, the controversial basketball stalwart who refused admission to the Hall of Fame, and Curt Flood, the baseball stalwart who helped to breach the sports' slave laws and open the floodgates to free agentry.

ROBINSON, JACKIE

Before he broke the major leagues' color barrier, in 1947—in his third season he would be the National League's most valuable player and one of the game's most exciting gate draws—this heroic man had been preceded in the headlines by his brother Mack. In the 1936 Olympics, in Berlin, Mack Robinson broke the 200-meter dash record, yet finished in second place, four-tenths of a second behind the new world-record dash (20.7 seconds) of Jesse Owens. Mack Robinson resides today in California, where he is raising funds to build a statue commemorating his legendary brother. Jack Roosevelt Robinson was a four-star athlete at the University of California at Los Angeles, a first lieutenant in the Army, a phenomenon with the Kansas City Monarchs of the Negro National League. Branch Rickey, president of the Brooklyn Dodgers, picked him to be the first black player in the biggies. (The St. Louis Cardinals voted not to take the field if Robinson played.) Robinson spent a year with the Dodger farm team in Montreal—he burned up the International League, hitting .349, stealing 40 bases. He retired with a .311 career average when the Dodgers, after the 1956 season, announced they were trading him to the Giants. In 1962, he became the first black in the Hall of Fame.

ROB ROY

His full name was Rob Roy MacGregor Campbell, and he was a Scottish Robin Hood and the title character in Sir Walter Scott's 1818 historical romance. Title character, but not the hero—that's Frank Osbaldistone, son of Mr. William Osbaldistone, of the firm of Osbaldistone & Tresham. Rob Roy weaves in and out of the novel, helping Frank Osbaldistone out of jams and pickles. The story, which takes place in 1715 in Northumberland and Glasgow, has been dramatized several times and was the subject of an opera by Flotow. The Scottish Scott, the father of the historical novel, was a lawyer, a sheriff-deputy, a balladeer, a poet, a court clerk, and, ruinously, a publisher. He was made a baronet in the wake of his "Waverly novels," which include *Rob Roy, The Black Dwarf,* and *The Bride of Lammermoor. Ivanhoe* (1820) was set many centuries earlier. The drink Rob Roy is a tough man's combination of scotch, sweet vermouth, and angostura bitters.

ROCKEFELLER CENTER

"The Heavens themselves, the Planets and this Center observe degree, priority, and place." It's a group of twenty-one office buildings, theaters, underground streets, and open public spaces in midtown Manhattan, a coordinated group of commercial buildings under unified control. Here, as the architectural critic Carol Herselle Krinsky has observed, the concept of a skyscraper city was realized in practice for the first time. After World War II, the original fourteen buildings were joined by seven more beyond the original site. At the end of 1973, the last of its three newest buildings that were planned in 1963 was finished. Sean O'Casey, never at a loss for words, said that "the newcomer to New York City, American or foreigner, doesn't spend a glance on St. John's of Morningside Heights, or on St. Patrick's on Fifth Avenue, or on the Russian basilica on Fourth Avenue, or thereabouts; but makes for Rockefeller Center where he can get an eyeful worth seeing."

ROCKEFELLER, JOHN D.

He was born when Martin Van Buren was President and he died in Franklin Roosevelt's second term. In ninety-eight years, he became as rich as, well, Rockefeller, America's first billionaire. He was the son of a peddler who struck it rich by establishing centralized control in the oil industry through Standard Oil—he ruthlessly crushed his foes and accumulated large capital reserves. He helped to found the University of Chicago, and he gave away more than half a billion dollars. His only son, John, Jr., bought the land for construction of the United Nations in New York City, planned Rockefeller Center, and restored the historic Virginia city of Williamsburg. His grandson Nelson was for fourteen years governor of New York State and for going on three years Vice-President, filling the vacancy created when Gerald R. Ford succeeded Richard M. Nixon in the Oval Office. John D. had a younger brother, William (1841–1922), a stock market manipulator and financier.

ROCKEFELLER, NELSON

How rich as Rockefeller is rich as Rockefeller? Informed guestimates had run as high as $10 billion. During the confirmation hearings on Nelson Rockefeller's nomination to be Gerald R. Ford's Vice-President, the family's chief financial adviser testified before the Judiciary Committee that the assets of the Rockefellers—eighty-four persons—totaled not quite $1.3 billion. The governor had an annual income of $4.6 million per year if he did nothing more than open his mail from the two trust funds set up for him by his father. At first, he did not pay an income tax in 1970; transactions in one of his trusts had legally spared him any payment; he later paid $6,250,000 in capital gains taxes and $814,701 in other federal imposts. When he was asked in a television talk show what he would have done if he hadn't been born with a fortune, Mr. Rockefeller answered unhesitatingly, "I would think of making one."

ROCKNE, KNUTE KENNETH

He went out flying—literally. The last Notre Dame team he coached, in 1930, had an unblemished record, winning all ten of its games, making his 13-year record 105 wins against twelve losses and five ties. The Studebaker Company was planning a car called the Rockne and Hollywood was talking deal, a football movie that the dean of sportswriters, Grantland Rice, would write. But—the airplane taking Rockne to the Coast to meet with RKO crashed in Kansas. As a player, he had been outstanding. In 1913, he led the Fighting Irish to a still-talked-about upset of heavily favored Army—they employed a legal but little-used football tactic: the forward pass. On graduation, he became a chemistry teacher at his alma mater. Four years later, in 1918, he took over the gridiron reins. His novel, *The Four Winners,* upheld sportsmanship, honor, and the proper place for athletics in life.

ROCKS

The major classes of rock: igneous—volcanic rock; rock formed under intense heat, as by volcanic action; metamorphic—rocks that have changed from their original constitution; sedimentary—rocks formed by the deposit of sediment, matter deposited by water, ice, or air.

ROCKWELL, GEORGE LINCOLN

The founder of the American Nazi party, the son of a vaudeville comedian and a toe dancer, claimed that he had "a truly superior mind, which can apprehend the mightiest facts and ideas in the universe—facts which are unthinkable to the millions and billions of human beings. Such a great mind can surely realize its own attitude with regard to the wormlike minds which squirm and crawl by the billions in the mud of life." When a grateful nation elected him President in 1972, he would ship all Negroes to Africa and gas all Jews; he called the Wailing Wall in Jerusalem "that glorified gentlemen's pissoir." He never quite forgave his mother for making him wear short pants when other boys his age were in knickers. He was a pilot in the Navy, married and divorced twice, and a failure at just about everything he tried, which included publishing a magazine for servicemen's wives. A priest who met with Rockwell told William F. Buckley, Jr.: "He is oddly personable, in a heavy, rude way, and not incapable of winning over single people of the same stripe. But that is the end of it. He is gross, fanatical, and urges criminally insane suggestions. . . . He is a Nazi of the true, vulgar, 1937 variety. His mind is a disaster area. Under pressure, he admits that the only relationship between his movement and *National Review* conservatism is that both are anti-Communist." To woo extreme racists, Rockwell renamed his group the National Socialist White People's Party. (Communist Jewry was spurring the Negro to mongrelize the white race.) He was shot by his Minister of Propaganda while backing his car away from a laundry in Arlington, Virginia. His last words were, "I forgot my bleach."

ROCKY MOUNTAINS

There are few cities of size in the 3,200-mile-long, 100–400 mile wide Continental Divide separating the basins of streams draining into the Atlantic Ocean from those draining into the Pacific Ocean: Kelowna, Kamloops, Prince George in British Columbia; Butte, Missoula, Helena in Montana; Casper in Wyoming; Santa Fe in New Mexico. When pale faces arrived from the East, the Shoshoni were in Idaho, the Blackfoot in Montana, the Utes in Colorado. The first white man to cross the Rockies was the Scottish explorer Sir Alexander Mackenzie, who passed through Canada's Peace River Valley in 1793. The Rockies were created primarily by folding and faulting, or cracking, of the earth's crust, and by tectonic activity, the movement of large crustal plates which leads to the uplifting of some areas and the sinking of others. The highest peak is Mount Elbert, 14,431 feet, in Colorado. Passes across the mountains include South Pass, at the southern end of the Wind River Range, in southwest Wyoming, and Kicking Horse and Yellowhead Pass in Canada.

RODGERS AND HAMMERSTEIN

They were always turning down ideas for shows. One became *Fiddler on the Roof.* Another became *My Fair Lady.* They wrote *Pipe Dream, Flower Drum Song,* and *Me and Juliet.* They became partners when Lorenz Hart, Rodgers' collaborator, died. Their first venture, *Oklahoma!* —its original title was *Away We Go*—broke fresh ground in the musical theater. *South Pacific* ran for years and was honored with a Pulitzer

Prize. *The Sound of Music* ran for years. *The King and I* ran forever. Their song "It Might as Well Be Spring," in the motion picture *State Fair*, was honored with an Oscar. Somewhere in the world at this very moment—no matter what the moment is—there is the sound of their music—someone is producing a Rodgers and Hammerstein show or humming or singing a Rodgers and Hammerstein song: "Bali Ha'i," "People Will Say We're in Love," "June Is Bustin' Out All Over," "Wonderful Guy," "I Enjoy Being a Girl," "I Whistle a Happy Tune," "Mister Snow," "Do-Re-Mi," "Oh, What a Beautiful Mornin'." Can you imagine a nightingale without a song to sing? (Six years before Rodgers and Hammerstein's *South Pacific* opened on Broadway, a drama called *South Pacific* opened at the Cort Theater. It starred Canada Lee, it was directed by Lee Strasberg, it ran for five performances.) Rodgers composed the score for forty Broadway shows.

ROENTGEN, WILHELM KONRAD

X is the usual mathematical symbol for the unknown. Because the German physicist at the University of Wurzburg in Bavaria had no idea of the nature of the radiation that was emerging from a cathode-ray tube, a radiation that was highly penetrating and yet invisible to the eye, he called it X-rays. The unit of X-ray dosage is called the roentgen. The first public demonstration of X-ray photography took place in 1896: Roentgen made a picture of a hand of an 80-year-old volunteer. Roentgen was honored with the first Nobel Prize in physics, in 1901. He did not attempt to patent any aspect of X-ray production or to make any financial gain from his discovery that was so vital to industry, medicine, and science.

ROGERS, WILL

The cowboy-lariatist-columnist-humorist-philosopher-flying fanatic may have been the most beloved man in the world in his day. When he died in an airplane crash in Alaska in 1935, he was the nation's top motion-picture box office attraction (he was succeeded by Shirley Temple) and the most popular after-dinner speaker in history. He told the truth: "Swinging a rope is all right—when your neck ain't in it. Then it's hell. . . . Our municipal election ran true to political form. The sewer was defeated but the councilmen got in. . . . On account of us being a democracy and run by the people, we are the only nation in the world that has to keep a government four years no matter what it does. . . . It's awful hard to get people interested in corruption unless they can get some of it. . . . The Democrats take government as a joke, and the Republicans take it serious but run it like a joke." He belonged to no organized party

—"I am a Democrat." His weekly syndicated column appeared on the front page of *The New York Times* and he made $500,000 a year during the Depression. He described himself as a poor-born "Injun cowboy," but his father actually was a prosperous rancher-politician in the Oklahoma territory. Billed as "the Cherokee Kid"—the man who could lasso the tail off a blowfly—Rogers drifted into show business—in South Africa—and presently was a vaudeville star in the United States. "The Senate passed a bill appropriating $15 million for food, but the House of Representatives has not approved it. They must think it would encourage hunger." On his tombstone is his best-remembered remark: "I never met a man I didn't like."

ROLLER COASTERS

Americans have been screaming their heads off on roller coasters for more than a hundred years. The first was opened in Coney Island on June 16, 1884, by the millionaire-inventor of seamless hosiery, La Marcus Thompson—his Switchback was strictly a gravity ride 600 feet in a straight line. The 1920s was the golden age of the roller coaster—more than 1,500 were built—the thriller's had its ups and downs since then. One expert believes that the Cyclone at Coney Island's Astroland is the best roller coaster because of how it drops and how the turns are put together, the element of surprise. The highest and hence fastest and also the longest roller coaster in the world is at King's Island near Cincinnati —"The Beast" is exactly that, two drops of 141 feet and 135 feet and a top speed of 64.77 miles per hour. Eeeeeeeeeeeeeeeeeeeee-EEEEEEEEE

ROLLER DERBY

A big wheel in the promotion of six-day bicycle races in Chicago, in 1935, the sports entrepreneur Leo Seltzer sketched out on a restaurant's checkered tablecloth his ideas for a new sport that would be on roller skates. The first version of Roller Derby was an endurance race over several days on a banked track. In the Trans-Continental Roller Derby, twenty-five teams of two skaters each (a man and a woman) skated the equivalent of the distance between New York and San Francisco; mileage was posted on a gigantic map of the United States. It has been said that a participant in a roller derby should have the quickness and the endurance of a speed skater, the reflexes of a skilled martial artist, the flexibility and the acrobatic skills of a gymnast, and the physical strength of a football player or a hockey player. Among the outstanding women skaters were Gerry Murray and Midge "Toughie" Brasuhn, Josephine "Ma" Bogash, and Joan Weston.

ROLLER SKATES

If he was like most inventors, Joseph Merlin was a pane in the glass to his friends. The Belgian is credited with the first patented roller skate (in 1760), but he soon shattered public interest in his wheeled invention by crashing into an expensive plate-glass mirror during a demonstration. In Paris in 1849, the composer Giacomo Meyerbeer commissioned Louis Legrange to put the cast of his opera *Le Prophete* on roller skates so they would look as though they were ice-skating outdoors. Each man's skate had only two wheels, in a line, with a space between; each woman's skate had two pair of wheels, one in front, one in back, Skates mounted on wooden rollers date from the 1860s, and J. L. Plimpton, of New York, made a roller skate in which one could actually turn. At the turn of the century, a Milwaukee inventor added ball bearings and installed round rubber cushions as shock absorbers. It is not known who suffered the first skinned knees, but it was probably that good-skate Merlin, the way *he* did things!

ROMAN NUMERALS

Symbols, they are a crude way of writing numbers: I, II, III, IV, V, VI. They seem to be related to the use of fingers in counting digits—the Latin *digitus* means "finger." V may be the open hand, X may be two open hands. There was no Roman numeral for zero. I stood for the figure 1, X stood for the figure 10. To get IX, both 1 and 10 had to be used. The day of the Roman numeral was numbered.

ROOD, FLOYD

A couple of decades ago, the retired fiftyish golf pro from Lake Charles, Louisiana, spent a year hopping out of and into a gas-engine golfmobile and driving a golf ball across the United States. He had figured that par would be 200,001. His first shot was a nine iron out of the Pacific waves at Santa Monica, California. His last, or 114,737th, shot was a drive into the world's second-largest water hole, the Atlantic, at Miami, Florida. At the very start of the sojourn, he was bitten by a black widow spider and spent seventeen days in hospital. Snakes were a hazard. A helicopter lowered him into the Grand Canyon so he could play through. It was all to raise funds for Rood's Youth in Sports Foundation, combating juvenile delinquency in Arizona City, Arizona.

ROOSEVELT, FRANKLIN D.—ASSASSIN'S TARGET

He almost didn't become the most elected President of the United States —the only President to be elected a third time *and* a fourth time. After running as the Democratic Party's Vice-Presidential nominee in 1920— James M. Cox and he lost to the Republicans' Warren G. Harding and Calvin Coolidge—F.D.R. was stricken with poliomyelitis and never walked again. In November 1932, he was elected President. Three months later—the inauguration was to be in March—he was shot at five times as he sat immobilized in an open touring car in Bay Front Park in Miami. Chicago Mayor Anton Cermak, sitting next to the President-elect, was killed and several people were injured. Mr. Roosevelt had just returned from an eleven-day fishing cruise on Vincent Astor's yacht *Nourmahal* and made a brief speech to the crowd gathered at dockside: "I am not going to attempt to tell you any fish stories, and the only fly in the ointment on this trip has been that I have put on about 10 pounds." A five-foot-one brick mason named Giuseppe Zangara who had been "in constant torment from a stomach operation" stepped on the running board of Roosevelt's car, shouted "Too many people are starving to death!" fired five shots from the $8 gun he had bought, was crushed by a policeman's nightstick, slumped to his knees, and rolled to the pavement. He later claimed that he had wanted to kill King Victor Emmanuel of Italy ten years earlier and President Herbert Hoover. In New York, Mrs. Eleanor Roosevelt, informed of the attack on her husband, said, "These things are to be expected," and, accompanied only by a maid, boarded a late-night railroad train for Ithaca, New York, and a speaking engagement. Zangara was electrocuted two weeks after F.D.R.'s first inauguration. It took 23 years for a commission to agree on both a site in the capital and an architectural plan for commemorating F.D.R.

ROOSEVELT, FRANKLIN D.—THIRD, FOURTH TERMS

The Twenty-second Amendment is known as the anti-F.D.R. amendment: No person shall be elected to the office of President more than twice, and no person who has held the office of President, or acted as President, for more than two years of a term to which some other person was elected President shall be elected to the office of President more than once. (Which also would have left out cousin Theodore Roosevelt, who succeeded the slain William McKinley in 1901 and was then elected in his own right three years later. He pledged he would retire at the end of a single full term, which he did, momentarily. He ran again in 1912, finishing second to Thomas Woodrow Wilson but ahead of the incumbent, William Howard Taft, who had been T.R.'s hand-picked successor.)

George Washington had planned to serve only one term but agreed to serve a second term (thereby setting the precedent) when his nonpartisan government seemed about to splinter. Washington has been named the greatest President of the United States. Abraham Lincoln has been named the second greatest; he had just begun his second term when he was murdered. The polio-stricken F.D.R. is considered to be the third greatest; his theme was "happy days are here again," and he pledged a new deal in the wake of the collapse of the stock market. He easily defeated Herbert Hoover in 1932 and swamped Alf Landon (523 electoral votes to 8) in 1936 and broke Washington's precedent by maneuvering successfully for a third term. He easily set back Wendell Willkie in 1940, then won a *fourth* term by defeating Thomas E. Dewey in 1944. He was the victim of a cerebral hemorrhage—"I have a terrific headache" were his last words; his long-time paramour, Lucy Mercer Rutherford, was nearby, in their retreat in Georgia—less than three weeks before Adolf Hitler committed suicide (poison, pistol) and Germany surrendered to bring the European phase of World War II to a close. In a fireside chat in 1934, Mr. Roosevelt had asked the American public, "Are you better off than you were last year? Are your debts less burdensome? Is your bank account more secure? Are your working conditions better? Is your faith in your own individual future more firmly grounded?"

ROOSEVELT, THEODORE

The only President born in New York City has also been the youngest to take office—he was only forty-two when he succeeded the assassinated William McKinley. He had been assured that McKinley was recovering from gunshot wounds. During the 1900 campaign, Roosevelt had stumped the country, delivering 673 speeches in 567 cities and towns. Old Rough and Ready lost the sight of his left eye during a boxing exercise in the White House. For mediating the peace treaty ending the Russo-Japanese war, he became the first American to be honored with the Nobel Peace Prize. For aesthetic reasons he tried to have the slogan "In God We Trust" removed from U.S. coins. He appointed the first Jewish cabinet member, Commerce and Labor Secretary Oscar S. Straus. Campaigning for the presidency on the Progressive, or Bull Moose, ticket in 1912, after four years out of office, "that damned cowboy" was shot while speaking in Milwaukee; he continued his speech for an hour before being treated by doctors. In 1913, he successfully sued a magazine editor for having called him a drunk in print. His mother and his first wife died on the very same day. "A really busy person never knows how much he weighs," the dynamic, rotund twenty-sixth President said. He wrote thirty-seven books. Among the titles: *African Game Trails. Life of Thomas Hart Benton. Through the Brazilian Wilderness. America and the World War.*

Hunting Trip of a Ranchman. The Foes of Our Own Household. History as Literature, and other Essays. The Naval War of 1812. The New Nationalism. Fear God and Take Your Own Part. T.R. spoke softly and carried a big pen.

ROOSEVELT, THEODORE—TEDDY BEAR

The twenty-sixth President was a favorite of cartoonists: He wore rimless glasses and had a bushy mustache, prominent teeth, and a jutting jaw. In 1905, he was drawn protecting a bear cub. Soon, toymakers were producing stuffed bear cubs that caught on as "teddy bears." In 1912, Old Gung Ho was the Bull Moose candidate for another presidential term; he lost.

ROSE BOWL

Fourteen years passed between the first postseason college football game in Pasadena, California, in 1902, and the second, but it's been played annually since 1916, the year before the United States entered World War I. But the Rose Bowl hasn't always been played in Pasadena. It was played once in Durham, North Carolina. It was less than a month after the Japanese sneak attack on Pearl Harbor and the United States entry into World War II. There was a fear that the Japanese would seize the distraction of the popular gridiron clash to attack the West Coast, maybe even Pasadena itself. North Carolina was considered to be out of harm's way, and so the game was shifted. Oregon defeated Duke, 20–16. Later that year, the state of Oregon *was* bombed. Nobuo Fujita took off from a Japanese submarine, *I-25*. A bomb ignited a forest fire on Mount Emily which was extinguished quickly by forestry personnel.

ROSE MARIE

Nelson Eddy the Canadian Mountie got his man—and a lady, Jeanette MacDonald, in the backwoods romance, "as blithely melodious and rich in scenic beauty as any picture" that had come from Hollywood up to 1936. The man who almost got away, an escaped prisoner who was the brother of Rose Marie, was played by Jimmy Stewart. A concerted effort and extremely pleasant concertizing against the magnificent back- and fore-grounds of mountain trails, shimmering lakes, and cloud-flecked skies: "Rose Marie, I Love You," "Song of the Mounties," "Indian Love Call." The stars also made beautiful music together in *Naughty Marietta, Maytime, New Moon,* and *Bitter Sweet.*

ROSE, PETE

Charlie Hustle (in every one of his record of more than 3,400 games played) is closing in on Ty Cobb's mark of 4,191 major league hits. He starts the 1985 season 94 hits shy of a tie. In 1978, Rose came within 12 games of tying Joe DiMaggio's historic consecutive-game hitting streak of 56 games as he set the National League record at 44. The three-time N.L. batting champion is the only baseballer to play at least 500 games at each of five different positions: first base, second base, third base, left field, and right field. He received $300,000 in severance pay when he was let go by the Philadelphia Phillies after the 1983 World Series.

ROSENCRANTZ AND GUILDENSTERN ARE DEAD

The witty, erudite British dramatist Tom Stoppard wasn't the first to have fun with *Hamlet*. Mark Twain's biographer Justin Kaplan has noted that Twain wanted to write a burlesque without altering the text: "His solution was to invent an extra character who made humorous comments on the other characters but was totally ignored by them. The character he hit upon . . . was a subscription book salesman named Basil Stockmar (the last name borrowed from Victoria and Albert's *éminence grise*) whose mother was supposed to have been Hamlet's wet nurse. 'They're on the high horse all the time,' Basil mutters about court life at Elsinore. 'They swell around and talk the grandest kind of book-talk, and look just as if they were on exhibition.' " The project died aborning. Twain came to believe that Shakespeare was merely another claimant, not the author of the tragedy (1601). Stoppard took two nonentities—two of Hamlet's school friends—and elevated them to the center of dramatic action. Guildenstern: "Death followed by eternity . . . the worst of both worlds. It *is* a terrible thought." The idea that was the impetus for *Rosencrantz* (entitled in its earliest form *Rosencrantz and Guildenstern Meet King Lear*) came from Stoppard's new agent, Kenneth Ewing.

ROSETTA STONE

On permanent display in the London Museum, it is a basalt slab, about a meter high, that was inscribed in the spring of the year 196 B.C. with the same message in hieroglyphic, demotic, and Greek by priests of Ptolemy V and unearthed in 1799 by a French soldier working on the fortification of the north Egyptian city of Rashid in the Nile River delta. The French Egyptologist Jean François Champollion, fluent in ancient Greek, could read that the stone had been inscribed to commemorate Ptolemy's coronation. Through his knowledge of Greek, Champollion established the principles for deciphering the Egyptian hieroglyphics. (By the age of thirteen, Champollion had mastered Greek, Latin, Hebrew, Arabic, Syrian, Chaldean, and Coptic, the Greek-based language of the early Egyptian Christians.) In his presentation of what he calls "encyclopaedia galactica," Carl Sagan says what a joy it must have been for Champollion to walk the Great Hypostyle Hall at Karnak and casually read the inscriptions, which had mystified everyone else, ". . . what a joy it must have been to open this one-way communication channel with another civilization, to permit a culture that had been mute for millennia to speak of its history, magic, medicine, religion, politics, and philosophy." Sagan himself is seeking messages from another ancient and exotic civilization, this time hidden from us not only in time but also in space.

THE ROYAL AND ANCIENT GOLF CLUB, ST. ANDREWS

The most famous golf layout is a links, not a course. A golf links is eighteen holes adjacent to a major body of water; in the case of St. Andrews, the North Sea. A golf course is eighteen holes totally surrounded by land; it may touch a lake or a river. Golf's earliest surviving written rules were drawn by St. Andrews linksmen for their inaugural competition, in 1754. At first, they played eleven holes out, then played the same eleven in reverse order, a round of twenty-two. In 1764, the first four holes were reduced to two and a round became eighteen, which it is to this day. The public may play at St. Andrews but not enter the clubhouse. (One of the charges that teed off the English tribunal against Mary Queen of Scots; she had been observed playing golf within days of the murder of her husband, Darnley.) Scottish officers played golf in America in 1779.

RUBBER

The geographer Charles La Condamine discovered a peculiar tree sap called caoutchouc during an amazing exploration of the Amazon territory in South America in the early eighteenth century and shipped quantities back home to France. The controversial English chemist Joseph Priestley gave it a utilitarian name when he observed that it could be used to rub out pencil marks like all get out. By the turn of the century, Paris had the world's first rubber factory. (Long before La Condamine and Priestley, the German mystical theologian Meister Eckhart perceptively noted, "Only the hand that erases can write the true thing.") La Condamine also discovered and introduced curare into Europe. Priestley, breathing the air 'round Tom Paine, discovered dephlogisticated air, or oxygen, carbon as an electrical conductor, and seltzer water.

RUBY, JACK

The "schwanz who yearned to be a mensch" lay dying in Dallas, in January 1967. He had a blood clot in the lungs and extensive adeno-carcinoma, which had spread through the body's ducts and cavities. No matter the award promised to his heirs, Lee Harvey Oswald's murderer stuck to his story: He had not known Oswald, he simply had made an illegal turn behind a bus and found himself in the parking lot of the Dallas jail, he was not part of a conspiracy, he had no recollection of the moment he killed the handcuffed Oswald—"It happened in such a blur . . . before I knew it . . . the officers had me on the ground." He demanded to be given a lie detector test, so he could prove that he had acted alone in the slaying of President John F. Kennedy's assassin, but his physical condi-tion (it was said) precluded the examination. Ruby had been sentenced to death in the electric chair. The conviction was reversed and he was being held in the Dallas County jail awaiting retrial, probably in Wichita Falls, when he became fatally ill. As a teenager, he had been a message-runner for Al Capone, the Chicago gangster. In Dallas, Ruby operated sleazy nightclubs and, for fun, pistol-whipped drunks.

RUDOLPH, WILMA

She was crippled as a child. She had been stricken with scarlet fever and double pneumonia, and couldn't walk without braces until she was eleven years old. As a sixteen-year-old, she ran to a bronze medal in the Olym-pics; as a twenty-year-old, in 1960, in Rome, she became the first Amer-ican woman to win three gold medals in Olympic track and field: 100-meter and 200-meter dashes and the anchor leg of the 400-meter relay.

RUGBY

Scrum, or huddle, is a play in rugby in which the forwards of each side crouch side by side, typically in 3–2–3 formation. With locked arms the two front lines meet shoulder to shoulder. Play starts by the placing of the ball between the front lines of the two sides. The hooker is a player in the front row of the scrum who hooks the ball and tries to gain posses-sion of it for his team. He is the only player who can use his foot to hook the ball out of the scrum. The scrum-half puts the ball into scrums and, when it is hooked, or heeled, gives it to his stand-off half, who will run and get the three-quarter backs under way. Frequently, the fullback is involved in three-quarter movements. (This may be why rugby has not been popular in some parts of the United States.)

RUGBY—NORTH DAKOTA

From Rugby, a little town in north-central North Dakota, you would need to travel 1,500 miles north to reach the Arctic archipelago, 1,500 miles south to reach the Gulf of Mexico, 1,500 miles to the east to reach the Atlantic Ocean, or 1,500 miles to the west to reach the Pacific Ocean. Rugby, some 54 miles from the Canadian border, is the geographic center of the North American continent. There's a stone cairn there to mark ground zero. (Central America is not part of the North American continent nor part of the South American continent. It's an isthmus connecting the two.)

RUNYON, DAMON

He was born in Manhattan—Kansas—and became the voice of Manhattan—New York—his favorite New York hangout was Lindy's restaurant, called Mindy's in his stories about the guys and dolls of Broadway and the track. His movie scripts included *Little Miss Marker* (Shirley Temple) and *Lemon Drop Kid*. He was only fourteen years old when he served in the Spanish-American War. He was a sports reporter—he relished heavyweight championship fights—and a war correspondent: the revolution in Mexico in 1912, World War I. Runyon was right: When you see a guy reach for stars in the sky, you can bet that he's doing it for some gal.

RUSSELL, BILL

One of professional basketball's greatest stars isn't in the Hall of Fame. He refused induction. He apparently wants nothing to do with the honor because he and other black players long suffered discrimination at the hands of white coaches, owners, and the public. The Hall says he has given no explanation. A tremendous shot-blocker and rebounder, Russ led the University of San Francisco to fifty-five straight court victories and the Boston Celtics to eight straight National Basketball Association championships and to ten in all. From 1965 to 1969, he was also the Celtics' playing coach, the first black to skipper a major professional team in the history of U.S. sport. He was the N.B.A.'s most valuable player six times.

477

RUTH, BABE

When the eager youth reported to manager Jack Dunn of the minor league baseball team the Baltimore Orioles, in 1914, someone piped up, "Well, here's Jack's newest babe now." So George Herman Ruth became Babe Ruth. He was not an orphan, but he did live in St. Mary's Industrial School, an institution staffed by brothers of a Catholic teaching order in Baltimore. The Sultan of Swat's hitting heroics helped to boost the national pastime's integrity in the wake of the "Black Sox" scandal of 1919. His 44-ounce "Black Betsy" belted 714 home runs. When Japanese soldiers attempted to storm U.S. Marine lines on Cape Gloucester, New Britain, in April 1944, they charged to their deaths with the battle cry "To hell with Babe Ruth!"

RYAN, CORNELIUS

More than 1,000 Allied and German survivors, French underground workers, and civilians were the principal sources of information for his book about D-Day, the invasion of Europe by Allied forces on June 6, 1944, *The Longest Day.* "Believe me, Lang," German Field Marshal Erwin Rommel said to his aide in April 1944, "the first twenty-four hours of the invasion will be decisive . . . the fate of Germany depends on the outcome . . . for the Allies, as well as Germany, it will be the longest day." Ryan believed that the D-Day casualties will forever remain estimates: Americans—6,603, including 1,465 killed; the Canadians, 946 casualties; the British, at least 2,500 to 3,000 casualties. The German total ranged from 4,000 to 9,000. Ryan wrote two more books about the Allied defeat of Nazi Germany: *A Bridge Too Far,* about the battle at Arnhem, where over twice as many Allied soldiers fell than during Operation Overlord at Normandy, and *The Last Battle,* about the taking of Berlin.

S

SACCHARIN

I. Remsen and C. Fahlberg accidentally discovered $C_7H_5NSO_3$ in 1879. The white, crystalline, aromatic compound has no nutritive value. In its pure form the artificial sweetener tastes several hundred times as sweet as sugar. It contains no carbohydrates. Its sodium salt is what's sold commercially.

SADE, DONATIEN ALPHONSE FRANÇOISE, COMTE DE

The pervert said, "The ground over my grave shall be sprinkled with acorns so that all trace of my grave shall disappear so that, as I hope, this reminder of my existence may be wiped from the memory of mankind." Sade will be too much with us always. If you inflict pain upon a love object as a means of obtaining sexual release, you are practicing sadism. If you get satisfaction of outwardly directed destructive impulses as a source of libidinal gratification, you are sadistic. Anal sadism, id sadism, oral sadism, larval sadism, phallic sadism, and bondage and discipline are right up the sadist's alley. "Because both sexual deviation and criminal acts exist in nature," Sade averred, "they are therefore natural." The deranged French writer was in the Seven Years' War, and he spent twenty-seven years in confinement in various institutions for sexual offenses. He took his last mistress when he was seventy-two years old and incarcerated again; she was fifteen. He was said to have persuaded her to shave her pubic hair, for the thrill of one last sexual aberration. It was a sade, sade day for masochists when the eponym went the way of all flesh.

SAFFRON

The costliest spice in the world, about $70 an ounce. It takes the stigmas (pistil tips) of 75,000 *Crocus sativus* blossoms to make a single pound when dried. It is native to the Mediterranean area, and is widely used in

479

French, Spanish, and South American cookery. Saffron is an essential ingredient in *arroz con pollo, paella,* and *bouillabaisse.* Homer knew its golden hue: "a saffron-robed morning." Constantine presented a gift of saffron to the Bishop of Rome. The crocus can also be employed medicinally.

SAGAN, CARL

His earliest extensive set of memories is from age four, when he was taken to the 1939 World's Fair in New York. When he was twelve, his grandfather asked him what he wanted to be when he grew up. The boy answered, "An astronomer." His grandfather then asked, "But how will you make a living?" "Even today," Sagan has written, "there are moments when what I do seems to me like an improbable, if unusually pleasant, dream: To be involved in the exploration of Venus, Mars, Jupiter, and Saturn; to try to duplicate the steps that led to the origin of life four billion years ago on an Earth very different from the one we know; to land instruments on Mars to search there for life; and perhaps to be engaged in a serious effort to communicate with other intelligent beings, if such there be, out there in the dark of the night sky." He believes that in half a century the preliminary reconnaissance of the solar system, the search for life on Mars, and the study of the origin of life will be completed. In 1975 he received the Joseph Priestley Award "for distinguished contributions to the welfare of mankind," and in 1978 the Pulitzer Prize for literature. In a remarkable 13-part television series, he reminded his millions of viewers that the cosmos is all that is or ever was or ever will be. He shares a birth date with Edmund Halley.

SAHARA

From the Arabic word *sahra* meaning "desert"—it is about 3.5 million square miles, slightly smaller than the area of the United States, 3,500 miles across northern Africa from the Atlantic Ocean to the Red Sea, 1,200 miles from north to south, touching twelve countries in all. Some dunes are as high as sixty-story buildings. The annual rainfall average is less than eight inches. About 4000 B.C., the climate was wet. Daytime temperatures are high. The highest official temperature ever recorded in the shade was 136°F. in Azizia, Libya, in September 1922. But it's a dry heat: Relative humidity is often in the 4 percent to 5 percent range. There are major deposits of oil and natural gas under the desert in Libya and Algeria.

SAINT ANDREW

He is the patron saint of Scotland, and Scots have organized Saint Andrew's societies dedicated to helping the poor. He is also the patron saint of Russia and Greece. His feast day is November 30. One of the twelve disciples, and the brother of Peter, he is said to have been a missionary in Asia Minor, Macedonia, and southern Russia. He was martyred at Patras, in Greece, and may have died on an X-shaped cross—Saint Andrew's cross. Scotland's oldest university is the University of Saint Andrews, founded in 1411, and the community of Saint Andrews on the East Coast between Edinburgh and Dundee is the world capital of golf—the Royal and Ancient Golf Club was founded there in 1754 and established many of the rules for the sport.

SAINT CHRISTOPHER

Christopher in Greek: "Christ bearer." William Caxton's *Golden Legend* made famous the patron saint of travelers and protector of all against perils from water and storms: "Christopher before his baptism was named Reprobus, but afterwards he was named Christopher, which is as much as to say bearing Christ, for that he bare Him in four manners: he bare Him on his shoulders by conveying, in his body by making it lean, in mind by devotion, and in his mouth by confession and preaching." Little is definitely known about him, not even his exact dates. He may have suffered martyrdom in Asia Minor in the third century. His name was dropped from the liturgical calendar in 1969.

SAINT GEORGE

He is the patron saint of both England and Portugal. By the 1300s, he had replaced Edward the Confessor as England's most popular saint. The facts of his life are hidden in legend. He may have been born in Lydia of Cappadocian parents, he may have been a soldier. It is said his open profession of Christianity led to his arrest, torture, and murder, in Nicomedia in 303 A.D., on April 23, which is his feast day. Saint George was highly venerated by the Crusaders. The red cross of Saint George on a white background appears in the British Union flag.

ST. LOUIS

The United States won seventy of the seventy-five medals awarded in track and field in the 1904 Olympics in the Missouri city. Few foreign nations had sent representatives. Archie Hahn, a football star at the University of Michigan, won three sprints: 60, 100, and 200 meters. Harry Hillman and James Lightbody also won three golds in track. The United States won all seven golds in boxing. Los Angeles is the only other U.S. city to host the Olympics: in 1932 and again in 1984. Denver refused by referendum—it didn't want Colorado torn up—to be the host city for the XII Winter Olympics; the Games were held in Innsbruck. (Denver is now the Smog Capital of the country.)

SAINT NICHOLAS

The most popular non-Biblical saint in Christendom, he is the patron of children, sailors, merchants, bankers, thieves, scholars, Greece, Sicily, Russia, and New York City. Traditionally, he is identified as a fourth-century bishop of Myra in Asia Minor. His relics were stolen from Myra in the Middle Ages and removed to Bari, Italy. In southern Italy in the early eighteenth century, wives wishing to get rid of their husbands used phials of poison inscribed "Manna of Saint Nicholas of Bari." Saint Nicholas legends have been said to represent sexual dream symbolism. The English in colonial New York adopted from the Dutch the now unrecognizable saint, calling him Santa Claus, a contraction of the Dutch Sint Nikolaas, and moved St. Nicholas's feast day, December 6, to the English gift holiday, Christmas. Fat and jolly are recently acquired characteristics.

SAINT VALENTINE

Greeting-card companies will always love Esther A. Howland. In the 1840s, she produced the first commercial valentine greeting cards and Americans took them to their hearts. February 14 is the feast day of the Roman martyr-priest, who died in 270 A.D. In medieval days, St. Valentine's martyrdom came to be associated with the union of lovers under conditions of duress.

SALIVA

The watery fluid is secreted by glands in and behind the mouth and is discharged into the mouth to aid in tasting, chewing, and swallowing, and in the digestion of starchy foods. And then what happens to make possible the passage of masticated (chewed) food from the mouth through the throat and the esophagus (gullet) and into the stomach? Dr. Morris Fishbein has summarized the complicated reflex of swallowing: It begins under the control of the brain by muscular action and then is propelled the rest of the way automatically. The mouth cavity is shut off by the position of the tongue against the hard palate and by the contractions of the muscles in the upper part of the throat. The nasal cavity is shut off by elevation of the soft palate against the postnasal openings. The opening into the larynx (voice box) is closed by the vocal cords and the epiglottis (trap door of the larynx), to keep the food from getting into the lungs. The passage through the gullet is entirely automatic, propelled by the wavelike contractions of its muscles.

SALK, JONAS

The director of the Salk Institute for Biological Studies, at the University of California, San Diego, developed a vaccine against poliomyelitis from killed monkey virus. A year earlier, in 1952, a polio epidemic had struck more than 50,000 Americans and killed 300. The immunologist believes that man needs to become increasingly conscious of the whole of which he is a part, as a species, so that he may function fully, though individually, and in a more healthful way as an element in that whole: This consciousness can be applied to the larger spectrum of man's concerns. Dr. Salk is married to one of Picasso's former wives.

SALT

The importance of salt to your life should not be taken with a—well, with a grain of salt. It is a vital constituent in your internal sea. Its concentration in the extracellular fluids—both the interstitial and the plasma—is enough to fill several salt shakers. Salt, or sodium chloride, is necessary for muscle contraction and for the digestion of proteins. It helps to regulate the flow of water between cells and the surrounding fluid. It is present in tears, saliva, breast milk, semen, and prostatic secretion. From antiquity salt has been venerated—and fought for—and taxed. It was once rare and expensive. Salt is mentioned tens of times in the Bible. Jesus' Apostles were "the salt of the earth . . . the light of the world." The word "salary" comes from the Latin word for salt. The Confederacy suffered when salt sources were captured by Union forces. Dante observed, "Thou shalt prove how salt is the taste of another's bread and how hard is the way up and down another man's stairs."

SALVATION ARMY

"One unending slum"—that's how Jack London was to describe London's East End, where the Methodist minister "General" William Booth in the 1860s initiated his nonsectarian Christian organization for evangelical and philanthropic work. The East London Revival Society was renamed the Christian Mission, then the Salvation Army. Its "warfare against evil" called for uniforms. There are officers and soldiers, and men and women share rank and responsibility equally. Members believed they are "saved to save." Their motto is "blood and fire." Unquestioned obedience is required in the ranks. The sacrament of baptism is not essential to salvation. The "war cry" is preached in nearly 200 languages. Booth's daughter Evangeline had read the Bible eight times before she was a teenager. In 1934, she became "general" of the International Salvation Army. Displaced persons have come under the wing of the Army.

SAN ANDREAS FAULT

With its branches and related faults, the principal crustal discontinuity in the broad transform zone where the Pacific plate moves relatively northwest with respect to the North American continent causes tremors and sometimes severe earthquakes from Point Arena, north of San Francisco, to the southern part of California, about 600 miles. The crust is moving at rates between three-quarters of an inch to two inches every year.

SANCHO PANZA

In Cervantes' original, Sancho Panza's donkey didn't have a name. Smollet's translation of *Don Quixote* called it Dapple. Panza in Spanish means "paunch." Panza is a paunchy, runty rustic who is persuaded by promises of the governorship of an island to become squire and attendant to the Knight of the Sorrowful Countenance. He is the best drawn of the 669 characters in the 461,000-word classic. He gets his island, but abdicates upon news of the approach of a hostile army. Sancho Panza was known for his common sense. The long-winded Don Quixote roamed the world tilting at windmills, righting wrongs, wronging wrights. The name of *his* nag was Rocinante.

SANDBURG, CARL

The poet-balladeer-historian wrote six volumes, a million and a half words, on Lincoln—"and I don't know yet what to make of him," the biographer admitted. Edward R. Murrow asked Sandburg why he had spent so much time with the sixteenth President. "Oh, the straight-off simplest answer to that is: because he was such good company . . . he still is good to brood about. He still has laughter and tears that are good for a fellow. . . . He was pre-eminently a laughing man, and he used to say that a good story was medicine." He read to Murrow what someone else had written about why Lincoln lasts: "There is no new thing to be said about Lincoln. There is no new thing to be said of the mountains or of the sea or of the stars. The years go their way but the same old mountains lift their granite shoulders above the drifting clouds. The same mysterious sea beats upon the shore. The same silent stars keep holy vigil above a tired world. But to the mountains and sea and stars, men turn forever in unwearied homage. And thus with Lincoln, for he was a mountain in grandeur of soul. He was a sea in deep undervoice of mystic loneliness. He was a star in steadfast purity of purpose and services. And he abides." Murrow asked Sandburg if he would rather be known as a poet, a biographer, a historian—or what? "I'd rather be known as a man," Sandburg said. "What I need mainly is three things in life, possibly four: To be out of jail, to eat regular, to get what I write printed, and then a little love at home and a little outside."

SAN FRANCISCO

It's been San Francisco, in honor of St. Francis of Assisi, since being seized in 1846 by a naval force under U.S. Commodore John D. Sloat in the Mexican War. Before that, the settlement in California was Yerba Buena. The name Puerto de San Francisco was applied late in the sixteenth century to the area and to an uncertainly located bay. A mission founded in 1770 was similarly named. San Fernando, in California, got its name from the mission dedicated in 1797 to St. Ferdinand (i.e., King Ferdinand III of Spain). San Jose—for the husband of the Virgin Mary. San Juan Capistrano—the mission was dedicated to St. John Capistran, the Franciscan hero of the siege of Vienna in 1456.

SAN FRANCISCO—QUAKE-FIRE

The forty-eight-second earthquake was bad enough (8.3 on the Richter scale of 9) when the San Andreas fault settled violently, horizontally *and* vertically, at 5:13 A.M. on April 18, 1906—tall structures, ribbed and rocked with steel, swayed like trees in a windstorm . . . there was a sickening sensation as if everything were toppling . . . heavy furniture moved about and banged upon the floor; and then the brick walls gave way . . . the earth tremors increased in violence . . . the ornate city hall came tumbling down, 15 million gallons of wine burst—but it was the

485

three-day fire that followed that all but destroyed the city: The center of San Francisco burned down—an area of 521 blocks, 28,188 buildings. Three hundred and fifteen people known dead, 352 forever unaccounted for. Part of the city was destroyed to save it: Dynamite blasted to rubbish the long line of mansions at Van Ness Avenue—the fire line there held, the tide was turned. For two months, San Francisco was the best-behaved city in the world, the phoenix had to rise again. But with the opening of makeshift saloons, things began to return to normal. Enrico Caruso and Jack London were in the city when the quake struck. In 1851, two fires had destroyed 2,000 buildings and killed about 30 persons.

SAN MARINO

The world's smallest and "most serene" republic, 23.5 square miles, a population of 22,000, landlocked in the calf of the Italian boot, the last of the independent secular republics that once existed in Italy. Its main sources of income are the sale of postage stamps and tourism. In 1861, President Abraham Lincoln was made an honorary citizen. (Twice, Lincoln offered generalship of a Union army to Giuseppe Garibaldi and twice the redshirted legendary hero of the Italian Risorgimento—he had once lived in Staten Island, New York—turned down the President's appeal.)

SAN SIMEON

William Randolph Hearst owned eighteen newspapers in twelve cities, and nine magazines. His penny journalism, his "yellow" journalism, helped to drive the United States into the Spanish-American War of 1898. (Almost as many American servicemen were blown up on a Sunday in Beirut in 1983 as were killed when the battleship *Maine* exploded mysteriously in Havana Harbor, the spark that ignited the war.) He was a Congressman, 1903–07, and a failed aspirant for both the mayorship of New York City and the governorship of New York State. The magnate ran his newspaper empire from his castle, San Simeon, in California, the largest monument to one man since Cheops. It was spread over 200,000 acres, with 50 miles of ocean front. It had the largest art collection ever owned by one man and a zoo that rivaled Noah's. It is said that everybody who was anybody—that included Bernard Shaw, Winston Churchill, President Calvin Coolidge—dropped by for a look and a drink. Hearst was a teetotaler and allowed only one drink per person in the Assembly Room before dinner. San Simeon was the model for Orson Welles's Xanadu in the motion picture *Citizen Kane,* as Hearst was the model for Welles's Charles Foster Kane. "In Xanadu did Kubla Khan A stately pleasure-dome decree: Where Alph, the sacred river, ran Through caverns measureless to man Down to a sunless sea. So twice five miles of fertile ground With walls and towers were girdled round: And there were gardens bright with sinuous rills Where blossom'd many an incense-bearing tree: And here were forests ancient as the hills, Enfolding sunny spots of greenery.''

SANTA CLAUS'S REINDEER

The eight that fly like the down on a thistle are listed only once in Clement Moore's poem "A Visit from Saint Nicholas": "More rapid than eagles, his coursers they came, and he whistled and shouted and called each by name: 'Now, Dasher, now, Dancer, Now, Prancer, now, Vixen! On, Comet! On, Cupid! On, Donner and Blitzen!' ''

SANTA MARIA

Christmas Eve 1492. The sea was as calm "as a mirror." Columbus was tired. The crew was tired. They retired, entrusting the helm to a lad. The flagship ran into the north coast of Hispaniola and toppled over. Local Indians helped the Admiral of the Ocean Sea unload and move quarters to the *Niña*: "So loving, so tractable, so peaceable are these people," Columbus wrote in his journal, "that I swear to your majesties there is not in the world a better nation, nor a better land. They love their neighbor as themselves, and their discourse is ever sweet and gentle, and accompanied with a smile; and though it is true that they are naked, yet their manners are decorous and praiseworthy." They were "nature's Christians." The *Santa Maria* was turned into a fortress which Columbus named La Natividad, or the Nativity, commemorating the birth of Christ. It was commanded by aide Diego de Arana and manned by thirty-seven sailors left behind. The *Niña,* its souvenirs including six red men, raced Martin Alonzo Pinzon's *Pinta* through the winter storms of the Atlantic to be first to announce in the Old World news of the New World. When Columbus returned to Hispaniola, he found none of his former crew— they had vanished.

SÃO PAULO

The capital of the tropical, coffee-wealthy state of São Paulo in southeast Brazil—and the largest city in South America (the population is more than 5 million)—is three times bigger than Paris. The traffic pattern is exasperating; it is necessary at times to drive ten blocks out of the way to reach a point half a block away. It was founded by Jesuit priests in

1554 and served as the base for *bandeiras* (expeditions) seeking Indian slaves and mineral wealth in the Brazilian interior.

SATURN

The sixth planet from the Sun—the mean distance is about 886 million miles—takes nearly thirty years to spin around the Big Broiler. Rings of billions of tiny ice-coated rocks that circle Saturn are about ten miles thick. (There are also rings around Uranus and Jupiter.) The volume of Saturn is more than 700 times the volume of Earth, and its mass is nearly 100 times that of Earth. It is the only one of the nine planets with a density less than that of water. The largest of Saturn's ten moons is Titan, the only satellite in the solar system that holds a dense atmosphere; prebiological organic chemistry may be in progress. Because of a moderately dense atmosphere and low gravity, Titan might be the easiest object for a spaceship to land on in the Universe.

SAVAK

An acronym of the Persian words Sazeman Etelaat va Amniat Keshvar —Security and Information Organization. Iran's brutally repressive secret police force was founded by General Teymour Bakhtiar when Parliament, responding to American pressure, enacted the secret police law in 1956 to keep misguided Iranians in line. Bakhtiar was the son of a noble khan of the Bakhtiari tribes and educated in French lycées and at Saint Cyr. He was murdered in 1970—by SAVAK agents. SAVAK torture: a soft-drink bottle forced up the rectum, electric prods on the genitals, skull-squeezers, shoulder-breaking weights, rape in front of family members, and the bedspring tour de force—the victim was tied to bedsprings that were then heated from warm to hot to searing. Before Ayatollah Ruhollah Khomeini's revolution brought down the Shah and broke up SAVAK, *Hamlet* could not be taught in Iranian schools because it dealt with the killing of kings. The spies and informers and torturers were so busy ferreting out the "Communists" whom Muhammad Reza Shah Pahlevi presumed were his foes that they did not hear, or report, the bubbling discontent in the mosques.

SCALLOP

It can swim, it can leap about by snapping its limy, hinged shells, which are controlled by a powerful adductor muscle, the only part of the marine bivalve mollusk that is eaten. A close relative of the oyster, the scallop has rows of steely blue "eyes." The common scallop is about two inches long and is more common on the East Coast of the United States than on the West Coast. Giant scallops of up to five inches in length are found in deep waters from Labrador to New Jersey.

SCHMELING, MAX

First, Jesse Owens kicked up his heels. Two years later, Joe Louis dealt the knockout blow to Adolf Hitler's thesis on the superiority of the Aryan race. The Brown Bomber kayoed Germany's heavyweight champion, and former world champion, in the very first round of their return bout in 1938. Two years earlier, Schmeling had scored a 12-round knockout, the first time that Louis was beaten. During World War II, Schmeling was a Nazi paratrooper. When he jumped on Crete, with the First Battalion Pararegiment, he suffered such a severe case of diarrhea that he had to be hospitalized.

SCIENCE FICTION AWARDS

The Nebula and the Hugo are awarded annually for excellence in science fiction writing. The Nebula is given by the Science Fiction Writers of America. The Hugo is named for the founder (in 1926) of the first sci-fi periodical, "Amazing Stories," Hugo Gernsbach. His novel *Ralph 124C 41 +* is considered to be a classic of predictive sci-fi. Published in 1925 and set in A.D. 2660, the book predicted televised phone calls, space flight, artificial cloth, sound movies, voiceprints used for identification, wireless power transmission, synthetic milk and foods, sliding doors that are automatically controlled. Gernsbach also predicted that most instruction would be absorbed by pupils while asleep, complete weather control, antigravity machines, streets fashioned of stainless steel alloys, the disappearance of money as a means of exchange, and invisibility machines.

SCOPES, JOHN T.

The American Civil Liberties Union advertised for someone willing to help challenge the new Tennessee law forbidding the teaching of Darwin's theory of evolution in contradistinction to the biblical interpretation of man's creation. A friendly, shy teacher of general science and coach of athletics volunteered. As I have noted in my book *America at Random,* Scopes never gave the lecture on evolution. The day that his class reached that part of the text, an athletic event kept him from teaching. Pupils who testified against him in the historic freedom-of-speech "monkey trial'' (1925) that ensued had to be crammed by the prosecution on what evolution was. When the case went on appeal before the Tennessee Supreme Court, Scopes was so engrossed in his studies of geology at the University of Chicago (where grateful scientists had established a scholarship for him) that he did not bother to return to the state. The higher court reversed the decision that Scopes be fined one hundred dollars. The Tennessee law that Scopes challenged was not repealed until forty years after the trial.

SCOTCH FOURSOME

A golf match. John and Jane vs. Dick and Dot. John and Jane have a ball. Dick and Dot have a ball. John and Jane take turns hitting their ball. Dick and Dot take turns hitting their ball. Very simple. Jane tees off and the ball goes 70 yards. John then hits the ball. See Jane then hit the ball. Roll, ball, roll. And so it goes—if all goes well. The name Scotch foursome has nothing to do with the nineteenth hole.

SCOTLAND YARD

It is not the headquarters of the national police force in England, my dear Watson. There is no national police force in England. Scotland Yard is the headquarters of the Criminal Investigation Department of the London Metropolitan Police. London's first police office was situated at No. 4, Whitehall Place. The rear entrance was along a narrow lane called Scotland Yard, and from that day to this day—even when today's New Scotland Yard is in Victoria Street—the headquarters of the C.I.D. of the Metropolitan Police has been called Scotland Yard. Before becoming a police center, it was the site of a palace used as a residence of visiting Scottish kings in the 1100s. The Black Museum of Scotland Yard—the term ''black'' was coined by a reporter who liked the negative emotionalism of it—was created as a detective training aid—to show today's investigators mementos of famous criminal cases and to prove that there may not be anything new under the sun.

SCOTT, GEORGE C.

The nominees for the best-actor Oscar in 1970 were Ryan O'Neal, George C. Scott, Jack Nicholson, James Earl Jones, and Melvyn Douglas, and the winner was George C. Scott, for *Patton*. He had announced that he didn't want the Oscar, it was ''degrading for actors to compete against one another," and he didn't show to receive it. In 1972, the nominees for the best-actor Oscar were Marlon Brando, Michael Caine, Laurence Olivier, Peter O'Toole, and Paul Winfield, and the winner was Marlon Brando, for *The Godfather*. He didn't want it, either. A starlet by the name of Maria Cruz, calling herself Sacheen Littlefeather, went to the stage and refused the Oscar for Brando, who wanted attention for his view that the American Indian did not get a fair shake in the visual media. Brando had accepted the best-actor Oscar in 1954 for *On The Waterfront*.

SCRIPPS INSTITUTE

Want to read how a tuna sees a net? Want to know the possibility of a helium flux through the ocean floor, the origin of manganese nodules on the ocean floor, data on speed and underwater exhalation of a humpback whale accompanying ship or about magnetic prospecting in southern California, the color of "pure" water, T phases from eighty Alaskan earthquakes? Subscribe to the scientific journal *Contributions* published by Scripps Institute of Oceanography, the world's largest institution of oceanography. (The Scripps is for the late newspaper publisher E. W. Scripps.) Its beginnings as a biological station were humble: a rented bathhouse for a lab, a gasoline launch for a ship, back in 1892. Today, its vessels and marine laboratories are the nucleus of the San Diego campus of the University of California. "Icing the pole or in the torrid clime, Dark—heaving—boundless—endless and sublime"—Byron, whose best friend drowned.

SCROOGE McDUCK

Donald's uncle, and Huey, Dewey, and Louie's great-uncle, is the world's richest duck, "the richest coot in the world." He plunges around in his money like a porpoise. "People that spend money," he quacks, "are saps. They don't know how to enjoy it." If he lost—he'd never *spend* them—a billion dollars a minute, he'd be broke in 600 years. "Great snakes!" First seen in a 1947 film, *Christmas on Bear Mountain,* Carl Barks's creation for Walt Disney was at first not the world's wealthiest duck. He was a decrepit, despicable old miser who grumbled and bah-humbugged about Christmas. "I just needed a rich uncle for the story that I was going to do," Barks has said. "I thought of this situation of Donald getting involved with a bear up in the mountains. Somebody had to own this cabin he was going to, so I invented Uncle Scrooge as the owner." Within a year, Uncle had new characteristics, a lucky dime, and 250 umtillion dollars—"gravy, boys!"

SEARS TOWER

There's nothing 5 & 10 about the tallest office building in the world, the national headquarters of Sears Roebuck & Co., in Chicago. 110 stories and the TV antennae on the roof make it 1,559 feet to the tippy-top. A gross area of 4.4 million-square feet—101 acres. 103 elevators. 18 escalators. 16,000 windows. The employee population is 16,700.

SECRETARIAT

It's a photo finish—which has been America's greatest race horse, Man o' War or Secretariat? Probably Man o' War, "Big Red," by a nose—he lost only one race, upset by Upset, at Saratoga in 1919, when he was roughly handled by a rookie starter. Secretariat made money in all but two of his twenty-one starts. He won the Triple Crown (1973) and set track records in the Belmont Stakes and the Kentucky Derby and probably in the Preakness as well—the clock in Baltimore malfunctioned. At Belmont in 1973 he set the thoroughbred record for the mile and a half with a breathtaking thirty-one-length whirlaway in 2 minutes 24 seconds. Man o' War was retired to stud for $5,000, a record at the time, and sired 379 foals, which won a total of 1,300 races. Secretariat raised the record stud price to $6,080,000.

SEOUL

The modern capital of South Korea will be the host city of the 1988 Olympics. In 1992, it will celebrate its 600th anniversary. Sights: three gates of the ancient wall that once surrounded the city and three imperial palaces and a gigantic bronze bell which was cast in 1468 and sits in the center of the city of 6 million. Seoul was the capital of the ruling Yi dynasty until Japan made Korea a colony in 1910; the Japanese governor general made the city his headquarters. Control of the city seesawed through the Korean War in the 1950s, and most of it was rubble when peace came.

SEQUOIA

The world's largest flora, with a trunk of 20 to 25 feet and a height of up to 385 feet. The evergreen tree was once widespread in temperate regions of the Northern Hemisphere, then nearly exterminated by ice sheets of the glacial ages. There are thirty-five groves in Sequoia National Park, in east central California. The sequoia is named for the Cherokee giant, Sequoyah—who was known as George Guess to most Americans and Sogwali to the Cherokee; missionaries pronounced him Sequoia. Out of his head, in a phenomenal achievement, he created the Cherokee syllabary, making the tribe literate. He was president of the Western Cherokee, serving as arbiter between his group and the Eastern Cherokee, who had been moved at gunpoint by U.S. troops to the Indian territory, now Oklahoma. Sequoyah loved his calumet.

SEVEN DEADLY SINS

Pride, avarice, lust, anger, gluttony, envy, and sloth—capital sins in theology, the wrongful desires or vicious affections that are the source and origin of habitual vice. Charles E. Sheedy, C.S.C., of Notre Dame University, has written that "these perverted desires, inclinations, or habits are basic to man's capacity for evil." There is no mention of them in the Bible, but in I John 2:16 all of the world's evil is attributed to "the lust of the flesh, the lust of the eyes, and the pride of life." Cardinal virtues are faith, hope, charity, courage, justice, temperance, and wisdom.

"THE SHADOW"

"The weed of crime bears bitter fruit. Crime does not pay. The Shadow knows." He laughs, and there is a commercial for Blue Coal. In the beginning of the radio mystery series, the Shadow served merely as the narrator. The Lamont Cranston character evolved in 1936. A mysterious wealthy man about town, Cranston—the Shadow—learned while in the Orient the secret of a hypnotic power to cloud men's minds so they could not see him. With this power, he aided the forces of law and order. Only one person knew criminologist Cranston's ability to become the Shadow —his lovely friend and companion, Margot Lane, no relation to Lois Lane. One of the four actors who knew "what evil lurks in the hearts of men" was Orson Welles. One of the actresses who played Margot Lane was Agnes Moorehead. Lamont's friend the cab driver, Shrevie, has been played by Keenan Wynn, and the Police Commissioner by Dwight Weist, Ken Roberts, and Kenny Delmar.

SHAH

Muhammad Reza Shah Pahlevi was shah (king) of Iran from 1941 to 1979, when he was booted off the Peacock Throne by the Muslim religious leader Ayatollah Ruhollah Khomeini. He had succeeded his father, who had refused to cooperate with the Allies during World War II and was forced to resign. Muhammad allowed the Allies to station troops in Iran and to send supplies through the country to the embattled Soviet Union. In the 1960s he began using oil revenues to promote social and economic development at the same time he was denying freedom of speech and using secret police and military force to silence opponents. Fleeing Iran, he became "the Flying Dutchman," a man without a country. When the United States admitted him for cancer treatments, Iranian radicals took hostage American officials in Teheran and held them for 444 days, until President Jimmy Carter was one minute out of office. The Shah died of cancer in Egypt, in 1980.

SHAKESPEARE

The Bard was a cunning linguist—coining words left and right to express his own special meanings in his own special passages. "Or to the dreadful summit of the cliff, That *beetles* o'er his base into the sea." (*Hamlet,* i.4.) "Beetle-brows," to express prominent brows, was an old epithet; Shakespeare framed the expressive verb "beetles" to indicate a cliff's summit that juts out prominently, that projects beyond its wave-worn base, like the head of a wooden beetle or mallet. "That, face to face and royal eye to eye, You have *congreeted*." (*Henry V,* i.2.) The single word expresses "greeted each other," "met together." "With *cadent* tears fret channels in her cheeks." (*Lear,* i.4.) From the Latin *cadens,* "falling," "trickling," "pouring down." Shakespeare used 17,677 different words in his plays, sonnets, and narrative poems, and he is the first known user of over 1,700 of them—in other words, one-tenth of his vocabulary was new to the language. Some examples: frugal, generous, laughable, lonely, majestic, courtship, aerial, hurry, monumental, road, lapse, assassination, pious, accommodation, apostrophe, castigate, perusal, seamy, submerge, critic. He also inspired dozens of titles of books, plays, and movies: *The Moon Is Down, Brave New World, Cakes and Ale, The Dogs of War, Call Me Madam, Fortune and Men's Eyes, Remembrance of Things Past, Something Wicked This Way Comes, The Sound and the Fury, Kiss Me Kate, Taken at the Flood,* and *Undiscovered Country.* Two of his thirty-eight plays were probably written in collaboration with John Fletcher: *Henry VIII* and *Two Noble Kinsmen.* The source of the latter was Chaucer's "The Knight's Tale." For someone with "small Latin and less Greek," Shakespeare is known as the world's greatest playwright.

SHAMROCK

The three leaves of what has become the national emblem of Ireland were used (according to legend) by St. Patrick to explain the doctrine of the Trinity. He had a vision that called him back to his native Ireland to Christianize it. He challenged paganism. He introduced the Roman alphabet. He modified the traditional laws of Ireland and mitigated the harsh ones that dealt with slaves and taxation of the poor. When the missionary died, in 461, after elevation to the bishopric of Ireland by Pope St. Leo I, the country was almost entirely Christian. There is no mention of the shamrock analogy in Jocelyn of Furness' twelfth-century biography of Christianity's most successful missionary, nor even in Patrick's own *Confessions*.

SHANGHAI

The largest city in the world (11,900,000 residents) was only a century and a half ago a sleepy fishing village near the East China Sea at the mouth of the 3,000-mile-long Yangtze River. A few thousand British marines and a few corrupt Chinese warlords opened China to a flood of opium via the port: It was like feeding poisoned milk to children. The white "barbarians" carved out choice areas for themselves: The French Concession and the International Settlement had their own laws and justice, and no Chinese (or dogs) were allowed. The metropolis was wicked, mysterious, debauched—the grossest of appetites could be gratified with impunity. Murderers, thieves, smugglers, slave traders, pirates, rum runners, gamblers, political dissidents, prostitutes by the thousands, and a million Chinese fleeing the Japanese army in the 1930s —the welcome mat was out for all. As I wrote in the nonfiction novel *Deliverance in Shanghai,* even 20,000 European Jews fleeing Hitler's lethal grip found refuge among his Asian ally; it wasn't until 1943 that they were forced by Hirohito's commanders into a square-mile ghetto in a Chinese slum. Noel Coward wrote *Private Lives* in four days in a hotel in Shanghai, and W. H. Auden and Christopher Isherwood enjoyed the baths there. Shanghai is a verb.

SHANNON RIVER

There once was a river named Shannon,
That rose in the Ulster county of Cavan,
    The longest in the Isles,

Brought a thousand smiles,
From the myriad who survived the great famine.
Waltzing through beautiful lakes (loughs), the Shannon at 240 miles is 30 miles longer than the British Isles' second longest river, the Thames. Limerick, the Republic of Ireland's third largest city, founded by Vikings, is on the 50-mile-long mouth of the Shannon at the Atlantic.

SHARIF, OMAR

"The only full-blooded romantic hero at present working in the English-speaking cinema" (wrote Kenneth Tynan) and "a movie star by an act of nature . . . a walking love scene" (Pauline Kael) wants to make enough money through acting so he can retire and play bridge for the rest of his life. "I bore so easily," the former Michael Shalhoub (of Syrian-Lebanese descent) has said, "so I taught myself to do something between scenes sitting around on movie sets and now I have become an expert on bridge." His bridge team was called "The Bridge Circus." He had excelled in mathematics, and his teachers in Egypt urged him to become a physicist; he went into the family lumber business. Egypt's movie queen, Faten Hamama, wanted him for *The Blazing Sun,* in 1952, and they discombobulated the Arab world by kissing on the silver screen; they also married. (The success of an Egyptian movie is determined by the amount of tears the audience sheds. A five-gallon picture is a smash.)

SHAW, GEORGE BERNARD

The greatest British playwright since Shakespeare, he was a master of English prose—on the stage and in his music and theater criticism. In 1925, he was awarded the Nobel Prize in Literature. His plays include *Heartbreak House, Back to Methuselah, Too True to Be Good, The Millionairess, Androcles and the Lion, Major Barbara* (poverty is the cause of all evil), *Mrs. Warren's Profession, Candida, The Devil's Disciple, Caesar and Cleopatra,* and, of course, *Pygmalion,* which became even better known when it was transformed into *My Fair Lady.* He was an ardent socialist. And he had some *piskt* on him: "I am a millionaire. That is my religion." "He who can, does. He who cannot, teaches." "There are two tragedies in life. One is not to get your heart's desire. The other is to get it." "One man that has a mind and knows it can always beat ten men who haven't and don't." "A lifetime of happiness? No man alive could bear it: It would be hell on earth." "Assassination is the extreme form of censorship." "With the single exception of Homer, there is no eminent writer, not even Sir Walter Scott, whom I can despise so entirely as I despise Shakespeare when I measure my mind against his. . . . It would positively be a relief to me to dig him up and throw stones at him." "The true artist will let his wife starve, his children go barefoot, his mother drudge for a living at seventy, sooner than work at anything but his art." "How can what an Englishman believes be heresy? It is a contradiction in terms."

SHEPARD, ALAN B.

At least we know who the first duffer on the Moon was—the fifth man on the Moon. The United States's first half-astronaut—he was the pioneer pilot in the Mercury program (1961)—had collected ninety-seven pounds of Moon stuff in the Fra Mauro area, in company with Edgar D. Mitchell, executed a heart-pounding ascent almost to the top of the 400-foot-high Cone Crater, and was back at the clubhouse, the lunar module *Antares*. There, he produced the head of a No. 6 golf iron and jury-rigged it to the handle of one of his tools. He "teed" up a golf ball, presently iron met ball and away it went. And went. And went.

SHIRER, WILLIAM L.

The literary critic Naomi Bliven has observed, "Some Americans—unfortunately, some in government—forget that freedom of the press and freedom of information and expression are not frills or electives or accessories; they are not privileges bestowed but rights essential to the working and the preservation of modern political democracy. [William L.] Shirer has produced an exceptionally powerful argument for these freedoms: In his prose, we live through what happens without them." He was an American foreign correspondent in Nazi Germany: In his Berlin diary, August 24, 1939, he wrote, "It may well be that Hitler will go into Poland tonight. Many think so. But I think that depends upon Britain and France. If they emphasize they will honor their word with Poland, Hitler may wait. And get what he wants without war. With Russia in his bag, Hitler is not compromising, apparently. Russia in his bag! What a *turn* events have taken in the last forty-eight hours. Bolshevik Russia and Nazi Germany, the arch-enemies of this earth, suddenly turning the other cheek and becoming friends and concluding what, to one's consternation, looks like an alliance. . . ." His thousand-page *The Rise and Fall of the Third Reich* was a best seller.

SHOEMAKER, WILLIAM LEE (WEE WILLIE)

Horse racing's winningest jockey—more than 8,000 first-place finishes and $90 million in prize money for his steeds—"the Shoe" weighed in at only two and a half pounds at birth and rode at just under 100 pounds. He began to ride at the age of seven, to work with racing horses at fourteen, and to win at eighteen, in 1949. He won the Kentucky Derby on Swaps in 1955, on Tommy Lee in 1959, on Lucky Debonair in 1965, but lost on Gallant Man in 1957 when he misjudged the finish line and stood up too soon. He was inducted into racing's Hall of Fame in 1958.

SHOES

It's best to buy a new pair of shoes in the afternoon. Otherwise, you're apt to put your foot in it. When you walk around, your feet begin to swell. In the afternoon, they are a bit bigger than they are in the morning. A pair of shoes bought for morning feet may be too small or tight for afternoon feet. On the other hand, shoes bought for afternoon feet can be worn comfortably by morning feet.

SHOGUN

The principal figure of John Blackthorne in James Clavell's novel and TV miniseries of seventeenth-century feudal Japan was inspired by the life of William Adams. As pilot of a Dutch ship, Adams was the first Englishman to visit the floating kingdom, in 1600. He became a retainer to the brilliant Tokygawa Ieyasu (Toranaga in the book), advising the lord on navigation, trade, and Western affairs. He was given the Japanese name Anjin Sama—Mr. Pilot. In the Clavell work the lord strives and schemes to seize ultimate power by becoming Shogun—the supreme military dictator—uniting warring sumarai fiefdoms. If lopped heads, severed torsos, assassinations, intrigue, war, tragic love, overrefined sex, excrement, torture, high honor, ritual suicide, hot baths, breathless haikus, and hundreds of italicized Japanese words are your cup of saki, the 500,000-word tome is irresistible, maybe unforgettable. The tone of the book was here and there way off course: A Dutch sailor says "Shut your face," when he isn't saying how he could use a cold beer. Japanese had also figured in the English-born American novelist's *King Rat*—they held American and Japanese POWs in a World War II camp in Southeast Asia.

SHREW

The smallest insectivorous mammal, the most plentiful mammal in the eastern United States, about two inches long, weighing no more than a few grams, it eats insects and slugs that harm crops, and even larger animals, such as mice, and starves to death if deprived of food for even half a day. No other animal has a higher metabolic rate; the heart of the masked shrew beats 800 times a minute. It is high-strung and nervous, and may die of shock from a sudden fright or a clap of thunder. Its array of teeth, in a sharp-pointed face, are formidable. The shrew lives everywhere except Australia, part of South America, and the polar regions.

SHRIVER, R. SARGENT

Democratic Presidential nominee George S. McGovern's first three choices for a Vice-Presidential running mate in the 1972 campaign turned him down: Florida Governor Reubin Askew, Senator Edward M. Kennedy, and Senator Abraham Ribicoff, who would have been the first Jew to be a candidate for the second highest national office. Senator Thomas F. Eagleton, of Missouri, accepted but was dumped after the convention when it was learned that he had undergone electric-shock therapy for mental depression. Sargent Shriver, Peace Corps director under President John F. Kennedy and JFK's brother-in-law, was chosen by the Presidential nominee and named by the Democratic National Committee. It was the Watergate campaign, and the Democratic ticket didn't have a chance—it won the electoral votes of only one state, Massachusetts, and the District of Columbia—even Senator McGovern's home state, South Dakota, and Shriver's, Maryland, didn't fall into line as Richard M. Nixon (with eighteen-to-twenty-year-olds voting for the first time) swept 61 percent of the popular vote. The President was viewed as more "open and trustworthy" than Senator McGovern.

SHROVE TUESDAY

It is the day before Ash Wednesday, the first day of Lent, the seventh Wednesday before Easter. It is a day of tumultuous celebration in Catholic countries. In New Orleans, carnival (from the Latin for "put away the meat") is the Mardi Gras (French for "Fat Tuesday"). "Shrove"— from the custom of confessing (being *shriven*) on that day. Shrove Tuesday in 1985 is on February 19; in 1986, February 11; in 1987, March 3.

SIAMESE TWINS

Today, they would be known as the Thai twins. Chang and Eng were the original Siamese twins, born in Siam of Chinese parents in 1811. Siamese twins are identical and physically joined, often sharing some internal organs. They remain attached at the abdomen, chest, back, or top of the head, depending on where the division of the ovum has failed. Some have been separated successfully by surgery. Chang and Eng were joined all their lives by a ligament from breastbone to navel. For many years they were on display in Barnum's circus. Each of them married and "between them" they fathered twenty-two children. At the age of sixty-three, Chang and Eng died within two hours of each other.

SIDECAR

By whom and for whom it was first concocted is still debated through the night at bars around the world. Was it dreamed up in Harry's New York Bar in Paris in the middle of the Depression? Or at a neat little *rive gauche* bistro during the Great War by a Yank who would rather have been Over Here rather than Over There? Talk it over, over a sidecar, which is 1 part Triple Sec, 1 part Cognac, and 1 part lemon juice shaken together with ice, strained, and served in a cocktail glass. A few sidecars and you don't need a motorcycle.

SIERRA NEVADA

Spanish for "snowy saw-toothed range," it's the highest mountain range in Spain, extending about 60 miles west and east, roughly parallel to and some 20 miles north of the Mediterranean Sea. Its highest peak, Mulhacen, 11,411 feet, is covered with snow all the time. The highest peak in eastern California's 400-mile-long scenic Sierra Nevada is 14,496-foot Mount Whitney, the highest U.S. coterminous peak. Thirty to 40 feet of snow is normal near Lake Tahoe and the Donner Pass, the principal way across the mountains—there was cannibalism among California-bound immigrants and gold-seekers stranded in Donner Pass in the late 1840s. It is home to the *Sequoia gigantea,* or "big tree," the largest member of Earth's flora, named for the Cherokee who single-mindedly created an alphabet. The eastern front of the Sierra Nevada is the largest tilted fault-block in structure in the country.

SIESTA

For many people, the best time of the day, an afternoon or even a morning nap or rest, popular in brutally hot Latin countries, and in some places so customary that business is suspended to allow for it. But count the English out—in the words of Noel Coward, they detest a siesta—like mad dogs, they go out in the midday sun.

"SILENT MAJORITY"

Alexis-Charles-Henri-Maurice Clérel de Tocqueville, after observing the American penal system, returned to France and wrote his classic of political literature, *Democracy in America*. He didn't think it would have a readership. He discussed the tyranny of the majority: "When I refuse to obey an unjust law, I do not contest the right of the majority to command, but I simply appeal from the sovereignty of the people to the sovereignty of mankind. Some have not feared to assert that a people can never outstep the boundaries of justice and reason in those affairs which are peculiarly its own; and that consequently full power may be given to the majority by which it is represented. But this is the language of a slave. A majority taken collectively is only an individual, whose opinions, and frequently whose interests, are opposed to those of another individual, who is styled a minority. If it be admitted that a man possessing absolute power may misuse that power by wronging his adversaries, why should not a majority be liable to the same reproach? Men do not change their characters by uniting with one another; nor does their patience in the presence of obstacles increase with their strength. For my own part, I cannot believe it; the power to do everything, which I should refuse to one of my equals, I will never grant to any number of them." President Richard M. Nixon made his historic, tide-turning "silent majority" speech on November 3, 1969—the "us" against "them" speech on the Vietnam War. If he had thought it would be picked up as a rallying description, he said later, he would have capitalized the silent majority in the text: "Let historians not record that when America was the most powerful nation in the world we passed on the other side of the road and allowed the last hopes for peace and freedom of millions of people to be suffocated by the forces of totalitarianism. And so tonight—to you, the great silent majority of my fellow Americans—I ask for your support. I pledged in my campaign for the Presidency to end the war in a way that we could win the peace. I have initiated a plan of action which will enable me to keep that pledge. The more support I can have from the American people, the sooner that pledge can be redeemed; for the more divided we are at home, the less likely the enemy is to negotiate at Paris." William Safire, a speech writer for the Nixon administration, has recalled that the "silent majority" phrase did not grab him, either: "We had used a similar construction early in the 1968 campaign—the 'silent center,' and 'the new majority'; and then, frequently, candidate Nixon would exhort the 'quiet Americans' and the 'quiet majority.' In May 1969, Vice-President Agnew used 'silent majority' several times in a speech . . . it had never taken hold. No catch phrase, I thought, but no harm done."

SIMON, NEIL

He even jokes about his epitaph. Where some might gravely jest, "What the hell was that all about?" or "I don't have time to die," Doc Simon says what's up: "I guess I'd like mine to say, 'This is a mistake—he's not due here for 10 more years.' " In the 1966–67 season, the comedic Midas had four shows raking in gold at the same time on the Great White Way: *Barefoot in the Park* (without George), *The Odd Couple, Sweet Charity,* and *The Star-Spangled Girl*—comedy and reality; extremely distorted but recognizable, not zany behavior. He (and the brother Danny) broke into the biz with a sketch in which a Brooklyn usherette describes a Joan Crawford movie: "She's in love with a gangster who is caught and sent to Sing Sing and given the electric chair and she promises to wait for him." He says working with Mel Brooks and Carl Reiner on "Your Show of Shows" was like going to a marvelous cocktail party every afternoon. The sunshine boy was also the author of *Fools, God's Favorite,* and skits for the revue *Catch a Star.* He's never won a Tony, not even for *Brighton Beach Memoirs.* "If comedy is about something worthwhile and pertinent," the multi-multimillionaire has said, "it's as important as drama."

SIMPSON, O.J.

The Heisman Trophy winner (University of Southern California) had rickets as a kid and wore braces. 1973 was the Juice's record-breaking year as a ball carrier in the National Football League. "My first years [in the game] were wasted because I had no goals," he said. "So I set a few goals, and I set 'em high." In '73, the Buffalo Bill gained 2,002 yards on 332 carries. He had eleven 100-yards-gained games and three 200-yards-gained games. In the 1975 campaign, he scored a league-record twenty-three touchdowns.

SINATRA, FRANK

He's been married four times—to Nancy, Ava, Mia, Barbara. When she learned that Ol' Blue Eyes, the Bony Baritone, the Chairman of the Board had married Mia Farrow, Ms. Gardner was quoted as saying, "I always knew he'd get in bed with a boy." A friend of Ms. Farrow's says the marriage went wrong because "Mia wanted to go to discotheques and Frank wanted to go to Jilly's and let them kiss his ring." Sinatra courted Lauren Bacall, who has been quoted as saying, "He behaved like a complete shit." Sinatra has been quoted as saying, "If I've had all the

affairs I'm given credit for, I'd be in a jar at Harvard Medical School."
He will be seventy years old in 1985.

SINATRA, FRANK, JR.

His father paid a quarter of a million dollars ransom to kidnappers, who
had held the young man for fifty-four hours in 1963. The money was
"bugged," and the police arrested two former classmates of Junior's
sister. The kidnappers bragged that they had played Monopoly with the
money, making the game "more interesting."

SINGAPORE

And why are you going all the way to Singapore, sweetheart? "Shopping.
And the bar at Raffles. Where better for a Singapore sling?" The Japanese went there in early 1942 to conquer it, and they did: The Brits' long-
range guns were frozen in place, aiming out to sea, so Hirohito's bicycle
corps wheeled down the Malay Peninsula and soon had the "Malta of the
East" in hand, hands up. (The Japanese didn't take many moons to
conquer the Road to Mandalay, Burma, and the infinite natural resources
of the south Near North.) Britain had controlled the crown colony (about
sixty islands) from 1824; it's been an independent nation since 1965. Sir
Thomas Stamford Bingley Raffles, a benevolent, liberal founder of the
British empire in the Far East, secured from Johore in the Malacca Sul-
tanate the transfer, in 1819, of Singapore to the East India Company and
effected policies that contributed to its role in the bourgeoning, lucrative
China trade. Raffles founded the modern city of Singapore, which today
is the capital of the 225-square-mile Republic of Singapore. Its population
is extremely dense—about 10,000 people per square mile—and extremely literate. There are four official languages: Tamil, Malay, English,
and Chinese—75 percent of the 2 million residents are Chinese.

SIRHAN, SIRHAN

"He was such an intelligent boy," his father said. "I had no worries
about him. I was sure he would do well." Said a neighbor: "He was an
A-1 boy, quiet, clean, and considerate. He'd come over to play Chinese
checkers with us, there just hasn't been a nicer boy." A former employer:
"He was a man with principles. He didn't smoke. He didn't drink. And
he always said he wouldn't lie." Robert F. Kennedy's assassin—Sirhan
means "wanderer" in Arabic—was treated after a bad fall from a horse
and was described by a doctor as "a fairly explosive personality." (Lee

Harvey Oswald had been similarly described; both killers also studied Russian.) He was a Jordanian citizen with permanent resident status in the United States. He flew into blind rages against Israel and Jews. When he was immediately seized after shooting Kennedy at point-blank range in a kitchen in the Los Angeles hotel where Kennedy had just acknowledged winning the California primary in the contest for the 1968 Democratic Presidential nomination, Sirhan had in his pocket an article by David Lawrence taking Kennedy to task for opposing U.S. involvement in the war in Vietnam while simultaneously increasing military aid to Israel. He also had four $100 bills. (Oswald was dead broke.) Sirhan insisted that he preferred "to remain incommunicado." He is serving a life sentence in a California prison but could be paroled.

SIRIUS

"Hail, mighty Sirius, monarch of the suns! May we in this poor planet speak with thee?" The brightest star in the night sky, it is about twice the size of the Sun and has about twenty times the luminosity. The Egyptians, probably the first people to adopt a predominantly solar calendar, noted that the annual flood of the Nile River would occur soon after the Dog Star reappeared in Canis Major. Pegging their calendar to Sirius, they soon had a year of 365 days, with each of 12 months having 30 days and the last month having an extra fifth. Because an extra fourth of a day was not included, the calendar drifted into error. Roman farmers sacrificed to the dog star a fawn-colored dog at their three festivals in May when the Sun began to approach Sirius. Sirius is "only" 8.7 light-years away. In 1862, a hunch was proven—Sirius had a companion, a white dwarf star, Sirius B.

SIROCCO

It's not just so much hot air when someone says that periods of the sirocco or the *foehn* or the harmattan or the chinook are associated with marked increases in restlessness and irritability. Occurrences of "ill wind" have been correlated with increased suffering and death among the physically and emotionally ill. The ionic balance of the atmosphere changes with the arrival of a hot, dry wind like the sirocco. Excess positive ions from the atmosphere are trapped at ground level. The effect on humans of excess positive ions is to bring about an increase in serotonin, one of the body's neurotransmitter substances. Excessive serotonin can make a person nervous, irritable, and depressed. If an individual is ill already or is predisposed toward emotional outbursts, the effect can have serious consequences. Conversely, an excess of negative ions brings on a feeling of well-being. Plunging water generates negative ions, one reason so many people enjoy lengthy showers and being near great waterfalls. The sirocco—an Italian word from the Arabic *sharq,* meaning "east"—is a hot, dust-laden, dry, southerly wind originating in the North African desert, usually in the spring, and blows all over Italy and nearby Mediterranean areas. The *foehn* is a warm, dry wind that blows down the side of a mountain, such as the Alps. A harmattan (from an Arab word for "forbidding" or "evil thing," and akin to "harum") is a dry, dust-laden wind blowing from the interior on the Atlantic coast of Africa in some seasons. The chinook is a warm, moist, southwest wind of the Pacific coastal region of North America from Oregon northward; it's also the name for the warm, dry, *foehn*like wind that descends the eastern slopes of the Rockies.

SIX-DAY WAR

Denied by Egypt the right of passage through the Red Sea and the Suez Canal, Israel attacked Egypt, Jordan, and Syria. In less than a week, in June 1967, it occupied the Gaza Strip and the Sinai peninsula of Egypt, the Golan Heights of Syria, and the West Bank and the Arab section of Jerusalem (both under Jordanian rule). The United Nations Security Council's request for Israeli withdrawal and Israel's call for direct negotiations for peace, secure and recognized boundaries, and right of passage were all ignored. Six years later, on October 6, Yom Kippur, the Day of Atonement, Egypt and Syria attacked Israeli positions in the Sinai and the Golan Heights. By war's end, three weeks later, Israel had troops in force across the Suez Canal, Egypt's Third Army was encircled on the East Bank, and Syrian forces were in retreat toward Damascus. On December 21, 1973, in Geneva, the first Arab-Israeli peace conference opened.

SKIN

It's your body's largest, fastest-growing organ. If you are an average-sized adult, your skin covers an area of about 18 square feet, including your feet, of course, and weighs 8 to 10 pounds. The palms of your hands and on the soles of your feet have the thickest sections of skin on your body, your eyelids the thinnest. The epidermis is the surface of your skin, the dermis is the lower layer. (Dermatology is the science that treats the skin and its diseases. Stuffed derma is allied, but that's something else again.) The dermis contains blood vessels, hair roots, fat, elastic fibers, and oily glands; the skin is lubricated by these glands. Your skin's chief role: to protect you from outside influences. You are sometimes saved by the skin of your skin.

SKUNK

What if you get sprayed by that amber-colored, blinding, stinging, stinking fluid called, technically, butylmercapton? Several washings with gasoline or a bleach are an antidote. Also recommended: chloride of lime, ammonia, tomato juice, diluted solution of sodium hypochlorite, or equal parts oil of citronella and oil of bergamot. Some victims have been known to bury their clothes—and themselves. Where does the spray come from? This mammal of the weasel family has a unique pair of secretory glands embedded in muscle tissue on either side of and slightly below the rectum. The fluid, or musk, is expelled through retractable ducts that end in gristle-like papillae. The skunk is not always a little stinker: It raises its tail as a warning.

SKYDIVING

The crazed person jumps from an airplane with a parachute and delays the opening of the chute for a free-fall period during which he (or she) floats or glides through the air (185 mph) or performs various stunts and maneuvers. The chute is opened at about 2,500 feet. In accuracy competition, the diver tries to land on a small disk in the center of a 6½-yard circle. Dwight Reynolds scored 105 dead centers at Yuma, Arizona, in March 1978. Research produced model chutes that have a drift or forward speed inherent in the motion of the canopy as it descends. The first world championships were held in Yugoslavia in 1951, when parachuting became a regulated sport. Skydiving is one sport truly shared by the genders.

SKYLAB

What goes up these days doesn't have to come down, ever. NASA's plan had been to rocket the abandoned, behemothic space laboratory into a higher orbit. But the uninhabited, $293 million, nine-stories-tall *Skylab* reentered Earth's atmosphere in July 1979; friction with air molecules burned and broke the "house" into hundreds of pieces. The bigger pieces, numbering about 500, some more than a thousand pounds in weight, roared through the southern sky and crashed into the South Atlantic, the Indian Ocean, and the sparsely populated desert of western Australia. No one was hit. Lucky. *Skylab*'s orbital limits had included all major population centers except those in the northern parts of Europe, Canada, and Siberia. Over six years, *Skylab* was home to three different astronautical crews. It had orbited the planet 34,981 times and cruised 874 million miles.

SLAVERY

"That peculiar institution"—Abraham Lincoln struck upon a compromise: Free the slaves right away and pay off their owners with a large loan floated for the purpose. His stroke of genius—it would be cheaper than a civil war—was thought to be merely a political gimmick, and that was that. Adoption of the Thirteenth Amendment, banning slavery constitutionally, was necessary because the Emancipation Proclamation had not prevented Southern states, on readmission to the Union, from reinstituting slavery: "Neither slavery nor involuntary servitude, except as a punishment for crime whereof the party shall have been duly convicted, shall exist within the United States, or any place subject to their jurisdiction." The rabid abolitionist William Lloyd Garrison had burned a copy of the Constitution at a public ceremony near Boston on the Fourth of July, 1854, declaring it a "covenant with death and an agreement with hell . . . a compromise with tyranny." Four decades after the end of the Civil War, 29 militant black intellectuals from fourteen states were not allowed to meet in a New York manor—none would accept them as guests—so they gathered on the Canadian side of the Niagara Falls. "The Niagara Movement" declared that America's 10 million blacks, "stolen, ravished, degraded—struggling up through difficulties and oppression—need sympathy but receive criticism, need help but are given hindrance, need protection but are given mob violence, need justice but are given charity, need leadership but are given cowardice and apology, need bread but are given a stone." The time was ripe for organized, determined, and aggressive action that would lead to immediate black freedom and growth in the United States.

SLEUTH

It's a group of bears. It's a hound, specifically a bloodhound, that tracks by the scent. It's also a detective. From the Middle English *slooth:* "trail," "track." Sleuths have been known to trail or track a sleuth. It's also the name of a diabolical two-man mystery drama by Anthony Shaffer.

SMITHSONIAN INSTITUTION

"America's attic" was founded "for the increase and diffusion of knowledge among men" by the last will of the bastard son of an English lord who had no acquaintances in America and seemed to have only a couple of books relating to America. It took Congress ten years—Senator John C. Calhoun: "it was beneath . . . dignity to receive presents from anyone"—before the English chemist James Smithson's gift of half a million dollars was accepted. First director was Joseph Henry, the Albany, New York, physicist who had invented the electromagnetic telegraph. Everything from soup to nuts, and including the kitchen sink, has been on display in the huge complex of museums and galleries in the nation's capital. Among the historic Americana, treasures, and trivia: Francis Scott Key's star-spangled banner, Davy Crockett's hatchet, Eli Whitney's cotton gin, the simple wooden cross that marked Casey Jones's grave, a lock of President Millard Fillmore's hair, a silk purse made from a sow's ear (a triumph of chemistry over conventional wisdom), a film clip of a World Series game in which an outfielder drops a flyball, a dowdy dress that Bess Truman wore to a White House dinner, a section of a "balloon-frame" farmhouse, paper money issued by Massachusetts in 1690, the Wright Brothers' first heavier-than-air flier, a nose-thumbing machine used in Warren G. Harding's Presidential campaign, a harpoon from a whaling boat, a space capsule, a Bowie knife, a streetcar, a ship's radio room of the early 1920s, a gravitational radiation antenna.

SNAIL

There are approximately 40,000 species of the univalve mollusk in marine or freshwater or terrestrial habitats. Many, including all land snails, are hermaphroditic, but the majority of the marine species have separate sexes. The male snail of the family *Helicidae* injects delicate calcareous darts ("love arrows") into its partner. Some snails eat both plant and animal matter, others eat only one type of food. To get around, the land snail secretes a slimy path over which it progresses slowly by rhythmic contractions of the muscular base, or foot. A few terrestrial species have returned to the sea, and must rise to the surface to breathe.

S. N. C. F.

The initials are for *Société Nationale des Chemins de Fer Français*—the national railroad organization that runs France's railroads and 22,000 miles of track. The lines form a cobweb pattern spinning everywhichway out of several terminals in Paris.

SNOW WHITE AND THE SEVEN DWARFS

Jakob and Wilhelm Grimm, the German folklorists, didn't bother to give them names in the tale they titled "Little Snow-White." The dwarfs were merely called the first, the second, the third, the fourth, the fifth, the sixth, the seventh. Even Walt Disney's wife was dubious about the project some called "Disney's Folly." When he told her he was going to do an animated story involving dwarfs, her immediate reaction was one of repulsion: "There's something so nasty about them." But Disney went back to his looking-glass and asked, "Looking-glass, looking-glass, on the wall, Who in this land is the fairest of all?" And the looking-glass again answered, "Thou, O Walt, *art* the fairest of all!" Such *was* his art that Frank S. Nugent, a movie reviewer for *The New York Times,* was to write, "If you miss *Snow White and the Seven Dwarfs,* you'll be missing the ten best pictures of 1938." Oscar voters agreed and honored Disney with a full-sized statuette and seven dwarf-sized copies. Disney had given each of the miner-dwarfs a different personality: happy, dopey, grumpy, sleepy, and so on. (Doc, Sneezy, Bashful.) The outline of the Grimm brothers' "Little Snow-White" was followed most faithfully, except for the ending. The Grimm ending: "And now the King's son had [the coffin] carried away by his servants on their shoulders. And it happened that they stumbled over a tree-stump, and with the shock the poisonous piece of apple which Snow-White had bitten off came out of her throat. And before long she opened her eyes, lifted up the lid of the coffin, sat up, and was once more alive. . . ." In Disney's version, three years to create, the Prince comes, kisses Snow White, and they ride off singing.

SOCCER

It's the most popular sport in the world. A billion people have watched the televised final match for the World Cup. Fans are rabid. Fields in South America are surrounded by a moat. Soccer is a simple game: Players can use any means other than their hands to get that ball into that rectangular goal at the other end of that field. (Goalies can touch the ball with their hands.) World Cup Competition was initiated in Montevideo, Uruguay, in 1930. Brazil has copped the cup a record three times. Brazil's Pele—Edson Arantes do Nascimento—is considered the greatest player in the history of the game. He led his team to the three titles, scoring an average of a point a game in international matches. The

509

world's highest-paid athlete, he was engaged by the New York Cosmos to put some kick into the North American Soccer League.

SOCRATES

The wisest man in Greece—others professed knowledge without realizing their ignorance; he said he at least was aware of his own ignorance. (The Socratic method, the dialectic, tends to expose ignorance by showing that many things people assume are true are false.) The Athenian philosopher was famous for courage in military battles. He lived by his principles, and died by them. In his search for wisdom about right conduct, he discussed virtue, justice, and piety. "Clear knowledge of the truth is essential for the conduct of life. Action equals knowledge. Rulers should be men who know how to rule, not necessarily those who have been elected. Man ought to take courage and look after his soul, dressing it in the beauty of harmony and righteousness and courage and generosity and truth—it is how one lives that counts." He defended the foundations of democracy, but appeared dangerous to Athenian democracy. In 399 B.C. he was charged with religious heresies and corrupting youth. Obscure political issues surrounded the trial. One reason the jury may have condemned him to death: the unbending pride with which he conducted his defense. Several times, Socrates turned his back on opportunities to escape. He carried out the death penalty by drinking a cup of hemlock poison.

SODOM AND GOMORRAH

"And the Lord said, Because the cry of Sodom and Gomorrah is great, and because their sin is very grievous; I will go down now and see whether they have done altogether according to the cry of it, which is come unto me; and if not, I will know And the Lord said, If I find in Sodom fifty righteous within the city, then I will spare all the place for their sakes. . . . the Lord rained upon Sodom and upon Gomorrah brimstone and fire from the Lord out of heaven. And he overthrew those cities, and all the inhabitants of the cities, and that which grew upon the ground. And Abraham gat up early in the morning to the place where he stood before the Lord: And he looked toward Sodom and Gomorrah, and toward all the land of the plain, and beheld, and, lo, the smoke of the country went up as the smoke of a furnace. And it came to pass, when God destroyed the cities of the plain, that God remembered Abraham, and sent Lot [Abraham's nephew] out of the midst of the overthrow, when he overthrew the cities in the which Lot dwelt." Lot had retreated to Zoar, which was spared.—Genesis 18,19.

SOLO, NAPOLEON

He was the man from U.N.C.L.E.—the television wheel on the James Bondwagon. Once again the impresario was Ian Fleming, who had created 007. Once again he got the right number—"The Man from U.N.C.L.E." 's sophisticated contretemps with its specter, T.H.R.U.S.H., were first-class escapist-spy-secret-agent adventures. Good-guy U.N.C.L.E. was the United Network Command for Law Enforcement, with headquarters in the bowels of New York City—the secret entrance was behind a fake wall in a dry-cleaning store. Bad-guy T.H.R.U.S.H. was the Technological Hierarchy for the Removal of Undesirables and the Subjugation of Humanity. Solo was played by Robert Vaughn and he went it alone at first. His partner, Illya Kuryakin, played by David McCallum, appeared for only five seconds in the pilot episode for the series, then rose from flunky to popular equal.

SOLOMON GRUNDY

John Bartlett—if we may quote *him*—says that the rhymes of Mother Goose originated with *Mother Goose Tales* as *Contes de ma mère l'Oye*, published in 1697 by Charles Perrault—Father Goose? *The Tales* were first translated in 1729, the rhymes as *Mother Goose's Melody* in 1781, by Robert Samber, and published in London by John Newbery, who established children's books as part of the publishing industry. Jack Sprat. Little Jack Horner. Old King Cole. Cock Robin. Simple Simon. Tom Tucker. Humpty Dumpty. Peter Piper. Miss Muffet. Tommy Tittlemouse. Jack and Jill. Bobby Shaftoe. And Solomon Grundy. What more fun way to learn the days of the week: Solomon Grundy, born on Monday, christened on Tuesday, married on Wednesday, took ill on Thursday, worse on Friday, died on Saturday, buried on Sunday. Which was the end of Solomon Grundy.

SOLOMON'S TEMPLE

The cedar of Lebanon used in building the Temple and the house of Solomon may not have been cedar of Lebanon, may not have been from the historic groves of the Lebanon mountains at all. It may have been that of the deodar cedar, native to the Himalayas; its durable and fine-grained fragrant wood is venerated by the Hindus, who call it Tree of God. The wisdom of Solomon is proverbial, but the two chapters of I

Kings (6–7) about building in Jerusalem with cedars of Lebanon are among the most difficult in the Old Testament to fathom, partly by reason of the technical terms whose precise meanings are no longer known. The Temple has played a central role in the memories and the hearts of Jews throughout the thirty centuries. The only remnant is the Wailing Wall.

SOMNAMBULISM

From the Latin words *Somnus* "sleep" + *ambulare* (−*atus*) "to walk." The sleepwalking disorder occurs during delta-wave sleep. The individual sits up in bed, picks at the blanket, then gets out of bed and walks about. He may open doors or eat or do other things for a half hour. He will stare blankly and unresponsively if challenged; it is only with great difficulty that the somnambulist can be awakened. The next morning, the stroll and activity will not be recalled. (Victor Hugo described Napoleon as "the mighty somnambulist of a vanished dream.")

SONNET

Developed from medieval songs and cultivated during the Renaissance, it is composed of fourteen lines of iambic pentameter with some form of alternating rhyme and a turning point, usually after the eighth line, that divides the poem into two parts: "Devouring Time, blunt thou the lion's paws,/And make the earth devour her own sweet brood;/Pluck the keen teeth from the fierce tiger's jaws,/And burn the long-lived phoenix in her blood;/Make glad and sorry seasons as thou fleet'st,/And do whate'er thou wilt, swift-footed Time,/To the wide world and all her fading sweets;/But I forbid thee one most heinous crime:/O, carve not with thy hours my love's fair brow,/Nor draw no lines there with thine antique pen;/Him in thy course untainted do allow/For beauty's pattern to succeeding men./Yet do thy worst, old Time: despite thy wrong,/My love shall in my verse ever live young." Words-worth and Shelley wrote long poems using the sonnet as the basic stanza. The curtal sonnet contains fewer than fourteen lines and as many as seventeen; its chief characteristic is signaled by a turn that comes between the problem and the resolution. Some other poetry forms: the villanelle, usually nineteen lines divided into five tercets and a quatrain—the third line is repeated in the ninth and the fifteenth lines—"Rage, rage against the dying of the light." Haiku, three lines of five, seven, and five syllables each. Ottava rima: an eight-line stanza of iambic pentameter, rhyming *abababcc*, e.g., Lord Byron's *Don Juan*.

SORBONNE

The distinguished Paris center of learning, named for its founder, Richard de Sorbon, opened more than 700 years ago as a house for impoverished theological students. Sorbonne is now often used as a name for the University of Paris, which in 1970 was reorganized into thirteen units by the French government.

SOUSA, JOHN PHILIP

America's march king was also a novelist. He wrote five works of fiction as well as his autobiography, *Marching Along*. He earned his dough-re-me with the composition of a hundred marches, many of them popular to this day: "Semper fidelis," "The Washington Post March," "The Stars and Stripes Forever," "Hands across the Sea." He also stole a march on other composers with the popular comic operettas *El Capitan, The Bride Elect,* and *The Free Lance*. He had learned band instruments as an apprentice in the United States Marine Band (his father was a member) and he became its conductor, in 1880, for a dozen years, one-two. He toured the world for years with his own band and was decorated with the Victorian Order by King Edward VII.

SPANISH-AMERICAN WAR

The battleship *Maine* was in Havana harbor to help protect American life and property during Cubans' revolution against Spain, in 1898. To this day it is not known exactly what happened—was there a submarine mine? an explosion in the forward magazine? The *Maine* blew sky-high and sank, and 260 sailors were killed. (Almost exactly the same number of United States Marines peacekeepers were killed in an explosion in Beirut, Lebanon, in 1983.) The jingoistic press in the U.S. had a war cry at last: "Remember the *Maine!*" The U.S. military moved in to help boot another European power out of the hemisphere, but not to exercise sovereignty, jurisdiction, or control. At one point, the United States occupied Cuba; Lieutenant James Moss's 25th Infantry helped to maintain order—it was a bicycle corps and all 100 soldiers were black. Theodore Roosevelt's troops were not mounted when he led the charge of "Rough Riders." The Spanish-American War became far-ranging—Manila Bay, the Atlantic, Puerto Rico. Cuba got its freedom and the U.S. got the Philippine Islands, Puerto Rico, and Guam. It took the U.S. two years to gain control of the Philippines, whose nationalists engaged in bloody resistance. Spain had acquired more new territory in one generation than

Rome had conquered in five centuries, and once owned all of South America and Central America—from Cape Horn to the Rio Grande—*plus* much of what is now the United States.

SPANISH STEPS

The monumental staircase in Rome connects the Piazza di Spagna and the French Church of Trinita dei Monti. Construction in 1723 was the idea of a French minister, design was by Specchi, and financing was partially by French funds. In May, the 138 steps are blanketed with huge azaleas in bloom, one of the city's most gorgeous sights. At the foot of the steps is the house in which the English poet John Keats succumbed to tuberculosis.

SPARTACUS

The best known of the many thousand runaway slaves—the Thracian broke away from a gladiator school—who defeated Roman forces, over-ran southern Italy, fought their way toward the safety of the Alps, only to turn south again for more plunder and the possible safety of Sicily between 73 and 71 B.C. Spartacus fell in a pitched battle, and General Pompey the Great, back from Spain, helped to put down the revolt. Six thousand of the recaptured slaves were crucified along the Capua-Rome way, though 3,000 captured Roman soldiers were found unharmed in the humane Spartacus' camp. Spartacus was not a revolutionary in the modern sense of the word, but he has become the patron saint of revolutionaries. His name inspired the Spartacus party, or Spartacists, a radical left-wing group of German Socialists formed in 1916 and led by Rosa Luxemburg and Karl Liebknecht—theirs was a revolt of modern "wage slaves." On the last day of 1918, the Spartacists founded the Communist Party of Germany (KPD).

SPEED OF SOUND

Mach—for the speed of sound—depends where the vehicle is. At sea level, at 32° F.—temperature figures in the definition—the speed of sound is 740 miles per hour. It is not as fast at higher altitudes. It is about 660 m.p.h. at 40,000 feet. Mach 1 represents the speed of sound; Mach 2, or supersonic flight, is twice the speed of sound, Mach 3 is three times the speed of sound, etc. "Mach" is for the Austrian physicist Ernst Mach, the first to note, in 1887, the sudden change in the nature of airflow over a moving object as it reaches the speed of sound—this was before powered flight. Mach studied the action of bodies moving at high speeds through gases. Mach numbers were first used in 1925, nine years after Mach's death. Mach believed that all knowledge of the physical world was derived through the five senses—sight, feeling, smell, hearing, taste —a view that challenged science's traditional claim of yielding absolute knowledge. Test pilot Chuck Yeager was the first to break the sonic barrier, in 1947.

SPELUNKER

It's from the obsolete English word spelunk, meaning "cave." A spelunker is one who makes a hobby of exploring and studying caves— speleology. For about ten minutes in July 1984, President Ronald Reagan was a spelunker, taking a gander in one of the longest-known caves in the world, Kentucky's Mammoth, surely with the caveat to watch his head.

THE SPHINX

Thousands of the mythical beasts were carved from rock in ancient Egypt —usually the head of a man, sometimes that of a ram, with the recumbent body of a lion. *The* sphinx is the Great Sphinx at Al Jizah, 240 feet long, 66 feet high, guarding the Great Pyramid of the pharaoh Khafre. Its head is that of Khafre; its headdress represents a striped "nemes" cloth worn as a type of crown by pharaohs in the Old Kingdom. Its nose was shot away by Arab vandals. The 40-story-high Great Pyramid was one of the seven wonders of the ancient world. In Greek mythology the Sphinx was a bird-winged monster with the head and the breasts of a woman and the body of a lion.

SPICE ISLANDS

Zanzibar—low-lying, coral Zanzibar off the east coast of southern Africa —its maximum elevation is 390 feet—is a Spice Island, one of the world's two main sources of cloves. (Its first European visitor was the Portuguese navigator Vasco da Gama, in 1499, the first European to reach the spices of the east by sailing around the Cape of Good Hope.) The Moluccas are *the* Spice Islands, the original home of nutmeg and cloves, and they, too, were first explored by Portuguese, including Ferdinand Magellan a decade before he tried to sail around the world. The Dutch conquered the islands, which are in East Indonesia, between Celebes and New Guinea, and became a power in cloves. In 1890, Germany traded Zanzibar for England's Helgoland in the North Sea.

SPIELBERG, STEVEN

You know how Hollywood is: Sometimes the rumors *are* true. Maybe the director of *E.T. did* get a royalty check for seven figures. And that it was merely the first of dozens. *E.T.*—the idea was turned down by studio after studio before Universal put up the money. Spielberg says the only time he feels totally happy is when he's watching films or making them. He's directed some of the top-grossing movies of all time: *Jaws, Close Encounters of the Third Kind, Raiders of the Lost Ark, Indiana Jones and the Temple of Doom,* and *E.T.:* "I never want to stop entertaining." He once said that he would like to have Richard Nixon paged over a public-address system, "just to watch heads turn." He got his break with *Amblin',* a 22-minute film about a boy and a girl hitchhiking from the Mojave Desert to the Pacific Ocean; it won awards at two film festivals. His first assignment for the biggies was directing Joan Crawford in the pilot of *Night Gallery.*

SPITZ, MARK

The sensational American swimmer in the bullet-riddled 1972 Olympics in Munich no longer holds the record for most medals won by an individual. Spitz won seven: four individual gold medals, in the 100-meter freestyle, the 200-meter freestyle, the 100-meter butterfly, and the 200-meter butterfly; three team gold medals, in the 4 × 100-meter freestyle relay, the 4 × 200-meter freestyle relay, and the 4 × 100-meter medley relay. Four years later, in Montreal, the Russian gymnast Nikolai Andrianov tied Spitz' mark of seven medals. The joint record was then busted in Moscow in 1980 by Andrianov's teammate Alexander Ditiatin, who leaped and vaulted to the new record of eight medals. He was the first man to score a perfect 10 in a gymnastics event.

SPLEEN

A versatile, ductless, glandular organ—it filters blood, it is the "graveyard" of old red blood cells, it produces blood cells, it is a blood reservoir —the spleen is not essential. It can be removed (e.g., in hemolytic anemia when too many red cells are being destroyed) without producing a disability. Excision of the gallbladder is also sometimes necessary for improved health. About five and one-half inches long and three inches wide, the spleen is situated directly below the diaphragm, above the left kidney and behind the stomach. It is classified as a lymphoid organ—in some respects, the spleen resembles an oversized lymph node. Yes, you can still vent your spleen even if you've had a splenectomy.

SPOCK, BENJAMIN McLANE

The gold medal that he won in rowing in the Olympics in Paris in 1924 is his proudest possession. His enormously popular book *Baby and Child Care*—parents know more than they think they know—was completed while he was on active duty as a psychiatrist in the U.S. Naval Reserve in World War II. He resigned his professorship in child development at Western Reserve University to devote his full time to the campaign against the Vietnam War. He was given a two-year prison sentence, later reversed, for conspiring to violate Selective Service laws.

SPRING

When spring came back with rustling shade and apple blossoms filled the air, Alan Seeger had a rendezvous with Death at some disputed barricade. For others when spring trips north again: for the fisherman, the first day of spring is one thing and the first spring day is another—the difference between them is sometimes as great as a month; for the young man, his fancy lightly turns to thoughts of love. Homer observed that a generation of men is like a generation of leaves: The wind scatters some leaves upon the ground, while others the burgeoning wood brings forth—and the season of spring comes on. So of men one generation springs forth and another ceases. Which may be why William Browne had the best idea of all: "There is no season such delight can bring, as summer, autumn, winter and the spring."

SPUTNIK

Jimmy Hoffa was elected head of the Teamsters. Governor Orville Faubus, of Arkansas, was standing firm on school segregation—he was for it. The flu epidemic spread in New York City. Warsaw was crushing still another protest. And the Soviet Union was changing the ways of the world forever. On October 4, 1957, it launched at seven miles per second the first man-made satellite to orbit the Earth, which *Sputnik* ("traveler") did every ninety minutes; there were passes over the United States. Back on Earth, in Washington, D.C., science became the most important subject. Nearly four months after Sputnik went out, the U.S. launched its first artificial satellite, *Explorer I;* it discovered the radiation belts that surround the planet.

SQUARE ROOT

It is a factor of a number that when squared gives the number. For example, $+3$ or -3 is the square root of 9. In other words, when a number is multiplied by itself, it equals a second number—the square root is the original number. Some more examples: 6 is the square root of 36: 6×6. 7 is the square root of 49: 7×7. 18 is the square root of 324.

SQUID

The carnivorous marine mollusk is a highly developed invertebrate, well adapted to its active, predatory life. It has a muscular funnel just below the head which expels water in jets. Two of its ten sucker-bearing arms used to steer while swimming are also tentacles that can snatch prey. Because there is no common ancestor, the eyes of the squid—which are remarkably similar to those of man—are an example of convergent evolution. A squid can be only two inches or up to giant-size, fifty feet, the largest of all invertebrates.

SRI LANKA

Sinhala for "resplendent land," which it is. Its beauty has earned the pear-shaped Indian Ocean island the sobriquet "pearl of the Orient." Before 1972, Sri Lanka was called Ceylon, from the Portuguese *Selen,* derived from the Indian name for the island, *Sinhaladvipa.* The former former former name was *Serendip;* the mineral serendibite occurs there in irregular blue grains. An independent republic within the Commonwealth of Nations, Sri Lanka is practically linked to southeast India by a bridge of shoals. Other new names for some old places: Iran–Persia. Zaire–Belgian Congo. Ethiopia–Abyssinia. Volgograd–Stalingrad. Belize–British Honduras. Botswana–Bechuanaland. Chicago–Fort Dearborn, Indian Territory.

STAINLESS STEEL

Credit for its invention is in dispute. Did the British metallurgist Harry Brearley do it alone, in 1913? Or did Brearley, F. M. Becket of the United States, and Benno Strauss and Eduard Maurer of Germany develop it more or less together, between 1903 and 1912? Stainless steel has a high tensile strength and resists abrasion and corrosion because of its high chromium content.

STALIN, JOSEPH

The Man of Steel was arrested six times. Five times, he escaped. The sixth time, in 1913, he was exiled to Siberia for life. "Life" turned out to be the amnesty after the February Revolution of 1917. He traveled to Petrograd (formerly St. Petersburg) and carved out a niche in the Soviet cabinet as people's commissar for nationalities, then as general secretary of the central committee of the Bolshevik Party. Lenin admired Stalin's administrative skill but not his theoretical acumen, and recommended that he be removed. But the revered power behind the revolution ("It is true that liberty is precious—so precious that it must be rationed"; "Communism is Soviet government plus the electrification of the whole country") died before he could pull the plug on his successor. By 1928, Stalin ("You cannot make a revolution with silk gloves") had gotten rid of other contenders for supreme power, particularly the brilliant Leon Trotsky ("The dictatorship of the Communist Party is maintained by recourse to every form of violence"), playing them off one against the other. Stalin became dictator, stepped up modernization of the disorganized eleven-time-zone-wide country with Five-Year Plans, signed a non-aggression pact with Hitler, suffered a nervous breakdown when Hitler attacked on a 3,000-mile-long front in the summer of 1941, and ruled with a steel fist (tens of millions of political prisoners were killed in the Gulag —"A single death is a tragedy, a million deaths is a statistic") until he died of a cerebral hemorrhage in March 1953. A recorded performance of a Mozart concerto by the pianist Mariya Yudina was on a turntable in Stalin's room when he was found dead. Stalin's mother had miscarried many times because of beatings by her husband, who would strike her even more when she was pregnant. A priest advised her that the next time she conceived she must offer the child to God: "If he doesn't become a priest, God will get very angry and terrible things will happen to your family, to Russia, and to the whole world." The next child was a boy, not a bad student in the seminary, but his ordination never took place. He became a revolutionary—an enemy of God and the czar. Stalin!

STANLEY CUP

The National Hockey League's holy grail is safe for another four years from the consecutive-year co-ownership mark. The New York Islanders failed in the spring of 1984 to cop the Cup for a fifth straight year, falling in the finals of the playoffs before the Edmonton Oilers. And so the Montreal Canadiens of 1956–60 still hold the record of five all alone. They also won the Cup four straight times 1976–79. (In 1938, the Chicago Black Hawks put the "Big Mug" in their trophy case after having won a mere 37 points and finishing sixth in the overall league standings.)

STANLEY STEAMER

The identical twins Francis E. and Freeland O. Stanley produced the first steam motor car to go successfully. Two years later, in 1899, they drove the "flying teapot" to the top of 6,288-foot-high Mount Washington, the highest peak in New England, in two hours and ten minutes; five years later, they got the time down to twenty-eight minutes. The driver of a steamer had to light his boiler, wait for the water to heat (maybe twenty-five minutes, while he got hot under the collar), and open the right valves. But once he got going, he could surpass the speed of 100 miles per hour —backward or forward—with minimal pollution. In 1925, the Stanleys gave up their enterprise. They dressed identically, from derby hats to socks, and both sported long beards.

STARR, BART

For two years before the National Football League and the American Football League merged and there was a Super Bowl by name, there was a championship pigskin clash between the titlists of the two leagues. Before there was a Tony Eason or a Joe Montana, there was a Bart Starr —*the* impeccable Bart Starr. He was the championship game's most valuable player, quarterbacking Vince Lombardi's Green Bay Packers to breezy 35–10 and 33–14 triumphs over the Kansas City Chiefs in 1967 and the Oakland Raiders in 1968. He suckered the Chiefs' defense and passed for two touchdowns. He completed 13 passes against the Raiders. In a sixteen-year career, he completed 57.4 percent of his passes (1,808 of 3,149) for 24,718 yards—that's more than 14 miles—and 152 touchdowns. He's ranked as pro football's sixth best all-time passer. Dallas' Roger Staubach rates tops.

THE STAR-SPANGLED BANNER

Congress stipulated that after July 4, 1818, the flag should have thirteen stripes, symbolizing the thirteen original states, and that whenever a new state was admitted a new star should be added on the July 4 following admission. No law designates the permanent arrangement of the stars. In all, there have been twenty-eight versions of Old Glory: twenty-seven official, one unofficial, which was the first, 1775–77. The forty-eight-star flag was first raised on July 4, 1912, after the admission of New Mexico and Arizona, and was in use the longest of all. On July 4, 1960, at Fort McHenry National Monument, in Baltimore, Maryland, the current fifty-star flag was raised for the first time officially. The fiftieth star had been added for Hawaii; a year earlier the forty-ninth star had been added for Alaska.

STATE FLOWERS

A sampling. Washington: western rhododendron. Alabama: camellia. Michigan: apple blossom. Maryland: black-eyed susan. Vermont: red clover. Nevada: sagebrush. Indiana: peony. New Hampshire: purple lilac. Wisconsin: wood violet. Oklahoma: mistletoe. Kansas, the Sunflower State: native sunflower. Connecticut: mountain laurel. Ohio, whose motto is "With God, all things are possible": scarlet carnation. Colorado: Rocky Mountain columbine. Arizona: blossom of the saguaro cactus. The country is blossoming.

STATE NICKNAMES

A sampling. Minnesota: Gopher State. Hawaii: Aloha State. Georgia: Empire State of the South. Nevada: Battle Born State. North Carolina: Old North State. North Dakota: Sioux State. Virginia: Old Dominion. South Dakota: Coyote State. Montana: Treasure State. Louisiana: Pelican State. Alabama: Heart of Dixie. Illinois: Inland Empire. Idaho: Gem State. Massachusetts: Old Colony. Maryland: Free State. Rhode Island: Ocean State. South Carolina: Palmetto State. The 209 square miles of the possession of Guam: The Pearl of the Pacific.

THE STATES

Four were admitted to the Union in a space of nine days in 1889: the two Dakotas, Montana, Washington. Five have been admitted in this century: Oklahoma in 1907; New Mexico and Arizona in 1912; Alaska in 1959; Hawaii, the fiftieth state, August 21, 1959. Delaware is the First State, having been first to ratify the Constitution, on December 7, 1787; Pennsylvania came in five days later; New Jersey, six days after that. Four states border Mexico: Texas, Arizona, New Mexico, California. In the Treaty of Guadalupe Hidalgo, ending the Mexican War, 1846–48, the

United States acquired from Mexico the regions of California, Nevada, and Utah, most of Arizona and New Mexico, parts of Colorado and Wyoming. Texas had revolted against the Mexican government in 1835, and became a state in 1845 after torrid abolitionist opposition. United States Army officers who fought in the Mexican War included Ulysses S. Grant, William Sherman, George B. McClellan, George Gordon Meade, Robert E. Lee, Thomas "Stonewall" Jackson, and Jefferson Davis.

STATUE OF LIBERTY

The inspiration of a French historian after the United States Civil War, it was a gift from France honoring America's centennial celebration of 1876. It was unveiled on Bedloe's Island in New York harbor on October 26, 1886. Her original name was Liberty Enlightening the World. In her left hand is a lawbook inscribed "July 4, 1776." Emma Lazarus' sonnet *The New Colossus* was inscribed on the bronze plaque on its pedestal in 1903: "Send these, the homeless, tempest-tost to me, I lift my lamp beside the golden door." Liberty is 151.1 feet tall and weighs 225 tons, is draped in classical robes, and wears sandals and a crown with seven spokes. The exterior copper shell was designed by the French sculptor Frederic Auguste Bartholdi, who was present when Ms. Liberty was dedicated by President Grover Cleveland. The wrought-iron pylon inside was designed by Gustave Eiffel, who went on to build the Eiffel Tower with its love-nest aerie. The stone and concrete pedestal was planned by Richard Morris Hunt, an American architect. A century later, Liberty still carries the torch for freedom—even when it's in a warehouse for repairs.

STEIN, GERTRUDE

It was in the poem "Sacred Emily" that the bold wordsmithy wrote "Rose is a rose is a rose is a rose." The literary cubist felt that in poetry "You can love a name and if you love a name then saying that name any number of times only makes you love it more." Poetry, to her, was "really loving the name of anything." She also remarked, "Remarks are not literature," and, "In the United States there is more space where nobody is than where anybody is. This is what makes America what it is." And "Pigeons on the grass alas." And "Before the Flowers of Friendship Faded Friendship Fades." At Radcliffe, she wrote across the top of her examination book: "Dear Professor [William] James, I am so sorry but really I do not feel like an examination paper in philosophy today," and she walked out of the room. Professor James, by post, responded: "Dear Miss Stein, I understand perfectly how you feel. I often feel like that myself." She got the highest grade in the course. She did advanced work in brain anatomy at Johns Hopkins University. She bought early Picassos; when she couldn't afford them anymore, Picasso gave them to her without payment. He painted her portrait. She protested: "I don't look like that." Picasso said, "You will," and she eventually did. "America is my country," she wrote in 1936, "and Paris is my home town and it is as it has come to be. . . . I am an American and I have lived half my life in Paris, not the half that made me but the half in which I made what I made." For more than a lost generation, her Paris address, 27 rue de Fleurus, was a magnet for artists, writers, philosophers, and critics. Her last words, to her long-time friend Alice B. Toklas, were: "What is the answer?" Miss Toklas remained silent. "In that case, what is the question?"

STENGEL, CASEY

After winning ten pennants and seven world championships in twelve seasons at the helm of the New York Yankees, Casey at age seventy-one moved across the East River to manage the fledgling New York Mets. He proved the obvious: The Mets finished 60½ games out of first place, the modern "worst" record in the National League. The Mets finished in last (tenth) place in each of their first four seasons. The Mets also hold the lowest winning percentage by a pennant winner: .503, in 1973. Casey's fifty-four-year professional career included fourteen seasons as a player. He hit .284. In the 1923 World Series, he accounted for both Giant victories with home runs. His funeral in 1975 was delayed nearly a week so that it could take place on an off-day during the pennant playoffs, baseball people traveling west to the American League playoff in Oakland would be able to attend: funeral postponed because of game. His biographer Robert W. Creamer believes the Hall of Famer might have enjoyed the humor in that.

STEVENSON, ADLAI EWING

The grandson of a Vice-President (Grover Cleveland's second) and the father of a senator wasn't much of a reader. He described experience as "a knowledge not gained by words but by touch, sight, sound, victories, failures, sleeplessness, devotion, love—the human experiences and emotions of this earth and of oneself and other men; and perhaps, too, a little faith, and a little reverence for things you cannot see." As he was being pressured to be the Democratic Presidential candidate in 1952, the Illinois Governor blurted, "This will probably shock you, but at the moment I

523

don't give a damn what happens to the country," yet ran twice, and lost twice, under the banner "We must look forward to great tomorrows." He said in the pre-TV days that the Presidential primary season was "a very, very questionable method of selecting Presidential candidates, and actually it never does. All it does is destroy some candidates." He was a string-saver. He was a virgin when he was married at exactly 4 P.M. on December 1, 1928, in a Presbyterian chapel on Chicago's Gold Coast with a seating capacity of thirty people; the walls of the chapel were covered with greenery. The marriage was a disaster. As President John Kennedy's ambassador to the United Nations, he drove home with angry eloquence and unanswerable photographic evidence the facts of the Soviet deployment and deception in the Cuban missile crisis (1962). An old and devoted friend, the eminent George Ball, found Stevenson's closing year "unattractive and terribly sad. Why should he spend his time with Marietta Tree and Ruth Field and Mary Lasker?" He was fat as a slug when he dropped dead in a London street. When he was thirteen, he had accidentally shot and killed another child.

STONEHENGE

A playground for Druid kids? Garbage left behind by extraterrestrials? Calendrical devices, astronomical laboratories? A religious center? Some archaeologists dismiss the theory that Stonehenge was used to measure solar and lunar movements and eclipses—it would have been too exotic an astronomical instrument for the Bronze Age culture that existed in England when the huge stones were raised on Salisbury Plain, Wiltshire, during the sixteenth century B.C. What is known for certain about the enigma of Stonehenge is that nothing is known for certain as to how the huge stones were transported, why the architecture of Stonehenge differs from that of other stone circles in Britain, and how, or whether, the builders may have indeed detected the Moon's long cycle fully 2,000 years before the Greeks. John Fowles has noted that any innocent approaching the subject will soon feel like the ram-in-a-thicket of another ancient culture. But it *is* a great place to get stoned at summer solstice.

STONE MOUNTAIN

Six hundred and fifty feet high, northeast of Atlanta in northwest Georgia, the largest mass of exposed granite anywhere in the world. Riding out of the northern face are the titanic carved equestrian figures of heroes of the Confederacy: Robert E. Lee, Stonewall Jackson, and President Jefferson Davis—a memorial to the Confederacy, commissioned in 1916 by the Daughters of the Confederacy. The original designer, Gutzon Borglum, destroyed his models over a disagreement, and went on to sculpt the Presidential faces at Mount Rushmore. When the state of Georgia purchased the mountain and established a state park there in 1963, the monument was completed by Walter Hahock.

STRAIT OF GIBRALTAR

In mythology its east entrance was flanked by the Pillars, or Gates, of Hercules—by the Rock of Gibraltar in Europe and by Mount Acha at Ceuta in Africa; the Jebel Musa, west of Ceuta, was probably a Pillar, too. The 8- to 23-mile-wide Strait joins the Mediterranean Sea with the Atlantic Ocean; at its eastern end is the Jurassic limestoned three-mile-long British tank, i.e., Gibraltar, a peninsula in southern Spain, now at odds with the British over ownership. Spain officially ceded Gibraltar to occupying Britain in 1713 in the Peace of Utrecht, which concluded the War of the Spanish Succession (the treaty also gave Britain exclusive control of the slave trade in Spanish America). The German Air Force pounded Gibraltar fruitlessly during World War II. It's still a strategic British air and naval base (and European colony). Her Majesty's Government still ignores one of the provisions of the Utrecht agreement; out of respect for Spanish sensibilities at the time, it declared that no Jews and no Muslims could live on Gibraltar. The only wild monkeys in Europe, the Barbary apes, still call it home. (As part of an agreement to open the border between Spain and Gibraltar, Britain and Spain will meet in 1985 on the future of The Rock.)

STRAIT OF JUAN DE FUCA

In the 1500s, a Greek navigator named Juan de Fuca in the service of Spain falsely claimed that he had discovered the waterway—the Strait of Juan de Fuca, natch—100 miles long and 11 to 17 miles wide—that separates Vancouver Island, British Columbia, and the state of Washington. Ships from Seattle, Vancouver, and Victoria, British Columbia, pass in and out of the Pacific through the strait. But what about that little island of San Juan at the eastern end of the strait, in Puget Sound? There was a rivalry between American settlers in Washington territory and the Hudson's Bay Company in Victoria, and there was joint occupation from 1860 to 1872, and the British-American treaty of 1846 fixing the boundary of Canada and the western United States wasn't precise here and there. Someone's got to *own* it, right? Okay, who? The United States? Canada? A third party? Let's get Emperor Wilhelm I of Germany in here as the arbitrator. And it came to pass, the little island of San Juan at the eastern end of the Strait of Juan de Fuca should belong to—the state of Washington. San Juan National Park was established in 1966 to commemorate the peaceful relations between Britain and the United States since settlement of the dispute.

STREET, DELLA

Not once, not twice, not three times, not four times, but five times the most famous secretary in mystery and detection, perhaps in all of fiction, turned down her boss's hand in marriage. Her boss: the most famous attorney in mystery and detection, perhaps in all fiction, Perry Mason, Esq. "I wouldn't want to live unless I could work for a living," she announced nearly a half-century ago (1936) in *The Case of the Stuttering Bishop*, and that was that, for she knew that if she were Mrs. Perry Mason, Mr. Perry Mason would not let her continue working at the office. (He wasn't about to lead Miss Street down the primrose path.) Mason, who will be one hundred years old in 1991, still takes only those cases in which he is convinced the client is not capable of committing the crime charged.

SUDAN

Gold is the only mineral wealth in Africa's largest country (967,494 square miles, or one-fourth the size of the United States), and Egyptian pharaohs directly north really dug it. The Sudd region in the south is swampland, central Sudan is grassy plain and savannah, the north is mostly desert. Northeast Sudan was once called Nubia, its Negroid tribes forming a powerful empire in the Middle Ages. Muslims inhabit the northern two-thirds of the democratic republic, blacks speaking Nilotic languages live in the south. The Nile courses northward into Egypt and communities center around water supplies. The capital, Khartoum, is on the Nile in central Sudan. Summers are hot—100°F. temperatures are typical. Sudan is also known for producing about 90 percent of the total world production of gum arabic.

SUDETENLAND

Most of the German population of 3 million was expelled from the mountainous region in northwestern Czechoslovakia after the district had been recovered by Czechoslovakia following World War II. The original German settlers arrived there in the twelfth and thirteenth centuries, but the region was traditionally part of Bohemia. In late 1938, with British and French approval (Czechoslovakia was not consulted), the Sudetenland was annexed by Hitler on the pretext that the Germans there were being "persecuted"—the British Prime Minister unfurled his umbrella and insisted that the grab and the appeasement would lead to "peace for our time."

SUDETENLAND—"PEACE FOR OUR TIME"

William L. Shirer was in Berlin on September 27, 1938, three days before Neville Chamberlain and Edouard Daladier, in Munich, gave Hitler the Sudetenland (there was no consultation with Czechoslovakia about the sacrifices it had to make), a deal that prompted the British Prime Minister to boast, "There has come back from Germany to Downing Street peace with honour. I believe it is peace for our time." Shirer remembers that a motorized division rolled through the Berlin streets just at dusk in the direction of the Czech frontier: "The hour was undoubtedly chosen to catch the hundreds of thousands of Berliners pouring out of their offices at the end of the day's work. But they ducked into the subways, refused to look on. . . . It was the most striking demonstration against war I'd ever seen. Hitler was reported to be furious . . . grim, then angry, and soon went inside, leaving his troops to parade by unreviewed." A year later, *The New York Times* carried a full-page-wide headline in the space above the masthead on page one. It was a device rarely used. This time it roared, "Chamberlain Announced Britain Is At War With Germany." Chamberlain's appeasement stance had been dictated by his belief that the Fuhrer was a rational statesman and, ergo, would not want a general war.

SUEZ CANAL

Twenty-five thousand Egyptians dug out 97,000,000 cubic yards of earth over a decade under the supervision of French engineer Ferdinand de Lesseps, who wanted to "break down the barriers which still divide men, races, and nations." The 105-mile-long ditch connecting the Mediterranean Sea and the Gulf of Suez and the Red Sea cut by 41.2 percent the nautical miles between London and Bombay, 25.8 percent between London and Hong Kong. Napoleon had been advised by a French survey team that construction of a sea-level canal would be impossible. Verdi wrote *Aida* to celebrate the opening of the Suez Canal. The night before the opening, an Egyptian frigate ran aground, blocking the passage completely; it was removed only a few minutes before a flotilla carrying the celebrating Empress Eugénie and representatives of most of the royal houses of Europe set off along the canal. When Egyptian President Gamal Abdel Nasser nationalized the canal in 1956, Great Britain, France, and

Israel tried to take it over. A cease-fire was occasioned by an atomic threat from the Soviet Union and by U.S. pressure through the United Nations. The canal was closed for eight years after the six-day Israeli-Egyptian war of 1967—Egypt sank ships to block the waterway. Israeli shipping rights were restored in 1979.

SUMO

There are thirty-two key techniques and approximately 200 movements (head throws, leg sweeps, slapping) to force an opponent out of the ring or to the floor with any part of his body above the knee, thereby achieving victory in this quasi-religious wrestling. Rikishi (the wrestlers) are conditioned through diet and training to reach gargantuan size. They wear only a silken loincloth (mawashi) wrapped four to seven times around the waist. Titles range from novice to grand champion. The referee (gyoji) wears a kimono and carries a fan, the color of its tassel indicating rank. A bow ceremony closes the sumai (struggle).

THE SUN

It has a diameter of 864,000 miles. At its center it has a density of over a hundred times that of water and a temperature of 10 million to 20 million degrees centigrade. The pressure there is about 700 million tons per square inch. It's enough to smash atoms, expose the inner nuclei, and allow them to smash into each other, interact, and produce the radiation that gives off light and warmth. During an eclipse of the Sun in 1868, spectral lines were located that were attributed to an unknown element that observers named "helium," from the Greek word for "sun." Thirty years later, helium was discovered on Earth. The Sun's total lifetime as a star capable of maintaining a life-bearing Earth (93 million miles distant) is about 11 billion years. Nearly half that time has passed. It takes about 8 minutes, 20 seconds for sunlight to reach the third planet from the Big Furnace.

THE SUNSHINE BOYS

The models for Neil Simon's stage and movie hit were Smith and Dale, vaudevillians originally Joe Sultzer and Charlie Marks. They became Joe Smith and Charlie Dale when they needed business cards and the printer had extra "Smith and Dale" cards on hand—the original Smith and Dale, whoever they were, had changed *their* names to Moran and Mack. Joe remembered that he had met Charlie literally by accident. "It was on the

Lower East Side, Eldridge and Delancey, one Sunday afternoon. We were both on bikes and we bunked into each other. . . . the way we argued reminded the bikestore owner of Weber and Fields. He said we should be friends and offered us a tandem to ride for a halfhour for free so we could get acquainted. And we did.'' Their routine was based on malapropisms and other word play, never more so than in their Dr. Kronkhite (Dale) routine. "Are you the doctor?" "I'm the doctor." "I'm dubious." "I'm glad to know you, Mr. Dubious." "What do you eat? What kind of dishes?" "Dishes? What am I, a crocodile?" They planned a Dr. Kronkhite sketch for television—Barbra Streisand was the nurse— but it never got on. "Excuse me, is this the doctor's office?" Smith asks. The nurse says, "Yes, I'm his nurse." "His nurse? Is the doctor sick, too?" She says, "No, I'm a trained nurse." "Oh, you do tricks? [*That* may be why it didn't get on.] What are the doctor's office hours?" The nurse says, "Twelve to three, three to six, six to nine, nine to twelve, twelve to three." Smith says, "With such hours he must be a horse doctor." In the doctor's waiting room, Smith learns that Dr. Kronkhite charges five dollars for the first visit, three dollars for the second visit, and one dollar for the third. Greeting the doctor, Smith says, "Well, doctor, here I am again, for the fifth time. If I come here again, you'll owe me eight cents."

SUPER BOWL

The New York Jets (11–3 on the season) scored the biggest upset in Super Bowl history in the very first official Super Bowl championship game in the National Football League, a 16–7 skunking of the heavily favored, Earl Morrall–led Baltimore Colts (13–1) in the Orange Bowl in Miami, in 1969. The Jets were the American Football Conference champs, the Colts the National Football Conference champs. The conferences were formed for the 1968 season to accommodate the merger of the National Football League and the upstart American Football League. After both the 1966 and the 1967 campaigns, there had been a championship game between the top teams of the two leagues. The Green Bay Packers (N.F.L.) won both Big Games. The January 1969 battle, after the 1968 season, was the first to be called the Super Bowl. The Green Bay victories were back-named and are today known as Super Bowl games I and II. Quarterback "Broadway Joe" Namath predicted that his Jets would win the '69 clash —"I'll guarantee you"—and they did, when back Matt Snell played the best game of his career: He scored on a short run, and Jim Turner booted three field goals. The Super Bowl reportedly got its name when the billionaire sportsman Lamar Hunt stumbled on a toy ball, about the size of a soccer ball, in the vestibule of his home in Dallas. (Billionaires have vestibules.) "What's this?" he asked his small son. "That's my super ball," the child answered. Hunt clicked on the phrase "Super Bowl" and jotted it down immediately on a used envelope. (It may be the most important message ever written on an envelope, because the Gettysburg Address wasn't.) The Super Bowl trophy has been named for the late Vince Lombardi, the premier N.F.L. coach who piloted the Packers to those first two "Super Bowl" triumphs. Green Bay hasn't been in the championship game since. Minnesota has lost the most Super Bowls—4.

I	1967	Green Bay (NFL)	35	Kansas City (AFL)	10
II	1968	Green Bay (NFL)	33	Oakland (AFL)	14
III	1969	New York (AFL)	16	Baltimore (NFL)	7
IV	1970	Kansas City (AFL)	23	Minnesota (NFL)	7
V	1971	Baltimore (AFC)	16	Dallas (NFC)	13
VI	1972	Dallas (NFC)	24	Miami (AFC)	3
VII	1973	Miami (AFC)	14	Washington (NFC)	7
VIII	1974	Miami (AFC)	24	Minnesota (NFC)	7
IX	1975	Pittsburgh (AFC)	16	Minnesota (NFC)	6
X	1976	Pittsburgh (AFC)	21	Dallas (NFC)	17
XI	1977	Oakland (AFC)	32	Minnesota (NFC)	14
XII	1978	Dallas (NFC)	27	Denver (AFC)	10
XIII	1979	Pittsburgh (AFC)	35	Dallas (NFC)	31
XIV	1980	Pittsburgh (AFC)	31	Los Angeles (NFC)	19
XV	1981	Oakland (AFC)	27	Philadelphia (NFC)	10
XVI	1982	San Francisco (NFC)	26	Cincinnati (AFC)	21
XVII	1983	Washington (NFL)	27	Miami (AFC)	17
XVIII	1984	Oakland (AFC)	38	Washington (NFC)	9
XIX	1985	San Francisco (NFC)	38	Miami (AFC)	16

LAKE SUPERIOR

The largest freshwater lake in the world is about thirty times as large as the state of Rhode Island and is of course the superior of the Great Lakes: It is the largest, the highest, the deepest of the five. It can be rough, and it does not freeze completely in winter. Several large islands make the lake their home: Isle Royale, Isle St. Ignace, and Simpson and Michipicoten. The city of Superior, in Wisconsin, is not the largest community on the lake—the largest city is Duluth, in Minnesota, with a population of 100,000. Chicago is the largest city on the Great Lakes.

SUPERMAN

In the beginning, on the doomed (atomic fire) planet Krypton, his name is Kal-El, the son of Lara and Jor-El. When his one-baby rocket ship lands near Smallville, Illinois, he is adopted by John and Martha Kent and he is named Clark. He is Superboy, then—faster than a speeding bullet—he becomes Superman. The difference between Krypton's red sun and Earth's yellow sun is credited with bestowing him with his powers. Action Comics No. 1, June 1938, featured the debut of the modern Hercules, the brainchild of two teen-agers, Jerry Siegel and Joe Shuster.

SUPERSTITION

Tossing salt over a shoulder. Not stepping on cracks in the sidewalk. Crossing oneself before attempting a foul shot in a basketball game or submitting a manuscript to a publisher. Edmund Burke called superstition the religion of feeble minds. Joseph Conrad: "... as to superstition, beliefs, and what you may call principles, they are less than chaff in a breeze." John Tyndall: "Superstition may be defined as constructive religion which has grown incongruous with intelligence." Burke also said, "Freedom and not servitude is the cure of anarchy; as religion, and not atheism, is the true remedy for superstition." To a profession steeped in superstition, the Shakespeare tragedy *Macbeth* is considered an exceedingly unlucky play among the theatrick. Its presentation, it is claimed by stagefolk, is invariably marked by misfortune and disaster. The witches' brew—"fair is foul"—has the power of working evil. It's even bad luck to say "Macbeth" in a theater. More show biz superstitions: A show is doomed if the actors applaud the playwright's first reading of his work. Don't whistle in a dressing room—you'll be asked to go outside, turn around three times clockwise, and say, "I am a fool." A black cat is the last thing any actress wants to see on an opening night. Even the makeup box is a source for superstition. Which all just goes to show.

SUPREME COURT

Only one justice has been impeached—the brilliant Samuel Chase, political leader in the American Revolution, signer of the Declaration of Independence—by the House of Representatives in 1804 for discrimination on the bench against Jeffersonians. When he was tried by the Senate, he was found not guilty. There have been only fifteen chief justices—none became President, only one was a former President, William Howard Taft, who had wanted the position for many years but declined it for various reasons each of the three times that it was offered by his predecessor in the Oval Office, Theodore Roosevelt. (He accepted President Warren G. Harding's appointment in 1921.) Warren E. Burger, appointed by Richard M. Nixon, has been chief justice since 1969. When first formed, in 1789, the court had six members. The size was increased to seven in 1807, to nine in 1837, to ten during the Civil War. In 1866, the number was reduced to eight to prevent President Andrew Johnson from filling any vacancies. It has been a nine-member court since Ulysses Grant's administration. The Woodward-Armstrong examination of the Burger Court—*The Brethren*—reveals that the chief justice has many times withheld his opinion until he knew what the majority held. Once, he changed his vote five times in one day.

SURFERS

In the search for the endless summer and the perfect wave, surfers have developed a feat they named for Quasimodo, the hunchback in Victor Hugo's novel *Notre-Dame de Paris* (1831). The surfer squats on the board, leans forward, and extends one arm straight forward and the other straight back. Surfing originated centuries ago in Hawaii. Duke Kahanamoku was the "grandfather" of modern Hawaiian surfing, which the novelist Jack London called "the sport of sports." Kahanamoku was "a brown mercury riding the swiftness of the sea." Tom Wolfe's "pump house gang" were Californians born to the polyurethane board.

SWAN

It is the offspring of a cob and a pen—the cob is the male, the pen is the female. They are old English terms to describe the large, stately waterbirds. A cygnet is a young swan. Game is a flock of swans privately owned. Herd is a flock of wild swans. Swanherd is a keeper of swans for a private owner. Swan master is a royal swanherd. Busking is the position of the swan's raised wings when it is swimming. A swan dive is a fancy dive in which the diver keeps his legs straight and his arms stretched out sideways, moving them forward before hitting the water. The Bard was the sweet swan of Avon.

SWISS FAMILY ROBINSON

Who wrote the internationally popular children's classic? Johann David Wyss? Or his son Johann Rudolf Wyss? Authorship is often wrongly attributed to the son, who *did* edit and popularize the book (and composed the Swiss national anthem). Johann David Wyss's account of a family's life on an uninhabited desert island was inspired by another Robinson, Crusoe, and stresses obedience to parental wishes and love for family. The family was a shipwrecked Swiss gentleman, his wife, and their four sons; an English girl, Emily Montrose, was shipwrecked with them. The first English translation was published in a small edition in

1814 by Mary Jane Godwin, who eloped with Percy Bysshe Shelley about the same time; Shelley's former paramour, with whom he had two children, presently committed suicide, and Shelley and Mary officially married. All very Frankensteinish.

SWITZERLAND

One reason that the roads of war do not pass through the Swiss Confederation of nineteen cantons and six half cantons is that it's the most mountainous country in Europe. The principal chain of the Alps extends in an arc of some 700 miles from the Tenda pass, above Nice, northeastward to the environs of Vienna. Mont Blanc is 15,771 feet tall and many peaks rise above the snowline between 8,000 and 10,000 feet. Glaciers form the headwaters of many Alpine rivers. North of the Alps is predominantly wet and colorful, and forests and grasslands prevail. South of the Alps, Mediterranean Europe is warm and dry, with infrequent rainfall and precarious vegetation. Switzerland's principal natural resource is water power. The former Helvetian Republic has four official languages: German (or more properly Schwyzerdütsch, the Swiss variant of German, though high German is also spoken), French, Italian, and Romansch, which is spoken only in the cantons Grisons and Engadine, in the southeastern corner of the country—Romansch is a dying language, artificially preserved. Sixty-five percent of the people speak Schwyzerdütsch. Notices in public places are printed in French, German, and Italian. The *lingua franca* of the modern world, English, is spoken widely, including by the gnomes in the international banking community there.

T

TABASCO

A sultry, exceedingly rainy state along the Gulf of Campeche, it is the largest site of petroleum in Mexico. Its expansive forests produce hardwoods, rubber, chicle, resins, and dyes. The Olmecs of Tabasco were the Sumerians of the New World; they, too, provided artistic, technical, and religious instruction for the civilizations that followed. Cortes crossed Tabasco in 1524 and Francisco de Montejo conquered it six years later. For more than a hundred years, Spain and England wrangled over it, and from 1921 to 1935 the *caudillo* Tomas Garrido Canabal considered it a virtual fiefdom. Tabasco is an Indian name meaning "damp earth"—and it sure is. (Tabasco is also the trademark name for a pungent condiment sauce made from capsicum berries.)

TABEI, JUNKO

The first woman to reach the 29,141-foot-high summit of Everest, the world's highest peak, she spent three years preparing for the ascent, raising $5,000 for expenses by giving piano lessons. She was thirty-five years old, five feet tall, she weighed ninety-two pounds, and was nearly killed by an avalanche. It took five hours to climb from the camp at the 24,885-foot level to the summit. Twenty-five men had already conquered Everest. Sir Edmund Hillary of New Zealand and his Sherpa guide, Tenzing Norkay, did it first, in May 1953. Mrs. Tabei, who lived in Saitama, a prefecture near Tokyo, entered the record book in May 1975.

TAGUS RIVER

Tejo in Portuguese, Tajo in Spanish, Tagus in English, the longest river in the Iberian Peninsula—or is it? the Ebro has its adherents—flows 585 miles through gorges and over waterfalls and through fertile fields from eastern Spain into the Atlantic Ocean at Lisbon, Portugal's capital city.

It forms part of the Spanish-Portuguese border. Spanning a Tagus estuary in south Estremadura province, between Lisbon and Setual Peninsula, is the longest suspension bridge in Europe—the main span is 3,323 feet, one of the longest in the world—the Salazar, named for the long-time (thirty-six years) Portuguese dictator Antonio de Oliveira Salazar. The harbor there is one of the finest on the continent.

TAJ MAHAL

The monument to love in Agra is one of the world's most beautiful buildings—it speaks a language of its own to the soul when seen by moonlight —it was scheduled for demolition in the 1830s so that its marble facing could be shipped to London for sale by auction to the landed gentry. Wrecking machinery was on the grounds when word came from England that the first auction of marble facades of Indian monuments and edifices had been a bomb—on second thought, it wouldn't pay to tear down the 200-year-old mausoleum. In a $70 million venture, the stricken Shah Jahan had imported craftsmen from Persia, Turkey, France, and Italy to build a memorial to his favorite wife, Mumtaz Mahal, "the Exalted of the Palace," who had died in childbirth. Shah Jahan had conceived of a twin structure to be built in black marble directly across the river from his wife's resting place, but he was placed by his son and heir in the Taj. Both Moghul monarchs are in a crypt in obedience to the tradition that no one should be able to walk over their graves. There is controversy as to whether airplanes are permitted to fly over the building. The Agra airport is far away, and there is no flight path over the monument.

TANGIER

It became a free city, an international zone, when France and Spain divided Morocco in 1912, and it lost that status when the North African country became independent after World War II. The port, nineteen miles from Spain, had been established by Phoenician sea traders by the twelfth century B.C. In turn, it was occupied by Carthaginians, Romans, Vandals, Arabs, Portuguese, British, and Spanish. In the present century, Tangier became a wild place, a paradise for shady dealers, writers of spy novels, and real spies. For many visitors, a few hours in Tangier suffice for a quick tour of the entire continent: It's enough time to hit the casbah and haggle for bargains and snap Polaroids of turbaned merchants, veiled women, and Berber farmers along the crowded Boulevard Pasteur. Residents are called Tangerines. Tangerines are also the reddish-orange-colored fruit native to China and are rich in vitamin C. The United States (principally Florida), Brazil, Spain, Italy, Mexico, and Japan produce most of the world's tangerines. The fruit is not grown in Tangier.

TANK

The first tanks were built during World War I at the insistence of Britain's First Lord of the Admiralty, Winston Churchill. He wanted an armored car that could smash right over German trenches on the western front. What he got was "Winston's folly"—rumbling, weird contraptions on a caterpillar tread. They made their debut in the battle of Flers-Courcellette, on the Somme River, in September 1916, and appeared to be a failure. Fourteen months later, at Cambrai, 300 British tanks changed modern warfare. In a dawn attack, they liquidated the German defenses. The Nazis used tanks to overrun Poland in a month at the start of World War II.

THE TARLETON TWINS

Stuart and Brent had known Katie Scarlett O'Hara for years. She had been their favorite playmate when they were kids—she could ride horses and climb trees almost as well as they. "Now [19 years old, six feet two inches tall, long of bones, hard of muscle] they were both in love with her. . . . Just what the loser would do, should Scarlett accept either one of them, the twins did not ask. They would cross that bridge when they came to it." They would probably think of it tomorrow. "For the present they were quite satisfied to be in accord again about one girl, for they had no jealousies between them." During the Civil War, Stuart got it in the knee and a minié ball went through Brent's shoulder. Presently, the Tarletons, Lieutenant Brenton, Corporal Stuart, were on a list of the dead . . . "the lazy twins with their love of gossip and their absurd practical jokes . . . [Scarlett] could not read any more. She could not know if any other of those boys with whom she had grown up, danced, flirted, kissed were on that list. . . . Oh, Rhett, why do there have to be wars? It would have been so much better for the Yankees to pay for the darkies—or even for us to give them the darkies free of charge than to have this happen." President Abraham Lincoln had the same idea. Shortly after being sworn, in 1861, he struck upon a stunning compromise: The slaves would be freed right away and their owners would be paid off with a large loan floated for the purpose. Secession or the threat of secession would be silenced once and for all, and the borrowed money would not have to be liquidated until the 1910s. Amortizing slavery would be vastly preferable to a war between the states. His was a stroke of genius and profound political resourcefulness, but The Great Emancipator could not inspire his fellow Americans to accept such farsighted and flexible good sense. His proposal was seen as a political gimmick, and was doomed.

TASMAN SEA

It lies in the southwest Pacific Ocean in the belt of westerly winds known as the "roaring forties" between the southeast coast of Australia (Sydney is the largest city on the sea) and Tasmania on the west and New Zealand on the east. A stormy body of water about 1,400 miles wide and 900,000 square miles in area, it merges with the Coral Sea to the north. Sighted (1642) by, and named for, the Dutch explorer Abel Janszoon Tasman in the service of the Dutch East India Company. He was the first westerner to circumnavigate Australia and demonstrate it's an island continent.

TAYLOR, ELIZABETH

No. 1. Nicky Hilton: "She let the dogs mess up all over." 2. Michael Wilding: "She has very little of the housewife about her. She is untidy to the point of disaster." 3. Mike Todd: "She believes thirty carats would be vulgar and in bad taste." 4. Eddie Fisher: "Just a little $50,000 diamond would make everything wonderful for up to four days." 5. Richard Burton: "Before Elizabeth, I had no idea what total love was . . . I don't approve of divorce as a blanket thing, but if two people are absolutely sick of each other or the sight of each other bores them, they should be divorced or separated as soon as possible." 6. Richard Burton: "Before Elizabeth, I had no idea what total love was . . . I don't approve of divorce as a blanket thing, but if two people are absolutely sick of each other or the sight of each other bores them, they should be divorced or separated as soon as possible." 7. Senator John Warner: "Being a senator's wife is not easy. It's very lonely. I wouldn't wish it on anyone. There was nothing for her to do except sit home and watch the boob tube." E.T.'s funniest experience? She was playing a scene with Mickey Rooney in *National Velvet*. "I was in his room watching him pack clothes into a suitcase. The cameras were rolling, but suddenly Mickey dried up. The words disappeared and there was a sinking feeling for me as well as for him. Nobody likes to have egg on his face, so Mickey stopped throwing clothes into the suitcase and got into it himself and closed the case tight from inside so nobody could see him." That "funniest experience" was more than forty years ago!

TELEVISION

Herbert Hoover appeared on an AT&T experimental telecast in 1927, but he was Secretary of Commerce, not President, at the time. It would be another twelve years before a sitting President appeared on television. On April 30, 1939, Franklin D. Roosevelt, who, like his fifth cousin, President Theodore Roosevelt, did so many things first, helped television make its long-awaited public debut. He was televised delivering a speech at the Federal Building on the exposition grounds overlooking the Court of Peace at the opening session of the New York World's Fair, in Flushing, New York. Two N.B.C. mobile vans were used, one handling the pick-up, the second the transmission. There were few sets: nine-inch and twelve-inch screens for the most part. Two months earlier, there had been an experimental transmission from the unfinished fair grounds: *Amos 'n' Andy* in blackface makeup. A test of an atomic explosion was first televised on February 1, 1951. A camera on Mount Wilson picked up the blast at Frenchman Flats, Nevada, 300 miles away.

"TELSTAR"

Earth's first communications satellite inspired a hit single record, an instrumental (no lyrics) composed by an English recording engineer, Joe Meek, and recorded off the cuff by the Tornadoes, a studio group that specialized as backup at recording sessions by others. "Telstar" was a hit in both Britain and in the United States, in 1962, as was another Tornadoes single a year later, "Ridin' the Wind."

TEMPLAR, SIMON

Virtue is its own reward. No service is too much trouble, and he doesn't have his hand out. A good, clean fight. A quick kiss. A Boy Scout's Bond. A saint. *The* Saint, Simon Templar, the smooth, suave, sophisticated, haloed hero of dozens of adventure-mystery novels by Singapore-born Leslie Charteris. The versatile actor Roger Moore was The Saint in scores of syndicated television shows and he later played Bond in the movies. He was to the manner born—he's the son of a policeman.

TEMPLE OF KARNAK

Hereeeeeeeeeee's Amon-Re, the chief god of the Egyptian Empire. The Great Temple in his honor is the finest example of New Empire religious architecture, its Great Hypostyle Hall, decorated by King Seti I about 1300 B.C., the largest columned hall ever built. The thick walls of the towering temple slope gently toward the top. Karnak is on the Nile in central Egypt, a mile east of Luxor; it occupies part of the site of necropolitan Thebes, popular with pharaohs, dead and alive.

THE TEN COMMANDMENTS

Moses destroyed the two tablets bearing the Ten Commandments written with the finger of God. Angered at seeing Aaron's sculpture of the golden calf—a false idol—he smashed the tablets to pieces and made the children of Israel drink of the powder made from the calf. He then returned unto the Lord for a second set of the tablets "and said, Oh, this people have sinned a great sin, and have made them gods of gold. Yet now, if thou wilt forgive their sin; and if not, blot me, I pray thee, out of thy book which thou hast written. And the Lord said unto Moses, Whosoever hath sinned against me, him will I blot out of my book."—Exodus 32.

TEN DAYS THAT SHOOK THE WORLD

November 1917. With the Bolsheviks in the majority in the Petrograd soviet, with the voices of the peasant and the working classes being heard throughout the land, the biczar Lenin urged the soviet to seize power from the czarist government. It was done in ten days that shook the world —the armed coup d'état by cossacks and White Guards was masterminded by Leon Trotsky. In Moscow, the Kremlin was taken after bloody fighting. Control of most of the cities countrywide was wrested. Lenin became chairman of the Council of People's Commissars; Trotsky, foreign commissar; Stalin, commissar of nationalities; Rykov, interior commissar. The dead revolutionaries were carried through Red Square in 500 coffins. The American journalist-poet John Reed's authoritative eyewitness account of the uprising indicates he didn't blink. Reed and the Wobblie-union leader William D. Haywood are the only Americans buried in the wall of the Kremlin.

TENERIFE

At the Los Rodeos airport on this Canary Island, aviation's worst disaster occurred. Five hundred and seventy-four people were killed when a KLM Royal Dutch Airlines Boeing 747 taking off in dense fog slammed into a Pan American World Airways Boeing 747 taxiing off the runway to an access ramp. All 234 passengers and 14 crew members aboard the chartered KLM jumbo jet were killed. Seventy passengers in the front section of the chartered Pan Am jet survived the collision. Both planes had been diverted from Las Palmas on Grand Canary Island. Los Rodeos was not equipped with ground radar, and the KLM plane apparently had not received final clearance for takeoff.

A.D. 1066

At least two, maybe three important things happened that fateful year in addition to, and as a result of, William the Conqueror's invasion and the Battle of Hastings, and not because Halley's comet was scaring the hell out of Earthlings again. The Norman invasion led to the loss of prestige for the English language. Norman (Romanesque) architecture was initiated. William was crowned on Christmas Day.

TEXAS

The "father of Texas" once argued that it should remain a state of Mexico—Stephen Austin believed that it did not have the resources either to win or to maintain its independence. He had founded the first Anglo-American community there, in 1822. His mottoes: redemption of Texas from the wilderness, fidelity and gratitude to his adopted country, true inflexibility to the interests and just rights of his settlers. When Mexico abolished slavery, Smith supported a contract-labor law allowing slaves to be brought into Texas, technically as indentured servants. When Santa Anna became dictator of Mexico in 1835, Texans rebelled; the next year, he wiped out defenders of the Alamo. Sam Houston's small army surprised the siestaing Mexican force at San Jacinto, near the present-day city of Houston, captured Santa Anna, and compelled him to recognize the independence of Texas. Abolitionists vigorously opposed statehood for Texas—the Texas constitution recognized slaveholding—and so it remained an independent republic under its Lone Star flag for nearly a decade. Houston served twice as its president and the city of Austin was the capital. President John Tyler, as his term was ending, maneuvered the admission of Texas through Congress, making it the twenty-eighth state. Annexation was the immediate cause of the Mexican War, in which the United States took by force what it had been unable to gain through diplomacy. (The United States had wanted California before the British or the French took possession, but Mexico had not been willing to negotiate.) The area of the Lone Star State—its motto is friendship, its flower is the bluebonnet, its bird is the mockingbird, its tree is the pecan, its song is "Texas, Our Texas"—has flown six different flags: the Fleur-de-lis of France, the Lions and Castles of Spain, the Eagle and Snake of

Mexico, the Lone Star of the Republic of Texas, the Stars and Bars of the Confederacy, and the Stars and Stripes of the United States.

TEXAS SCHOOL BOOK DEPOSITORY BUILDING

Lee Harvey Oswald's sixth-floor lair on November 22, 1963, is becoming a historical and educational exhibit which could rival the Alamo as a tourist attraction in the nation's second-largest state. Three areas are being recreated: the window from which the assassin fired his misaligned Mannlicher-Carcano into President John F. Kennedy's convertible limousine; the floor where the antiquated mail-order rifle with its defective scope was discovered; and a lunchroom, originally on the second floor, where the lumpen Oswald was seen swigging a Coke just after the shooting. The Dallas County Historical Foundation has conducted a public drive to raise $3 million to pay for the restorations. When he fled his workplace, Oswald went to his coffin-sized rented room, retrieved a pistol, shot police officer J. D. Tippet in the street, and was captured in a movie theater (*War Is Hell*). Delegates to the Republican National Convention in Dallas in the summer of 1984 were formally invited on a tour of sites connected with the assassination, but someone had the good sense to order its cancellation.

THATCHER, MARGARET

The first woman to lead a European democracy (1979–   ) held only one great office of state before she became Britain's Prime Minister—she was Minister of Education and Science. The "Iron Lady" emerged as a major Parliamentary figure and was elected leader of the Conservative Party in 1975. As a young person, she took part in piano competitions, she took elocution lessons, she was an enthusiastic, competitive hockey player and a team captain, and she took five years of Latin in one.

"A THING OF BEAUTY"

John Keats was in his early twenties when he recalled that the imagination of a boy is healthy and surmised that the mature imagination of a man is healthy; "but there is a space of life between, in which the soul is in a ferment, the character undecided, the way of life uncertain, the ambition thick-sighted: thence proceeds mawkishness, and all the thousand bitters which those men I speak of must necessarily taste. I hope I have not in too late a day touched the beautiful mythology of Greece, and dulled its brightness: for I wish to try once more, before I bid it farewell''—which he did, within three years, at the age of twenty-five. Rich in imagery and color, the long poem *Endymion:* "A thing of beauty is a joy for ever: Its loveliness increases; it will never Pass into nothingness; but still will keep A bower quiet for us, and a sleep Full of sweet dreams, and health, and quiet breathing."

"THINK"

The motto of wildly successful International Business Machines—IBM. The Thinker is one of the world's most distinguished sculptures. "What makes my Thinker think," The Thinker's creator said, "is that he thinks not only with his brain, with his knitted brow, his distended nostrils and compressed lips, but with every muscle of his arms, back, and legs, with his clenched fist and gripping toes." Auguste Rodin worked twenty-one years perfecting *The Thinker.* Until it was given by subscribers as a gift to the city, Parisites had to visit cemeteries to see Rodin's best work.

THE THIRD REICH

"Reich" in German for "empire," "realm." The Third Reich was officially proclaimed after President Paul von Hindenburg died, in 1934, and Chancellor Adolf Hitler declared himself *der Fuhrer,* the Leader. The Reich was to last 1,000 years. It lasted 11. The First Reich was the German Empire—or Holy Roman Empire, from 800 to 1806. Then came the Second Empire, 1871–1918. Emperor William II fled to Holland and abdicated; the Dutch government refused to extradite him. (Hitler met with him after conquering the Low Countries in 1940.) The Third Reich was built on the speeches of a demagogue who stirred genitalia and rattled ovaries: "The one means that wins the easiest victory over reason: terror and force. Mankind has grown strong in eternal struggles and it will only perish through eternal peace. Strength lies not in defense but in attack. The great masses of the people . . . will more easily fall victims to a big lie than to a small one. Germany will be either a world power or will not be at all. If the German people despair, they will deserve no better than they get. If they despair, I will not be sorry for them if God lets them down."

THE THIRTY-NINE STEPS

He wrote a four-volume history of World War I and biographies of Caesar (Julius), Scott, and Cromwell. He was elected to Parliament and was a popular governor general of Canada in the 1930s (promoting good relations with the United States). But the Scottish statesman John Buchan will probably be best remembered for this thriller, published in 1915. During the Great War, he wanted to write detective fiction "and take real pains with it. Most detective story-writers don't take half enough trouble with their characters, and no one cares what becomes of either corpse or murderer." He started on the story in lodgings at the seaside. Mrs. Buchan has recalled that nearby was a private beach, a small cove that was reached by a rickety wooden staircase. "How many steps there were I do not know, but John hit on the number thirty-nine as one that would be easily remembered and would catch people's imagination." When the staircase was replaced, the Buchans received a small block of wood in the shape of a step and bearing a minute brass plate with the title "The Thirty-Ninth Step." The author, always the statesman, said that he enjoyed the film version (1935); he did not even mind the introduction of a woman into the story and other drastic alterations to the plot.

THOR

The widely popular Norse god of thunder, the patron and protector of peasants and warriors, had a magical thunderbolt—a boomeranging hammer that returned to him after he threw it. The hammer warded off evil spirits and smashed giants and demons to pieces. (The Vikings boasted that they were the people of Thor.) He was very tall, very vigorous, and he had a big red beard—streaks of lightning. His palace was called Bilskirnir: It had 540 rooms. His servant Thialfi was an advisor. Thor was destined to fight and never to conquer until the end of time his eternal enemy the Midgard Serpent, which enveloped the Earth with its coils and caused terrible sea storms.

THOREAU, HENRY DAVID

He was a parcel of vain strivings tied by a chance bond together. He believed that this world is but canvas to our imaginations, that dreams are the touchstones of our characters, the bluebird carries the sky on his back, the perception of beauty is a moral test, and that any man more right than his neighbors constitutes a majority of one. The New England naturalist and philosopher quit teaching school in Concord because he would have had to employ corporal punishment. He lived with Ralph Waldo Emerson and then for two years alone at Walden Pond, an experiment in living the simple, self-reliant, contemplative life of a free spirit: "I have never found the companion that was so companionable as solitude. We are for the most part more lonely when we go abroad among men than when we stay in our chambers. A man thinking or working is always alone, let him be where he will. If a man does not keep pace with his companions, perhaps it is because he hears a different drummer. Let him step to the music which he hears, however measured or far away." It was only long after his death that Thoreau came to be thought of as one of the great figures of American literary and intellectual history. In 1953, E. B. White wrote, "*Walden* is the only book I own, although there are some others unclaimed on my shelves. Every man, I think, reads one book in his life, and this one is mine. It is not the best book I ever encountered, perhaps, but it is for me the handiest, and I keep it about me in much the same way one carries a handkerchief—for relief in moments of defluxion or despair."

THORPE, JIM

"The greatest athlete of the half-century" (Associated Press) wore a "slightly illegal" football shoulder pad with an outer covering of sheet metal that crushed opposing ball carriers. He was stripped of his 1912 Olympic gold medals in both the decathlon and the pentathlon when it was discovered that he had played semiprofessional baseball. In 1973, the International Olympic Committee voted to restore the Indian's amateur status for the period 1909–12, eliminating a major obstacle to the posthumous return of his records and medals. Thorpe played major league baseball for six years, batting .252, driving in 82 runs with the Giants, Reds, and Braves. His football exploits put the Canton (Ohio) Bulldogs on the map. He became an alcoholic and died penniless. In 1954, the towns of Mauch Chunk and East Mauch Chunk, Pennsylvania, were united and renamed Jim Thorpe in his memory.

THE THREE MUSKETEERS

Alexandre Dumas's best historical romance, published in 1844, is ablaze with adventure and intrigue. Athos, Porthos, and Aramis were the three best blades in the ranks of the Musketeers of the Guard in the service of Louis XIII, in 1626. Athos looked like a nobleman. Porthos squired dames, bragging incessantly of his loves. Aramis, dressed always in black, claimed that he was a churchman at heart. They were joined by a young, penniless Gascon, D'Artagnan by name, who had shown his mettle by fiercely challenging to a duel a stranger who seemed to be laughing at his orange horse. "All for one, one for all." At melodrama's end, Athos returns to his estate, Porthos marries a rich widow, Aramis becomes a monk, and D'Artagnan—known as the Fourth Musketeer—becomes a famous soldier and a good friend of the stranger with whom he had dueled when he appeared on the scene.

THE THREE WISE MEN

The Gospel According to St. Matthew 2: "Now when Jesus was born in Bethlehem of Judaea in the days of Herod the king, behold, there came wise men from the east to Jerusalem, Saying, Where is he that is born King of the Jews? for we have seen his star in the east, and are come to worship him. . . . Then Herod, when he had privily called the wise men, inquired of them diligently what time the star appeared. And he sent them to Bethlehem, and said, Go and search diligently for the young child; and when ye have found him, bring me word again, that I may come and worship him also. When they had heard the king, they departed; and, lo, the star, which they saw in the east, went before them, till it came and stood over where the young child was. When they saw the star, they rejoiced with exceeding great joy. And when they were come into the house, they saw the young child with Mary his mother, and fell down, and worshipped him: and when they had opened their treasures, they presented unto him gifts; gold, and frankincense, and myrrh. And being warned of God in a dream that they should not return to Herod, they departed into their own country another way." Magi were a priestly caste or fraternity of ancient Persia. The word "magic" is derived from "magi." St. Matthew didn't say how many Magi visited the infant Jesus; Eastern tradition contends there may have been at least twelve. There were three gifts mentioned, and so legend has assumed there were only three wise men, or kings, or Magi. The names Gaspar and Melchior and Balthazar that have become traditional for the Magi were not bestowed, it seems, until the sixth century.

U.S.S. *THRESHER*

"Minor difficulties . . . test depth"—and then a rather muted, dull thud, a breaking-up noise: the last messages, the last sound from the world's fastest-moving and deepest-diving nuclear-attack craft, a blue-black $45-million war machine. On a test run after nine months of overhaul, the 278-foot-long *Thresher,* named for a shark and styled for attack with a shark-shaped hull, sank to the bottom of the Atlantic Ocean some 220 miles east of Boston, in April 1963—drowning its 129-man crew, the worst submarine disaster in history, and the first to strike any of the United States's thirty (at the time) atomic-powered underwater craft. A Navy Court of Inquiry concluded that there had been a pipe failure in the salt-water system and a torrential rush of the Atlantic had flooded the engine room, disrupting electrical circuits and power: "Within moments she had exceeded her collapse depth [classified] and totally flooded." The highest previous toll in a submarine disaster: 102 died when the U.S.S. *Argonaut* was lost in the Pacific in 1943. Another *Thresher* was the first U.S. submarine attacked by *friendly* forces in World War II. Surface vessels and aircraft accidentally fired on it near Pearl Harbor shortly after the Japanese sneak-attacked the U.S. naval base and airfield there on December 7, 1941. Four months later, the *Thresher* served as a weather-reporting station for the Doolittle sneak-air raid on several Japanese cities.

TIDES

There is indeed a tide in the affairs of men. Our Moon weighs 81-plus-18-zeroes tons and it is that body's gravitational attraction that causes the rhythmic, worldwide rising and lowering of the sea level. The Bay of Fundy in eastern Canada has the greatest tidal range in the world—44.6 feet. (The world average is about 2.5 feet.) There would be no tides if our heavenly body attracted every point within Earth with equal force. The first Greek to observe tides also produced the correct explanation for them, about 300 B.C. But it took 2,000 years before his explanation—that the Moon did it—was accepted, and then only when Isaac Newton explained lunar attraction in his grand scheme as to how the Universe ticks. There are about 12 hours and 25 minutes between tides. There are also biological tides. They affect human emotions. Millions of people experience ups and downs in the relentless, restless grip of the lunar effect—it is a lover's moon, it is a killer's moon.

TIERRA DEL FUEGO

"Land of fire" in Spanish, so named by Ferdinand Magellan when he sailed by the southernmost south of South America in 1520 in his historic circumnavigation of the globe. The Onas, the Alakalufs, and the Yahgans kept fires going to keep warm against the appalling, icy climate—they have since been extinguished by disease. The English naval person Robert FitzRoy picked up three of the natives—York Minster, Jemmy Button, and Fuegia Basket—educated them at his own expense in England, and returned them, on the Darwin odyssey, to spread Christianity and civilization among their countrymen. Even though the *Beagle* arrived at Tierra del Fuego in midsummer, it "had to battle for a month against mountainous seas as she tried to round the Horn [Alan Moorehead summarizing Darwin]. Darwin's first thought on catching sight of the native Fuegians was that they were much closer to wild animals than to civilized

546

human beings. . . . They were huge creatures, with long matted hair and dark cadaverous faces which they painted in stripes of red and black, with white circles round their eyes. . . . Except for a short mantle of guanaco skin thrown over their shoulders, they went naked. The color of their skin was copper, and they coated themselves with grease." The archipelago is separated from the mainland by the Strait of Magellan. The Andes extend through the western part, which belongs to Chile, and the plateau of Patagonia continues into the eastern section, which belongs to Argentina. The city of Ushuaia is the world's southernmost seat of government.

TIJUANA

Sixteen miles south of downtown San Diego, California, a wide-open brassy northwest Mexican (Baja) city during Prohibition in the United States, horse races, jai alai, bullfights, nightclubs, restaurants, shops shops shops—and half-a-million swinging residents—it's the foreign city most visited by Americans, it may even be the foreign city most visited more than once by most Americans. The ambience is more American than Mexican. The dollar, not the peso, is the common unit of monetary exchange. "Tijuana today, tamale the world."

TIMBUKTU

At its zenith, 1400–1600, the west African city in the Republic of Mali was the intellectual center of Islam and the Songhai empire (100 Koranic schools and a university centered at the Sankore mosque). It was the terminus of a trans-Saharan caravan route famous for gold trading. When the Sultan Ahmad al-Mansur of Morocco sacked the city at the end of the sixteenth century, the scholars were arrested on suspicion of disaffection; some were killed, others were exiled to Morocco. Today, small caravans arrive in winter, but they carry salt, not gold. No railway or tarmac road runs to Timbuktu, still most easily accessible by camel or boat.

TIME ZONES

There are eleven in the Soviet Union, the world's largest country, almost 7,000 miles from west to east, 2,500 miles from north to south—more than 2 million square miles are in Europe, 6.5 million square miles are in Asia. *Soyuz Sovietskikh Sotsialisticheskikh Respublik,* abbreviated *CCCP* in Cyrillic characters, is larger than the face of the Moon that is seen from Russia. It takes an express train a week to run from Moscow to Vladivostok. There are three time zones in the mainland United States. When it is noon in Washington, D.C., it's seven in the morning in Honolulu and Anchorage—and one o'clock tomorrow in Hong Kong. China, the second largest country in the world, has decided to have one, nationwide. Eight o'clock in Shanghai could be pitch dark while eight o'clock on the western border with Afghanistan could be broad daylight.

TIMOTHY

It is a valuable grass for hay. In its growing state, it is too rough to be eaten, but it dries well and makes a good winter food for livestock. Timothy was once a hefty cash crop, because the chief propulsion for farm machines in those days was the horse and the horse wasn't going anywhere without fuel. In 1711, the grass was found growing wild along the Piscataqua River, in New Hampshire, by Jonathan Herd [sic]. It got its name from the first farmer to promote grass for hay—a guy who didn't let any grass grow under his feet, Timothy Hanson by name. Some other grass names: beach, blue-joint, bristly foxtail, ticklegrass, downy chess, Japanese brome, deer-tongue, Fall Witch, field garlic, velvet, broom sedge, toad rush, and sheep fescue.

TITANIC

The ill-fated, "unsinkable" White Star liner had an ill-fated sister vessel, the *Olympic,* which had entered service a year before the *Titanic.* The *Olympic* had three notable collisions in her long career, including one, at the start of her fifth voyage, with the Royal Navy cruiser H.M.S. *Hawke* in full daylight on a calm sea within sight of land—two normally operated vessels steamed blithely to a point of impact as though mesmerized. Fourteen years before the *Titanic* sailed on an April day in 1912 on her maiden voyage from Southampton to New York, a novel called *Futility* was published. I summarized the work in *Isaac Asimov's Book of Facts:* the *Futility* was about an unsinkable and glamorous Atlantic liner, the largest in the world. Like the *Titanic,* the fictional vessel is triple-screw and can make 24–25 knots; at 800 feet, it is a little shorter than the *Titanic,* but at 70,000 tons its displacement is 4,000 tons greater. Like the *Titanic*'s, its passenger list is the *crème de la crème,* and of course there aren't enough lifeboats. On a cold April night, the fictional "unsinkable" vessel strikes an iceberg and glides to the bottom of the Atlantic. [As you have guessed,] the name of this liner, in the story by Morgan Robertson

—*The Titan*. About 1,500 people drowned when the *Titanic* struck an iceberg near Newfoundland on the night of April 14, 1912.

"TO ERR IS HUMAN"

Alexander Pope, about whom Samuel Johnson said, "A thousand years may elapse before there shall appear another man with a power of versification equal to that of Pope," declared in his "Essay on Criticism" (1711) that "To err is human, to forgive divine," playing off Seneca's memorable *Humanum est errare* Plutarch said, "For to err in opinion, though it be not the part of wise men, is at least human." James Shirley, in "The Lady of Pleasure" (1635), wrote, "I presume you're mortal, and may err." In 1787, Robert Burns, in "Address to the Unco Guid," wrote, "Then gently scan your brother man, Still gentler sister woman; Though they may gang a kennin' wrang, To step aside is human."

TOFFLER, ALVIN

The original title was *The Future As a Way of Life*. Fortunately, the social commentator changed it to *Future Shock*. (Fortunately, George Orwell changed the title of *The Last Man in Europe* to *Nineteen Eighty-Four*.) Culture shock, Toffler wrote in the late 1960s, is relatively mild in comparison with the much more serious malady, future shock. Future shock "is the dizzying disorientation brought on by the premature arrival of the future. It may well be the most important disease of tomorrow. . . . Future shock is a time phenomenon, a product of the greatly accelerated rate of change in society. It arises from the superimposition of a new culture on an old one. It is culture shock in one's own society. But its impact is far worse. Change is avalanching upon our heads and most people are grotesquely unprepared to cope with it." Change, he said, "is essential to man, as essential now in our 800th lifetime as it was in our first. Change is life itself. But change rampant, change unguided and unrestrained, accelerated change overwhelming not only man's physical defenses but his decisional processes—such change is the enemy of life." Toffler's sequel, *The Third Wave*, echoes Marshall McLuhan's dictum that technology shapes how a society lives.

TOILET PAPER

"Gayetty's Medicated Paper—a perfectly pure article for the toilet and for the prevention of piles"—the world's first toilet paper, invented in 1857, by Joseph C. Gayetty, who was never known to take a back seat to anyone when it came to marketing a new idea. Gayetty put his watermark on every sheet, which was made of unbleached, pearl-colored, pure, manila hemp.

TOKYO ROSE

An American citizen, a graduate of the University of California at Los Angeles, Iva Ikuo Toguri d'Aquino was in Tokyo when Japan attacked the United States in December 1941. First under the name Ann, short for Announcer, then Tokyo Rose, she was a propaganda broadcaster for the Japanese during World War II. She was pardoned by President Gerald R. Ford on his last day in office, in January 1977. (*Tokyo Rose* was also the name of the U.S. reconnaissance plane that made more than 700 photographs in thirty-five minutes over Tokyo on November 12, 1944—the first U.S. aircraft to fly over the Japanese capital since the Doolittle raid in April 1942.) The German version of Tokyo Rose was Axis Sally, whose real name was Mildred E. Gillars.

TOMATOES

All roads lead to Rome, and one day on one of those roads came the plant *Lycopersicon esculentum* of the family *Solanaceae,* related to the potato and eggplant, first cultivated as a food crop by the Indians of South America and exported to the Old World by way of Mexico, probably by conquistadors. The Italians named their early yellow variety *pomi d'oro,* "apple of gold." Inevitably, it was distorted elsewhere on the continent, becoming pomme d'amour, or "love apple." Today, most people love this fruit, which it is technically, but for a long time it was feared as being poisonous—tomato leaves and stems *are* toxic. Thomas Jefferson was bold enough to plant a crop in 1781. It's become the superstar of the vegetable world. There are more than 4,000 varieties. California grows upward of 400 million boxes of tomatoes every year—a box equals 32 pounds. (An inferior boxer is called a tomato, as is a ripe, attractive girl.)

TOM THUMB

P. T. Barnum went to great lengths, not to mention extremes, to put on the greatest show on Earth. The impresario who believed there was a sucker born every minute imported a 6½-ton elephant from the London zoo and dubbed it Jumbo, and made a quick deal in Bridgeport, Connecticut, for a midget whom he dubbed General Tom Thumb—both the pachyderm (later a stuffed pachyderm at Tufts University) and the Yankee mite were favorites of Queen Victoria. Charles Sherwood Stratton's three siblings were of normal stature, but Charles stopped growing from the age of six months (less than 24 inches tall, fifteen pounds) to his teens, when he spurted to a peak of 33 inches and put on about fifty pounds. He was a showoff—a marvelous entertainer: dancing, singing, joking—small talk was not his style: A mimic, he did a terrific Napoleon. His marriage in 1863 to Miss Mercy Lavinia Warren Bumpus, another small person, all but bumped the un-Civil War from the front pages. The Thumbs lived happily and wealthily ever after. There's a life-size statue of the four-star attraction in his home town.

TONGUE

It's your strongest and most flexible muscle. It helps you to chew your food. It helps you to shape the sounds you make, especially the consonants (*b, c, d, f, g, h, j, k,* etc.). Take a bite of a piece of toast. Your tongue will mash it against the roof of your mouth and mix it with saliva so that you can experience the sensation of taste. It then positions the food for additional chewing, finally moving it to the back of your mouth so you can swallow it. Different parts of your tongue are sensitive to different tastes. The front and the sides of your tongue are particularly sensitive to sweet tastes. The back of your tongue responds especially to bitter tastes.

TORNADO

Its winds can be the most violent on Earth—speeds of more than 300 miles per hour have been recorded. In 1925, 689 people were killed when a twister plowed through Missouri, Illinois, and Indiana. Scientists still do not know exactly how the dark, funnel-shaped, gyrating tornado develops, but conditions are ripe on a hot, humid afternoon or early evening in the spring in a Plains state when cool, dry air from the north collides with warm, humid air from the Gulf of Mexico. Tornados occur throughout the world but principally in the United States. If you hear a loud, louder "freight train" noise and there hasn't been railroad trackage for miles around for years, head for shelter.

THE TORRENTS OF SPRING

"YOGI JOHNSON WALKING DOWN THE SILENT STREET WITH HIS ARM AROUND THE LITTLE INDIAN'S SHOULDER. The big Indian walking along beside them. The cold night. The shuttered houses of the town. The little Indian, who has lost his artificial arm. The big Indian, who was also in the war. Yogi Johnson, who was in the war too. The three of them walking, walking, walking. Where were they going? Where could they go? What was there left?" To "cool out" before revising *The Sun Also Rises,* Ernest Hemingway spent a week in November 1925 writing *The Torrents of Spring.* His publisher, Horace Liveright, turned it down; he had little or no choice, Hemingway's novel minced Liveright's best-selling author, Sherwood Anderson. Scribner's gladly accepted the manuscript and published it, unaltered, in May 1926—Hemingway's first published novel. Said one reviewer, "as a contribution to the literature of satire, it falls noiselessly among Dr. Johnson's crab apples." Said another: "Hemingway has caught a glint of Anderson's professional naivete. Beyond that, however, parody is a gift of the gods. Few are blessed with it. It missed Hemingway. He is better as a writer of short stories." Later in the year, Scribner's (the publisher Hemingway preferred) issued the novel that made famous the former journalist, ambulance driver, and infantryman in the Italian army as the spokesman of the "lost generation," *The Sun Also Rises.*

TOTALIZATION

Invented by the son of an archbishop and Primate of New Zealand, the tote board revolutionized the sport of horse racing. It is the machinery through which parimutuel, or pooled, betting is carried on. It dispenses tickets and it automatically records wagers and calculates odds. In other words, the tote board is an aid to the making and the winning of bets on the relative values of horses in a race. A central computer instantaneously records the wagers, computes the odds, and displays moment-to-moment wagering on an electronic board in the track's infield facing the grandstand.

TOULOUSE-LAUTREC, HENRI DE

The French painter and lithographer's parents were first cousins, his father a wealthy nobleman. Henri's legs were frail, so even two mild falls at the age of fourteen were too much for him. He slipped on a polished floor and broke his right leg. A second fracture was caused by a bad spill as he was walking along with his mother, near Bareges; he tumbled into the dried up bed of a torrent, no more than one or one-and-a-half meters in depth. The miserable, stunted cripple was dragged to spas, but his leg bones never joined normally again. He haunted the night haunts of Montmartre, painting the true "and not idealized. Perhaps that is a fault, because I don't spare the warts and I enjoy adding the hairs that sprout from them." His whores and lesbians were painted without commentary. Dancers and personalities of the Moulin Rouge cabaret, the Moulin de la Galette, the Cirque Fernando, the Divan Japonais, the Café Weber, the Comédie Française, and the brothels were painted true. He suffered a mental and physical collapse—alcohol was first his solace, finally his nemesis—hospitalization did not help—and he died at the age of thirty-seven in his mother's arms at the Château de Malrome, sobbing with his last breath, "Mama, you, only you."

TOUR DE FRANCE

They circle the country, starting at Rennes in Brittany, winding in and out of Belgium, Luxembourg, Germany, Monaco, and Andorra, and finally home to the Parc des Princes stadium in southwest Paris. Another time, they start out in Cologne, cross the northern part of France, head south along the Atlantic Coast, cross the Pyrenees into Spain, then north and east, along the Mediterranean coast, through some of the worst mountain passes of the Alps. The Tour de France—the most important cycling race in the world—about 2,600 miles in thirty-one daily stages. The individual stages are timed. The racer with the lowest overall time is the winner. The leader wears a yellow T-shirt. Seconds, not minutes, not hours, have separated the winner and the second- and third-place finishers. The driving force? What pumps them up? Money. Every pedal-pusher is a movable billboard. His shirt, his pants, his cap, and his bike are emblazoned with advertising labels for seemingly myriad products.

TOWER BRIDGE

It spans the Thames immediately below the Tower of London. A 2,000-ton drawbridge, it is about 800 feet long between the abutment towers. Latticework footbridges connect the tops of the towers. The original steam machinery was a marvel of Victorian engineering. In 1951, the drawbridge started to raise while a bus was crossing it. The driver accelerated and successfully jumped the widening gap. (Between the tenth century and construction of Westminster Bridge in 1750, London Bridge was the only bridge to span the Thames.)

TOWER OF LONDON

The White Tower, the initial structure in the ancient fortress, in London's East End, was built on the site of a Roman bulwark during the reign of

William the Conqueror. There are fifteen other towers. Kings spent the night there before their coronation. *The* Tower has been infamous: Sir Thomas More, Anne Boleyn, Catherine Howard, Lady Jane Grey, and Sir Walter Raleigh were among many men and women who were beheaded there. The children Edward V and his brother, the Duke of Kent, were murdered in the Tower by Richard III. Since 1967, the Crown Jewels have been exhibited in a depository below the Wakefield Tower. The 300-year-old St. Edward's Crown is the oldest king's crown still in existence. Queen Victoria's royal scepter is decorated with the largest diamond in the world, more than two inches long, more than one inch wide: 516.5 carats. The Tower is patrolled by Yeomen of the Guard, or Beefeaters, in Tudor garb. Because legend says that the Tower will crumble if its ravens fly away for good, the birds' wings are clipped.

TRACY, SPENCER

He said he had a face like a beat-up barn door. His advice to other actors was, "Know your lines and don't bump into the furniture." Seventy films over a thirty-seven-year period and the only actor to win two consecutive Oscars as best actor: as the stoic Portuguese fisherman Manuel in *Captains Courageous* (1937)—the statuette was mistakenly engraved "Dick Tracy," and Tracy didn't bother attending the awards ceremony—and as Father Flanagan in *Boys Town*. He was nominated for the eighth time for his portrayal of an incorruptible Maine judge in *Judgment at Nuremberg*. He was on the screen alone for almost an hour of the 86-minute *The Old Man and the Sea*. It took so long to make the financially disastrous movie that the joke was that the original title was *The Young Man and the Sea:* "If I'd known what trouble it was going to be," Tracy said, "I never would have agreed to it. This is for the birds." Of Hollywood's growing interest in politics, the gruff, outspoken actor scoffed, "Before you ask more actors to get into politics, remember who shot Lincoln."

TRANS-SIBERIAN RAILROAD

Russian settlement of Siberia on a gigantic scale was made possible by construction, beginning in 1892, of the world's longest railway—4,607 miles from Vladivostok on the Pacific Coast to Chelyabinsk in the Urals, 5,973 miles (and a total of seven days), with a connecting line to Leningrad. Thirty-eight tunnels were punched through mountains along the shores of Lake Baikal, the largest fresh-water lake of Eurasia and the world's deepest lake (more than a mile). A second track has been added alongside the original.

TRANSVAAL, ORANGE FREE STATE

Two of the four founding provinces of the Republic of South Africa at the turn of the century. They had warred against Great Britain—the nasty Boer War, the nasty South African War—and accepted British sovereignty in exchange for responsible government in the near future, which they got, sort of, in the Union of South Africa, in 1910. (The Boers were European settlers, their language was Afrikaans; Boer is "farmer" in Afrikaans.) The two provinces have a common border in the Vaal River. Much of the world's gold has been mined in the highveld Transvaal, whose capital is Pretoria (also the legislative capital of South Africa) and whose largest city is Johannesburg. There has been much gold, diamond, and coal mining in the plateau Orange Free State, whose capital and largest city is Bloemfontein (which is also the judicial capital of South Africa). Foreigners have been magnetized by the areas' mineral resources. South Africa's two other provinces are Natal and Cape Province. About 14 percent of the land has been designated for black Africans in ultimately independent territories.

TRANSYLVANIA

Pardon me, boy, is this the Abraham (Bram) Stoker item? You were maybe expecting Zsa Zsa? Twenty-one thousand two hundred ninety-two mineral-rich square miles (Transylvania) in central Rumania; they were "in" Hungary for 900 years, before the Treaty of Trianon after World War I. Reference points familiar to true-blue redblooded Transylvanians: Cluj, Brasov, Sibiv, Tirgu-mures, Moldavia, Bukovina, Carpathian Muresul, Magyar, Teutonic Knights, Vlachs, Ausgleich, Alba Iulia. Transylvania's "golden age" was more than 300 years ago. The region's best-known figure is the madeup Dracula, the vampirish Count Dracula, the brainchild brought to life by the English novelist (and actor-manager) Bram Stoker, in 1897. Time for a silver bullet.

TRAPP FAMILY

He had seven children, together they had three more. He was the widower Baron Georg von Trapp, a much-decorated German submarine commander in World War I, she was the tomboyish Maria Augusta Kutschera, a teacher who was planning to take the veil at the Nonnberg Benedictine Convent at Salzburg. The family fled Nazism and began singing in America the great religious and secular music of the Renaissance and baroque periods. Their debut in October 1938 was at Lafayette

College, Easton, Pennsylvania. Their manager urged that the Trapps make their concerts more lighthearted, informal, and he dubbed them the Trapp Family Singers. ("How I hated this country at first," Maria Trapp has said. "Oblong envelopes and mayonnaise on pears.") Their farewell tour in 1955 ended with three Christmas concerts in New York. Mrs. Trapp reluctantly agreed to let Richard Rodgers and Oscar Hammerstein make her a fortune in royalties to use in missionary work. Since the autumn of 1959, *The Sound of Music* has been the sound of jingling cash registers. "Seeing Mary Martin as me made me feel funny—sort of awkward. But when the Baron [Theodore Bikel] came on in his captain's uniform, it took my breath away. Because this was exactly the way it was. It all really happened that way."

THE TREASURE OF THE SIERRA MADRE

It was all in the family: The toothless actor Walter Huston won an Oscar in 1948 for his male supporting performance in *The Treasure of the Sierra Madre*—he "supported" Humphrey Bogart and Tim Holt—and his son John won two, for his screenplay and his direction of the motion picture about gold prospectors. *Hamlet* was judged best picture of the year (1948) and Sir Laurence Olivier was the best actor. Best actress was Jane Wyman, the deaf-mute in *Johnny Belinda,* who said, "I accept this award very gratefully for keeping my mouth shut once. I think I'll do it again."

TREATY OF VERSAILLES

The six-month peace conference in 1919 closing World War I was held in France's Palace of Versailles, where forty-eight years earlier William I of Prussia had been crowned German emperor. The treaty was a bitterly contested compromise between President Woodrow Wilson's Fourteen Points and the "Carthaginian" terms of the implaccable French premier, Georges Clemenceau. Germany was not included in the consultation and was held responsible for the terrible war. It was stripped of its colonial possessions and its sphere of influence in China. East Prussia was split into two parts. The Free City of Danzig was established so Poland would have access to the Baltic Sea. Alsace and Lorraine were returned to France. The coal mines of the Saar Valley in Germany would be run by the French for fifteen years. The German army and navy were drastically reduced. Later, a reparations commission assessed Germany about $33 billion in forty-two annual payments; Germany defaulted during the Depression, in 1931. An English historian called the treaty "crushing and severe to a high degree." Because the Treaty embodied formation of the League of Nations, the United States Senate did not ratify it; in 1921, the

United States merely declared that its war with Germany was over. The rise of Hitler and National Socialism, or the Nazi movement, was fueled by Germans' dissatisfaction with the peace terms.

TRIFFIDS

In John Wyndham's science fiction novel *The Day of the Triffids,* the triffids were Indonesian (Sumatran) plants with intelligence and mobility which had been developed by men in search of a new source of vegetable oil.

TRINITY

At dawn on July 16, 1945, dawn of the atomic age—the first atomic bomb (code named Trinity, in an allusion to a John Donne sonnet!) was tested in the desert at Alamogordo, New Mexico. The physicist Enrico Fermi had said that there was one chance in thirty that the bomb, dubbed Fat Man, would destroy New Mexico and one chance in one thousand it would blow up the world. The director of the atomic research project, J. Robert Oppenheimer, argued that the bomb should be dropped without warning on a Japanese city—nothing could rival the impact—but not on Kyoto; its value was historical, and destruction might stiffen Japanese resolve. A nonmilitary demonstration would be a waste of one of the two bombs the United States still had; a test would not necessarily convince Hirohito's military that only a single weapon had been detonated. Oppie vigorously opposed the development of the far-more-lethal hydrogen bomb on both technical and moral grounds. A hydrogen bomb is triggered by the explosion of an atomic bomb.

TRIPOLI

"From the halls of Montezuma to the shores of Tripoli"—to the shores of Libya, the seat of the Karamanli dynasty, where Barbary pirates clashed with American ships at the end of the eighteenth century and the beginning of the nineteenth. In those days, the piratical Barbary states—Tripoli, Algiers, Tunis, Morocco—extracted annual payments from merchantmen who wanted to travel unmolested through the Mediterranean Sea, the pirates' "turf." In 1800, the United States warship *George Washington* was captured by forces of the Dey of Algiers and forced to sail under escort to Constantinople, where the captain and the crew were presented as slaves to the Sultan. In 1801, Tripoli seized several American vessels. Three years later, the recklessly brave, stubbornly patriotic

American naval officer Stephen Decatur stole into Tripoli harbor and destroyed the captured American frigate *Philadelphia*. In 1805, Tripoli agreed to abolish protection money. In 1815, Captain Decatur forged a treaty humiliating to the Algerian piratical state: No payments were required, all American property was restored, all Christian slaves escaping to American men of war were considered emancipated.

TRIVIAL PURSUIT

Okay, spermologers, why are Scott Abbott and the brothers Chris and John Haney the most popular Canadians in the world? On a rainy Saturday afternoon in Montreal in 1979, the journalists Abbott and Chris Haney challenged each other to a game of Scrabble. Haney asked, "Why don't we invent a game?" Within an hour, they had designed a basic structure. After looking through many almanacs, encyclopedias, and old newspapers, and with a scrounged bankroll in hand, they produced 1,100 units that were successfully test-marketed within a couple of weeks. Word of mouth did the rest for Trivial Pursuit. A fact checker was engaged to head off mistakes in the Genus II United States edition. The following wonders sought out and checked facts for *Beyond Trivia:* Cynthia Coffey, Pat Fitzpatrick, Trevor Jackson, Richard Greenberg, Jim Weldon, Melissa Mizel, Linda Marr, Mark Smith, John Betancourt, and Walter Glanze.

TROPICAL ZONE

Hanoi, Bogota, Honolulu, the Solomon Islands, Ceylon, Nigeria, Peru, El Salvador—some of the cities and some of the countries that are in "the tropics," between nearly 24° north of the equator (the Tropic of Cancer) and nearly 24° south of the equator (the Tropic of Capricorn)— the farthest points north (June 21) and south (December 21) at which the Sun is directly overhead at noon. Torrential showers, often with thunder and lightning, are a late-afternoon hallmark of the tropics. Nighttime is the "winter" of the tropics. The selvas of the Amazon Basin in South America, parts of Indonesia, and the Congo basin of Africa are tropical rain forests.

TROPIC OF CAPRICORN

Capricorn from the Latin *caper,* meaning "goat," and *cornu,* meaning "horn." The constellation of stars known as Capricorn used to be directly above the imaginary line that traces the southern boundary, or

Tropic of Capricorn, of Earth's tropical zone—the line is 1,600 miles south of the equator, as the northern boundary, or Tropic of Cancer, of Earth's tropical zone is 1,600 miles north of the equator—the 3,200 miles between are the tropics. Cancer is "crab" in Latin, and the constellation of stars known as Cancer used to be directly above the imaginary line that became the Tropic of Cancer. The vertical rays of the Sun shine down on the Tropic of Cancer at noon on the day of the summer solstice and on the Tropic of Capricorn at noon on the day of the winter solstice. The Tropic of Cancer crosses the Pacific Ocean north of Hawaii, southern China, northern India, Arabia, the Sahara, passes between Cuba and Florida, and crosses Mexico. The Tropic of Capricorn passes through the middle of Australia, and crosses Madagascar, South Africa, southern Brazil, and northern Chile.

TROTSKY, LEON

Up to a point, the superlatively intelligent, indomitably aggressive Lenin aide and Russian Communist revolutionary was lucky. A marked man since breaking with Stalin, he was refused admission by most countries and expelled from others. Seventy-three bullets were fired into the bedroom of his house in a suburb of Mexico City—Trotsky and his wife, thanks to a moment's warning, hid under their bed and emerged unscathed. Later in the same year (1940) a man who had worked his way into the Trotsky entourage killed him with an ice pick. A trial never proved that the assassin was a Stalinist agent; he was released from prison after seventeen years. Trotsky had been one of the chief organizers of the October Revolution, which brought the Bolsheviks to power. He was expelled from the politburo in 1926 and from the party the next year, and ordered to leave the Soviet Union.

TROY

The city of the Trojan war was Phrygia, the center of an ancient region known as Troas in central Asia Minor (now central Turkey), best known to the Greeks as a source of slaves and as a center of the cult of Cybelle. The son of a Protestant minister in Germany amassed a fortune in the California goldrush and devoted himself to proving that the blind Homer had sung a true story. Heinrich Schleimann began digging at Hisarlik in the spring of 1870 and discovered seven Troys stacked one on top of the other, plus two other layers, also Troys. The Troy in the bard's history was the sixth—the names of Priam, Patroclus, Achilles, Ulysses, Hector, Astyanax, Agamemnon, Helen are burned into the fabric of Western culture.

TRUMAN, HARRY S

And so baby boy Truman was born on May 8, 1884, in the little Missouri village of Lamar, at the northern edge of the Ozarks, about 100 miles from Grandview. Should he be named Harry Shippe Truman—Shippe for his paternal grandfather—or Harry Solomon Truman—Solomon for his maternal grandfather? So, with Occam's razor, they sliced away the "hippe" and the "olomon" and ended up with a simple S—and a headache for proofreaders. The Missouri Mule went to bed on election night in 1948 with the nation pretty much convinced that he had been voted out of office. (On Election Day 1876, Samuel J. Tilden, also the Democratic nominee, went to bed believing that he would be the next President. As it turned out, he indeed won the popular vote, 51 percent to Rutherford B. Hayes's 48 percent. But Hayes, who told friends that he had lost, was to win the 19 contested electoral votes—and then the election, by one electoral vote, 185 to 184. Congress' fifteen-man electoral commission voted 8–7 strictly along party lines to award all disputed states—and the election—to Hayes. Tilden restrained his followers, and Hayes further mollified them with an agreement to end military occupation of the South.) Truman carried twenty-eight states (303 electoral votes), defeating heavily favored New York Governor Thomas E. Dewey, who had lost four years earlier to Franklin D. Roosevelt's fourth successful bid for the Presidency. The nation's thirty-third President believed that the buck stopped with him. After authorizing the atomic bombing of Hiroshima, Truman retired to family quarters in the White House and "slept like a baby." He did not seek reelection in 1952.

TRUTH OR CONSEQUENCES

The people of Hot Springs, New Mexico, voted 4 to 1 to tell the truth and to take the consequences, though consequences they did not consider them to be. On March 31, 1950, they voted to change the name of their community to Truth or Consequences, which entitled it to be host to the tenth-anniversary broadcast of the Ralph Edwards radio program.

TUDOR

England's remarkable Tudor dynasty of 118 years got its name, but not its lineage, from Sir Owen Tudor, a handsome Welsh chieftain and a squire at the court of Henry V; he won the heart and the hand of Catherine of Valois, the young widow of Henry V. Henry VII, crowned in 1485, was the first Tudor, and Elizabeth, who died in 1603, was the last.

Between them were Henry VIII, who became king in 1509; Edward VI, 1547; Mary, 1553. It was a period of distinguished English literature (Shakespeare, for one) and scholarship, the rise of England as a naval power (the defeat of the Spanish fleet, for one), Reformation of the English church, and governmental reorganization that strengthened the monarchy. The Tudor dynasty was succeeded by the house of Stuart, whose claim to the throne was derived from Margaret Tudor.

TUNNEY, GENE

The world heavyweight boxing champion (1926–28; he retired) drew an SRO crowd when he lectured on Shakespeare at Yale University in 1928. The boxer had mastered Shakespeare's *The Winter's Tale* by reading it ten times. His favorite play was *Troilus and Cressida*. "Why have I been invited to speak at Yale?" he asked rhetorically. "Surely not because I have anything important to say about Shakespeare. I have been invited because I am the champion boxer of the world. I am that *now,* and there is great interest in everything I do and say. I am followed around by crowds. But how long do you suppose that will last? It will last just as long as I am heavyweight champion. Ten years from now, nobody will care what I do or what I say. It is important for me, therefore, to make the most of the present moment, for the present moment is all I have." Later that year, the modest intellectual heavyweight took long walks on the island of Brioni, in the Mediterranean, with George Bernard Shaw and Richard Strauss; later, Shaw complained that newspapermen weren't interested in what he had to say to Tunney, they were interested only in what Tunney had to say. He was the lightheavyweight champion of the American Expeditionary Forces. He lost only one professional fight, to Harry Greb, in defense of the American lightheavyweight title in 1922; he regained it from Greb the next year. He wrested the heavyweight crown from Jack ("I forgot to duck") Dempsey and held on to it in the famous "long count" return bout in 1927.

TURCOTTE, RON

Every jockey's dream came true for him in 1973, as it has for only ten jockeys in the history of the Triple Crown—he won the Kentucky Derby, the Preakness, and the Belmont back to back to back, on Secretariat. Since 1978, the Canadian has been a paraplegic. For months, he and other jockeys "complained about careless riding to New York stewards. But the stewards weren't doing anything about the loose riding. The jocks were getting away with murder." On a July afternoon at Belmont, Turcotte rose in the saddle of his half-ton horse Flag of Leyte Gulf (which could run a sixteenth of a mile in six seconds) in an effort to keep the horse from running into the young jockey Jeff Fell's mount, which had floated into his path. Turcotte's horse clipped the heels of Fell's and he fell to the turf. None of the horses touched Turcotte, but he hit hard on his neck. Fell won the race and Turcotte's career (3,033 winners, $29 million in prize money) was over.

TURKEY

The dumbest domesticated animal, related to the grouse and the pheasant, got its name from its "turk-turk" call. There were turkeys in the Western Hemisphere 40 million years ago. It's a good flier but is nonmigratory. It is also polygamous. It loafs during the middle of the day and appears to be fascinated or bewildered by fire. It tends to roost in bare trees, and will not fly off even if shot at. A well-known turkey-watcher has written, "Everyone who has kept tame turkeys must have noticed the dilatory and ridiculous performances attendant on getting to roost each night. Though each has roosted on the same branch for months and knows exactly the best way to get to it, he will go round and round the tree, noting each branch and favorable alighting place with critical eye, seemingly intent on finding some new way to arrive at the old end. Now he thinks he has found it, squats and almost stretches out his wings, then he thinks better of it, and walks on to do the same thing over and over again." In slang, the word turkey means, well, the thing's a turkey.

TURKEY MEAT

Four ounces of raw, dark turkey meat have 92 mgs. of sodium and 85 mgs. of cholesterol. Four ounces of raw, light turkey meat have 58 mgs. of sodium and 68 mgs. of cholesterol. Raw dark's four ounces have 4.9 grams of fat; raw light's have 1.4. So you'll be adding 44.1 calories with the dark meat, only 12.6 calories with the light. One gram of fat yields approximately nine calories to the body. Fats, or lipids, are the most concentrated source of energy in the diet. When oxidized, fats furnish more than twice the number of calories per gram furnished by carbohydrates or proteins. Carbohydrates are the chief source of energy for all body functions and muscular exertion, and are necessary to assist in the digestion and assimilation of other foods. Next to water, protein is the most plentiful substance in the body. It is one of the most important elements for the maintenance of good health and vitality, and it is of primary importance in the growth and the development of all body tissues. It is the major source of building material for muscles, blood, skin, hair, nails, and internal organs, including the heart and the brain.

TUSSAUD, MADAME

Visitors to Tussaud's Waxwork Museum in London in the 1970s voted for the persons, present or past, real or fictional, whom they most hated. The losers, in order from one to five: Hitler, Amin, Nixon, Dracula, Mao. Marie Gresholtz Tussaud was Swiss-born and learned to model in wax in her uncle J. C. Curtius' workshop in Paris, where he had wax museums. During the Reign of Terror, she was suspected of having sympathy for the king. She was imprisoned and forced to model the heads of victims lopped off by the guillotine. She inherited her uncle's museums and moved to London with a son and established a waxwork there as well.

TUTANKHAMEN

Practically nothing was known of the Egyptian boy king (c. 1350 B.C.) of the XVIII dynasty when the archaeologist Howard Carter and financier Lord Carnarvon in 1922 found his burial place in the Valley of the Tombs near Luxor. Undisturbed for 3,265 years, Tut's was the first royal sepulcher found intact there. It took six years for excavations and work within the tomb to be completed. Lord Carnarvon contracted a fatal illness a few months after the tomb had been opened: Had he broken the powerful law that forbade the disturbance of the kingdom of the dead? Carter lived another decade.

TWAIN, MARK

The twain is meeting. The Sage of Hannibal may be the best-known, most-translated author in China today. He may have been the best-known author in the United States in the late nineteenth century but he wasn't the most read. His books were constantly banned. *The Adventures of Tom Sawyer,* for example, was excluded from the children's room in the Brooklyn Public Library. *The Adventures of Huckleberry Finn* was assaulted by Louisa May Alcott and banned as "trash and suitable only for the slums" by Concord, Massachusetts, which had had Henry David Thoreau to contend with. Twain the publisher successfully put out Ulysses S. Grant's memoirs and lectured his way around the world. He also formed the anti-Roosevelt (Theodore) Anti-Doughnut Party: "I think the President is clearly insane in several ways, and insanest upon war and its supreme glories. I think he longs for a big war wherein he can spectacularly perform as chief general and chief admiral, and go down in history as the only monarch of modern times that served both offices at the same time." The Democratic Party was that "good and motherly old benevolent National Asylum for the Helpless." It seemed to Twain that "an Anti-Doughnut Party that won't take office is just what is wanted in the present emergency. Whenever the balance of power shall be lodged in a permanent third party, with noncandidates of its own and no function but to cast its whole vote for the best man put forward by the Republicans and Democrats, these two parties will select the best they have in their ranks. We hold the balance of power."

TWAIN, MARK—"DAN'L" (THE JUMPING FROG)

Dan'l Webster was the name of the celebrated jumping frog of Calaveras County in Mark Twain's first short story: ". . . and quicker'n you could wink he'd spring straight up and snake a fly off'n the counter there, and flop down on the floor ag'in as solid as a gob of mud. . . . Jumping on a dead level was his strong suit, you understand. . . ." A stranger "prized his mouth open and took a teaspoon and filled him full of quail-shot— filled him pretty near up to his chin—and set him on the floor . . . Dan'l give a heave and hysted up his shoulders—so—like a Frenchman, but it warn't no use—he couldn't budge; he was planted as solid as a church, and he couldn't no more stir than if he was anchored out. . . . The feller took the money [from the bet]. . . . At the door I met the sociable Wheeler returning, and he buttonholed me and recommenced: 'Well, thish-yer Smiley had a yaller one-eyed cow that didn't have no tail, only just a short stump like a bannanner, and—' However, lacking both time and inclination, I did not wait to hear about the afflicted cow but took my leave." Twain boasted, "It is the best humorous sketch America has produced yet. . . ." It is indeed a comic classic.

TWAIN, MARK—DEAD?

"If Mark Twain very ill, five hundred words," the reporter in London was cabled by the Associated Press in New York. "If dead, send one thousand." A new-found cousin, Dr. Jim Clemens, had fallen ill, and the news-wire service back home had the facts wrong. Twain (Samuel Clemens) told the inquiring reporter at the cousin's door, "You don't need as much as that. Just say the report of my death has been grossly exaggerated." The joke flashed all over the world. Clemens had been born under Halley's comet, in 1835, and he said he was going out under it, in 1910, and he did, on return from a sojourn in Bermuda.

TWAIN, MARK—*LIFE ON THE MISSISSIPPI*

The river was within him. Sam Clemens left Hannibal (125 miles north of St. Louis, Missouri) at the age of twenty-one, but in middle age, as Mark Twain, he recalled in *Life on the Mississippi* "the annual processions of mighty rafts that used to glide by Hannibal when I was a boy—an acre or so of white, sweet-smelling boards in each raft, a crew of two dozen men or more, three or four wigwams scattered about the raft's vast level space for storm quarters . . . we used to swim out a quarter or third of a mile and get on these rafts and have a ride. . . . When I was a boy, there was but one permanent ambition among my comrades in our village on the west bank of the Mississippi. That was, to be a steamboatman . . . the great Mississippi, the majestic, the magnificent Mississippi, rolling its mile-wide tide along, shining in the sun. . . ." Hannibal has remembered its most famous son: Mark Twain Dinette and Drive-In, Tom & Huck Motel, Becky Thatcher Nursing Home, Injun Joe Lodge, Mark Twain Beverage Co., Inc., Mark Twain Mental Health Center, the Huck Finn Conoco Station. "God's fool" would have had a word for all that: Either "There's millions in it!" or "I do not want Michael Angelo for breakfast —for luncheon—for dinner—for tea—for supper—for between meals."

TWAIN, MARK—RE BOARDINGHOUSE FIRE RESCUE

The humorist listed twenty-seven people and things to be rescued from a boardinghouse fire. First to be saved were fiancees, persons toward whom the rescuer felt a tender sentiment but had not declared himself; sisters, stepsisters, nieces, first cousins, and cripples. At the bottom of the list: female domestics, male domestics, the landlady, the landlord, firemen, furniture, and—last and least, as expected—mothers-in-law.

TWIGGY

Leslie Hornby was a teen-age manicurist when she was discovered in the 1960s. Fashion-designer Mary Quant called her the "knock-out beauty of our time." She looked like a marionette. She had the haircut of a four-teen-year-old boy and looked like a waif and weighed ninety-one or so pounds. She made lots of money being a model, but she got sick of being asked what she ate and what her measurements were (30-23-31), and retired at the age of nineteen and knitted a lot and went shopping a lot. She played Polly Browne in Ken Russell's movie version of *The Boy Friend*. "I made a big mistake after *The Boy Friend*," Twiggy says. "I should have capitalized on the success of the film and sought out excellent movies. Instead, I approached the whole thing lackadaisically. I really blew a great opportunity.'' (She was in *There Goes the Bride* with Tommy Smothers and in something called *W.*) She was 'S Wonderful in the Broadway hit *My One and Only*, and weighs nearly eight stone these days.

TWINS

It's not doubletalk: Five possible types of twins have been theorized. Monozygotic: A fertilized egg splits into two fetuses. Uniovular dispermatic: One egg is fertilized by two sperms. Secondary oocytary: The egg divides just before fertilization—a second-stage division. Dizygotic: formed from two eggs and two sperms. Primary oocytary: The egg divides into equal portions before fertilization. Twins are born more often to older mothers. Women between the ages of thirty-five and forty are more apt to have twins than are women in any other age group. Among whites, twins occur in about one percent of all live births. Among blacks, twins occur once in every seventy-nine births. In Nigeria, fraternal twins occur once in every twenty-two births. The study of the phenomenon of twins is called gemellology. Alexander Graham Bell, who was also a eugenicist, and never sheepish about new ideas, developed a type of sheep that would consistently bear twins and have enough functional nipples to nourish them. ''Ewe do something to me.'' By 1939, the twinning rate of the Bell flock had increased so much that the lambing of 100 ewes produced 184 young. ''As twinn'd lambs that did frisk i' the sun, and bleat the one at the other.''

TYPEWRITER

The only correctly spelled ten-letter word you can write using only the top line of letters on the typewriter keyboard is ''typewriter'' itself. The first practical commercial machine was invented in the United States in 1867 by Christopher Latham Sholes and two associates. It had understrike type bars that registered an impression beneath the platen. The letters were all capitals. A shift-key model was produced in 1878. Thomas Edison, of course, was granted a patent for the first electric typewriter, in 1872, but the electric typewriter came into use only in the mid-1930s. In 1961, IBM introduced the Selectric (with which this manuscript was typed); a metal globe that moves across the surface of a stationary paper holder replaced the usual type bars, and there is no moving carriage. Interchangeable globes, or balls, provide a variety of typefaces and special symbols, allowing a single typewriter to be utilized for scientific writing, foreign languages, choreography notations, etc. Mark Twain was the first author to submit a typed manuscript to his publisher.

U

U-BOATS

Nazi submariners claimed they had sunk 2,828 Allied merchant ships and 145 warships during World War II. The Allies claimed they had sunk 785 of the 1,162 U-boats. The first major U-boat success was the sinking of the British aircraft carrier H.M.S. *Courageous* off the coast of Ireland less than three weeks after Britain and Germany had declared war, in September 1939. Another major U-boat hit was the U.S.S. *Reuben James,* the first United States combat ship to be sunk during the war— the United States wasn't even in the conflict officially. Nearly three weeks after Hitler had attacked its former ally the Soviet Union on a 3,000-mile-long front (summer 1941), the U.S. occupied Iceland at the tardy invitation of a sulky Icelandic government, and the Navy began escorting Allied merchant ships in convoys from East Coast ports to Iceland, where the Royal Navy took over. The U.S. destroyer *Greer* and the Nazi submarine *U-652* played a cat-and-mouse game with depth charges and torpedoes. President Franklin D. Roosevelt then issued orders to shoot on sight any ship interfering with American shipping. The Germans torpedoed the U.S. destroyer *Kearny* and a naval oiler, the *Salinas*—both survived. But Lieutenant Commander H. L. Edwards's *Reuben James,* escorting a convoy from Halifax, went to Davy Jones's locker on October 31, 1941, blasted by *U-562,* with a loss of 115 officers and men. Pearl Harbor was thirty-seven days later. The Navy sank its first U-boat on April 13, 1942, off Wimble Shoal, near Hatteras, North Carolina. The destroyer U.S.S. *Roper* sank *U-85,* then depth-charged the survivors. Torpedoed crewmen in the North Atlantic died of heart attacks in the frigid waters—before they could even drown.

UNCLE TOM'S CABIN

Harriet Beecher Stowe, "the little lady," in President Abraham Lincoln's estimation, "who made the great war" with the publication of her mild abolitionist tract (the villains were Northern renegades and Mrs. Stowe emphasized the evil social effects of slavery, such as the separation of black families), then wrote a novel about economics. *Dred, A Tale of the Great Dismal Swamp* stressed that the base of the moral evils of slavery was economics: Free markets, such as there were in the North, were so much better for the businessman than was slavery. The utopian life on a Canadian farm was the setting, as an abolitionist guided his slaves toward gradual freedom.

UNIFORMS

In official competition, table tennis players must wear dark-colored shirts. In tennis, men must wear shirts and shorts, women short dresses or tops with skirts and shorts. Cricket: white or cream shirts and pants, a sweater if the weather is cool, a peak cap or protective helmet; boots may be spiked. Judo: the costume (judogi) must be white or off-white. Boxing: "The belt" (an imaginary line between the top of the hips and the navel) must be shown clearly by a contrast in color. Fencing: Clothing must be white, strong material, not so smooth that a weapon point will glance off it, without buckles or openings in which a weapon could be caught. Equestrianism (dressage 1): A whip may be carried only by ladies riding sidesaddle. Handball: Wet shirts must be changed at the request of the referee.

UNITED NATIONS SECRETARIES GENERAL

The world organization, chartered in 1945, between V-E and V-J days, has had five: Trygve Halvdan Lie, Norwegian, 1946–52; Dag Hammarskjold, Swedish, 1953–61; U Thant, Burmese, 1962–71; Kurt Waldheim, Austrian, 1972–81; Javier Perez de Cuellar, Peruvian, who began his five-year term on January 1, 1982. The United States contributes 25 percent of the U.N.'s regular budget; the Soviet Union, 11.33 percent; Japan, 8.66 percent; West Germany, 7.74 percent; and France, China, and Great Britain, about 5 percent each. There are 159 member nations.

UNSER BROTHERS

Bobby and five-years-younger Al are the only brothers to win the Memorial Day Indianapolis 500 automobile race; between them they have won it six times, three times apiece. Bobby: 1968. Al: 1970, 1971. Bobby: 1975. Al: 1978. Bobby: 1981. Bobby has twice been the champion of the U.S. Auto Club; Al, once. But neither Unser holds the record for most Indy wins: A. J. Foyt was champ in 1961, 1964, 1967, 1977. In 1982, Gordon Johncock won by less than a second: .16 seconds to be exact, at

162.026 miles per hour, just shy of Mark Donohue's record Indy time of 162.962 set in 1972.

URALS

The 1,500-mile-long "Stone Belt" across the Soviet Union from the Arctic tundra to the deserts north of the Caspian Sea is the traditional boundary between Europe and Asia. It separates the Russian plain from the west Siberian lowlands. The low range—general elevation is about 2,000 feet—is the repository of the Soviet Union's great natural resources: iron ore, coal, copper, manganese, gold, aluminum, potash, emeralds, chrysoberyl, topaz, amethyst, bauxite, asbestos, zinc, lead, silver, platinum, nickel, chrome, tungsten—in the west Urals, oil. Russian industry in Europe was moved to the haven of the Urals during World War II.

URANUS

Discovery of the seventh planet from the Sun by the German-English astronomer William Herschel in 1781 doubled the extent of the known solar system. At first it was called "George's Star," for the then king of England, George III, then "Herschel" by some astronomers. It finally was named for the father of Saturn—in Greek, Cronos—it spins far outside the orbit of the planet Saturn. According to gravitational theory, Uranus was 1.5 minutes of arc away from where it should be. This led astronomers in 1846 to discover the object that was exerting a gravitational force on Uranus' orbit—the giant planet Neptune. Only one more planet has been discovered—Pluto, in 1930, by an American astronomer, Clyde W. Tombaugh. It takes Uranus slightly more than 84.01 years to revolve around the Sun. Its day is only 10 hours, 48 minutes. The largest of Uranus' five known natural satellites, Titania, is about a quarter the size of Earth's moon. Uranus' visible cloud cover may be of ice crystals.

U.S. CAPITOL

What used to be called Jenkins' Hill was, as Pierre L'Enfant said, an obvious "pedestal waiting for a monument." On September 18, 1793, President George Washington climbed the hill to lay the cornerstone of the U.S. Capitol: "He heads a short procession over naked fields, he crosses yonder stream on a fallen tree, he ascends to the top of this eminence where original oaks of the forest stood as thick around as if the spot had been devoted to Druidical worship, and here he performed the appointed duty of the day." The original plan for the Capitol was by Dr.

William Thornton, an amateur of architecture. He was chosen among the seventeen entrants to receive the prizes of $500 and a city lot when Washington recommended his design: "The grandeur, the simplicity and the beauty will . . . I doubt not, give it a preference in your eyes as it has in mine." The first part of the Capitol was completed in 1800. A square, two-story section held the 32-member Senate, the 106-delegate House, the Library of Congress, the Supreme Court (1801), and the District of Columbia Circuit Court. The first joint session of the Congress was held on November 22, 1800.

U.S. CONSTITUTION

Drafted in secret by the Constitutional Convention in Philadelphia and signed on September 17, 1787, by thirty-nine of the fifty-five delegates, it became the supreme law of the land when it was ratified by the ninth state, New Hampshire, on June 21, 1788. It is the oldest written document of its kind. The Preamble begins "We, the people of the United States . . ." The actual grant of power is set forth in seven articles. Article One creates Congress. Article Two creates the executive department headed by the President. Article Three: the federal court system. Article Four: federal-state relations. Article Five: amendments. Article Six: the Constitution is "the supreme law of the land; the judges in every State shall be bound thereby, anything in the Constitution or laws of any state to the contrary notwithstanding." Article Seven: states when the Constitution becomes effective—the only original article with no present-day significance. Rhode Island was the only one of the original thirteen states not represented at the Convention. Not until 1941 were the first ten amendments ratified by the last three of the fourteen states in the Union at the time the amendments were drawn up: Georgia, Massachusetts, and Connecticut. The Bill of Rights had become law by one vote in 1791. Debates had been kept secret because the delegates did not want differences to be exaggerated by the public, thereby undermining acceptance of the final documents.

U.S. OPEN

It took tennis superstar Martina Navratilova eleven years to capture her first U.S. Open championship. Arthur Ashe was an amateur when he won the first Open title, in 1968, while still in the Army. (He was also the first American tennis player to earn more than $100,000 a year.) The men's title has been won seven times by three men: three-time Wimbledon champ Big Bill Tilden—he later was jailed twice for homosexual activity—Richard Sears, and Bill Barnes. Jimmy Connors is closing in on a tie: he has five U.S. titles. John McEnroe has four. Tilden was an extraordinary champion in spite of a handicap on his racquet hand: Part of the middle finger was amputated when it became gangrenous.

UTERUS

In Latin, "womb," "belly," perhaps akin to the Greek *hoderos,* "belly," and to the Sanskrit *udara.* The uterus is cut out in a hysterectomy—in Greek, uterus is *hystera.* The etymologist John B. Bremner has observed that ancient medical men concluded that the source of the vapors was the malfunction of an organ not possessed by the males. Hence, our word "hysteria" for wild emotionalism, "surely an etymological misconception." In the bad old days, women were considered more likely to be emotionally disturbed than men.

UTOPIA

In Greek, "no place," which is exactly where the ideal state founded entirely on reason is. Sir Thomas More is a principal character in his own book, which he wrote in Latin in two parts, the second part first, in 1515, the first part second, the next year. The two other principals are Peter Giles, a citizen of Antwerp and a friend of Thomas More, and Raphael Hythloday, a traveler and an acquaintance of Peter Giles. Utopia is somewhere in the oceans of the Western Hemisphere. Crescent-shaped, about 500 miles in perimeter. King Utopus isolated and protected the island from the encroachments of warlike and predatory neighbors. There are fifty-four shires, or counties. The central city, Amaurote, is home to the prince, who is Utopia's nominal ruler. To avoid hasty or rash decisions, the people's council makes no decision on a problem on the same day the problem is presented for solution. Everyone works, except the unusually talented, who are selected for training and service in the academy of learning. The workday, at craft or trade, runs six hours. Gold and silver are used for chamber pots. There is no violence, bloodshed, or vice. The Utopian criminal is enslaved. The welfare of the family is a state matter. The noble Sir Thomas, an ardent humanist, was beheaded for not impugning the Pope's authority or acknowledging Henry VIII as the head of the English Church.

U-2

So routine had United States high-flying spy missions over the Soviet Union become that the President, the Secretary of State, the acting Secretary of State, and the Secretary of Defense did not know that Francis Gary Powers was on such a flight on the eve of a summit meeting between the two superpowers. May 3, 1960: The United States issues a "cover story" that a weather-observation plane is missing on a mission over Turkey. May 5: Soviet Premier Nikita Khrushchev announces that the Soviet Union shot down a United States plane on May 1. May 5: The United States repeats its cover story, adding that the plane may have drifted over Russia. May 7: The Soviet Union reveals it has the wrecked plane, the pilot, and the pilot's confession. The United States responds: The flight probably went over Russia but was not authorized by top officials. May 9: The United States announces that the May 1 flight was one of a long series of reconnaissance flights over Russia authorized under directives from President Dwight D. Eisenhower. May 16: Premier Khrushchev calls the U-2 flights "aggression" and shoots down the summit conference scheduled for Paris. Senator William J. Fulbright: "I believe the prestige and influence of our country on the affairs of nations has reached a new low . . . little or no consideration was given to the international consequences of a failure on May 1." Powers was exchanged for a Soviet spy trapped in New York, and later died in the crash of a radio-station helicopter in California. On the morning that President John F. Kennedy was assassinated in Dallas, Texas, 13 months after the Cuban missile crisis, a U-2 fell into the Gulf of Mexico. Presumably, it had been on a secret overflight of Cuba. (President Kennedy had announced that U-2s were grounded.) Assassinologists who argue that Cuban Premier Fidel Castro commanded the rubout of his archenemy to the north have never linked the murder with the U-2 incident; they may not even know about it.

V

VACUUM

Latin for "empty." A space absolutely devoid of matter. (William Blake: "flames . . . mounting on high into vacuum, into nonentity.") United States Air Force experiments with chimpanzees and dogs prove that man can live exposed to vacuum for a brief time. Vacuum is also defined as a state of isolation from outside influences or factors. W. S. Maugham noted that there are people who live in a vacuum . . . so that the world outside them is of no moment. A true vacuum does not exist on this planet.

VALENTINO, RUDOLPH

Hollywood's first "Latin lover" had only a couple of weeks earlier scored another success, this time in *The Son of the Sheik,* when he was stricken with appendicitis. He underwent surgery. His condition was pronounced good. He was on his way to recovery. He suffered a relapse. Pleurisy developed. The silent-screen star who had let his style do the talking died a few minutes after noon on August 23, 1926, in Polyclinic Hospital, New York City. Women around the world became hysterical. A few shot themselves. In Japan, two girls clasped hands and leapt into a fiery volcano. There were "grief riots." Valentino's funeral was turned into a carnival. Mobs paid their last respects. It took fifteen days to get the body to California for burial. "The Sheik of Araby's" last words were rewritten and rewritten. Did he really say, "Let the tent be struck!" —hyping his last movie, in which he had wooed Vilma Banky, the "Hot Paprika" from Hungary? Or did he say, "I want the sunlight to greet me —don't pull the shades!"? Had he really been engaged to the tempestuous Polish film star Pola Negri? Would Valentino's older brother, Alberto, be able to follow in such large footsteps? (No!) Through his agent, the former Rodolfo Alonzo Raffaelo Pierre Filibert Guglielmi Di Valentina d'Antonguolla sent word from heaven that he had many valuable friends there and was happy: "Caruso likes me. So does Wally Reid and Sarah Bernhardt, both of whom are doing well in the movies up here.

Sarah has been particularly kind to me. These spirits do the same thing as they did on earth, but, of course, in a different way: They act with more soul now."

VALLEE, RUDY

How green was this Vermont-born crooner? Not very. He got into show biz at an early age and for twenty years his time was our time in the Heigh-Ho Club in New York City and on national radio. He succeeded in the biz by really trying: the "Stein Song," the "Whiffenpoof Song," "Vagabond Lover." On his eightieth birthday, in 1981, he said that he didn't see a future for the song-writing industry and the portion of the recording industry that deals in popular songs: "What used to be a truly sound and very fine part of show business is ruined. Composers now just don't have depth of inspiration for melody. Most of the lyrics of the pop songs you hear today are repetitious. They're almost nursery rhymes, as if written by children—which they are." Vallee says that he received the first singing telegram, in the early 1930s. He was singing at the Brooklyn Paramount Theater at the time and a young woman whose name he remembers as being Lucille Lips did what no one before her had done.

VAMPIRE

Want to keep your neighborhood vampire at bay tonight? Put a little wreath of garlic around your neck—it is said vampires find garlic as odorous as the rest of us do. Charms and amulets also do the trick temporarily. To kill off the reanimated bloodsucker once and for all, drive a stake through its heart or cremate it. Belief in vampirism is rife among Slavonians—Count Dracula was a Slovak. The next time you're in a graveyard and you see several holes about the breadth of a man's finger in the soil above a grave, you might just want to vamp right out of there —there may be a vampire on the rise. Want to find a vampire's grave in Siberia? Find a virgin boy. Place him upon a coal-black stallion that has never served a mare. Note the spot where it will not tread. Dat's de place.

VAN GOGH, VINCENT

A few days before he killed himself, in 1890, the Dutch post-impressionist painter made *Crows in the Wheatfield*. Art historian Meyer Schapiro says that for all its abstractness of composition it "represents with a tormented veracity an experienced landscape. But it is also a moment of crisis in which contrary impulses away from reality assert themselves with a wild throb of feeling." Van Gogh painted "as a means to make life bearable. . . . really, we can speak only through our paintings." *Crows:* an intense blue sky, yellow wheatfields, deep purple paths, green grass, an endless progression of zig-zagging black crows, like figures of foreboding death. Turbulence and disarray. Van Gogh, who had been unable to sell a single painting, made *Crows* in a mental hospital. He saw his art as "the lightning conductor for my illness."

VATICAN CITY

Within the city of Rome, the world's smallest sovereign state (108.7 acres, ⅙ square mile), with the Pope absolute ruler. Its independence was determined by Italian dictator Benito Mussolini and Pope Pius XI in the Lateran Treaty of 1929: Absolute sovereignty over the plot ceded to the Holy See west of the Vatican (the residence of the Pope) would be vested in the Pope; the inhabitants (about 1,000 priests, a few hundred lay persons) would be subjects of the Supreme Pontiff, not of the king of Italy; the Italian treasury was to pay the Papal treasury 1 million lire in reparation for seizures of Papal property when the troops of King Vittorio Emanuel I thrashed the swashbuckling army of Pope Pius IV in 1870; the Papal state and the Italian state would recognize each other formally and exchange ambassadors. In vibrant tones of pious emotion, His Holiness exclaimed when negotiations were completed, "It gives God back to Italy and Italy to God." The Pope and about 1,000 aides live behind the city-state's leonine walls.

V-E DAY

May 8, 1945, the war in Europe was over. Götterdämmerung had come like collapsing jackstraws. On April 30, Adolf Hitler (and his bride of a day) had committed suicide in his submarinelike bunker under the Reich chancellery—he may not have seen the light of day in the last four months of his life. Two days earlier, Benito Mussolini and his mistress had been captured and executed by Italian partisans. Soviet armies stormed into Berlin. The German armies in Holland, Denmark, northwest Germany, and Austria raised white flags. The Americans were at the Brandenburg Gates. General Alfred Jodl and Admirals Hans von Friedeburg and Karl Doenitz surrendered the Fatherland unconditionally to the Allies. Propaganda Minister Paul Joseph Goebbels killed himself and Reichsmarshal Hermann Goering (The Gas Bag, The Ironn Hermann) was captured. The Third Reich that was to have been the glory of the world for a thousand years was kaput after only eleven. V-J Day was

August 14, eight days after Hiroshima, six days after the Soviet Union kept its Yalta promise and attacked Japanese forces in Manchukuo, and five days after Nagasaki. It is estimated that 60 million people died in the six-year worldwide conflict involving every major power on earth.

VENETIAN BLIND

The bad-taste joke started a long time ago in the floating kingdom. "How do you make a Japanese blind, Molo-san?" "Well, Fon-san, you take these bamboo rods and a roll of tape and some cord and these two fingers here—" Making window blinds of slats became a popular vocation in the floating city of Venice in the 1600s. Today's Venetian blinds have horizontal slats made of sturdy material such as wood or metal that are turnable so as to admit or exclude light and/or air.

VENUS

The second planet from the Sun is the only one that rotates in a direction opposite from its orbiting motion. It's the brightest planet out there. We see it as a morning star and sometimes as an evening star, because it is never more than forty-eight degrees from the Big Furnace. In many respects, Venus and the Earth are similar: in surface gravity, mass, volume, density, diameter. But it's not our twin. Its crushing atmosphere of carbon dioxide cannot be penetrated optically, but radar has depicted a pockmarked surface with craters up to 600 miles in diameter. United States fly-bys and Russian satellites on its surface report winds between 170 miles and 250 miles per hour and temperatures up to 900° F. Venus' day is 5,832 hours long.

VERMONT

The only New England state that doesn't border the Atlantic Ocean was the first state beyond the original thirteen to join the Union, in 1791. Its name is from the French *vert mont,* "green mountain," and it is the Green Mountain State. Ethan Allen and the Green Mountain Boys, in cahoots with Benedict Arnold, captured Fort Ticonderoga from the British across Lake Champlain, in 1775, and sought to control their land back home rather than submit it to the jurisdiction of others: "We owe no allegiance; we bow to no throne. Our rule is law. The law is our own." (Allen, a giant of a man, could put away more liquid hellfire Stonewalls at a sitting than any man—hard cider liberally laced with rum—and chew

576

up nails and spit them out as buckshot.) When Vermont finally achieved statehood—it went long unrecognized by the Continental Congress—Allen's family lost all its land. Famous Vermonters have included the first publishers of the *New York Herald* and *The New York Times,* John Dewey, Admiral George Dewey, Stephen A. Douglas, and the only President to be born on the Fourth of July, Calvin Coolidge.

VERRAZANO-NARROWS BRIDGE

It is no longer the world's longest suspension bridge. The Humber Estuary Bridge near Hull in England is 4,626 feet. The Verrazano bridge connecting Staten Island and Brooklyn, New York, is 4,260 feet. The Golden Gate is 4,200 feet. The Salazar Bridge is 3,323 feet. The main span of the Mackinac Bridge is 3,800 feet. The Severn Road Bridge in England is 3,240 feet. Still to come, the world's longestest, the 5,840-foot Akashi-Kaikyo Bridge in Japan.

VESPUCCI, AMERIGO

You're reading this in America rather than in a country named _____, because of this Italian contemporary of Christopher Columbus, whom he probably greeted in Seville when Columbus returned from that historic first voyage to the "Indies" and whom he *did* help to outfit for the second expedition. Vespucci discovered and explored the mouth of the Amazon for Spain. Under Portuguese auspices, the navigator in 1501–02 charted the coastline of South America, probably as far as Patagonia. He became convinced that these lands in the western Atlantic were not a part of Asia but a separate land mass. In 1507, the humanist mapmaker Martin Waldseemuller wrote about the new lands: *"ab Americo Inventore . . . quasi Americi terram sive Americam"*—"from Amerigo the discoverer . . . as if it were the land of Americus or America." At first, the name was applied only to South America; it was extended later to North America. Spain made Vespucci the prestigious Pilot Major in 1508. He evolved a system for computing nearly exact longitude, and arrived at a figure for the Earth's equatorial circumference only fifty miles short of the correct measurement.

VESTAL VIRGINS

Probably a whiter shade of pale, they were at first two, then four, and finally six in number, maidens consecrated for thirty years to the Roman

577

hearth goddess Vesta and to the maintenance on her altar of the sacred fire burning eternally—it better had! The punishment for letting the fire go out and for other offenses was scourging; for violating the vow of virginity, entombment alive. They could marry after expiration of service, which also included preparation of sacrifices, but marrying a former vestal was considered to be unlucky. Vestals, picked from unblemished candidates between the ages of six and ten with prominent, freeborn, living parents, were a privileged group, it says here.

VICTORIA CROSS

It is Britain's foremost medal "For Valor," and like so many things between 1837 and 1901 it was named for Queen Victoria. During World War II, it was awarded 183 times, including to an eighteen-year-old, John Hannah. The United States' highest war medal, the Congressional Medal of Honor, was awarded upward of 500 times in World War II.

VIETNAM WAR

Tet, the final turning point in American public opinion, was a self-inflicted defeat. A blazing, continuing controversy developed over reportage of the New Year's battle across Vietnam in 1968. Dr. Humphry Osmond and I have asked (in our book *Predicting the Past: Memos on the Enticing Universe of Possibility*) why the successful military defense in Vietnam by armies of the United States and South Vietnam was transmuted into a political and psychological defeat by strident, ill-informed efforts of the media in the United States. Several American generals and journalists and, it is said, one North Vietnamese general believe that this was so. Simply stated, the United States news media did not believe United States generals' claims of victory. Whatever one believes about Tet, it is difficult to believe that the hordes of uncensored correspondents—overrunning the little country, looking for the unexpected angle, reporting their own prejudices—made it easier for American and South Vietnamese commanders. Battlefield reports whirled off presses and were beamed into American living rooms during the dinner hour only a few hours, sometimes only a few minutes, after the reported events had occurred. Hanoi's General Vo Nguyen Giap fought the Tet flop without such "advantages." In retrospect, he may well consider that the absence of the media on his side was the crowning mercy of the Vietnam war and his distinguished career. Suppose General Giap had been given the same fervid attention by the media that General William Westmoreland could not avoid. Would North Vietnam, which suffered huge losses in men and arms, have survived Tet? As it was, or so accounts have gone, the United States and South Vietnam were able, thanks to the media, to snatch defeat from the jaws of victory. In his $120 million libel suit against CBS, General Westmoreland said that the television network was wrong and reckless in its 1982 documentary that he says defamed him. "The Uncounted Enemy: A Vietnam Deception" depicted what CBS called "a conspiracy at the highest levels of American military intelligence" to understate to President Lyndon B. Johnson and the Joint Chiefs of Staff and the American public what officers knew to be the size of the Vietcong and North Vietnamese forces before the Tet offensive. Peace negotiations in Paris were delayed for seven months over seating arrangements at the "peace" table so that the Saigon and the National Liberation Front (NLF) delegations could avoid face-to-face recognition and discussion. The North Vietnamese demanded a square table so the guerrillas' claim to independent status would be enhanced. The Allies saw it the same way and therefore wanted two rectangular tables, with the United States and the South Vietnamese representatives seated at one, the North Vietnam and the NLF representatives seated at the other—the provisional revolutionary government thus would not have a whole side of one table to itself. The NLF was a signator to the peace agreement on January 27, 1973. A decade later, all but one or two of the prospective jurors in the Westmoreland-CBS trial in New York admitted that they did not recall the names of Richard Helms, Robert McNamara, and Dean Rusk.

VIKING

The United States spaceship that touched down on Mars a couple of weeks after the 200th anniversary of the Declaration of Independence from England had to travel 440 million miles on an elliptical orbit, though the red planet at its closest approach to Earth is only 34.6 million miles distant in a straight line. Viking was a miniaturized automated laboratory. It was only 1 cubic foot of space, but the biology unit that examined soil for signs of life contained the following: 3 automated chemical labs; a computer; ovens for heating samples to 1,100°F.; counters for radioactive tracers; filters; sun lamp; gas chromatograph to identify chemicals; 40 thermostats; 22,000 transistors; 18,000 other electronic parts; and 43 valves. Carl Sagan has reported that two of the three microbiology experiments seemed to yield positive results. Something in the Martian soil, "when mixed with a sterile organic soup from Earth, chemically broke down the soup—almost as if there were respiring microbes metabolizing a food package from Earth. Second, when gases from Earth were introduced into the Martian soil sample, the gases became chemically combined with the soil—almost as if there were photosynthesizing microbes, generating organic matter from atmospheric gases."

VIOLIN

The best violins were crafted about two centuries after the instrument first appeared as the *viola da bracchio* (arm viol). The Italian Antonio Stradivari produced at least 1,116 instruments, of which 540 were violins, most of them in the first third of the eighteenth century. Some of the world's best violinists have included the composers Niccolo Paganini (he revived the practice of diverse tunings of the strings) and Antonio Vivaldi (*The Four Seasons*), and the greats of this century, Isaac Stern and Jascha Heifetz.

VIRGINIA

Virginians took the lead in winning freedom for the United States and in organizing the government: George Washington, Thomas Jefferson, Richard Henry Lee, Patrick Henry, John Marshall, and George Mason. Mason was the revered elder statesman of the state and a moving force at the Constitutional Convention; because it lacked specific guarantees of human rights, he did not endorse the document produced there. Presidents from Virginia: George Washington, Thomas Jefferson, James Madison, James Monroe, William Henry Harrison, John Tyler, Zachary Taylor, Woodrow Wilson—eight in all. Six First Ladies were born in Virginia. Other famous Virginians include Robert E. Lee, Richard E. Byrd, Walter Reed, Meriwether Lewis and William Clark, Joseph E. Johnston, Edgar Allan Poe, Booker T. Washington, James B. Cabell. Richmond became the capital of the Confederacy when Virginia seceded from the Union in 1861; in 1862, one third of the state split away and became West Virginia, loyal to the Union.

VIRGIN ISLANDS

Britain has held the British Virgin Islands since 1666—more than thirty islands, 59 square miles, immediately to the northeast of the Virgin Islands of the United States, formerly the Danish West Indian Islands, purchased by the U.S. from Denmark on March 31, 1917, for $25 million —133 square miles, 68 dots, in the tropical Lesser Antilles. The United States had been interested in the islands since the Civil War, when the Confederacy used the islands' harbors and shipping facilities to circumvent the blockade imposed by the Union. On the eve of America's entry into World War I, President Woodrow Wilson was persuaded that the islands would be militarily useful—for protecting the Panama Canal to the west, for one. The United States still wanted to buy, Denmark now wanted to sell—a deal after fifty years of off-again on-again discussions! The islands, of volcanic origin, were discovered and named by Christopher Columbus. Charlotte Amalie on St. Thomas is the capital of the Virgin Islands of the United States; the two other large islands of importance are St. Croix and St. John. Most of St. John is the Virgin Islands National Park. The British Virgin Islands have been a colony since 1970. The capital is Road Town, on Tortula.

VIRGIN MARY

Jesus' mother has appeared more times than any other woman on the cover of *Time* magazine—10! She gave birth to at least four other sons and to at least two daughters. Mark 6:3: "Is not this the carpenter, the son of Mary, the brother of James, and Joses, and of Juda, and Simon? and are not his sisters here with us? And they were offended at him. But Jesus said unto them, A prophet is not without honour, but in his own country, and among his own kin, and in his own home." There is no mention of the Virgin Birth in the Gospels according to either Saint Mark or Saint John. Jesus' mother witnessed the Crucifixion. John 19: "When Jesus therefore saw his mother, and the disciple standing by, whom he loved, he saith unto his mother, Woman, behold thy son! Then saith he to the disciple, Behold thy mother! And from that hour that disciple took her unto his own home."

VITAMINS

The word "vitamin" is rooted in *vita*—the Latin noun for "life." Fifteen vitamins have been discovered. They were first isolated only as recently as the second decade of this century, by the Polish biochemist Casimir Funk. The B vitamins are a family, or complex, because they are found in approximately the same foods and perform similar functions in the body; a deficiency in one of the B vitamins is often indistinguishable from the symptoms of deficiency in another. The Bs are active in providing the body with energy basically by converting carbohydrates into glucose, which the body burns to produce energy. They are the single most important factor for the health and normal functioning of the nervous system. All the B vitamins are natural constituents of brewer's yeast, dessicated liver and other organ meats, wheat germ, whole grains, brown rice, legumes, nuts, lean meats, poultry, fish, and leafy green vegetables. The best-known Bs are B-1 (thiamine), B-2 (riboflavin), B-3 (niacin or nicotinic acid or niacinamide), B-6 (pyridoxine), B-9 (folic acid), B-12 (cyanocobalamin), pantothenic acid, choline, inositol, and biotin. The renowned orthomolecular specialist Allan Cott, M.D., of New York City, uses vitamins, plus minerals, amino acids, and dietary reform, to help learning-disabled children to improve their performance.

VON BRAUN, WERNHER

In 1930, the German engineer read an article speculating on travel to the Moon that "filled me with a romantic urge to soar through the heavens and explore the mysterious universe." He helped to develop Hitler's V-2 flying bomb that rained death on England in the months before V-E Day: The 3,600 missiles had a five-minute, 190-mile flying span with nearly a ton of explosives. He was arrested and imprisoned when he refused to let Heinrich Himmler, the Gestapo chief, take over command of the V-2 program; Hitler ordered his release. When Russian armies came within 100 miles of the missile-launch site at Peenemunde, in 1945, von Braun fled to Bavaria and arranged to be captured by Americans. He was flown to the United States with a contract with the Army to direct guided-missile development. His staff included 117 German scientists, engineers, and technicians who had worked with him in the Third Reich. His expertise in supersonic aerodynamics helped to land man on the Moon in 1969. After applying for U.S. citizenship, he said, "I go to church regularly now . . . as long as national sovereignty exists, our only hope is to raise everybody's standard of ethics."

VOSGES MOUNTAINS

The vineyards on the Alsatian slopes of the crystalline and sandstone mountain range in eastern France, between the Alsatian plain in the east and the plateau of southern Lorraine to the west, produce Riesling and other wines. The highest point is the Ballon de Guebwiller (4,672 feet), and there's a seven-mile-long railroad tunnel through the Vosges.

WAILING WALL

The Muslim quarter, in the eastern part of Jerusalem, contains a sacred enclosure, the Haram esh-Sherif. Its wall incorporates the only extant piece of the Temple of Solomon; the western wall, or Wailing Wall, is Jewry's most hallowed religious and historic site. The Temple, a permanent house of the Lord, superseding the custom of using a movable tabernacle, is the only known massive structure of the ancient Hebrews. Over the years, it was looted, burned, pillaged, restored, and again stripped.

WAKE ISLAND

The three-square-mile atoll with three islets (Wake, Wilkes, Peale) was a commercial air base on the route across the central Pacific and a United States military base when the Japanese raided Hawaii in December 1941. U.S. Marines commanded by Major James Devereaux repulsed several Japanese invasion attacks before surrendering to superior forces. The last Marine off Wake was also the first American to return there after V-J Day. The Mercury astronaut Scott Carpenter said that he had been inspired to become a Navy pilot by the Hollywood movie *Wake Island* (1942), which recreated the only bright spot for the United States in the early days of the Pacific war.

WALCOTT, JERSEY JOE

Rocky Marciano's blockbusting right to the jaw in the thirteenth round knocked out the world's oldest-ever (thirty-eight) heavyweight boxing champion, Jersey Joe Walcott, in Philadelphia, in 1952. (Twenty-six years earlier, Gene Tunney had knocked off Jack Dempsey's crown in the same arena.) Walcott sank against the ropes, then slid head first to the canvas, and was counted out of the title he had triumphantly won slightly more than a year earlier. In the first round, Marciano had been knocked down for the first time in his career. Fans stormed the ring to celebrate the first white heavyweight to gain the title since Jim Braddock was shellacked by the Brown Bomber, Joe Louis, fifteen years earlier, in Chicago. Louis was the first black boxer to hold the title in twenty-two years, or since the days of Jack Johnson. The iron-fisted Marciano retired undefeated in 1956, at the age of thirty-one. Louis was twenty-three years old when he became champion. Muhammad Ali was the youngest boxer to wear the crown. He was only twenty-two—loud-mouthed, bragging, insulting, floating like a butterfly, stinging like a bee—when he upset a bleeding, injured Sonny Liston in 1962 in Miami Beach. Ali was then known as Cassius Clay, and immediately after the bout yelled to the newsmen at ringside, "Eat your words." Only three of the forty-five sportswriters had picked him to win.

WALKER, MOSES FLEETWOOD

The brothers Walker, Moses and Weldy, may have been the first black baseball players in the major leagues. They played a few games in 1884 with Toledo when the American Association had major league status. Moses was an above-average catcher. The black pitcher George Stovey won thirty-three games for Newark in the International League in 1887; three years earlier, the national pastime's first big star, infielder-manager Cap Anson, said he would refuse to field his Chicago White Stockings against Newark if Stovey played. As many as two dozen blacks played on teams in the professional leagues before the turn of the century. The very first organized league, the National Association of Base Ball Players, in 1867, established the barrier against blacks. The governing committee recommended that all teams "which may be composed of one or more colored persons" be denied admission. The Negro National League was formed in Kansas City in 1920.

WALLOONS

They were among the first settlers in New York, Huguenot refugees. Generally speaking, they have been the French-speaking people of southern Belgium. Flemings are the Dutch-speaking people of northern Belgium. (Brussels is bilingual.) The Walloons are lineal descendants of "Gallic Belgae," or Celtic people. Their section of Belgium contains major mining areas and heavy industries. The Flemish engage mainly in agriculture, shipping, and manufacturing (mostly textiles). The interests of these learned men, with high standing and powerful influence in the neighboring Netherlands, led to explorations for a Northwest Passage.

WALTON, IZAAK

"Gone fishing"—the sign's been up since the middle 1600s—"I have laid aside business, and gone a-fishing," the father of fishing wrote in one of the most famous books in the English language, *The Compleat Angler; or, the Contemplative Man's Recreation.* Amid the civil wars of the time, Walton quoted his friend the poet Sir Henry Wotton as to why angling mustn't be done on the fly: "It was an employment for his idle time, which was then not idly spent . . . a rest to his mind, a cheerer of his spirits, a diverter of sadness, a calmer of unquiet thoughts, a moderator of passions, a procurer of contentedness; and that it begat habits of peace and patience in those that professed and practiced it." Angling didn't have to fish around for compliments from Walton: "Doubt not but angling will prove to be so pleasant that it will prove to be, like virtue, a reward to itself. . . . You will find angling to be like the virtue of humility, which has a calmness of spirit and a world of other blessings attending upon it." Walton also tested the upstream publishing waters with biographies of his friend Wotton, who himself wrote *Character of a Happy Life,* and the metaphysical poets John Donne ("But God, who is able to prevail, wrestled with him, as the Angel did with Jacob, and marked him; marked him for his own") and George Herbert.

WAMBSGANSS, BILL

The Cleveland Indian second baseman made the only unassisted triple play in World Series history. In the fifth inning of game five of the 1920 championship against the Brooklyn Dodgers, Wambsganss caught a Mitchell liner, stepped on second base before Kildruff could duck back, and tagged Miller running from first on the pitch. In that strange and memorable game, Cleveland's Elmert Smith hit the first grand slam home run in a World Series game. Cleveland won the game, 8–1, and two days later iced the Series, five games to two.

WAR OF THE ROSES

The red rose: the noble house of Lancaster. The white rose: the noble house of York. At stake in the intermittent thirty-year clash that was to end feudalism: the throne of England. The crucial tilt took place at Bosworth Field in 1485. Lancaster's Henry, Duke of Richmond, routed and slew Richard III (who had been willing to trade his kingdom for a horse) and ascended the throne as Henry VII, the first Tudor. He united the houses of Lancaster and York by marrying Edward IV's daughter Elizabeth.

THE WAR OF THE WORLDS

Announcer: "Ladies and gentlemen, this is the most terrifying thing I have ever witnessed!. . . . . Wait a minute! Someone's crawling out of the hollow top. Someone or . . . something. I can see peering out of that black hole two luminous discs . . . are they eyes? It might be a face. It might be. . . ." Its mouth was "V-shaped with saliva dripping from its rimless lips that seem to quiver and pulsate." America was scared out of its pants in 1938 by Orson Welles's Halloween eve radio broadcast— "Invasion from Mars" in the format of a news show—based on H. G. Wells's *The War of the Worlds*. Hundreds of thousands of terrified people ran into the streets believing that Earth was being invaded by Martians with "minds that are to our minds as ours are to the beasts that perish, intellects vast and cool and unsympathetic," extraterrestrials who themselves perished because they had no resistance to Earth microorganisms. The next day, a Nazi Party newspaper blamed the nation's panic on the Jews. The columnist Dorothy Thompson wrote that Welles had proven how easy it could be to ignite panic in time of war. Princeton University undertook a study. The Federal Communications Commission issued a law forbidding that kind of broadcast in the future.

WARREN COMMISSION

President Lyndon B. Johnson induced the Chief Justice of the Supreme Court, Earl Warren, three times governor of California, to head a commission to "explore all avenues and true facts and prove that Lee Harvey Oswald alone murdered President John F. Kennedy" in Dallas on November 22, 1963. The commission's star witness, in 1964, was the widow of the accused assassin. Marina Oswald couldn't explain why her husband would shoot a man he esteemed and then deny the celebrity he had long sought: "I feel in my own mind he did not have President Kennedy as the target. Lee must have staked everything on one card." She asked if anybody else important was in the President's limousine. Psychiatrists in sealed and never-published testimony alleged that shooting the President would have been the farthest thing from Oswald's troubled mind. Another interviewee said that the only person he had ever heard Oswald say he wanted to kill was his wife, "and, gentlemen, I can't say I blame him." The Warren Commission, without ascribing a motive, concluded that Oswald had killed the President. He had acted alone. There was no conspiracy. Attorney General Robert Kennedy, JFK's brother, stimulated conspiracy theories when he informed President Johnson the day after the manacled Oswald had been slain that the Kennedy family was satisfied that Oswald had acted alone and the case should be closed. One door he wanted kept locked and bolted was the government's sundry plots to murder Fidel Castro—secretly, JFK had been in the assassination biz.

WASHINGTON

The Evergreen State is the only state named for a President. One year before the American Revolution, Spain's Bruno Hezeta sailed the coast. Three years after George Washington became the President, the American Robert Gray sailed along the Columbia River. In 1811, the fur trader John Jacob Astor established a post at Fort Okanogan. The United States and Britain agreed in 1846 on the border of Washington and neighboring Canada—the United States had threatened war with Britain ("Fifty-four forty or fight" was a theme of the 1844 Presidential election; they settled for the boundary at latitude 49°N.)—but Washington didn't join the Union until November 11, 1889—the forty-second state. The state song is "Washington, My Home." The state bird is the willow goldfinch. The state tree is the western hemlock. The state flower is the western rhododendron. The motto is By and By. The acres of forested land are 23,181,000. Washington is one of four states with active volcanoes: Mount Rainier and Mount St. Helens. Well-known Washingtonians have included William O. Douglas, Bing Crosby, Theodore Roethke, Mary McCarthy, and Edward R. Murrow.

THE WASHINGTON POST

The winner of the Pulitzer Prize for "meritorious public service" for its investigation of the Watergate break-in and cover-up at first, in the summer of 1972, covered the story as a mystery story, a crime. Announcements of Democratic press conferences on the subject would go to the national desk, where, as often as not, an editor would spike the notice, preferring to let the wire services cover it. Democratic Party boss Lawrence O'Brien called Watergate a political crime, "but that did not make it one." In 1973, White House aide Jeb Magruder testified that ". . . there was no question that the cover-up began that Saturday when we realized there was a break-in. I do not think there was ever any discussion that there would not be a cover-up." Attorney General John Mitchell believed that the "White House horror stories" could have destroyed President Richard M. Nixon's political career: "I still believe that the most important thing to this country was the reelection of Richard Nixon. I was not about to countenance anything that would stand in the way of that reelection.'' His noble defense of the President did not keep Mitchell from going to jail.

WATERFORD

The small seaport city on the Suir River in the county of the same name in the province of Munster in the Republic of Ireland became famous in the 1700s for making Waterford glass. It was blown for about a century, then became a glass darkly until the 1950s, when production was rejuvenated. Waterford was first known as Cuan-na-ah, "haven of the sun," and was the only Irish community that resisted Oliver Cromwell successfully; it was taken the next year, 1650, by Henry Ireton. The most prominent relic—it dates from 1003—is the fort Reginald's Tower.

WATER POLO

It's played with an inflated leather-covered ball in either an indoor or an outdoor pool twenty to thirty yards long, up to twenty yards wide. It can be a violent sport. It was in the 1870s that the English broke the ice of this aquatic game which encompasses features of soccer, hockey, football, basketball, and drowning. Two teams, seven players to a team, four seven-minute quarters (five-minute quarters in international play). All movement is by swimming. Only the swimmer with the ball may be tackled. A goal is scored by throwing, kicking, or heading. In the 1972 Olympiad, the pool was tinged with blood as Yugoslavia defended its title against Cuba. The United States has won only one Olympic gold medal in water polo, and that was in St. Louis, in 1904. Hungary is the perennial power.

WATER TAPS

When in Spain, do what the Spanish do. If you want cold water from your tap or faucet, you turn the knob labeled "F"—for "frio," cold. For hot water (sometimes), turn the knob labeled "C"—for "caliente," hot. In France, also "C" for hot, "chaud," and "F" for cold, "froid."

WEBER, RICHARD ANTHONY

He is bowling's leading money-winner—more than half a million dollars to go with his titles and championships. He is celebrated for being able to adjust or correct his delivery at the foul line. Weber gave up a postal clerkship to be anchorman with the St. Louis Budweisers. Other big names in bowling are Tom Baker, Marshall Holman, and Joe Berardi.

WEBSTER, NOAH

The lexicographer and philologist had a word for just about everything, including 70,000 headwords, 12,000 of which had not appeared in such a work before, for his *American Dictionary of the English Language,* a 20-year labor of love that was published in 1828, a scholarly achievement of the first order. He instituted reforms that were largely responsible for the differences between American and British spelling—his *Blue-backed Speller* became the authority. He believed that grammar is formed on language, not language on grammar. The polymath wrote the *Brief History of Epidemic and Pestilential Diseases, Ten Letters to Dr. Joseph Priestley,* and *Experiments Respecting Dew.* He founded and edited Federalist newspapers supporting George Washington's presidential administration. He was principally responsible for the adoption in 1790 of a national copyright law. Yes, Webster's *Third New International Dictionary of the English Language*—nearly 3,000 triple-columned pages, with definitions from A to zyzzogeton—is the most recently revised form of Webster's seminal work. You can look it up.

"WEE WILLIE WINKIE"

Another Mother Goose rhyme: "Wee Willie Winkie runs through the town, Upstairs and downstairs in his nightgown, Rapping at the window, crying through the lock, 'Are the children in their beds, for it's now eight o'clock?' " Tom, Tom, the piper's son, was also all over the place: "He stole a pig and away he run: The pig was eat, and Tom was beat, And Tom went howling down the street. . . . [He] Learned to play when he was young; But the only tune that he could play, Was 'Over the hills and far away.' "

WEIGHTLIFTING

"The strongest man in the world" muscled his way to eight Olympic gold medals and hoisted over 100 world records. In the 1972 Olympics, in Munich, "the Russian bear" Vasily Ivanovich Alekseyev weightlifted a total of 1,410¾ pounds. Four years later, in Montreal, his winning Olympic lifts were "only" 969¾ pounds.

589

WEISSMULLER, JOHNNY

The greatest swimmer of the first half of the century (Associated Press) took the plunge at an early age. By the time he retired from competition after the 1928 Olympics, he had won fifty-two national championships, three Olympic gold medals, and set sixty-seven world records. In Hollywood, the buoyant 190-pounder played a monosyllabic "Me, Tarzan" in loincloth in nineteen films, then Jungle Jim in sixteen. He was the first inductee into the swimming Hall of Fame.

WEST, MAE

Every young man should have gone West. She was the original two-fer. Her first name should have been Can. Or Will. She sure was able. She was the unparalleled (barring none) mistress of double entendre. "A man in the house is worth two in the street." "It is better to be looked over than overlooked." "It's not the men you see me with, it's the men you don't see me with." "When I'm good, I'm very good, but when I'm bad I'm even better." "It's not the men in my life, it's the life in my men." "Is that a pistol in your pocket, big boy, or are you just glad to see me?" Everyone wanted to go up and see her. Except maybe W. C. Fields. "I can't see Bill Fields as a two-gun man," she said when they were planning *My Little Chickadee*, "but his dexterity as a two-bottle man is common knowledge. He'll shudder with horror when I make it part of my agreement to do the picture that he lay off all alcohol while we are shooting." "Not even a small beer?" Fields is said to have whimpered as he signed on the dotted line. (Whenever he slipped off the wagon, W. C. would tell the kid actors to go out and play in the traffic.) Miss West wrote this exchange for *My Little Chickadee* (two earlier titles: *The Lady and the Bandit* and *The Jayhawkers*): Fields's Indian valet, referring to West, asks, "Big Chief gottum new squaw?" Fields retorted, "Ya-as, brand new. I haven't even unwrapped her yet." Ya-as, she was some little chickadee. (A chickadee is a titmouse.)

WESTMINSTER ABBEY

Officially the Collegiate Church of St. Peter in Westminster, in London, it is both the crowning place and the burial place of most English sovereigns. Monuments throughout the Gothic church–national shrine commemorate many men who are not buried there. In the middle of the nave (the loftiest in England) a slab of green marble is inscribed "Remember Winston Churchill." It was placed there in accordance with the wishes of the Queen and the Parliament on the twenty-fifth anniversary of the Battle of Britain; the former Prime Minister's body rests at Bladon. The Poets' Corner in the south transept honors many, including Tennyson, Eliot, Byron, Browning, Shakespeare, Blake, Longfellow, and Dryden. Also commemorated in the Abbey: John André, who was hanged by General George Washington as a British spy during the American Revolution. A prize fighter (Jack Broughton) is buried in Westminster Abbey, as are Charles Darwin and England's "unknown warrior" in World War I—his remains were brought from Flanders and interred in earth brought from the battlefields.

WHALES

The aggregate weight of thirty average-size elephants, the blue whale is the largest animal known: about 200 tons, about 100 feet—longer than from home plate to first base. It is larger than was even the largest prehistoric animal! The whale is a mammal that has returned to the sea and taken on a fishlike form. It no longer has external hind limbs, and its front limbs have evolved into flippers. It propels itself by moving its massive tail flukes up and down. The valve of the blow hole closes and keeps out seawater when the whale dives. The sperm whale can descend more than 3,000 feet and remain underwater for more than an hour. The long, deep dive is the whale's most striking adaptation to the sea. Some of the sounds on the humpback whale's sonic scale cannot be heard by humans. Some sounds at high intensity turn into heat and can kill prey.

THE WHITE HOUSE

At 1600 Pennsylvania Avenue, the oldest public building in Washington —the cornerstone was laid in 1792—has 132 rooms and a bomb shelter and occupies 86,184 square feet. In the original plans, it was called "the Palace." John Adams was the first President to hang his hat there. It was burned on the night of August 24, 1814, by British troops, in the War of 1812. The interior had to be rebuilt completely. The name "White House" developed about this time but didn't become official until the twenty-sixth President, Theodore Roosevelt, had it engraved upon his stationery. (Martha Washington's estate was called the White House.) The most famous object there is the Lincoln Bed; it is nine feet long and made of solid rosewood. Lou Henry Hoover set the best table. When he had lived in the White House for only two days, John Adams wrote, "I pray heaven to bestow the best of blessings on this house, and on all that shall hereafter inhabit it. May none but honest and wise men ever rule under this roof."

THE WHITE HOUSE: 202-456-1414

Telephone switchboard operator: White House.
J.A.: May I speak with President Reagan, please?
Operator: He's out of the country.
J.A.: May I leave my name and number and ask that he return this call?
Operator: No, sir, You'll have to call his office on Monday after 9 A.M.
J.A.: Thank you.
(Mr. Reagan *was* out of the country. He plays Trivial Pursuit.)

WHITEMAN, PAUL

At one time, there were more than fifty Paul Whiteman bands touring the nation, putting the roar into the Roarin' Twenties, the jazz into the Jazz Age. In 1924, he conducted the first symphonic jazz concert, at Aeolian Hall, in New York City—introducing *Rhapsody in Blue,* which George Gershwin had written for the occasion in merely three weeks. The conductor had his own radio program for eighteen seasons and introduced the Dorsey brothers, Bing Crosby, Jack Teagarden, and Bix Beiderbecke. He also was the first to conduct Ferde Grofe's *Grand Canyon Suite.*

WHITNEY, ELI

The inventor introduced mass production to American industry by figuring out how to make standardized, interchangeable parts. No longer did every device consisting of more than one part have to be made by hand; a machine-made part could replace any other one of that type. He fulfilled a government contract for 10,000 muskets through his revolutionary system, and personally demonstrated to President John Adams how disassembled muskets could be put together quickly. He prospered on numerous government contracts. He did not reap financial reward for inventing the cotton gin ("gin" being short for "engine"), which separated short-staple upland cotton from its seeds, rejuvenated slavery, and prompted the South to go to war rather than to give up its "peculiar institution." Most historians agree that the Civil War would not have happened but for Whitney's cotton-cleaning machine.

WHITWORTH, KATHY

It's enough to tee them off, but neither Kathy Whitworth nor Sam Snead —the professional golfers with the most career victories—has won the

Women's Open or the United States Open, respectively. Miss Whitworth became the professional golfer with the most career victories—eighty-five—when she defeated Rosie Jones in a sudden-death playoff in the Rochester International golf tournament on July 22, 1984. (Ten weeks earlier, she had finished seventieth in the United Virginia Bank Classic.) Miss Whitworth, who began playing professionally in 1958, and Snead had been tied at eighty-four for most victories since she won the Kemper Open in March 1983. She's been seven times the Ladies' Professional Golf player of the year, 1966–69, 1971–73, and was the first LPGA member to make over a million dollars.

"WHY DID THEY DO IT?"—AND SOME LAST WORDS

It's what Pope John Paul II exclaimed after being shot in Vatican City. Fortunately, "Why did they do it?" were not to be the Pontiff's last words. "Last words are not samples of the best, which involve vitality at its full, and balance, and perfect control and scope," Walt Whitman said. "But they are valuable beyond measure to confirm and endorse the varied train, facts, theories, and faith of the whole preceding life." Whitman's last words may have been "O I feel so good!" when the pain he was suffering was relieved. Franklin Roosevelt's last words were "I have a terrific headache." Theodore Roosevelt's: "Please put out the lights." Charles Darwin's: "I am not the least afraid to die." Florenz Ziegfeld's, in a delirium: "Curtain! Fast music! Lights! Ready for the last finale! Great. The show looks good. The show looks good!" Warren G. Harding's: "That's good. Go on; read some more." George Washington's: " 'Tis well." William Henry Harrison's: "I wish you to understand the true principles of the government. I wish them carried out. I ask nothing more."

WILDE, OSCAR

He finally yielded to Lord Alfred Douglas's exhortation and sued Douglas' father for criminal libel. But it backfired: Two trials later, Wilde was found guilty of sodomy with young Douglas and spent two years at hard labor at Reading Gaol and writing recriminations to his co-sodomizer. But he maintained an unconquerable gaiety of soul, proving the importance of being Oscar. Earlier, the Aesthetic Singer had paid a call on America, stating on arrival that he had "nothing to declare but my genius." There was widespread hostility to his languid poses and aesthetic costume of velvet jacket, knee breeches, and black silk stockings. He paid a visit to the Camden, New Jersey, home of the Good Gray Poet,

Walt Whitman, who told Wilde to continue his mission of shattering the ancient idols. They spent an afternoon together, drank a bottle of wine, and proceeded upstairs on a thee and thou basis. Laying a hand on the poet's knee, Wilde said, "I can't listen to anyone unless he attracts me by a charming style or by beauty of theme." Whitman, stroking his silvery beard, later said, "Wilde seemed to me like a great big splendid boy." Wilde married the daughter of a prominent Irish barrister and fathered two children. His only novel was *The Picture of Dorian Gray*. (Lord Douglas was also a poet, and he lived until 1945.)

WILHELM, HOYT

He knuckleballed for more than a score of years in baseball's big leagues —twenty-one in all—but he always talked about his very first at-bat. He hit a home run. He didn't hit another one in more than 400 more times at the plate. In his second season, he hit a triple, and never hit another. He also hit two doubles in his second season, and in nineteen more campaigns hit only one more. The first relief pitcher in the Hall of Fame registered 143 wins and 227 saves.

WILLIAMS, TED

Major league baseball's greatest feat has been Joe DiMaggio's 56-game hitting streak in the last campaign before Pearl Harbor. Yet in that same nearly-two-month period the Yankee Clipper was eclipsed in batting percentage by the Boston Red Sox's Ted Williams, .412–.408. The Splendid Splinter finished the season with a .406 batting average, the first .400-plus BAV since 1930—there hasn't been a .400-hitter since—but he didn't win the American League's most valuable player award—DiMag did. Williams didn't feel "robbed or cheated." DiMaggio "was a great player on a great team that won the pennant," easily. In 1942, Williams won the triple crown—and Joe Gordon of the Yanks was MVP. In 1947, Williams outhit DiMaggio, .343–.335, clubbed 32 home runs to DiMag's 20, and drove in 114 runs to DiMag's 97—DiMag was voted MVP, again, when a Boston writer didn't place Williams anywhere in the top ten on his ballot. Williams *was* voted MVP in two other seasons. Typically, he has said that the honor should be above personalities: "It is something one accepts graciously or loses graciously. I never made any bones about it one way or the other. I was happy when I won it, but never flabbergasted when I lost." Williams' last at-bat—typically, he blasted a home run—is celebrated in an account by Martha "Genius" Updike's husband, John.

594

WILLIAMS, TENNESSEE (THOMAS LANIER)

The two-time Pulitzer Prize winner for drama (*A Streetcar Named Desire, Cat on a Hot Tin Roof*) "didn't go to the Moon, I went much further —for time is the longest distance between two places." The "genitalman of letters" stirred compassion for the lost souls, the deformed and the outcasts of a self-congratulating society. "Some things are not forgivable," he said. "Deliberate cruelty is not forgivable. It is the one unforgivable thing in my opinion and it is the one thing of which I have never, never been guilty." He was a monumental hypochondriac, and he drank and took pills immoderately. In his book *Memoirs* he wrote in detail about his homosexuality; his art was private. In 1942, M-G-M rejected his screenplay for *The Gentleman Caller*. He transformed it into his Broadway debut, *The Glass Menagerie*. "Once you fully apprehend the vacuity of a life without struggle, you are equipped with the basic means of salvation." Williams once said that his own creed as a playwright was fairly close to that expressed by the painter in Shaw's play *The Doctor's Dilemma:* "I believe in Michelangelo, Velasquez, and Rembrandt; in the might of design, the mystery of color, the redemption of all things by beauty everlasting and the message of art that has made these hands blessed. Amen." Amen.

WILSON, WOODROW

Broken by the fatigue and the strain of campaigning for United States entry into the League of Nations, and then by an incapacitating stroke, the twenty-eighth President was virtually detached from the Oval Office in the last seventeen months of his second term. He died in the year he left office (1921) and is the only President buried in the District of Columbia. (Two Presidents are buried nearby in Virginia's Arlington National Cemetery—William Howard Taft and John F. Kennedy.) When he became governor of New Jersey in 1911, Wilson had never before held public office. A year and ten months later, he was elected President. He broke a century-old precedent, in 1913, by appearing before Congress— he wanted to emphasize his determination to lead in legislation and to use all his powers as the President and the leader of the Democratic party.

WINCHELL, WALTER

"Good evening, Mr. and Mrs. North and South America and all the ships at sea, let's go to press. FLASH!" At 215 words a minute, "Mrs. Winchell's little boy" rat-a-tat-tattled his news of the week as he fiercely tapped a set of telegraph keys. "Other columnists may print it—I make it public," the creator of modern gossip writing boasted. He loved to coin words: terpsichorines, Ratzis, infanticipate, Renovated, giggle-water, phfft. He had such clout that he arranged the surrender of Louis (Lepke) Buchalter, a New York City hood, to J. Edgar Hoover himself. "Mr. Hoover," said the columnist, "this is Lepke." "How do you do," Mr. Hoover said. "Glad to meet you," the gangster said. When the erstwhile song-and-dance man retired from radio, he narrated the television series "The Untouchables" for four years. In New York his column appeared in the *Mirror*. Thousands waited for the early-bird edition, flipped to Winchell, the track results, and the numbers, then threw it away. His biggest scoop: F.D.R. would go for it a third time!!!!!!! (President John F. Kennedy talked faster than Winchell—325 words per minute.)

WINDSOR CASTLE

English rulers since William I have lived there, in south central England, by the Thames River. And some have been buried there, including Queen Victoria and Prince Albert, in the royal mausoleum, Frogmore. One of the most splendid churches in the land is there, St. George's Chapel; its construction was initiated by Edward IV. It is where Knights of the Garter are installed with medieval ceremony. The castle has been besieged only twice. Its original purpose as a fortress has long been subordinated to the need for comfort in the royal quarters. Chaucer was a clerk of works there.

WINE—CONSUMPTION

Italians consume the most wine per capita—110.5 liters per person every year. (A liter is 1.06 quarts, so that's 117.13 quarts or 234.26 pints.) The French are also in triple digits: 103.04 liters per person every year. The next big eight wine-consuming nations per capita are: Portugal, Argentina, Spain, Switzerland, Luxembourg, Chile, Hungary, and Austria. The leading beer-drinking countries are Czechoslovakia (*152.7* liters per capita per year), West Germany, Australia, Belgium, Luxembourg, and New Zealand.

WINGS

With but one exception—the insects—the wings of all flying animals (the bees with their four wings, the birds, the modern bats, the extinct flying reptiles) are simply modified front legs. Insects have both their old legs and their new wings. The organs of flight evolved from folds of the integument, paranotal lobes, extended from the sides of the back on the second and third thoracic segments.

WITCH TRIALS

There were 150 "witches" and "wizards," and they were charged with having been possessed by the devil. The nineteen persons condemned to death in the infamous trials in Salem, Massachusetts, in 1692, may have been suffering hallucinations after eating contaminated bread. One of the colonial judges, Samuel Sewall, was so certain that the convictions had been a mistake that through the last thirty-three years of his life he accepted "blame and shame" for the verdict, and spent a day each year in fasting and prayer.

THE WONDERFUL WIZARD OF OZ

In the movie version (1939) of the book *The Wonderful Wizard of Oz* (1900), the Cowardly Lion, the Scarecrow, and the Tin Woodsman rush to Dorothy's rescue. In Lyman Frank Baum's novel, Dorothy was so very angry that the Wicked Witch of the West had taken one of her pretty silver shoes, she picked up the bucket of water that stood near and dashed it over the Witch, wetting her from head to foot. "Didn't you know water would be the end of me?" asked the Witch, in a wailing, despairing voice. "Of course not," answered Dorothy, "how should I?" "Well, in a few minutes I shall be all melted, and you will have the castle to yourself. I have been wicked in my day, but I never thought a little girl like you would ever be able to melt me and end my wicked deeds. Look out—here I go!" In the movie, the Wicked Witch (Margaret Hamilton) writes "Surrender, Dorothy" across the sky, a visual not in the book, which also became a successful musical-stage extravaganza. While Baum was editor of a periodical for window decorators, *Chicago Show Window,* at the turn of the century, he wrote *Father Goose: His Book,* an instant success (a thousand copies a day nationally for ninety days), and the first of fourteen *Oz* books. Other *Oz* titles including *The Woggle-Bug Book, Ozma of Oz,* and *Tik-Tok Man of Oz* helped to take Baum over the rainbow and down the yellow brick road to a large home in California with a flower garden in which he kept an enormous cage full of rare songbirds. Dorothy's surname was Gale.

WONDERS OF THE WORLD

They were the Great Pyramid of Khufu (or all the pyramids with or without the Sphinx); the Hanging Gardens of Babylon, with or without the walls; the Mausoleum at Halicarnassus; the Artemision at Ephesus; the Colossus of Rhodes; the Olympian Zeus, statue by Phidias; and the Pharos at Alexandria. Lewis Thomas, director of Sloan-Kettering Memorial Hospital in New York and the author of several science books, including *Lives of a Cell*, has compiled a list of seven modern wonders of the world: the Oncideres, a species of beetle that Thomas says keeps reminding us how little we know about nature; the infectious agent known as the scrapie virus: it "seems the strangest thing in all biology"; the olfactory receptor cell, located in the epithelial tissue high in the nose: "how it makes sense of what it senses, discriminating infallibly between jasmine and anything else non-jasmine, is one of the deep secrets of neurobiology"; the termite: a mass of them, a thoughtful, meditative brain on a million legs that does its architecture and engineering by a complex system of chemical signals; a human child—he makes language; and the first of all wonders of the modern world, Earth itself: "There is nothing to match it anywhere, not yet anyway."

WOOD, GRANT

The Iowan studied painting in Paris and Munich and was influenced by the precise details and the realism of Flemish and German paintings. When it came time for him to make his mark, he was as American as one could be—a leader in the regionalism movement. His most famous—and most parodied—painting is called, appropriately, *American Gothic.* (Quick: Which of the couple holds the pitchfork?) *Arbor Day, The Midnight Ride of Paul Revere* (the patriot rides through a hilly *Iowan* landscape), and *Daughters of Revolution* are top notch. Who better to be the director of WPA art projects in Iowa?

WRESTLERS

Some of them are incredible hulks—Andre the Giant, for instance, stands seven foot four and weighs well over 400 pounds. Some are masqueraded —the Masked Marvel wears a black stocking cap with holes for his eyes and mouth. Some are pretty—Gorgeous George dyed his hair blond and set it and he had a valet spray Chanel No. 5 perfume around the squared circle before a match. Some are called weirdos—the Angel says he strengthens his neck muscles by putting a noose of thick rope around his neck and hanging from a limb of a tree for an hour every day. Professional wrestlers are show biz—"all the traffic will allow"—and their job is to keep fans's hatred boiling and the bucks pouring into the big arenas. "I'm in it for the money, no question," says The Body, Jesse Ventura. Adrian "Golden Boy" Adonis has said, "People need to take out their frustrations. The American people are sickies who love violence and the sight of blood." Is it all a charade? It is said that that's a question most safely asked by phone of wrestlers a continent away.

WRESTLING—HOLDS

The nelson is a wrestling hold in which a wrestler exerts leverage in different directions against an opponent's upper arm and head. There's the full nelson, the double nelson, the quarter nelson, the three-quarter nelson, and the half nelson. The latter is applied by placing one arm under the corresponding arm of the opponent and reaching up to push against the back of the opponent's head. The half nelson is sometimes called simply the nelson.

THE WRITING WALLACES

Let's make a list: *The Chapman Report, The R Document, The Fabulous Originals, The Prize, The Man, The Seven Minutes, The Square Pegs, The Word, The Fan Club, The Fabulous Showman, The Pigeon Project* are some of Irving Wallace's more than twenty works of fiction and nonfiction. Son David: *The People's Almanac, The Book of Lists, Chico's Organic Gardening and Natural Living, Laughing Gas,* and *What Really Happened to the Class of '65.* Daughter Amy: *The Book of Lists, The Two, The Psychic Healing Book.* Wife Sylvia: *The Fountains.* (David is known by the family's pre-Ellis Island name, Wallechinsky.) Now you know how to fill your home with works by Picasso, Magritte, Toulouse-Lautrec, Rivera, Miro, Braque, Matisse, Modigliani, and Gauguin—and that's just a part of the collection. Screenwriting helped, too: *The West Point Story, The Big Circus, Meet Me at the Fair, Split Second.* Screen adaptations and a percentage of the box office helped, too. To Irving Wallace, Hollywood is "a plush hell, an infernal region dominated by double-dealing, politics, feuds, pettiness, thievery, cretinism, where the writer suffers indignity, disrespect, disdain, and where he can make more money than he could possibly make in any other salaried medium of writing."

WRIGHT BROTHERS

Their serious study of flight began in 1899. They tested man-carrying gliders in 1900. They designed and tested some 200 shapes of wings in a homemade wind tunnel (six feet long, sixteen inches square) in 1901. They made record-setting glider flights in 1902. On December 17, 1903, they did it—they made man's first powered heavier-than-air flight in a "crate" driven by a lightweight, twelve-horsepower gasoline engine. Orville Wright's first flight, near Kitty Hawk, North Carolina, lasted twelve seconds. The longest of four flights that day was fifty-nine seconds. Later in the day, a gust of wind overturned and wrecked the wooden flyer. The brothers stuffed the pieces and the fabric covering into barrels and shipped them to their bicycle shop in Dayton, Ohio. Nearly two years later the Wrights were in the air for as long as thirty-eight consecutive minutes, and they ascended and descended at will, and actually *turned*. It took U.S. Army officials eight years to agree to observe a demonstration of powered flight. When the Smithsonian Institution would not acknowledge the Wrights's achievement, the pioneers sent their historic first plane to the Science Museum in London. The Smithsonian changed its mind and the flyer is now on display in Washington. Wilbur Wright died in 1912. Orville Wright lived until 1948.

"WYNKEN, BLYNKEN AND NOD"

"Dutch Lullaby" was another title for this verse by the late nineteenth-century journalist, author, and poet Eugene Field, a whimsical newspaper columnist (the *Denver Tribune*, the *Chicago Record*) and an inveterate practical joker of great ingenuity and wide renown. He also wrote "Little Boy Blue" and "The Rock-a-By Lady from Hushaby Street." Wynken, Blynken and Nod one night Sailed off in a wooden shoe—Sailed on a river of crystal light Into a sea of dew. "Where are you going, and what do you wish?" the old Moon asked the three. "We have come to fish for the herring fish That live in this beautiful sea; Nets of silver and gold have we," said Wynken, Blynken and Nod. The old Moon laughed and sang a song, As they rocked in the wooden shoe; And the wind that sped them all night long Ruffled the waves of dew; The little stars were the herring fish That lived in the beautiful sea, "Now cast your nets wherever you wish—Never afeard are we!" So cried the stars to the fishermen three. . . . All night long their nets they threw To the stars in the twinkling foam—Then down from the skies came the wooden shoe, Bringing the fishermen home. . . . Wynken and Blynken are two little eyes, And Nod is a little head, And the wooden shoe that sailed the skies Is a wee one's trundle-bed; So shut your eyes while mother sings Of wonderful sights that be, And you shall see the beautiful things As you rock on the misty sea Where the old shoe rocked the fishermen three—Wynken, Blynken and Nod.

X

The fewest number of words in English begins with the twenty-fourth letter of the alphabet. In Webster's *Third New International Dictionary, Unabridged*, there are 345 words beginning with X. Among them: xenolith (a fragment of a rock included in another rock); xiphophyllous (having sword-shaped leaves); xoanon (a primitive image of wood sometimes recalling in shape the block or tree trunk from which it was cut); and x-ray.

Y

YAHTZEE

This dice game can be played by one to four persons. Five dice are thrown—five of a kind is a yahtzee. Even a YAHTzee!!! In each turn, a player may roll the dice up to three times in order to get a scoring combination. There are thirteen scoring rounds in each game. The object is to obtain the highest score for one or more games. The player with the highest total score for all games (up to six games) is the winner.

YAK

Over six feet high at the shoulders and weighing more than half a ton, the Asian wild ox can slide down icy slopes, swim swift rivers, and traverse steep rock grades—and that's just your typical yak, the mammal that lives at the highest altitudes. With his nose almost touching the earth, the yak roams the cold, dry plateaus of Tibet more than three miles above sea level, which is why God covered him with black or brownish-black hair. The domesticated yak, usually called the grunting ox, is sometimes white or even piebald, and gives pink milk.

YALE UNIVERSITY

The distinguished hall of ivy was named for a bescandaled governor of the British East India Company who had been born in Boston and taken to England when he was three years old, never to return to the colonies. The educational institution in Saybrook, Connecticut, was the fledgling Collegiate School of Connecticut when Jeremiah Dummer and Cotton Mather persuaded Elihu Yale in England to donate religious books, a portrait of George I, and £200. There was a subsequent donation yielding £562. The school changed its name to Yale College in 1718. When Yale died a rich man, in 1721, he did not bequeath an additional gift to Yale, which had moved to New Haven five years earlier. The £562 was the largest single gift to the college before 1837.

YALTA

Not until 1947 was the complete text published of all the agreements of the Big Three Yalta Conference in February 1945. President Franklin Delano Roosevelt, Prime Minister Winston Churchill, and host Soviet Premier Joseph Stalin, meeting at Yalta, reaffirmed that Germany must surrender unconditionally. Stalin pledged that the Soviet Union would enter the war against Japan two to three months after Germany surrendered—it did, three months to the day after V-E Day and two days after Hiroshima and six days before V-J Day. Germany was to be divided into four separate zones of occupation; there would be war crimes trials and reparations; the Soviet-Polish frontier would be drawn to the west of the prewar frontier; China and France would be invited to sponsor the founding conference of the United Nations; Manchurian railroads would be under joint Chinese-Soviet administration. Churchill believed that Stalin would readily forego Roosevelt's good will should Soviet interest so demand. During the Cold War and subsequently, the late American President was accused of turning over Eastern Europe to Communist domination. In the Allies' first postwar meeting—at Potsdam, in the summer of 1945, Harry S Truman was now the U.S. President, Clement Attlee British P.M.—the Yalta agreements were clarified and implemented. Japan was informed that it must surrender unconditionally or face total destruction.

"YANKEE DOODLE"

A mocking verse composed by a British army surgeon, a Dr. Shackburgh, who was quartered among the Dutch colonists along the Hudson River at the time the colonial troops were mustering for the French and Indian War in 1754: Yankee Doodle went to town, riding on a pony, he stuck a feather in his hat and called it macaroni. Yankee is probably a rendering of the Dutch *Janke* (Johnny). Doodle may also have been a Dutch word but already employed in English in the sense of "a foolish fellow." Edward Gates, a professor of English at Indiana State University, speculates in *Test Your Word Power* that the British marching to Lexington and Concord on April 19, 1775, may have sung "Yankee Doodle." Yes, "Lucy Locket lost her pocket" was the familiar folk tune to which "Yankee Doodle" was set.

YAZSTREMSKI, CARL

What can you possibly win in the major leagues with a .301 batting average for the whole season? In 1968, at least, it was good enough for the Boston Red Socker to cop the batting title in the American League. It was his second consecutive batting title—his .326 was tops in the league in '67, when he won the triple crown and paced the Beantowners to the league championship. He loved playing baseball. "I absolutely loved it. I loved stepping into the batter's box." He hung up his spikes at the close of the 1983 campaign, having played 3,308 games (twenty-two seasons), more than anyone else ever has. He also holds the record for having been walked intentionally the most times: 187. (Zack Wheat, of the Dodgers, won the batting title in the National League in 1918 without hitting a home run.)

YELLOW RIVER

Nine hundred thousand northern Chinese were drowned (sacrificed) in 1938 when Chiang's retreating army dynamited dikes along "China's sorrow" in order to flood 20,000 square miles and hundreds of cities and villages and to dam the onrushing Japanese military tide. The Yellow, or Huang Ho, is China's second-longest river—nearly 3,000 miles. It gets its name from the loess, a loamy yellowish-brown earth, it collects as it passes south through the Great Wall and eventually into the Yellow Sea. Lan-chou is the largest city along the way. Peking is expending much energy channeling the Yellow into peaceful purposes.

"YELLOW ROSE OF TEXAS"

She may have been an Indian. She may even have been Chinese. Or a light-skinned black. She was the sweetest rose of color a fellow ever knew. Her eyes were bright as di'monds. They sparkled like the dew. "You may talk about your dearest maids, and sing of Rosy Lee, but the Yellow Rose of Texas beats the belles of Tennessee." No one knows who wrote the song, but when it appeared in the mid-1850s the author was identified only by the initials "J.K." It was a marchin' song for both the Union and the Confederate armies in the Civil War and a standard with minstrel shows. Franklin Roosevelt loved it, the Texas Rangers adopted it as their official song, and Mitch "Sing Along" Miller repopularized it in the mid-fifties.

YELLOWSTONE NATIONAL PARK

In the old days you could set your watch by Old Faithful—every 64.5 minutes the ancient "geezer" would shoot about 11,000 gallons of water some 150 feet into the air. But geysers they are a-changin'. Nowadays, its timing is off—something about being under the weather, which it always is, it doesn't go with the flow, which has been altered by civilization. It pops up irregularly. Yellowstone—3,400 square miles, mostly broad plateau, in northwest Wyoming, Montana, and Idaho—is Earth's most prolific geyser area; it has about 200 gushers and 10,000 hot springs. Enter on its thousand miles of hiking trails through the Roosevelt Arch and enter primitive America: ice-blue lakes and ponds, wild mountain country, bears and other dangerous animals, thermal heat, snow, rain, windswept Mount Washburn, the "black glass" Obsidian Cliff, glacier-carved canyons that are grand. Other incomparable geysers: Grand, Castle, Beehive, Riverside. Two years after General Henry Washburn discovered the area, in 1870, Yellowstone was set apart as the world's first national park. Today, it's the third largest in the United States's national park system.

YELLOW SUBMARINE

Al Brodax, of King Features, needed an idea that the Beatles would "buy." They had already turned down two years's worth of ideas, and Brodax was desperate to make an animated movie with them. "Hey, how's about Minoff? Maybe he could think of something." Lee Minoff had adapted the comic strip "Mandrake the Magician" as a feature film for Brodax (it was never made) and he had a comedy heading for Broadway, *Come Live with Me*. Minoff, who had been an aide to Stanley Kubrick on *Dr. Strangelove*, listened to "Sgt. Pepper's Lonely Hearts Club Band." After a hard day's night, he was given a ticket to ride when he hit on the idea pegging the script to the song "Yellow Submarine." Paul McCartney loved the outline, the Beatles loved the outline. Minoff did an original story, the first draft of the screenplay, the second draft of the screenplay, and then it was hello, goodbye, everybody's friends were all aboard, and the band began to play. Proving once again that we all live in a yellow submarine.

YEW

It is a hard tree, somber of aspect and frequently of great size and girth (as much as thirty feet) and age (up to 1,000 years)—and absolutely hollow. It is commonly found in English churchyards, from Kent to Devon and in Monmouth, Hereford, Merioneth, and Denbighshire. It is revered for its evergreen longevity and for its vital contribution to the defense of England—yew wood makes a bow that can take bows—boughs? Sir Arthur Conan Doyle noted, "The bow was made in England;

of true wood, of yew wood, the wood of English bows." The genus spreads across the Northern Hemisphere and is geographically distinguishable as six species. The common yew *(Taxus baccata L.)* can be found in Europe, Algeria, and in Asia Minor. Yew does something to poets. "Bring(s) me yew to deck my grave: such end true lovers have," William Blake rhymed in deathless poesy.

YIDDISH

"Klutz" rhymes with "butts," and, yes, it's Yiddish, from German: (a) log, or block of wood, (b) a heavy person, (c) a strong man or giant. A klutz is a clod, a clumsy, slow-witted, graceless person; an inept blockhead. The men sat slurping their borscht. After a while, the first man says, "Life is like a beet." "Like a beet?" asks the other. "Why a beet?" "How should I know," the first man says. "What am I, a philosopher?" What he definitely is is a klutz. In Yiddish, a goniff is a thief; a noodge is a pest; zoftig means plump, almost fat; a nebish is a drab, pathetic loser; a shloomp is unkempt, slobby; schlock is a, well, a schlocky, cheaply made article; shmata is a rag, raggedy clothes; k'nocker is a big shot, a bragger; a nudnik is a pest, an obnoxious person; a kvetch is a self-indulgent complaint; kvell, to feel great satisfaction at the success of a loved one, especially of a son or a daughter; nachas, pleasure earned from the success of a loved one—one draws or "sheps" nachas; shmuck, "ornament," from a number of possible German words meaning neat, smart, or to decorate; in Yiddish slang, shmuck is a penis; in American slang, a shmuck is a fool. The novelist I. B. Singer delivered part of his Nobel Prize for Literature-acceptance speech in Yiddish. "In a figurative way," he said, "Yiddish is the wise and humble language of us all, the idiom of a frightened and hopeful humanity."

YOM KIPPUR

The most solemn date in the Jewish year, the day of atonement, when God seals the fate of every person for the ensuing year. It is a day of fasting. It is also forbidden to have marital relations, to anoint with oil, or to wear leather shoes. In ancient times, the day was the occasion of a solemn Temple ceremonial, the only occasion when the high priest entered the Holy of Holies. "And this shall be a statute for ever unto you: that in the seventh month, on the tenth day of the month, ye shall afflict your souls, and no work at all, whether it be one of your own country, or a stranger that sojourneth among you. For on that day shall the priest make an atonement for you, to cleanse you, that ye may be clean from all your sins before the Lord. It shall be a sabbath of rest unto you, and ye shall afflict your souls, by a statute for ever. And the priest, whom he shall anoint, and whom he shall consecrate to minister in the priest's office in his father's stead, shall make the atonement, and shall put on the linen clothes, even the holy garments: And he shall make an atonement for the holy sanctuary, and he shall make an atonement for the tabernacle of the congregation, and for the altar, and he shall make an atonement for the priests, and for all the people of the congregation. And this shall be an everlasting statute unto you, to make an atonement for the children of Israel for all their sins once a year. And he did as the Lord commanded Moses.''—Leviticus

YORK, ALVIN

At first a conscientious objector, the back-country Tennessee farmer finally joined the army and in October 1918 found himself in the Argonne Forest—World War I was in its fourth year. The advance of his regiment across the valley beyond Hill 223 was being held up by heavy fire from German machine guns on the wooded slope at one end of the valley. Corporal York was sent out in a patrol of seventeen soldiers to silence the enemy. He is credited with mowing down—from a kneeling position, he used his rifle like a machine gun—twenty-five German soldiers and stopping a charge by a Hun platoon. He also captured 132 others, including five officers. Sergeant York became a popular hero when he was awarded the Congressional Medal of Honor. He let Hollywood make a movie of his heroism only when Gary Cooper agreed to play the role.

YORKTOWN

The last battle of the American Revolution. With his back to the wall, British General Charles Cornwallis bit the bullet and sent out an officer with a white flag. General George Washington at the Rock Redoubt signed the surrender papers, "done in the trenches before Yorktown in Virginia, October 19, 1781." The Father of His Country was generous but decreed that the British army must march out with colors cased and its bands playing only British tunes instead of the traditional "honors of war." Cornwallis was "too ill" to hand over his sword personally at Surrender Field and Washington chose not to receive it from Cornwallis' deputy; an aide did. The world was turned upside down. The war dragged on for two more years—the British didn't surrender New York until 1783 —General Washington didn't ride triumphantly back into the city until December 4. But Yorktown had assured American independence.

YOUNG, BRIGHAM

"Do you think that I am an old man?" the fifty-six-year-old Mormon leader asked the congregation. "I could prove that I am young; for I could find more girls who would choose me for a husband than can any of the young men." Discussing polygamy, a Mormon tenet, with Vice-President Schuyler Colfax, Young said, "I never saw the day that I wanted to be henpecked to death, for I should have been if I had married a rich wife." The doctrine of plural marriage was based on a vision of Joseph Smith, who founded the Church of Jesus Christ of Latter-Day Saints, commonly called Mormon. For more than thirty years Young was the chief influence on Mormonism. Two of the twenty-seven women he made his wife were Joseph Smith's widows whom he married in an obligation to support them in their old age: "They already had engagements with the Prophet for eternity." He fathered fifty-six children—thirty-one daughters, twenty-five sons—believing that cohabitation was solely for the purpose of procreation. He was survived by seventeen wives. The Edmunds Act of 1882 deprived any polygamist of the right to vote or to hold office. The history of Utah has been the history of Mormonism; it entered the Union as the forty-fifth state, in 1896, after the church withdrew sanction of polygamy. Utah is the Beehive State—the beehive is a symbol of the Mormons, known for their great industry.

YOUNG, CY

He's been baseball's winningest pitcher—and losingest pitcher. The Red Sox lefthander for whom baseball's pitching award is named scored 511 victories in 828 decisions, for a .617 winning percentage. He pitched a perfect game in 1904, he pitched a no-hitter when he was 41 (1908), he holds the record for consecutive hitless innings pitched (24). Cy was the moniker for Denton True. The Cy Young award was inaugurated in 1956 by Commissioner Ford C. Frick to focus more attention on moundsmen. For the first eleven years, it was given to only one pitcher in all of baseball, not to one in each of the two leagues as has been the case since 1967. The first eleven winners were: Don Newcombe, Warren Spahn, Bob Turley, Early Wynn, Vernon Law, Whitey Ford, Don Drysdale, Sandy Koufax, Dean Chance, and, in 1965 and in 1966, for the second and the third times, Sandy Koufax. The only four-time winner has been taciturn southpaw Steve Carlton, of the Philadelphia Phillies, in '72, '77, '80, '82.

YO-YO

The toy resembling a flat spool that may be made to spin and move down and up a string wound around it was discovered in the Philippines by Donald Duncan and introduced to civilization in 1929. It was originally a jungle weapon that could be bounced off the head of an enemy and swiftly drawn up out of sight by someone hiding in a tree. In slang, yo-yo means a stupid, incompetent, or undesirable person; a jerk; a gullible person; a dupe. In other words, a yo-yo.

Z

ZAÏRE

Zaïre since the early 1970s—the Democratic Republic of the Congo and the Belgian Congo and the Congo Free State and the Kongo kingdom before Zaïre—deep in the heart of Africa, three times as vast as Texas and about one-quarter the size of the entire United States. The equatorial rain forest in the north (average daytime temperature: 90°F.) is so thick that parts of its floor haven't seen the Sun, or vice versa, since who knows when. Zaïre has 60 percent of the globe's reserve of cobalt and it's had Joseph D. Mobutu (Mobutu Sese Seko) as president since 1965. The first inhabitants were probably Pygmies. About 1500, the Kongo kingdom adopted Roman Catholicism, and Portuguese businessmen began enslaving and exporting hundreds of thousands of blacks. The explorer Henry Morton Stanley, who had served both sides in the United States Civil War, crossed the Congo from east to west in 1876. In the 1880s, King Leopold II of Belgium fiercely, harshly, cruelly exploited the country, people, and minerals. The motto of Zaïre is Justice, Peace, and Work. A variety of gods and spirits are worshipped still by a majority of the 30 million residents.

ZAMBEZI

Africa's fourth-longest river (1,700 miles) spills over the lopsided Victoria Falls in southcentral Africa, on the Zambia-Rhodesia border, throwing up a mist and a roar perceptible from a distance of about 25 miles. The river drains more than 500,000 square miles and empties into the Mozambique Channel of the Indian Ocean, near Chinde. Both the river (in 1851) and the falls (1855) were discovered by the Scottish missionary and explorer David Livingstone, who was looking for the source of the Nile River when he was "found" in 1871 by the *New York Herald*–sponsored Henry Morton Stanley: "Dr. Livingstone, I presume?" Stanley later explored the Congo River from its source to the sea and established outposts for the Belgian monarch. Livingstone died in the village of Chief Chitambo in 1873 and was buried in Westminster Abbey.

ZAPRUDER, ABRAHAM

The Dallas businessman happened to film the assassination of President John F. Kennedy in Dealey Plaza. The first 6.5-mm bullet from Lee Harvey Oswald's misaligned rifle nicked and traumatized the President's spine and tore out his throat and an overlapping part of his shirtfront immediately below the Adam's apple. In one four-hundredth of a second the shot then ran through his chest, right lung, fifth right rib, and right wrist, and then ran into the right thigh of Governor John Connolly sitting on a jump seat in front of the President. Kennedy's elbows flashed upward in supplicatory motion, and a quizzical expression rolled across his face. Four seconds later, the President, still upright in his rigid steel-ribbed corset, was nearly decapitated by Oswald's second hit. Pale blue tissue flew every which way from a gaping wound that a moment earlier had been the right side of Mr. Kennedy's head. Heavy brain matter jetted through the massive exit cavity and ineluctably lashed backward the remaining half of his head. The unscathed First Lady at J.F.K.'s left was swamped with brains and scalp and hair and blood erupting from the demolished body of her husband. Mrs. Kennedy crawled across the trunk of the open convertible limousine . . . she reached out . . . and pulled aboard a Secret Service agent. When she learned the identity of her husband's assassin, she reportedly exclaimed, "Killed by some harebrain little runt! It makes it all so meaningless."

ZERO

Calculation with large numbers is not possible without the zero. Astronomy, physics, and chemistry would be a cipher today without the zero. Greek math was nothing because it didn't know from the zero. The zero didn't exist in Roman numerals. When Italian businessmen figured out how convenient Arabic numerals were, they abandoned Roman numerals. But they still needed something to stand for nothing—they just couldn't stand nothing. "Nothing" is not just nothing—it's vital. The Arabic word *sifr* was changed to *zepiro*. The Hindus and the Mayas seem to have been the first to develop the zero. Addition of zero to any number leaves it unchanged. Subtraction of zero from any number leaves it unchanged. Multiply any number by zero and you get zero. Division by zero, however, is still undefined. There is no number that is the value of a number divided by zero.

ZERO DEGREE LONGITUDE

The prime meridian (or longitude) passes through the original site of the Royal Greenwich Observatory, in Greenwich, England, and all points along it are at 0° longitude. Because there can be no latitude in determining where you are or where you are going—if you have to know exactly —lines of longitude (meridians) and lines of latitude (or parallels) have been mapped on the globe—longitude runs from north to south, from Pole to Pole, latitude runs from east to west so that all points along a parallel are the same distance from either Pole. The North Pole has a latitude of 90° north and the South Pole a latitude of 90° south. Longitudes range from 0° to 180° west and from 0° to 180° east. The international date line lies along the 180° meridian, except where it is rerouted to account for population areas. This book was written at 73.59 west longitude and 40.46 north latitude.

ZIPPER

Something had to be done to cut down on the time—*all that forever*—it was taking women to lace up their shoes and their boots. And so Whitcomb L. Judson, of Chicago, put his mind to it and invented—the zipper. But it was a zip. There were design defects—the fastener came apart easily, for one. It needed more zip in its zip. And zip it got, from a Swedish engineer in Hoboken, New Jersey, Gideon Sundback; he was granted a patent for "separable fasteners" in 1912. It was the first zipper to work on the principle of identical units mounted on parallel tapes—the zipper we know and couldn't part with.

ZOMBIE

It's a knock-your-socks-off rum drink which, it is said, threatens to paralyze one's vital spirits. It's American slang to describe a disagreeable and unwanted human being whom the ingroup wishes to ostracize. In voodoo, it is a person believed to have been raised from the grave by a priest (a houngan), who uses him for drudge work and to implement evil schemes. The term originated in West Africa.

ZOONOSIS

It's a disease communicable from animals to man under natural conditions. Rabies, brucellocis, tuberculosis, pittacosis (parrot fever), and tuleramia (rabbit fever) are examples of a zoonosis disease. Eskimos have contracted brucellocis from eating the bone marrow and the uncooked liver and kidney of freshly killed reindeer; Peruvians, from consuming fresh cheese made from unpasteurized goat milk; Mongolians, from drinking *airig,* or fermented mare milk.

ZOOT SUIT

It was banished by the War Production Board as a glaring example of wasteful manufacture during World War II—the zoot favored by "hep cats" had a very long jacket, flared at the bottom, exaggeratedly padded (six inches of stuffing), boxy shoulders; trousers with pleats at the waistline, cut very wide over the hips and tapering down to such narrow bottoms that men with big feet had trouble slipping the trousers on; pockets were slash, sleeves pegged. Accessories were equally flamboyant. Hat brims were wide, very wide, shoes were extremely pointed, cuff links were enormous, and there just had to be an extra-long key chain fastened to the belt loop of the trousers. The first zoot suit of record was bought by a busboy for $33.50 from a store in Gainesville, Georgia, in February 1939. The zoot suit orbited when cartoonist Al Capp had Lil' Abner trade in his too-small, too-tight suit for one cut full and roomy— the excess cloth was a sign of affluence. In the opinion of one fashion writer, it was "extremely unfortunate that the zoot suit became a sign of disorder in the eyes of certain sections of the trade. If nothing else, the zoot suit showed the concern of the young man for clothes and fashion— no matter what the fashion might be." To others, there was more zoo than zoot in the outfit.

"ZORRO"

The secret identity of Don Diego de la Vega, a swashbuckling character in Johnston McCulley's novel *The Curse of Capistrano.* As a black-garbed masked avenger who signed his exploits with a sworded "Z," he championed oppressed peasants against tyrannical Spaniards in Old California. *Zorro Rides Again* and *Zorro's Fighting Legion* were legendary Hollywood movie serials. The feature film *The Mark of Zorro* (1940) is still relished for the clash of steel between Zorro, played by the dashing cutup Tyrone Power, and Captain Esteban (Basil Rathbone).